INSIDE THE
FASHION
BUSINESS

Jeannette Jarnow
Edwin Goodman Professor and Professor Emeritus,
Fashion Merchandising
Fashion Institute of Technology

Miriam Guerreiro
Professor, Fashion Merchandising
Fashion Institute of Technology

INSIDE THE
*F*ASHION
*B*USINESS

TEXT AND READINGS

Fifth Edition

Macmillan Publishing Company
New York

Collier Macmillan Canada
Toronto

Production Supervisor: Charlotte V. Hyland
Production Manager: Sandra Moore
Cover photographs: Preston Lyon
Photo Researcher: Meredith Davenport
Illustrations: Fineline Illustrations, Inc.
Photo credits appear on page 553.

This book was set in Palatino by Digitype, Inc. and was printed and bound by
Halliday. The cover was printed by Phoenix Color Corp.

Macmillan Publishing Company
866 Third Avenue, New York, New York 10022

Collier Macmillan Canada, Inc.
1200 Eglinton Avenue East
Suite 200
Don Mills, Ontario M3C 3N1

Library of Congress Cataloging-in-Publication Data
Jarnow, Jeannette A.
    Inside the fashion business : text and readings / Jeannette A. Jarnow ; Miriam
Guerreiro.—5th ed.
       p.   cm.
    Includes bibliographical references.
    ISBN 0-02-360002-0
    1. Fashion merchandising—United States. 2. Clothing trade—United States.
I. Guerreiro, Miriam.   II. Title.
    HD9940.U4J3 1991
    338.4′7687′0973—dc20   90-30859
                                      CIP

Printing: 1 2 3 4 5 6 7   Year: 1 2 3 4 5 6 7

To the readers of the previous
editions whose enthusiastic
acceptance of this book encouraged
us to undertake this new and
revised edition.

Preface

Inside the Fashion Business is a book for those who have a particular interest in what is called the "fashion industry"—that complex of enterprises that is concerned with the design, production, and marketing of men's, women's, and children's apparel and accessories.

Volatile, exciting, challenging—that is the fashion business. It is a business that, like fashion itself, is ever-changing—thus this new revised edition. This new, fifth edition has been completely updated and, like the previous editions, is a combination of text and industry readings. Our objectives are twofold: to develop an understanding of the workings of an industry that is a major segment of the U.S. economy and to expose the reader to its inner workings as perceived through the eyes of recognized authorities and practitioners in the field.

By providing this knowledge, we also hope to help fashion business aspirants crystallize their career objectives and reach their own specific goals in the wonderful world of fashion.

ORGANIZATION

The plan that we have followed is simple and consistent. An introductory overview of the fashion business is followed by chapters that each deal with one particular segment of the industry. These chapters are divided into two parts. First comes an organized fact-filled body of knowledge. Next comes a series of industry readings carefully selected to complement, supplement, and illustrate the subject matter of the chapter. These readings describe the operations of leading companies in their respective fields. Then, to facilitate further research, each chapter has a bibliography, a list of trade associations, and a listing of trade periodicals related to its subject. In each case the chapter concludes with a series of suggested student learning activities that require review, interpretation, and application of knowledge. Following the final chapter are three appendixes and a fashion business language guide.

CONTENT

Chapter 1, "The Business of Marketing Fashion," presents an overview of the U.S. fashion industry and its scope, economic importance, and marketing practices. It also discusses the power of fashion and the role of the ultimate consumer.

Chapter 2, "Principles of Fashion," discusses the generally accepted definitions of fashion and the principles governing its origin and dynamics, along with the implications for the marketers of fashion. It also discusses the role of designers today.

Chapter 3, "The Materials of Fashion," examines the industries that provide the raw materials from which apparel and accessories are made: fibers, fabrics, leathers, and furs. Each is discussed in terms of its economic importance, its method of operation, and its strategies for meeting present conditions.

Chapter 4, "Women's and Children's Apparel—U.S.A.," discusses the design, production, and marketing of women's and children's apparel. It includes the history, development, growth, and practices of this segment of the fashion business, along with the methods used to meet present-day challenges.

Chapter 5, "The Menswear Industry," reviews the growth of this industry, its adaptation of the influence of fashion, and its changing methods of operation.

Chapter 6, "Fashion Accessories and Intimate Apparel," deals with the economic importance and operations of the specialized industries that produce accessories and intimate apparel.

Chapter 7, "Imports," is concerned with the extensive penetration of foreign-made merchandise into the United States, the reasons therein, the procedures involved, and applicable government import regulations.

Chapter 8, "Foreign Fashion Producers," discusses the foreign fashion producers that supply us with goods, ranging from internationally famous foreign designers to contractors in low-wage countries.

Chapter 9, "The Retailers of Fashion," explains the different types of retail operations, the circumstances and period of their origin, the part that each plays in the business of fashion, and how retailing is changing.

Chapter 10, "Auxiliary Fashion Enterprises," covers the service enterprises that contribute to the effective functioning of the fashion business, such as news media, fashion advisory and information services, advertising and publicity agencies, and resident buying offices, among others.

Appendix A is an annotated list of influential designers. Appendix B, "Sources of Current Statistical Information," provides information for those who wish to keep current and update the figures presented in this edition. Appendix C, "Career Opportunities in Fashion" is a road map for those seeking a niche in the fashion business. Entry-level opportunities are discussed in terms of personal qualities, skills, and preparation.

The authors feel strongly that readers need statistical yardsticks against which to measure the importance of the various industries, trends, and individual enterprises in the fashion business. This we have sought to provide in the text, within the limits of what was available up to the time of publication.

A Fashion Business Language Guide follows the appendixes.

ACKNOWLEDGMENTS_ _ _ _ _ _ _ _ _ _ _ _ _ _ _ _ _ _

We both wish to stress that this book, as with its predecessors, reflects the thoughts of many other people. We are grateful to the business leaders who shared their knowledge of experience with us and to the publications and organizations that granted reprint permissions for readings. Also, we thank the faculty members, students, and library staff of the Fashion Institute of Technology for their continuing support and suggestions. A special acknowledgment is due Beatrice Judelle, our co-author of earlier editions, whose many contributions to this book are still in evidence. Finally, we thank the many friends in the academic and fashion worlds who gave advice and counsel. These people helped us shape the previous editions and encouraged and guided us once again in this revision.

Jeannette A. Jarnow
Miriam Guerreiro

Contents

1 THE BUSINESS OF MARKETING FASHION 3

The Business of Fashion: An Overview 4
The Consumption of Fashion Goods 8
The Marketing of Fashion 11
Penetration of Imports 14
Federal Legislation Affecting the Fashion Business 15

READINGS 23

Welcome to the 21st Century, Ready or Not 24
What Is Perfume but Water and a Bit of Essence? 27

Endnotes 32
Selected Bibliography 32
Trade Associations 33
Trade Publication 33
Chapter Review and Learning Activities 33

2 PRINCIPLES OF FASHION 35

The Language of Fashion 35
The Constant in Fashion Is Change 38
Fashion: A "Follow-the-Leader" Process 41
How Fashions Develop 47
The Prediction of Fashion 53
American Designer Awards: The "Oscars" of Fashion 59

READINGS 61

The Subject Was Fashion 62
Calvin Klein: In the Midst of Change, a Certain Style 64
Donna Karan: Hot and Getting Hotter 68
Ralph Lauren: Telling Stories 70
Adrienne Vittadini: From Esthetics to Reality 73
Beyond Fashion: Mary McFadden 75
Geoffrey Beene's Amazing Grace 78

Endnotes   79
Selected Bibliography   80
Trade Associations   82
Trade Publications   82
Chapter Review and Learning Activities   83

3   **THE MATERIALS OF FASHION   85**

From Fiber to Fabric   85
Fiber Producers   86
Textile Producers   92
Fashion Research and Development   99
Electronics: The New Technologies for the 1990s   105
Competition from Imports   109
Furs and Leathers   110

   READINGS   119

   Over the Rainbow   120
   This Is Springs   122
   Burlington's New Weave: Smaller and Tighter   124
   At Cone Mills Quick Response Spells Survival   126

Endnotes   127
Selected Bibliography   128
Trade Associations   129
Trade Publications   130
Chapter Review and Learning Activities   130

4   **WOMEN'S AND CHILDREN'S APPAREL — U.SA.   133**

Economic Importance   133
History and Growth of Women's Industry   134
From Design Concept to Retailer   140
Nature of the Industry   153
Location of Fashion Market Centers   163
Children's Wear   174
Competition from Imports   177

   READINGS   178

   The Wizard of the Working Woman's Wardrobe   179
   Levi's Makes Push in Women's Wear   183
   King of the Copycats   188
   Designers Still Put Stock in Trunk Shows   191
   OshKosh Defined   193

Endnotes   195
Selected Bibliography   196
Trade Associations   197
Trade Publications   197
Chapter Review and Learning Activities   198

5   THE MENSWEAR INDUSTRY 201

Economic Importance   202
History and Development   202
Nature of the Industry   206
Design and Production Procedures   210
Marketing of Menswear   221
Competition from Imports   232
Fashion Explosion in Men's Accessories   232

READINGS   233

Brooks on Precedents and Presidents   234
Suit Wars   235
Two-Day Sales Trip to Up Sales: Focus on Customer
    Service   240
Greif Companies: Megastore Trend Gives Rise to Merchandise
    Coordinators   243
How Hartmarx Brands America   245

Endnotes   248
Selected Bibliography   248
Trade Associations   249
Trade Publications   250
Chapter Review and Learning Activities   250

6   FASHION ACCESSORIES AND INTIMATE APPAREL 253

The Accessories Industries   254
Shoes   257
Hosiery   264
Handbags and Small Leather Goods   268
Gloves   272
Millinery   274
Jewelry   276
Other Accessories   280
Accessories Designers   281
Intimate Apparel   281

READINGS   286

Carolee: Taking Risks, Moving Ahead   287
Nike's Bright Knight   290
Inside Grandoe   292
Hanes Hosiery: Runs, Hits & Errors   294
An Industry Focus: The Business of Intimate Apparel: What's
   Next?   298

Endnotes   303
Selected Bibliography   305
Trade Associations   305
Trade Publications   306
Chapter Review and Learning Activities   307

7   **IMPORTS   309**

Import Penetration by Foreign Producers   310
Regulation of Imports   311
Who Imports and Why   320
Protectionism versus Free Trade   326
Global Sourcing: An International Fashion Mix   327
U.S. Penetration of Foreign Markets   329

READINGS   333

Allure of Asia Continues High for U.S. Firms   334
Caribbean Sourcing Poised to Take Off   336
A Visit with Vittadini in Hong Kong   339
Why Made in America Is Back in Style   340
A European Push by Robert Janan   343

Endnotes   346
Selected Bibliography   347
Trade Associations   347
Trade Publications   348
Chapter Review and Learning Activities   348

8   **FOREIGN FASHION PRODUCERS   351**

Different Types of Foreign Producers   351
Paris Haute Couture   352
Ready-to-Wear Fashion Centers   360
Overseas Contractors in Low-Wage Countries   372
Fashion: A Global Business Today   379

READINGS   380

La Creme de la Hem: An Insider's Guide to the Exclusive
    World of Haute Couture   381
Italy's Fashion Trillionaire   386
Investing in the Nineties   392
The Business of Chic   395
Gotta Have Gottex   399

Endnotes   402
Selected Bibliography   403
Trade Associations   404
Trade Publications   404
Chapter Review and Learning Activities   404

9 THE RETAILERS OF FASHION 407

Fashion Retailing in the Past   407
Different Kinds of Retail Operations   408
Department Stores   409
Apparel Specialty Stores: Large and Small   412
Chain Store Retailing   415
Mail-Order Houses: Nonstore Retailing   419
Discount Retailing: Underselling Operations   424
Franchised Retailing   429
Shopping Centers and Malls   430
Other Types of Retail Operations   431
The Changing Dimensions of Fashion Retailing   433

READINGS   445

Watch Out Macy's, Here Comes Nordstrom   446
Wal-Mart: Will It Take Over the World?   450
Standout in the Land of Catalogues   456
Charivari: New York's Hottest Boutique Causes an
    Uproar   458
Tomorrow's Buyer: A Production Expert   461
The Limited: Speeding into the Nineties   463

Endnotes   465
Selected Bibliography   466
Trade Associations   467
Trade Publications   468
Chapter Review and Learning Activities   468

10 **AUXILIARY FASHION ENTERPRISES 471**

Fashion Information and Advisory Services   471
Resident Buying Offices: Market Representatives   474
Fashion in the News Media   482
Advertising and Publicity Agencies   489
The Fashion Group   492
Other Fashion Enterprises   492

READINGS   493

T.F.S. — The Fashion Service   494
The Tobé Report   498
We Are AMC   500
The Fashion Group   505
Mademoiselle: Editors and Departments and
What They Do   507

Endnotes   511
Selected Bibliography   511
Trade Associations   512
Trade Publications   512
Chapter Review and Learning Activities   512

APPENDIXES   514

A. The Influential Designers   514
B. Sources of Current Statistical Information   522
C. Career Opportunities in Fashion   524

FASHION BUSINESS LANGUAGE GUIDE 542

INDEX 555

INSIDE THE
FASHION
BUSINESS

1

The Business of Marketing Fashion

Fashion in the United States today is big business. Its component parts—the design, production, and distribution of fashion merchandise—form the basis of a highly complex, multibillion-dollar industry. It is a business that began with small entrepreneurs at the turn of the century and today is a huge, many-faceted business. It employs the greatly diversified skills and talents of millions of people, offers a multitudinous mix of products, absorbs a considerable portion of consumer spending, and plays a vital role in the country's economy. It is, moreover, a business of curious and exciting contrasts. On one hand, there is the rarefied air of Paris couture salons presenting collections of exorbitantly priced made-to-order designer originals; at the other extreme are giant factories that mass produce and distribute endless quantities of low-priced apparel to towns and cities across the country. It is also international in nature, since the United States both imports and exports fashion merchandise.

This chapter presents an overall view of the U.S. fashion industry—its scope, economic importance, and marketing concepts. It also introduces the reader to the person who occupies the key position in the entire group of enterprises that constitute this business: the consumer. The readings that follow illustrate general marketing concepts and strategies.

Subsequent chapters discuss in detail the various segments of the industry that are involved in the design, production, and distribution of fashion merchandise: fibers and fabrics, apparel and accessories production, foreign sources of supply, retailing, and related auxiliary services.

THE BUSINESS OF FASHION:
AN OVERVIEW_____

The impact of fashion is all-pervading, but when we speak of the *fashion business*, that term is generally understood to refer to all companies and individuals concerned with the design, production, and distribution of textile and apparel goods. Unlike industries such as tobacco and automotive products manufacturing, the fashion industry is not a clearly defined entity. It is a complex of many different industries, not all of which appear at first glance to have anything of fashion among their products.

Scope of the Fashion Industry

Plainly recognizable as part of the fashion business are industries devoted to the making of inner- and outerwear articles of women's apparel; those involved in the production of men's wear; those that make children's apparel; and those that make accessories such as scarfs, jewelry, handbags, shoes, gloves, wallets, and hosiery. Some of these industries serve one sex or the other; some serve both sexes.

When one moves back to an earlier stage of production—to the fibers, fabrics, leathers, furs, metals, and plastics from which the finished products are made—the line between what is and what is not the fashion business becomes harder to draw. Some textile mills that produce dress and coat fabrics also produce bedsheets, carpets, or industrial fabrics. Some chemical companies that produce fibers that are eventually spun and woven to make garments are also producers of explosives, fertilizers, and photographic film. Some producers and processors in fields normally remote from fashion find themselves temporarily with one foot in the fashion business when prevailing styles demand such items as industrial zippers, decorative chains, quilted fabrics, or padding materials, for example. A season or two later, these people may be as far removed from the fashion business as ever, but for the time being, they too are part of it.

The fashion business also includes different types of retailers, such as stores that sell apparel and accessories, and mail-order catalogs from which many consumer purchases are made. It includes businesses that neither produce nor sell merchandise but render advice, assistance, or information to those that do.

In this last category are consumer publications that disseminate news of fashion, ranging from the daily newspaper to magazines devoted primarily to fashion, such as *Seventeen, Details, Vogue, Harper's Bazaar,* and *Gentlemen's Quarterly.* Also included in this category are trade periodicals that carry news of fashion and information on production and distribution techniques to retailers, apparel manufacturers, and textile mills. It includes also publicists and advertising specialists, fashion consultants, and buying offices that represent retail stores in the vast wholesale centers.

All these and more are part of the business—farms and mills and factories, blue-collar and white-collar workers, tycoons, and creative artists. All play their parts in the business of fashion.

Economic Importance

The business of fashion contributes significantly to the economy of the United States both through the materials and services it purchases and through the wages and taxes it pays. In assessing the importance of this contribution, it helps to consider **consumer expenditures**, the number of people employed, and the amount of wages and salaries paid to them.

In 1989 Americans spent $200.1 billion for clothing, shoes, and accessories —an amount that constituted more than 5 percent of what they spent for all purposes from food to foreign travel.[1] The outlay for fashion goods ran well above that for furniture, household equipment, or tobacco, for example. A further index of the importance of fashion goods is reflected in department store figures. Typically, the sales of men's, women's, and children's apparel and accessories account for well above half the total volume of such stores.[2]

Still another indication of the industry's importance is the number of jobs it creates—and it creates them in every state of our country. Of the millions of people employed in factory work in the United States, better than one in every eight is employed either in those industries that produce apparel for men, women, and children or in the textile plants that produce the materials from which the garments are made.[3]

Apparel production alone employs more people than the entire printing and publishing field and more than the automobile manufacturing industry. Additional millions are employed in producing such items as fur and leather garments and in staffing the retail organizations that distribute these goods. To this total, add some share of the employment in finance, transportation, advertising, utilities, and other essential services that devote part of their efforts to the fashion industry, and it becomes obvious that the industry has an astounding impact on our economy.

The Fashion Pipeline: Channels of Distribution

There are three main links in the production and distribution of fashion products: (1) the **primary markets**, which provide the raw materials of fashion, such as fibers, fabrics, leathers, and furs; (2) the **secondary markets**, which manufacture finished products of apparel and accessories; and ultimately (3) the retail distributors. All three links are interdependent. The primary markets depend on the secondary markets for the sale of their products; the secondary markets depend on the primary markets to provide the materials from which to fabricate finished goods; both markets depend on the retailer to present and sell the merchandise to the ultimate consumer. It is the retailer who is the final link between the consumer and the vast network of the fashion-producing industry. Within that network are enterprises of many different types. A flow chart in this

The Fashion Pipeline

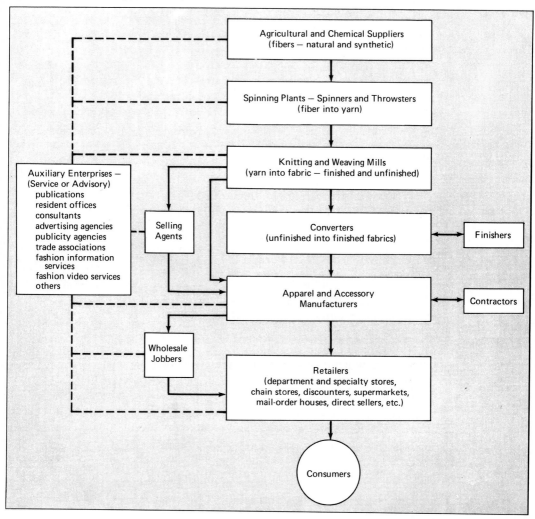

chapter illustrates the main segments and the interrelationships of each. Subsequent chapters discuss the activities of each in detail.

PROLIFERATION OF VERTICAL OPERATIONS

In recent years, the fashion pipeline has become more varied. Manufacturers have expanded into the retail business and retailers have entered the manufacturing area.

Vertical operations are not new in the fashion industries; manufacturer-owned retail stores have existed for decades in the menswear industry. What is new is that vertical ventures have been proliferating in women's wear and accessories, and are currently pervading the fashion business.

Today, many yarn spinners, knitters, weavers, apparel producers, and retailers, who formerly were mutually exclusive and distinctive segments of the fashion industries, are losing their familiar identities and have taken over some of each other's roles.

Examples exist at all levels of the industry, but it is most obvious and visible at the manufacturer–retailer interface. Some of the most successful companies on both sides of this divide are taking over functions that once were performed exclusively by their suppliers or customers. For example, a retailer such as The Limited is involved actively in designing and producing some of the merchandise it sells; the manufacturing company of Liz Claiborne has opened its own retail outlets.

These vertical operations, which have created an intensely competitive market as both producers and retailers fight it out for a greater share of consumer dollars, are further discussed in the appropriate chapters.

Timing of Product Development and Showings

Each link in the fashion industry chain periodically presents its new styles very early to those in the next level of production, so that producers and sellers may in turn prepare their collections well in advance of the consumer buying periods. For example, the colors, weaves, and fabrics that are expected to receive consumer acceptance are researched and decided on a year to two years before the consumer will see them.

By consensus and custom, each branch of the industry sets its opening dates by balancing many factors against one another: the change of season, the time required to produce goods after trade buyers have placed their orders; and the time required by product developers (whose titles may be fashion director, designer, stylist, retail buyer, or creative director) to assess the pulse of the market. Attempts to change customary dates have been made in some branches of the industry, with no success. Despite the fact that consumers today are more knowledgeable, sophisticated, and more inclined toward seasonless dressing, tradition and custom seem to prevail. Still, everyone in the fashion industry chain seems to produce collections earlier and earlier — possibly motivated by a desire to reach customers with something new a jump ahead of competitors, or possibly to forestall expensive overtime costs when production runs late, or even to avoid the premium charges for super-fast delivery services on last-minute orders and shipments.

The accompanying chart shows the time patterns for the average workings of major links within the fashion industry.

Timing of Product Development within the Fashion Industry

Activity	Length of Time before Consumer Buying Season
Development of new fiber variants	4 to 5 years (continuous)
Development of fabrics by fiber companies and mills	2 years
Color prediction at fiber level	2 years
Development of new fabric lines by textile producers	1 year
Apparel companies shop fabric lines	10 months to 1 year
Development of apparel designs by apparel producers	7 to 9 months
Lines shown to retail buyers	3 to 6 months
Production of garments by manufacturers	2 to 5 months
Retail selling season	Before and at the beginning of the actual selling season

THE CONSUMPTION OF FASHION GOODS_____

The fashion industries, like most other consumer goods industries in the United States today, have a productive capacity beyond what the public actually needs. At the same time, most consumers have incomes in excess of what their households require for such absolute necessities as food and shelter. This combination of ample productive capacity and ample discretionary spending power means that consumers have a wide choice as to how they will spend their money. A woman, for example, does not merely choose between one dress or another; she may also choose between a new dress and a new household appliance. Likewise, a man may choose between one jacket or another, or he may choose between a jacket and some new golf clubs.

The Role of the Consumer

The role of the ultimate consumer in the fashion business is an important one and, in the final analysis, controlling. This is a fact recognized by all successful fashion professionals. Ordinarily the part that consumers play is a passive one. People do not actually demand new products and designs of which they have little or no knowledge; neither do they demand change. Their individual and collective power is exercised in the selections they make, on the one hand, and in their refusals to buy, on the other. It is by their acceptance or rejection that they influence the goods that will be presented for their favor and even the methods of presentation.

The controlling role of the consumer is not unique to the fashion industry.

Selected Components of Consumer Expenditures (Add 000,000)

| Year | Total | Clothing and Accessories | | Shoes and Other Footwear |
		Men's and Boys'	Women's and Children's	
1970	$ 52,396	$15,539	28,794	$ 8,063
1975	70,021	20,807	38,519	10,695
1980	102,831	30,142	56,909	15,780
1989	200,100	55,900	115,100	29,100

SOURCE: Department of Commerce, Bureau of Economic Analysis.

Every business that serves the public has to guide its operations in light of consumer demand. The fashion industry, however, moves at a fast tempo. The rewards of success are great and the cost of failure correspondingly high. As the late Dr. Paul H. Nystrom put it:

> Consumer demand is the guide to intelligent production and merchandising. . . . A knowledge of the fundamental facts of what consumers want and why, is clearly of the first importance . . . to those who plan the policies, design the product, determine the price lines, prepare the advertising and sales promotion, sell the goods and make the collections, in fact all who deal with the problems of the consumer.[4]

The Power of Fashion

Few words in any language have as many different implications as the word *fashion*. To the layman, it implies a mysterious force that makes a particular style of dress or behavior acceptable in one year but quite the reverse in another. Economists view fashion as an element of artificial **obsolescence** that impels people to replace articles that still retain much of their original usefulness even though the new articles may not greatly differ from the old ones. To sociologists, fashion represents an expression of social interaction and of status seeking[5]; psychiatrists find indications of sex impulses in patterns of dress.[6] But whatever fashion may mean to others, it represents billions of dollars in sales to the group of enterprises concerned with the production and distribution of apparel and accessories. As one fashion scholar said, "Everything that matters, everything that gives their trade its nature and place in the world must be ascribed to fashion."[7]

Fashion, in and of itself, does not create consumer purchasing power, but wherever there is such purchasing power, there is interest in fashion. In times past, when purchasing power was concentrated among the wealthy few, they alone pursued fashion. Today, with widespread ability to spend, the great masses of people follow fashion, and thus fashion determines both the character and the direction of consumption. Although such factors as price, durability, convenience of use, and quality of workmanship are also of concern to the consumer, they mean relatively little unless the purchased articles are also clearly identified with the prevailing fashions. Fashion is also an important factor in the replacement market for such utilitarian items as household goods; it is often more important than wear and tear in motivating discard and replacement of furniture, kitchen utensils, and automobiles, for example. Businesses that serve the consumer succeed when they go with the fashion, but are doomed to fail whenever they go against the tide.

Socioeconomic Factors That Affect the Consumption of Fashion

The growth of the fashion business in the United States directly reflects the vast social and economic changes that have taken place in this country's lifetime. As one noted social commentator has expressed it, "Few societies in history have been as fashion conscious as the American, and there have been few in which styles and clothes changed so often. Students of human society know that changing fashions are an index of social change within a society."[8]

Keeping up with the changing social and economic trends is not a one-time or a once-in-a-while research project for fashion professionals. Instead, it is necessarily as much a part of their day-to-day activity as keeping sales and inventory records. The fashion industry is aware of the various social and economic factors that influence the needs and wants of consumers; it is aware also that, as consumers react to these influences, their fashion needs and wants change. The industry is constantly fine-tuning its awareness of these changes and its responses to them.

The consumer market is the source of all ultimate demand. Significant changes that take place in the consumer market have had and will continue to have significant impact on the fashion industries. For example, the age mix of the population, both present and projected into the future, has a definite bearing on the current fashions and on those to come. The baby boom that followed World War II gave us the rise of the "Yuppies" — or young, upwardly mobile urban professionals — who became a major economic and fashion force in the 1980s. It is among their numbers that we find the strong thrust of women into the work force, and especially into executive positions. This trend not only changed the status of women but has also affected the way they dress. By the same token, the young men of this age group increasingly participated in home and leisure activities, and accordingly adopted more varied styles in dress. Earlier generations, it is true, had working wives and husbands who participated in home activities, but not in the numbers or with the impact of this group.

In virtually no aspect of life does the United States of the 1990s resemble that of the 1960s. The consuming population in general is growing older and the 35–54 age group is growing more rapidly than any other U.S. population group. Family life has been turned inside out by the rush of married women, many of them mothers, into the work force. Households made up of single individuals, once a rarity, are fairly commonplace today; so are single-parent households, in which the unmarried or divorced parent drops the child off at a day-care center and spends the major part of the day in the business world rather than in the nursery and the kitchen. Customers have changed from the conventional mother-at-home shopping during the week in downtown or sub-urban stores to the working woman, the senior citizen, and the single adult, each with his or her preferences in clothing, food, and lifestyles in general.

America is changing. Nowhere is it more evident than in **demographic** shifts largely wrought by the population bulge created by the "baby boom" following World War II combined with a variety of other social and economic considerations. As society fragments and becomes more diverse, a new con-sumer is emerging with a group of different socioeconomic and geodemogra-phic measurements being developed and applied to better zero in on targeted consumer groups. However, broad demographic trends are vital when viewing future U.S. markets for a wide variety of goods and services. Marketing and media decisions will be heavily influenced by several major demographic shifts perceived to be taking place over the next 20 years.

The statistics of population changes that are presented at the end of this chapter provide an indication of how fashion's customers will change. Ob-viously, the American consumers of today differ vastly from those of yesteryear—just as those of tomorrow, and their fashions, will inevitably differ from those of today.

THE MARKETING OF FASHION_____

Producers of fashion traditionally have been backward in many of the market-ing techniques that have sparked growth in such other industries as, for exam-ple, packaged foods. In recent years, however, there has been a major change in fashion marketing philosophy. Sophisticated research techniques have been applied to the study of consumer wants; emphasis has been put on product development geared to meet these wants; and vast amounts of promotional funds have been spent to establish the identity and enhance the demand for specific brands and designer name products.

These marketing activities take place at all levels of the fashion industry—from the producers of fibers, fabrics, and apparel to the retailers of fashion merchandise. A basic difference is that producers are concerned with what to manufacture, whereas retailers are concerned with what to select and purchase for resale.

The Marketing Concept: Consumer Orientation

To understand the marketing concept, it is only necessary to understand the difference between marketing and selling. Not too many years ago, most indus-tries concentrated primarily on the efficient production of goods, and then relied on "persuasive salesmanship" to move as much of these goods as possible. Such production and selling focuses on the needs of the seller to produce goods and then convert them into money.

Marketing, on the other hand, focuses on the wants of consumers. It begins with first analyzing the preferences and demands of consumers and then producing goods that will satisfy them. This eye-on-the-consumer approach is known as the **marketing concept**, which simply means that instead of trying to sell whatever is easiest to produce or buy for resale, the makers and dealers first endeavor to find out what the consumer wants to buy and then go about making it available for purchase. Every step—design, production, distribution, promotion—is geared to consumer demand.

Much can be done to stimulate that consumer demand, but to do this effectively one must first recognize that fashion itself is a democratic phenomenon: the sellers nominate and the consumers elect. Customers therefore must be perceived as the motivating force behind the marketing process. Without them, there would be no business.

This concept does not imply that business is benevolent or that consumer satisfaction is given priority over profit in a company. There are always two sides to every business transaction—the firm and the customer—and each must be satisfied before trade occurs. Successful merchants and producers, however, recognize that the surest route to profit is through understanding and catering to customers. A stunning example of the importance of catering to the consumer presented itself in mid-1985, when Coca Cola changed the flavor of its drink. The nonacceptance of the new flavor by a significant portion of the public brought about a prompt restoration of the Classic Coke, which was then marketed alongside the new. King Customer ruled!

Market Segmentation: Targeting Consumers

Since no business can be all things to all people, it must select one or a few groups of customers as its target. Everything that follows in the marketing process is then geared to the target group, or market segment. To understand market segmentation, it is first necessary to know what a market is. In general terms, a **market** means a meeting of people for the purpose of buying and selling. Such a meeting is not necessarily physical or personal. Specifically, a market for fashion merchandise refers to people with money (some more, some less) and with an inclination to buy fashion-related goods. Fortunately, the potential consumer fashion market in the United States is so large that there is enough business for a company to operate successfully by satisfying even a small percentage of that market.

A *segment* is any part of a whole market. According to the American Marketing Association, **market segmentation** means dividing the heterogeneous market into smaller customer divisions that have certain relatively homogeneous characteristics the firm can satisfy.[9] The segment will consist of a group of customers (not necessarily physically in one community) who react in a similar way to a given set of market stimuli. The segment may be based on such characteristics in common as income level (high, middle, upper middle, etc.), lifestyle (suburban, city), fashion preferences (*avant garde* or classic), special interests (jogging, aerobic dancing, disco), sizes (extra large, petite, junior, miss), occupation (career executive, homemaker), and so on. The potential categories are many more than can be illustrated here, and the kinds and types within each category are also more numerous than our necessarily limited examples.

Usually, a market segment includes a combination of two or more of such characteristics as were mentioned here. The individuals who constitute a segment may differ in other respects, but they have a commonality of interest and wants that makes each one a potential customer for the business concern that is courting that particular market. A market segment can even be large and powerful enough that producers and retailers prepare whole new categories of clothing for it. For example, in the 1980s as the baby boomers born in the 1950s and early 1960s entered the work force, they created a market segment for executive career apparel.

If a business, either manufacturing or retailing, is large enough, it may cater to several different market segments at once, creating separate divisions or departments for each. An obvious example is the special shops, both free-standing and within department stores, for "big is beautiful" women and for extra-tall, extra-large men.

It must be realized that segments do not always remain static. One of the costliest errors a business can make is to take its market for granted. Economic and social conditions change; competitors develop new market strategies; new products arise and affect consumer purchasing patterns. The only way for a business to expand or even maintain its market position is to keep up with, and even ahead of, such changes. Products, services, and pricing policies must continuously be reevaluated in terms of changing market influences.

The need to target consumer groups is threefold: (1) to identify consumer characteristics most suited to the goals and capabilities of the firm; (2) to provide a basis for formulating and, if necessary, adjusting the firm's policies and products to satisfy these characteristics; and (3) to pinpoint consumer characteristics that affect patterns of buying behavior.

Market segmentation in itself will not ensure success in the fashion business, since it is only one of a combination of many factors in the equation. Not to segment, however, is to choose a sure way to failure. The principle of segmentation is based on the fact that people are different and that, to make the point again, no one company can be all things to all people. A choice must be made as to which segment of the market a particular business or division or department can most effectively serve.

As a great fashion retailer once put it: "Each store has to edit and present what best fits its own audience. Fashion is not the same for every store. Hot numbers in one store can fall flat in the competitor's."[10]

PENETRATION OF IMPORTS_____

The growth in American consumer expenditures for apparel has not provided a proportionate growth for the U.S. apparel manufacturing industry. Beginning in the 1970s, imported apparel has been increasingly accounting for a rising share of consumer expenditures. As an example, during the 1980s imports increased at an annual rate of 12 percent, as compared to an increase in consumer apparel spending of about 1 percent per year.[11] It is quite obvious from these two divergent growth rates that not only do Americans respond favorably to foreign-made goods but imports reduce the share of the consumer markets that the domestic industry holds.

Although the garment industry shares many problems with other import-troubled U.S. industries, its relatively simple technology and smaller capital

Projected Domestic Production, Imports, and Consumption of Apparel

1982–1995

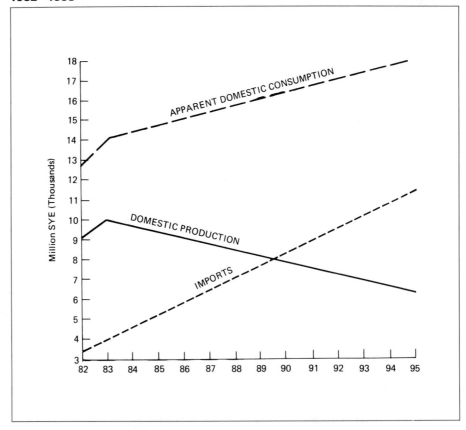

SOURCE: U.S. Commerce Department.

requirements coupled with its labor-intensive dependence on low-skilled workers make it particularly vulnerable to imports from low-wage foreign countries. The major impact of imported apparel is stiff price competition.

Although it is generally agreed that international trade is in the long-range interests of our country and of the world, the prospect of further dislocations due to increased foreign competition is not pleasant for the industry to contemplate. The government makes efforts to respond to the needs of the apparel industry by regulating the flow of imports, but it is limited by foreign policy considerations and the possibility of other countries' retaliating against what they consider American protectionism.

Since the subject of imports is dealt with in further detail throughout this book, it is sufficient to state here that this increasing degree of foreign penetration into the American fashion business has created an economic problem for all segments of the U.S. industry, which it has been unable to offset by corresponding increases in exports.

FEDERAL LEGISLATION AFFECTING THE FASHION BUSINESS

Under the American systems of government and economy, businesses enjoy certain rights and freedoms. Although business in America originally operated in a *laissez-faire* economy (i.e., noninterference by government), the emergence and abuses of trusts and monopolies in the late nineteenth century, which minimized competition and made it difficult for small business to survive, created the need for regulation. Two basic categories of federal legislation affect the fashion industry: (1) laws that regulate competition and (2) labeling laws designed to protect consumers.

Federal Laws Regulating Competition

Sherman Anti-Trust Act—1890: This was our first law enacted to restrain unfair competition. It outlawed monopolies and practices that restrained competition.

Clayton Act—1914: This law reinforced the Sherman Act by spelling out some specific restraints pertaining to price fixing, price discrimination, and interlocking directorates.

Federal Trade Commission (FTC) Act—1914: This law created the **FTC** to serve as a "policing" agency to enforce the Sherman and Clayton acts, to investigate alleged unfair methods of competition, to conduct hearings, and to issue cease-and-desist orders. This law was amended by the Wheeler–Lea Act of 1938 and gave the FTC authority to prohibit fake advertising and made it an additional offense to injure the general public.

Robinson–Patman Act—1936: According to this law, which was aimed primarily at giant retailers, large purchasers of goods may not be given so large a discount as to give them monopolistic advantage. This act makes price discrimination between purchasers of like grade or quantity illegal (e.g., it outlawed "phony" advertising allowances).

Celler-Kefauver Act—1950: This law made it illegal to eliminate competition by creating a monopoly through the merger of two or more companies.

Product Labeling Laws to Protect Consumers

In addition to regulating business to promote competition, the federal government has enacted various product labeling laws intended to protect consumers by requiring that the materials used be listed, that they be safe and accurately identified, that the percentage of natural and synthetic fibers be shown, and that clear instructions to consumers about the care and maintenance of articles be provided. Examples of these labeling laws are as follows:

Wool Products Labeling Act—1939
Fur Products Labeling Act—1951
Flammable Fabrics Act—1953
Textile Fiber Products Identification Act—1966
Fair Packaging and Labeling Act—1966
Care Labeling of Textile Wearing Apparel Act—1972

Demographics that Affect the Fashion Industry

Expected Trends in U.S. Population by Major Apparel Markets, 1990, 1995, 2000, and 2005 (Figures in millions)

Markets		1990	1995	2000	2005	Percentage Change 1990–2005
Infants	Ages 0–2	11.0	10.5	10.0	9.9	−10%
Children's						
Boys'	Ages 3–7	9.5	9.5	9.1	8.7	−8%
Girls'	Ages 3–7	9.0	9.1	8.6	8.4	−7%
Boys & Girls						
Boys'	Ages 8–17	17.7	19.0	19.5	19.1	+8%
Girls'	Ages 8–14	12.0	12.8	12.9	12.4	+3%
Adult Total						
Male	18+	89.4	93.2	97.6	102.0	+14%
Female	15+	101.8	106.0	110.6	115.1	+13%
Adult Markets by Age						
Male	Ages 18–24	13.2	12.3	12.8	13.6	+3%
	25–34	22.1	20.6	18.7	18.1	−18%
	35–44	18.8	21.1	21.9	20.5	+9%
	45–54	12.4	15.3	18.3	20.6	+66%
	55–64	10.1	10.1	11.6	14.,3	+42%
	65+	12.8	13.8	14.3	14.9	+16%
Female	Ages 15–24	17.8	17.2	18.1	19.0	+7%
	25–34	21.8	20.4	18.4	17.9	−18%
	35–44	19.1	21.2	22.0	20.5	+7%
	45–54	13.1	16.0	18.9	21.0	+60%
	55–64	11.3	11.2	12.6	15.4	+36%
	65+	18.7	20.0	20.6	21.3	+14%
Total All Ages		250.4	260.1	268.3	275.6	+10%

SOURCES: U.S. Department of Commerce; Bureau of the Census.

Coming Soon: Age of the Aged
As the old get older, the percentage of young gets dramatically smaller.

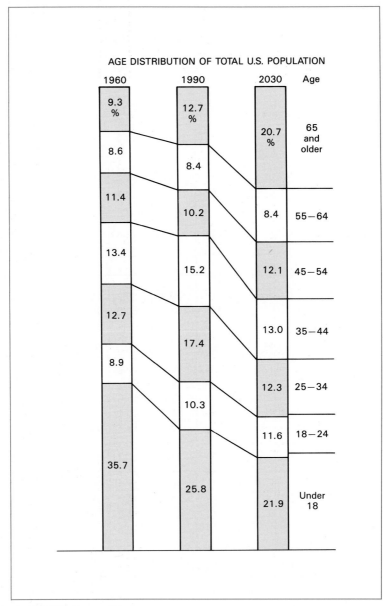

SOURCE: U.S. Census Bureau.

50 and Over, a Growing Force

Line shows projection to the year 2020 for the number of people in the U.S. 50 years old and older, starting with an estimate for July, 1986, in millions. Bars show the percent of the population 50 years old and older.

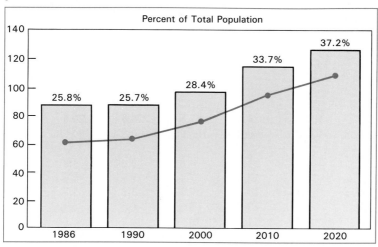

Percent of Total Population

SOURCE: U.S. Department of Commerce; U.S. Census Bureau.

Projected Growth in Households

In thousands.

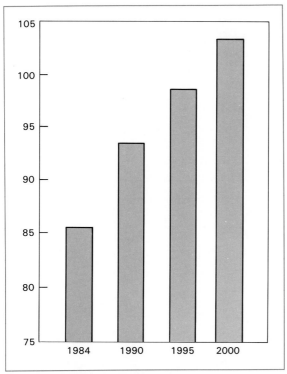

SOURCE: The Dynamics of Americas Housing, Hughes/Sternlieb.

Projection of Households by Income and Age: 2000 (Income in 1984 dollars)

| Income Class | Total | Age of Head | | | | | |
		Under 25	25–34	35–44	45–54	55–64	65 and over
		Projection: 2000					
Total Households (millions).......	102.4	4.3	17.5	24.0	20.6	13.8	22.2
Percent Distribution	100.0%	100.0%	100.0%	100.0%	100.0%	100.0%	100.0%
Under $5,000.....	6.1	11.1	4.8	3.8	4.4	6.2	10.0
$5,000–$10,000...	10.4	16.0	7.4	5.5	6.0	9.3	22.0
$10,000–$15,000..	9.1	14.8	7.7	5.5	5.7	8.5	16.6
$15,000–$20,000..	8.4	13.8	8.5	6.0	6.1	8.1	12.3
$20,000–$25,000..	8.4	11.7	10.1	7.2	6.6	8.0	9.7
$25,000–$30,000..	8.1	9.3	10.6	8.5	7.0	7.9	6.7
$30,000–$35,000..	7.4	6.8	9.9	8.3	6.9	7.0	5.1
$35,000–$40,000..	6.5	4.8	8.6	7.8	6.7	6.3	3.9
$40,000–50,000...	10.8	6.3	13.1	14.1	12.4	10.8	5.0
$50,000–$60,000..	8.2	3.0	8.7	11.3	10.6	8.5	3.1
$60,000–$75,000..	7.4	1.3	6.1	10.3	11.9	7.2	2.3
$75,000 and over..	9.1	1.1	4.6	11.7	15.8	12.1	3.4

SOURCES: U.S. Department of Commerce; The Conference Board.

Distribution of Families and Income by Income Class: 1990
Based on constant 1980 dollars.

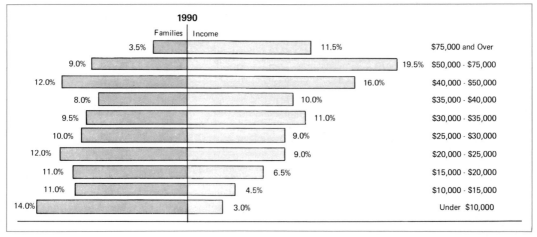

SOURCE: U.S. Census Bureau.

Composition of the Labor Force, 1995–2000

Millions of persons.

	1995	2000
Male, Total	70.4	73.1
16–19	4.0	4.5
20–24	6.9	7.0
25–34	18.3	16.6
35–44	19.4	20.1
45–54	13.7	16.3
55–64	6.4	7.2
65 and over	1.6	1.4
Female, Total	61.2	65.6
16–19	3.9	4.4
20–24	6.5	6.7
25–34	16.0	15.1
35–44	17.1	18.4
45–54	11.6	14.2
55–64	4.9	5.7
65 and over	1.2	1.0

SOURCE: U.S. Department of Commerce; U.S. Census Bureau.

As the Pool of Young Workers Shrinks, Women will Fill the Gap

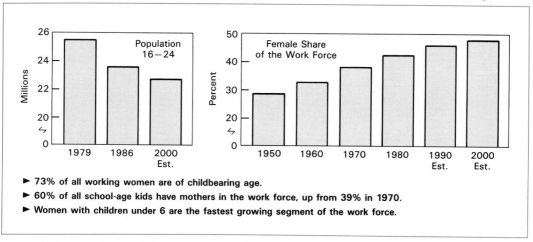

► 73% of all working women are of childbearing age.
► 60% of all school-age kids have mothers in the work force, up from 39% in 1970.
► Women with children under 6 are the fastest growing segment of the work force.

SOURCE: U.S. Census Bureau; U.S. Department of Labor.

Who's Minding the Children?

Even with the sharp rise in working mothers, most children are still cared for at home — their own or someone else's.

Day Care

Who looks after children under age 5 while their mothers work?

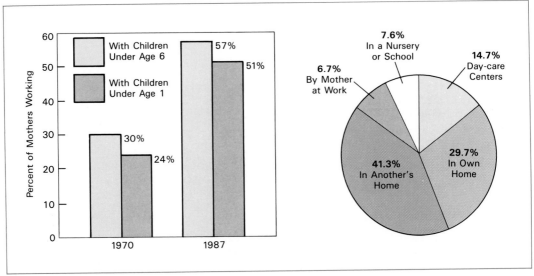

SOURCE: Childcare, Inc.

SOURCE: U.S. Census Bureau.

Comparison of Female Population Growth between Ages 14–34 and 35–54 "Prime Spending" Groups, from 1995–2000

Year	Total "Prime Spending" Population	Ages 14–34 Number	Ages 14–34 % of Total	Ages 35–54 Number	Ages 35–54 % of Total
		Population			
1995	76,498	39,260	51.3	37,238	46.9
2000	79,356	38,463	48.5	40,893	51.5

Years	Total "Prime Spending" Population Total Period	Total "Prime Spending" Population Compound Annual	Ages 14–34 Total Period	Ages 14–34 Compound Annual	Ages 35–54 Total Period	Ages 35–54 Compound Annual
			Rate of Change			
1995–2000	3.7	0.7	−2.1	−0.4	9.8	1.9

SOURCES: U.S. Department of Commerce, Bureau of the Census.

Readings

Consumer demand is the guide to successful production and marketing of fashion merchandise. Throughout the fashion industry, all eyes are on meeting the consumer's wants and needs.

Welcome to the 21st Century, Ready or Not

A changing consumer market has led to the creation of many new market segments. In order to succeed, individual companies must focus on specific segments and create specialized niche businesses.

What Is Perfume but Water and a Bit of Essence?

The ticket of admission to a select "community of customers" is the wearing of the correct designer name. Pierre Cardin was the first renowned designer to capitalize on this trend.

Welcome to the 21st Century, Ready or Not

by Herbert Blueweiss

On the calendar Dec. 31 was just another move for the apparel industry from one year to the next. Actually, retailers and apparel/textile suppliers have already been beamed into the 21st Century . . . ready or not.

The sense of being transposed into a new time frame is proving quite disturbing to the business community. But then anything that changes the status quo is upsetting, especially for those settled very comfortably into a way of doing business that has varied very little over the years.

As shocking as many of the changes may appear to be, they should not be surprising. The first signs of the old order's breaking up in men's wear began in the mid-1960s . . . when the mod explosion created the mainfloor fashion customer.

That customer may not have been sophisticated and chic, but his importance was less in how he scored in taste than in the fact that his shopping patterns created the twilight zone for the white shirt-blue suit syndrome.

Fashion on a broad, mass scale . . . propelled by sportswear . . . expanded the role of department stores, and made them a major channel of distribution in men's wear, challenging the position held by specialty stores.

An all-too-familiar pattern ensued and change began to accelerate at an ever faster pace. Customers began to follow their own instincts instead of those of designers . . . and designers began to pay attention to that brand-new concept of "lifestyles."

Retailers went on an expansion binge and in the process lost the loyalty of their customers . . . (they also lost control of inventory and service). Customers had more stores and more merchandise to choose from than ever before.

The retail scene began to change dramatically as did consumer shopping patterns . . . each interacting with the other. As changes intensified, the fact became inescapable that retailing and its suppliers were being restructured into a shape and form hitherto unforeseen.

Today there are many believers whose eyes have been opened by the changes . . . probably very few who are not. And the process goes on.

Now that changes and restructuring are commonplace in the industry, there is a universal need to know where the industry is heading. This became apparent during the past year, with the big questions revolving around fashion and distribution . . . what to make, what to buy, where to sell it, for which consumer.

Oddly enough, much of this thinking and its impact on the marketplace had been telegraphed to us some time ago.

In 1984, Donald O'Brien, then senior vice-president of marketing at Jordan Marsh in Boston, described to an NRMA audience how and why J.M. moved from a staid, MOR (middle of the road) department store to one that was strong on fashion, was exciting and was a desirable store to shop. The move was motivated by a shift in population in the New England area . . . as basic industries moved away . . . and a

Source: Daily News Record, Fairchild Publications, January 2, 1989. Reprinted by permission.

consequent loss in share of market. High-tech industries moved in, bringing with them younger and more sophisticated customers, and Jordan Marsh shifted its marketing and merchandising focus.

In December 1986, Vern Page of Sears Roebuck, speaking at an AAMA seminar, said, "Up to the middle 1960s there was a predictability to consumer patterns. There was a singular value system with a high level of conformity. Terms like 'brand' and 'store loyalty' were commonplace.

"A target household could be described confidently: married couple, one or two children, suburban home, two cars, single income, with the husband working.

"Today, less than 10 percent of American households meet those criteria. Today's shopper is, in fact, many different shoppers as a result of the dynamic changes in the demographics of our society."

And more than 10 years ago, Stanley Marcus, former chairman of Neiman-Marcus, observed in an interview, "In many cases, department stores have become mere depots for manufacturers, with little ability to tailor stocks to meet the requirements of individual communities . . . Any objective observer visiting a modern shopping center where the major stores of the community are in close juxtaposition must get a sense of fatigue from seeing virtually the same goods and colors and textures in store after store. Exclusivity in a mass-production market, even when legally possible, is hard to come by."

Try that one on and see what conflict it forecasts . . . and confirms . . . in a highly fragmented consumer market.

And just last month at the AAMA marketing seminar, Peter Thigpen, in his presentation, brought it all up to date with his description of how Levi Strauss is changing its approach to the marketplace. Thigpen, president of Levi's TJC (The Jeans Company), is soon to become head of a new domestic operations unit at Levi's.

Suggesting going back before taking a look forward, Thigpen said, "At Levi's, we look back with a great feeling and nostalgia at the halcyon days of the late 1960s and 1970s."

Showing a slide, he pointed out, "This is Woodstock . . . 350,000 typical customers, typically doing their thing. No complication here. Two prime colors . . . indigo blue and flesh. Half the population was under 25 and busy being uniformly different. . . . It was also before cable, and there was network TV enabling us to get the same message to the broadest possible audience."

Again, a demonstration with slides, and Thigpen went on, "The biggest problem for us was how to get more denim and more sewing machines. The concentration was not on how to sell more but on how to make more. The complexity was not in marketing, certainly not in customer relations."

After recalling what that period brought, including the price wars of 1976 and the growth of specialty stores such as the Gap, he emphasized the changes taking place brought about by many demographic factors like diversity of the work force, aging of the baby boomers, increases in leisure and entertainment options.

He noted there is now a declining peer group mentality toward clothing, while the age and racial composition of the population are changing.

"While 18- to 24-year-olds will continue to decline until the year 2000, 18- to 24-year-old Hispanics will increase 40 percent in the work force, and by 2015 Hispanics will surpass blacks.

"How do we market to such a diverse society and variety of consumer segments?"

When Peter Thigpen described measures taken by Levi Strauss to make the company compatible with demographic changes under way, the AAMA marketing audience broke into spirited applause as the new ads were run through on the screen.

Thigpen, head of a new operations unit at Levi's, was speaking at AAMA's annual marketing seminar last month, introducing "new age" concepts that may very well be guideposts, in one way or another, for apparel executives as they proceed through the present and into the future.

"There is no homogeneity left (in the marketplace)," said Thigpen, "and Maginot Line marketing fights the last war, and will be outflanked with flexible target marketing in the future.

"Marketers who recognize the explosion in diversity . . . in consumers, in media and in the means available to connect the two . . . will win what promises to be an increasingly sophisticated and professionally fought battle in the future."

During his talk, he spotted some TV ads prepared for Levi's that reflect the new thinking. The first is aimed at the Spanish-speaking population, which Thigpen had already demonstrated will continue to be an important source of new customers.

Levi's has already begun marketing to this customer group in its advertising, and the TV spot shown was prepared for six cities, entirely in Spanish, with young Hispanics dancing and singing . . . wearing Levi's jeans.

In its marketing analysis, Levi's learned "that we need each of our consumer targets and we need to speak to them directly . . . in forms that are relevant to them. But with all the diverse audiences we have to reach, we still have to maintain some sense of Levi's-ness. Our marketing people have worked with our agency to create messages that have a feeling of unity despite the diversity.

Thigpen showed the TV spots that project this mood, and noted that in the 1970s, network TV "allowed us to market our message to the broadest audience in a homogeneous market . . . but now cable, in 57 percent of homes and projected to reach 87 percent by mid-1990s, allows us to use rifles not shotguns.

"Once identifying the consumers we want, it's easy to locate them in the US . . . by city, by neighborhood. We can focus on existing stores because besides knowing who we want and where they live, we also know product style preferences."

It can reach the point, he added, that "we're able to tell them individually where what we hope they want can be located."

In still another talk, demonstrating a major apparel company's efforts to bring its image into greater conformity with the dynamics of the marketplace, Harris Hester, president and CEO of Cluett, Peabody, showed an Arrow TV spot that drew laughs and cheers . . . "and awards at Cannes."

It showed a group of choirboys and young men in dress shirts transposed into sport shirt wearers as the music changes and the beat is stepped up. "It increased awareness of our dress shirts, but did nothing for our sportswear," Hester commented wryly.

Hester also pointed out that methods like Levi's have increasingly made selling an executive decision.

"Fewer and fewer road salesmen can be effective, considering the world we live in. Executive selling has become a way of life, and key marketing is driving the business."

Observations of both Thigpen and Hester mirror some of the forces at work that are leading the entire supply side and all retail channels of distribution into new directions. For suppliers particularly . . . who are a step or two removed from consumer market fragmentation . . . these are very difficult times.

If focus and target marketing are appropriate tools for manufacturers as well as retailers, then the manufacturer with the one right product would be most successful . . . until the product falls out of favor. Unless, of course, the resource is prepared to follow up with winner after winner . . . a very demanding procedure.

Manufacturers whose images have been established in the explosive growth category of sportswear are going to have a less difficult access to the market than those whose profiles have been built on the dress classifications of tailored clothing and dress furnishings.

Retailing, especially volume retailing, is much more tuned in to the faster-turning sportswear market. And faster turns come out of the rapid fashion changes that are the basis for ready-to-wear in men's wear.

Manufacturers and retailers alike are shifting course in response to fragmentation of the marketplace and changing taste levels. In the process, the relationship itself, between suppliers and store, is undergoing change.

What at one time was an easygoing, arms-around-each-other relationship . . . and that's ancient history now . . . has turned into one that at best is at arm's length. In fact, mega-retailing is creating mega-problems . . . even for manufacturers who might like to consider themselves as mega-suppliers.

Just when signs indicate that Quick Response has brought a more cooperative mood between store and supplier, the harsher aspects of the relationship have surfaced. Business pressures have forced many of the big store groups to promote significantly beyond plan, and gross margins in many cases have been depressed.

According to reports from some suppliers, stores have been asking resources to help them recover excess promotional costs and help bring gross margins back to plan.

This is not an industrywide condition, but enough of it exists to disturb manufacturers who themselves are under severe pressures to maintain their own profit margins.

What Is Perfume but Water and a Bit of Essence?

by Richard C. Morais

Mort Sahl summed it all up: "Ask a Californian who he is and he points to his car." That was in the Sixties. Today the Californian—or any trendy person anywhere in the world—might just as well point to his underwear. Or to his frying pan. Thank you, Pierre Cardin.

In 1950 Pierre Cardin, an Italian-born Frenchman, founded his own haute couture house. Nearly bankrupt a half-dozen years later, he had—rather, he adapted— a brilliant marketing idea. Why limit the market for designer-name clothing to the handful of women who could afford the then princely sum of $500 or more for a dress? Why not slap his name on off-the-rack, ready-to-wear dresses? Why not license factories to use his name and his designs? The idea wasn't original. Cardin launched his career at Christian Dior, where he had witnessed the first licensing agreement in 1949. Wasn't the idea of a ready-made "designer" dress a contradiction in terms? The prestigious Chambre Syndicale de la Couture Parisienne, the governing body of the 23 haute couture houses, certainly thought it was an outrage. In 1959 it expelled Cardin from its ranks, but it couldn't stop the trend he had started. Walk through any store anywhere in the world and try to find clothing that does not bear a designer label; it takes some doing. "Cardin," says Kurt Barnard, publisher of Barnard's Retail Marketing Report, "started this whole designer craze." Today, mass-produced items ranging from men's underpants to frying pans, penknives, alarm clocks and luggage bear designer labels, and people happily pay a few pennies or many dollars extra for the comfort of those labels.

At 65, the man who started it all basks in the rosy glow of fame and an estimated personal income of $20 million or so a year. FORBES interviewed him recently in his ostentatiously modest offices at No. 59, rue du Faubourg St. Honoré.

Let others have sleek, expensive-looking offices. Despite the fashionable address, Cardin's offices are dingy, with threadbare carpets and smudged walls. His own dress makes a similar statement. He is modishly attired in a luxurious cashmere jacket and silk foulard, but his loafers are stained, unpolished and scuffed. Both office and dress suggest a man who does things to please himself, the rest of the world be damned. How rich are you we ask? Cardin pulls his overcoat collar over his face, almost as if he's trying to protect himself from the questioning. "I never count what I earn," he says.

The facts suggest that the latter statement isn't entirely true, but Cardin is careful to present himself as an artist as well as a moneymaker. With a dégagé demeanor of an aging boulevardier, Cardin slouches in a circular foam chair he designed back in the 1970s. "I have the most important name in the world," says Cardin in a monotone reminiscent of Truman Capote's "I give my name only to the best products." Allowing his name to be used, he adds, "is like a queen or a president honoring a cocktail reception."

Such deliberate immodesty goes hand in hand with a shrewd business sense. With 840 licenses to use his name in effect worldwide, Cardin has far more agreements than Christian Dior (300 licenses), Yves St. Laurent (200) or Calvin Klein (12). In 98 countries, from Argentina to the Soviet Union, the PC initials confer status for everything from belts to bidets, from fragrances to frying pans. Under the Maxim's of Paris name, which he bought in 1981, Cardin also peddles hotels, crystal and dinner jackets.

Taken together, Cardin-inscribed products gross around $1.2 billion at wholesale, perhaps $2 billion or more at retail. From those sales, Cardin receives royalties of around $75 million. Businesses he owns outright bring his total estimated annual revenues to around $125 million. Cardin's overhead is small in relation to his take: a small licensing staff, some designers, cramped offices.

Although the Chambre Syndicale de la Couture Parisienne has now accepted him back, and although many of its members now compete with him in mass merchandising, he is still resented in the trade. "The difference between us and Cardin," says Geoffroy de Seymes, Christian Dior's international director of licensing, "is that Dior never sells its name. We negotiate a creation and only when the licensee understands the creation do we give the licensee a contract."

To which Cardin snaps: "It's snobbish stupidity. Why am I bad if I sell a frying pan, but if I sell perfume I'm an aristocrat? What is perfume but water and a bit of essence?"

That's a good question. Another is this: Why do consumers around the world happily pay extra for apparel, cigarettes, fragrances and frying pans simply because the products come emblazoned with a designer's initials? Historian Daniel J. Boorstin, now the Librarian of Congress Emeritus, helped us to understand the labeling phenomenon 25 years ago with the publication of his concise book *The Decline of Radicalism: Reflections on America Today.*

If Cardin got there first in a business sense, Boorstin was among the first to understand how the spread of affluence and modern communications were changing the world. Once upon a time, Boorstin wrote, people thought of themselves in ethnic, political and religious terms. Sample: I am a middlewestern Republican Presbyterian. Or: I am a southern Baptist Democrat of Scotch-Irish descent. And so on. They still do. But superimposed upon that older sense of identity is a new sense of identity born of the consumer age: I am a white-wine drinking, Rolex-watch-wearing Volvo driver. In such a world where bourgeois tastes transcend national and cultural boundaries, use of designer names is a natural. I am a Pierre Cardin type. Or a Ralph Lauren type. I identify with their style. I am with-it.

Boorstin spoke of "consumption communities" replacing the older communities. "A consumption community," he wrote, "consists of people who have a feeling of shared well being, shared risks, common interests, and common concerns that come from consuming the same kinds of objects." Porsche drivers, FORBES readers, Gucci loafer-wearers — these are just a few of many thousands of consumption communities.

The nice thing about consumption communities is that they are democratic. Anyone can join. You don't need family connections or diplomas from the right schools to drink Chivas Regal or drive a Mercedes or collect art. All you need is the right amount of money.

"The designer label," Boorstin says, "is the application of the concept of celebrity to the consumption community. That is, a designer label is a community of consumers on whom some of the celebrity of the name rubs off."

And so it is that underwear by Jockey or Hanes is just underwear. But underwear by Pierre Cardin or Perry Ellis is a personal statement: I am an avant-garde fellow like Pierre. I am proud to associate with like-minded people, and I don't mind paying extra for the privilege.

For Cardin all this is more than just an academic concept. He wrings it for all it's worth. He receives a royalty of between 7% and 10% of the wholesale price on clothes and 3% to 7% on everything else.

And what can Cardin do for his licensees? Consider Taroma Inc., a subsidiary of the $180 million (revenues) Swiss tobacco company, F.J. Burrus. The family-owned company, with a 23% hold on the Swiss tobacco market, decided in 1982 to export its two market-leader cigarettes, Select and Parisienne. The international cigarette business is cut-throat, and Taroma's management realized it needed something special to get the brands moving. Rather than go to the enormous expense of trying to create an internationally famous brand name, Taroma's executives signed a licensing agreement for the Cardin name. Like all Cardin's licensees, Taroma had to guarantee minimum annual royalties.

"We needed a door opener," says Francois Janet, Taroma's managing director. It seems to have worked: Smokers in the Pierre Cardin consumption communities responded. "Now that we have the distributors' attention," says Janet, "we then ask whether they want one of our middle-range products." This year Janet expects to sell 200 million of the premium-priced Pierre Cardin cigarettes. Cardin's reward? Around $225,000 annually — and Cardin bears no capital risk.

"Designer" appeal is almost universal today. Cardin first visited Japan in 1957. At that time it took 48 hours to fly from Paris to Tokyo (versus 14 hours today), and the Japanese were still digging out from the war's destruction. Today sales of Cardin-licensed products are as high in Japan as they are in the U.S. or Europe.

Cardin discovered the world in good part because he was losing out in Paris. Cardin's heyday as a designer rather than as a licenser and businessman was in the 1960s. The world gasped at his space age 3-D shift, astronaut men's look and "white breasts" dress. He launched the first designer men's line in 1960. He was also the first postwar designer to move aggressively into products unrelated to fashion. In 1970 he designed his own line of furniture.

By the 1970s, however, Paris had found new darlings—designers like Kenzo and Claude Montana. So Cardin packed his bags and headed abroad, to less advanced countries, where the middle classes were growing fast but where designers had scarcely penetrated. To Paraguay he went, to Korea, Cyprus and Venezuela. Today 40% of Cardin's business is done outside Europe, the U.S. and Japan. Says Cardin, "I never go where oil has already been discovered."

Cardin's kind of oil is only just being discovered in the communist countries. Cardin first approached the Soviets under Andropov. Since then he has spent about $10 million wooing party bosses, even bringing the glasnost rock opera *Junon & Avos* to his Paris theater. In 1986, after some well-publicized kissing of Raisa Gorbachev's well-manicured hand, Cardin closed a deal that already is bringing him $180,000 in royalties quarterly from the Soviets. "The Soviet Union," says Cardin, "could become one of our biggest markets."

In 1978 Cardin shocked China's top party chiefs with a closed-door fashion show. Today he gives shows to thousands of Chinese, in stadiums. Cardin spent his

own money opening a Maxim's of Paris in Beijing in 1983. All in all, he has dropped some $20 million developing China. "My name is now the most important French name in China," Cardin says. Building on the recognition, Cardin in early 1988 signed an agreement with the Italian apparel firm Grupo GFT, a state-run Chinese company and a Hong Kong firm to manufacture a complete line of Cardin clothes in China.

If the U.S. market is not Cardin's largest, it is nothing to be sniffed at. Cardin products here gross about $240 million at wholesale. Some 32 licensees, including Hartmarx Corp. and Swank Inc., manufacture 54 product categories sold from Brooklyn's Abraham & Straus to Los Angeles' Broadway. U.S. manufacturers pass on about $12 million a year in royalties to Paris and are also obliged to spend close to $10 million a year on local advertising and public relations. That helps keep the Cardin name before the public and retain its value.

Cardin runs his empire by instinct and guesswork. During an 18-hour workday Cardin will jump from signing checks to producing a play, authorizing a perfume ad to threatening a licensee, to sewing on a button. There's no lawyer, no chief financial officer, not even a general manager. No employee has ever seen a business plan or a budget. Cardin's licensing directors can negotiate any deal they want. The only real financial control chez Cardin is the one that counts most: Cardin himself must sign every agreement and check that leaves the house.

According to licensing director Herve Duquesnoy: "Cardin invests on impulse after minimum research. Instead of losing time on two-year studies that cost a lot, he prefers to do it directly and see if it works. When Picasso did a painting, he didn't have a five-year business plan. Cardin is the same."

Critics, most of them competing designers, say that with 840 licenses worldwide Cardin is little more than a legal office, with little concern for, or control over, quality. "The Pierre Cardin name has an enviable recognition factor, but it's threadbare around the edges," agrees Kurt Barnard. "He has so many licenses that the name has become diffused. There's no distinctive individuality, no fingerprint."

Cardin heatedly rejects this view. "I have never lost my couture clients," he insists. But his actions suggest he is concerned. According to licensing director Edouard St. Bris, Cardin cut the number of PC licensees by about 10% in the early 1980s. A few years ago he bought a factory outside Paris so he could control the manufacturing of his new Prestige and Maxim's labels for dresses and suits that retail at between $1,000 and $2,000.

Having created one of the modern world's most franchisable names, can Cardin repeat the trick? So he hopes.

In 1981 Cardin paid Louis Vaudable $20 million for the three-star restaurant Maxim's de Paris, which has been in business since 1893. Where once King Edward VIII and Mrs. Simpson dallied, Japanese tourists can now have their photographs taken and dine on $35 asparagus to the sounds of a strolling violinist. A full dinner with a decent bottle of wine costs about $200 a person. Yet with a staff of 150, Maxim's de Paris earns only about 6% on its sales of about $8 million a year. This profitability hardly seems worth the purchase price — until you remember that included in the price were the perpetual, worldwide rights to the Maxim's name. And who better to know what's in a name than Pierre Cardin?

"Maxim's is like haute couture was 30 years ago," says licensing director Duquesnoy. "High fashion was so expensive that if you didn't have ready-to-wear and accessories you were killed. Same with Maxim's today. You need diversification to earn some returns." And if Cardin wants to keep growing, he probably has no other choice. Boorstin thinks Cardin has so democratized the Pierre Cardin label that it is in danger of losing its prestige value. If everyone has a Cardin pan, why buy one more?

There are now seven Maxim's de Paris restaurants, including franchised ones in London, Mexico City and Tokyo. The failed Maxim's in Brussels has been written off, Rio's is reopening and there are plans for restaurants in Moscow and Bombay. Bombay, with its hungry millions and choking poverty? Why not? Cardin rightly sees India as a fast-developing nation with an already huge and still growing middle class. Cardin's basic idea is to have a super luxury Maxim's presence in every large population center in a country so the name establishes itself locally. Then Cardin moves downscale to introduce Maxim's clothes and food products to the local market.

Maxim's, however, is being kept upmarket from PC products. Cardin is carefully marketing Maxim's licenses for hotels. The Maxim's label is on clothes, accessories, gourmet food and tableware lines but, unlike PC belts and shirts, these are not items you will find at Abraham & Straus.

However, never one to miss a trick, Cardin is also experimenting with a downmarket knockoff of Maxim's, called Minim's. If you don't try, you will never know.

Après Cardin? No one knows. A lifelong bachelor, Cardin has no progeny to whom to pass the business. Cardin told FORBES he realized that it's time for him to reflect on his own mortality, and he vaguely suggested he might even sell the name one day.

What would the name be worth? A quarter of a billion dollars? Probably more. It's a wonderful world.

Endnotes

1. U.S. Department of Commerce, Bureau of Economic Analysis, *Survey of Current Business*, June 1990.
2. "Merchandising and Operating Reports," published annually by National Retail Merchants Association.
3. *U.S. Industrial Outlook*, 1990.
4. Paul H. Nystrom, *Economics of Consumption*. New York: Ronald Press, 1929.
5. See Bernard Barber and Lyle Lobel, "Fashion in Women's Clothes and the American Social System," *Social Forces*, December 1952; and R. K. Merton, *Social Theory and Social Structure.* Glencoe, Ill.: The Free Press, 1949.
6. See Edmund Bergler, *Fashion and the Unconscious*, New York: R. Brunner, 1953, for a provocative work based on his psychoanalysis of many fashion professionals.
7. Dwight E. Robinson, "The Economics of Fashion Demand," *Quarterly Journal of Economics*, Vol. 75, August 1962.
8. Max Lerner, *America as a Civilization.* New York: Simon and Schuster, 1957.
9. American Marketing Association, *Definition of Terms.*
10. "Fashion, the Heartbeat of Retailing," address by Hector Escobosa, at the annual convention of the National Retail Merchants Association, New York, January 7, 1963.
11. Industry Surveys, Standard & Poor's, September 1990; and *Focus: An Economic Profile of the Apparel Industry*, AAMA, September 1990.

Selected Bibliography

Baker, Michael John. *Dictionary of Marketing and Advertising.* New York: Macmillan, 1984.

Calvin, Robert J. Profitable Sales Management and Marketing for Growing Businesses. New York: Van Nostrand Reinhold, 1984.

Category, Philip R. *International Marketing*, 5th ed. Homewood, Ill.: Irvin, 1985.

Doroff, Ralph. *Marketing for the Small Manufacturer.* Englewood Cliffs, N.J.: Prentice-Hall, 1983.

The Fashion Guide. Published by the Fashion Guide, 1989.

Kotler, Philip, and Gary Armstrong. *Principles of Marketing*, 4th ed. Englewood Cliffs, N.J.: Prentice-Hall, 1989.

Langer, Judith. *Consumers in Transition: In-Depth Investigation of Changing Lifestyles.* New York: American Management Association, 1982.

Mitchell, Arnold. *Nine American Life Styles: Who We Are and Where We Are Going.* New York: Macmillan, 1983.

Rogers, Dorothy S., and Linda R. Gamans. *Fashion, A Marketing Approach.* New York: Holt, Rinehart and Winston, 1983.

Smith, Sweetman R., and Rona Ostrow. *The Dictionary of Marketing.* New York: Fairchild Publications, 1988.

Tedlow, Richard. *New and Improved, the Story of Mass Marketing in America.* New York, Basic Books, 1990.

Trade Associations

American Marketing Association, 310 Madison Avenue, New York, N.Y., 10017.

Direct Marketing Association, 6 East 43rd Street, New York, N.Y. 10017.

Trade Publications

American Demographics, P.O. Box 6543, Syracuse, N.Y. 13217.

Direct Marketing, 224 7th Avenue, Garden City, N.Y. 11530.

Marketing Communications Magazine, 475 Park Avenue South, New York, N.Y. 10016.

Sales and Marketing Management Magazine, 633 Third Avenue, New York, N.Y. 10022.

CHAPTER REVIEW AND LEARNING ACTIVITIES

Key Words and Concepts

Define, identify, or briefly explain the following:

Channels of distribution
Consumption expenditures
Demographics
FTC
Market
Marketing
Marketing concept

Market segmentation
Obsolescence
Primary market
Robinson–Patman Act
Secondary market
Sherman Anti-Trust Act
Vertical operations

Review Questions on Chapter Highlights

1. Name the different types of industries involved in the business of fashion and explain the interrelationships.
2. Explain the importance of the fashion business to the economy of the United States.
3. Name the three main links in the production and distribution of fashion merchandise and explain their interrelationships.
4. What is meant by vertical operations?
5. Give examples of current social and economic factors that are affecting the consumption of fashion.
6. What are the demographic factors that affect the business of fashion? Why?
7. What is the marketing concept? Define *market segmentation* and give specific examples. Explain its importance.
8. What is the relationship between the marketing concept and market segmentation?
9. Name the two basic categories of federal legislation that affect the fashion industries and give examples of each.

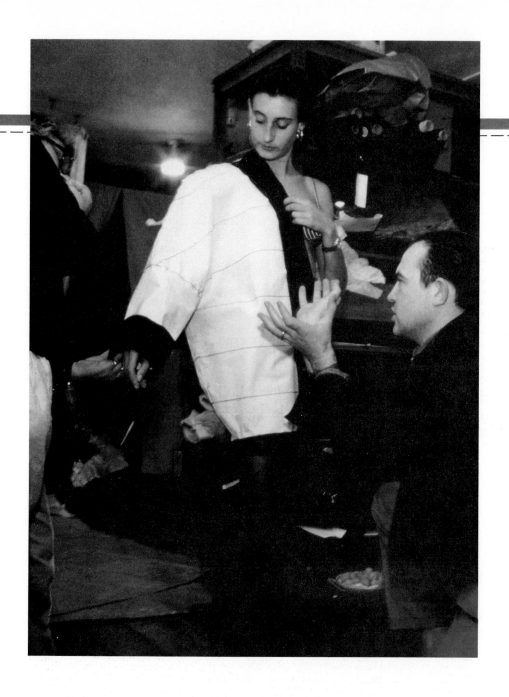

2

$\mathcal{P}$RINCIPLES OF $\mathcal{F}$ASHION

Fashion, which is as old as time and as new as tomorrow, is one of the most powerful forces in our lives. It influences what we wear, the way we talk, the foods we eat, the way we live, how and where we travel, what we look at, and what we listen to. Fashion is what leads us to discard a product that is still useful but is no longer "in." It is also what makes us sometimes wear more clothes than we may actually need, and sometimes less than is needed to protect us from the cold or the sun.

The intensity with which changes in fashion are followed by people everywhere on all levels of society is evidence of its social significance and its impact on human behavior. To be "out of fashion" is indeed to be out of the world.

This chapter discusses the generally accepted definitions of fashion and the principles governing its origin and dynamics. It also suggests some of the many implications of the fashion process for the producers and sellers of fashion goods. The readings that follow the text profile some leading American designers of fashion.

THE LANGUAGE OF FASHION

Many definitions of fashion have been given by wise and witty or learned men and women. For example, to Oscar Wilde, "fashion is a form of ugliness so intolerable that we have to alter it every six months." And according to Ambrose Bierce, "fashion is a despot whom the wise ridicule . . . and obey." Thoreau philosophized that "every generation laughs at the old fashions but follows religiously the new." And Shakespeare wrote that "fashion wears out more apparel than the man."

Since an understanding of fashion is obviously of primary importance for fashion practitioners, let us begin by defining the terms that are used by everybody and confused by some. Although the definitions that follow are formulated largely with respect to textiles and apparel—the subject of this book—it must be emphasized that they apply equally to music, painting, architecture, home furnishings, automobiles, telephones, and any other consumer goods or services that one can think of.

A Style: Distinctive Characteristics

The terms **fashion** and **style** are confused by many people who say, "That's the style," when they really mean "That's the fashion." There is a world of difference in the meanings of these two terms. A *style is a type of product that has one or more specific features or characteristics that distinguish it and make it different from other products of the same type.* For example, a crew neck is one style of neckline and a turtle neck is another. All blazer jackets have certain features in common—features that make them different from, say, safari jackets—just as bow ties differ from four-in-hands. Baggy jeans have a common characteristic —fullness—that distinguishes them from other types of jeans. Shirtwaist dresses have a distinctive feature that makes them different from wrap, sheath, or other types of dresses.

Similarly, there are different styles of fabrics, each of which has its own distinctive features, such as denim, gabardine, chiffon, and seersucker, to name but a few. In automobiles, there are such styles as convertibles, station wagons, and vans. Art has such styles as pop art, art deco, and impressionism; houses may be colonial, ranch, Victorian, or other styles. There are styles in penmanship, interior decoration, advertisements. In any one category of product, there is usually an endless variety of styles.

A Design: Variations of a Style

Within a specific style, there can be many variations in trimmings, texture, decoration, or other details. A cardigan sweater, for example, is a distinctive style, but within that style, individual variations could include different types of knits, embroideries, pockets, and necklines, to name but a few. *These individual interpretations or versions of the same style are called **designs**.* Compared with the number of styles in any given product, the possible variety of designs is limitless. Each design is different from the others in detail; they are all individual interpretations of their respective style.

In the fashion industry, when a style becomes popular, many different designs or versions of that style may be produced. In the trade, each producer assigns a **style number** to each design in the firm's line, which is used to identify it in production, selling, and shipping.

Fashion Means Consumer Acceptance

Among the countless definitions of fashion, the one from Webster's latest unabridged dictionary comes very close to what professionals mean when they use the word: *the prevailing or accepted style in dress or personal decoration established or adopted during a particular time or season.* The most widely recognized fashion authority, the late Dr. Paul H. Nystrom, defined fashion in similar words as "nothing more or less than the prevailing style at any given time."[1] Thus, a fashion is always based on a specific style. A style, however, does not become a fashion until it gains consumer acceptance, and it remains a fashion only as long as it is accepted.

For example, bow ties, tapered jeans, crinoline skirts, and chemise dresses are and will always be styles, but they can only be called fashions if and when they become prevailing styles. It is clearly possible, moreover, for a particular style to come in and go out of fashion repeatedly. Some examples of such "ins and outs" of fashion are peasant blouses, sheath dresses, padded shoulders, and circular skirts, to name but a few.

The element of social acceptance is the very essence of fashion. Acceptance, however, does not mean that a style is necessarily worn by everyone or even by a majority of the public. Acceptance can be and usually is limited to a particular group of people or to a particular location. For example, what New York men and women wear is often unacceptable in other parts of the United States that have markedly different climates or mores. Furthermore, what is popular among a particular age or occupational group may not be accepted by those of different ages or occupations.

Other Key Fashion Terms

There are, of course, many more key words commonly used in the fashion business, and it is necessary to understand their precise meanings to understand fashion itself and follow a discussion of fashion principles.

CLASSICS AND FADS

A classic is a style that continues to be accepted, to a greater or lesser degree, over an extended period of time. In the fashion world, this means that its acceptance endures for several seasons, or even longer. Typical of classics are blazer jackets, crew-neck shetland sweaters, and men's oxford cloth button-down collared shirts. From time to time, some classics can achieve a peak in popularity and become a mass fashion. That happened to the examples just cited, which in 1983 constituted the "preppy look."

In contrast to classics, there are styles that sweep suddenly into popularity, are adopted with great fervor, and then just as quickly disappear. Their acceptance is generally for a brief period and among a limited following. *These short-lived fashions are called fads*, and they seldom have any lasting impact on future fashions. An example is the Nehru collar, which was adopted by men almost overnight several years ago and died as abruptly as it was born. Often there is a capricious aspect in a fad, as in the case of "pet rocks" and "mood rings," which were briefly and suddenly seen everywhere, and then just as suddenly were gone. Fads go up like rockets and sink without a trace once their brief popularity is over.

LIMITED AND MASS FASHIONS

The term **high fashion** is commonly used to describe a *very new style, whose acceptance is limited to those who want to be first to adopt the very newest fashions and can afford their often astronomical prices.* Some of these styles are limited in appeal primarily because of the high prices they command. Their intricate design and costly workmanship keep some of them out of reach of all but people in top income brackets. Other styles may be limited because they are too sophisticated or extreme to be attuned to the needs of the average man or woman. In either event, high fashion styles are generally introduced, produced, and sold in relatively small quantities, until their newness wears off. If the style has the potential for appealing to a broader audience, it is generally copied and sold at lower prices. The originator and the early purchasers, meanwhile, have gone on to something new.

In contrast with high fashion, which accounts for a relatively small portion of the fashion industry's business, there are **mass fashions** or **volume fashions**. These are *styles that are accepted and worn by a large number of people.* Mass fashions are produced and sold in large quantities at moderate prices and constitute the bread and butter of the fashion industry.

FASHION TREND

Fashions are not static; there is always movement, and that movement has a direction, discernible to careful observers. *The directions in which fashions are moving are called fashion trends.* For example, skirt lengths may be moving up from the calf to the knee — perhaps almost imperceptibly from one season to the next, but generally in an upward direction. Short jackets, as another example, may gradually be gaining at the expense of hip-length styles. Men's ties may be getting wider or narrower; women's shoes may be getting clunkier or more elegantly slim; the athletic workout look may be getting more or less popular in other leisure-time clothes; and so on. The changes from season to season may be slight, but they generally have a direction. The ability to recognize that direction or trend is vital to fashion practitioners. Since these people must work far ahead of consumers' buying periods, much of their success depends on their ability to read the signs and recognize promptly the incoming and outgoing trends in fashion. The terms *"prophetic," avant garde*, and *forward fashions* are often used to describe styles that are gaining in acceptance.

THE CONSTANT IN FASHION IS CHANGE _____

If there is one absolute constant pertaining to fashion, it is the fact that it is always changing — sometimes rapidly, sometimes slowly, but it is never static or dormant. This element of change is recognized in the definitions of fashion itself cited earlier, by the use of such words as *prevailing* or *a given period of time.* To ignore the element of change is like looking at a still photograph in place of a motion picture. The still tells you what is happening here and now; the motion picture shows you what came before and what may lie ahead.

Why Fashions Change

To understand the constant changes in fashion, it is imperative to understand that fashions are always in harmony with their era. As a famous designer expressed it, "Fashion is a social phenomenon which reflects the same continuing change that rides through any given age." Changes in fashion, he emphasized, "correspond with the subtle and often hidden network of forces that operate on society. . . . In this sense, fashion is a symbol."[2]

PSYCHOLOGICAL REASONS

Men and women are complex creatures whose actions are seldom governed by reason alone. Change comes about for psychological reasons. People grow bored with what they have; the eye wearies of the same colors, lines, and textures after a time; what is new and different appears refreshing; and what has been on the scene for a while appears dull and unattractive. Thorstein Veblen, writing at the beginning of the present century, made this clear in his *Theory of the Leisure Class.* As he pointed out: "A fancy bonnet of this year's model unquestionably appeals to our sensibilities today more forcibly than an equally fancy bonnet of the model of last year; although when viewed in the perspective of a quarter of a century, it would, I apprehend, be a matter of the utmost difficulty to award the palm for intrinsic beauty to one rather than to the other."[3]

Changes for such psychological reasons occur also in the fashions for products other than clothing. For example, nothing could be more utilitarian than a broom, a refrigerator, a telephone, a tea kettle, or a hand tool. Yet people about to buy such things will be attracted to, for instance, a broom with a coppertone handle to go with a similarly colored refrigerator that has recently been purchased to replace a quite adequate white model that they discarded. This element of change for the sake of change — artificial obsolescence, in fact — touches nearly all products today. Along with boredom, human curiosity or an innate desire for new sensations leads to change for its own sake.

RATIONAL REASONS

Changes in fashion are also caused by rational reasons, such as environmental factors that create new needs. A classic example of a social change that brought about a drastic change in fashions occurred in the early decades of the twentieth century, when women sought, gained, and enjoyed new political and economic freedom. Their altered activities and concepts of themselves encouraged them to discard the constricting garments that had been in fashion for centuries and to adopt shorter skirts, relaxed waistlines, bobbed hair, and other fashions more appropriate to their more active lives. Generations later, as women moved into top executive positions in the business world, the tailored suit, femininely soft blouse, and attaché bags became the "dressing for success" fashion among career women.

Similarly, in the decade following World War II, when the great trek to the suburbs began, those who joined the exodus from the city found themselves needing cars and car coats, garden furniture, and casual clothes for backyard barbecues. The physical fitness movement in the 1970s and 1980s brought about a need for exercise clothing, and as the interest in jogging, hiking, tennis, and aerobic dancing mushroomed, so also did the need for new and different fashions appropriate to each of these active sports.

Changes in Fashions Are Gradual

Although fashions change constantly and new ones appear almost every season, a full-scale changeover is never completed at any one time. In studying the pattern of change in fashions, scholars have observed that changes in fashion are **evolutionary** in nature, rather than revolutionary.

It is only in retrospect that fashion changes seem marked or sudden. Actually, they come about as a result of a series of gradual shifts from one season to the next. For example, when women's skirts began inching up from midcalf in the 1960s, this gradual shortening was not particularly noticeable at first. It was only when skirts moved thigh-high, in the form of minis and micro-minis, that people took notice of the approaching extreme. Similarly, when men begin to abandon ultranarrow ties and suit lapels in favor of more and more width, the changes are not noticed at first. Then, when wide ties and lapels begin to lose their appeal and progressively narrower styles make their appearance, people again mistake their belated recognition of these gradual shifts for a sudden change in fashion.

Even today, when the rate of fashion change has accelerated sharply, the pace of change is really slower than it appears to the unskilled observer who has failed to notice the early evolutionary movements in a new direction.

The evolutionary nature of fashion change is a fundamental principle that is recognized by fashion practitioners; it provides them with a solid, factual foundation for forecasting and identifying incoming fashions. When planning and developing new styling ideas, they always keep the current fashions and evolving directions in mind. Thus, the acceptance of a particular coat or dress fashion during a current season becomes a straw in the wind for experts in search of clues to next season's trends. The degree of its acceptance provides needed clues as to what will or will not be welcomed by the consumer in the next season. Knowing that people do not respond well to sudden changes, the fashion experts build gradually, not abruptly, toward new ideas.

A lone exception to this principle occurred just after World War II. During that cataclysm, fabrics were in decidedly short supply; fashion was at an enforced standstill; women's clothes were built along straight, skimpy lines. By 1947, however, fashion was on the move and making up for lost time. Dior introduced his famous "new look," with long, full skirts and pinched waists. The radical change was accepted overnight. This unique event in fashion history was possible because the years of wartime shortages had precluded the gradual changes that would otherwise have taken place.

Even the slowest, most gradual of evolutionary changes in fashion, however, do change direction eventually. Once an extreme has been reached, shifts begin to occur in a new and different direction—often a complete reversal, like the returning swing of a pendulum. "All fashions end in excess" is a saying attributed to Paul Poiret, an outstanding couturier of the 1920s, and his remark carries as much weight today as it did then.

Examples are readily found in both history and recent times. Eighteenth-century hoopskirts and the crinolines of the nineteenth century ballooned to diameters of eight feet. Later, both exploded into a fragmentation of trains, loops, and bustles that nevertheless provided a far slimmer silhouette. Similarly, when the miniskirts of the 1960s moved up to the micro-minis of the 1970s, hems began inching downward. Whether it be skirt lengths, silhouettes, suit lapels, or general fashion looks, all fashions tend to move steadily toward an extreme, at which point a new direction develops.

FASHION: A "FOLLOW-THE-LEADER" PROCESS

In the constant change and movement of fashion, there is a definite orderliness about the pattern of acceptance. Styles become fashions through a "follow-the-leader" process. Understanding the acceptance pattern is a key to understanding fashion movements; it explains how a look or idea begins with a few and spreads to many.

The Fashion Cycle

Every fashion has a life span, known as a **fashion cycle**. This consists of three major stages: a beginning, or rise; a peak or very popular stage; and a declining stage. The acceptance patterns of individual styles and of overall fashion looks both fall into this pattern.

In its first or beginning stage, the fashion is adopted by people who like or can afford to be first with what is new, or who are highly motivated by a desire to dress differently from others. These pacesetters are relatively limited in number. In this first stage, the new fashion is often called a "high fashion," as explained earlier in this chapter.

If and when the new fashion idea spreads and is widely imitated by the greater number of people who tend to follow rather than lead, we arrive at the

Fashion Cycles Differ

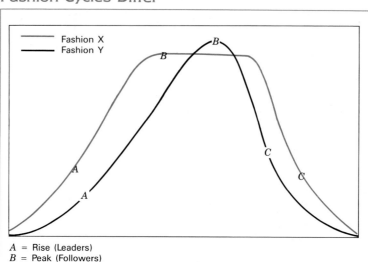

Fashion X
Fashion Y

A = Rise (Leaders)
B = Peak (Followers)
C = Decline (Laggards)

second stage of peak or mass acceptance. The fashion is then in such demand that it can be mass produced and distributed at prices within reach of many consumers.

Ultimately, each fashion moves into its third or declining stage—usually the result of consumer boredom arising from seeing too much of the same thing. Some consumers will still be wearing it at this stage, but they are no longer willing to purchase it at regular prices. Meantime, other, newer fashions are going through the earlier stages of their cycles.

This pattern of acceptance and decline has been explained thus by sociology professor Neil J. Smelser:

> It is important to (style leaders) to be among the first in order to reap the psychological rewards of being in the forefront of fashion, and it is almost as important to flee from a new style when it is assumed by the masses. Further back in the procession, among the followers, the motivation is more purely sociable—persons adapt to styles to avoid being conspicuously traditional, rather than to be conspicuously original.[4]

These stages of public acceptance tend to occur in all products that are subject to changes in fashion—not just in dress. Similar cycles can be traced in home furnishings, architecture, food, and even manners, but the pattern shows up most obviously in what we wear.

Different fashions vary in their life spans, in the degree of acceptance they attain, and in the rate at which they move through their various stages. The length of time a particular fashion may remain in any of its three stages depends on the extent to which it is gaining or losing public acceptance. Some fashions may endure for a year or more; others for a season; and, indeed, some may never get beyond the first stage of acceptance by small groups of people. Therefore, if one were to draw a fashion cycle, it would include the three stages, but its shape would be different for different fashions. The rise and fall may be gradual or sharp; the peak may be narrow or wide. Although no one graph can depict the life story of all fashions accurately, all would have a wavelike appearance.

Academically minded students of fashion have sought to chart the ups and downs of fashions in an effort to determine the length of time a fashion movement takes to run its course. The time intervals, however, elude measurement. The spread of fashion, as of every new idea, is a complicated social phenomenon. The public's needs and interests do not change by clockwork.

The problem of applying the stopwatch technique to an analysis of fashion movements is also complicated by the fact that price differentials, which at one time tended to mark the different stages of style acceptance, have virtually disappeared. Moreover, while some cycles are in their peaks, their successors are already in the growing stage. Many new fashions often reach full growth without ever entirely displacing those that preceded them. A further complicating factor is that, owing to the evolutionary nature of changes, clearly definable shifts in fashion do not occur at a given time, and it is impossible to pinpoint the exact beginning or end of a specific fashion.

APPLICATION TO MERCHANDISING FASHIONS

An understanding of the fashion cycle is basic to successful merchandising of fashion goods, at wholesale or retail. Because very few concerns, if any, can successfully serve under one roof both the pacesetters and the followers, each firm must have a clear-cut policy on which fashion stages it wishes to deal in.

The main volume of business, in manufacturing and retailing alike, is done in fashions that are widely accepted or well on their way to the top or peak of the fashion cycle. A business that aims to attract a mass customers audience must concentrate on widely popular fashions, or on those that show promise of rising into the mass acceptance stage. These volume fashions constitute the major portion of the business done by the giant firms in the fashion industry. Conversely, those manufacturers and retailers that concentrate on being the first to carry the newest, the most individual, or the most extreme fashions cannot expect to do a large volume of business. Their appeal is to the limited group of customers who adopt such fashions. Their volume contributes only a small part of the total business done in the fashion industries, but a vital one indeed.

Merchandising the Fashion Cycle

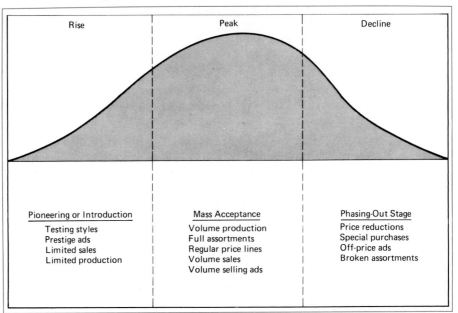

Rise	Peak	Decline

Pioneering or Introduction	Mass Acceptance	Phasing-Out Stage
Testing styles	Volume production	Price reductions
Prestige ads	Full assortments	Special purchases
Limited sales	Regular price lines	Off-price ads
Limited production	Volume sales	Broken assortments
	Volume selling ads	

Theories of Fashion Leadership

Social scientists explain the follow-the-leader element in fashion cycles in terms of an individual's desire to achieve status by choosing apparel similar to that chosen by an admired individual or group. This association through choice of fashion is a means of bridging the gap between social classes — that is, becoming in one's mind like "them" by wearing what "they" wear. Imitation and conformity in dress are also explained in terms of insecurity, since it takes more social courage than most of us possess to be conspicuously different from others in the appearance we present to the public. Thus, fashion gives expression to two basic human needs: the need for social status and the need to conform.[5]

Three academically accepted theories categorize the admired groups or individuals from whom fashion leadership flows. These theories are "trickle down," "horizontal, or trickle across," and "bottom up." Each has its own claim to validity with respect to specific fashions and the fashion cycle.

TRICKLE-DOWN THEORY

The **trickle-down theory** maintains that new styles make their first appearance among people at the top of a social pyramid and then gradually move down to progressively lower social levels.

Centuries ago, the persons at the top of the pyramid and therefore the setters of fashion were royalty. Fashions trickled down through the ranks of the nobility and those of the middle classes who had the means. The lower classes, of course, had neither the means nor the temerity to copy, or were even prohibited by law from doing so.

These days, royalty has practically disappeared, and the position at the top of the pyramid is held by individuals at the top of the economic, social, entertainment, and political ladders. Many such people make it their business to dress well, and their activities and appearance are highly publicized. To the large majority of the public, the fashions accepted by the glittering personalities at the top constitute a guide to what to wear, within the limits of their own more restricted budgets and social activities. For most consumers, innovation is risky but imitation is safe. Thus, fashions trickle down from higher to lower echelons, just as they did in the days of royalty.

Simultaneously, those at the top seek to dissociate themselves from those whom they consider socially inferior. They abandon a fashion once it has achieved popularity at less distinguished levels and introduce a new and different idea.

This type of social behavior was recognized and its implications for fashion were propounded by such early economists as Thorstein Veblen, John Roe, and Caroline Foley,[6] and by such sociologists as George Simmel, who spelled it out, step by step, in a paper published in 1904.[7]

TRICKLE-ACROSS THEORY

As the twentieth century progressed, it became clear that fashion was no longer a matter of imitating any single social or economic class, but of choosing one's own role models—and not necessarily from among individuals with glittering genealogy or fabulous wealth. This phenomenon gave rise to another theory of fashion emulation: the **trickle-across theory**, enunciated by Charles W. King in 1963.[8] He observed that fashions spread horizontally within and across homo-

Theories of Fashion Leadership

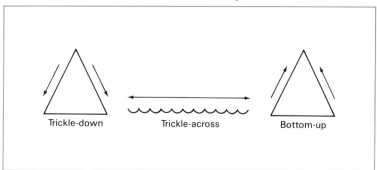

Trickle-down   Trickle-across   Bottom-up

geneous groups, rather than merely vertically from one social level to another. He believes that each segment of our pluralistic society has its own leader or leaders whom it emulates. For example, a ''Big Man'' on campus may favor white sweaters and thus set a fashion for them among other students. In the business world, aspirants to the executive office tend to dress as the upper echelons do, be it the gray flannel suit of the 1950s or the attaché cases of the 1980s. Even in so small a group as a suburban country golf club, the dominant members subtly influence the dress of the other members by the fashions they favor.

BOTTOM-UP THEORY

The third and most recent theory espoused by many students of fashion and by fashion practitioners themselves is that the traditional trickle-down movement has reversed itself and many fashions now filter up. This **bottom-up theory**, as advanced by Greenberg and Glynn, maintains that young people are quicker than any other social group to initiate new and different fashions and that fashions filter up, not merely from youth to older age groups, but also from lower to upper economic classes.[9] Typical of fashions initiated by the young and less than affluent are jeans, sneakers, tee shirts, military surplus and safari clothes, black leather pants and jackets. Each of these started in the streets with young people of modest means and streamed upward to well-to-do middle-aged adults. The male espousal of flowing hair and beards similarly was initiated by the young in the 1960s, and that fashion spread to gray-haired, balding men as well. When younger men became reacquainted with razors, their elders soon followed suit.

MARKETING IMPLICATIONS

These three different theories of how fashions spread have major significance for practitioners in the field, since they confirm that there is no single homogeneous fashion public in our pluralistic society. A number of distinctly different groups make up the fashion public, and each has its own leaders and its own perception of fashion. Although we continue to see many new styles introduced at high prices and eventually becoming fashions, this is less often the case than it once was. One successful new style may originate in the studio of a prestigious designer, but another may come into fashion from the stock of an Army-Navy store.

Leadership in fashion these days has less and less to do with price and high-priced merchandise. Therefore, producers and retailers can no longer look only to an elite group of traditional fashion leaders for incoming trends. They must also be aware that some fashions flow upward and others flow across within special groups. Dominant individuals and dominant influences, wherever they reveal themselves within our society, are important influences on fashion. Success depends on identifying and watching these, not just the patrons of elite restaurants, resorts, and entertainments.

HOW FASHIONS DEVELOP_____

There is no question that it is far easier to recognize what is fashionable at a given time and place than to say why or how it became a fashion. When we search for the influences that brought forth such fashions as the hobble skirts and crinolines of the past, or some of the fashions of the present, we are confronted with a complex question indeed. Several things we do know, however. One is that esthetic appeal alone does not produce a fashion. Veblen made this point when he observed that there is no intrinsic difference between the gloss of a patent leather shoe and the shine of a threadbare garment. People, he observed, are ready to find beauty in what is in vogue; therefore the shine on the shoe is beautiful and the garment's shine is repulsive.[10]

Another thing we know is that promotional efforts by designers, producers, or retailers cannot in themselves dictate what customers will accept. If there were such dictators in the past, there certainly are none today. And a third factor that we know is that a fashion does not just happen without a reason. It is a response to many things: attitudes, social changes and movements, major events on the world stage, and new technological developments, for example. Which of these is the most important, no one can say; their relative strengths vary with the times.

The Role of Designers

There are countless styles, each of which has its own distinctive characteristics and most of which have, at one time or another, or more than once, been a fashion. It is a common misconception, however, that all have been "created" by designers and only by them.

It is true, indeed, that many new fashions have been introduced by famous designers. Some examples include the boxy jackets of Chanel's 1920 suits; the bias cut dresses of Vionnet in the 1920s; Dior's "new look" in the 1940s; and the bodysuits of Donna Karan in more recent times.

Often, however, it is a functional garment rather than an individual designer that generates a new fashion. Some examples that have taken the fancy of the public and become fashions in their time are the bomber jackets of aviators, the pea coats of sailors and the trench coats of soldiers, the leg warmers of dancers, and the protective overalls of farmers. Similarly, denim pants. The ultrapractical style created by Levi Strauss in gold-rush days inspired the jeans that have enjoyed worldwide popularity in the second half of the twentieth century. And let us not forget that many examples of "street fashions" that started among young people and moved out to a wider following. A classic case is the miniskirt: the miniskirt and boots that London working girls adopted in the 1960s attained widespread popularity before being shown in Paris by Courreges.

Designers who acquire a reputation for "creating" fashion are simply those who have been consistently successful in giving tangible expression to the shapes, colors, fabrics, styles, and looks that are wanted and accepted by a substantial number of customers. The fact that a style may be widely heralded as a new fashion does not make it one. Even among the greatest of designers, it is recognized that it is only when customers accept a style, new or old, that the particular style becomes a fashion. Paul Poiret, one of the greatest Paris couturiers, once told an American audience the following:

> I know you think me a king of fashion. It is a reception which cannot but flatter me and of which I cannot complain. All the same, I must undeceive you with regard to the powers of a king of fashion. We are not capricious despots who wake up one fine day, decide on a change in habits, abolish a neckline or puff out a sleeve. We are neither arbiters or dictators. Rather we are to be thought of as the blindly obedient servants of woman, who for her part is always enamored of change and a thirst for novelty. It is our role and our duty to be on the watch for the moment at which she becomes bored with what she is wearing, that we may suggest at the right instant something else which will meet her taste and her needs. It is therefore with a pair of antennae and not a rod of iron that I come before you, and not so much as a master that I speak, but as a slave . . . who must divine your innermost thoughts.[11]

Poiret was at his peak in the early decades of this century, but designers today still see things as he did—although they express themselves in less flowery language. Here is Halston, very much a designer for a part of this century: "I have always felt that all the designers can do is suggest; it is the consumer who accepts or rejects and is the ultimate maker of fashion."[12]

Fashions Reflect Their "Times"

Fashions in clothing have always been more than merely a manner of dressing. A study of the past and a careful observation of the present will make it apparent that fashions are social expressions; they document the taste and values of their era just as painting, sculpture, and other art forms do. Fashions are a fact of social psychology. They reflect the way people think and live, and are therefore influenced by the same environmental forces that act on any society. Every fashion seems completely appropriate to its era and reflects the spirit of an age as no other symbol of the times does. This is true both for widely accepted fashions and for those that flourish only within small isolated or counterculture groups. To illustrate: Mennonite garb reflects Mennonite ideals; punk dress and hair styles reflect the attitudes of punk rockers.

NEWSWORTHY EVENTS AND PERSONALITIES MAKE FASHIONS

Fashions are made by outstanding personalities and major happenings in the fields of entertainment, sports, art, and politics. Almost anything or anyone of newsworthy importance in the world of entertainment from prominent personalities to major television or motion picture productions has an effect on the fashions of the times. To cite but a few examples from the 1970s and 1980s: the Indian inspired fashions influenced by the widely watched television production of "Jewel in the Crown" and the Indian art exhibits in New York and Washington; the tremendous impact on hair and clothing styles of superstars whose personae are as closely identified with their clothes as with their music; the career fashions that received impetus from a new wave of television and movie productions that starred women in positions as business executives; the popularity of the black leather look, skull and crossbones imagery, and decorative metal studs resulting from the enthusiasm for "heavy metal" music.

Many new fashions have also emerged from the public's participation in sports and physical fitness activities. Each activity usually creates a need for different types of functional garments, many of which develop into everyday fashions. For example, sweatsuits and sweatshirts are an outgrowth of the functional running suits worn by joggers. A relatively short-lived fashion for dancers' leg warmers and cut-off tee shirts was generated by the active interest in aerobic dancing. Similarly, the fashions that developed for the brightly printed jams worn by surfers and skateboarders, and for the skin-tight bicycle pants of bicycle enthusiasts.

Emulation of personalities in the public eye, whose clothing and activities are featured in the media, also plays a part in the development of fashions. For instance, the pillbox hat and bouffant hair style of Jackie Kennedy, the young and much admired "first lady" in the 1960s, were widely imitated, as were the classic styles of dresses worn by Nancy Reagan in the 1980s and the faux pearls of Barbara Bush in the 1990s.

SOCIAL MOVEMENTS CREATE FASHIONS

Fashions develop in response to social movements. For example, the focus on career fashions and specialized career shops for women in the 1980s was a direct response to the rise of women in the ranks of corporate executives. Similarly, the anti-establishment fashions of the 1960s—cut-off jeans, long hair, beards, the "hippie" look—were visible expressions of the anti-establishment attitude that developed as a reaction to the unpopular Vietnam War of the 1960s.

In ways uniquely their own, hair styles have reflected social movements. In the Gay Nineties, women enhanced the luxurious look of their hair with pinned-on puffs, curls, rats, and other devices that have gone the way of tight

Fashions Reflect the Times

Events	Entertainment 1910s	Looks	Events	Entertainment 1950s	Looks
Modern Art	"Birth of a Nation"	The Gibson Girl goes modern	Television	"Rebel without a Cause"	The trapeze
Costumes for plays	"Intolerance"	Looser waists	The "Beat" generation	"Some Like It Hot"	The chemise
Ballet and fine art influence fashion	"Peg O' My Heart"	Gossamer fabrics	Abstract expressionism	"Gigi"	The shirtdress
	"Let Me Call You Sweetheart"	Hobble skirts	Sock hops	"Singing in the Rain"	Pennyloafers
	"Alexander's Ragtime Band"	Empire waist silhouettes	"My Fair Lady" on Broadway	"Psycho"	Bobby sox
				"High Society"	Capri pants
				"Hound Dog"	Ponytails
				"Three Coins in a Fountain"	The sheath
				"I Love Paris"	Saddle shoes
				"Standing on the Corner"	Princess dresses

Events	Entertainment 1920s	Looks	Events	Entertainment 1960s	Looks
Prohibition	"The Jazz Singer"	Short skirts	Woodstock	"2001: A Space Odyssey"	Ironed hair
The Charleston	"The Shiek"	Flapper chemises	Pop art	"The Sound of Music"	Nehru jackets
Art Deco	"City Lights"	Bobbed hair	Psychedelics	"Bonnie and Clyde"	Love beads
Bootleg liquor	"Tea for Two"	Powdered knees	The Beatles	"The Graduate"	Teased hair
"Showboat" on Broadway	"Ol' Man River"		Flower children	"Z"	Go-Go boots
The Cotton Club in Harlem	"Swanee"		"Hair" on Broadway	"Let the Sun Shine In"	Miniskirts
	"The Man I Love"			"Strangers in the Night"	Dark eyes, pale lips
	"I'm Just Wild about Harry"			"Moon River"	Pillbox hats
				"I Want to Hold Your Hand"	Prints

1930s — first column:
- Hollywood glamour influences fashion
- Café society
- "Our Town" on Broadway
- Jazz

1930s — second column:
- "Gone with the Wind"
- "The Wizard of Oz"
- "It Happened One Night"
- "42nd Street"
- "10¢ a Dance"
- "I Got Rhythm"
- "Night and Day"
- "Putting on the Ritz"

1930s — third column:
- Streamlined silhouettes
- Body-conscious shape
- Bias cut
- Shirtwaists
- Draping and shirring
- Halters and hip wraps
- Hats and gloves
- Fox trimmed coats

1970s — first column:
- Roller skating
- Disco
- "A Chorus Line" on Broadway

1970s — second column:
- "The Godfather"
- "The Great Gatsby"
- "Annie Hall"
- "Rocky"
- "Butch Cassidy and the Sundance Kid"
- "Cabaret"
- "Send in the Clowns"
- "The Way We Were"
- "Losing My Mind"
- "Killing Me Softly"

1970s — third column:
- Granny dresses
- Platform shoes
- Message tee shirts
- Midis
- "The Great Gatsby"
- "Annie Hall"
- Hot pants
- Designer jeans
- Punk

1940s — first column:
- WW II ends
- Nylon stockings available
- "Death of a Salesman" and "Street Car Named Desire" on Broadway

1940s — second column:
- "Casablanca"
- "Citizen Kane"
- "Adam's Rib"
- "Born Yesterday"
- "Notorious"
- "The Red Shoes"
- "So in Love"
- "If I Loved You"
- "Some Enchanted Evening"
- "Moonlight Serenade"

1940s — third column:
- Short hemlines to long
- Dior's "New Look"
- Hepburn pants
- Sarong drape
- Peplum jackets
- Uniform style suits
- Hats with veils
- Platform shoes

1980s — first column:
- MTV
- New wave music
- Michael Jackson
- Postmodern art and architecture
- "Cats" on Broadway
- Madonna
- Heavy Metal
- "Phantom of the Opera"
- "Les Miserables"

1980s — second column:
- "Rambo"
- "Born in the U.S.A."
- "Flashdance"
- "We Are the World"
- "Eraserhead"
- "Murphy Brown"
- "thirty-something"
- "LA Law"
- "Cosby Show"
- "Golden Girls"
- "Wheel of Fortune"
- "Batman"

1980s — third column:
- Menswear
- Sweaters
- Preppy
- Leggings
- Punk hairdo
- Torn jeans
- Sweat clothes
- Athletic shoes
- Earrings
- Bodysuits

corseting. In the 1960s, alongside the unkempt locks of the hippies, blacks let their hair grow long and full in the Afro styles that proclaimed that black was beautiful. In the 1970s many blacks, looking back to their roots, adopted corn-row hair styles and dreadlocks—two African hair styles almost impossible for Caucasians to copy. In the 1980s, Mohawks and spiky pink and green hairdos were part of punk rock's way of thumbing its collective nose at the establishment.

SOCIAL VALUES AND ATTITUDES
CREATE FASHION

There is, of course, no one universal way of life in America today, even among those who constitute the mainstream. Except within fragmented groups, like those mentioned earlier, our values are varied. Some of us are hedonistic; others are antimaterialistic. Some are conservative; some are futurists. Whatever our values and lifestyles, our dress reflects that choice, consciously or otherwise. As one commentator points out, clothes nowadays are viewed "sometimes with almost mystical fervor, as the most basic expression of life style, indeed of identity itself."[13] Thus, fashions are a language that communicates self-identity and group identity with instant impact. When youth ideas are dominant, there is a tendency for people of all ages to dress, act, and think like, and to make believe, they are young. The expanding use of hair dyes and face lifts by both sexes reflects the desire to appear young, no matter what nature may say to the contrary. The wearing of pants by women for many occasions is not merely a matter of dressing practically; it is also an expression of their freedom from the conventional restraints that they and their mothers had accepted in earlier years. When women, even those who wear trousers for most occasions, prefer to express their femininity, they move into fashions that are frillier, lacier, and sexier. When ostentation is seen as an expression of success, then rich clothes and elaborate home furnishings are "in." At other times, a revulsion against "conspicuous consumption" will express itself in understated clothes and home furnishings. And so it goes.

TECHNOLOGICAL DEVELOPMENTS
CREATE FASHION

New technological developments often father new fashions. So simple a thing as a digital clock, for instance, makes it possible to depart from the round-face design that prevailed for centuries. Some apparel fashions seem to have their origins in the development of new fibers and fabrics, new processes for utilizing familiar ones, and other fruits of the chemist's genius—plus a waiting need for the new or a weariness with the old. For example, the synthetic fibers that made wash-and-wear fabrics possible, and thus influenced fashion, might not have had such a rousing welcome if they had come on the scene early in the century, when domestic help was plentiful and when the stiffly starched, beautifully ironed garment was a symbol of a well-run household.

Other examples abound, such as the popularity of skintight bodysuits in the 1980s resulting from the development of stretch fabrics; and the proliferation of graphics on tee shirts, which were made possible by the advances in heatsetting technology. Plastics in their infinite variety influenced the development of such fashions as raincoats in gay colors, and the leather look of suede-like fabrics that offered the flexibility, easy care, and lightweight qualities of cloth.

THE PREDICTION OF FASHION

Analyzing and predicting which styles will become the fashions for coming seasons has been called an occupational guessing game for the fashion industry, with millions of dollars at stake. Fiber, textile, and leather producers must work from one to two years ahead of the consumers' buying seasons; apparel and accessory designer/manufacturers must prepare their lines from nine months to a year ahead in order to show them to retail buyers three to six months in advance of the consumers' wearing season. Without accurate forecasts and projections of what looks, colors, fabrics, silhouettes, and design details are likely to be acceptable to customers, they would not be able to produce and sell the massive quantities of textiles and apparel that they do.

Such forecasts and predictions of fashion are neither guesswork nor a game, nor a matter of intuition. Rather, prediction is one of the most vital activities in the fashion industries. The successful forecaster recognizes that fashion is neither haphazard nor mysterious, but a tangible force whose progress can be charted, graphed, understood, explained, and projected. Basically, what fashion practitioners do is examine past experiences for clues as to what will happen today, and then analyze and evaluate today's activities for indications of what may happen tomorrow.

Determining Targeted Customers: Market Segmentation

Whether one is designing, producing, or selling, the first step is to have a clear picture of the customer segment that constitutes the firm's targeted customers. A noted economist has said that "the central function of the entrepreneur in a fashion industry is far less the efficient organization of the production of a given commodity and much more the shrewd anticipation of the changing preferences in his numerically restricted clientele—his own small niche in the great neighborhood of women."[14] Just as there can be no universal weather forecast, but only one that is pinned down as to time and area, in our pluralistic society there are city, suburban, and small town; there are young and not-so-young; there are the blue-collar and white-collar background; there are middle-income and well-to-do; there are followers and leaders; there are the conservative and the *avant garde*; and so on. What one forecasts for, say, the young juniors in a wealthy suburb of the West may be all wrong for the same age group in a poor neighborhood of an Eastern city.

With a specific targeted customer group in mind, the next step is to collect all the facts one can get. What are they buying this season? What are the activities and occasions for which they need clothes? What are their priorities? Are they innovators or imitators? What people, periodicals, or environmental influences will affect their choice? And so on. The more answers one has to such questions, the clearer the picture becomes, and the easier it is to forecast. Perhaps the essential element in the **prediction of fashion** is best pinpointed by one successful merchant's definition of fashion as "a conception of what your customers want."[15]

Analysis of Customers' Fashion Preferences

There is in the fashion industry a constant flow, back and forth, of information about the styles that the customer is buying. The systems that producers and retailers have today for this purpose are extremely rapid and accurate, thanks to the development of the computer. In most retail stores, a record is kept as to the styles, colors, fabrics, and so on, that have been purchased for resale. On this record are also entered the day-to-day sales. Every garment bought by a consumer thus becomes a ballot cast by the customer for the wanted size, color, fabric, silhouette, and style.

From the records, retailers can discern sudden or gradual changes in the preferences of their own customers. These changes become apparent whether the same customers are turning to different fashions, or whether there is a change in the kind of people who make up the store's clientele. In either case, the proprietor or buyer sees that there is less demand for this, and more for that.

These variations in what consumers are buying at that store are reflected in what the store buys from the manufacturers of fashion merchandise. Multiply that store's experience by the hundreds or even thousands of stores that buy from one manufacturer, and you see that producers have a pretty broad spectrum of consumer response as represented in the rate at which their various styles are sold. If they have countrywide distribution, they may see that certain areas are buying certain colors, styles, or fabrics faster or more slowly than others. If they have no reason to believe that this is due to special effort (or lack of effort) on the part of their retail outlets in those areas, they can assume that a regional difference is influencing sales. Typical of such differences are the West Coast's quickness to accept what is new, and especially what is casual and relaxed, or the Middle West's fondness for shades of blue to go with the blue eyes that predominate among the German and Scandinavian groups who have settled there.

From the manufacturer of the finished garment, information about customer preferences, as expressed in customer purchases, flows in several direc-

Analyzing Fashion Purchases at Point of Sale

Retail sales ticket showing manufacturer, style number, classification, season, size, and price. This information is fed into a point-of-sale (POS) register and the data appear on sales and inventory reports.

Bar-code ticket.

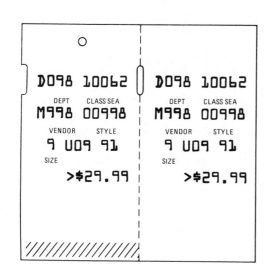

(1) A number system character that identifies the product category. There are currently seven categories.

(2) A five digit number that identifies the manufacturer . . . assigned by the Uniform Code Council, Inc.

(3) A five digit product code number that is assigned and controlled by the manufacturing company. This number is unique for each of the manufacturer's products including each size, flavor, color, etc.

(4) A check digit.

tions. One flow is back to the retail stores, by means of the manufacturer's salespersons, to alert them to trends they may not have noticed for themselves. Another flow is to the fabric producers, in the form of the garment maker's reorders for the most accepted fabrics and colors.

Information about the customer and the balloting that he or she does from day to day at the retail cash register is also collected by other people in the fashion field. Editors of consumer magazines, for instance, check regularly on trends with manufacturers of raw materials and finished products. They do this to see whether their own previous editorial judgments of fashion trends have been right, and to establish a basis on which to select styles to be featured in future issues. What the customer does or does not buy is watched as closely in the fashion industry as the ticker tape is watched by stockbrokers.

Often the customer is a guinea pig on whom the experts test their judgment. Sometimes he or she is a member of a committee formed by retailers or editors to represent a particular section of the public and to be available for consultation or reaction to new ideas, or just to sound off on any subject. Consumer surveys are also conducted by stores, producers, and publications. More often, the customer serves unknowingly as a test subject. When a new style, color, fabric, or silhouette is introduced, makers and retailers usually proceed on a "sample, test, reorder" system. This means that only small quantities are made up and placed for sale in retail stores. At the first inkling of customer reaction, the retailer reorders the acceptable styles and discontinues whatever other styles may have evoked little customer enthusiasm. The manufacturers, meanwhile, are watching the retail reorders to see which styles they should cut in quantity and which ones should be discontinued.

No one, least of all the customer, may fully understand why one style is chosen in preference to another, but everyone in the fashion industry is observing their selections and thus determining what the current fashions are and evaluating their degree of popularity and their directions.

Recognizing and Evaluating Trends

The logistics of projecting current fashions are relatively simple. Whatever styles have been steadily rising in popularity during the last few months may be expected to continue to rise for a few months more—or at least, not to decline abruptly for some time. For instance, a rising trend for fur-trimmed coats at the end of a fall season is very likely to be followed by a high demand for fur-trimmed coats at the beginning of the next fall season. Likewise, whatever has been steadily declining in popularity up to the present offers little favorable prospects for the future. People in the fashion business seem to develop almost a sixth sense for weighing various factors and judging probable ups and downs of trends. Their apparently instinctive skill arises from years of experience in studying signs that may escape the untrained observer, just as a weather forecaster observes signs the rest of us may not have noticed and becomes adept in this work.

Sources of Information

Fashion practitioners base their predictions not only on their own selling records and preliminary sales tests, but also on facts and observations that are available from other segments within the fashion industry.

The fact-gathering procedure, to continue the analogy to weather forecasting, is similar to preparing a meteorological map, with its isobars, temperature readings, pressure systems, and other indicators of present and future conditions. On the fashion forecaster's mental map of present and future customer

The Looks from 1920 to 1990

preferences are the factors below—in addition, of course, to a knowledge of the movement of fashions.

With respect to the firm's targeted customer group, the fashion forecaster calls on the following:

- Careful observation of current events that have captured or are likely to capture the imagination of customers and affect the styles they will prefer.
- Awareness of the current lifestyles and dress of those men and women most likely to influence what the firm's own customers will ultimately adopt.
- Study of sales trends in various sections of the country, not only for the forecaster's own company, but for competing companies to whatever extent is possible.
- An intimate knowledge of the fashion opinions of their sources of supply.
- Familiarity with professional sources of information, such as fashion reporting services, fashion periodicals, opinions of consultants, analyses offered by resident buying offices, and the like.
- Exchange of information with noncompeting concerns.
- Understanding of and constant awareness of the inevitable and evolutionary nature of changes in fashion.

Thus, a forecaster, whose official title may be designer, fashion director, product developer, magazine editor, or store buyer, may decide that brighter and gayer colors will be more acceptable than they were in the previous year, that oversized tops have run their course for the time being, or that sleek hairdos are coming in.

A fashion forecast, once made, whether in one's own mind or in print, is seldom final and immutable. The unexpected can often happen when some new factor enters the picture. In any forecasting, whether it be weather or fashion, all that can be hoped for is a high percentage of successful projections. Even the best informed and most successful designers, producers, buyers, and fashion reporting services make errors, resulting in merchandise that must be disposed of in some way—usually unprofitably.

Consumers have given proof often enough that they have minds of their own and will reject a so-called fashion before it can even get going if it does not appeal to them. And if the industry had any doubts about this, it has only to look back a bit. Efforts to induce customers to wear hats when they preferred to go hatless achieved nothing. Similarly, an effort in 1970 to switch customers from miniskirts to the so-called midi, or midcalf length, met with disastrous results.

The importance of the customer in determining the course of fashion was stated effectively by Bill Blass, the American designer whose leadership has been legendary for decades. He said, after the "midi" fiasco:

> I have never felt for one minute that the designers or the press or the industry could force or impose a new fashion on the customer, and that's never been more evident than now. The designer can only propose; the customer decides. This is a time of great individuality in customer buying, so the store merchant must pay more attention than ever to what his or her customers are looking for, and then find the designers who are making clothes that relate to their customers.[16]

AMERICAN DESIGNER AWARDS: THE "OSCARS" OF FASHION

American designers, like professionals in the American theater, television, and motion pictures, are given awards when their work earns the admiration of their peers. These awards are generally made on the basis of ballots cast by designated panels which usually consist of members of the fashion press and other selected fashion practitioners. Given annually from 1956 to 1984, the Coty American Fashion Critics Award recognized excellence in design. The first to win Hall of Fame eminence was the late Norman Norell. Other recipients have included Geoffrey Beene, Bill Blass, Anne Klein, Ralph Lauren, Calvin Klein, Mary McFadden, James Galanos, and Oscar de la Renta.

In 1984 the Coty Awards were discontinued and a group of leading designers formed the Council of Fashion Designers of America (CFDA) in order to present their own annual awards to individuals in the areas of the arts and industry who have made outstanding contributions to American fashion. The CFDA hosts an annual awards dinner at which it presents winners from such varied fields as publishing, retailing, photography, jewelry, and television. It also presents the Lifetime Achievement Award to an individual who has made an outstanding contribution over his or her lifetime. Winners of this award have included James Galanos (designer), Katherine Hepburn (actress), Eleanor Lambert (publicist), Horst (photographer), and Alexander Liberman (publisher).

Another award has been the Cutty Sark Award, given under the auspices of the Men's Fashion Association. This award was given annually from 1979 to 1988 to the most innovative menswear designers of the year. As of the time of this writing, the latest winners have included Jeffrey Banks, Bill Robinson, and Alexander Julian, among others. In 1989, the Cutty Sark Company, which had originally established this award, was replaced as a co-sponsor by the Wool Bureau and the name of the award changed to the Woolmark Award. When this change was announced, the president of the Wool Bureau said that sponsorship of such an award program "is in keeping with the Wool Bureau's leading role in fashion development and promotion."[17]

Although there are other awards given from time to time by various business organizations, the three awards discussed above are considered to be the "Oscars" of fashion.

Readings

These readings show that successful designers do not consider themselves arbiters or dictators of fashion. Those at the top make it very clear that their success owes a great deal to analyzing what their targeted customers want.

The Subject Was Fashion

Fashion has a magic element that goes beyond the intrinsic value of its material—it makes women feel beautiful.

Calvin Klein: In the Midst of Change, a Certain Style

Fashion designer Calvin Klein believes that although fashions are always changing, his customers expect a certain style from him—pure, clean, and modern clothes that are very American.

Donna Karan: Hot and Getting Hotter

Whether it be jeans, cashmere sweaters, bodysuits, hosiery, or sunglasses, to Donna Karan it's all one wardrobe. In her opinion, fashion designing is not about clothes— it's about how they go together, how a woman moves in them, and how they make her feel.

Ralph Lauren: Telling Stories

Ralph Lauren's designs—and his advertisements—tell a story about his customers' lifestyles. He designs for his own lifestyle and for the people whose lives he understands.

Adrienne Vittadini: From Esthetics to Reality

Adrienne Vittadini describes herself as the woman for whom she is designing—an active woman, a homemaker, a woman involved in the arts, a woman who travels. It is her own needs that inspire her.

Beyond Fashion: Mary McFadden

Mary McFadden knows her clientele well. They are affluent, travel a lot, and want to look educated, feminine, and a little mysterious. For them, she ransacks the distant past for her timeless evening dresses.

Geoffrey Beene's Amazing Grace

Although many of Beene's designs seem to flout tradition like putting diamonds on a plastic bracelet, he has won eight Coty Awards and is considered by many to be the most creative American designer.

THE SUBJECT WAS FASHION

by Woody Hochswender

Being in fashion is one great feeling money can buy. But most of us sense a real gulf, if not an existential chasm, between the price of beautiful clothes and the cost of their materials and labor. Consider, for instance, a $300 evening dress by Victor Costa, which may be nearly a line-for-line copy of another designer dress costing $3,000. In the Costa, will you feel only 10 percent as beautiful?

Granted, the workmanship and fabric in more expensive clothes are often very different. Perhaps the more costly dresses are silk-lined, the seams finished by hand. But there is something else, a hidden premium. What you are paying for, essentially is *fashion*.

Fashion to people is like feathers to a bird. We need clothes, and yet such plumage performs surplus functions, from signaling one's status to inviting seduction. These extra benefits, which may be embodied in an ultra-luxurious series of details or

a high-style design, cost something. And, oddly, the more we pay and the more alluring the fashion is, the less enduring it seems to be. Look at last year's chic: The pouf went poof. Now, its as hot as yesterday's mashed potatoes.

Nevertheless, we come up with all kinds of rationalizations for buying fashion, for choosing the $1,300 coat over the $300 one:

"It goes with everything."

"It's really well-made."

"The prices are only going to go up."

"There are a whole lot of things I won't buy if I buy this one thing."

"If I'm not worth it, who is?"

There is also a special allure that comes from a garment's newness. From childhood on, it has been deeply ingrained in us that in the fall, we buy new books and new clothes. Our garments, like our books, seem to have magical elements that go beyond the intrinsic value of their materials. From the dazzling frivolity of Christian Lacroix to the serene town-and-country looks of Ralph Lauren, the idea of fashion both compels and repels, depending on the delicacy of your eye and the state of your pocketbook.

Men have an easier time than women with these considerations. Men's wear has a lot of intrinsic value. Many of the features of fine men's dress have a functional origin, often derived from playing field and battlefield rather than cutting room or salon.

Napoleon, for example, had buttons put on soldiers' coat sleeves to prevent his men from wiping their noses on their jackets. Likewise, jacket lapels go back to early military tunics, which soldiers were in the habit of folding back on hot days. It was a simple step to design this quirk into the garments themselves. Jacket vents derived from the sport of riding horses; button-down collars from the polo field; trouser cuffs from walks in the woods, and so on.

But with women's clothing, fashion has traditionally superseded utility. In the past, custom demanded that women wear a stiff corset, a whalebone bodice, a padded bosom. Superfluous superstructure inside, pure adornment outside. Vestiges of this approach appear and reappear with the cycles of fashion. What good is a pouf? Does a pencil skirt facilitate movement?

In the aftershock of such pure whimsy, some women's fashions are shifting toward the solid ground of "investment dressing," otherwise known as career dressing. (Even the "ladies who lunch" wear suits these days.) Flamboyance and fantasy are out; simple, understated clothes are in. Vendors who specialize in such sensible, practical garments, at various price points, are booming, from the sort of good, solid American retailer like Ann Taylor to the more expensive Armani and Chanel.

Coco Chanel was one of the first to bring function to fashion. Credit her with discarding the corset and various other linings that restricted movement and with adapting the conventions of men's wear — sweaters, blazers and pants — to make women's clothing less rigid and more practical. Her collarless cardigan jacket, often made of tweeds purloined from the great traditions of British men's wear, and accompanied by a straight skirt and strands of artificial pearls or gilt chains, is again a forceful and fashionable look 70 years after its conception.

Yet no matter how practical these designs may be, they have an element of fashion. Today's working women still assume that they will spend a substantial part of their income on their wardrobes, at least partly because of changing styles. To Henry David Thoreau's famous line, "Beware of all enterprises that require new clothes," the Seventh Avenue reply — reinforced in television and films, from "L.A. Law" to "Big Business" — is, "Your career is only as good as the clothes you get to wear to it."

But while this movement toward investment dressing is changing the face of fashion, it will never wipe away its smile. For all women — even the most intellectual — want to look beautiful. We consider it axiomatic that someone who is beautiful is dressed well. There is a kind of ineffable synergy between an attractive woman and what she wears.

A canny woman, for instance, will buy an inexpensive straight black skirt and a $1,000 Armani jacket, and she will be fashionable with something left to dine on. Fashion is broad, style is individual. A woman brings a lot to the value of clothes. If style enhances who you are, fashion allows you to become something more.

When a woman buys a designer dress or suit, she is buying the illusion of what that dress or look means, whether it is the secret thrill that heads will turn, or the quiet confidence that they will not. She is buying emotional rather than material value. It's a form of social security.

"We are not really used to asserting ourselves just on the basis of our character, the way men do," explains one woman. "So we assert ourselves through clothes. We're changing, but there are vestiges of that attitude."

In the end, most of us don't need more clothes. We've all got closets jammed with the stuff. What we *want*, which is quite different, is to look dashing, indomitable, sultry, soigné, neat.

Fashion, then, is the price we pay for wanting to be beautiful.

CALVIN KLEIN: IN THE MIDST OF CHANGE, A CERTAIN STYLE

by Kathleen Boyes

New York—"It starts with a philosophy of design that is always changing and evolving," explains Calvin Klein, referring to his creative process. "But there's a certain style, an attitude that is expected of me—pure, modern clean clothes that are very American. It's what I love and what I do best."

That "certain style" is the foundation of the Calvin Klein empire—an empire that, including the whole range of Klein products, licensed and unlicensed, has been pulling in at least $1 billion in annual retail sales for several years. It has made him a household name and a media phenomenon, carrying him way beyond the world of Seventh Avenue.

It is no accident that Klein is still receiving accolades—the recent CFDA salute, to name one—on his company's 20th year anniversary, which falls this month. Rather, it is his keen understanding of himself, of what he stands for, and of what others expect of him that keeps Klein at the top of American fashion.

Sitting on a black pillow back couch in his office at 209 West 39th St., Klein looks like he just stepped out of one of his ads. He is wearing a beige cashmere turtleneck, a houndstooth jacket and brown trousers. His office looks like a comfortable living room, rich in neutral colors, with leather bound books and magazines lying about. Propped up against the wall are his ads, matted and framed. The wooden blinds are drawn, giving the room a quiet ambience.

Occasionally, Klein sips coffee from the white cup and saucer on the coffee table. To make a point, he leans forward, often talking with his hands, his legs comfortably crossed.

"If I can't do something with the right enthusiasm and the right precision, I'd rather not do it. If I get tired of something or get bored, I might compromise myself, so I'd rather give it up," says Klein.

Source: *Women's Wear Daily*, February 22, 1988.

What also has kept Klein on top is his continuing evolution. "Designing clothes for American women is the most challenging, the most rewarding thing I do. Yet there's so much change—if you go through the last 20 years of my work, you'll see the changes. There has to be a change in order to last. Otherwise people move on to someone else. So an essential part of the creative process is always thinking of something new."

Inspiration for Klein is less discernible than for other designers. "I don't work within themes. It's not like I go to a Picasso exhibit and then show a 'Calvin-interprets-Picasso collection.' I'm not doing costumes; I'm doing very real clothes for the modern woman," explains Klein.

"If I am inspired by a book on the Masai, you won't know it. I once did some photos at Luis Barragan's, the Mexican architect's house—I love his work and sense of color. I used those colors in a collection. Sonia Caproni, who was then with I. Magnin, sent me a book of his work after the collection and said, 'I thought you might want to see this,' not knowing it had been my inspiration."

"Sometimes a woman will inspire me," continues Klein. "One time it was Katharine Hepburn. At one spring show my daughter thought every girl on the runway looked like Kelly (Klein's wife). Sometimes it's a model, like Jose. Or inspiration could come from someone like Grace Coddington, my design director. She has a strong sense of style.

"There isn't a set routine to my designing. I start with the fabrics and go from there. I'll have a feeling about what I want to do before I go to Europe and I'll look for fabrics conducive to that feeling. An example would be wanting a fabric with a lot of structure, that is stiff enough to make jackets or evening dresses. Or, it might be a flowing fabric that I can drape with. If I don't find it, then I might find something else that inspires something altogether different. I'm completely open, though I know right away if something isn't me."

Typically, Klein will take his design staff with him on his European fabric trips. The staff is comprised of three assistants, including Klein's associate of ten years, Zack Carr, who last fall returned to the Klein operation after a 2½ year hiatus, which included a short-lived venture with his own label.

Working as a closely knit team, Klein and staff come back to New York and start "sketching like mad" before the fabrics even arrive.

Klein communicates verbally with his assistants, telling them the "feeling" he's having about the season. "I'll tell them I'm thinking tight, or I'm thinking pants. I might ask them to get out a piece I did several years ago because it feels right for now."

"Then the fabric comes in and we have drapings and fittings and the feeling of a collection starts emerging. Shapes and silhouettes emerge and you know where you're going," adds Klein.

Sometimes a collection does not come so easily. "We have to be creative on a deadline. I have to do a show and I have to do a collection even if I don't have a show. Naturally there are highs and lows. Sometimes your assistants are just better and more excited and you can lean on them more. Other times everyone is feeling a little bit lost," says Klein. "That becomes a sign of a real pro, just pulling it together. I'll just get in there and make it happen."

Once a collection is designed, Klein starts preparing for his show. This is where the fine tuning and Klein's devotion to detail are most evident. Every model is assigned to specific looks. The models are then called in and the garments are refit on the particular girl who will be wearing them. Klein also decides their hair and accessories at that time.

"Of course, inevitably it changes. The girl will come in and not look right in what I envision her in and then we'll start all over again," explains Klein. "But nothing is left to chance. I don't even have to be at the show, things are that exact. There's no excuse for not being perfect, not being precise."

With Klein, the creative process does not end with the show. "I remain involved to the point that before any stock goes out a selection must come to my office for me to look at. If I think something is wrong, it doesn't get shipped," says Klein. "What good is being creative if the end product isn't what you showed on the runway?"

The Collection is just the beginning of Klein's creative odyssey which extends to exclusive collections, jeans, licensees, and advertising.

Though Klein designs exclusives for Bloomingdale's, Saks Fifth Avenue and Neiman Marcus, it is in the special collection that he does for Bergdorf Goodman that the designer can luxuriate with a couture approach.

"Ira Neimark and Dawn Mello approached me and asked if I would like to do a special collection. I could take as many risks and use the highest quality fabrics available. They gave me free rein and included me in the designing of the shop," says Klein. "Designing this collection pleases me aesthetically and it adds to the overall image of the Calvin Klein business."

At the other end of the spectrum, a key part of the Calvin Klein business is Puritan Fashions, which includes Calvin Klein Sport, women jeans and casual sportswear, Calvin, the contemporary jeans collection, and Calvin Klein Sport for Me.

"The jeans started out as a fun thing, a way to design inexpensive clothes," says Klein. "I had no idea it was going to turn into a $250 million sportswear company.

The key link between Klein and Puritan Fashions is Leann Nealz, the director of design. "She has to be my eyes. She knows when it's me and when it simply isn't. It's so important to have that trust. I'd call her and say 'I feel strongly about stretch,' and she'll have already ordered it. Sometimes I need to spend more time with her, and other times it's smooth sailing."

Klein works much the same way with his Puritan men's wear business, and licensees, which include coats, hosiery, underwear and sleepwear, cosmetics, shoes, furs and a new accessories collection.

Arthur Cook, vice president and creative director of licensees, directs on Klein's behalf. "When I can't personally see everything, Arthur can speak for me. I try and see as much as possible. I know right away if it's right. If it's not, it doesn't matter how much they tell me it will sell, they can't make it."

"I'm more involved with some licensees just because I enjoy them more or they need more attention. Shoes are a good example. I love shoes and have very strong points of views on footwear, from the expensive group to the Sport shoes to the new performance shoes."

Image is one area where Klein insists on absolute control. Anytime a product bearing his name is to be photographed for advertising or sent to a fashion magazine, he decides which piece is used.

Klein opened an in-house advertising agency, CRK Advertising—The R is for Richard—when he felt he did not have enough control with an outside agency. "It was easier to find people and do it myself," explains Klein. The "eyes and ears" of Klein at CRK is Sam Shadid, vice president and creative director.

"It's more difficult for me to explain the creative process of the advertising than anything else. I sit with Sam, Dick Avedon, Bruce Weber or Irving Penn and discuss what it is I want to say," explains Klein.

"A few years ago it started with a portrait of Greta Garbo that was in my office. We were working with Jose at the time and I told everyone I wanted portraits. Whether it was portraits of my clothes, jeans or someone in their underwear, I wanted portraits. That direction has been relatively easy to continue." "Commercials are another matter," he continues. "You really want to get people's attention, to really shake them up. So you go for it, you be provocative."

In 1989, Klein will be doing 13 commercials. "It's a lot," he acknowledges. "But it's all so much fun. I don't go on locations like I used to. With commercials everything is so laid out—what she's going to be wearing, who is directing—it's all done in advance. The only surprise is if we like it more than we thought we would."

"With print, there's more leeway. Whether it's with one model or a group shot, things can change—maybe you planned to do it indoors but it looks better outdoors. You have to give the photographer and stylist freedom. I used to be the stylist years ago, now I'd rather sit and be involved in the conceptualization than go on the actual shoot."

Klein is about to embark on a new adventure—retailing. In April he will open his first store in Dallas. "It's incredible how much work goes into a store. It's been a great learning experience working with Peter Marino (the store's designer)." Klein's been busily at work choosing furniture, displays and fixtures. In the future, Klein plans retail expansion. He intends to target cities where there are no major stores carrying Calvin Klein merchandise.

Another new project for Klein is his accessories collection that will be manufactured and sold through his cosmetic company, Calvin Klein Cosmetics, a division of Minnetonka. This collection, being produced in Europe, will be marketed very much like his cosmetics, with in-store boutiques with representatives. Klein's accessories will include handbags, luggage, gloves and scarves.

"The variety of what I do is the best part. When I was in school, I never dreamed I would be involved in so many creative areas, from television to fragrance to shoes," says Klein. "I love working on the conceptual end, but I don't want to spend my life doing one thing. That's the beauty of working with people who know you so well—they can carry through with something so you can move on."

At this point in Klein's career, enjoyment seems to be his primary motive. "I don't need the money, I haven't for a long time. So unless it's fun and I really believe in it, it's not worth it. If you really enjoy something, you'll produce something that's valid."

Surprisingly enough, Klein does not work long hours. Except for two weeks before his spring and fall shows, Klein does not work late into the night or on weekends. "I can do a lot in a day, I have to. If I need to decide something quickly I will," says Klein.

"But I'm thinking about work all the time. You can't turn off fashion. I can be looking at a film and think, 'she looks great' or, 'what wonderful photography'. Somehow it always comes back to something I'm involved in."

"Whether you're talking about me, Bill or Oscar, it's so much more than just designing clothes. There's just so **much going on**."

DONNA KARAN: HOT AND GETTING HOTTER

by Kathleen Boyes

New York—It's no surprise that Donna Karan designs in layers; she thinks that way. Try to get her to focus on DKNY, and she'll tell you how great her jeans look with one of her cashmere sweaters. Or bring up her hosiery, and she'll talk about dressing from head to toe, starting with the right eyewear. And mention her main collection, and she'll tell you how it has the comfort of DKNY.

Even as her business sizzles in a number of directions, the fact is Karan cannot separate any of her collections because she sees them as one.

"I'm designing one wardrobe. Whether you're talking about a sable coat or a pair of jeans, it's one mindset," explains Karan during a recent visit to her office. "When I first used washed silk, people were shocked—how can I use the same fabric as Go Silk? Well, it feels delicious. I don't care who else uses it, because it will have my trademark. Believe me."

The Karan trademark is celebrating its fifth year with this fall collection. In that time, the company has grown from its original five employees to 105, and has outgrown its two floors at 550 Seventh Ave.

The Donna Karan label is owned equally by Karan and her husband Stephan Weiss with Takihyo Inc., which is owned by Tomio Taki and Frank Mori. Besides her collection, DKNY and the accessory line, all produced by Karan, there are licensees in furs, sunglasses, hosiery, shoes, cashmere and DKNY jewelry.

According to company executives, total wholesale volume expected for the Donna Karan umbrella in 1989 is $141 million, of which $32 million will come from the licensees and $58 million from DKNY—a substantial growth, considering last year's wholesale revenue came in around $49 million.

Sitting in her black and white office, Karan looks exhausted. She has just come from the showroom, during market week for DKNY, where she has been arguing with retailers because she is not able to ship as much as they want.

Stock demands are just one problem facing a company bursting at the seams. Karan is currently moving production to another building and is planning to reorganize. With all this, finding time to design is one of her biggest concerns.

"Quite honestly, I may have bitten off a bit more than I can chew," she says. "Knock on wood, everything is going great. We're all on a high which makes the chaos fun."

So why does she keep adding new dimensions, like the recent cashmere collection or the DKNY jewelry line?

"There's never been a comfort level for me. It's an obsession," explains Karan. "I love conceptualizing new businesses."

DKNY filled an important void for Karan. She needed jeans and could not find a pair that were made for a woman's body. Also, she wanted a vehicle to offer her "fashion essentials"—like cotton Ts and white shirts—year round.

"There was no sportswear line designed for a woman," says Karan. "Every-

Source: *Women's Wear Daily*, April 3, 1989.

thing out there was junior-looking or dress-for-success."

DKNY grew out of Karan's Collection. "I was trying to do it all at once and at the same time not have it look schizophrenic," she points out.

As a result, DKNY allows her more freedom with Collection.

"I put my heart into DKNY," she explains. "Afterwards, all I could think was what was going to happen to Collection? Well, I discovered that the glamorous, creative side of me, took over. I'm turned on by the sheer luxury and the experimental art form that I'm able to indulge in."

Karan's new cashmere line is also rooted in Collection. "My cashmere is not about fashion. It's about my signature pieces—but all in cashmere."

A product's suitability is more important to Karan than its cost.

"I don't think that everything has to be in cashmere. But I also don't worry about the expense when putting a shearling coat on DKNY," says Karan. "I think a Keds sneaker is every bit as valid as a crocodile belt.

"Price doesn't matter when something is good, even when you're talking about a pair of tights," says Karan.

Putting her leg on the table, she tugs on her black hose and adds, "I couldn't find this tight anywhere. With me, the underpinnings are as important as the clothes. When Hanes came to me to do my tights, I was very clear: these are the tights I want. If you can make them, fine."

At this stage in her business, Karan designs everything. Two of her three assistants, Jane Chung and Edward Wilkerson, have been with her since she was working at Anne Klein. Chung works on DKNY, and Wilkerson, with Istvan Francer, works on Collection.

"There is nothing I don't touch," emphasizes Karan. "I work extremely hard on fabrications, often researching and developing my own. I do all the draping and all the fittings."

Accessories are designed with Collection. With the exception of eyewear, no product is designed independently.

Explains Karan, "I don't do hosiery colors, or anything else, to complement other people's clothes."

It's not just the clothes that form a network; all of Karan's creative endeavors are connected. Many include Peter Arnell, of Arnell Bickford agency, who has collaborated with Karan since the inception of the company. Arnell is responsible primarily for advertising, though his influence is felt in several promotional areas, including the current project of designing future Donna Karan stores.

"What's great about working so closely with the same people is they really know you and what your message is," says Karan.

Karan's advertising reflects the essence of her design message. Dennis Piel is the photographer, and Rosemary McGrotha is Karan's steady model.

"I try to capture an expression or a moment," says Karan. "For me, it's not really about clothes, but how the woman moves in them and how they make her feel. That's why I put bare legs in my hosiery ads."

Part of Karan's design impetus is her own criticism. "I never feel a collection is right," she explains. "I do the best job I can within the time limit, but I always feel I need another collection to complement the one I'm doing. If I ever feel this is it, I'll close my doors."

But Karan has a lot of voids to fill before that happens. "When I think of the things I haven's done yet, I get crazy. Retail stores, swimwear, underwear, cosmetics, International . . . the list is endless," she says, holding her head in exasperation. "Bergdorf's is opening a men's store. It makes me nuts. I'm dying to do men's wear. Every time I shop for fabrics I think how easy it would be for me—I mean the jackets . . ."

Before the Designing Whirlwind finishes that thought she's off on another. ". . . and cosmetics? I have a concept in my mind about that. I won't just be another designer perfume; that's the last thing we need."

RALPH LAUREN: TELLING STORIES

by Kathleen Boyes

New York—"Paris designers are often thought of as the best tailors in the world. That may be. However, they are making a dress. I am writing a story," explains Ralph Lauren, describing his design philosophy. "While the dress is important, it's just one part of the story."

Thus, apparently, lies the key to Lauren's storybook success. This year Ralph Lauren products are expected to generate $2 billion in worldwide retail sales. The women's collections, licensed by Bidermann Industries, USA, will be responsible for over $300 million of those sales. Lauren is owner and chairman of Polo/Ralph Lauren which includes his men's wear collection and his Madison Avenue store. His licensed products, in addition to women's apparel, include footwear, boy's wear, girl's wear, eyewear, scarves, hosiery, fragrance, handbags, luggage and leather goods.

Lauren's midtown office is a cab ride away from the frenzy of SA. Looking tan and relaxed in his de rigueur uniform of a denim jacket, workshirt and jeans, Lauren takes a visitor on a tour of his office. He points out such personal mementos as the needlepoint pillows made by his former model Clotilde that proclaim him the best

designer in the world, a painting done by a Santa Fe friend, a photograph taken by his wife, Ricky, of an old barn on their ranch in Colorado, and his collection of model race cars.

Calmly sipping a cup of coffee, he leans back into the tan suede couch and speaks softly of his creative process. To punctuate certain ideas, Lauren moves forward, bracketing the air with his hands.

"I work like a writer, with a theme that connects everything I do," explains Lauren. "The story starts with a girl. Who is she? What is she doing?

"I imagine her life: she get up in the morning, she goes to work, maybe she's a lawyer, whatever. Or maybe she's horseback riding or she's driving a car in the country. In my mind I create a world based around this girl."

For Lauren, who has often expressed an interest in acting, and worked on the wardrobes for both "The Great Gatsby" and "Annie Hall," there is an important relationship between movies and fashion.

"I think there's a degree of acting in fashion. You play different roles with your clothes, whether you're lunching at Le

Source: *Women's Wear Daily*, October 24, 1988.

Cirque or watching a tennis match. The clothes make you feel differently," says Lauren. "That's when the clothes come alive, not when a jacket is lying on the bed."

Lauren prefers to talk about style rather than fashion. "The words fashion and designer have always bothered me," says Lauren. "The kind of girl I design for is stylish in a quiet way; she's not always shopping or looking for the latest trend that she might have seen on the cover of a magazine. She's not fashionable in that sense."

Tradition is another favorite Lauren word. "I think clothes have to have a sense of tradition. I don't design clothes to be thrown out after each season; instead they should add to an existing wardrobe. Look at anything I designed in the past and it's still valid today. I design things to last."

Lauren is well aware of his critics who say that he is so caught up in tradition that he doesn't design anything new or even original.

Says Lauren: "Sure there are fashion editors who think I'm not creative and that I only copy L.L. Bean and Brooks Bros. My answer to that is you don't stay around for so many years if you have nothing new to say.

"The clothes I make may look familiar," continues Lauren, "but go and try to find the right jacket with the right shoulder in the right fabric. Or go to Vermont and try to find everything from my new country store. It's not that you've never seen this stuff before, or that I discovered a new concept. It's that I pulled all the right elements together.

"There is a consistency to my work and it's not because I want to be safe or that I can't do other things. It's because I feel it, it's who I am. It's successful, it keeps going."

Though Lauren is "writing stories" when he designs, clearly he is always the central character. "I design for my world, for the people I know, whose lives I understand. Someone like me," says Lauren.

"For me to put my name on anything I have to want to own it. I have to want to wear it or want my wife to wear it. I have to want it in my home. That's how I work."

Ricky Lauren is an important influence. "My wife serves as a barometer," says Lauren. "She tells me what she needs and what she's tired of wearing. She's also my toughest critic; what could be worse than having the woman in your life not want to wear the clothes you design?"

Lauren keeps a tight rein on the design of his products. Though he has small design teams of about two or three people for each category, he plays commander-in-chief in every design session, regardless of the product.

In each area, there is a senior vice president who works directly with Lauren both creatively and organizationally. Buffy Birrittella oversees both the women's collections and advertising; his brother Jerry, men's wear and Nancy Vignola, home furnishings. Mary-Randolph Carter, who is a vice president works on advertising. All are employed by Polo/Ralph Lauren and based in the West 55th Street office.

"At any given moment I am working on many different things. In some ways, I design by appointment; I can go from a meeting on men's wear to one on home furnishings and then on to Roughwear," explains Lauren.

Deadlines dictate Lauren's priority list. "If Classics is about to open, I clear the calendar and just work on that," says Lauren.

To prepare for his Collection, Lauren often travels for both inspiration and practical reasons, such as buying fabrics. Often he will bring a few design associates with him, including a sketcher.

Lauren begins each collection with a

mood or a feeling. "I'll sit down with my design team and tell them what I'm thinking. I might say, for example, that I want it clean, without frills," explains Lauren. "Or I might start a collection based on something specific like a color. I did that with my fall collection which began with a sculpted red jacket.

"I set the tone and then we begin pulling out fabrics, old photographs, movie stills or old books. We keep searching for things that fit into that mood," says Lauren.

"Sometimes it all falls together, other times you keep looking," he continues. "But it all goes back to the deadline. It's like writing a book: you may have great ideas floating in your head, but if your editor tells you it's due next week, you focus and make it happen.

"Where it really starts to happen is on the fitting model," he points out. "I'll have a tailor and a few other people with me and we'll work directly on the girl. Maybe I'll realize that everything I originally envisioned was wrong, that it doesn't work.

"That's when I start molding the collection like a sculpture. I can tell at a glance if there's a mistake. I might take off a collar and all of sudden the jacket will click."

Flexibility is essential at this point. Says Lauren: "Sometimes a mistake will work, so you go with it. You stay open and see what happens."

Perhaps Lauren's most important deadline is his show. "Right before the show is pressure time. The machine starts to roll, because it has to. It comes together at the very end when the clothes are coming in. I will try unexpected combinations, like suede pants with a tapestry jacket. That's when it comes alive."

When asked how he works with his licensees, Lauren's answer is simple: "I design the products and maintain total control.

"Some designers who license their name only care about the Collection, with everything else not being quite as significant," he continues. "Everything that I do is important to me. I work on it and I control it. It's not like someone else does the work and says here it is.

"For example, when it comes to my shoes, I worry about the sole, the quality of the suede, the color of the laces. Everything is part of the whole; it's the details that set my things apart.

"With my clothes, I'm concerned about the shape of the pocket, the stitch, the flap, all of it. Those are the elements that I think have made me," states Lauren.

What also has made Ralph Lauren is the world he creates with his advertising.

"My ads are my stories come to life. They are about a lifestyle, the world that I am thinking of when I'm designing," says Lauren.

The ads, which are photographed by Bruce Weber, often depict family life. Using both models and non-models, Weber will take the cast on location, where they will be given Lauren's clothes to wear all day. Weber then spontaneously photographs them, creating a natural effect.

For Lauren, identification with role models in advertising, like in movies, is critical. "Someone can show you a jacket that you think is okay. Then you see it on an actress in a movie. You like her, you like her style. You start identifying with her and start thinking that you can wear her jacket and have that same style. We all do that," explains Lauren. "'Annie Hall' was a good example of that. There was an attitude: a cute girl . . . New York . . . a great style. Women reacted and wanted to dress like her."

But, as with designing, Lauren remains flexible about his advertising.

"Last fall, I decided that I wanted my

advertising to be as clean and simple as the clothes. I didn't want a lot happening in the background, or many props. I wanted it to be stark, graphic, like a great piece of artwork," says Lauren. "Bruce disagreed. He said I always needed to have something there, even if just a lamp. I asked him to try it both ways.

"Later on we were taking photos of me by my red race car. Then it clicked. The car matched the starkness of the clothes. All the elements came together successfully."

Lauren is not one to rest on his laurels. "There will always be a new challenge ahead, something to learn about," says Lauren.

"I love discovering new worlds. Like race car driving; I didn't know anything except that I liked race cars. So I did research. I went to the raceway, I went to racing school, I bought cars. Little by little I learned."

Lauren feels he is still learning about his business. Says Lauren: "I want to perfect my craft; better quality is something you're always striving for. You can never sit back and think you've done it. There will always be room for improvement."

ADRIENNE VITTADINI: FROM ESTHETICS TO REALITY

by Kathleen Boyes

New York—"I am a hands-on designer," says Adrienne Vittadini. "I am totally involved in each product, from the original sketch, to the development of the fabric and the print, right on down to the button."

Adrienne Vittadini, who with her husband Gianluigi Vittadini owns the nine-year-old company that bears her name, is responsible for approximately 1,000 designs each season and sets the design direction for five licensees. Industry sources estimate the 1987 wholesale volume for Vittadini products, including licensees, to be $100 million.

"Nine years ago we started the company as a hobby for me, a professional hobby, while my husband worked in his family's pharmaceutical company. We had

no idea how this would grow," explained Vittadini.

When the company first opened, Vittadini was the sole designer with no assistants. To design she would lock herself up in her country house for two weeks and emerge with a fully designed collection. Said Vittadini, "It was an ideal state, with no interruptions." The creative process became more complicated as the company grew. "It's no longer possible for me to physically remove myself from it all," sighed Vittadini.

It also became impossible for Vittadini to design her collections by herself. Over the years, she developed a design studio that includes five major design assistants — one each for the main collection, the sport

Source: *Women's Wear Daily*, April 3, 1989.

collection and dress collection—and two that work exclusively with licensees. Vittadini's licensee categories include swimwear, socks and hosiery, leather, lingerie and accessories.

Like most female designers, Vittadini says she is her best customer. "I am my customer," said Vittadini. "I design for an active woman, a homemaker, a woman involved in the arts, a woman who travels. It is her needs, my needs, that inspire me."

Vittadini approaches each collection thematically. "First I come up with a mood, a feeling. What would I like to wear? It could be anything from a 1960s feeling to a romantic, soft look," said Vittadini. "My collection last spring was inspired by Grace Kelly in 'To Catch a Thief.'"

Art plays a key role inspiring Vittadini, who attended Philadelphia's Moore College of Art and whose father was a sculptor. The sense of sculpting is apparent when Vittadini talks about the creative process. She constantly says the word "chiseling," as if clothing itself were a work of art. Vittadini also derives ideas from traveling and culture. Her themes can focus on an individual artist, as with the collection inspired by Miro, or embrace a country, such as the one based on Spain.

"Once I focus on an area, I start researching. I live in libraries and museums. I also buy as many books on the subject. Every trip I come back with a suitcase full of books," said Vittadini. "In so many ways, it's like going back to school."

With themes and images in mind, Vittadini starts creating concept boards, which is where her assistant designers come in. "I start with my main collection. Verbally we go over the ideas and colors. We set the color board and get specific," said Vittadini.

Since the samples are made in Italy and Hong Kong, Vittadini sketches must be very specific. Said Vittadini, "If I use a logo or a passementerie look, it all must be drawn here in excruciating detail. Complex knits have to be mapped out. We can't leave anything to chance, or interpretation."

It is at this point that Vittadini the designer becomes Vittadini the merchandiser. "Initially I'm only concerned with esthetics, but then I envision how the clothes will look in the store and start chiseling and revising," said Vittadini.

She then travels to both Italy and Hong Kong where she completes the creative process. "I try on all the clothes, which is key to determining if something looks and feels right. I keep chiseling until it's right."

A supportive team allows Vittadini to focus on designing. Though the company is owned by Vittadini and her husband, it is with Richard Catalano, the chief executive officer, that the Vittadinis manage the company.

"The three of us are the perfect balance," points out Vittadini. "Gigi and Richard are the business end and I am the creative. We have a tremendous respect for one another and make all major decisions together."

Yet while the three form a close-knit team, Vittadini's design studio is on a separate floor and they seldom see each other in the day. "When I am designing, I don't take phone calls and don't welcome visitors. Richard and Gigi respect my privacy." When the three do meet, it is seldom in the office; rather it is in the Vittadinis's upper Eastside apartment or a three day jaunt to Bermuda.

"If it weren't for Gigi's support, none of this could have happened. He had more faith in me than I had in myself," adds Vittadini.

Vittadini management style extends to her five licensees. "I need to like the people I work with. There has to be that trust, that sense of integrity of product with anyone I deal with. I can't be limited as to how many samples I can make. If I feel something isn't right, or not of a certain quality, I must be able to start all over," said Vittadini. "I get so involved with each collection. I must feel that same sense of dedication."

It is that sense of dedication that makes Vittadini reluctant to delegate to others, though she is slowly learning that she must. "It is very difficult for me to delegate. Gigi and Richard keep telling me I must let go, but I find it painful, really painful," said Vittadini.

In November, Vittadini opened her first store on Rodeo Drive and plans to open more stores in the future. Having just completed decorating her Manhattan apartment and starting renovation on her new Hamptons home, Vittadini now finds herself thinking seriously about expanding into the home furnishings market.

Has the growth of her company changed her at all? "Not really, I've become more organized and committed to a schedule than I was before. But I still think of it as just a little company."

BEYOND FASHION: MARY MCFADDEN

by Diane Rafferty

Early Bronze Age clothing preserved for ages in the bogs of Denmark and now displayed at Copenhagen's National Museum is, basically, pure Mary McFadden. The prehistoric T-frame sleeved jacket with embroidery, the long braided cord at the waist, the large hammered-metal disk at the navel, the vertical string skirt, even the remnants of a snood are all signatures of McFadden's designs—if you translate the strings into her trademark, Fortunyesque pleating.

Mary McFadden may be the only fashion designer who thinks like an anthropologist. Unlike other designers, who strive to come up with something new every year, McFadden looks to the past—ancient history, in fact—for her inspiration and has rarely varied her forms. It is a surprisingly successful approach: McFadden gives new meaning to the American fashion buzzwords "classic," "timeless," and "durable." Gloria Steinem, who collects McFadden

evening wear, says, "I like the idea that after I'm gone someone will find something of hers in a thrift shop and be able to wear it."

"I think the simplest things are the most beautiful," says McFadden. "The most refined forms were worked over for hundreds of years to achieve their perfection. They're classic, because we already know they work. The silhouettes—the T-frame, the column, the A-line—were perfected, unlike some of the new silhouettes today that are not yet quite corrected. In understanding so-called primitive people, who evolved these clothes, reading Ruth Benedict's *Patterns of Culture* and Lévi-Strauss was important for me, as were the years I've lived in Africa."

McFadden went to Foxcroft, in Virginia, L'École Lubec, in Paris, the Traphagen School of Fashion, the New School for Social Research, and Columbia University,

Source: *Connoisseur*, October 1988.

where she studied anthropology for her sociology degree. In 1965 she moved to South Africa (her husband was a DeBeers executive) and wrote and edited for *Vogue*. McFadden had known *Vogue*'s editor Diana Vreeland since she was a child in Southampton on Long Island, and Vreeland's exuberant global fashion view undoubtedly made its mark on her. In 1968 McFadden moved to Zimbabwe (then Rhodesia), where she founded a sculpture workshop for African artists and helped get their works into museums in Paris and New York. She returned to New York in 1970, serving as special-projects editor at *Vogue*. During her travels, she collected African and Chinese silks and with them made up three tunics for a *Vogue* fashion shoot. Bendel's bought them immediately and commissioned many more from her.

Since she started designing, in 1973, McFadden has presented twice-a-year collections based on an historical culture — Pompeii, Egypt, the twelfth-century world of the Saracen Saladin, that of pre-Columbian Central America. This fall's collection draws from Lady Murasaki's eleventh-century epic *Tale of Genji*, particularly the twelfth-century illustrations attributed to Fujiwara Takayoshi. "It was a great challenge to me," says McFadden. "Japanese culture is the most sophisticated and the one I understood the least. And this period was the most important because the Japanese had just dismissed their Chinese ambassadors. They became very insulated and started developing their own style."

With the Genji collection, McFadden has truly come into her own: her preoccupation with the beginnings of a culture, with elaborately feminine indoor dressing, with stark black-and-white outfits, with simple forms (tunic, kimono, fencing jackets; loose, flowing Empire gowns and wide-cut pants), her love of rich, detailed adornment (embroideries, jewel-encrusted bodices, hand-painted motifs on

quilted jackets), the whole Vreeland "Japanesey" image, even McFadden's own penchant for white makeup and jet black, geometrically cut hair — all mesh beautifully with the Heian period.

So do the nature-inspired motifs with which she adorns her fabrics. Ornamental figures in the Genji collection include kishi flowers, lotuses, wisteria, golden clouds, thunderbolts, butterflies, snow crystals. McFadden has drawn in the past from Chinese, Burmese, Islamic, and Sanskrit designs. "I use all the symbols of the sun, the moon, the earth, clouds, and sea formations in abstraction," she says. "The spiral as a symbol of life and death. For jewelry, tree-growth symbols, astrological disks. I never use birds, though. They scare some women."

But McFadden is guided by hard-headed practicality, not by the stars. She anchors her fanciful fashion designs in an easily cared-for fabric. It is a concern she has had for years. In the early 1960s, long before Burberry raincoats became as common as blue jeans, she approached Gloria Steinem on a New York bus to ask if she could buy the beat-up British trench coat she was wearing. This very American appreciation of the durable and comfortable is as much a key to her success as her recognition of the need for magic in women's evenings. With her creation of "marii" pleating, McFadden has done for evenings on yachts what Levi Strauss, the jeans man, did for hanging out on campus.

Marii, like denim, travels easily, respects all seasons and climates, and is virtually indestructible. McFadden found the fabric seventeen years ago in Australia. "I took it to Japan to convert," she says, "because at that time it was very difficult to find a good poly that would have the same properties as silk when pleated and still be permanent." Like the Venetian Fortuny's pure, pleated silks, McFadden's polyester satin folds up like a handkerchief, forms a column on the body, and feels like liquid gold. But Fortuny pleating has to be re-pressed, and silk is perishable. Marii pops back into shape when unfolded. One McFadden devotee finds the dresses perfect for travel. "When you arrive at a hotel and find the steam room closed after four, you're in big trouble—unless you have a personal maid! But Mary's things come out of the suitcase like new."

McFadden has made the material her signature. "She's really taken a stand on this Fortuny-like pleating," says the fashion doyenne June Weir. "And she's developed it. Certainly, Europeans have done crystal pleating since Fortuny, but you identify it today with Mary McFadden."

Her ubiquitous use of marii is encour-aged by her studies of women's habits, their need for both comfort and glamour. Unlike many Seventh Avenue designers, who pro-duce for a mass market, or the French, often accused of working in an ivory tower, McFadden keeps her range small—ex-pensive, special-occasion dressing and, more important, knows her clientele well. "Mary talks to her clients," says Lynn Man-ulis of Martha on Park Avenue, a salon that has represented McFadden from the start. "She knows what they want and thrives on that feedback."

McFadden's customer is well off, travels a lot, and wants to look educated, feminine, and a little mysterious. Apart from the ever practical Steinem, who finds McFadden too expensive (gowns retail for $2,500 to $3,600) and buys the model's samples at the showroom, McFadden's cus-tomers include Patty Hearst, Sigourney Weaver, Margaux Hemingway, and Barbara Walters. "One of the secrets of Mary's suc-cess," says Manulis, "is that her clothes work on small figures like Mary's [size 4] and on more ample bodies too."

In many ways, the world traveler Ruthie Leffall, barely five feet tall, who is the wife of Howard University's chief of surgery, LaSalle Leffall, is a typical client. "I hear that this year she's doing something Japanese," she says. "But I don't get that involved in the theme. I tend to want the top from one year and the bottom from another. I remember going to a state dinner in Africa. Before I left, I decided at the last minute to take one of her pleated tops with a little chiffon skirt—a dress from some years ago. And it was just right for the oc-casion. And all through South America I wore her quilted jacket either over a gown or with a silk skirt of hers. If it was cool, I wore it with a wool skirt. It always worked. And because there's always some interest-ing detail, you get a compliment. Then you feel much nicer! I have some wonderful pa-jamas from her first collection. I think they're coming back into style. I'll recycle them."

McFadden is not an innovator in fash-ion design. She sets herself outside the fashion system and slowly elaborates her original statement, which evolved from studies of "primitive" forms. Like the im-mensely successful Ralph Lauren, she strives for timelessness. But unlike Lauren, who keeps adding details to a photographic vision of a vaguely prewar English landed gentry, McFadden taps the primordial ooze of fashion and varies the details, drawing from far-flung sources. She puts her cre-ative energies into these details and insists on quality: her embroideries and shadow lace (chikenwok) are done in India, color-ations in Japan, macramé and tailoring in New York—all under her supervision. She is an individualistic designer, but her de-signs will never look quaint. McFadden makes clothes to be treasured centuries from now.

GEOFFREY BEENE'S AMAZING GRACE

by Jay Cocks

His house is miles from Manhattan, out in Oyster Bay, on the north shore of Long Island. From the large home to the rolling acreage and the bounteous orchid gardens, this is Gatsby territory, a place of retreat. But in his work Geoffrey Beene is not interested in insulating himself or in evoking a Pololand of faux nostalgia and privileged period froufrou. Since he began his own label in the spring of 1963, Beene has kept a pace and set a standard that has made him, gradually and quietly, one of the most intrepid of fashionmakers.

The lovingly assembled career retrospective of 138 garments, which opened last month at New York City's National Academy of Design, is an eye-popper. The interplay of color and fabric is, as usual, dazzling. Heavy-duty industrial zippers are used with both leather and lace; effulgent Hudson's Bay blankets from L.L. Bean are trimmed with satin and turned into evening coats; a snazzy sequined evening dress is shaped and decorated like a football jersey. Vintage cartoon characters such as Felix the Cat and the Little King undercut and complement the high seriousness of a swank evening gown. The revelation of the show, which combines work from his first collection to his very latest, is its restless response to convention, its adventurousness about shape. "I love standards," says the designer, 61, "but I don't mind breaking rules. The only standard that finally matters is taste."

Beene can sculpt a dress with sensual simplicity or fill out a coat so that it seems to loft from the body. His rule breaking—like putting diamonds on a plastic bracelet—is focused, almost casual, and helps shatter stereotypes. In the fashion world, Beene has resisted and neatly refuted the caricature of Americans as the slightly slaphappy innovators of sportswear and merchandising trends. A long black wool coat from 1983, with flowing gold satin insets along its back and sleeves, constructed of curved seams, is a masterly combination of *grand luxe* and offhand invention, a subtle experiment in enlarging the possibilities of wearable form. Beene calls it "probably the single most significant piece of clothing I ever designed."

Like all of Beene's best work, this coat does not flout tradition, it teases it. Beene keeps rebellion firm but marginal, just as he did as a young medical student, when he sketched dresses on the page borders of his *Gray's Anatomy*. The year after Geoffrey Beene, Inc., was launched, Beene won the first of an unprecedented eight Coty Awards, the industry's Oscars, for his women's fashions. By the early '70s, he had made a wedding dress for Lynda Bird Johnson and had become one of the country's best-known and most sought-after designers, specializing in a kind of over-embellished chic. A *New Yorker* review of a 1972 collection nailed him for excesses of design that were "indulging fancifully in styles that women have never dreamed of simply because they have no earthly use for them."

Beene took all this to heart. "It made me rethink clothing and change my career," he says. He abandoned heavily structured clothes for looser, more accommodating shapes, knowing all the while that he was flirting with commercial disaster. "It was a rough period for me," he recalls. "We could have gone under." But Beene, who was raised in Louisiana and still speaks with a Southern lilt, has a certain flintiness to match his creativity. Says Issey Miyake, who apprenticed with Beene for five months in 1969: "His design is clean and clear and strong, just the way he is in life. He always keeps creativity No. 1 and business No. 2. He never compromises."

His experiments with looser, lighter forms gradually coincided with the radical incursions Miyake and others were making into the fashion mainstream, and the Beene business soon flourished again. "Someone once told me, 'Your clothes are always so wearable,'" he recalls. "And I said, 'If they're not, there should be another name for them. They couldn't be clothing.'" His instincts about the flexibility for styling can occasionally lead to confusion, however. "I've been thrown out of many places for inappropriate dress," Beene laughs, remembering the time he and a friend turned up for a swank lunch and were rebuffed by the maître d'. Beene's loosely tailored jacket of his own design did not pass the restaurant's dress code. He turned to his companion, borrowed her tailored blazer, passed his jacket to her, "and we sailed into the restaurant, with me in a woman's jacket, and that was that."

Beene's styling continues to be fluid, although he is now cutting some of his clothes closer to the body—a few of his evening dresses for the current season will not forgive an extra pound—but ease and sensuality remain constant, as does his fixation on the future. He wants to remove the stigma of synthetics ("They work; they don't wrinkle; they take less care") and dreams of designing a whole couture collection of man-made fabric. "If it was appreciated," he says slyly, "then I'd tell everyone what the material was. After the show."

One of the best pieces in the National Academy exhibition is a simple dress of black wool and white hammered satin, draped and hung in back with trompe l'oeil suspenders that rise to the neck and form a small collar in front. It is from Beene's current collection and shows that his hand is stronger than ever. "When you think of something as very American," observes Miyake, "you think of something as very new." By this definition, Beene continues to be the most American of designers and very likely the country's best too.

Endnotes

1. Paul F. Nystrom, *Economics of Fashion*. New York: Ronald Press, 1928, p. 4.
2. Cecil Beaton, *The Glass of Fashion*. Garden City, N.Y.: Doubleday, 1954, pp. 335, 379–381.
3. Thorstein Veblen, *The Theory of the Leisure Class*, Mentor Edition. New York: New American Library of World Literature, 1963, p. 97.
4. As quoted in Molly Ivins, "The Constant in Fashion Is the Constant Change," *New York Times*, August 15, 1976.
5. Edward Sapir, "Fashion," *Encyclopedia of the Social Sciences*, Vol. VI. New

York: Macmillan, 1931, pp. 139–144; and Gabriel Tarde, *The Laws of Imitation*. New York: Henry Holt & Co., 1903, p. 313.

6. Veblen, *The Theory of the Leisure Class*; John Roe, *The Sociological Concept of Capital*. London: Macmillan, 1834, Chapter 13; Caroline R. Foley, *Economic Journal* (London), Vol. 3, 1893, p. 458.

7. George Simmel, "Fashion," *American Journal of Sociology*, Vol. 62, May 1957, pp. 541–558. Reprinted from the *International Quarterly*, Vol. 10, October 1904, pp. 130–155.

8. Charles W. King, "Fashion Adoption: A Rebuttal to the 'Trickle Down' Theory," Reprint Series 119. Reprinted from American Marketing Association Winter Conference, 1963, by Purdue University, Krannert School of Business Administration.

9. Allan Greenberg and Mary Joan Glynn, *A Study of Young People*. New York: Doyle, Dane, Bernbach, Inc., 1966.

10. Veblen, *The Theory of the Leisure Class*, p. 97.

11. Quentin Bell, *On Human Finery*. London: Hogarth Press, 1947, pp. 48–49.

12. RAM Reports to Retailers, January 1977.

13. Charles E. Silberman, "Identity Crisis in the Consumer Markets," *Fortune*, March 1971, p. 95.

14. Dwight E. Robinson, "Economics of Fashion Demand," *Quarterly Journal of Economics*, Vol. 75, August 1961, pp. 395–396.

15. Alfred H. Daniels, "Fashion Merchandising," *Harvard Business Review*, May 1951.

16. RAM Reports to Retailers, January 1977.

17. Wool Bureau Special Report, January 1989.

Selected Bibliography

Adburgham, Alison. *View of Fashion*. London: Allen and Unwin, 1966.

Anspach, Karlyne. *The Why of Fashion*. Ames: Iowa State University Press, 1967.

Batterberry, Michael and Ariane. *Mirror Mirror: A Social History of Fashion*. New York: Holt, Rinehart and Winston, 1977.

Beaton, Cecil W. H. *The Glass of Fashion*. Garden City, N.Y.: Doubleday, 1954.

Bell, Quentin. *On Human Finery*, 2d ed. London: Hogarth Press, 1976.

Bergler, Edmund. *Fashion and the Unconscious*. New York: R. Brunner, 1953.

Boehn, Max von. *Modes and Manners*. Philadelphia: J. B. Lippincott, 1932.

Bond, David. *The Guinness Guide to 20th Century Fashion*. Middlesex, England: Guinness Publishing Ltd., 1988.

Boucher, Francois. *2,000 Years of Fashion*. New York: Harry N. Abrams, 1967.

Broby-Johansen, R. *Body and Clothes: An Illustrated History of Costume*. New York: Reinhold, 1968.

Calasibetta, Charlotte. *Dictionary of Fashion*. New York: Fairchild Publications, 1976.

Carter, Ernestine. *Magic Names of Fashion*. London: Weidenfeld and Nicolson, 1980.

Coleridge, Nicholas. *The Fashion Conspiracy*. New York: Harper and Row, 1988.

Contini, Mila. *Fashion: From Ancient Egypt to the Present Day*. New York: Odyssey, 1965.

Cunningham, Cecil W. *Why Women Wear Clothes*. New York: Gordon Press, 1979.

D'Assailly, Gisele. *Ages of Elegance: Five Thousand Years of Fashion and Frivolity*. London: MacDonald, 1968.

Diamonstein, Barbara. *Fashion: The Inside Story*. New York: Rizzoli, 1985.

Everyday Fashions of the Twenties as Pictured in Sears and Other Catalogs. New York: Dover Publications, 1981.

Fairchild, John. *Chic Savages*. New York: Simon and Schuster, 1989.

Flugel, John C. *The Psychology of Clothes*. New York: International Universities Press, 1966.

Hall, Carolyn. *The Twenties in Vogue*. New York: Harmony Books, 1983.

Harris, Christine, and Moira Johnston. *Figleafing through History: The Dynamics of Dress*. New York: Atheneum, 1971.

Hollander, Anne. *Seeing through Clothes*. New York: Viking Press, 1978.

Horn, Marilyn J., and Lois M. Gruel. *The Second Skin: An Interdisciplinary Study of Clothing*, 3rd ed. Boston: Houghton Mifflin, 1981.

Khornak, Lucille. *Fashion, 2001*. New York: Viking Press, 1982.

Kidwell, Claudia Brush, and Valerie Steele. Washington, D.C.: Smithsonian Institution Press, 1989.

Kohler, Carl. *A History of Costume*. New York: Dover Publications, 1963.

Lagner, Lawrence. *The Importance of Wearing Clothes*. New York: Hastings House, 1959.

Laver, James. *The Concise History of Costume and Fashion*, rev. ed. New York: Oxford University Press, 1983.

Laver, James. *Dress*. London: J. Murray, 1950.

Laver, James. *Modesty in Dress*. Boston: Houghton Mifflin, 1969.

Laver, James. *Taste and Fashion*. New York: Dodd Mead, 1938.

Laver, James. *Women's Dress in the Jazz Age*. London: H. Hamilton, 1964.

Laver, James, and Christina Provert. *Costume and Fashion*, rev. ed. New York: Oxford University Press, 1983.

Lurie, Allison. *The Language of Clothes*. New York: Random House, 1981.

McDowell, Calin. *McDowell's Directory of Twentieth Century Fashion*. Englewood Cliffs, N.J.: Prentice-Hall, 1985.

Milbank, Carolyn R. *The Evolution of American Style*. New York: Harry Abrams Pub., 1990.

Moore, Jonathan. *Perry Ellis: A Biography*. New York: St. Martin's Press, 1988.

Murray, Maggie Pexton. *Changing Styles in Fashion: Who, What, Why*. New York: Fairchild Books, 1990.

Nystrom, Paul F. *Economics of Fashion*. New York: Ronald Press, 1928.

O'Hara, Georgina. *The Encyclopedia of Fashion*. New York: Harry N. Abrams, Pub., 1986.

Perna, Rita. *Fashion Forecasting*. New York: Fairchild Books, 1987.

Roach, Mary Ellen, and Joanne B. Eicher. *Dress, Adornment and the Social Order*. New York: John Wiley & Sons, 1965.

Rudofsky, Bernard. *The Unfashionable Human Body*. New York: Doubleday, 1971.

Solomon, Michael R. *The Psychology of Fashion*. Boston: D. C. Heath, 1985.

Stegemeyer, Anne. *Who's Who in Fashion*. New York: Fairchild Publications, 1988.

The Designing Life. Staff of Washington, edited by Lois Persceetz. New York: Clarkson N. Potter, Inc., 1987.

Tortora, Phyllis, and Keith Eubank. *A Survey of Historic Costume*. New York: Fairchild Books, 1989.

Tozer, Jane. *Fabric of Society: A Century of People and Their Clothes, 1770–1870*. New Jersey: Laura Ashley, 1985.

Trachtenberg, Jeffrey A. *Ralph Lauren: The Man behind the Mystique*. New York: Little, Brown, 1988.

Wilcox, Ruth Turner. *The Mode in Costume*. New York: Charles Scribner's Sons, 1983.

Yarwood, Doreen. *The Encyclopedia of World Costume*. New York: Scribner's, 1978.

Trade Associations

Council of Fashion Designers of America (CFDA), 1412 Broadway, New York, N.Y. 10018.

The Fashion Group, 9 Rockefeller Plaza, New York, N.Y. 10020.

International Association of Clothing Designers, 7 East Lancaster Avenue, Ardmore, Penna. 19003.

New York Fashion Designers, 1457 Broadway, New York, N.Y. 10036.

Trade Publications

Daily News Record, Fairchild Publications, 7 East 12th Street, New York, N.Y. 10003.

Women's Wear Daily, Fairchild Publications, 7 East 12th Street, New York, N.Y. 10003.

CHAPTER REVIEW AND LEARNING ACTIVITIES

Key Words and Concepts

Define, identify, or briefly explain the following:

A style	Fashion prediction
Avant garde	Fashion trend
Bottom-up theory	Forward fashion
Classic	High fashion
Design	Mass fashion
Evolutionary	Style
Fad	Style number
Fashion	Trickle-across theory
Fashion cycle	Trickle-down theory

Review Questions on Chapter Highlights

1. Give examples of each of the following: a style, fad, classic, design, fashion, fashion trend. Explain the differences and relationships between these terms.

2. "The only thing constant about fashion is change." Explain why fashions change and cite examples.

3. Cite examples of products other than apparel and accessories that are currently being affected by fashion.

4. Do you agree or disagree that there are different fashions for different groups of people? Give examples to prove your answer.

5. Does your current wardrobe represent one or more stages of the fashion cycle? Which stage or stages and why?

6. Explain the following statement: "There are three accepted theories that categorize the admired groups from which fashion leadership flows." Give examples.

7. Do designers originate all fashions? Prove or disprove.

8. Explain how fashions reflect their "times" and cite specific current examples.

9. Is there a relationship between market segmentation and the prediction of fashion? Explain.

10. Describe the factors that must be considered by fashion professionals in predicting coming fashions.

11. What awards in the American fashion industry are comparable to the "Oscars"? To which current American designers would you give an award, and why?

3

$\mathcal{T}$HE $\mathcal{M}$ATERIALS OF $\mathcal{F}$ASHION

The expression of every fashion in the form of a garment or accessory owes as much to the fabrics, furs, or leathers that are available as it does to the idea that inspires its birth. As Christian Dior once said, "Many a dress of mine is born of the fabric alone."[1]

To grasp the importance of the producers of the raw materials in the business of fashion, one must recognize that many of the changes are primarily variations in colors, textures, or fabrics rather than changes in style.

This chapter is concerned with the *primary* fashion markets that provide the fibers, fabrics, leathers, and furs that enable designers to give substance to their ideas. The text discusses the most important segments of the primary markets and indicates how each of these influences fashion and is influenced by it. The readings that follow illustrate the operations of leading companies in the field.

FROM FIBER TO FABRIC _____

The making of fabrics involves a great many processes, uses machines of many different types, and employs the skills and knowledge of a variety of producers and processors.

No matter what the end result, every textile product originates as fiber. Fibers fall into two main categories: (1) **natural fibers**, such as cotton, wool, ramie, silk, and flax, which come from plant and animal sources and have been used for thousands of years, and (2) **man-made fibers**, which are basicly chemical products and whose development and utilization are twentieth-century phenomena. Whether fibers are natural or man-made, however, they undergo the same basic fabrication processes in the course of their transformation into textile products: the spinning of fibers into yarns, the weaving or knitting of yarns into fabric, and the finishing of fabric to impart color, texture, pattern, or other characteristics. *Weaving* is the interlacing of two sets of yarns, vertical and horizontal. *Knitting* involves machines that make fabric by inter-looping of either vertical or horizontal sets of yarns.

Before being made into a fabric, fibers must first be spun into yarns. **Yarn** is produced by twisting together strands of fiber into a continuous thread or filament. This may be as coarse as rug backing or finer than sewing thread. To manufacture cloth, the yarns are knitted or woven together.

Some natural fiber yarns are dyed before being made into fabric. This is particularly true of wool, but sometimes man-made fibers receive similar treatment. In the latter case, the fibers are **solution-dyed**, which means that dye is introduced into the chemical "dope" from which the fiber is made. In **yarn dying** the yarn is first spun, then put on cones, then dyed on the cone prior to the fabric production process. More commonly, however, yarns are employed in their undyed state to produce **greige goods**, which is undyed, unfinished fabric that is later dyed in the piece and subjected to a variety of finishing processes. At every step of the way, from fiber production to finished product, fashion is the primary influence in determining what materials will be used, how they will be treated, and what the end product will be.

FIBER PRODUCERS _____

Much of the fashion industry's ability to respond promptly and accurately to changes in consumer preferences for apparel and accessories is due to the immense variety of textile products available for use. In turn, the textile industry can more readily present its impressive range of textures, colors, weights, lusters, and other characteristics because the fiber producers are also aware of and responsive to fashion's requirements. That responsiveness, this far back in the production process, was slight in the days when only natural fibers were available, but it has reached enormous proportions now that man-made fibers have opened new doors in the industry.

Suppliers of Natural Fibers

The natural fibers are cotton, wool, silk, ramie and flax. The amounts and qualities available at any given time and place are influenced by environmental conditions, such as climate and terrain suited to the animals and plants that are their source. Suppliers of natural fibers are many, are located all over the world, and tend to be relatively small in size. They generally sell their products in local markets to wholesalers who, in turn, may sell them to other wholesalers in regional markets. In the case of cotton and wool, commodities dealers may buy these fibers from central wholesalers throughout the world and sell them to mills. Thus, it is possible for an American textile producer to create a shirting fabric from Egyptian cotton, or a Japanese knitter to offer a sweater of Australian lambswool.

Before the entrance of man-made fibers, the suppliers of natural fibers were scarcely a part of the fashion industry. Their traditional role was only to

Examples of Natural Fiber Logos

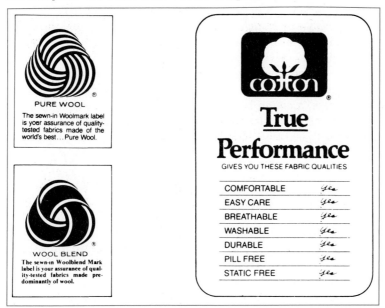

PURE WOOL

The sewn-in Woolmark label is your assurance of quality-tested fabrics made of the world's best...Pure Wool.

WOOL BLEND

The sewn-in Woolblend Mark label is your assurance of quality-tested fabrics made predominantly of wool.

True Performance
GIVES YOU THESE FABRIC QUALITIES

COMFORTABLE	Yes
EASY CARE	Yes
BREATHABLE	Yes
WASHABLE	Yes
DURABLE	Yes
PILL FREE	Yes
STATIC FREE	Yes

produce and sell their raw materials. They were not concerned with the making of these raw materials into yarns for weaving or knitting fabrics, and they had no relationship with the garment makers or ultimate consumers. They certainly were not attuned to fashion. All of this changed with the entrance of man-made fibers into the business of fashion.

The need to compete with man-made fibers forced the cotton and wool growers into reevaluating their marketing procedures. They were impelled to take a more aggressive role and move out to reach the textile producers, the garment makers, and the ultimate consumers. In addition to improving the desirable properties of their fibers, the suppliers of wool, cotton, and other natural fibers each began united efforts to compete more favorably with the man-made fibers. Today natural fiber producers, through their trade associations, act as a source of information about the fabrics processed from their respective fibers and about fashion in general. They also promote their fibers to the trade and to the general public by directing attention to the virtues of their product.

For example, there is an International Wool Secretariat supported by wool growers from all over the world. Their headquarters, which are located in London, are staffed with fashion specialists who advise fabric manufacturers of new developments in weaves, patterns, and colors. This association also publicizes wool in all media and by all means—films, fashion presentations to the trade and to the press, and cooperative advertising programs with makers and sellers of wool garments. There is also a very active cotton association, Cotton Incorporated, which is headquartered in New York City and acts as an information and promotional center for cotton. They prepare and distribute advance information about fashions in cotton and cotton-blended fabrics to designers, manufacturers, the fashion press, and retail stores. They also advertise cotton fashions in consumer and trade publications. In addition, both associations encourage producers and retailers to use their distinctive logos (a ball of yarn in the one case, a cotton boll in the other) in the advertising of fashion garments made of their particular fibers. The promotional activities of their trade associations have drastically changed the part played by natural fiber producers in the world of fashion.

Man-Made Fiber Producers

As defined by the Textile Fiber Products Identification Act, man-made fiber is "any fiber derived by a process of manufacture from any substance which, at any point in the manufacturing process is not a fiber." This is in contrast to the term *natural fiber*, meaning a fiber that exists as such in the natural state.

For hundreds of years, man had toyed with the possibility of duplicating the work of the silkworm by mechanical or chemical means. These small creatures feed on mulberry leaves and are able to produce a thick liquid, which they force out through tiny openings in their heads in the form of silk fiber. Thus, in 1855, a Swiss chemist named Audemars attempted to produce synthetic silk by using the fibrous inner bark of the mulberry tree.

It was not until 1891, however, that the French Count Hilaire de Chardonnet built the first "artificial silk" plant in France. He eventually earned the title of "father of the rayon industry" when, in 1924, artificial silk was renamed *rayon*: "ray" to suggest sheen and "on" to suggest cotton. Rayon was followed by a deluge of man-made fiber experiments and developments in the 1920s and 1930s. The giant breakthrough came with the first public showing of nylon hosiery, introduced by Du Pont, at the 1939 Golden Gate Exposition in San Francisco. Not only did nylon hosiery immediately become one of the most wanted articles of feminine apparel, but nylon itself played a significant role in World War II for such uses as parachutes and uniforms.

With the development of man-made fibers, the importance of natural fibers declined dramatically, whereas the growth of the man-made fiber industry was phenomenal. These figures illustrate the point: At the end of World War II, man-made fibers accounted for only 15 percent of all fibers used in the textile mills of the United States. By 1965, the man-made fiber industry was providing 42 percent of the nation's fiber needs. By 1989 the man-made fibers accounted for 64.5 percent of the total fiber consumption used by American mills. Cotton in that year provided 29.3 percent of the fiber; cellulosics provided 4.8 percent; and wool provided 1.4 percent.[2]

Impact of Chemical Fiber Producers

The continuing development of an unending procession of new man-made fibers took place and continues to do so in the laboratories of giant chemical companies such as Du Pont, Hoechst-Celanese Fiber Industries, Dow Chemical, Monsanto, and Eastman Chemical, for example. The entrance of these chemical producers into the fashion industry has brought about many changes in the fashion business, along with a whole new world of textiles. Since few in the textile industry know how to handle new synthetic fibers, the man-made fiber producers have to teach and guide spinners, weavers, and knitters in the processing and fabrication of new fibers. They also have to create a demand among garment producers for the fabrics made with their fibers and provide them with guidance and encouragement. Finally, they have to educate and create a demand among consumers as well. In short, they not only supply their fibers to yarn makers, but with their enormous facilities for financing and research, they assume a dominant role in how these fibers are used in yarns, fabrics, and fashion apparel. Unlike the suppliers of natural fibers, the man-made fiber producers made fashion their business from the start.

The entrance of giant chemical companies into the business of fashion has added new dimensions to the fashion industry. The concept of creating whatever kind of fiber is needed or wanted to develop new and different fabrications opened up a whole new world of textiles such as "stretchable," "wash and wear," "durable press," "heat-set pleats," and "wrinkle-resistant," with more to come. The promotional funds provided by man-made fiber producers to help

U.S. Total Fiber Consumption
1950 compared to 1989.

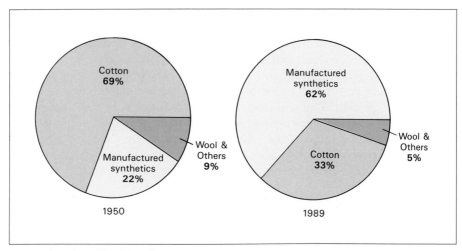

SOURCE: American Fiber Manufacturer's Association.

finance the advertising of fabrics and/or garments that feature their fabrics generate more fashion advertising than would otherwise be possible. The financial resources of giant chemical companies are such that they can support continuing research and development of new concepts in technology, merchandising, and fashion, the results of which are made available to fabric and apparel producers.

FLEXIBILITY OF MAN-MADE FIBERS

Two basic types of man-made fibers are used for apparel: cellulosic and noncellulosic. Cellulosics are produced from cellulose, the fibrous substance found in plants, such as softwood trees, and are made with a minimum of chemical steps. They include rayon, triacetate, and acetate. Noncellulosic fibers are made from chemical derivatives of petroleum, coal, natural gas, air, and water. Fiber chemists link the molecules from these sources into long chains called polymers. In this category are nylon, acrylic, and polyester fabrics.

Man-made fibers have been improving the quality of fashion goods by offering a variety of characteristics unavailable in natural fibers. Their production, moreover, is not affected by the vagaries of weather or other natural conditions. They can be manufactured in quantities as large or as small as anticipated demand requires, and they can be endowed with desirable characteristics not necessarily found in natural fibers. For example, triacetate can be used to produce fabrics that are washable and wrinkle-resistant, or with pleats that are heat-set for permanency; it can also be used in fabrics with brushed or napped surfaces and textured effects. Acrylic fibers can be employed in pile fabrics that are used in fleecewear, and that simulate furs. Modacrylics, inherently flame-resistant, are excellent for use in children's sleepwear, upholstery, blankets, and draperies.

An example of how a fiber can constantly be improved to meet changes in consumer demand is offered by nylon and polyester. Today, high-filament nylon is blended with stretch fibers such as spandex to create new swimwear, exercise wear, and dance clothing. Nylon reflective yarn is used in clothes that reflect the headlights of oncoming cars when worn by nighttime joggers and bicycle riders. In the home, nylon has become the leading fiber for carpets; 99 percent of all domestic carpets are made of it. In 1990, a new yarn of microfiber polyester spun in filaments of less than one denier — two or three times thinner than a human hair — was introduced by Du Pont and Hoechst-Celanese. This new yarn has greater softness and silk-like characteristics, and will lead to a totally new generation of polyester textile products.

EMPHASIS ON BRAND NAMES

Under the Textile Fiber Products Identification Act, the Federal Trade Commission establishes generic names for synthetic fibers. A **generic name** is one that designates a general group of fibers with similar chemical composition and properties. Of the more than 20 generic names established, however, relatively few are used for apparel fabrics. Polyester, nylon, and rayon, in that order, are the most widely used for clothing; other fibers used include acrylic, acetate, modacrylic, and triacetate. Within any of the basic broad categories, fiber producers can modify the basic chemical and physical composition to produce a new fiber. Although the same generic names may apply to the newer creations, these *variants*, as they are called, are usually identified by a **brand name** given them by the manufacturer.

From the first, the producers of man-made fibers have been very aggressive in promoting their brand names. A *brand* is a device, sign, trademark, or name that is used to identify and distinguish products as a means of building a market for them. Each company uses its brands to build recognition and acceptance of its product, to differentiate it from other similar products in the customer's mind, and to lessen price competition. To accomplish these ends, producers of man-made fibers advertise their brands in trade and consumer magazines and

Man-Made Fibers and Major Trade Names

Acetate	Nylon	Olefin	Polyester (cont.)
Acetate by Avtex	A.C.E.	Herculon	Strialine
Ariloft	Anso	Herculon Nouvelle	Trevira
Avron	Antron	Marvess	Ultra Glow
Celanese	Blue "C"	Patlon	Ultra Touch
Chromspun	Cadon		
Estron	Cantrece	**Polyester**	**Rayon**
Loftura	Caprolan	A.C.E.	Absorbit
	Captiva	Avlin	Avril
Acrylic	Celanese	Caprolan	Absorb
Acrilan	Cordura	Crepesoft	Beau-Grip
Bi-Loft	Courtaulds Nylon	Dacron	Coloray
Creslan	Cumuloft	Encron	Courcel
Fi-lana	Eloquent Luster	Fortrel	Courtaulds HT
Orlon	Eloquent Touch	Golden Glow	Rayon
Pa-Qel	Enkacrepe	Golden Touch	Courtaulds Rayon
Remember	Enkalon	Hollofil	Durvil
So-Lara	Enkalure	Kodaire	Enkaire
Zefkrome	Enkasheer	Kodel	Enkrome
Zefran	Lurelon	KodOfill	Fibro
	Multisheer	KodOlite	Rayon by Avtex
Aramid	Natural Luster	KodOsoff	Zantrel
Kevlar	Natural Touch	Lethasuede	
Nomex	Shareen	Matte Touch	**Spandex**
	Shimmereen	Natural Touch	Lycra
Modacrylic	Softalon	Plyloc	
SEF	T.E.N.	Polyextra	**Triacetate**
	Ultron	Shanton	Arnel
	Zefran	Silky Touch	
	Zeftron		**Vinyon**
			Vinyon by Avtex

SOURCE: *Man-Made Fibers—A New Guide*, Man-Made Fiber Producers Association, Inc.

other public media in their own names, or in conjunction with fabric firms or makers of finished products. Anything from a multipage advertisement in a trade paper to an elaborate fashion presentation on TV may be used. In addition, their cooperative advertising money pays for much of the trade and consumer advertising of textiles and apparel in which their branded fibers are employed and identified. They also arrange or participate in fashion presentations staged by textile firms that identify their fibers, and they distribute free educational booklets to both retail employees and the consumer to acquaint people with the properties and names of their fibers. Some branded fibers are sold under a licensing arrangement that restricts the use of the brand name to products that comply with standards set by the fiber producer. An example of such a brand is Fortrel. At the other extreme are fibers that are sold as unbranded products, with no specified or implied performance standards or restrictions on their end use.

TEXTILE PRODUCERS

Textiles is a broad term that describes fabrics made from fiber by any of a number of different methods. Thousands of yards and millions of pounds are produced annually in the United States, in infinite variety: wovens and knits,

End Use by Type of Textile, 1989

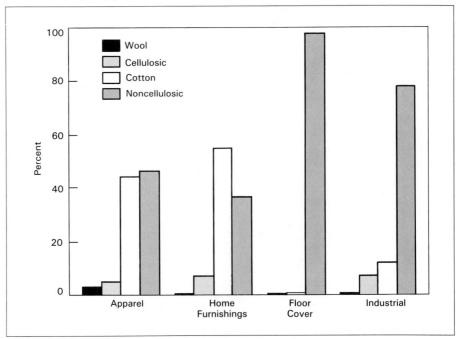

SOURCE: Textile Organon, Textiles Economic Bureau.

polka dots and stripes, reds and blues, chiffons and seersuckers, and on and on, in every kind and color and texture fashion can demand. In providing the materials with which to express the designers' ideas, textiles are the very essence of fashion. Without denim, for instance, the fashion for jeans could not have come into being. Nor could there be sweatsuits and jogging outfits if the appropriate sweatshirt materials were not available.

Economic Importance

The basic function of the textile segment of the fashion industry is the transformation of fibers—natural or man-made—into yarns and then into finished fabrics. At one end of the industry spectrum are thousands of manufacturing plants that perform one or more of the three major processes involved in the production of fabrics: spinning fibers into yarns, weaving or knitting yarn into fabric, and finishing fabric to provide color, pattern, and other desirable attributes. At the other end of the spectrum are the sales offices that market the finished cloth to apparel and accessories producers, fabric retailers, and the home furnishings industry.

The textile industry plays a vital role in the economy of the United States. It encompasses companies operating approximately 2,500 plants and gives employment to more than 680,000 people. Its output was valued at the manufacturing level at almost 68.9 billion in 1989.[3]

Although the bulk of the manufacturing facilities are on the East Coast, some phase of textile activity is carried on in nearly every state of the union, with the largest concentration in the South. Marketing, styling, and design activities are centered in New York City as the number one location, with Los Angeles second, but selling activities reach into many other major cities.

The textile industry consumes fibers and dyes, machinery and power, services and labor to produce cloth that finds its way into a myriad of end uses—fashion apparel and accessories, to be sure, but also such diverse products as inflatable buildings, tire cord, space suits, sheets, carpets, and diapers. Clothing and accessories take up more than one-third of the industry's output, with products for the home ranking second and increasing rapidly.

History and Growth

Although the U.S. textile industry today is the largest in the world, textile production by factory methods had its beginnings in England. During the eighteenth century, while the United States was becoming aware of itself and struggling for its independence, a series of inventions, each a closely guarded trade secret, had mechanized the spinning of yarn and the weaving of cloth in England and had moved production from the home to the factory in that country. The American colonies were, as England intended, a dependent market for one of the mother country's major products.

Colonial America imported most of its fashion materials: silks from Italy, China, and France; woolens, calico, and cashmere from England; feathers and artificial flowers from France. Prosperous settlers took full advantage of such imports; those who were less prosperous produced their own crude materials with which to clothe themselves. The men raised and sheared sheep, grew flax, tanned leathers, made shoes, and cured furs. Women did the spinning, weaving, dyeing, cutting, and sewing of the family garments.

EIGHTEENTH CENTURY: FROM HAND TO MACHINES

The transition from handcraft to factory production of textiles had its start in the United States when the first cotton **spinning mill** was built in 1790 at Pawtucket, Rhode Island, by **Samuel Slater**.[4] Slater was a young Englishman who had worked in one of England's leading mills and memorized the machinery his country refused to export. Declaring himself a farmer rather than a mechanic, he was allowed to emigrate to the United States, carrying his knowledge in his head. In 1793, Slater expanded his plant to house all the processes of yarn manufacture under one roof. That same year Eli Whitney introduced his cotton gin, a machine that pulled fibers free of seeds and helped to make a bountiful supply of cotton available to Slater and other early American textile producers.

Slater's spinning mill, now a textile museum, not only was the first successful spinning or yarn-making plant in this country but was also considered to have started the **Industrial Revolution** in America. His contribution to the industrialization of this country was recognized by President Andrew Jackson, who called him the "Father of American Manufacture."[5]

RAPID GROWTH IN THE NINETEENTH CENTURY

The nineteenth century saw a period of great development in textile manufacturing activity. The country was growing rapidly and the continuing improvement of textile machinery and factory methods made it increasingly economical to produce textiles outside the home. Fundamental to this development was the introduction and perfection in 1814 of the power loom by **Francis Cabot Lowell**, a Boston merchant, importer, and amateur scientist, who visited England and memorized the system in factories there.[6] Lowell's factory in Massachusetts was the first in America to handle all operations from raw cotton to finished cloth under one roof. Before Lowell, spinning mills contracted out the weaving of yarn into cloth to individuals or small groups of workers. Spinning was thus a factory industry, and weaving a cottage industry before Lowell.[7] The nineteenth century also saw the rise of a domestic wool industry as a result of the introduction of Merino sheep into America early in that century. By 1847, more Americans worked in textiles than in any other industry.[8]

Additional impetus was given to the industry by the Civil War, which made great demands on American mills for fabrics for soldiers' uniforms, over and above the country's normal requirements. By the end of the war, the textile industry was firmly established and mass production of fabrics, although not yet of top-quality goods, was well on its way. As late as 1858, England and France were still our sources for better grade textiles, notably fine broadcloth, and the New York Chamber of Commerce reported "that American wool, when used alone, cannot produce cloth of equal quality and finish as that made of foreign wools."[9]

By the end of the nineteenth century, however, woolens became available in a great variety of patterns and in great quantities, and cotton fabrics were even more abundant and variegated. In the relatively small silk industry, in which imports dominated the market as late as the 1860s, domestic production provided the overwhelming share by the turn of the century.[10]

PUBLICLY OWNED GIANTS THROUGH THE MID-1980s

Spurred on by the booming postwar economy in the late 1940s and an increasingly affluent consumer market, leading firms in the industry began to expand by means of mergers and acquisitions and to "go public" by offering shares in their companies on the stock exchanges. For some companies, the objective was diversification, such as by acquiring carpet and hosiery mills in addition to those that produced garment fabrics. Burlington Industries, for example, originally specialized in weaving rayon fabrics. In 1939, it moved into hosiery production. During World War II it made nylon parachute cloth. After the war it continued to expand, acquire new plants, buy up other companies, and diversify. At present, as one of the largest textile producers, it produces many different types of fabric and is a vertically integrated operation.

The drive toward integration and diversification that began in the 1940s continued in the 1950s and 1960s. Between 1955 and 1966, when acquisitions were perhaps at their height, the Federal Trade Commission reported that about 365 textile companies were acquired by other companies.[11] In the 1970s, the Federal Trade Commission moved against excessive mergers and acquisitions,

Sales of the Largest Textile Firms

Company	1989 Sales (Add 000)
Milliken	$2,900,000
Burlington Industries	2,200,000
Springs Industries	1,909,000
Fieldcrest	1,338,200
West Point Pepperell[a]	1,253,800
Guilford Mills	619,663
Dixie Yarn Company	570,840
Delta Woodside	569,052

[a]Represents Household Fabrics Financial Summary Form 10-K.
SOURCES: Companies' annual reports, 1990.

in this and many other industries, to avoid the lessening of competition that could result.

From the mid-1980s on, one saw a total restructuring of the American textile scene. Many public companies went private either through leveraged buy-outs, or as a result of acquisitions by other textile companies or major investment companies. Of the top 15 U.S. textile companies that were publicly held in 1981, only a handful among them (Springs Industries, Guilford Mills, Westpoint Pepperell, and Fieldcrest Cannon) remain. At this writing, their future fate remains uncertain as the entire industry continues to experience a restructuring.

MERGERS AND CONSOLIDATION

Merger mania in the textile industry has been encouraged in part by the flood of imports of fabrics and also by a desire on the part of many giant companies to increase market share and thus their ability to compete against other giants by combining similar products.

Some of the mergers include Springs Mills, which bought converter M. Lowenstein and also consolidated their Springmaid with Wamsutta Brands. Burlington Industries had a leveraged buy-out; Fieldcrest bought Cannon; Collins and Aikman was purchased by Wickes Co.; Cone Mills, together with Odessey Partners, purchased J. P. Stevens and Forstman and Co.; Farley Inc. bought West Point Pepperell; and the list goes on.

This consolidation has changed the nature of the textile industry from a manufacturing-driven industry into a more marketing-driven posture with huge market shares now in the hands of fewer and stronger players. Burlington is no longer in the home furnishings area. Stevens is out of the converter fabrics and yarn business, which consisted primarily of greige goods for apparel fabrics, carpeting, automotive fabrics, and industrial fabrics. However, Odessey Partners (which now own J. P. Stevens) purchased Burlington's domestics business, which now makes Stevens a major presence in the home furnishings area. Burlington is concentrating all of its effort into expanding its importance in the marketing of fabrics for men's and women's apparel producers.

Most textile companies have seen the marketing advantages of specializing in either home furnishings and domestics and apparel textiles and of becoming a more important presence in one or the other. Milliken and Dan River remain the major holdouts that continue to market to both areas.

Geographic Location

Throughout the nineteenth century, the industry was located principally in New England, where it began. Cotton, however, was grown in the warm southern states, and the transportation northward to the mills was slow, inconvenient, and costly. Industry leaders began to turn their eyes southward but, although there were small textile mills in virtually every southern state in the early nineteenth century, they were not especially welcome. Plantation owners found industrialization repugnant, perhaps seeing it as a threat to their way of life and as competition for slave labor.

After the Civil War, however, southern leaders recognized the need for industrialization and offered textile companies special inducements, such as low taxes and utility rates, if they would build plants in the South. The movement of cotton manufacturing plants gained momentum after World War I, and by 1920 more than half the spinning and weaving capacity of cotton textile manufacturing was found in the South.[12] Woolen and worsted plants, attracted by an improved spinning system developed in the South for woolen manufacture, followed suit shortly after World War II. Today, the three southern states of North and South Carolina and Georgia employ a majority of the textile industry's labor force.

Along with the growth of the industry came changes in the selling and distribution of its output. Merchants who had originally started as importers of European fabrics gradually became selling agents for the domestic mills or bought their goods outright for resale. The expansion of domestic output after the Civil War stimulated the establishment of a textile center in downtown Manhattan, on and near Worth Street, that became the heart of the textile trade. The name *Worth Street* became synonymous with the body of textile merchants on whom American mills depended for their orders and often for the financing. After World War II, however, when fashion's impact hit the industry, the textile showrooms began moving uptown, where they are still located, right on the doorstep of the women's apparel industry.

Today, the textile mills are largely situated along a broad arc reaching from New England through the Southeast, but their designing, styling, and sales activities are heavily concentrated in New York City.

Different Types of Textile Producers

In its early history, the U.S. textile industry was highly fragmented. Different companies specialized in different stages of production, each of which required different machines, processes, and skills. Spinning mills bought fibers, which they spun into yarn. Fabric mills purchased such yarns and performed the weaving or knitting into cloth. Much of what the fabric mills produced was greige goods, or unfinished cloth. At this point, finishing plants took over, doing the dyeing, printing, or whatever other treatments were required. In the case of yarn-dyed fabrics, commonly woolen cloth, the fabric usually required less finishing than piece-dyed fabrics.

Today more and more fabric producers seem to be utilizing a wider range of fibers or combinations of fibers, and more companies are producing more diversified product lines.

VERTICALLY INTEGRATED FIRMS

During and immediately after World War II, problems of scarcity and price made the prewar production and marketing procedures of fragmented operations infeasible. The industry began to integrate itself. In some cases, fabric mills ceased to rely on spinning mills, selling agents, and finishing plants, and acquired or set up their own operations. Burlington Industries was one such company. In other cases, independent selling agents such as J. P. Stevens acquired textile mills and finishing plants. In still others, converting firms such as Cohn Hall Marx bought mills to be sure of having fabrics to sell.

Today the textile industry includes companies that engage in all processes of production and distribution—spinning, weaving, knitting, finishing, and selling. This all-encompassing operation is called **vertical integration** and it enables a company to control its goods through as many processes as are potentially profitable. Nevertheless, even in these integrated firms, operations are specialized in their different plants, each of which performs a single function in the production of fabric, and different products are distributed by their different specialized marketing divisions.

SPECIALIZED FIRMS

There are still, however, many more companies that specialize in a single phase of production. Some are large firms that employ hundreds of workers, such as spinners like Dixie Yarns and Wintuk Yarns; weavers such as Dan River; giant converting companies such as Concord Fabrics; and printers such as Cranston. There are also many small firms, some of which limit themselves to narrow product lines, such as velvets and velveteens, or to such dressy fabrics as chiffons, taffetas, and silk failles. Other firms deal only in knits, brocades, metallics, or novelty fabrics. Their limited specialization seems to make them invulnerable to penetration by very large firms.

CONVERTERS

Converting is a specialized textile operation whose function it is to style greige goods and arrange to have it finished. The unfinished goods are contracted out to finishing plants for processing as ordered by the **converter** (i.e., dyeing, printing, waterproofing, etc.). The finished goods are then sold by the converter to apparel and home furnishings manufacturers or to fabric retailers. The converter may be either a division of a vertically integrated textile company or an independent company that owns neither fabric mills nor finishing plants but serves as a middleman between these two stages of production. In that capacity, the converter specifies all aspects of the finished fabric, such as design, color, and other treatments considered necessary to make the goods salable to apparel producers or fabric retailers. Independent converters are usually relatively small operators, but there are big names among them, such as Concord, Loomskill, Erlanger Blumgart, and Pressman-Gutman.

There are three basic types of converting organizations, each of which performs essentially the same functions. One is the *independently owned converting company*, which has contractual relationships with the mills from which it purchases greige goods, or the finishing plants it uses, or both. A second is the *converter-jobber*, also independently owned, who does not have any contractual arrangements. The third is the *integrated converter*, which is a division of a vertical textile firm. Such a converter works primarily with greige goods from mills of the parent organization and, as a general rule, has the finishing done in its own plants. It may also use outside sources, however, for greige goods or finishing.

Converters fulfill an important function in the textile industry. Since they enter the fabric production process in its end stages, they can work quite close to the time of need and adjust quickly to changes in fashion. Converters (company or independent) keep in contact with clothing producers, seeking indications of colors, patterns, and finishes that are likely to be wanted. For this reason, most of them are located in major apparel markets, with more than 90 percent located in New York City. The successful converter is a keen student of fashion, observes trends, anticipates demand, and is one who senses and responds to fashion directions.

FASHION RESEARCH AND DEVELOPMENT

Apparel designers say that fabric is the designer's creative medium, just as pigment is the painter's. A good designer responds to new fabric and searches for the quality that will make it—and his or her designs—come alive. To make possible fabrics that will evoke such response and that will ultimately be acceptable to the consuming public, fiber and textile producers must keep many fashion steps and several years ahead of the design and production of apparel. By the time fashions are featured in stores and magazines, they are old hat to textile designers and stylists, because these are the people who have created these patterns and colors at least a year earlier. And probably two years before the public sees the fashions, the fiber companies and their associations were working with fabric mills on the kinds of cloth to be presented. At that time or even earlier, fiber companies were working on color projections and fiber variants for seasons still further ahead.

Specialized Fashion Staffs

Fiber and textile producers invest a great deal of time and money in fashion research to guide the development of salable fabrics, blends, textures, colors, finishes, and whatever other properties are expected to be wanted. All of the large producers, textile as well as fiber, maintain specialized fashion staffs in menswear and women's wear to research and report on trends in fashion.

Although their individual responsibilities and titles—fashion merchandisers, creative directors, fashion coordinators, stylists, and others—vary from one company to another, the recommendations of these fashion experts guide their company's design and production activities. These fashion specialists tour the world fashion centers looking for fashion inspiration and direction, observe what fashion leaders are wearing, exchange ideas with apparel designers and manufacturers and fashion editors, and generally use every resource available to anticipate what will be wanted by their customers and eventually by the public. At the same time, many large producers conduct market research in order to analyze consumer attitudes and their ever-changing tastes and preferences as to performance characteristics. Thus armed with their research findings about the performance and fashion features that are likely to be wanted, producers design, develop, and produce fibers and fabrics long before they become available to ultimate consumers.

Early Color Decisions

Fashion decisions in the primary markets begin with color. Color is a sensation —a mood—and one of its attributes is that it helps sell clothing. Fairly typical of the procedures followed in determining the colors to be used are those described by Ed Newman, then vice president and creative director of Dan River, Inc., in the comment:

> When putting together a color line we review the best and worst sellers of the last season, check computer readouts, have informal discussions with manu-facturers and check the racks of department and specialty stores. We think of what colors have been missing from the palette for a while and which shades seem "new again." Many colors make the natural progression through the seasons; a wine becomes purple, the purple moves to magenta and the ma-genta to a pink. No mystery—just logic. The final choice of a color line is logic, research and "gut feeling." With it lies the success or failure of your next season.[13]

The Color Association of the United States (CAUS), a major force in guiding industry color decisions, has been issuing color projections for textiles and apparel for more than 74 years and has been forecasting home furnishings and appliance colors for nearly 30 years. It is a nonprofit service organization whose board of directors consists of top industry executives, each from a different industry, and all of whom donate their time. Seasonal forecasts for women's wear, menswear, children's wear, and the interior design industries are developed by committees of experts from each industry segment from fiber producers to retail. These forecasts are arrived at by committees of volunteers who evaluate what they call the "color climate." To arrive at their decisions, they consider everything from politics to the economy to cultural events and movements. Among the members of their committees are such distinguished persons as Mary McFadden, the well-known fashion designer, and Jack Lenor Larsen, a famous textile designer.

CAUS makes its predictions at least two years in advance and sends them to 1,500 subscribers, including design companies, textile mills, and paint manufacturers. The choice of colors will rule everything from women's fashions to desktop accessories.

Intercolor, an association of representatives from the worldwide fashion industry, arranges meetings in Paris twice each year. There, these experts analyze color cycles and the natural evolution of color preferences to determine specific color palettes for their target season two years in the future. Another color prediction service offered to textile and apparel producers is the **International Color Authority** (ICA). They, too, meet twice a year to establish their color predictions for fiber, yarn, and fabric producers. Six months later, they send a modified version of their selected colors to member apparel producers.

Textile Design

In addition to the color story, fabric stylists must also be aware of the silhouettes coming into fashion, so that the fabrications they recommend will be appropriate. For example, if the trend is toward a tailored or structured look, firm fabrications are necessary, whereas soft, light fabrics are needed for a layered look.

Once the stylists have their color story set and the fabrications determined, the next step is designing the fabric. Textile designers, unlike apparel designers, are primarily concerned with two-dimensional surfaces, rather than with the three-dimensional human form. A further consideration is the capabilities of the knitting machines or weaving looms to be used. If a printed design is to be applied to the fabric, the designer must also consider any problem the pattern may present to the garment cutter. The pattern, usually a continuous repetition of a motif, is planned so that it does not entail unnecessary waste or difficulties in the cutting of garments.

Textile designers tend to specialize in either print, woven, or knitted design. Some are full-time employees of fabric mills, converters, or textile design studios. Others work free-lance and sell their sketches to textile companies.

Fashion Presentations

Fiber and fabric producers have developed considerable skill in utilizing their fashion expertise to sell their products. And through the fabrics they make available and the fashions they promote, they exert an important and continuing influence on the fashion industry's chain of production and distribution.

Large producers (both fiber and fabric) are very active in disseminating the fashion information they have collected to all segments of the industry. Most maintain fabric libraries in their showrooms that contain swatches of fabrics currently available or scheduled for production for an upcoming season. In addition, producers and retailers are invited to visit, inspect, and consult special displays of new yarns and fabrics that are set up periodically. These libraries and exhibits are used by apparel makers and their designers, retailers, and fashion reporters as sources of information about future fabric and color trends.

Some conduct seasonal clinics and workshops at which they visually present their fashion projections and illustrate them with garments they have had made up for this purpose and in which their fibers or fabrics are featured. These clinics are open to all segments of industry: producers, retailers, and fashion reporters.

Seasonal Lines and Sales Presentations

Once a fabric line is set and sample yardage is in process, the work of the sales and merchandising staff is put into motion. In the primary markets, two new seasonal lines a year are customary. Fabrics for seasonal apparel lines are shown from six to nine months in advance.

The actual selling of piece goods is broken down into two phases. The first of these, called "preselling," is a presentation by the textile company's merchandising staff to its key accounts — the decision makers. Presentations take the form of color swatches (small fabric samples made on sample machines), croquis (painted samples on paper), color puffs, and sketches set up on story boards for approval. Presentations are made either in the fabric mill's own showroom or in the showrooms of their customers. At this point, all samples shown are **open-line** goods, available for selection. If a customer chooses to have a particular sample "confined" and not available to others, and agrees to purchase an amount of yardage considered adequate by the mill, then no other customers may purchase it. Exceptions are sometimes made, however — for example, for a very prestigious designer label.

The second phase of fabric selling is the sales presentation to all other customers, regardless of size. Appointments are made six to eight weeks in advance of these customers' market weeks (selling periods), and presentations are made to apparel designers, stylists, and even the apparel companies' marketing staffs. Sample yardage is then ordered by the apparel producers for use in making up sample garments. After such garments have been shown to retail store buyers, apparel producers decide how much goods to buy and place their fabric orders. By the time this takes place, the textile creators are well into work on the next season's goods.

Textile Trade Shows

American producers participate in trade shows both in the United States and abroad. Held semiannually, these shows are attended by designers, manufacturers, and retailers who come to look at and perhaps buy the new fabrics. At this writing, the most comprehensive such shows are the **Interstoff** Textile Fair held in Frankfurt, West Germany; the **Première Vision** in Paris, France; the **Ideacomo** in Como, Italy; **Texitalia** in Milan, Italy; the **New York Fabric Show**; and the **Canton Trade Fair** in Canton, China. Each host country presents the latest lines of textiles developed within its own borders, along with whatever else producers from other countries choose to exhibit. Other, smaller shows

include the Knitting Yarn Fair in New York City, which features new yarns, dyeing, and knitting techniques; and Cotons de France in New York City.

In addition to stimulating sales of fabrics, these shows result in further benefits. First, they make all related industry branches aware of changing fashions. At the same time, they unify and coordinate the thinking of related areas within the industry, so that they change in phase with one another and thereby facilitate the mass production that mass demand requires.

ELECTRONICS: THE NEW TECHNOLOGIES FOR THE 1990S

Although we still have a long way to go before we can produce a million yards of fabric by a simple verbal command, the fashion industry has been in the process of modernizing itself with new electronic capabilities that are reshaping its present and its future.

The textile industry has been spending more than $1.5 billion a year in modernization. Textile productivity has increased by an average of 5 percent a year compared to 2.4 percent for all manufacturing. "The result is that no one in the world can produce textiles as efficiently." [14]

Quick Response (QR): Computerized Partnerships

The end of the 1980s witnessed the introduction of a new industry-wide strategy called Quick Response. No recent industry development has created as much interest, publicity, and reams of printed materials as QR.

QR is a strategy whose aim is to achieve quick and precise replenishment of fast-selling merchandise by means of computerized partnerships between fabric suppliers, apparel producers, and retailers. Companies that participate in this strategy are linked electronically to each other so that each can speedily exchange, in computer language, information about the merchandise that is currently being purchased by the ultimate consumers. Its purpose is to considerably shorten the time it takes for currently wanted merchandise to arrive in retail stores and to keep inventories at each level in balance with consumers' current needs and wants. Its development was spearheaded by the textile industry in order to meet the competition from apparel imports that involved the use of foreign-made fabrics.

A QR program begins with an agreement among a textile company, an apparel producer, and a retailer to participate in a computerized partnership after the fabric producer has shown its line to an apparel producer who then prepares and shows his or her line to a retailer. The preparation and presentation of these lines are done many months in advance of a retail selling season. At this point, the retailer decides only on the styles and fabrications to be produced and establishes the quantities that will be needed for specific time periods, subject to timely revision. Colors and sizes, however, are not yet specified.

After the apparel manufacturer knows the styles, fabrics, and quantities, he or she works with the fabric supplier and establishes the types of fabrics to be used and the estimated quantities of as yet unfinished fabrics to be held in reserve and finished as needed for future use. Before the garments are put into production, the retailer establishes model stocks by style, fabric, size, color, and quantities for specified time periods, all of which are subject to needed revisions. The apparel producer now details the ordered fabrics by the colors and quantities wanted by the retailer for his or her opening inventories, and goes into production.

When the merchandise is received by the retailer, it is ticketed with an identification code. When a sale is made, a scanner at the cash register decodes the ticket and records the key elements of the sale such as the price, the vendor number, and the size, color, and classification. This information is relayed to the store's central computer, where a running inventory of goods on hand is maintained. It is also transmitted through electronic data interchange (EDI) to the apparel manufacturer's computer, which enables the producer to replenish the styles, colors, and sizes that are needed, based on planned stock levels. Now that the producer knows which fabrics and colors need replenishing, this information is then quickly transmitted to the textile company's computer; the company will finish and quickly deliver the unfinished goods that have been reserved for the apparel producer.

This preplanning at all market levels makes it possible to stock smaller lots of goods close to the time of consumer purchases, thereby eliminating heavy inventories of untested goods at all market levels. The advantages to all participants are increased sales as a result of being able to respond quickly and accurately to consumer wants, reduced investments in raw materials and finished goods inventories, and a reduction of markdowns due to a surplus of slow-moving stock.

Expediting the movement of information about consumer purchases back through the production system involves a great deal of computer input and cooperation at each level. Although the concept of Quick Response involves many companion developments such as electronic mailboxes, merchandise information systems (MIS), automatic reorders, electronic message and answering centers, automatic warehousing and inventory controls, and voice activators, its basic components are as follows:

- **Electronic Data Interchange (EDI):** A method of transmitting computer data from one company to another into an electronic mailbox that unscrambles the data and makes it usable by the recipient, and vice versa.
- **Bar coding:** A series of 11 black-and-white vertical bars printed on a ticket or label that is attached to merchandise. These bars are a code that identifies the merchandise category, the manufacturer, and the individual item down to the details of size and color.
- **Scanners:** Devices that read the bar code at the point of sale (POS), trans-

form it into numbers, and transmit the product code into a computer. By means of EDI, retailers and producers can instantly keep track of all sales data on individual purchases and thus monitor styles and current or emerging trends.

- **Universal Product Code (UPC):** The Uniform Code Council is a nonproduct trade association that sets standards for transmitting information by computer and administers a Universal Product Code. The UPC is an 11-digit numeric code that identifies the product. The first digit in the UPC code is a number system that serves to key the other numbers as to meaning and merchandise category. The next five digits are the manufacturer's identification number, which is assigned by the Uniform Code Council. The item or product code is the next-to-the-last five digits which are assigned and controlled by the supplier and are unique to his or her item. The last bar is a checking digit.

This QR strategy, using high technology data exchange and inventory controls, and based on industry-to-industry cooperation, and coordination has proven to be successful, especially in more basic merchandise. The formation of two industry groups has contributed to its success, and both groups contributed to the development of the third.

TALC

The Textile-Apparel Linkage Council comprises companies such as Haggar Apparel Company, Oxford Industries, Maidenform, Milliken, Levi-Strauss, and Burlington Industries, among others. These firms have established and accepted bar coding uniformity, Electronic Data Interchange standards, shade values, ticket design, and other standards necessary to transmit uniform and accurate information from computer to computer.

VICS

Voluntary Interindustry Communications Standards is an outgrowth of the Crafted with Pride organization. This committee includes representatives from K mart, Sears, Bullocks, Dayton-Hudson, Blue-Bell, V. F. Corporation, Levi-Strauss, Milliken, and Wal-Mart. Their efforts are directed toward improving customer service through voluntary standards for identifying and marking products, and communicating across all industry segments involved in bringing goods to consumers in a more timely manner.

ANSI X 12: AMERICAN NATIONAL STANDARDS INSTITUTE

ANSI X 12 is the result of a committee, cutting across many major industries, that was formed to apply a set of conventions that establish the format of an electronic document. For electronic data interchange to take place, a commonly accepted format or set of conventions must be uniformly established and accepted by all. This enables all companies, regardless of size, computer type, or computer language used, to accept and understand each other's data. Using a specific set of data keys with its accompanying dictionary, all businesses (both big and small) can receive and interpret the numbers transmitted. For example, the first three-digit number describes the type of document being transmitted (purchase orders, invoice, etc.); the next 10 digits give the sender's identifying code for its own name; and so on through the document. This system has already been accepted by the automotive, electronics, textile, apparel, retailing, and footwear industries, for a total of 44 industries.

Thus ANSI X 12 is the backbone of QR since it makes the industry capable of both receiving and sending immediate electronic information to its customers, be they General Motors, Levi-Strauss or Wal-Mart.

Computer Aided Design (CAD)

The introduction of computer aided design (CAD) systems in textile designers' studios provides the capability to experiment with weave, color, and yarns directly on a computer monitor. The additional use of high definition computer printers makes possible the printing of fabric designs in color on paper that are so realistic as to be confused with an actual swatch of fabric. Once a fabric printout is accepted, the computer can prepare and deliver exact instructions for replication in the sample weaving department if needed.

This provides a textile company with the ability to offer an endless supply of new and innovative designs tailor-made to each customer's particular wants and needs.

Computer Aided Manufacturing (CAM)

The computer aided manufacturing (**CAM**) system is used to guarantee that the colors on the CAD printout of the design are identical to those used in the weaving of an actual sample fabric, or blanket. A "textile" industry blanket is a series of preselected color combinations all in the same pattern. Data from dyeing used to calibrate color matching programs can be fed into color simulation computers. (Calibration data defines the dye's coloristic attributes. This, along with the colorant's performance specifications, produces an "electronic shade card.")

Shuttless Weaving

The high-speed shuttless loom has increased productivity dramatically, with each new shuttless loom capable of weaving more than twice as many yards per hour as the old shuttle loom.

There are different types of these looms, and each offers different benefits.

- *Projectible looms.* These looms weave a broad assortment of fabrics from basic poplins and twills to a variety of fibers and blend levels.
- *Rapier shuttless looms.* More versatile and less productive than the others, they can take all types of colored yarn for many end market uses.
- *Air jet shuttless.* The workhorses of all of these types of looms, these are the most productive and widely used shuttless looms. They cannot weave multi-color or decorative fabrics.
- *Water Jet looms.* These looms produce synthetic silk-like fabrics for blouses, characterized by good productivity and fine quality, but they lack flexibility.

The next generation of shuttless looms are likely to be fully robotic, with the ability to insert several different colored yarns into the weave. When combined with CAD-CAM, the future holds superior fashion styling with shorter required minimum yardage, and shorter production times at competitive prices.

Holograms

These are metallic-like designs which are placed on the surface of materials and which seem to change colors and move when the surfaces that they adhere to change. Already widely used on credit cards, hangtags, and novelty jewelry, holograms are now used in apparel textiles. They can also be less expensively produced through the use of diffraction foils which, instead of using a complete picture or image that moves, use essentially a prism that refracts many colors when moved.

COMPETITION FROM IMPORTS

The U.S. textile industry as a whole continues to be the largest textile industry in the world.[15] Nevertheless, the United States imports a considerable amount of textile fibers, yarns, and complete textile fabrics from abroad. In 1989 the U.S. dollar value of textile imports amounted to more than $6.4 billion. This is more than the amount produced by the top three textile producers in the United States combined.[16]

Our purchases abroad include such fibers as wool from the United Kingdom and Belgium, cotton from China and Egypt, flax from Ireland, ramie from India, and man-made fibers from Japan and Korea. The fabrics we import include silks from China, Japan, and Italy; laces from France; and woolens from Italy and West Germany. In addition, we import a variety of other fabrics from the Far East. Some of our imports are from countries that have traditionally produced superior fibers and fabrics of a particular kind; others are simply a matter of importing from countries whose labor costs and costs of factory operation make it possible for them to sell more cheaply in the American market than domestic producers can.

We do, of course, export some of our own output. In 1989 our textile export figure was $3.9 billion, with the United States the number 1 world supplier of cotton and synthetic yarns. This, however, leaves us with an export trade deficit in the textile area of more than $2.5 billion. The downward trend in textile employment from 848,000 in 1980 to 687,000 in 1989 has, to a large extent, been caused by the drastic inroads made by textile imports.[17]

FURS AND LEATHERS _____

Furs and leathers were used for garments long before textiles were developed, and they are still major raw materials in the fashion industry. Both materials share certain basic qualities: they utilize the skins of animals; the natural habitat of the individual animal determines the part of the world in which the material originates; high degrees of skill are required in selecting, treating, and making garments and accessories of the material; there can be great variations over the years in the availability of a particular animal skin; there has not yet been a way to produce truly equivalent materials in laboratory or mill.

The qualities with which nature has endowed both furs and leathers make them uniquely desirable in today's sophisticated, mechanized age, just as they were in the dawn of history. In the fashion field, dominated by textiles and other machine-made products, each of these two materials occupies a small but important place. Although both materials require skilled handling and slow processing, the fashion industry curbs its appetite for speed when dealing with fur and leather. It has no real choice.

The Fur Industry

The wearing of fur as a status symbol goes back to the ancient Egyptian priests, if not further. Present-day use of fur for prestige and fashion is evidenced most clearly in the parade of sable, chinchilla, mink, and other expensive furs on such occasions as inaugural balls, opera openings, and other gatherings of the socially and financially elite.

NATURE OF THE INDUSTRY

Sales of fur garments within the United States reached a historic high of $1.8 billion set in the 1986–1987 season, about triple the sales of 10 years previously of $612 million.[18] Since then, however, sales growth has leveled off. The gain was attributed largely to the rise of discount fur merchandisers that market to young working women. Recently there have been intensified protests from animal rights groups, a decline in mink pelt prices—the furrier's mainstay— and a growing number of inexpensive imported coats entering in the United States. About 75 percent of mink coats sold in America now cost less than $5,000, a level not prevalent since the 1960s.[19] The boom in less expensive minks has reduced the market for higher priced garments, and as a result New

York manufacturers are consolidating, combining showrooms, and diversifying, often becoming importers as well as manufacturers.

Ninety-eight percent of domestic factory production of fur garments takes place almost entirely in New York City.[20] There, one finds a great concentration of dealers in raw skins, as well as *dressers*, or firms that prepare skins for use by the garment producer. In the United States there are currently about 350 plants devoted to making fur garments. These are mostly small and family owned; only 7 percent have 20 or more employees.[21]

The demand for fur garments in the United States and worldwide seems to be continuing, but the manner in which that need is met is changing. The bulk of the annual American production of 4.5 million mink pelts, considered the finest in the world, is now exported. Eighty percent goes overseas, with Japan now the number one consumer of finished American mink coats. The United States in turn imported $423.9 million of finished fur garments in 1988, principally made from less expensive Scandinavian, Russian, and Chinese pelts.[22]

In New York City the industry employs 1,900 people, down from 3,600 in 1979 according to figures from the U.S. Bureau of Labor Statistics.[23] Along Seventh Avenue, New York City's fur district, names like Fortune Furs (from Hong Kong), Sam Yang Enterprises (Korea), and Ronlee apparel (a division of Jindo, the largest importer of furs in the United States) appear next to William Rosenfeld Furs and other domestic fur manufacturers.

MANUFACTURING OF FUR GARMENTS

At every step of the way, from the living animal to the finished fur garment, the industry requires specialized knowledge, plus skills that are acquired through a long learning process. In many phases of the work, hand operations prevail. Mass production methods have little application.

The process begins with a trapper who obtains animals in the wild by methods that do not damage the **pelts**, or with a breeder who raises certain species under controlled conditions on a fur ranch. According to the Fur Information and Fashion Council, about 80 percent of the furs used in the United States are from ranch-bred animals, notably mink and fox. The fur business is necessarily worldwide in scope, with each country offering pelts of animals indigenous to its area. To secure desirable pelts, fur traders attend auctions all over the world: in Russia and Finland; Oslo, Sweden; Montreal, Canada; and Frankfurt, Germany.

Once purchased, the raw skins are prepared for use by dressers. These companies first immerse skins in a salt-water solution, then scrape off excess fat and flesh from the hide. Next, the pelts go into revolving, sawdust-filled drums that remove grease and dirt. Oils are then added to keep the skins soft and pliable. Finally, the fur itself is combed and blown to raise its pile. Only after the furs become part of a finished garment is the last step taken—glazing, to add to the natural luster by drawing the oils to the surface.

To enhance their natural beauty, some furs are subjected to other steps.

Fur Industry Flowchart

Auctions are arranged by permanent trade associations (e.g., the Emba Mink Breeders Associates). Some skin dealers sell directly to retailers. Commission merchants often sell directly to manufacturers.

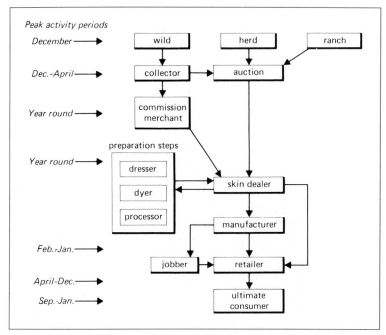

SOURCE: Reprinted with permission of Fairchild Publishing Company.

Beaver or nutria, for instance, may be plucked, to remove the guard hairs and enhance the underfur. On furs like beaver or nutria, shearing may also be used to clip the fur into an even pile.

Colors, too, may be subjected to change. White furs may be bleached to remove stains or discolorations, at least until a few years of exposure to air causes them to yellow. Other furs may be given a dye bath, to change the color entirely. In such cases, a federal law, the Fur Products Labeling Act, requires appropriate labeling. Other beauty treatments are tip dyeing or blended color. The latter is a matter of brushing dye over the fur to even out the color or give additional color depth. All this before the making of a garment begins!

Production of the actual garments involves a number of skills. First comes the selection and matching of bundles of pelts for each individual garment. Then the skins are cut individually by hand, sewn together in garment sections, and wetted, stretched, and nailed by hand, fur side down, to a board and allowed to dry in the desired shape. Only then are the sections sewn together to complete the garment.

For some expensive furs, like sable and mink, the expensive **letting-out** process precedes the garment construction. Again, this is a hand operation that requires great skill. Each skin is cut in half through the dark center stripe. Diagonal cuts are then made down the length of the skin at intervals of ⅛ to ³⁄₁₆ of an inch apart. When the resulting strips are sewn together at a different angle, a longer, narrower skin is formed, presenting the striped effect that is wanted, for example, in mink garments.

MARKETING FUR GARMENTS

There is one major market period when fur garment producers present their wares to retailers—the period from May 15 to June 15—in New York City. Showings are usually held in the manufacturers' showrooms, generally on live models in the larger companies. The majority of fur wholesalers are located on or near Seventh Avenue, between 27th and 30th streets. In that area, messengers carrying thousands of dollars worth of furs and fur garments stroll through the streets as casually as if they were bringing a bag lunch to the office.

There are approximately 4,000 fur retailers in the United States, of which about 1,000 are specialized fur shops. The overall figure includes small mom-and-pop local retailers, fur boutiques, and large department stores.[24] Because of the huge investment in merchandise required to present an adequate assortment to the consumer, the practice of consignment selling is common in the fur trade. This means that the manufacturer ships a supply of garments to the retailer and is paid for them only when they are sold; unsold garments are returnable at a specified date.

Department stores and large specialty shops almost universally lease out their fur departments, thus calling upon the capital and the expertise of the lessee. Under such an arrangement, the lessee supplies stock, hires and trains salespeople, and pays for the advertising. All activities are subject to store policy and approval. The lessee benefits by the drawing power of the store's name and location, and pays a percentage of sales plus rent. Evans & Co., of Chicago, is the largest such leased fur department operator, with more than 800 retail operations all over the United States. In 1988 they launched a new specialty store division of their own called Arctic Dream, catering exclusively to lower priced furs.

In addition to the advertising done by retailers, the industry launches advertising and publicity through its trade associations, many of which concentrate on a single type of fur, for example, EMBA (the Eastern Mink Breeding Association), GLAMA (Great Lakes Mink Association), SAGA (Scandinavian mink and fox breeders), the Canadian Majestic Mink Association, and the British-Irish-Dutch conglomerate. Speaking for furs in general and the fur garment manufacturers as a whole is the American Fur Information and Fashion Council, the industry's trade association.

THE IMPACT OF FASHION

Many factors influence the fashion for furs. When there is a fashion for opulence, furs are "in." When there is a revulsion against ostentation, or against wanton killing of animals for their skins, people swing away from furs. When the fashion world, as it has done in the past, goes overboard for an exotic fur to the point that the animal involved is threatened with extinction, the conservationists and sometimes the government itself will bring pressure to bear against the use or importation of such furs. This happened with leopard, which zoomed into prominence in the 1960s, causing such indiscriminate slaughter that by 1969 the animal was an endangered species. Similarly, revulsion against the use of certain types of seal fur, for which trappers kill very young pups, curtails the market to some extent—but not enough to stop the annual slaughter. These days, a retailer may add a footnote to the store's advertising, stating that no endangered species are among its offerings.

A fashion development since the late 1970s has been the introduction of major American apparel designers into the fur business. Through licensing arrangements with major fur producers, Valentino, Oscar de la Renta, and Adolfo, among others, now have their names on a variety of high priced fur garments. Where formerly terms such as *quality* and *luxury* got major emphasis in the industry, today a new fashion dimension has been added—designer names.

IMPORTS AND EXPORTS

Once a fur garment gets into the channels of trade in the United States, it is not easy to identify its source. The Federal Fur Products Act requires that a garment be tagged with the following information: the name of the fur in plain English, the country of origin of the pelts, any processing such as dyeing or shearing, and whether full, partial, or pieced pelts were used. In addition, secondhand furs must be marked as such. However, it does not require information about where the garment was made. It could be presented or even labeled "U.S.A." yet have been made in, say, Korea. Industry experts say that the lower the selling price compared with that of similar garments, the greater the likelihood that the coat or jacket was imported. For example, the labor cost of manufacturing a full-length mink coat in the United States is about $1,000, whereas the same coat made in Hong Kong would have a labor cost of $300 to $400; in Korea, $125 to $175; in China, less than $100. So far, the finest furs at the top of the price range have no problem with imports. When Russian sables and white lynx garments sell at wholesale for as much as $75,000 to $100,000, they are above price competition. And the pelts used, moreover, are of too high a value to be entrusted to the less-skilled workmanship of cut-price operators at any stage of the game.

The Leather Industry

Leather is one of man's oldest clothing materials. Long before they learned to plant cotton and make fabrics, people were skilled in the tanning and use of leather for sandals and crude garments. Leather apparel in this country goes back to the American Indians, who made moccasins and cloaks out of deerskin. Renowned frontiersmen like Daniel Boone and Davy Crockett and other early settlers wore deerskin and buckskin pants, shirts, shoes, and jackets.

NATURE OF THE INDUSTRY

The leather tanning and finishing industry is made up of establishments primarily engaged in tanning, curing, and finishing animal hides and skins to produce leather. Also included are leather converters and dealers who buy hides and skins and have them processed under contract by tanners or finishers. The output of the leather tanning and finishing industry in 1989 was valued at $2.46 billion. There are some 130 establishments in the industry directly involved in tanning and finishing hides and skins whose employed workers total 14,700.[25] Since leather is a by-product of the meat packing industry, the industry tends to be cost-efficient. The packinghouses derive their primary reve-

Leather Industry Flowchart

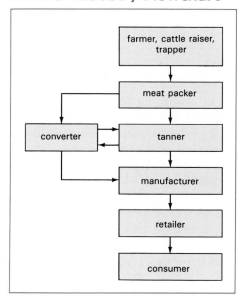

SOURCE: Reprinted with permission.

nue from the carcass; the skins and hides, which have no food value, are sold to the leather trades.

Processing of the hides and skins is done largely in small plants located mostly in the North Central and Northeastern states. Three major types of companies are involved: (1) converters, who buy the hides and skins from meat packers and contract them out to tanneries for finishing, (2) contract tanners who finish skins but do not market them directly, and (3) regular or complete tanneries that purchase and process skins and hides and sell finished leathers.

Like the fiber and fabric producers, the leather industry promotes and sells its products to manufacturers of apparel and accessories. Yet, unlike fiber and fabric companies, the tanning companies do not make their names known to the consuming public. Advertising for leather garments and accessories may include the name of the fashion designer, the manufacturer, and the type of leather, but never the name of the producer of the leather.

HIDES AND SKINS

These terms, used interchangeably by the layman, have very specific meanings within the leather industry. **Hides** come from animals whose skins weigh more than 20 pounds, such as cattle, horses, and buffalo. These hides are so thick they are frequently split into two or more layers, called **splits.** Under Federal Trade Commission regulations, the under pieces must be identified as splits and cannot be called genuine leather or genuine cowhide. **Kips** is a term applied to skins weighing between 15 and 25 pounds. The term **skins** designates still smaller skins, from such animals as calves, pigs, sheep, and goats.[26]

PROCESSING OF LEATHERS

There are three basic steps in processing leather: pretanning, tanning, and finishing. **Pretanning** is basically a cleansing process in which the leathers are soaked and rid of all flesh, hair, and dirt. Next is **tanning,** which both preserves the skin and improves its natural physical properties. The varied tanning methods employ such substances as oil, vegetable substances, alum, formaldehyde, zirconium, and, most commonly used in the United States, chrome. The technical term "in the blue" refers to hides, skins, or kips that have been chrome-tanned but not yet finished. Final steps after tanning include dyeing and a variety of finishes. Among these is aniline, the most expensive, used only on the finest, smoothest skins to impart a highly polished surface. Other finishes include embossing, which presses a pattern onto the leather, often to simulate expensive alligator or snakeskin; also sueding and napping to raise the surface; or pressing, to give a shiny glazed finish. That last, called glacé leather, is often used for accessories.

LEATHER MARKETING

Because of the length of time required to purchase and process its raw material, the leather industry is among the earliest to research and anticipate fashion trends. Its decisions as to colors, weights, and textures are reached early and are presented early. The industry as a whole participates in this process through its strong association, Leather Industries of America (LIA). The LIA offers color seminars semiannually and sells swatches of its colors to industry members at nominal cost, some 18 to 24 months in advance of the season concerned. Other functions of the LIA include a Hide Training School for persons engaged in the buying or selling of either hides or leathers; sponsorship of an annual contest among U.S. design schools to select six Student Design Award winners for creative use of leathers in fashions; and publication of an industry-wide weekly entitled *Council News* to cover all pertinent information of interest to its members.

As experienced observers of fashion signals and early forecasters of trends,

Leather Industry Trade Show

visit IAG LEATHER SHOW new location!

The NAMSB Show
(National Association of Men's Sportswear Buyers)

♦ ♦ ♦

Section 3A
Jacob K. Javits Convention Center
39th St. & 11th Ave.   New York City

Sponsored by

LEATHER
INDUSTRIES OF AMERICA INC.

1000 Thomas Jefferson Street, N.W., Suite 515
Washington, DC 20007
(202) 342-8086   Fax: (202) 342-9063
Twx: 710-822-0130 TANNERCIL WSH

♦ ♦ ♦

The Show For Accessory and Garment Leather

*Now Presents a Wider, More Exciting Array of Leather
Than Ever Before!*

the leather industry is looked to for guidance by other segments of the fashion industry.

At least one to one and a half years before the ultimate consumer sees the finished products in retail stores, there are leather trade shows at which tanners show and sell their latest products to professional buyers. For example, the *Semaine du Cuir* is a long-established major annual show in which tanners from around the world participate, and to which buyers come from all over the world, along with the fashion press. This show is held in Paris, usually in September.

The Hong Kong International Leather Fair is a more recently established trade show. It is held in June in Hong Kong and attracts buyers and sellers from many countries, including the United States.

The Tanners' Apparel and Garment (TAG) Show is held in New York City in October of each year and attracts garment manufacturers, suppliers, and retailers, among others. In 1989 there were 82 exhibitors and 38 foreign countries represented.[27]

IMPORTS AND EXPORTS

Domestic cattle hides are a by-product of the meat packing industry, and a long-term downward shift in demand for red meat has discouraged growth in cow herds. Yet the weaker dollar and strength in demand increased U.S. leather exports in 1989 to $642 million. Canada was the largest importer, followed by Korea, Italy, Japan, and Taiwan.[28]

Imports of leather rose sharply in 1989 to $735 million, up from $124.4 million in 1975. The quantity of upholstery leather alone increased by 50 percent. Argentina was the largest supplier, followed by Brazil, Italy, and the United Kingdom.[29]

Readings

The greatest factor in the success or failure of any textile company is its willingness to change from the status quo to a broader vision of opportunities that offer a greater chance of profitability and survival.

Over the Rainbow

June Roche, the corporate fashion director of Milliken and Co., is considered to be the nation's most influential color expert. She forecasts winning colors at least 18 months before they show up, and her guidance is sought by producers of everything ranging from textiles to office furniture. Car makers are among her most devoted followers.

This Is Springs

Creativity in product design and innovations in marketing have made Springs one of the three largest manufacturers in the world of textiles.

Burlington's New Weave: Smaller and Tighter

Hoping that "smaller" would result in bigger profits, Burlington Industries, a $2 billion textile giant, closed or sold 34 of its 84 manufacturing plants, slashed $70 million from its overhead, and retired almost one-half of its top executives.

At Cone Mills Quick Response Spells Survival

In order to retain its position as a key supplier of denim and corduroy, Cone Mills entered into a Quick Response computerized partnership with major apparel manufacturers such as Levi, Wrangler, and Lee. Although the QR programs required a large capital investment for the new technology, expectations are that the benefits will eventually outweigh their costs.

OVER THE RAINBOW

by John Birmingham

June Roche predicts a bright future for America. There are already unmistakable glimmers—vivid reds and purples, emerging this fall as the key fashion colors for women's clothing. By next summer the amperage will rise even higher, as more swimsuits light up the beach in such fluorescent colors as hot pink and electric orange.

"And this is only the beginning," says Roche. "The nineties will be a color decade like none before. You'll see people wearing outfits all in one bright color, not just with a little color against a neutral background. And you'll see lots of different products in bright colors, and whole rooms painted in color, instead of off-white or beige."

Roche, the 50-year-old corporate fashion director of Milliken & Co., is the nation's most influential color expert. In choosing colors for the $1 billion textile firm, she picks winners at least 18 months before they show up on department store racks.

Granted, all of the top textile companies employ colorists who attempt to do that. But Roche takes unusually strong positions, identifying the one or two colors on the cutting edge. Moreover, she has a singular way of explaining her forecasts to the industry, in lively slide presentations during which she's as likely to talk about hairstyles, architecture, or Pee-Wee Herman as the colors themselves. On stage, Roche personifies the fashion theme of the moment. To herald a return to femininity, she walked on waving a large, feathery fan. When rugged looks were emanating from Australia, she appeared in an oilskin coat accessorized by a bush hat and whip.

Such showmanship—coupled with an uncanny record for accuracy—has made June Roche a hot ticket. Last year her ready-to-wear presentations drew some 3,000 buyers and designers, from such stores as Macy's and Bloomingdale's, as well as Milliken's manufacturer customers. Her guidance is also sought by many outside the fashion world, producers of everything from office furniture to Crayola crayons. "It's all connected," she says. "Whatever happens in fashion goes on to affect other products."

Even automobiles. In fact, car-makers are among Roche's most devoted followers. Once a year she meets with designers from General Motors, Ford, and Chrysler, who represent annual sales of about 6.5 million cars. As early as 1984 she began steering them toward "Marilyn Monroe colors"—pastels evoking Cadillacs and T-birds of the fifties, but less harsh, more sophisticated. Of course, Detroit moves more slowly than Seventh Avenue. But by 1990 roughly 30 percent of American automobiles will be pastel colored, according to consultant George Moon, former head of interior design at GM. "June Roche has a perceptible effect on our industry," says Moon.

How did Roche know that pastels were on the way? Each year she logs more than 40,000 air miles in her search for fashion news, cultural events, and anything else that might signal changes in consumer color preferences. But this time the tip-off came right to her mailbox, in the form of a lingerie catalog.

"This was back in the early eighties," she recalls. "I was struck by the Victoria's

Secret catalog, which seemed to be doing fabulously well. Yet women at that point were dressing like men, in necktie and burgundy shirts and charcoal-gray blazers. So I thought: Who's buying this sexy, feminine underwear? Is there some other desire that's been overlooked?"

Recently fashion designers have been hoisting the femininity banner to new heights.

"Right now we're reaching the exaggeration point," she says. "The first sign was the miniskirt. Then Christian Lacroix blew everything away; he made the ultimate feminine statement, with froufrous and flowers and petticoats. After that, the trend has nowhere to go. So it's time for the next phase."

Which brings us to the neon nineties. Last winter Roche dashed off to Hawaii and Bali to photograph the latest surfer looks, marked by blinding colors and bold decals. Later, speaking before a group of swimwear manufacturers, she touted a "nearly neon" palette—a bit lighter than traditional Day-Glo—which reflects the continuing trend toward brighter colors.

"For years we've worn a lot of neutrals because we feel safe in them. They enable us to blend in," says Roche. "But the nineties won't be about safeness and blending in. They'll be about *individuality*. And that means wearing colors that draw you out."

Roche, who grew up in New Bedford, Massachusetts (in a family "with whaling captains on one side and textile workers on the other"), joined Milliken soon after graduating from New Bedford Institute of Technology. She started out designing fabrics and developing color cards, but the job quickly expanded. Today Milliken grants

her an apparently flexible budget and schedule to operate as a sort of freewheeling ambassador for the company.

Not surprisingly, Roche shows an intuitive knack for uncovering the sources of future color trends. She explored Egypt two years before the much-hyped "Treasures of Tutankhamen" exhibit reached the United States, inspiring a wave of gold and bronze. Her Australian trip predated the superstardom of Mel Gibson and the release of *Crocodile Dundee*. But Roche made her proudest prediction a decade ago—for purple.

"That was a real breakthrough," she says. "It took courage, because until then everybody thought purple had funeral connotations and just wouldn't sell."

By 1979 plum was the most popular color for GM cars, and purple, in one shade or another, has remained a Milliken bestseller ever since.

Now that Americans have overcome such taboos, they are open to a wide variety of colors. Still, Roche keeps scouting for the common denominators. One of her recent trips was to France, for the Cannes Film Festival. "My job is simply to have my antennas out, knowing what to pick up on and what to filter out," she says.

"A lot of it is a matter of timing," she adds. "For instance, when the menswear look for women came in, I was one of the first to go to Milan. But now that that's over, I don't even *look* at Armani and Versace."

Meanwhile, she listens to music. And peers in store windows. And watches TV. "And don't forget junk mail," she says. "If you really examine junk mail, you'll find the pulse of what's happening in the country."

THIS IS SPRINGS

With this 1988 annual report, we introduce a program called "The Springs of Achievement." This program sets forth our company's long-standing basic values: quality, service, creativity, personal and family development, education, history and the future. Each is an area where we have made commitments, want to raise our standards and achieve new levels of excellence.

"The Springs of Achievement" describes our tradition, now more than a century old, of striving for quality in our work, our products and services and in our lives.

We are a major manufacturer and marketer of home furnishings, finished fabrics and industrial textiles. Consolidated 1988 sales were $1.8 billion.

We operate 39 manufacturing plants in six U.S. states, England and Belgium, with a minority interest in a joint venture in Japan. Of these, 24 are in South Carolina, where we are the largest industrial employer. Sales, distribution and administrative offices are located throughout the U.S. and Canada. Approximately 23,300 people are associated with Springs.

Home furnishings sales were $772.6 million in 1988. Products include sheets, pillowcases, bedspreads, comforters, draperies, towels, bath mat sets, bed and bath accessories, tufted area and scatter rugs, woven area rugs, ceramic bath accessories, table linens, shower curtains, drapery hardware, window shades and blinds. Most of these products are sold directly to retailers.

Finished fabrics sales were $638.5 million in 1988. Our fabrics include a broad range of colors, weights, fibers, finishes and printed designs. These woven and nonwoven fabrics are sold to manufacturers of apparel, decorative home furnishings, furniture and specialty products, as well as to the home sewing and couture markets.

Sales of industrial fabrics were $413.7 million in 1988. Through Clark-Schwebel Fiber Glass Corporation, we are one of the world's largest producers of woven industrial fiber glass fabrics used for printed electronic circuit boards, aircraft parts, sporting goods, reinforced plastics, dust filtration bags and electrical insulation. We produce aramid fabrics for antiballistic vests, protective helmets, reinforcement of aircraft parts and marine applications. We also produce a variety of specialty fabrics for other markets.

Springs' major brand names are Springmaid®, Wamsutta®, Ultrasuede®, Skinner®, Pacific®, Graber®, Performance™, Fashion Pleat®, Custom Designs™ and Pacific Silvercloth®.

In preparation for this year's annual message, we reread the chairman's letter in our annual reports since 1980. We were either prescient or lucky, depending on one's views of these matters, in that nearly all items reported or projected have turned out as described, which may say more about our ability to write than to manage. But we are particularly pleased that in the 1981 report we wrote, "We believe the decade of the 1980s can be one of the best in the company's long history."

Such has been the case, and 1988 adds to this record. Sales reached a record $1,825,000,000. Though earnings of $52.8 million, or $2.98 per share, were down slightly from the previous year, they were the second best in the history of the company. Importantly, without the special charge for a restructuring reserve created in 1988, our earnings would have been $3.61 a share, a record level for the company.

Source: Springs annual stockholders' report, 1989.

These sales and earnings before the special charge were double the rate of 1980's $800 million in sales and $1.82 a share, adjusting for stock splits.

At a time when "smokestack" America generally and the textile industry particularly looked as if they were both going to be shipped overseas, Springs, among others, continued to show remarkable resiliency and strength during a period of enormous change in our industry, our country, and in the world. Much has been written about the internationalization of the U.S economy, but one needs to experience the dynamics before he truly understands what that means. Springs people have.

It is to the credit of all Springs people that over the last ten years Springs' total return to shareholders through February 6, 1989 averaged 22.3 percent as compared to 17.0 percent for the S&P 500. So much for "dead" industries!

During 1988 we made a number of changes consistent with plans and objectives described in earlier years. We completed a thorough analysis of all of our textile manufacturing facilities and increased in a major way the amount of dollars to be spent in enhancing these facilities with state of the art technology. Having completed all of the planning and most of the work on modernization of our Home Furnishings Manufacturing facilities, during 1988 we completed a similar review of and plan for our Finished Fabrics Manufacturing facilities. The implementation of these plans bodes well for our customers and for our people as we continually strive to find ways to make Springs a world-class company with the ability to compete anywhere.

Additionally, we commenced construction of a fabrication plant in Fort Lawn, South Carolina, to meet more promptly the needs of our customers. It is anticipated that this facility will begin production in the late spring of 1989. By focusing our facilities on proprietary or unique products rather than commodity products, we believe that we will serve the best interests of our customers, the ultimate consumers, and our shareholders. The strengthening of our business in this manner makes us less vulnerable to imported fabric and, in all likelihood serves a greater purpose for our customers.

As part of this review, we made organizational changes that further strengthen our group concept. M.L. Fontenot, previously president of our Consumer Fashion Division became an executive vice president of Springs and president of our Finished Fabrics Group. Jules Lasnick, a director and executive vice president of Springs, became the president of the Home Furnishings Group, a new position. We believe these changes more nearly meet the needs of the time and the requirements of the future.

Creativity

Springs' creative approach to business has been most visible in our product design and marketing initiatives.

Graber Industries won its second "Roscoe" award from The Resources Council for creative achievement in interior design, for a metallized backing for light-colored pleated shades.

In textiles, we received 10 nominations for "Tommies," the top award of the American Printed Fabrics Council. We won two, one for the Wamsutta reversible sheet pattern "Valencia," and one for a Springmaid quilt pattern, "I Love Country." It was the third "Tommy" in six years for the Wamsutta/Pacific Division and the second in a row for our Retail and Specialty Fabrics Division. Springs also received nominations in the womenswear, sleepwear, over-the-counter and technical excellence categories.

Bill Blass produced his 18th Springmaid collection. The Blass line now coordinates with bed and bath accessories. Lawrin Lamps and Masterlooms chain-stitched area rugs.

Andre Richard Company joined Springs early in 1988 as part of our Consumer Fashion Division, adding an array of high-fashion ceramic bathroom accessories, shower curtains and table linens. Creative design skills came, too. "Anastasia," an art deco pattern developed for Springs by Andre Richard, was the best-selling Springmaid sheet for the second year in a row.

Our Performance Products Division is expanding its line of Fisher-Price products to encompass a full range of juvenile bedding, while the division's novelties continued to set the industry pace for innovation.

At the top of the line, the "Mirabelle" pattern was added to Wamsutta Supercale Elite, our 250-thread count cotton luxury sheet ensemble, while the Springmaid 230-count sateen line was augmented with two new patterns.

In a kind of cultural exchange, Finlay-son, a noted Scandinavian home furnishings firm, began designing Springmaid bed and bath fashions while Vantona, a leading British firm, began using Springmaid designs for the upscale department store trade in the United Kingdom.

Elsewhere, Wamsutta introduced a dozen new curtain designs, Minnie Mouse joined Mickey in the Pacific brand sheet lines and Graber developed vinyl vertical blinds that simulate marble, clay and other textures.

A number of proprietary products have been developed at our Research and Development Center, which continues to increase its active role in new product development, customer service and exploration of new ventures.

Our report is not intended to be exhaustive, merely illustrative. Product innovation and creativity are hallmarks of Springs, and our achievements—particularly in branded products—grew during 1988.

BURLINGTON'S NEW WEAVE: SMALLER AND TIGHTER

It wasn't what you'd call great timing. Not three weeks after Burlington Industries Inc. issued junk bonds to finance its leveraged buyout, the crash of '87 hit on Oct. 19. The bonds' price sank to 88¢ on the dollar, double the drop of comparable paper. And the LBO, crafted by Morgan Stanley & Co., looked like the Deal Most Likely to Fail. The $2.9 billion price was 26 times the textile giant's earnings, and the summer deadline

for raising $650 million through asset sales appeared to be impossibly tight.

But while other LBOs are stumbling or collapsing, Burlington is shaping up as the year's surprise survivor. The scaled-down, $2.2 billion company has paid down 45% of its buyout debt, and it's churning out record cash flow from its remaining operations. In fact, the textile giant, based in Greensboro, N. C., is so healthy that on Sept. 6 it called in $312 million in bonds paying 15.25%. Analysts estimate that Burlington, by substituting cheaper bank debt, will save $17 million in annual interest payments.

Austere Culture

Burlington didn't do anything fancy. It just cut. And cut. The company slashed $70 million from overhead, sold or closed 34 of its 84 plants, and had 6 of its top 13 executives take early retirement. All told, Chairman Frank S. Greenberg trimmed the payroll by 18,000—and even put an employees' pitch-and-putt golf course up for sale.

A firm market for Burlington's apparel fabrics didn't hurt, either. Nor did an industry consolidation that helped the company fetch premium prices for its industrial fabric plants. But the cyclical textile industry can turn around fast, so Greenberg isn't about to let his company return to its old, prodigal habits.

Under former Chairman William A. Klopman, whom Greenberg succeeded in 1986, Burlington seemed bent on bigness for its own sake. Klopman spent more than $2 billion on state-of-the-art plants, but critics contend the 10-year buildup was unfocused and disruptive. Even Greenberg admits that writedowns and worker retraining costs, which the accountants called nonrecurring, "recurred all the time" and ate into profits.

Greenberg has instilled a culture of austerity. Strategic and operational decision-making, once upper management's preserve, is now in the hands of division managers, and their deliberations are guided by the sober realities of the income statement. Greenberg himself spends two days a week on the front lines, reviving the laggard carpet division in Valley Forge, Pa. "We are less chivalrous and romantic and more prudent," admits Greenberg, 59.

If the romance has faded, so has the company's indifference to markets. Customers say the new Burlington is more likely to accept thinner margins to win new business. And despite lending covenants that restrict capital outlays, the buyout hasn't derailed product rollouts. One of the latest: a form of denim that lends itself more readily to stone-washing, the current *ne plus ultra* of chic.

The biggest winners may be Burlington's new investors. Charles J. Rose, an analyst with Oppenheimer & Co., estimates that by 1990, Morgan Stanley's initial 35% investment of $43 million should grow eightfold in value, to $340 million. And Burlington's executives will soon get the chance to buy a 14% stake.

'Probably Illegal'

Burlington's workers aren't so fortunate. The company no longer pays out pension money to them when their plants are sold. Instead, Burlington protects its cash flow by retaining the funds until workers retire. Unions estimate the change freezes more than $10 million in benefits for workers at two former Burlington plants in Erwin, N. C., alone. Burlington says selling so many plants makes the former policy untenable. Bruce Raynor, Southern director for the Amalgamated Clothing & Textile Workers Union, isn't sympathetic: "They're holding the retirement money. It's certainly immoral, and it's probably illegal."

But labor unrest is less worrisome to Burlington than its debt, which at $1.6 billion is still a perilous 96% of capital. And the company could be rocked by a slump in apparel sales, since it now derives 63% of its revenues from that business. Burlington is still a long way away from the comfort zone.

AT CONE MILLS QUICK RESPONSE SPELLS SURVIVAL

by Ray Clune

Greensboro, N.C.—To Dewey Trogdon, chairman and chief executive officer of Cone Mills, Quick Response is like marriage: It isn't cheap, it takes total commitment, and it's supposed to last forever. And like marriage, it's a two-way street with lots of give and take from the partners if it is to work.

"Quick response is not a quick fix," Trogdon said. "It's not a fad and it's not a program that will end. It's a process that goes on and on." Cone, one of the first major corduroy and denim producers to launch a Quick Response initiative, actually began its involvement two years ago, "in large part out of necessity," Trogdon explained.

"Big customers like Wrangler, Levi and Lee said, 'if you're going to be a key supplier this is what we want you to do.' So we started with large-tier customers and we ran into a lot of unexpected problems, but we also ran into some unexpected benefits."

Cone hasn't yet put a dollar figure to its overall costs and savings resulting from its QR initiative, but Trogdon says he is working on that.

Today, he estimates Cone is about 50 to 60 percent on its way to fully implementing its QR expectations but he feels it will take another two years to fully complete the drive.

The former president of the American Textile Manufacturers Institute outlined Cone's strategy of reaching its goals via four steps:

1—Communication with customers on their needs.

2—Developing the necessary infrastructure.

3—Beginning the Quick Response program.

4—Improving manufacturing technology, systems, and controls.

"What we want to do is to create value in manufacturing. Marketing is steering and service is supporting. Where we really want to score is in manufacturing."

Trogdon emphasized that customer service, production scheduling, data processing and fabric design have all got to be absolutely coordinated before a Quick Response strategy can work. "Even if that requires heavy capital investments in new technology."

But, he emphasizes there is more to Quick Response than new technology—there must be emphasis on people and their mindset. "For the whole process to work as it has been drawn up it must have the support of every employee in the company. The commitment in terms of strategies and policies must be 100 percent. In terms of achieving that commitment through our company, I think we're now about 75 or 80 percent of the way." The executive noted that Cone is going through an education process that has cost approximately $1 million over the past couple of years, and is expected to cost yet another $1 million over the next two.

Proud of its initiative, Cone made a video on Quick Response as a marketing tool to demonstrate to customers its total commitment to the process.

"But the major ruboff came from our

Source: *Daily News Record*, Fairchild Publications, May 1988. Reprinted by permission.

own employees since they recognized that our customers were going to see this video," he added quickly.

"QR is definitely a major marketing tool for Cone" Trogdon declared. "If you are going out for business today, QR must be a major part of your drive. That doesn't mean you are going to get paid more for doing it—customers expect it now."

In Cone's video, various employees from all divisions participate and discuss their job functions while emphasizing their commitment to the process.

Since it began its QR strategy Cone has added approximately 1,000 employees to its roster, bringing it to about 10,800 workers. In 1984 when the firm went private through a leveraged buyout, it had 9,400 employees. Although additional staff must be considered in the expense column along with new technology, new systems, and higher production and processing costs, eventually the real result is significant savings through reduced inventory and improvements in quality.

"Inventories and quality related things are the biggest savings," Trogdon said. "Our buzz phrase now is do it right the first time, so we are not making the same mistakes and redoing the same things twice. We're already realizing substantial savings because we are hitting right on target more times. This means savings in warehouse costs, inspection costs, and reduced damage from multiple handlings. Finally, quality problems are spotted four to eight weeks sooner than before."

Prior to implementation of its QR procedures, Cone inventory dwell time was running anywhere from four to eight weeks. That's been cut to about two weeks.

"We carried a lot of inventory, but that was basically done, I think, to excuse some poor performance on our part," Trogdon declared. "We've probably cut the customer's inventory from three to four weeks to three to four days because the cloth is going in when it's already scheduled on the cutting table," he explained.

In building its infrastructure, Cone centralized customer service—creating an information linkage with customers, centralized production planning, centralized fabric development, and focused data processing on marketing and manufacturing support systems.

Trogdon expects to reduce turnaround time by 60 percent later this year when it phases in its newest improvements in manufacturing.

So what's the bottom line?

"That's easy," he replies with a smile, "The game is survival—and ultimately prosperity for all—shareholders, employees, customers, suppliers, and communities."

Endnotes

1. Christian Dior, *Talking about Fashion.* New York: G. Putnam's Sons, 1953, p. 35.
2. *Textile Organon, U.S. Industrial Outlook,* 1990.
3. *U.S. Industrial Outlook,* 1990.
4. Frederick Lewton, "Samuel Slater and the Oldest Cotton Machinery in America." Smithsonian article for 1926.

5. *Textiles—An Industry, a Science, an Art.* Charlotte, N.C.: American Textiles Institute.

6. *Mankind's Magic Carpet.* Charlotte, N.C.: American Textile Manufacturers' Institute.

7. *All About Textiles.* Charlotte, N.C.: American Textile Manufacturers' Institute, pg. 5.

8. Ibid, p. 1.

9. Herbert Heaton, "Benjamin Gott and the Anglo-American Cloth Trade," *Journal of Economics and Business History*, Vol. 2, November 1929, p. 147.

10. E. B. Alderfer and H. E. Michl, *Economics of American Industry*, 3d ed. New York: McGraw-Hill, 1957, p. 417.

11. U.S. Department of Labor, *Technology and Manpower in the Textile Industry of the 1970s*, Bulletin No. 1578, p. 10.

12. Walter Adams, *Structure of American Industry*, rev. ed. New York: Macmillan, 1957, Chapter 2.

13. Ed Newman, "Development of a Fabric Line," *Inside the Fashion Business*, 3d ed. New York: John Wiley & Sons, 1981, p. 92.

14. Interview with Dewey Trogden, President of Cone Mills, *Women's Wear Daily*, June 1988.

15. C. O'Connor, chief statistician, American Textile Manufacturers' Institute, January 1989.

16. *U.S. Industrial Outlook*, 1990.

17. Ibid, and U. S. Department of Commerce.

18. *New York Times*, March 14, 1989.

19. Ibid.

20. Sandra Blye, executive director of American Fur Industry, Inc.

21. Ibid.

22. *New York Times*, March 14, 1989.

23. Ibid.

24. Sandra Blye.

25. *U.S. Industrial Outlook*, 1990.

26. Tanners' Council of America, *Dictionary of Leather Terminology*, 4th ed.

27. TAG Leather Show 1989 catalog.

28. *U.S. Industrial Outlook*, 1990.

29. Ibid.

Selected Bibliography

Corbman, B. *Textiles: Fiber to Fabric*, 6th ed. New York: McGraw-Hill, 1982.

Ewing, Elizabeth. *Fur in Dress.* England: Batsford, 1981.

Fairchild's Textile and Apparel Financial Dictionary. New York: Fairchild Publications, published annually.

Kaplan, David G. *World of Furs.* New York: Fairchild Publications, 1974.

Pizzuto, Joseph J., Arthur Price, and Allen C. Cohen. *Fabric Science.* New York: Fairchild Publications, 1984.

———. *Fabric Science Swatch Kit.* New York: Fairchild Publications, 1984.

Powers, Susan, and Rosemary Mitorja. *The Designer's Fabric and Trim Resource Guide.* New York: Trends in Progress, 1988.

Prentice, Arthur C. *A Candid View of the Fur Industry.* Bendley, Ontario: Clay Publishers, 1976.

Silbert, Viola. *How to Buy a Fur That Makes You Look Like a Million.* New York: Villaro Books, 1987.

Sinclair, John L. *The Production, Marketing and Consumption of Cotton.* New York: Praeger, 1968.

Textile Industry and the Environment, The. Research Triangle Park, N.C.: AATCC, 1973.

Walton, Frank. *Tomahawks to Textiles: The Fabulous Story of Worth Street.* New York: Appleton-Century-Crofts, 1953.

Ware, Caroline F. *The Early New England Cotton Manufacture.* New York: Johnson Reprint Corporation, 1966.

Wingate, Isabel B. *Fairchild's Dictionary of Textiles*, 6th ed. New York: Fairchild Publications, 1979.

———. *Textile Fabrics and Their Selection*, 8th ed. Englewood Cliffs, N.J.: Prentice-Hall, 1981.

Trade Associations

American Fabric Manufacturers Assoc., 1150 17th Street, Washington, D.C. 20026.

American Fur Industry, 363 7th Avenue, New York, N.Y. 10001.

American Printed Fabrics Council, Inc., 1040 Avenue of the Americas, New York, N.Y. 10036.

American Textile Manufacturers' Institute, Inc. (ATMI), 1801 K Street Northwest, Washington, D.C. 22037.

American Yarn Spinners Association, Inc., P.O. Box 99, Gastonia, N.C. 28052.

The Color Association of the U.S., 24 East 38th Street, New York, N.Y. 10016.

Cotton, Inc., 1370 Avenue of the Americas, New York, N.Y. 10019.

Emba Mink Breeders Association, 151 West 30th Street, New York, N.Y. 10001.

Fur Information and Fashion Council, Inc., 101 East 30th Street, New York, N.Y. 10016.

International Silk Association, U.S.A., 200 Madison Avenue, New York, N.Y. 10017.

Knitted Textile Association, 386 Park Avenue South, New York, N.Y. 10010.

Leather Industry of America, 2501 M Street Northwest, Suite 350, Washington, D.C. 20037.

Mohair Council of America, 1412 Broadway, New York, N.Y. 10036.

Textile/Clothing Technology Corp. (TC2), 706 Hillsborough Street, Raleigh, N.C. 27603.

Textile Distributors Association, Inc., 45 West 36th Street, New York, N.Y. 10018.

Textile Fabric Association, Inc., 36 East 31st Street, New York, N.Y. 10013.

Wool Bureau, Inc., 360 Lexington Avenue, New York, N.Y. 10017.

Trade Publications

American Fabrics and Fashions, 24 East 38th Street, New York, N.Y. 10016.

American Fur Industry News Letter, 363 7th Avenue, New York, N.Y. 10001.

America's Textiles, 106 East Stone Avenue, P.O. Box 88, Greenville, S.C. 29602.

The Business of Fur, 141 West 28th Street, New York, N.Y. 10017.

Daily News Record, 7 East 12th Street, New York, N.Y. 10003.

Fur Age Weekly, 127 West 30th Street, New York, N.Y. 10001.

Fur Publishing Plus, Inc., 141 West 28th Street, New York, N.Y. 10017.

Knitting Times, 51 Madison Avenue, New York, N.Y. 10018.

Leather Today, 19 West 21st Street, New York, N.Y. 10017.

Modern Textiles, 303 Fifth Avenue, New York, N.Y. 10016.

New York Connection, 1 Times Square, New York, N.Y. 10018.

T.D.A. News, 45 West 36th Street, New York, N.Y. 10018.

Textile Industries, 1760 Peachtree Road, Northwest, Atlanta, Ga. 30357.

Textile Month, 205 East 42nd Street, New York, N.Y. 10017.

Textile Week, 1221 Avenue of the Americas, New York, N.Y. 10020.

Textile World, 1221 Avenue of the Americas, New York, N.Y. 10020.

CHAPTER REVIEW AND LEARNING ACTIVITIES

Key Words and Concepts

Define, identify, or briefly explain the following:

Bar coding	Generic name
Brand name	Greige goods
CAD	Hide
CAM	Ideacomo
Converter	Industrial Revolution
Converting	Interstoff
EDI	Kips

Letting-out   Skins
Francis Cabot Lowell   Samuel Slater
Man-made fibers   Solution-dyed
Natural fibers   Spinning mill
New York Fabric Show   Splits
Open-line   Tanning
Pelt   Textiles
Première Vision   Universal Product Code
Pretanning   Vertical integration
QR   Yarn
Scanners   Yarn-dyed

Review Questions on Chapter Highlights

1. Give examples of current and past fashions that prove the following statement: "Many of the changes in fashion are primarily variations in colors, textures, or fabrics rather than changes in styles."
2. In their correct sequence, name the steps in the production of fabrics.
3. Explain the statement that "unlike the suppliers of natural fibers, the man-made fiber producers made fashion their business from the start."
4. What was Samuel Slater's role in the Industrial Revolution in the United States?
5. How has the domestic industry met the competition of imports?
6. What are the competitive advantages and disadvantages of a vertical operation?
7. Describe the function of a converter and explain the various ways in which different types of converters perform the same function.
8. Discuss the various fashion activities of the primary markets.
9. What are new technological developments in the textile industry, and what are their advantages?
10. List and explain the steps in the production of a finished fur garment.
11. What is there about the processing of leather that causes the leather industry to be among the earliest to research and anticipate fashion trends?
12. Select one or more of the readings in this chapter and explain their relationship to the content of this chapter.
13. Discuss and explain the relationships between apparel producers and the primary producers.

ATLANTA APPAREL MART

4

WOMEN'S AND CHILDREN'S APPAREL—U.S.A.

"And if it be true . . . that the condition of a people is indicated by its clothing, America's place in the scale of civilized lands is a high one. We have provided not alone abundant clothing at a moderate cost for all classes of citizens, but we have given them, at the same time, that style and character in dress that is essential to the self-respect of a free, democratic people."[1]

These words, spoken by a clothing manufacturer, William C. Browning, near the end of the 1800s, aptly capture the essence of today's American ready-to-wear industry. This industry has brought the mass production of fashionable clothing to its highest development and leads the world in the quality, quantity, and variety of its output. Known by many names (the apparel industry, the garment trades, the cutting-up trades, the needle trades) and once even characterized as "the Wild West of United States industrial society,"[2] the clothing-producing industry is a sizable force in our nation's economy.

This section deals with the development, location, operations, and economics of the women's branch of the American apparel industry, including that subdivision concerned with children's wear. The readings following the text, which discuss apparel companies, have been selected to give the reader a deeper insight into the unique nature of one of this country's major industries.

ECONOMIC IMPORTANCE

By any of a number of yardsticks, the importance of the women's fashion business is clear. In terms of how consumers spend their money, it is estimated that in 1989 the outlay for women's and children's clothing and accessories, exclusive of shoes, was $115.7 billion.[3] In terms of the value of its production, the women's fashion industry also ranks high. Using 1989 once more as a yardstick year, the value of factory shipments of apparel, accessories, and fabricated textiles for women and children was $32 billion. Another yardstick —employment in the apparel industry as a whole (men's, women's, and children's wear combined)—is more than 1 million, or about 5 percent of total factory employment.[4] The major divisions of the women's apparel branch, according to the authors' estimates based on government reports of employment, account for much more than half.

Numbers alone, however, do not tell the full story of the importance of the fashion industry as an employer. Historically, the industry has been a haven for the foreign-born and the ghetto resident in search of work; it is a vast source of jobs in all parts of the country for semiskilled labor; and it is notable for hiring and training unskilled workers.

Not only is the women's apparel industry, with which we are primarily concerned here, of considerable size itself, but its activities have great influence on many other business areas. Its productive facilities, as is discussed later in this section, are distributed throughout the United States. It provides an outlet for the talent of gifted, creative individuals and employment for workers who are happiest at routine jobs. In addition, it is an industry that has changed fashion from what was once the privilege of the Four Hundred to something within reach of all but the most deprived women in this country. It is in the United States that the development of mass markets, mass production methods, and mass distribution of fashion merchandise has been most rapid. It is to this country that manufacturers and retailers from other countries turn for the know-how of making and selling fashionable ready-to-wear merchandise.

HISTORY AND GROWTH OF WOMEN'S INDUSTRY

Until the mid-nineteenth century, ready-made clothing was virtually nonexistent, and fashionable clothing was something that relatively few people in the United States wore or could afford. The wants of these few were supplied by custom-made imports, usually from England or France, or by the hand labor of a small number of custom tailors and dressmakers in this country. The dressmakers worked at home, or in the homes of their customers, or in small craft shops. The fabrics they used for their wealthy clients were generally imported from Europe.

Ready-to-Wear in the Nineteenth Century

From colonial times to the end of the 1800s, the majority of American women wore clothes made at home by the women of the house; every home in modest circumstances was its own clothing factory. Aiding these home sewing operations were the instructions for constructing garments printed in such early American women's magazines as *Godey's Lady's Book* and *Graham's Magazine*. And in 1860, Ebenezer Butterick developed paper patterns that provided the home sewer with help with styles and sizes. Home dressmaking continued to prevail.

WOMEN'S READY-TO-WEAR IN 1860

In contrast to custom-made apparel, which is constructed to the exact measurements of the garment's wearer, the term **ready-to-wear** applies to apparel made in standardized sizes and usually produced in factories.

SOURCE: From a city directory, circa 1855.

As discussed in the chapter on menswear, the first ready-to-wear clothing in the United States was produced for men. Not until the U.S. Census of 1860 was the commercial manufacture of women's ready-to-wear deemed worthy of enumeration. In that year, mention was made of 96 manufacturers producing such articles as hoopskirts, cloaks, and mantillas. What was available was of poor quality and completely lacking in good design. Although once started, the industry grew rapidly, home dressmaking continued until into the early twentieth century, and it was not until well into the 1900s that the term *store clothes*, applied to early ready-to-wear, was used in other than a derogatory manner.

The women's ready-to-wear business in the United States is indeed young, and its early beginnings were anything but fashion inspired. In not much more than a century, the industry that once served only the lowest income levels of society has worked its way up to acceptance by the very richest of women.

FROM HAND TO MACHINE PRODUCTION

The major event that opened the way to ready-to-wear production was the development of the sewing machine by **Elias Howe** in 1845. Howe's machine was further perfected by **Isaac Singer**, whose improvements made it suitable for use in factories. Singer also promoted it aggressively, thus bringing it to public attention. These machines, first operated by footpower with a treadle and later by electricity, revolutionized production by making volume output possible in machine-equipped factories.

IMMIGRANTS: A SOURCE OF MANPOWER

A plentiful supply of labor is essential to growth of any industry. This is especially true of an industry like apparel production, which was, and still is, heavily dependent on hand-guided operations such as cutting and machine sewing. Workers to perform those tasks became available in vast numbers, beginning in the 1880s, in the person of immigrants from Central and Eastern Europe. Many of the newcomers were Jews, fleeing Czarist persecutions and bringing tailoring skills with them; others, without a trade and with no knowledge of the language, were ready and willing to master the sewing machine and work at it to survive in their new country. Hundreds of thousands of immigrants came each year, and the stream never slackened until restrictions were placed on immigration in 1920. This influx of immigrant labor, both skilled and unskilled, made possible an accelerated pace of industry growth.

Developments in the Twentieth Century

During the first two decades of the twentieth century, a number of developments combined to give additional impetus to the industry. In the 1920s, the industry came of age and the output of apparel passed the billion-dollar mark, representing one-twelfth of the country's total output of manufactured goods.[5]

IMPROVEMENTS IN TECHNOLOGY AND RETAIL DISTRIBUTION

Continuing improvements in textile technology in both Europe and America made available a wide variety of fabrics. Improvements in machines for sewing, cutting, and pressing made garment production faster, easier, and cheaper.

Along with the improvements in textile and apparel production technology, there were advances in mass distribution. Retailers began to learn the ready-to-wear business. Dry goods merchants learned to sell apparel; department and specialty stores that prided themselves on their custom-made operations began to establish ready-to-wear departments. Continuing innovation in retail salesmanship and advertising stimulated the demand for the industry's products and contributed to the further expansion of women's apparel manufacturing.

INCREASING NEED FOR READY-TO-WEAR

As manufacturing improved, ready-made clothing overcame the stigma of inferiority and cheapness that had originally been attached to it. It became an acceptable answer to a growing need for reasonably priced and respectably made apparel.

An important reason for this need was the changing role of women. Prior to 1900, there were relatively few women who looked beyond the confines of home and family. Many of those who did work held miserably paying domestic or farm jobs. To be well dressed was the privilege primarily of the wives and daughters of well-to-do men.

At the turn of the century, a whole new breed of busier and more affluent women began to emerge: women in colleges, women in sports, women in politics, and women in factories, offices, and retail stores. World War I further gave many women their first view of an occupation outside the confines of their homes, and stimulated the need for ready-made clothing. Their expanding interests and activities made ready-to-wear for themselves and their families a great convenience, and thus accelerated its acceptance among nearly all classes and incomes.

RECOGNITION OF AMERICAN DESIGNERS IN THE 1940S

In the early years of the twentieth century, the American apparel industry had demonstrated an awareness of fashion but had not yet reached the point of sponsoring or participating in its development. Instead, producers and retailers looked to Parisian couture designers for inspiration. Twice a year, heads of apparel-producing firms went to view the Paris collections and bought samples for copying or adapting into mass-produced garments. At the same time, buyers from leading retail stores also bought lavishly from the Paris collections and arranged for manufacturers to copy or adapt the garments chosen. American fashion publications also concentrated their publicity almost solely on what was being shown. The phrase *Paris inspired* was the key to fashions and their promotion.

Inevitably, however, American design talent had been attracted to the industry. By the 1930s, many capable and creative designers were at work in the trade, but so great was the enthusiasm for Paris that their names were rarely mentioned in the press or by the stores. In the war-ridden years of the 1940s, with Paris blacked out by the German occupation, Dorothy Shaver, then president of Lord & Taylor and an outstanding fashion merchant, smashed the tradition of idolizing Paris designers. Her store, for the first time in retail history, advertised clothes designed by Americans and featured their names: Elizabeth Hawes, Clare Potter, Vera Maxwell, Tom Brigance, and Claire McCardell, considered by many to have been the first true sportswear designer. The rule that only French-inspired clothes could be smart had been broken.

RISE OF PUBLICLY OWNED GIANT FIRMS IN THE 1960S

Until the 1950s, the women's apparel industry consisted almost entirely of relatively small, privately owned, single-product businesses, each concentrating its efforts on its own specialized product. Large or publicly owned firms were virtually nonexistent. In the late 1950s and throughout the 1960s, however, the situation changed and huge, publicly owned, multiproduct corporations made their appearance in the apparel field, usually by means of mergers with and acquisitions of existing companies. Many influences contributed to this phenomenon. Among them was the increase in consumer apparel spending resulting from an expanding economy. Another factor was the need to become large enough to be able to deal successfully with ever-larger textile suppliers, on the one hand, and enormously large retail distributors, on the other.

The rise of publicly owned giants in the apparel field during the 1960s is

Publicly Owned Women's Apparel Producers: Selected Examples

Company	1989 Sales (add 000)
Vanity Fair	$2,532,711
Liz Claiborne	1,410,000
Leslie Fay	786,257
Gitano	625,890
Warnaco	516,673

SOURCE: Companies' 1990 annual reports.

reflected in the fact that, in 1959, only 22 such publicly owned firms existed in the women's apparel field but, by the close of the 1960s, some 100 multiproduct apparel companies were listed on the stock exchanges and inviting public investment as a source of capital for further expansion.

GOING PRIVATE IN THE 1980S: LEVERAGED BUYOUTS

In the mid-1980s, the trend toward going public began to reverse itself and some large manufacturing firms began to "go private" again through **leveraged buyouts**. In a typical leveraged buyout, a group of investors, aided by an investment firm specializing in the field, buys out a company's public shareholders by leveraging or borrowing against the company's own assets. The investors put up between 1 and 10 percent of the total price in the usual case. The rest of the purchase price, up to 99 percent in some cases, is financed by layers of long-term loans from banks and insurance companies. The company's assets and cash flow are then used to pay back the loans, with or without the sale of bonds. The company's management has reclaimed their autonomy, albeit with a load of debt and interest payments, but without the need to submit their operating decisions to the review of outside stockholders. Some examples of leveraged buyouts were those of Levi-Strauss, Leslie Fay, and Puritan, among others.

THE ILGWU: GROWTH OF THE UNION

No history of the apparel industry would be complete without mention of the International Ladies' Garment Workers' Union (**ILGWU**) and its contribution to the industry's development. In the early days of the women's apparel industry, working conditions, as in many other industries of the period, were generally extremely bad. Men and women worked 12 hours and more a day, seven days a week, in damp, disease-breeding places, referred to in disgust as **sweatshops**. The hourly wage was five cents. Some provided their own machines, and paid for thread and needles, for the water they drank, and sometimes even for the "privilege" of working in the factories. Work was also taken home to dark, unsanitary tenements that often doubled as sweatshops, and in which children worked long hours side by side with their parents. It was in this environment in 1900 that the ILGWU, then representing fewer than 2,000 workers, was founded after two decades of desperate struggle.

But the union did not achieve strength until after several major strikes and the monumental disaster of the **Triangle Waist Fire** of 1911. This tragic event took place in a factory where 146 persons lost their lives because of locked exit doors, inadequate fire escapes, and one fire escape that actually ended in midair. The shock of this holocaust was the turning point in the sweatshop era,

ILGWU Logo

SOURCE: Reprinted with permission of the International Ladies
Garmet Workers Union (ILGWU).

because it awoke the public conscience to labor conditions in the garment
industry.

Since the 1920s, industry-wide strikes and lockouts have been all but
nonexistent. Today, labor–management relations are characterized by cooperation in research, education, and industry development, and the women's apparel industry–union pattern is held up as a model for others to follow.

FROM DESIGN CONCEPT TO RETAILER _____

There are three major processes in making and marketing apparel: design,
production, and sales. The designing department creates new styles; the production division produces them in the various sizes and fabrics required to fill
retail store orders; the sales division, acting as liaison between manufacturer
and retailer, markets the line. All are interdependent. The top executive (or team
of top executives) at the head of the company sets policies, coordinates these
functions, and makes all final decisions as to their activities. Throughout the
women's apparel industry, this is the basic pattern of operations.

Seasonal Lines

In the women's apparel industry, producers periodically prepare and present (or "open") new **seasonal lines** to be shown to retail store buyers. A line is a collection or group of styles designed for a specific season. In the women's apparel industry, four to six new lines or collections are customary: Spring, Summer or Transition, Fall I, Fall II, and Resort or Holiday. Additionally, many firms add new styles to their lines for a given season as that season progresses, and they may also withdraw some styles that are slow sellers.

The exact opening dates and number of new lines vary from one segment to another in the industry but, as a general rule, higher priced lines are presented before lower priced lines. Fall I (early fall) collections are shown early in March, Fall II in early April, Resort (or Holiday) in August, Spring in October or November, and Summer or Transition in January.

The Design Function

First of the many steps in the production of apparel is the designing process for an upcoming season. This work may be done by one person or a staff. It may also be performed by one of the owners in a small firm, or by free-lance designers who operate out of their own studios.

DESIGNERS: OWNERS OR EMPLOYEES

The authority, position, and name recognition of the designer vary greatly from one firm in the industry to another. In the majority of apparel firms, the designer is simply a hired talent, perhaps only one of several responsible for developing lines that will be presented under the manufacturer's firm name or brand name. Manufacturers generally hesitate to build up the name of a designer who could be working elsewhere next season. Therefore, the vast majority of the industry's designers are nameless as far as the public is concerned. Also in the industry are many small firms that do not even employ designers but rely on free-lance design services or on a patternmaker with a good sense of fashion.

Today the number of American designers whose names are well known to the public has increased. This is because they have become owners, partly or completely, of their own producing companies, operating in their own names, and featuring their names on labels, in national advertising, and in the fashion press. Among the best known and most successful are the companies of Calvin Klein, Ralph Lauren, Bill Blass, Oscar de la Renta, James Galanos, Caroline Herrera, Adrienne Vittadini, Arnold Scaasi, Donna Karan, and Liz Claiborne.

Typical of the way a designer wins recognition by operating his or her own company is the story of Liz Claiborne. During the many years she worked for Jonathan Logan, she was unknown to the consuming public. In 1976, in conjunction with several partners, she formed her own company under her own

1990 N.Y. MARKET DATES

TRANSITION, JAN. 16-27 • EARLY FALL, FEB. 27-March 10 •
COMPLETE FALL, APRIL 3-14 • RESORT, JULY 31-AUG. 11 •
SPRING, OCT. 23-NOV. 3

Executive Director: Ruth Finley, (212) 289-0420

ADELE SIMPSON
AFTER FIVE BY JULIE DUROCHE
AGNONA
AKIRA
APE LIMITED/ANNE PINKERTON
ASERET
AUGUSTUS
AYAKO
BALLANTYNE CASHMERE CO., LTD.
HARVE BENARD
RAUL BLANCO
BILL BLASS
BLASSPORT BY BILL BLASS
BOGNER
ELEANOR P. BRENNER
OLEG CASSINI
CASTLEBERRY KNITS
CHETTA B
CIAO LTD
PATRICIA CLYNE
VICTOR COSTA
CRISCIONE
MARY DADAS FOR PAULA
LEAMOND DEAN INC.
DIANNE B
PERRY ELLIS
ENCORE (DIV OF UMI)
ESCADA BY MARGARETHA LEY
GENE EWING BIS
FABRICE SILHOUETTE
HELEN FABRIKANT FOR H. FABRIKANT
LOUIS FERAUD
ALFRED FIANDACA
JULIE FRANCIS
DIANE FREIS
DIANE VON FURSTENBERG STUDIO
JIMMY GAMBA
JENNIFER GEORGE
GIANNI SPORT LTD.
CAROLINA HERRERA
HINO & MALEE
ICINOO LTD.
MR. JAX BY RON LEAL
JAYNA
JEANNE-MARC
JOANIE CHAR
ANDREA JOVINE
KANAE IKAI
DONNA KARAN
KEITLEN
KENAR
ANNE KLEIN AND COMPANY
ANNE KLEIN II
ANNE KLEIN DRESSES
CALVIN KLEIN
ANN LAWRENCE

LEONARD-PARIS COUTURE
LESLEIGH INC.
LUCILLE CHAYT
JESSICA McCLINTOCK
MARY McFADDEN
BOB MACKIE BOUTIQUE
BOB MACKIE ORIGINALS
MANNEQUIN DESIGNS, INC.
LOUIS MARINO
MATSUDA
MIGNON
RICHARD MISHAAN
MISS O BY OSCAR DE LA RENTA
FABIAN MOLINA
RINA DI MONTELLA
MICHII MOON FOR SANYO
HANAE MORI
M W MOSS
MORTON MYLES
CHARLOTTE NEUVILLE
ALBERT NIPON
N.R. 1
ANNE PINKERTON COLLECTION
STANLEY PLATOS
POGIA BY D. POLIMENI
CARMELO POMODORO
RENLYN
OSCAR DE LA RENTA
MARY ANN RESTIVO
RIAZEE/NIGHTS
RICHILENE
RIYOICHI LTD.
CAROLYNE ROEHM
ROUIE (U.S.A.) INC.
GLORIA SACHS
ST. GILLIAN
SCAASI BOUTIQUE
KIRSTEN SCARCELLI
JERRI SHERMAN
SOFIA & ANNE
STARINGTON
ALFRED SUNG
ROSE TAFT COUTURE FASHIONS
TAHARI
TAMOTSU
LINDA ALLARD FOR ELLEN TRACY
TRIGERE
UMI COLLECTIONS BY ANNE CRIMMINS
JOAN VASS
VICTORIA ROYAL
ADRIENNE VITTADINI
NORMA WALTERS
RICHARD WARREN
YEOHLEE
L'ZINGER INTERNATIONAL/GO SILK

SOURCE: Advertisement in Womens' Wear Daily.

name, and since then has become well known among manufacturers, retailers, the apparel-buying public — and even among investment strategists who take a lively interest in trading shares in her company. Her firm, moreover, is the largest and only designer-owned company with a sales volume of more than $1 billion a year.

Designer-name firms generate relatively small sales volume, because their products are aimed and priced for a limited, affluent group of customers. Their importance, however, goes far beyond the dollars in their respective tills, because of the impact of their ideas on the fashion business and the fashion consumer. They are like the icing on the cake — a small but important part of the whole, and a part without which the cake would have little appeal.

RESPONSIBILITIES OF DESIGNERS

The designer, whoever he, she, or they may be, is expected to develop a group of new designs at least two or three months in advance of a seasonal marketing period — which, in turn, is usually six months in advance of the consumer buying period. In many instances, because fashion is basically an evolutionary process, each seasonal collection may include "new" designs that are simply updated versions of the current or past season's best sellers. Also included may be copied or revised versions of some other company's best sellers.

The designer's responsibilities go beyond ideas alone, and there are many practical obstacles to overcome. In addition to creating styles that will fit into the firm's price range and type of merchandise, the designer is responsible for the selection of fabrics and must give consideration also to the availability and cost of materials, the availability of production techniques, costs of labor, and the particular image that the company wishes to present. Great designers are those who can apply their creative talents and skills to overcome business limitations and product saleable merchandise.

PREPARATION OF A LINE

Among the fashion innovators, designs originate on the drawing board or in the muslin; among the less original manufacturers, a design will often start life in the form of someone else's merchandise that has been sketched or purchased for copying.

In a very large company there will generally be a merchandiser, one of whose functions is planning the overall fashion direction for the coming season and giving directions to the design staff about seasonal themes, types of items to be designed, and colors and fabrics to be used. In a smaller company the owner or the designer will fulfill this function.

Once a design has crystallized, the next step is to execute an actual garment. This is generally done by a *sample hand,* an expert seamstress working closely with the designer, or an assistant designer. Revisions are made as needed until a satisfactory sample emerges.

Next, a company executive or team of executives check the garment for costs, production feasibility, sourcing for production, fabric requirements and availability, and profit possibility. At this point, the principals of the firm make the final decision as to which of the styles will or will not be included in the line. Some styles may require minor changes — as, for example, adding or omitting buttons, pockets, or pleats. Other styles may be discarded entirely.

If a design is to become part of a line, it is given a style number, and a highly skilled *patternmaker* makes a master production pattern for it — in one size only (whatever size the firm uses for its samples). From this pattern, one garment is made to see if correction is needed in the pattern, and to work out the final "costing." A change in the pattern or the stitching or the details of a garment, it should be understood, may affect the cost of production. Conversely, the need to reduce costs may require some change in the pattern, such as eliminating some of the width of a skirt, omitting pocket detail, or added seaming detail.

When the pattern is right, duplicate samples are made by operators known as *duplicate hands*, usually slightly less skilled than the original sample hands. The duplicate samples are for company salespersons to show in the company's main showroom, in any regional sales offices that it may have, on the road, and at any trade shows in which it participates. In some firms, however, especially those in the higher priced lines, the master production pattern may not be made until after enough orders are booked to justify production of the style.

Production of Apparel

Some producers may decide at once which numbers they will put into the line. Those less sure of themselves generally await retail buyer reaction before putting any numbers into production. Those styles and designs that do not achieve acceptance must be eliminated to avoid costly markdowns or "close-outs" later in the season. From an initial collection of, say, 100 styles, some will be discarded after they have been shown. Of the remainder, it may be only a relatively small percentage that will warrant continued production after initial orders have been obtained, produced, and delivered. The number of orders received or realistically anticipated that is considered sufficient for a **cutting ticket** (production requisition) varies with each firm's needs and price levels. For example, producers whose dresses retail at medium to higher prices say that they require orders of from 100 to 500 pieces of a number before cutting. On the other hand, one producer whose coats employ carefully hand-cut leather in their designs and whose retail prices are very high indeed has told the authors that he will put a number into production even with orders for as few as 10 pieces. For manufacturers that are producing for mass distribution, the number of pieces considered a minimum for a production order may be counted in the thousands. Each producer has to work out its own minimum, in terms of how many pieces can be expected to be sold to customers, and how much must be realized in profit on the sales of a given number to offset the costs of putting it into production, in addition to all other costs.

The Major Steps in Manufacturing a Garment

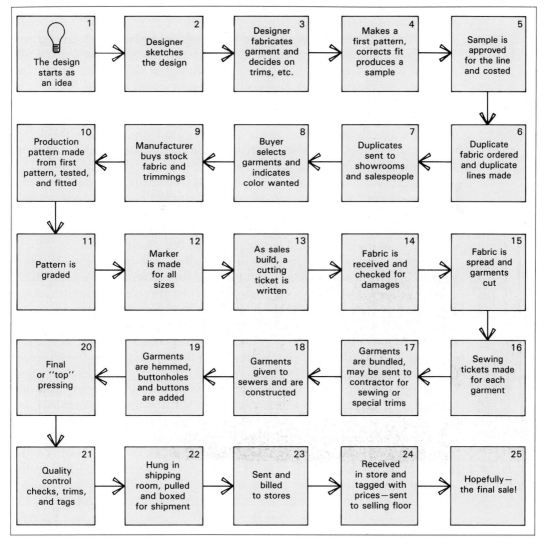

STEPS IN PRODUCTION

After it has been decided to produce a style in quantity, the master pattern for it is graded. **Grading** means that the pattern's various parts are "sloped" up and down to create separate patterns for each size that is to be cut. The process, which involves adding or subtracting fractions of an inch for each size, can be done by skilled patternmakers and graders with constant checking to ensure proper fit. Or it can be done mechanically by computers.

Next, after grading, comes the **marker**. This is a long paper guide that shows all of the various pieces and sizes of the pattern as they should be laid out in order to cut the cloth economically and with bias and straight where each is needed. For the actual cutting, layers of fabric are rolled out on long tables. The marker is placed on top. Guided by the marker, the cutter uses electrically powered knives that cut through a very substantial depth with speed and accuracy. The number of garments cut at one time varies with the thickness of the fabric, the cutter's skill, the price of the garment, the number of orders, and so forth. As many as 6,000 garments of a style can be cut on a long table in one operation. The newest use of technology in apparel production is the use of laser beam fabric-cutting systems that cut the fabric more quickly and more accurately than an electrically driven knife.

The cut parts of the garments are then collected, identified, and "bundled," to be passed along for the sewing operation. This may be done in the firm's own plant if it is an "inside" shop; more commonly, the bundles go by truck to a contractor's plant for the sewing. In some instances, contractors do the cutting, working from the marker and continuing from that point.

In some plants, a single operator does all of the machine sewing on a garment. This is the tailor system, still followed for garments that require highly skilled workers. More often, team or piece work prevails, and each operator does just one part. Where different machines or different adjustments of one machine are needed for the various elements of the garment, the team system makes for speed. Any hand sewing that is required comes under the heading of trimming, and is done by operators other than those who put together the main body of the garment.

Garments are then inspected, pressed, and readied for return from the contractor (if one is involved) to the original establishment, where they are finally inspected and distributed to the stores that bought them.

The period between design and delivery of a dress or similar fashion garment is a long one that the ultimate consumer knows little about. Yet the important decisions on what type of merchandise customers will find in the stocks of their favorite stores are made during this period.

The women's apparel industry in the United States is distinguished by the relative rapidity with which it produces and distributes its goods. In a business that must keep up with changing fashion, it is vital to surmount time and distance factors by speed and flexibility in production. No matter how early the industry starts preparing its lines, and no matter how early the retailers place their initial orders, the business of production, once started, becomes a race with the clock.

COMPUTER AIDED MANUFACTURING (CAM)

New automated devices are enabling the apparel industry to speed up the manufacturing process and reduce labor time per garment. For example, automated marker and patternmakers are being widely used. Computer inspection of fabrics, scanning and measurement of fabric width variance, and recognition of shading are becoming integral parts of a fully automated quality control system. Computerized systems are gradually replacing the time-honored way of cutting fabrics with manually operated machines. New automatic conveyor systems for handling in-process goods are reducing materials handling. Computer-aided design systems are constantly being upgraded and refined through improved software and faster computers.

Although sewing the garments together still accounts for the largest portion of the labor cost to an apparel item, even though 70 to 80 percent of the time spent is actually in handling and positioning the piece goods, new programmable sewing units that utilize microprocessors are reducing the labor content. New automatic conveyor systems for handling in-process goods are further reducing the handling of materials. Other technological developments are taking place in the areas of robotics and automated warehouse facilities.

As of the time of this writing, it is the larger firms that have been more active than small companies in adopting many of these electronic innovations. Smaller companies do not have the capital needed to install costly automated equipment. However, just as the invention of the sewing machine revolutionized the production of apparel in the nineteenth century, it seems inevitable that automated devices will become the *modus operandi* of all apparel producers in the century to come.

Behind the Price Tag of a $73.00 Skirt
Poly/cotton skirt: wholesale price, $35.00; retail price, $73.00.

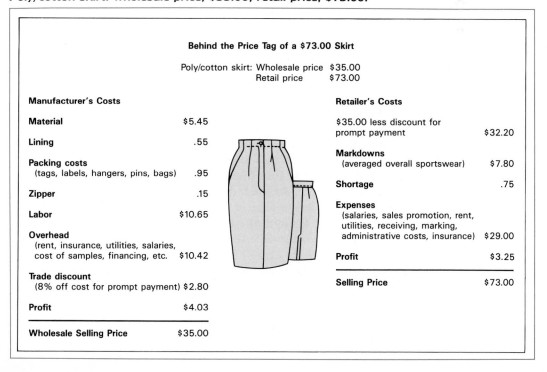

Behind the Price Tag of a $73.00 Skirt

Poly/cotton skirt: Wholesale price $35.00
Retail price $73.00

Manufacturer's Costs		Retailer's Costs	
Material	$5.45	$35.00 less discount for prompt payment	$32.20
Lining	.55		
Packing costs (tags, labels, hangers, pins, bags)	.95	Markdowns (averaged overall sportswear)	$7.80
Zipper	.15	Shortage	.75
Labor	$10.65		
Overhead (rent, insurance, utilities, salaries, cost of samples, financing, etc.)	$10.42	Expenses (salaries, sales promotion, rent, utilities, receiving, marking, administrative costs, insurance)	$29.00
Trade discount (8% off cost for prompt payment)	$2.80	Profit	$3.25
Profit	$4.03	Selling Price	$73.00
Wholesale Selling Price	$35.00		

QUICK RESPONSE: SPEEDING UP PRODUCTION TIME

As described in the previous chapter, **Quick Response** (QR) is an industry-wide computerized strategy for quick and precise replenishment of fast-selling merchandise. Today, many apparel companies are participating in computerized partnerships with retail customers and fabric suppliers, which is enabling them to accelerate their manufacturing process and provide customers with more timely delivery of currently wanted merchandise. By means of electronic data interchange, participating apparel producers receive an instant and continuing flow of information about what their "retail partners" are selling by style, sizes, and colors, and what needs to be replenished. This information enables them to predetermine production plans and schedules more precisely by discontinuing slow-moving styles and concentrating on best sellers, thereby reducing costly markdowns and increasing turnover. Also, by receiving retail reorders and giving fabric reorders directly into their interlocking computers, they can bypass the manual order entry process. For apparel producers, the implementation of a QR program requires a change in their traditional operational strategies and production planning which formerly focused on the reduction of production costs and is now focusing on the reduction of production time. It also requires a clear working relationship with their retail customers and their fabric suppliers.

As of this writing, the first QR partnerships that were formed have been between large-volume producers and retailers, each of which had the capital to invest in the necessary but costly electronic equipment. For example, Levi-Strauss, which has a computer-to-computer network with the giant Wal-Mart retail company, affixes identifying bar code labels on its merchandise and provides elaborate software services to track the sales in its stores. Dillard's, one of America's largest department stores, is linked to six suppliers of basic merchandise with which it electronically shares information to place reorders and to pinpoint trends. Among its suppliers are Hanes Hosiery and Haggar, a giant manufacturer of classic menswear. These and other QR participants claim that the program has increased their sales tremendously.

It must be noted that a great many fashion industry executives strongly believe that the Quick Response strategy for quicker replenishment of fast-selling merchandise is not quick enough to keep up with seasonal merchandise and ever-changing fashion trends. They argue that QR works only for basic goods that have a longer selling life. As one industry executive put it: "If something is selling out there, we say let's look at it and learn from it but maybe let's not repeat it. Time is moving fast and the big seller of today by next Tuesday is already in question. We are more interested in divining the next best seller than knowing what's the hot item today."[6]

There is no question that many other manufacturers are following the leaders in the Quick Response movement. Whether Quick Response strategies will become the working tool of the fashion industry — and how applicable it is to ever-changing fashion merchandise — still remains to be seen.

Marketing Procedures

Over the years, the women's apparel industry has established a pattern of selling directly to retailers, supplementing the efforts of producers' salespeople with advertising and publicity. This practice of direct selling, from producer to retailer, is related to the need for speed in the marketing time for ever-changing fashions. Since timing in fashion is of utmost importance, there is no real place for wholesale middlemen in the marketing of fashion goods. Such middlemen would have to buy, warehouse, and sell — distribution procedures too time-consuming to be practical except for staple items such as basic hosiery and undergarments, and any other articles in which fashion change is fairly slow.

PRESENTATION OF LINES

The methods of introducing new lines to buyers vary. Some firms show their new collections accessorized, dramatized, and professionally modeled in elaborate fashion shows. These shows may be staged in ballrooms, chic restaurants, discos, and other "in" locations. Other companies simply have their lines ready in their showrooms, where the garments are on racks, to be taken down and shown to individual retail buyers for inspection and possible purchase. Some firms stage press previews of their new collections, to which they invite fashion editors in order to get publicity to the consuming public. Others show their lines only to publications in which they are eager to have a "credit" — an editorial mention of one of their numbers. The method and timing of presenting new lines varies from firm to firm, and from one branch of the industry to another.

The initial presentation of a line, however, is only the beginning of a manufacturer's selling effort, since relatively few retail store buyers will be present at the opening. For the benefit of late-comers, the line will continue to be shown at the company's headquarters, although without the initial fanfare and probably without live models. For the benefit of retail store buyers who may not have seen the line while in the market, or who may not have come at all, the firm may send it out with traveling sales representatives, or exhibit it at regional showrooms and trade shows, or it may do all of these.

RELIANCE ON A SALES FORCE

By and large, women's apparel producers rely on their own salespeople to bring the products to the attention of retail store buyers. Most firms maintain selling staffs in their showrooms to wait on visiting retail store buyers and to build a following among retailers who are potential customers. Some firms also employ road salespeople who travel with sample lines to show their merchandise to retailers within their assigned territories. These men and women may also set up temporary display in any regional trade shows that take place in their territories. In addition, many of the larger firms supplement their headquarters showrooms with regional showrooms.

For those manufacturers who do not have their own sales staffs or regional sales offices, there are independent selling representatives that maintain permanent showrooms and represent several noncompeting lines in given areas.

The industry usually pays its salespeople on a commission basis, except for those who staff the showroom in the headquarters office.

ADVERTISING AND PUBLICITY: NATIONAL AND TRADE

Before the 1960s, the names of American designers and garment manufacturers were not generally well known to customers; apparel was purchased by a combination of approval of a garment's appearance and confidence in the retail seller. The source of a garment or accessory was considered the retailer's trade secret; the store's label was of paramount importance.

The rise of giant apparel firms in the 1960s gave impetus to the development of brand names and their promotion by national advertising campaigns. This advertising was aided by the **cooperative advertising** funds made available by the giant producers of man-made fibers such as Dupont, Celanese, Trevira, and Kodel, for example. These were (and still are) arrangements under which the manufacturer and fiber company share the cost of advertising which is run in the manufacturer's name and features the fiber brand in order to promote it to the consumer. The national advertising of "names" became increasingly important when designers of higher priced merchandise went into business for themselves, either alone or with partners, and established the manufacturing companies that today bear their names. The amount of brand- and designer-name national advertising done by the apparel industry today is very impressive in comparison with this almost nonexistent type of industry advertising prior to the 1960s, but it is still small alongside what is spent by such other major industries as food, drugs, autos, and electronics. In addition to the national advertising done by large brand- or designer-name companies, all fashion manufacturers make widespread use of trade publications as advertising media to bring their names and products to the attention of retailers. The small and specialized circulation of these publications brings their advertising rates far below those of consumer publications, and thus an apparel producer does not have to be large to make good use of them. Among those widely used are *Women's Wear Daily, California Apparel News*, and *Body Fashions/Intimate Apparel*. All of these are supported by the advertising of small and large producers.

Also common in the apparel business are cooperative advertising arrangements between retailers and apparel manufacturers. In these arrangements the advertising appears under the store's name and features the manufacturer's name or brand. In such an arrangement, the retailer enjoys more advertising space than is paid for out of pocket; the manufacturer enjoys advertising that is run in conjunction with the name of a locally known and respected retail store, and that is usually backed up by the store with a substantial stock of that maker's goods. The retailer, moreover, as a large and consistent purchaser of space in the local papers, pays a much lower rate for this space than the manufacturer could obtain for its occasional insertions. "Co-op" money buys the producer more space for less cost.

Other promotional techniques include providing retailers with selling aids: customer mailing pieces and newspaper advertising mats and photographs for use in store advertisements, for example.

Many of the larger firms also employ publicity agents. It is through their efforts that many of the fashion articles that appear on the lifestyle pages of newspapers have their origin. Press releases, often accompanied by fashion photographs of high quality, are sent directly to newspaper editors or, in some cases, to local stores for forwarding to the editors.

DESIGNER TRUNK SHOWS

Another marketing technique used by many well-known designers is the **trunk show**. A trunk show is a showing by a manufacturing company of its complete line to consumers assembled in a major retail store. A key company salesperson is in attendance, and often the designer makes a personal appearance. There are also live models to exhibit the garments. Such shows are backed by heavy local advertising and publicity. The consumer has the opportunity not only to see the manufacturer's complete line, but also to order through the store any styles, sizes, and colors not available in the store's stocks, since it is usually impossible for any store to stock an entire line. Designers get a firsthand view of consumer reaction; retailers observe consumer response to style numbers they did not select as well as to those already chosen for resale; producers and retailers gain sales from the impact of the promotion. Most designers say there is nothing like a trunk show for stimulating interest in and sales of their merchandise.

Manufacturers into Retailing

Today, many apparel-producing companies, dissatisfied with the capabilities of their retail customers to efficiently market their products, are taking an increasingly active role in retailing their own merchandise. Instead of depending exclusively upon retail accounts to buy and sell their products, more and more apparel manufacturers are also selling directly to the consumer through company-owned retail shops, factory outlets, and their own separately run shops within the retail stores that buy their merchandise. Usually these retail activities represent a small portion of the company's total sales, and there appears to be no intention on the part of these producers to abandon manufacturing in favor of retailing. Their aims are to seek a larger share of the consumer market, to "showcase" their entire line, and to be less dependent upon retailers to buy and distribute their merchandise.

MANUFACTURER-OWNED RETAIL STORES

The manufacturer-owned retail stores have long been an established channel of distribution in the menswear industry, as is discussed in the chapter on menswear. In the women's apparel field, however, the trend toward company-owned retail stores accelerated in the 1980s as more and more women's apparel manufacturers moved into their own retail operations in ever-increasing numbers. These company stores are located in prime shopping areas, carry a large and complete stock of the firm's products at regular prices, have an attractive environment, and offer many customer services.

Among the large and well-known American "name" companies that operate their own retail stores are Ralph Lauren on New York City's Madison Avenue, the Mickey and Co. stores owned by J. G. Hook, Betsy Johnson's stores in California and New York, the 13 stores through the United States that belong to Esprit, the 37 First Issue and 14 Liz shops of Liz Claiborne, and Calvin Klein's first store in Dallas and more to come. The list goes on and on.

Some industry observers believe that these company-owned stores essentially bring them into direct competition with their retail accounts. The top executives of these manufacturer/retail combines, however, concur with an explanation given by Jerome Chazen, an executive vice president of Liz Claiborne, that "rather than competing with Claiborne's retail accounts, their company stores will demonstrate to retailers how their products can be presented and merchandised more effectively."[7]

The relatively new company stores that have been discussed above should be distinguished from the manufacturers' underselling factory outlets that have been around for decades. These older factory outlets were usually sparsely located, in out-of-the-way factory town locations, and were stocked with an incomplete assortment of irregulars, seconds, and excess out-of-season merchandise—an inevitable by-product of mass-produced ready-to-wear that was unsalable at regular prices. The current proliferation of factory outlets is discussed in the retailing chapter.

MANUFACTURERS' SHOPS WITHIN STORES

Producers with strong images are further playing an increasingly active role in the presentation and sale of their own merchandise by means of their own separate "named" (i.e., brand or designer) shops within the large retail stores to which they sell. In cooperative operations such as these, the retailer provides the "real estate" (the space within the store) and is credited with the sales volume of the department. Although financial arrangements vary, the vendors participate in the design and fixturing of their department and pay all or part of

Crossing Over

Selected apparel manufacturers that operate retail stores.

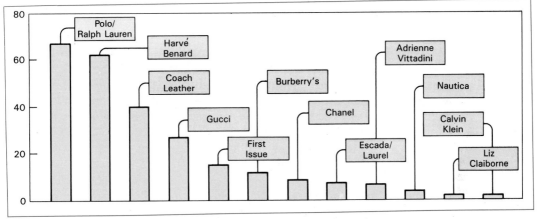

SOURCE: Company reports.

the cost for setting them up as well as the costs of advertising. The department's selling personnel either are employed and paid by the manufacturer directly or are the retailer's employees whom the manufacturer has specially trained. The quantity and quality of the merchandise assortment, as well as its presentation, are determined by the manufacturer.

In order for manufacturers to be given their own department within a store, their merchandise must appeal to the store's targeted customers and the vendor must guarantee the retail company that it can provide continuity as well as a minimum amount of sales on which the retailer will achieve a required gross profit. The ability to provide enough merchandise to keep the shop filled and to keep that merchandise moving is also a vital consideration for the retailer.

The companies of Liz Claiborne and Ralph Lauren have been leaders in this "shop-within-a-shop" concept with their creation of "Liz Shops" and "Polo" shops. It has been estimated that in their specific locations, their sales are up by 20 to 40 percent as a result of consumers' receptiveness to these "name" shops. Their success has encouraged other manufacturers to follow suit.

NATURE OF THE INDUSTRY_____

Apparel producers vary widely as to size, product, and type of operation. Small companies coexist with giant firms. Specialists rub shoulders with firms that, through their various divisions, can dress a woman from the skin out and for every conceivable occasion. Self-contained operations and plants that perform no more than a single step of the production process, publicly owned giant companies and small privately owned firms, fashion creators and flagrant copiers—all are found in the industry.

Different Types of Producers

Apparel manufacturers do not always handle the entire production of a garment in their own factories; they may contract out some of the work. The U.S. Census of Manufacturers, therefore, divides the industry's firm into three classifications according to the comprehensiveness of their production activities: manufacturers, apparel jobbers, and contractors. Common usage, however, employs different criteria and terminology.

MANUFACTURERS

Classified as **manufacturers** by the census are those firms that buy fabric and do the designing, patternmaking, grading, cutting, sewing, and assembling of garments in factories that they own. In the industry, factories that are wholly owned by a manufacturing company are known as **inside shops**, whether or not all steps in production are performed on the same premises. A major advantage of such integrated operation is that there is complete control over the production quality of the product. A disadvantage is that the necessary factory facilities and machinery require large capital investments.

APPAREL JOBBERS

What the census and also the ILGWU define as an **apparel jobber** is a firm that generally handles all processes but the sewing, and sometimes the cutting, and that contracts out these production processes to independently owned outside contracting facilities. The majority of women's apparel firms, both small and large, high priced and low priced, contract out their sewing and often their cutting, as well as any other highly specialized production processes such as embroidery, quilting, and pleating, which require special machinery. One advantage of using outside facilities in this way is that minimal capital investment is required. A disadvantage is that there is less quality control.

The term *manufacturer*, however, as it is generally used within the industry, refers to any firm that buys fabric, designs garments, maintains a showroom, sells to retailers, and ships and bills merchandise. Regardless of whether the firm is an "inside" shop or a jobber, the industry calls such firms manufacturers.

THE CONTRACTING SYSTEM: OUTSIDE SHOPS

There are independently owned factories that own their machinery and employ operators to sew and often cut goods from the designs, materials, and specifications of the apparel jobbers that hire them. Both the census and the industry refer to such factories as **contractors**.

The contracting system evolved early in the history of the industry. Prior to 1880, the manufacture of women's apparel was generally accomplished, in all its steps, under one roof. However, as ready-made clothing began to be produced in volume, it became common practice to perform in one place only such key operations as designing, patternmaking, grading, cutting, inspection, selling, and shipping. Most of the sewing tasks were contracted out to individual women who worked in their homes. This was a "cottage industry" procedure in which women added to the family income by doing piece work sewing at home. Eventually, this production shifted to privately owned factories that were devoted entirely to such work. This system of employing outside production facilities — the contracting process — continues to play an important role. The burden of seasonal idleness and production peaks can be shifted to entrepreneur contractors, along with the investment in sewing machines and the dealings with labor.

Contractors are used by both small and large firms, and an individual company may use as many as 40 different sewing shops at the height of the producing season. Even firms with their own "inside" production facilities hire independent contractors for extra capacity in busy periods; still others subsidize contracting shops. This system of using outside production facilities also enables manufacturers to diversify their product mix to meet changing consumer demands. For example, sportswear producers may one season need jackets in their lines and the following season need sweaters. The contracting system makes it possible for them to adjust and change their lines without making large dollar investments in new equipment. Most contractors specialize in a particular category of merchandise. Some of them work only for one company; others do contract work for several different firms.

Examples of the Contracting System

Contractors Wanted	Contract Work Wanted
Seeking low-priced sleep and loungewear maker who can cut, sew, ship. Call Bob 213 554-2725.	15 years exp in garment business. High quality, low price on evening wear. Call 505 277-0405.
Knitwear mfr. looking for contractor, women's and children's knitwear. Steady production and high volume. Contact: Box B35115, WWD.	NY contractor experienced in all types of knitwear, sportswear. Call 212 555-6677.
Seeking sewing contractors for full and half slips. Call 215 333-8585.	Shirt & blouse factory, very high quality, seeks top-quality mfr. Can handle small lots. Contact: WRC Bldg., 432 W. Spruce, Phila., PA 19111.
Cotton/linen line contractors sought. Small lots. Call 212 444-5656.	

SOURCE: Daily advertisements in Women's Wear Daily.

Today the women's clothing industry is a maze of inside and **outside shops**, of contracting and subcontracting and contracting beyond that. This system makes it possible for newcomers with salable ideas but limited capital to swing into large-scale production almost overnight, through the simple device of hiring the contractor's plant, labor, and production know-how. Contractors need not be located in the major market centers. Nowadays, they are located not only in every section of this country, but almost everywhere in the world where labor is abundant, facilities are available, and wages are reasonable.

Size of Apparel Companies

In matters of size, as in almost every other characteristic, the apparel industry presents enormous variety. There are huge companies that devote themselves entirely to the women's wear business; there are other enormous companies that have one or more divisions in this field; and there are the small fry. Despite the emergence of giant firms, the trend toward consolidation, the presence of conglomerates, and all the other indications of bigness, the women's apparel industry remains a stronghold of small business—more so perhaps than any other major industry.

DOMINANCE OF SMALL SPECIALIZED FIRMS

It has been estimated that the apparel industry consists of some 20,000 establishments, half of which employ fewer than 20 workers.[8]

Many of these firms are contractors whose very existence makes it possible for an enterprising and creative person with a flair for fashion and selling ability to set up an apparel company and hope to prosper. Except for the purchase of fabric, little else is needed in the way of capital outlay, since the cutting and sewing can thus be farmed out. The key to success is in producing styles that will find acceptance. In that respect, the small firm is viable and has an equal chance with a large one. The small entrepreneur has the further advantage of being able to move quickly to exploit sudden fashion shifts. On the other hand, a single poor season can wipe out a small, undercapitalized firm—and often does.

Today, small reputable specialized producers continue to set the fashion pace for the industry as some of the country's leading designers give splendid proof of how a small firm can flourish. The companies such as those of Bill Blass, Galanos, Calvin Klein, Anne Klein, Donna Karan, Geoffrey Beene, and Oscar de la Renta, for example, are relatively small; their individual sales volume figures exclusive of licensing royalties are less than $100 million. Although their target customers are women who spend a great deal on a single garment, their combined spending for fashion is a drop in the bucket compared with the volume done by moderate-priced apparel companies that cater to the great mass of American consumers. Dollar volume alone, however, does not measure the importance of the designers and their firms. The publicity they generate in the news media, plus the impact of the fashion news embodied in their garments and their licensed names, constitutes a major element in keeping the general public aware of fashion and the American fashion industry.

No matter how much the future holds for further merging and giantism in the apparel industry, one can be sure that there will always be a pool of small manufacturers that are innovative and flexible and have a clear view of what their small, special target customer group wants. As an element in the apparel industry, the small producer will survive. Those who fall by the wayside are sure to be replaced by newcomers.

MULTIPRODUCT GIANT COMPANIES

Although the greatest majority of apparel companies have an annual sales volume of less than $100 million, today there are some multiproduct giant companies involved in the production of apparel whose sales volume is far in excess of that figure. All have expanded either by diversification or by acquiring other companies. Two outstanding examples of giant companies that have diversified their product mix are Liz Claiborne, with sales in excess of $1 billion, and Levi-Strauss, whose business exceeds $2 billion.[9] Liz Claiborne, who began her business in 1976 as a sportswear producer, expanded into dresses, menswear, and accessories. Levi-Strauss added women's wear to their menswear.

A second type of diversified giant company, exemplified by Warnaco and Vanity Fair, each of which started as undergarment producers, moved into new fields by acquiring other companies already active in the area in which they

VF (Vanity Fair): A Multiproduct Company

Divisions	Product
Intimate apparel	
Modern Globe	Lollipop panties
Vanity Fair	Intimate apparel
Lee Underwear	Undergarments
Sportswear	
Basset Walker	Activewear
Jantzen	Men's and women's apparel
Jansport	Men's and women's activewear
Jeanswear	
Lee	Moderate to better jeans
Wrangler	Moderate-priced jeanswear
Girbaud	Up-market sportswear
Rustler	Discount brand
Occupational apparel	
Red Kap Industries	Industrial apparel
Big Ben	Workclothes

SOURCE: Annual report.

wished to function. For instance, under the $2 billion corporate umbrella of VF Corporation (i.e., Vanity Fair) one will find the following separate divisions: Lee Jeans, Wrangler Jeans, Girbaud, Jantzen, and Bassett Walker, among others.

A third type of giant company is composed of conglomerates whose business activities involve companies operating in widely diversified fields. For example, Sarah Lee, a food company, owns Hanes, L'Eggs, Coach Leathergoods, Isotoner, and Stedman Company, the third largest tee shirt manufacturer in the United States.

Giant apparel companies, however, are actually multiproduct aggregates of small and medium-sized business divisions, each of which concentrates on a range of products targeted to a specific consumer market segment and operates quite autonomously. In such setups, each specialized product division draws on the parent firm for financing and for policy decisions, but each one has its own name, its own clearly defined product area, its own design staff, its own contractors, its own selling force, and even its own advertising.

Specialization by Products and Prices

Traditionally there has been a high degree of product and price line specialization among industry firms. Small companies generally limit themselves to a particular category of garments such as sportswear, evening wear, bridal dresses, coats, or suits within a narrow range of prices, and also in particular size ranges, such as juniors, children's, misses, women's, and the like. Even multiproduct giant producers and retailers tend to follow this pattern by maintaining separate divisions or departments for different categories of merchandise. Although specialization still continues, over the years producers have tended to broaden their assortments as a result or changes in fashion.

PRODUCT SPECIALIZATION

The following are typical products in the women's apparel industry in which companies or divisions of multiproduct companies specialize:

- Outerwear—coats, suits, rainwear
- Dresses
- Sportswear and separates—active wear, pants, tops, sweaters, jackets, blouses
- After-five and evening clothes
- Bridal and bridesmaid attire
- Uniforms and aprons—career (other than office) apparel, daytime dresses
- Maternity
- Swimwear and beachwear
- Intimate apparel—foundations, lingerie, robes

- Blouses
- Sweaters and knitwear

WHOLESALE PRICE SPECIALIZATION

Within the wide spectrum of wholesale prices for garments, there are *price ranges* in which individual manufacturers specialize. Elements in the wholesale price of a garment are (1) the quality of workmanship, (2) the cost of labor, and (3) the quality and amount of fabric and trimmings. The women's apparel industry generally divides itself into the following five price ranges (or groups of individual prices per garment):

1. *Designer* (highest priced merchandise). This includes the lines of American name designers such as Calvin Klein, Bill Blass, Oscar de la Renta, Donna Karan, Ralph Lauren, Geoffrey Beene, and James Galanos (whose prices are the highest of all).
2. *Bridge* (high prices but lower than designer). This includes the lower priced or secondary lines of designers such as Anne Klein II and Donna Karan's DKNY. It also includes such lines as Ellen Tracy, Adrienne Vittadini, and Dana Buchman.
3. *Better* (medium to bridge prices). The lines of Evan Picone, Liz Claiborne, Jones New York, J. H. Collectibles, and Ciao would fall into this price range.
4. *Moderate* (or lower than better but higher than budget). This includes such lines as White Stag, Russ Togs, Jantzen, Levi-Strauss, and Gitano.
5. *Budget* (the lowest prices in which one would find advertised brand names). This includes firms such as Ship 'n' Shore, Judy Bond blouses, and Wrangler jeans.

Prevalence of Style Piracy

Apparel designs cannot be copyrighted; therefore, copying the work of creative designers is standard operating procedure for many firms, both large and small. Design and styling are such important competitive weapons in the fashion industry that **style piracy**, against which U.S. laws provide no protection, is considered a way of life in the garment business. In the language of the industry, however, a design is never "stolen"; it is "knocked off." It is copied, adapted, translated, or even pirated, but the "**knock-off**" is never considered as having been "stolen." This is not hypocrisy but simply the garment trade's way of acknowledging that copying dominates the industry; it is done openly and without apology. The late Norman Norell, who produced garments in very high price lines, indeed, and who was considered in his day the dean of American designers, expressed his philosophy about style piracy: "I don't mind if the knock-off houses give me a season with my dress. What I mind is if they bring out their copies faster than I can get my own dresses to the stores."[10]

Aside from the absence of copyright protection for apparel designs, there are several reasons for this copying practice. Plunging into a fast-selling style, regardless of whose design it was originally, is one way to make a modest investment work to the limit. Another reason style piracy is rife is the highly specialized nature of the firms themselves. If, for example, a dress intended to retail at $150 has features that would make it a fast seller at a lower price, the originator of the style is in no position to produce or market inexpensive versions. The originator's entire purchasing, production, and distribution are geared to customers who are willing to pay for the particular grade of material, workmanship, and details in which he or she has specialized. In addition, apparel firms' labor costs are established by the union, based on the companies' normal wholesale price lines, and they cannot be reduced. On the other hand, a maker specializing in garments to retail at $50 has much lower labor costs, enjoys access to sources for much less expensive fabrics, knows how to cut corners in production, and has established distribution among retailers catering to the price-conscious consumer. And if a style can be copied down to a still lower level, or can be marketed at some intermediate levels, makers specializing in those levels are likely to step in.

Occasionally, the copying process is reversed, and a style that originates in the lower priced lines will have features that make it desirable for higher priced manufacturers to adapt. Normally, however, the procedure is for a style that originally retailed for hundreds of dollars to be "knocked off" at successively lower prices, if it shows signs of popular acceptance by customers.

Proliferation of Industry Licensing Agreements

The 1970s witnessed the burgeoning of the "name game"—the licensing by prominent American apparel designers of their names for use by manufacturers of accessories and of lower priced clothing. **Licensing** is a legal arrangement covering a specific period of time, during which a manufacturer of goods in a particular generic category is given exclusive rights to produce and market a line of merchandise bearing the name of a licensor. For this privilege, the **licensee** pays a **royalty fee**—that is, a percentage of the wholesale sales of the goods concerned. Royalty fees generally range from 5 to 7 percent. In addition, a guaranteed minimum payment is usually specified.

The **licensor**, however, is not required to confine his or her name to only one product category. For instance, a licensing arrangement with a jewelry manufacturer does not preclude similar arrangements with producers of jeans, sunglasses, shoes, bed linens, scarfs, hosiery, fur coats, perfume, swimwear, or any other product that can profitably become part of the name game. Apparel and accessories, nevertheless, are a major field for such exploitation. It is estimated that in 1989 licensed apparel and accessories represented 35 percent of all licensed name products sold at retail, out of a total of $59.8 billion a year, an amount still on the rise.[11]

Licensing arrangements are not new to the European couture; some of the most famous among them have long had income of this sort from American manufacturers and stores. For American designers, however, this is a relatively new development and one that has grown enormously. Today, some designers are receiving royalty fees that equal and in some cases even exceed the total sales volume of their own apparel enterprises.

The proliferation of licensing by both American and European designers has arrived at the point that their names now appear on apparel priced well below the high prices level of the merchandise for which they became famous. Examples include the Calvin Klein jeans line manufactured by Puritan Inc. and the Halston name marketed by J. C. Penney, to name but two.

Apparel producers do not necessarily limit themselves to licensing one designer's name alone. They may have several arrangements during the same period. For example, Fairbrook Enterprises, a prominent coat producer, makes coat lines under licenses with Perry Ellis, Anne Klein II, and Calvin Klein while at the same time manufacturing other branded lines of their own.

The practice of licensing in the apparel industry is not limited to designer names. There are firms whose company names are so well known that they are able to license them to makers of other products. As but one example, Jordache produces and promotes its own line of jeans but licenses its name for some 46 other products to U.S. manufacturers and 55 to foreign producers. These range from women's undergarments produced by a lingerie company to sunglasses made and marketed by an optical company. Also into the licensing act today are legions of widely recognizable names such as cartoon characters, sports figures, movie and television idols, and corporate names and logos. Among the foremost is the licensing of the different characters of Disney Enterprises and those of Looney Tunes. For example, J. G. Hook licensed Mickey Mouse for the line of adult women's apparel and formed a division called Mickey and Friends, which in 1984 (its first year of operation) generated $211 million in wholesale sales.[12] The popular TV show "Dynasty" generated a Krystal perfume and Dynasty apparel and accessories. A company like Coca Cola climbed on the licensing bandwagon and licensed Murjani International to produce a line of Coca Cola leisure apparel. Even the beer company of Anheuser Busch is into the licensing game with its Spuds Mackenzie logo. A relatively recent development has been the entry of retail stores into exclusive licensing agreements of their own. For instance, Bloomingdale's has licensed Norma Kamali to design a line of swimwear and sportswear that it will have produced for their stores alone; Sears has entered into a licensing arrangement with McDonald's to produce McKids, a line of children's apparel.

The major value of a licensing arrangement to the licensees is that the merchandise carries a highly recognizable, presold name. To consumers, the name often symbolizes status, achievement, and quality. To the licensors, of course, it means additional income from royalty fees, and extended name exposure without the hassles and high cost of having to produce and market the goods themselves.

Among the most active American designer-name licensors are Bill Blass,

Licensing: Sales of Licensed Products by Category

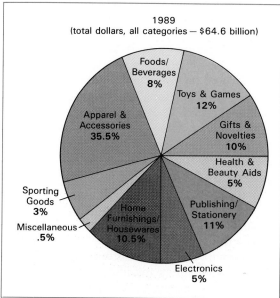

SOURCE: The Licensing Letter, 1990.

Anne Klein, Calvin Klein, Ralph Lauren, and Oscar de la Renta. The designer's input varies. For example, the Anne Klein company supplies its 28 licensees with color, fabric, design, and display ideas, and it retains final approval on all merchandise bearing its name. Others merely "edit" their licensed collections, reserving the right to approve such factors as color, quality, and design approach. With a few exceptions, very few actually design every item sold under their name. These items are more often than not designed by the unknown designer of the licensed company. What they all have in common is a very profitable royalty fee income amounting to many millions of dollars.

It must be remembered, however, that the licensing value of a designer's name is directly dependent on the success and prestige of the licensor. Almost any designer entrepreneur can have an unsuccessful collection. A series of unsuccessful collections can put any such firm out of business and also put an end to licensing, since licensees have no reason to renew an arrangement with a designer whose name has lost its glamour or status. No licensing agreement is forever.

Today, with the thousands of licensed names and licensed products plus the licensing brokers who serve as the liaisons between licensors and licensees, licensing has almost become an industry unto itself.

Financing by Factoring

Many garment manufacturers rely heavily on outside sources for operating capital. These sources are called *factors*. The manufacturer engages a factor to become its credit and collection department. Orders are submitted to the **factoring** company for approval and are shipped as designated. The invoices are assigned to the factor, who supplies immediate cash, usually equal to 90 percent of receivables' net value. (The 10 percent reserve of outstanding receivables is usually held to cover returns, allowances, etc.) The factor then proceeds to collect payment from the manufacturer's customers and takes the credit risk. For their services as a credit and collection department and guarantor of credit risks, factors receive a fee known as a factoring commission.

LOCATION OF FASHION
MARKET CENTERS _ _ _ _ _ _ _ _ _ _ _ _ _ _ _ _ _ _ _

Although some phase of apparel production (i.e., contracting and subcontracting) can be found in many states of the Union, the design and marketing activities of domestic apparel companies are concentrated in relatively few major cities throughout the United States. It is in these cities that one finds an enclave of apparel companies that produce and sell merchandise at wholesale level to retail buyers. Known as **market centers** in the trade, these centers are the very heartbeat of the industry since they are the marketing link between apparel manufacturers and retail distributors.

New York, the Leading Market Center

The oldest, largest, and best-known wholesale fashion center in the country is located in the heart of New York City. Whereas other sections of the country have been whittling away at its base, insofar as women's and children's ready-to-wear is concerned, it is still unquestionably the fashion capital of the world.

It is not entirely an accident that New York occupies this dominant position. When Elias Howe first perfected his sewing machine, factory production of garments was not limited to any one city or area. But then came the great wave of immigration, as mentioned earlier in this chapter. New York was a major port of entry for newcomers, eager to find work in the city where they landed. Their assimilation into the garment industry there was often immediate, with some manufacturers and contractors actually meeting incoming vessels to recruit whole families for work in their factories. This pool of labor, growing out of the steady stream of immigrants, was the circumstance that enabled New York to leave its rivals behind in the production of apparel.

New York had the further advantage of being close to both the cotton mills of the South and the woolen mills of New England. It was also the nation's largest city and the center of fashionable society. Once New York had gained dominance, it became a magnet, attracting such auxiliary businesses as embroi-

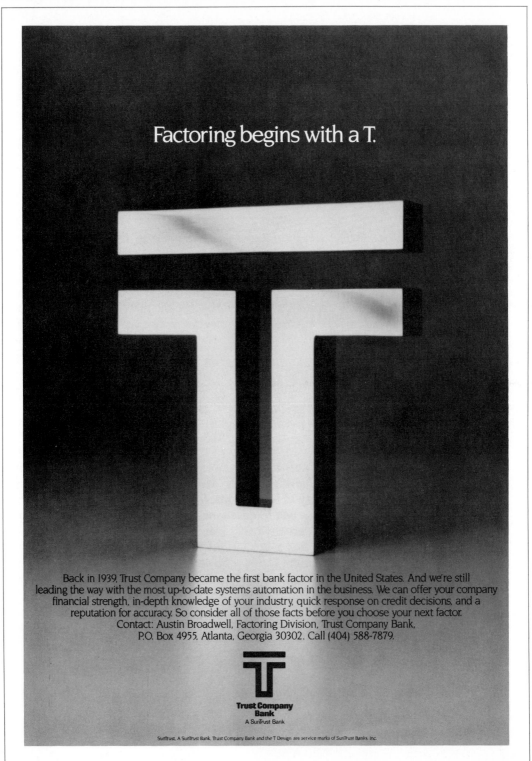

Factoring begins with a T.

Back in 1939, Trust Company became the first bank factor in the United States. And we're still leading the way with the most up-to-date systems automation in the business. We can offer your company financial strength, in-depth knowledge of your industry, quick response on credit decisions, and a reputation for accuracy. So consider all of those facts before you choose your next factor. Contact: Austin Broadwell, Factoring Division, Trust Company Bank, P.O. Box 4955, Atlanta, Georgia 30302. Call (404) 588-7879.

Trust Company Bank
A SunTrust Bank

SunTrust, A SunTrust Bank, Trust Company Bank and the T Design are service marks of SunTrust Banks, Inc.

dery, pleating, and trimmings, as well as textile showrooms, consumer and fashion periodicals, trade associations, and the like. With these advantages, the city became the hub of the women's garment industry.

Today, New York still remains and will probably continue to remain the dominant center of the U.S. fashion industry. It is only in that city that one can find the showrooms of an estimated more than 5,000 apparel firms, the showrooms of all major fiber and fabric producers, the headquarters of consumer and fashion magazines, and the offices of major trade associations. Add to that the countless opportunities for fashion practitioners to engage in New York's other important activity—"shop talk" with suppliers, friends, competitors, editors, and other sources of fashion information—and it becomes clear why the city retains its position as the hub of the fashion industry. Almost all of the leading American fashion designers work in New York–based firms because, as one major designer explained it: "Everything is here . . . you have to commute to see what kinds of clothes are needed for commuting and working. You have to live through the seasons to design clothes for the seasons. New York is just like fashion: dirty and clean, casual and uptight, alive and changing."[13]

Current estimates are that the area in and around New York employs more garment workers than any other center of the industry and that the production of women's and children's wear constitutes the largest industry in New York City and New York State.

SEVENTH AVENUE

So much of New York City's garment and accessories business is concentrated within a distance of one block east or west of **Seventh Avenue (SA)**, from West 41st Street south into the low West 30s, that the term *Seventh Avenue* has become synonymous with the women's fashion industry. The street itself was renamed Fashion Avenue in 1972. Within this area, there are literally thousands of showrooms presenting every known type and price line of women's ready-to-wear and accessories. These showrooms include not only those of New York firms, but also those of many producers whose headquarters are in other parts of the country and even in other parts of the world. There are other apparel centers elsewhere in the country where women's garments are produced and sold, but to those in the fashion business, no other center has the color, tension, activity, or merchandise variety of Seventh Avenue.

Individual buildings within the garment center tend to be specialized, each housing producers of more or less the same categories of merchandise and wholesale price ranges. For example, 1410 Broadway (the next street east of Seventh Avenue) is the market for moderate-priced sportswear, sweaters, and budget apparel; 1407 and 1411 Broadway house the showrooms of more than 2,000 sportswear companies; 1400 Broadway is the main building for medium-priced misses and junior dress firms; 1375 houses many bridal and evening dress firms; and 1350 contains many producers of lower priced apparel, of the type sold by the dozens, sometimes called "daytime" dresses.

The upper end of Seventh Avenue has a range of coat and suit firms and

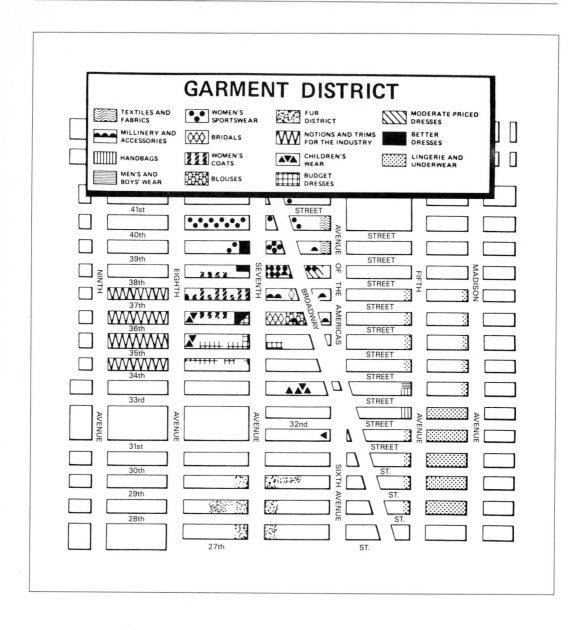

higher priced designer-name companies, with the overflow spilling into West 39th Street. Coat and suit firms are in 500 and 512 Seventh Avenue. Designer-name companies like Bill Blass, Trigère, Ralph Lauren, Geoffrey Beene, and their peers are in 530 and 550 Seventh Avenue. At the lower end of Seventh Avenue are makers of lower priced apparel whose names are generally unknown to the public. Children's wear showrooms are mostly on the south and west fringes of the area, with many of them concentrated in a specialized children's wear building at 112 West 34th Street.

The garment center's tenants, however, have been pushing out its boundaries. For example, two buildings on West 35th Street have attracted many young designer firms, and 1441 Broadway now houses three floors of the Liz Claiborne company, and other better-sportswear producers.

DECENTRALIZATION OF PRODUCTION

At one time, practically every New York–based firm had its design, showroom, production, and shipping facilities in the garment district, and even all in the same building. Increasingly in recent years, apparel firms locate their cutting and, to a larger extent, their sewing operations in areas outside the city, and even outside the country, whether these production facilities are owned by the companies or simply contracted for. This trend is noticeable not only in New York, but in other large cities as well. The high cost of rent, the unavailability of space that can be adapted to newer methods and equipment, the rising cost of taxes and labor, the almost unbelievable traffic congestion on city streets — all these have encouraged the establishment of factories in small towns in New York State and the surrounding states, in the Southeast, and in foreign countries — Hong Kong, Taiwan, and Korea, for instance. No matter where the goods are produced, however, the finished garments are sent back to the parent firm for selling and distribution. Seventh Avenue remains the nerve center of the design, marketing, and management operations, regardless of how far afield the production facilities may be.

Secondary Fashion Design Centers

There are other focal market centers outside New York City, but no one of them begins to compare with it in terms of the number of companies based there or the variety, quantity, and dollar sales. Each of these other centers tends to be fairly specialized as to the types and price ranges it produces. Many of the manufacturers in these **secondary design centers** have sales representation in New York City.

LOS ANGELES

Los Angeles, although not a very close second to New York City, has emerged as the second most important design and manufacturing center, known for its "California look." Once limited mostly to swimsuits and active sportswear, it now turns out a wide range of moderate-priced garments, including blue jeans, "trendy" junior-sized garments, and boutique items.

Los Angeles manufacturers have some advantages over New York: less expensive and abundant space, and a large pool of Mexican workers. Unfavorable factors include a shortage of the experienced patternmakers and small specialized fabric and findings firms that are plentiful in New York. California manufacturers, however, have developed their own "look" and are noted for their creative innovations in sportswear styling and colorations.

MIAMI

Of the more than 1,000 apparel manufacturing companies in Florida, the largest segment by far is made up of children's wear companies located in Miami. However, there are also an increasing number of swimwear, sportswear, and activewear manufacturers that are running small but successful businesses in Florida. The state government's fiscal policies are particularly attractive to manufacturers. The corporate income tax of 5 percent is among the lowest of any state in the United States, and there are no taxes on inventory. In addition, Florida attempts to stimulate employment by extending tax credits to manufacturers that create jobs in blighted areas.

Children's wear manufacturers were among the first to establish themselves in Florida — as early as 1940. In the 1960s, some 30 children's wear firms founded the Florida Children's Wear Manufacturers Guild, which now sponsors one of the most successful trade shows in the country. The show, held once a year, attracts well over 1,000 retail store buyers from major department and specialty stores countrywide.

An interesting point — the Miami manufacturers credit Cuban immigrants, fleeing from the Castro regime, for the growth of their industry. As one head of a children's wear firm expressed it, "The Cuban immigration of the Sixties was the catalyst that allowed us to grow. Once we got the Cuban labor working for us, we could take orders from major stores and know that we could deliver the merchandise."[14] Today, many Cubans have graduated from positions as machine operators to become principals in their own companies — a modern parallel to the European immigrant tide that helped New York City's apparel industry grow in an earlier day!

DALLAS

Once a design and production center primarily for lower priced polyester knit garments distributed through large-volume apparel chains, Dallas has changed. Most of the manufacturers headquartered in Dallas have made a shift to a mix of moderate-priced dresses and sportswear in a greater variety of fabrications to meet the changing demands of a large segment of mainstream customers. As one of Dallas's leading manufacturers explained it: "Dallas is a market that caters to middle America, only middle America has changed, and we've noticed. None of the merchandise we produce is faddish, because the middle American customer we're trying to reach isn't faddish."[15] In recent years, however, a cadre of young designers who live and work in Dallas are breathing new life into their local industry and are becoming known for their creative and innovative designs. To date, the best-known Dallas-based designer is Victor Costa.

CHICAGO

Chicago has changed. At one time it had a reputation for conservatively styled and well-made dresses for misses and women, at higher than moderate prices. But here is how an article describes the Chicago market:

> Gone are the days when traditional and polyester were the fashion watch-words here. Gone are the days when moderate-priced volume manufacturers and their multi-million dollar business along the crowded banks of the Chicago River were the ONLY game in town. Today Chicago is fashion. From the fresh young talent not long out of design school, like Richard Dayhoff, Kate Jones, and Peggy Martin, to the long established designers rapidly gaining a national reputation, like Maria Rodriguez, Mark Hester, and Gina Rossi, Chicago is making a new fashion statement.

OTHER FASHION DESIGN CENTERS

Some other secondary design centers, even more distant from New York in terms of both the value of output and the variety of merchandise, are Boston, whose local manufacturers have developed a reputation primarily for well-made, moderate-priced classic sportswear and rainwear; and Philadelphia, for moderately priced sportswear and children's wear.

Apparel Marts: Regional Selling Centers

An industry development that began in the late 1970s is the marketing importance of **apparel marts**, or large regional selling centers. Located in major cities throughout the United States, their purpose is twofold: (1) to reach out for and sell to small fashion retailers in the surrounding areas and (2) to serve as a wholesale selling facility for apparel producers, wherever the headquarters of the companies may be.

In addition to the lines of local producers, these marts house **regional showrooms** of hundreds of apparel firms from other parts of the country and even those of some foreign fashion producers. The showrooms bring the current and incoming seasons' lines of these companies within easy reach of the area's small retailers, most of whom do not have the time or money to go to New York more than once or twice a year, if that often. Buyers for nearby large retail organizations also find the marts a convenience, as it is often more practical to fill some of the special or urgent needs from a nearby source of supply.

Showrooms are leased both on a year-round basis and for temporary use during major seasonal buying periods. The temporary showrooms are particularly convenient during regional **market weeks**. Such weeks are scheduled periodically as a means of introducing the new lines of hundreds of out-of-town producers to the retailers of the area at the start of a buying season. Separate market weeks are usually held for different categories of merchandise and range in number from two to five a year. Merchandise categories include accessories, sportswear, intimate apparel, infants' and children's wear, and dresses, among others. A typical calendar of market weeks in major marts is included in this chapter.

The past two decades have seen Los Angeles, Dallas, Atlanta, and Chicago emerge as important regional selling marts, challenging what was once New York's exclusive domain. To attract buyers to market weeks, these marts stage many special events, such as fashion shows, merchandising seminars, and entertainment galas.

THE DALLAS APPAREL MART

Considered to be the largest of its kind, the Dallas Apparel Mart covers four city blocks on a 20-acre site—in addition to a recently opened menswear facility of 400,000 square feet. The mart houses more than 2,000 exhibitors of women's, men's, and children's apparel and accessories and shoes along eight miles of corridors. Among its occupants are many prominent designer-name companies. The showrooms are grouped by merchandise category, and annually book orders approaching $2 billion. Its showrooms include 1,600 that are permanently occupied, and another 300 that are taken by exhibitors on a temporary basis. To maintain a flow of customers for these exhibitors, the mart spends many millions on promotion.[17]

Although large Texas retailers such as Neiman Marcus may shop this mart, the typical and best customers of any mart are not the buyers from major stores, but a host of small independently owned specialty store retailers from the surrounding areas. Dallas draws these customers primarily from Arkansas, Louisiana, Oklahoma, and Texas as well as others from western and southern states. It is interesting to note that many New York firms "test" their new lines there just before presenting them in their New York showrooms.

THE CALIFORNIA APPAREL MART

Located in Los Angeles, the California Apparel Center contains some 1,200 permanent showrooms, plus 300 or so that are available for temporary rentals. This mart is not only a regional selling facility for New York manufacturers, but also the showcase for West Coast producers whose merchandise is not exhibited in other marts or even shown in New York. Retail buyers are drawn from the Southwest, the whole of California, Washington, Oregon, and New York.

Various incentives are offered to retail buyers to attract them to the mart: rebates on airfare or gasoline, free meals, and other inducements. Attendance is also promoted by means of a newsletter, a calendar of special events, and market directories. As a service to exhibitors, the mart also publishes a buyer registration list, which manufacturers can use as a mailing list.

THE ATLANTA APPAREL MART

The newest of these apparel selling centers is the Atlanta Apparel Mart, which opened in 1979 and contains some 1,200 permanent showrooms, plus several hundred temporary ones. The facility has 1.2 million square feet, on seven floors, each of which is assigned to a specific type of apparel. There are seminar programs, run by industry professionals and outside management consultants, in addition to fashion shows and entertainment specials. Besides using direct mail pieces and brochures and advertising in trade publications, the Atlanta

A Regional Mart

THE SOURCE

THE APPAREL CENTER IS ONE-STOP MARKET SHOPPING MADE EASY, WITH MORE THAN 8,000 LINES UNDER ONE ROOF. EACH YEAR WE ATTRACT MORE THAN 70,000 BUYER VISITS WITH FABULOUS FASHION, SEMINARS, NETWORKING EVENTS AND MORE. FOR RETAILERS WHO DEMAND SERVICE, SELECTION, AND ABOVE ALL, CONVENIENCE, WE DELIVER. SIMPLY PUT, THE CHICAGO APPAREL CENTER IS MID-AMERICA'S ULTIMATE MARKETPLACE FOR BUYERS AND SELLERS.

FALL II/ HOLIDAY

CHICAGO APPAREL CENTER
WOMEN'S & CHILDREN'S FALL II/HOLIDAY MARKET JUNE 1-5, 1990
LEASING INFORMATION (312) 527-7540 · RETAILER INFORMATION (312) 527-7755

mart sends leasing agents to New York to make direct contact with potential showroom occupants.

The primary draw for the Atlanta Mart is among the southeastern states, but attendees come from as many as 30 states to shop there. As in all the other marts, Atlanta's principal customers are small retailers.

THE CHICAGO APPAREL CENTER

The Chicago center, owned by the Kennedy family, is a 25-story building, opened in 1977. It has 11 floors of showrooms, plus a hotel, and a 140,000-

1990 market weeks

Below is the schedule of 1990 market weeks for women's apparel in the various regional markets and in New York. Unless a separate children's wear show is listed, the regional markets include women's and children's wear. Dates are subject to revision. Readers are advised to check with the marts prior to scheduled show.

	SUMMER	FALL I	FALL II	RESORT	SPRING
ATLANTA					
Atlanta Apparel Mart	Feb. 2-5	March 22-27	May 31-June 5	Aug. 23-28	Oct. 18-23
BIRMINGHAM, Ala.					
Birmingham Jefferson Civic Center	Jan. 21-23	March 18-20	May 27-29	Aug. 5-7	Oct. 28-30
BOSTON					
Bayside Expo Center	Jan. 14-17	April 1-4	June 3-6	Aug. 19-22	Oct. 28-31
Children's Market	Jan. 4-7	March 8-12	April 5-8	Aug. 9-12	Nov. 8-11
				Sept. 13-16	
CHARLOTTE					
Charlotte Apparel Center	Jan. 26-30	March 30-April 3	June 8-12	Aug. 17-21	Oct. 26-30
Children's Market (Charlotte Merchandise Mart)	Jan. 19-22	March 9-13		July 27-30	Oct. 5-9
CHICAGO					
Chicago Market Apparel Center	Jan. 20-24	March 17-21	June 2-6	Aug. 25-29	Nov. 3-7
DALLAS					
Dallas Apparel Mart	Jan. 25-30	March 22-27	June 7-12	Aug. 16-21	Oct. 18-23
DENVER					
Denver Merchandise Mart	Jan. 19-22	April 6-9	June 1-4	Aug. 10-13	Oct. 19-22
KANSAS CITY					
Kansas City Market Center	Jan. 6-9	April 6-10	June 2-5	Aug. 4-7	Oct. 12-16
LOS ANGELES					
California Mart Pacific-Coast Travelers	Jan. 19-22	March 30-April 3	June 1-5	Aug. 24-28	Nov. 2-6
California Kids Show	Jan. 21-24	March 18-21		July 29-Aug. 1	Oct. 14-17
MIAMI					
Miami International Merchandise Mart					
Southern Apparel Exhibitors, Inc.	Jan. 12-16	March 16-19	June 8-11	Aug. 10-14	Oct. 12-16
MINNEAPOLIS					
Hyatt Merchandise Mart	Jan. 14-14	March 4-7	April 1-5	Aug. 5-8	Oct. 21-25
			June 10-13		
NEW YORK	Jan. 8-19	Feb. 26-March 9	March 26-April 6	Aug. 6-10	Oct. 22-Nov. 2
PITTSBURGH					
Pittsburgh Expo Mart, Monroeville	Jan. 21-23	April 1-3	June 10-12	Sept. 9-11	Nov. 4-6
Children's Market	Jan. 31-Feb. 1	March 17-20		July 29-31	Nov. 17-20
PORTLAND					
Montgomery Park	Jan. 21-22	April 24-25		Aug. 5-6	Oct. 21-22
SAN FRANCISCO					
San Francisco Apparel Mart	Jan. 14-16	April 6-8	June 17-19	Aug. 19-21	Oct. 20-23
San Francisco Concourse, 635 Eight Street	Jan. 13-16	April 5-8	June 16-19	Aug. 18-21	Oct. 19-23
SEATTLE					
Seattle Trade Center	Jan. 27-30	March 24-27	June 9-12	Aug. 11-14	Oct. 27-30
VIRGINIA					
Old Dominion Fashion Exhibitors					
Radisson Hotel, Virginia Beach	Feb. 14-15	April 25-26	June 14-15	Sept. 5-6	Nov. 7-8
Embassy Suites Hotel, Tyson's Corner, Va.	Feb. 11-12	April 29-30	June 17-18	Sept. 9-10	Nov. 4-5

square-foot exhibition hall. There is also a 3,000-square-foot exhibit, set up as a model retail store, to offer ideas for store plans, fixturing, color effects, and the like.

Some 4,000 resources are represented on a year-round basis. These span all price levels and cover a wide spectrum of manufacturing firms from all over the world. Included are children's wear, furs, accessories, men's, and women's apparel. Among the year-round tenants are such designer firms as Oscar de la Renta, Geoffrey Beene, Yves St. Laurent, and others of similar stature. As in other marts, there are several hundred showrooms available for temporary rentals.

Among the Chicago Mart's promotional events is a center-sponsored "Chicago Is" fashion showing of Chicago-based, designer-named manufacturers' lines.

OTHER MERCHANDISE MARTS

In addition to the four major apparel marts described above, there is a smaller specialized apparel mart in Boston and a new Fashion Center in San Francisco. There are also general merchandise marts in other cities that have several floors devoted to apparel showrooms. Like the specialized marts, these more general ones aim to promote their local industries and house both permanent and temporary showrooms for local, national, and international producers. And like the apparel centers, the general merchandise marts hold regularly scheduled market weeks that are attended mostly by smaller retailers from the surrounding regions. Some examples are the Miami Merchandise Mart, the Carolina Trade Center in Charlotte, North Carolina, the Kansas City Trade Center, and the Radisson Center in Minneapolis.

Future of New York

Although more of the buying and selling action has moved to regional apparel marts, New York is still firmly entrenched as the key marketplace of the United States because it offers buyers their choice of more than 175,000 lines of goods, an amount that no other area can ever begin to match. It still remains to be seen whether the proliferation of regional selling offices will affect the frequency with which buyers for major stores throughout the country shop the New York market.

In any event, the marts have proved not only a boon to the smaller stores in the areas surrounding them, but also a source of sales to firms that lease showrooms in them. As a fashion executive once explained it: "There's no way we can show our clothes as well in Dallas as we can in New York, but they buy. Last year we sold half a million dollars worth that we wouldn't have otherwise sold."[18]

There is talk of possibly building an apparel mart on 42nd Street in New York City. Whether or not New York should have a mart of its own is a question that is causing controversy on Seventh Avenue. Some manufacturers believe such a mart would help New York business. A greater number, however, feel it would be a bad move to further concentrate showrooms in an already highly congested area. They believe, moreover, that such a building is not needed because the New York garment center is, in effect, just such an apparel market. Another argument against the idea is that, whereas other cities house only showrooms, New York firms still use their headquarters facilities as design rooms, sample rooms, for shipping, some cutting—as well as for showrooms.

As the executive director of the Federation of Apparel Manufacturers has put it: "The huge variety of apparel in the New York market, over 176,000 lines, is more than what is available in all the apparel markets around the world combined, from Hong Kong to Atlanta and more."[19] Nevertheless, more and more New York–based manufacturers continue to show their merchandise not only at home base, but also in facilities closer to its eventual destination.

CHILDREN'S WEAR _____

In the not-too-distant past, when children were expected to be seen but not heard, they were dressed in miniature versions of adult apparel. Parents chose their clothes. Today, largely as a result of their exposure to television, children have become customers in their own right and have definite opinions about the toys they want, the foods they eat, and the clothes they wear. This "liberation" of children has had a direct effect on the styling of children's wear.

Nature of the Industry

The development of the children's wear segment of the industry and its methods of operation, as far as the presentation of seasonal lines and the production methods used, follow the same pattern as the women's sector. However, the children's industry has a relatively small volume of output and many fewer companies, is less competitive and less aggressive in its marketing practices, and puts emphasis on the ages of the ultimate consumers.

There are close to 1,000 companies that produce children's wear. The total value of output is more than $4 billion.[20] With the notable exception of a few giant firms such as OshKosh, Carter, and Healthtex, the majority of companies are small. Most manufacturers produce three seasonal collections per year—Spring/Summer, Fall, and Holiday. Many children's wear firms are located in New York City, but there is a substantial contingent in the Miami fashion industry, many of which maintain sales representatives in New York.

Some large-scale multiproduct producers of adult apparel have entered into some phase of children's wear. Among them are such companies as Levi-Strauss, Russ Togs, Guess, and Esprit. As explained previously, these large producers set up separate divisions for each of their product categories, and their children's wear is no exception. The design, production and marketing of children's products has its own division in these firms.

Industry Specializations

As in the women's wear industry, manufacturers tend to specialize by price range, sizes, and types of merchandise. In terms of price levels, most companies fall into low, moderate, or higher priced categories. In regard to type, the most common specializations are by age or size groups rather than by merchandise categories. Children, it should be understood, have different body proportions at different stages of growth, and their garments must be designed accordingly. For example, two girls of the same height and weight may require garments from different ranges, because one still has toddler proportions and the other has small-girl proportions.

Thus, the size ranges are related to the age or stage of growth. The following sizes are the same for girls and boys:

Infants: 3 to 24 months
Toddlers: T2 to T4

From children's size 4, the sizes for the two sexes diverge. Children's sizes for girls go from 4 to 6x, then go on to girls' 7 to 14, and preteen 6 to 14. Boys' wear is sized 4 to 7 and 8 to 12, and their garments are made in the children's wear industry. When they pass this age and size, however, the boys move into the menswear industry, wearing boys' sizes 14 to 20, and going on to young men's and students' wear.

In a large retail store, each age or size grouping is often in a section of its own, usually within the infants' and children's department, and usually under one buyer unless the store is quite large. Clothes for boys who have outgrown the children's size ranges are generally bought, displayed, and sold with or near menswear.

Marketing Activities

Marketing practices are similar in many respects to those of the women's wear industry. For example, seasonal lines are presented in showrooms, at company headquarters, and sometimes also at regional marts. The merchandise, however, is not usually dramatized and accessorized as is done in the women's industry. Advertising and sales promotion are relatively minor, with the exception of the few very large firms, which have made their names well known through national advertising. Most producers in this industry leave consumer advertising to the retail stores.

The industry has its own specialized publications: *Earnshaw's, Girls and Boyswear Review,* and *Kids Fashions,* plus a weekly section in *Women's Wear Daily.* All of these focus on trade and product news and carry advertising to the retail trade.

There are three trade shows a year, held in New York; more than 300 lines are usually exhibited at each. These are the National Kids Fashion Shows,

Children's Wear Annual Market Show

SOURCE: Reprinted with permission of the Florida Children's Wear Manufacturing Guild.

which are in addition to the Florida Children's Wear Manufacturers' Guild Show, an annual trade show held in Miami.

As in the women's industry, the licensing "name" game is very prevalent. Character licensing is a practice so rampant in the industry that very few tee shirts, sweatshirts, sleepwear, and similar items are without the licensed names of a Mickey Mouse, Star Wars, Miss Piggy, Looney Tunes, Snoopy, Strawberry Shortcake, and *ad infinitum*. Also important is the licensing of sports figures and designer names. Today, many children's wear manufacturers have licensing agreements with both European and American designers. European luminaries such as Christian Dior, Pierre Cardin, Yves St. Laurent, and Givenchy have licensed their names to producers of higher priced children's wear, as have some well-known American designers.

It is interesting to note that in recent years many large retailers of adult apparel have gone into the children's wear business such as The Limited, Gap Kids, Benetton's 012, and Laura Ashley's Mother and Kids.

COMPETITION FROM IMPORTS

Until the 1960s, almost all ready-to-wear purchased by American consumers was produced in the United States by our domestic apparel industry. Imports of apparel products were not of significant size, in either quantity or value, and much of what was brought in from abroad was of poor quality, intended for the extreme low end of the market. Beginning in the mid 1960s and continuing at a rapidly accelerating pace through the 1970s and 1980s, apparel imports have gained at a rate appalling to the American industry. For example, by 1989 for every 1,000 garments produced in this country, an additional 550 were imported and in some categories even exceeded our domestic output. That is massive competition indeed, and it has caused the industry to call on the government to exert such pressure as it can to stem the tide.

Since the subject of import growth and penetration, and its implications, is discussed in great detail in a later chapter of this book, at this point it is sufficient simply to recognize that imports are an enormous problem for our domestic industry.

Readings

Success in the women's and children's apparel field means knowing what customers will buy. But it also means knowing when and how to expand its business.

The Wizard of the Working Woman's Wardrobe

By recognizing that there was an opportunity for more varied and more relaxed clothing for working women, Liz Claiborne's business has grown at a rate far exceeding that of the industry as a whole.

Levi's Makes Push in Women's Wear

Levi-Strauss, which built its billion-dollar business mainly on menswear, moved to broaden its customer base by developing a portfolio of apparel products for women.

King of the Copycats

Victor Costa has made his fame and fortune as a fashion designer by cashing in on the highest form of flattery — copying, adapting, and interpreting the designs of top European couturiers. Many of his loyal customers have appeared on the best-dressed list. Neither they nor he seems to mind his reputation as a veteran knock-off artist.

Designers Still Put Stock in Trunk Shows

Designers find trunk shows invaluable. Although the sales figures are significant, what they consider most important is that they learn from their direct contact with customers — what customers react to and how their clothes fit them.

OshKosh Defined

Originally a manufacturer of bib overalls for farmers and railroad men, OshKosh B'Gosh made the transition into children's wear in the 1950s. Today its children's line is in such demand that it is unable to produce all that can be sold.

THE WIZARD OF THE WORKING WOMAN'S WARDROBE

by Michele Morris

With her sleek helmet of black hair and bold silver jewelry, Elisabeth Claiborne Ortenberg could have stepped right out of a Cubist painting. She's dressed casually but elegantly in a black T-shirt and stirrup pants. Tangerine nail polish and a daffodil yellow jacket add jolts of color to what could have been a somber picture. Her handshake is firm, her smile wide and handsome, but it's her eyes, accented by large round eyeglasses, that linger in one's memory. The owlish frames, similar to those worn by Le Corbusier and Philip Cortelyou Johnson, highlight her role as fashion visionary. Bernard Chaus, one of her competitors, describes the woman behind the glasses, president and CEO of Liz Claiborne, Inc., the apparel company whose annual sales run about $1 billion, as "the great pathfinder."

The path she found has tugged at the heartstrings and opened the purse strings of America's working women. A dozen years ago Liz Claiborne, a respected dress designer, spotted an opening. Though the league of working women was growing, no one in the fashion industry was offering truly suitable clothes for these women. The next step up from the T-shirt and pants of the homemaker was the skirted navy blue MBA suit of the career woman. "I just felt there was an opportunity for more varied, more relaxed clothing and that every working woman wasn't ending up in the boardroom or aspiring to that," Claiborne, 59, explains in a firm voice.

Claiborne's employer at the time, Youthguild, the junior dress division of Jon-athan Logan, didn't share her belief that sportswear—coordinated separates that women could mix and match—was the wave of the future. In December 1975 Claiborne walked out. She and her husband Arthur Ortenberg, a veteran fashion executive, took $50,000 in savings and started a sportswear company. They recruited Leonard Boxer, a manufacturing expert, and Jerry Chazen, a marketing specialist, whose expertise rounded out their own, and raised $200,000 in seed money from friends, family and business associates.

The Gamble that Paid Off

Just as Claiborne suspected, the well of desire for the right clothes to wear to work was deep, wide—and untapped. Nine months later Liz Claiborne, Inc., was in the black. By the end of the first year the company had rung up $2.5 million in sales. And that was just the beginning. In 1981 the four partners took the company public for $19 a share, raising a $6.1 million pot.

Working women didn't just buy Claiborne's clothes; they bought stock in her company. At the company's annual meetings appreciative shareholders often give the president a standing ovation. Despite the deep dip in retail stocks since the October market crash, Claiborne stock has been a star on Wall Street. Return on shareholder's equity usually reaches 34 percent (the industry average is 14). Since the initial offering the stock has split 12 times and currently sells at around $17 a share. "If you invested $25,000 in Liz Claiborne when it went public and held it until today," says Jay J. Meltzer, an analyst with Goldman Sachs & Company, "your investment would be worth over $525,000."

Two years ago Liz Claiborne, Inc., cracked the Fortune 500 list. Ranked number 437, it was the first company started by a woman to make the grade. "1986 has been a year of fulfillment," Claiborne wrote in the company's annual report. "It has been the most emotionally gratifying period I have enjoyed thus far as President of our Company." Two years running the company has been named one of the nation's ten most admired companies by *Fortune* magazine. "It takes a far-seeing business ability to conceive of a strategy, execute it and make it work as they have," says Meltzer.

Key to Claiborne's success is her service approach to manufacturing. She has a vision of what others need and want. Time and again she's seen opportunities and created innovative systems to fill those needs. She is a designer, yes, but she also is selling real clothes to real working women. For her the design process doesn't start at the drawing board but at the closet. She imagines her customer's wardrobe and then builds on it. When working with retailers she listens to their concerns and comes up with ways to weld a strong partnership. And she's built a company whose strength lies in its sense of community.

An Old-Fashioned Upbringing

"Liz has always been ready to take command of a situation," says Omer Claiborne, her oldest brother, who owns a gallery in Santa Fe. That's a surprising statement about a woman whose strict parents kept her in pigtails and convent schools.

"I was brought up by a very old-fashioned father," Claiborne says. "He didn't think it was necessary for me to go to school. I never even graduated from high school." She spent her early years in Brussels, where her father was a banker with Morgan Guaranty.

From her mother, Claiborne learned a lot of practical things — sewing, cooking, as well as an eye for beauty. "If my mother needed a wastepaper basket and couldn't find one she liked, she would cover a little box with a piece of fabric," she says. "I was taught to look at things. You don't just buy a chair, you buy a pretty chair."

Claiborne's European childhood ended abruptly in 1939 when the Germans prepared to invade Belgium. The family returned to New Orleans, where they have deep roots.

Claiborne's father did not want her to go into fashion or business, so she studied painting. At 19, she won a *Harper's Bazaar* design contest for her sketch of a high-collared coat with a "military feeling." In 1951 she defied her father — cutting off her hair, she headed for New York. She landed a job on Seventh Avenue as a sketcher for Tina Lesser, one of the few sportswear designers at the time. "Tina was an extremely creative person, but she couldn't draw," Liz says. "I always used my art training as an entrée to get a job." She married Ben Schultz, a book designer, and changed jobs several times. "I wanted varied experience," she says. "I became Omar Khayam's assistant at a very expensive Seventh Avenue house. But it just didn't appeal to me. I wanted to go into sportswear."

In the 1950s, when a lot of women went home to have babies, Claiborne became a working mother. "I was very career oriented," she says. "I worked to the last day of my pregnancy and came back to the office two weeks later. In retrospect it's not such a smart thing to do."

The '50s will always be remembered as the decade of the dress. Despite her distaste for dresses (Liz prefers to wear pants), Claiborne earned a reputation as a great dress designer. "It's almost like being an actress. You get channeled into a certain area." One of the dress company executives who hired her, Arthur Ortenberg, would become her second husband after each of their first marriages ended.

In 1960 when Jackie Kennedy and her princess-style dresses moved to the White House, Liz Claiborne moved to Youthguild, where she stayed for 16 years. Her boss there, Arthur Lefkowitz, gave her the leeway designers cherish. "I learned that if you are given responsibility, you tend to take a job more seriously."

One responsibility Claiborne took seriously was her family. "I had to be the Rock of Gibraltar," she says to explain why she stayed put for so long. "Art was the one who was always experimenting and changing jobs. He had his own company and then that went out of business, and he'd try this and that." By the time the couple decided to risk launching their own company, Ortenberg had a range of entrepreneurial experiences to draw from and their children were on their own. Today Claiborne's son Alexander Schultz, 33, is a jazz musician in Los Angeles.

Partners in Success

Seated at the white table in Claiborne's serene white office overlooking New York's gaudy Times Square, Liz and Art look like pepper and salt. Her hair is dark, his white. Her clothes are dark and sleek, his are pale and rumpled. They're the personification of a corporate chiaroscuro. "Liz is highly artistic," says one former executive. "Art is highly organized."

Asked about the corporate culture, Art prefaces his reply with "Permit me another sports analogy. We turn to the great New York Knicks team of 1969–70. No one was a superstar, but it was probably one of the most glorious teams that ever existed," he says, leaning back in his chair. "When someone asked Walt Frazier what made the team so great, he thought for a while and said, 'Well, we always passed the ball to the open man.' That's what we try to do here."

The spotlight at Liz Claiborne, Inc., doesn't shine only on Her Lizness, as her husband playfully calls her. She and the other executives work hard at fostering an esprit de corps. Everyone at the company is on a first-name basis, including Liz and Art. Even the company directory lists its 3,400 employees alphabetically by first name.

"The company is an amalgamation of a mom-and-pop shop and sophisticated manufacturing company," says one analyst. "It's run like a Japanese company," says Ken Wyse, former corporate-marketing director. "People feel part of it."

"We decided from the start that we were going to be a very familial company," Claiborne says. "Since we were four partners doing everything ourselves, it just grew this way. I still spend part of every day with a division." From her first collection of sportswear, the company has spun off in many directions—jeans, shoes, accessories, dresses (Claiborne, ever realistic, quickly recognized that *other* women like them), menswear and fragrance. Today it has nine divisions.

The familial spirit begins in the executive suite, a dazzling white L-shaped loft shared by the Ortenbergs. Liz works at one end, Art at the other, and they often meet at the pair of exercise bikes near the windows. Or they call around the corner to each other. Their 30-year partnership evidently doesn't need doors for privacy. Bookshelves hold photos of family and friends at her three vacation homes—a beach house on Fire Island, a ranch in Montana and a cabana on St. Bart's—all talismans of her decade of success.

The three founders (Leonard Boxer is retired) and two other executives, Harvey Falk and Jay Margolis, form the policy committee that runs the company. Beneath them is the strategic planning committee, which maps out the company's future. As the company has matured, Claiborne has evolved from hands-on designer to top editor of other people's designs. With 15 designers under her wing, she now manages by teaching, not by doing. "I'm still learning how to manage creative people," Claiborne says. "You've got to show them that you can do it just as well as they can—or better."

Even though Claiborne's name is on the label as well as the company, she is not interested in fostering a cult. "Liz is a great nurturer of talent," Wyse reports. "She expects the best. The extra competition brings out the best in people" Last year she made the unusual move of giving one of her promising protegés, Dana Buchman, 36, her own label. Perhaps Claiborne remembered the sting of disappointment when Youthguild would not give her public recognition. She was not going to make the same mistake and lose a talented designer.

Launching the Dana Buchman division enabled the company to enter a lucrative new market without diluting the potency of the Liz Claiborne label. Buchman's line falls into what the rag trade calls bridge sportswear. These higher-priced collections are a bridge into big-ticket designer fashions.

Staying Close to the Customer

"I've watched Liz with customers," says Carol Allen, a fashion stylist in Seattle. "She really listens to their concerns." Claiborne's methods are corporate policy. "We go to the stores and bring back all kinds of information," Claiborne says. "Division presidents all travel in the US and sometimes bring along their designers."

"There are lots of very loyal Liz Claiborne customers," adds Allen. "You can build on her wardrobes; you don't throw out what you bought last year. Liz keeps current without being trendy. When you sell a beautiful blouse for $50, you'll get loyalty."

"Liz really believes it's important to give a woman good value at a price she can afford," says Buchman. Claiborne's blouses retail for about $60, skirts for $70, and jackets for $100. "If it isn't worth it to the customer, we'd throw it out and try again. We would never charge a 900 percent mark-up just because it looks good."

"Liz has an incredible ability to see what women want to wear," says Monika Tilley, a well-known swimsuit designer who has known her for 20 years. "She makes happy clothes. The proportion, the colors, the styles, the sizes, all have good spirit—they make people look 'up.'"

Changing the Ready-to-Wear Calendar

Just as Liz Claiborne designs clothes for the people who wear them, she designs collections for the people who sell them. The company has broken a number of traditions in the garment industry and has earned the respect of retailers.

Recognizing that the normal four design/retail seasons made it difficult to find a swimsuit in July or a wool coat in January, Claiborne added two collections to her annual offerings. Today there are six seasons in a Claiborne year — holiday, spring I, spring II, summer, fall I and fall II. "This means that every two months they're producing a new line. It's very difficult to manage. Bernard Chaus hasn't been able to do this," says Maggie Gilliam, a director at First Boston Corporation. But Claiborne pulls it off and keeps the sales floors fresh and the registers ringing. This pays off. Annual sales per square foot — a common industry yardstick — are estimated at $400 to $500, about twice the industry average.

Claiborne's service gospel is preached at malls across America. About 15 Liz Claiborne fashion consultants visit stores nationwide, talking with customers and training salespeople in how best to sell Liz Claiborne clothes. The company is even dispatching its own salespeople to the grass-roots level. At the Liz Claiborne boutique at Jordan Marsh in Boston, 12 clerks ring up sales — double the usual number.

Most apparel manufacturers track what the retail buyers are ordering and fine-tune their future lines accordingly. But Claiborne's focus on the consumer sparked the development of a computerized system called System Updated Retail Feedback. SURF tells the company what styles — in which sizes and colors — have sold in a cross-section of stores each week. "SURF gives them weekly reports on what's hot, what's not," says Ken Wyse. "No other company does it."

The Next Step

Pathfinder that she is, Claiborne is not about to rest on her laurels. The company is busy planning for the future. "Our goal is to perpetuate this company," she says. "And to turn it over to the young management. That's one of the reasons for spending so much time teaching, correcting, guiding these new division heads."

Today Liz Claiborne, whose father hated the idea of her going into fashion or business, has the thrill of walking to work and seeing crowds of women wearing clothes she envisioned a decade ago. Youthguild, she told you so.

LEVI'S MAKES PUSH IN WOMEN'S WEAR

by Blaise Simpson

San Francisco — Throughout its 138-year history, Levi Strauss & Co., the venerable apparel giant with headquarters here, has been perceived as a male-oriented company.

The images conjured up by the Levi's brand were primarily masculine — from the miners of the California gold rush for whom denim jeans were created, to celluloid heroes such as Marlon Brando and

Source: *Women's Wear Daily*, March 2, 1989. Reprinted with permission.

James Dean, who roared across the public imagination on motorcycles, clad in faded Levi's.

Now however, since going private in August 1985, the company has completely revamped its women's apparel business in response from retailers.

Steve Powers, a senior vice president and merchandise manager at the May Co., Los Angeles, said, "The 900 Series jeans have done very well. In fact, I've just gone over our reports for the last 120 days and we've sold out on virtually all of our orders. Where we've bought, say, 1,800 pieces, we've sold 1,680. Our business has been good with them." Powers said the 900s are sold in the Weekending department at May Co., alongside such lines as Calvin Klein Sport and Sync.

The Authentics, Big Tabs and 900 Series all carry the familiar red Levi's red pocket tab, although on Big Tabs it's slightly enlarged—hence the name. They are produced in domestic women's apparel factories and are marketed in four major releases per year by a network of about 75 women's apparel representatives.

Junior sizes run from 3 to 15, misses' from 6 to 18 and there are large sizes through 28. Prices range from $19 to $22 wholesale, depending on the finish.

Although neither Kasten nor Ferguson will disclose recent sales figures, Ferguson says her goal is for the women's jeans to become number one in the markets they serve.

"We don't serve all the distribution that the Lee Co. does," she emphasized. "They sell to discounters and mass merchants and we do not. So it's not reasonable for us to think in terms of number one overall in market share. But I hope we will become first as far as unit share, and perception in the market as being a brand that offers the newest looks and leads the market."

Levi's women's sportswear is divided into two categories, traditional and contemporary. Included in traditional are Bend Over, the original easy-care man-made fiber blend pants, and Levi's Sportswear, tailored trousers in polyester and cotton and polyester and rayon blends. Both are geared to an older customer, and are made in sizes 8 to 20 plus large sizes.

Kasten said that although Bend Over volume has decreased in recent years, there is still a significant main floor business and a loyal customer that has recently brought stores back to the line.

The news in sportswear is in the contemporary area, where Levi's Dockers for women, which were introduced just six months ago, have already outperformed the company's most optimistic expectations.

"Our Dockers area is exploding—it's incredible," said Kasten gleefully. "We've got some people who've been in our women's division 16 or 17 years and they've never seen anything like this. We are actually higher on the power (growth) curve than men's (Dockers) was at the same time in their history."

Dockers was a somewhat revolutionary concept in the men's market when it was introduced about 19 months ago. It was a line of relaxed fit, casual cotton pants and tops for men who wanted something a little dressier than jeans, and were not old enough to want the polyester blend casual slacks their fathers or grandfathers would wear.

Dockers quickly found its niche in the men's main floor area and racked up $40 million in sales within the first 1½ years in business. Kasten predicts an even faster growth for the women's Dockers, placing first-year volume of sales at about $40 million.

Susan Tighe, merchandise manager for women's sportswear and Dockers, explained that although the women's line has similarities to the men's, such as relaxed fit and all-natural fabrications—it is conceived separately for women by designer Constance Bennett.

"It's another extension of what a woman wants to wear for casual dressing as a jeans alternative. It's targeted to a 22- to 39-year-old misses' customer. She's a young professional who wants to be fashion-minded and contemporary without being gimmicky," asserted Tighe.

Up to now, Dockers has primarily been produced in Hong Kong and Taiwan, although Tighe says domestic sourcing is becoming increasingly prevalent. The main fabric in dockers is a garment-washed cotton twill.

Tighe reported Dockers are hanging in contemporary sportswear departments with labels such as Calvin Klein Sport, adjacent to Lizsport and Esprit.

Levi's won't discuss just how much of its total sales are in the women's area, but market analysts, including Jerard Less of Jerard Less, Inc., in New York, and Harry Bernard of Colton Bernard, Inc., in San Francisco, pin it at about 10 or 12 percent of the total volume, which places it about $300 million.

Prior to 1985, while Levi's was still publicly held, the organization of its women's apparel companies was fragmented. Women's jeans were part of The Jeans Co., which included men's and children's divisions as well as shirts and new brands.

Branded women's sportswear, such as Bend Over pants and other traditional sportswear, was grouped into Battery Street Enterprises, which also had non-Levi's brand lines such as Koret, Oxford, Rainfair, Resistol Hats and Frank Shorter Running Gear under its umbrella, as well as licensing agreements with Perry Ellis (for Perry Ellis America) and Andrew Fezza.

In the last two years the company has disbanded Battery Street and consolidated its women's business, in both jeans and sportswear, into the new Levi Strauss Sportswear division.

Although it sold off virtually all the non-Levi's brand companies that had been in Battery Street and discontinued its licenses with Fezza and Ellis, Levi's also moved to broaden its customer base by buying Brittania jeans in December 1986, and entered into a licensing contract in 1985 with Alexander Julian, Inc., for the Colours by Alexander Julian line, and Julian's higher-price collection. The rights to the latter were returned to Julian earlier this year.

Both the Brittania and Colours women's lines recently completed their first year of operation under the Levi's banner.

In an effort to go after rival VF Corp.'s Lee and Wrangler lines, Brittania is marketing its fashion-conscious junior and misses' bottoms at lower prices than Levi's and has geared the product for open distribution, an area Levi's has traditionally not wanted to venture into with its own brands.

Colours by Alexander Julian is a moderate-price misses' career sportswear line that is selling to better-price specialty and department stores at higher price points than Levi's sportswear carries.

Leo Isotalo is the president of Levi Strauss Sportswear and over all men's wear and women's apparel, with the exception of Brittania, which operates as a separate entity, its management reporting to Tom Tusher, chief operating officer of Levi's.

Isotalo is well qualified to reflect on the changes in the women's apparel effort. Before assuming his current title, he spent 11 years with Levi Strauss International and then headed Battery Street Enterprises. "When we went private we basically decided that we ought to focus more on those things that we understand," explained Isotalo.

He pointed out, however, that the term "back to basics" is wrong when applied to Levi's. "That's a misnomer, because it implies that we're a single-product company or that we've gone back to the kinds of things we used to do. What we have done is to examine the various kinds of markets and products that we understand and that make sense to the consumer coming from us. And we've focused on those. Maybe it's a return to fundamentals—to what we really do well."

Isotalo feels the term "fundamentals" applies as easily to the recently launched Levi's Dockers women's sportswear as it does to jeans. He is careful to point out that Levi's wants to be identified as a company with a variety of products to offer the consumer.

"You must have a jeans component, you must have a casual component and we still have a significant traditional sportswear element," he said. "Anyone who professes to be moderate, as we are, who doesn't have a portfolio of products is kidding themselves. We've positioned ourselves to flex while we go ahead, rather than just going along and pinning our hopes on one product."

When the women's jeans division was moved into Levi Strauss Sportswear 1½ years ago, it was placed in the hands of Tom Kasten, women's apparel president, who had spent 22 years in other posts with the company.

In response to poor sales, Kasten and his crew, including Kathy Ferguson, who was hired away from Lee to become vice president of merchandising, moved quickly to change the fit, fabrications and styling of the jeans product.

"We wanted to be distinctive," Kasten explained. "We wanted to be more the leading edge. We didn't want to market fabrications or finishes. So we looked at pushing our product more aggressively, and became a little more innovative in the way we attack the market."

There were obvious things wrong with the line when Kasten and Ferguson stepped in. Kasten recalls that the women's 501s were either too narrow in the hip or too wide in the waist and that jeans hems were too big at 15 inches, which he says "was just contrary to the market."

Once they had gotten the fit down, the jeans team went to work on paring the line into three easily understood categories: Authentics, which includes 501s, the original slim-fit button fly, and 505s, five-pocket zip-fly; Big Tabs, a young line for juniors, and the new 900 Series, which was created to showcase premium styling, fabrics and finishes for the fashion end of the misses' and junior market.

Although 501s remain the largest volume unit, the 900 Series is where the excitement is, according to Ferguson, who points out that although they made their debut less than a year ago, the 900s now account for 35 percent of the women's jeans business. The new line is also getting positive consumer responses.

In New York, Bob Wildrick, senior vice president in charge of buying for Belk Stores, said, "Dockers is the most exciting concept to come out of Levi's in at least five years. I think they're filling a niche other manufacturers have neglected. We were in on the rollout of Dockers for women. We've increased our buys, have done well with it and plan to do more. It's a good value and good for the customer that Belk has—the customer who likes Bass Weejuns, Top Siders and Dockers."

Wildrick said the line is sold in the moderate price misses' area in the Belk stores (there are 365 of them throughout the Southeast), and that shop concepts are being used in the larger stores.

At May Co., Steve Powers said, "We tested Dockers for women for holiday and it did very well. We've ordered it for spring, and we are planning to put the line into a shop concept. We have a very big business with Dockers for men, probably the largest in the country."

Dockers has already been seen on TV, worn by the actresses on "thirty-something."

In San Francisco, at Levi's Plaza, just across the street from the imposing seven-story glass and brick Levi's headquarters, sits a lower, more modest structure known as the Koashland Building. It is here that Brittania relocated just six months ago, after having been bought by Levi's in late December 1986.

Brittania, which started near Seattle, Wash., in 1972, was one of the first to offer designer jeans at a moderate price, making the company an overnight sensation. In 1980, sales peaked at $200 million in volume. But once the design boom ended, it was bust for Brittania, which was forced to file Chapter 11 in 1983.

Why did Levi's buy Brittania at a time when it was getting rid of other non-branded companies? Margie Hanselman, Brittania's women's apparel merchandise manager, explained, "It was a means of selling another brand and selling to open distribution. Originally it was a department store and better specialty store line, and we still sell it there, but we are also looking to develop big volume retailers and upscale mass merchants, places where we don't sell Levi's — like Bradlees and Target Stores. We know that it is a brand with a strong customer franchise, so it's really a chance to develop another market."

Brittania also brought with it the very large pants quota it owns in the Far East. Although the quota could be assigned by Brittania to another part of Levi's, Hansel-man said most of it will be used up producing Brittania's own lines.

Because Brittania's women's jeans are produced in Asia, using local fabrications, wholesale prices are low, ranging from $12.75 to $18.25. Right now three lines are produced annually, although there may be more in the future. Only three releases have been made since Levi's bought the company. Brittania's silhouettes are slightly more fashion forward than Levi's.

Jim Chriss, vice president of marketing at Brittania, is optimistic about the company's future, in spite of its past problems. "The customers only remember that they liked the product. They just couldn't find it. So we're redefining that and reintroducing it from that standpoint.

Although the company's Colours by Alexander Julian line is well established in the men's market, Colours for women, just entering its second year, is still evolving.

We have repositioned the line in the last year to be more career oriented," said Steve Fischmann, president of Colours for women.

"Over the first year, some areas were not so successful," he said. "We initially made a foray into the more casual area, and it has not worked out, whereas our career dressing has been very successful."

Colours in better-price career sportswear, he said, competes with lines such as Liz Claiborne, Evan-Picone and JH Collectibles. It emphasizes unusual textures in natural wool, silk and cotton, and the subtle color contrasts that Julian is known for. "We are working very closely with Alex's design team in both concept and execution."

In terms of what Colours for women has to offer Levi's, Fischmann, who reports to Isotalo, added, "I think that for the business at Levi's it provides a nice level of contact to have at department stores. We can pass on interesting perspectives to the other women's businesses. It gives them a level of intelligence at the next step up that can provide direction. And hopefully, they will get profits."

In the last few years, Levi's has managed to rid itself of unprofitable and out-moded businesses while simultaneously updating all its women's products.

"I think the best way to summarize," said Kasten "is to say that what will make us successful in the Nineties is to look at change as an opportunity, rather than some agony that we must go through."

KING OF THE COPYCATS

by Jennifer Foote

Lingering near a dress rack that overflows with opalescent ruffles, crisp netting, feathers and fishtails of floral fabric, designer Victor Costa plucks lovingly from the gems that he envisions as centerpieces of his fashion legacy. It is a confusing display, since each of the creations pays homage not to Costa's imagination but to that of other top couturiers, the sort who might someday enjoy museum retrospectives. As he caresses and smooths the exquisite jackets and lavish gowns, Costa reels off the names of the designers he "interpreted" for each of his designs. Valentino, Lacroix, Scaasi, Ungaro. Only one gown, a wild, wispy creation, doesn't look familiar. "This one isn't from anyone," says Costa, blushing a little. "It's just my fantasy and it didn't sell very well." But then, what is one fantasy when your wildest dreams have come true?

Victor Costa, a veteran knockoff artist who once labored in anonymity, is officially in vogue. Offering low prices in the world of high fashion, the affable Texan has found his way into the closets of women on the best-dressed list. His stylized renditions of Paris designs appear regularly on the heroines of the evening soaps and a recent polka-dot number had near-equal billing with Holly Hunter in "Broadcast News." Even Christian Lacroix, whom Costa copies slavishly, has a kind word for his thieving fan. "When I met him," says Costa, giddy with pride, "he hugged me and said, 'Victor, my friend!' It made me feel very good."

It has taken 30 years for Costa to emerge as a peer of his former classmates at the Ecole de la Chambre Syndicale de la Couture Parisienne. A poor kid from Houston's Fifth Ward, he was laughed at by fellow design students for his Southern drawl and fanciful tastes. But a fashion accent on the divinely feminine has conspired with economic disaster to draw Victor Costa out of the shadows, bringing with him prodigious collections of $300 dresses that have been mistaken for $5,000 exclusives. "The Black Monday ladies and the oil-impoverished ladies have husbands who have said '*Basta*'," says Costa. "They've had to re-educate their pocketbooks and they've discovered VC." They join the ranks of teenage prom queens and society women who have long relied on Costa for reasonably priced fantasy wear. He "tackles the fashion world like a Texan," proclaims his homestate magazine Texas Monthly. "He's a businessman first and an artist second." Topping Costa's list of notable clients are Ivana Trump, who orders 30 VC's at a clip, Betsy Bloomingdale and Charlotte Ford. Last year he did $30 million of business; this year he expects to hit $40 million. And he doesn't even have his own perfume. Yet.

Before his divorce several years ago, Costa was comfortable with obscurity. But when he broke up with his wife of 26 years, he decided to "give my whole life to my career," he says. He shrewdly raised the prices of his dresses, from the $90-to-$300 range to the $250-to-$800 level, just enough to get them on racks in better retail space; and he began to travel, staging fashion shows coast to coast on the charity circuit. Not in the least bashful about the more mercenary aspects of his craft, Costa talks about his strategy of "romancing" his customers at a show before lunch and then, while they eat, rushing to a store across the street to set up racks of his clothes for them to buy for dessert. "They can see it on the runway and walk out with it over their arms," he says. Unlike most designers, Costa can never be accused of fearing schmaltz, either; he serenades his high-society ladies during shows, crooning a beguiling mix of light opera and fashion commentary into a mike. "A lot of the names just sit in the corner and act like they don't know what's going on," says the designer, who regularly visits a vocal coach. "Victor is a very unassuming person," adds Bergdorf Goodman president Dawn Mello. "His ego isn't inflated, which is quite unique in this business."

'The Girl Inside'

Costa remains firmly entrenched in the real world when he designs, cutting and showing a wide size range of his dresses, which he tailors to camouflage flaws like "huge hips or upper arms that are gone forever." But fantasy is the key element of his high-fashion refinements, which he creates under the somewhat chauvinistic premise that "after 5 o'clock a lady wants to reflect and be a woman again." His design philosophy that "dressmakers are there to please not to dictate" is blasphemy in haute couture, but he is loved for it. "He makes all women, even size 14s, feel beautiful," says a Bergdorf sales associate of the VC's in her boutique. "My idea is always to make a dress that when a woman has it on, it becomes priceless," explains Costa. "Inside every woman there is a girl who really wants to be the prettiest in the room. I work for the girl inside the woman." Former Miss America and actress Mary Ann Mobley buys dozens of VC's every year for a packed schedule of pay-and-play charity events. "When you have to buy a large quantity of gowns, it's not going to kill you to buy Costas," she says. "My ambition when getting dressed is that I will look nice, not that someone will say. 'Look, she's wearing a $5,000 Chanel'." Costa himself has sharp words for those who indulge in high-fashion frivolity. "Any woman that spends thousands on a dress ought to be strung up," he says.

A self-described "indoor child," Costa began sketching paper-doll dresses and merchandising them on the playground at the age of seven. During high school, mingling with rich kids in the city's only Roman Catholic academy for boys, he designed extravagant prom dresses for the sisters of his school chums and made them in his garage. He was conducting a brisk business in wedding dresses by the time he decided to leave for the Pratt Institute in New York. But it was after a stint in the Paris fashion school, where Yves Saint Laurent and Karl Lagerfeld were classmates, that this training as a copycat began in earnest. A designer for the Suzy Perette label in New York, it was Costa's job to attend Paris fashion shows and "interpret" the designs for the SP line back home. "It was like graduate school," he says. "You had to be brainwashed by the pieces to bring those very expensive looks to your customer at her price point. After a number of years, it becomes second nature." So adept is Costa at high-fashion refinement that he can produce 250 designs five times a year for his collections, which are boiled down to 150 pieces for the runway. "It is my joy to see a $100,000 dress on the runway, giggle a little and then interpret and refine those kinds of looks for my ladies," he says.

'The Ultimate'

Costa doesn't mind his reputation as a copycat; he believes it is a gift to be able "to give women some measure of what the world is considering the ultimate." Many of the designers he interprets, however, consider Costa's talent a curse. Copies of Parisian hits can be made available to American shoppers before the originals reach the racks. But Costa's own instincts also are part of his success. He is a romantic whose drama and frills are signatures of high-pro-

file designers like Ungaro and Lacroix. "What I've been doing for 15 years, the world thinks is the epitome of fashion right now," says Costa. Though he lurks at the Paris debuts of most designers' collections, Costa's own dresses often reflect his private speculation about fashion trends. Thumbing through a copy of one fashion magazine, Costa talks about making other designers' dresses "palatable" for his own customers. "Is this reality?" he asks, pointing to a whirling hodgepodge of a gown from Paris. "It's a hoot. I'll take something of this and make it palatable so my lady can taste of it, like a rich dessert, and digest it."

Victor Costa enjoys his newfound glory, but is perfectly happy to remain outside the prestigious circle of designers he copies. "I don't think any of them think like I think, that it's good to give a woman a bargain," he says. And besides, there is longevity in staying on the sidelines, mimicking the mood and line of Paris from a studio in Dallas. "I don't want to fall into that pit of being popular today and nowhere tomorrow," says Costa. "I am comfortable in the background." Yet, even in the background, Costa has fallen prey to fashion larceny. He's being copied. "I'm furious about it," he says, but laughs quickly at the irony. "I suppose I'm seeing what it feels like with the shoe on the other foot."

DESIGNERS STILL PUT STOCK IN TRUNK SHOWS

by Kevin Haynes

New York — Designer firms agree that trunk shows are still an important forum for sizing up a collection and fortifying their relationships with individual retailers and customers. The promotions have also proven to be a wise business investment, said to account for anywhere from 15 to 45 percent of a designer company's annual business.

"Our trunk shows are phenomenally successful," raves Donna Karan, who sold more than $350,000 at a single show recently at Saks Fifth Avenue in Los Angeles. Karan says most shows take in about $150,000 when she's present, about $100,000 when she's not.

Since starting her own company [five] years ago, Karan has authorized about 125 trunk shows a year and appears personally at special shows in three stores: Bergdorf Goodman in New York, Saks Fifth Avenue in Los Angeles and I. Magnin, San Francisco.

"We try to affiliate the three shows with a charity event," says Karan, who usually times the event to coincide with the showing of her fall lines in June. However, the I. Magnin showing wasn't held until September because of the designer's cramped schedule.

Unlike the company trunk shows, which are generally open to the public during regular store hours, Karan's personal appearances involve a private in-store evening event for about 250 invited guests who see the entire 90-piece fall collection donned by 15 models.

The recent show at Magnin's was a departure for Karan, who prefers that her trunk shows be held before her fall collection is available in store. "Our system is a little different than other designers,' she explained. "We don't ship early. We don't ship fall until August 1 so all our trunk shows are done in June and July."

No matter when they're staged, the events have played a crucial role for the designer in gauging retail and consumer reaction first-hand to her latest work.

"Trunk shows are invaluable because I really understand and learn about the customer," says Karan, whose bestsellers for fall included stretch wool crepe high-rise skirts and her basic black jersey dress, which sold 2,000 units. "The sales are not insignificant but what I learn from the customer — what she reacts to, how the clothes are fitting her — those are the things I find most important."

The impact on the bottom line has also been positive: Karan says about 20 percent of the company's annual business is registered at trunk shows. "It's a chance for our customer to get a complete overall feeling for what the collection is all about," she said. "There's a woman out there who does not have time to shop, who can totally put herself together. We have the entire collection there, we show them how to accessorize it — we even have a representative from Hanes hosiery (a Karan licensee).

Other designer companies agree that the bottom line isn't just the day's sales, but the personal relationship that designers are able to establish with the store and its customers.

Source: *Women's Wear Daily*, October 26, 1988. Reprinted with permission.

"No matter what you do (in sales), it's worthwhile," says Gerald Shaw, president of Oscar de la Renta, Ltd. "A substantial show would be $100,000, but we've had shows where we did $50,000."

The company conducts about 35 to 40 trunk shows a year, about five featuring the designer. "Whenever Oscar is at a show it's a formal show—it's not just another trunk show," Shaw said. "It would be something hooked up with a charity, usually a black-tie dinner. If he stays over the next day and spends a few hours in-store, that's a plus, surely. It's always a plus if he's there."

Fall bestsellers emerging from de la Renta's trunk shows, with or without the designer, include a wool crepe dress with velvet sleeves, an Irish tweed three-piece suit with a cashmere sweater; leopard skirt with double-faced moss jacket, and a beige and white glen plaid dress with cape and fur collar.

Albert Nipon is another believer in the good will and business accomplished with a steady schedule of trunk shows and occasional personal appearances. "It gives us good exposure and identifies us with a home base store," explained Nipon, founder and chairman of Albert Nipon, Inc. "Secondly, we get an early reading of what the customer is going to buy—and it's not always what the retailer supports. We find we're surprised an awful lot."

Nipon said the company does about 40 trunk shows for each of its four seasons, including the resort/spring shows that got underway in October. Fall's bestsellers were the occasion dresses that retail for $800 to $900. "That's the top end of our line," he said.

Nipon said trunk shows account for about 15 percent of the company's business. "Our business is not based on the trunk show business," he said. "I do trunk shows and personal appearances to support

the business a retailer is doing with us already."

However, Nipon keeps close tabs on the bottom line at each show. "We want the cash registers to ring that day," he says. "A good day is $25,000. But I also measure what the store did that day. When I'm there I want to know what my department did, what the floor did and what the entire store did."

Nipon makes a handful of personal appearances that are usually tied in with a formal showing or a benefit. "This season I myself will do at least a half a dozen, including a museum benefit and a junior league benefit. I'm already booked out through next February."

After a hectic fall schedule, Bill Blass hasn't scheduled any personal appearances to promote his spring collection, which opens Nov. 2. "I think Mr. Blass does not want to travel as much as he used to," explains Harold Leigh Davis, executive vice president and sales director. "He did a tremendous amount for fall."

The first company trunk show for spring will be held Nov. 23 at Nan Duskin, Philadelphia, followed by shows in December for Saks Fifth Avenue and several Neiman-Marcus stores. "Starting Jan. 4, we do two shows a day through the middle of March somewhere in the country," Davis said.

The events always feature Blass' entire collection—about 110 pieces for fall and spring—and account for about 45 percent of the company's sales, he said. Sales at individual store shows average about $50,000 but usually increase about 15 percent if Blass is on hand. The company's best performance came during the fall of 1986 when a four-day event at Martha's netted $350,000 at retail, Davis said.

Blass did "extremely well" with suits for fall, Davis added. Other strong sellers were leopard skirts, tweed tent dresses with fur trim, cashmere sweaters and pastel coats.

Mary McFadden, Inc., runs two trunk shows a week throughout the year, though the designer says she limits her personal appearances to about two each quarter, including a recent stop at Saks Fifth Avenue in San Francisco, where the show coincided with a benefit for the San Francisco Symphony.

Sales range from $60,000 to $100,000, though McFadden said she once netted $150,000. "It represents an important part of our business," she said, estimating the share at one-third.

McFadden's said her fall bestsellers were the beaded dresses with elaborate jeweled inserts, retailing for $2,000 to $4,000.

Though the styles may change with the season, SA contends trunk shows will continue to prove a profitable business venture.

OSHKOSH DEFINED

by Loribeth Skigen

OshKosh B'Gosh. By golly, say that name 10 times fast. Then say $226 million in 1987 sales, and projected 1988 sales of $260 million. The name may be whimsical, but when it comes to apparel, OshKosh's signature items mean business.

Recently children's wear has grabbed much of the apparel world, as well as the 93-year-old company itself by the seat of the pants. With baby boomers having their own generation of babies, demand for pint-size apparel has grown. It has become the focus of the mix at OshKosh, representing more than 85 percent of the Wisconsin-based company's total.

It wasn't always so. Originally Osh-Kosh was a regional manufacturer of bib overalls for farmers and railroad men. Children's merchandise was added into the mix in the 1950's as a tag-along to the goods offered to adults. "Obviously the propor-

tion of children's products has dramatically increased," says Douglas W. Hyde, Osh-Kosh's vice president of merchandising.

Strategically, the transition to children's wear was a successful move. Since 1984—when net sales were $137.4 million —the company has seen volume increase 64.7 percent. During the next five years, Hyde expects his firm's volume to grow between 12 percent and 15 percent per year. But the unexpected boom in business generated from children's wear in recent years has caused the company its share of growing pains.

Like other firms that have enlarged rapidly in recent years, OshKosh has had to face the tough task of keeping up with its own expansion. The line is in such demand that securing adequate production has been troublesome. "We've gone through various points where we were on allocation, and

Source: *Apparel Merchandising Magazine*, July 1988. Reprinted with permission.

then during certain periods we caught up and actually had more product than we could sell," says the affable Hyde.

Staffers are working to increase the amount of goods they can produce in-house. Currently they contract about 30 percent of their production, but they hope to lower that to about 20 percent. To that end they are building two additional production facilities that will augment 12 existing plants. Under construction is a 124,000 square-foot factory in Tennessee which should be up to full capacity within two years. In May, OshKosh also bought a 180,000 square-foot operation in Tennessee which will consist of a receiving and distribution center, as well as a finishing plant.

Though they will continue to rely on outside contractors to a certain degree, OshKosh executives have no plan to relax their strict quality controls. "We've seen what's happened to others that were hot resources, and they went out and bought product from anybody that had a sewing machine. Subsequently, quality was sacrificed. We don't like to do things poorly, we would much rather pass up some business," says Hyde. He adds: "We look at a season and say we might be able to grow 30 percent, but to do that, we are probably going to be subcontracting our product to people we're not very comfortable with. So we plan on a growth percentage that we feel we can handle."

Harnessing their expansion will undoubtedly continue to cause OshKosh-enthusiastic retailers some dismay. But merchants indicate that OshKosh's items are worth the wait. "As trying as they are when it comes to deliveries, OshKosh is unquestionably my top children's wear resource because of quality and customer acceptance," says one Northwestern buyer.

Other retailers agree that putting up with delivery difficulties is a small price to pay to carry the line. "On an annual basis, OshKosh generally produces 20 percent increases for us. In the next 12 months to 18 months we expect them to continue to be an excellent supplier for us," says Roger Farrington, divisional merchandise manager at Chicago-based Marshall Field & Co.

OshKosh executives realize their attention to quality and styling has helped make them popular with both consumers and retailers. They consider these elements key in helping maintain an edge among their competitors, which include Health Tex, Buster Brown, Izod, Levi Strauss & Co. and even private label.

When you walk into a store, OshKosh's merchandise doesn't look like everyone else's. "Our designers have developed a sense of what the OshKosh look is, it's not the Levi look, it's not the Buster Brown look. It's a look that evolved from the bib overall and now is translated to other products. For instance we now carry knit tops, and bib overall mini-skirts," says Hyde.

In spite of expanding their line to include fashion goods, OshKosh executives have managed to keep prices sharp. Historically, OshKosh has tried to offer value. When the company opened in 1895, the price of a pair of men's overalls was about 30 cents. By today's department store standards the goods, at $18, are still quite reasonable. These prices also translate to children's wear — the average unit selling price for smaller-size goods is $15.

OshKosh's intrinsic value, not to mention consumer recognition, makes it a primary candidate for instore shops. Retailers have been requesting such shops, and OshKosh executives agree that the concept — which they plan to develop this year — could be beneficial. "Sometimes, our items are thrown in with everyone else's, and what we've tried to create with our product gets lost," explains Hyde, who foresees the infant, toddler and particularly 4–6X and 4–7 size ranges as the most viable categories for shops. Funding for the areas would be a cooperative effort, Hyde explains.

He also admits that should OshKosh be successful with individual shops within stores, freestanding units would be a logical next step. But the 37-year-old executive is quick to say that OshKosh does not want to compete with retailers.

However, like any manufacturer might during these merger-heavy days, OshKosh executives have measured their competitive worth against other vendors, but staffers aren't worried. "Actually, consolidation will probably help us," predicts Hyde. Basing his fortune-telling on past experience, he thinks that OshKosh is one of the brands that retailers will hold on to. "When May Co. had an influence on Robinson's and Lord & Taylor we immediately saw our business go up," says Hyde.

Although the OshKosh business is obviously strong, a weakness exists. The company, until quite recently, has done little to follow the demographics of its customers. "We're losing hundreds of thousands of kids once they're 5 years old. Then they're into Esprit or Bugle Boy or whatever the hot

junior resources are," says Hyde. He is also aware that by 1991 the birth rate is expected to slow. Subsequently, executives plan to address youthwear — lines for sizes 7–14 girls and 8–16 boys — in a bigger way. Youthwear now accounts for only about 5 percent of the children's wear mix. Executives expect to increase that to 13 percent in the next 5 years. Translated to dollars, youthwear would generate $50 million of the projected $360 million.

The company's first step in making youthwear more important was to hire Dutch-born designer Dorthée Van Mol in December 1986. She made her OshKosh debut with the holiday '87/'88 collection; her European-influenced designs helped bring more sophistication to girls sizes 7–14. Previously, OshKosh's older lines had copied the look, but not the sales results of younger lines. As a result of these styling changes youthwear sales increased by 50 percent.

Being fluid isn't new to OshKosh. Taking risks in the past is what brought them from a little town in Wisconsin to homes across the nation. With a continued focus on slow but steady growth, and an abiding adherence to fashion rather than fad, the OshKosh B'Gosh name could be tickling tongues for another 93 years.

Endnotes

1. Claudia Kidwell and Margaret C. Christman, *Suiting Everyone: The Democratization of Clothing in America.* Washington, D.C.: Smithsonian Institution Press, 1974.

2. S. Freedgood, "$100 Million in Rags," *Fortune*, 1962.

3. U.S. Department of Commerce, annual studies of personal consumption expenditures.

4. U.S. Department of Commerce; *U.S. Industrial Outlook*, 1990; Research Department, ILGWU.

5. U.S. Department of Commerce, *Long Term Economic Growth 1860–1965*, October 1966.

6. B. Konheim, president of Nicole Miller, *Retailing Technology*, February 1988.

7. *Women's Wear Daily*, May 20, 1988.

8. *Industry Surveys*, Standard & Poor's, September 1990.

9. Company annual reports, 1990.

10. "He's a Fashion Purist with the Golden Touch," *Business Week*, September 12, 1964.

11. *The Licensing Letter 1990*, Scottsdale, Arizona.

12. "Cartoons and Celebrities Showing Muscle," *Women's Wear Daily*, February 20, 1985.

13. "The City That Dresses a Nation," *New York Sunday News*, February 15, 1976. The speaker is Donna Karan, then a designer for Anne Klein, Inc.

14. "More Than Just Kid Stuff," *Women's Wear Daily*, May 26, 1985.

15. "Dallas, the Business of Fashion," *Women's Wear Daily*, October 15, 1985.

16. "Chicago Is," *Women's Wear Daily*, March 13, 1985.

17. "Regional Marts: Battling for the Buyers," *Women's Wear Daily*, June 3, 1988; also "Opportunity Calls beyond Seventh Avenue," *Advertising Age*, May 1986.

18. "Marts and Markets," *Stores Magazine*, April 1985.

19. Ibid.

20. U.S. Industrial Outlook, 1990.

Selected Bibliography

Dubinsky, David. *David Dubinsky: A Life with Labor.* New York: Simon and Schuster, 1977.

Fairchild Fact Files (fashion industry series). New York: Fairchild Publications, published annually.

Focus: Economic Profile of the Apparel Industry. Washington, D.C.: American Apparel Manufacturers' Association, revised annually.

Hall, Max. *Made in New York.* Cambridge, Mass.: Harvard University Press, 1959.

Kidwell, Claudia, and Margaret C. Christman. *Suiting Everyone: The Democratization of Clothing in America.* Washington, D.C.: Smithsonian Institution Press, 1974.

Stein, Leon. *The Triangle Fire.* Philadelphia, Penna.: Lippincott, 1962.

Women's Apparel Guide. New York: Fairchild Publications, 1988.

Trade Associations

Affiliated Dress Manufacturers, 1440 Broadway, New York, N.Y.

American Apparel Manufacturers Association, 2500 Wilson Boulevard, Arlington, Va. 22201.

American Coat and Suit Manufacturers Association, 450 Seventh Avenue, New York, N.Y. 10123.

Bureau of Wholesale Sales Representatives, 1819 Peachtree Road, North East, Suite 515, Atlanta, Ga. 30309.

California Fashion Creators, 110 East 9th Street, Los Angeles, Calif. 90015.

Childrenswear Manufacturers Association, 112 West 34th Street, New York, N.Y. 10120.

Costume Designers Guild, 11286 Westminster, Los Angeles, Calif. 90066.

Council of Fashion Designers of America, 1633 Broadway, New York, N.Y. 10019.

Federation of Apparel Manufacturers, 450 Seventh Avenue, New York, N.Y. 10001.

Infant and Juvenile Manufacturers Association, 100 East 42nd Street, New York, N.Y. 10017.

Infants' and Children's Wear Salesmen's Guild, 45 West 34th Street, Room 1102, New York, N.Y. 10001.

Infants', Children's, and Girls' Sportswear and Coat Association, 450 Seventh Avenue, New York, N.Y. 10123.

Ladies Apparel Contractors Association, 450 Seventh Avenue, New York, N.Y. 10001.

National Association of Blouse Manufacturers, 450 Seventh Avenue, New York, N.Y. 10001.

National Association of Uniform Manufacturers and Distributors, 1156 Avenue of the Americas, New York, N.Y. 10036.

National Association of Women's and Children's Apparel Salesmen, Inc., 401 Seventh Avenue, New York, N.Y. 10001.

National Dress Manufacturers Association, 570 Seventh Avenue, New York, N.Y. 10018.

National Knitwear and Sportswear Association, 51 Madison Avenue, New York, N.Y. 10010.

National Knitwear Manufacturers Association, 350 Fifth Avenue, New York, N.Y. 10018.

United Infants' and Children's Wear Association, 520 Eighth Avenue, New York, N.Y. 10018.

Trade Publications

Apparel Industry, 180 Allen Road, Atlanta, Ga. 30328.

Apparel News South, Atlanta, Ga. 30328.
Apparel World, 386 Park Avenue South, New York, N.Y. 10010.
The Bobbin, 1110 Shop Road, Columbia, S.C. 29202.
Boutique Fashions, 210 Boyleston Street, Chestnut Hill, Mass. 01267.
California Apparel News, 110 West 40th Street, New York, N.Y. 10008.
Discount Merchandiser, 641 Lexington Avenue, New York, N.Y. 10022.
Earnshaw's, 393 Seventh Avenue, New York, N.Y. 10001.
Infants' and Toddlers' Wear, 370 Lexington Avenue, New York, N.Y. 10010.
Kid's Fashions, 71 West 35th Street, New York, N.Y. 10001.
Teens and Boys Magazine, 210 Boyleston Street, Chestnut Hill, Mass. 01267.
Women's Wear Daily, 7 East 12th Street, New York, N.Y. 10003.

CHAPTER REVIEW AND LEARNING ACTIVITIES

Key Words and Concepts

Define, identify, or briefly explain the following:

Apparel jobber	Line
Apparel marts	Manufacturer
CAM	Marker
Contractor	Market center
Cooperative advertising	Market weeks
Cutting ticket	Outside shop
Elias Howe	Quick Response
Factoring	Ready-to-wear
Grading	Regional showroom
ILGWU	Royalty fee
Inside shop	Seasonal line
Isaac Singer	Secondary design center
Knock-off	Seventh Avenue (SA)
Leveraged buyout	Style piracy
Licensee	Sweatshop
Licensing	Triangle Waist Fire
Licensor	Trunk show

Review Questions for Chapter Highlights

1. Explain the economic importance of the women's and children's apparel industry to the United States.

2. In chronological order, give the major developments that contributed to the growth of the women's ready-to-wear industry and explain the importance of each.

3. What is a leveraged buy-out and give some examples.

4. What is a seasonal line, how many are there each year, and what steps are taken in preparing seasonal lines?

5. Give the specific steps, in sequential order, involved in the production of apparel.

6. How and why does Quick Response speed up production time?

7. Discuss the strategies that can be used by an apparel producer to market a line to retailers.

8. Discuss three methods by which manufacturers are selling directly to consumers and give an example of each.

9. Explain the differences between a manufacturer, an apparel jobber, and a contractor and discuss the advantages of each type.

10. Discuss the following statement: "As long as there is a free enterprise system, there will be room on Seventh Avenue for the small manufacturer."

11. Is the practice of style piracy good or bad for the fashion industry? Why?

12. Why is licensing so prevalent in the fashion industry?

13. Explain why New York developed into the fashion capital of the United States. Do you think it will retain its present status?

14. What is the role of the regional marts in the marketing of apparel?

15. If you were a children's wear buyer, what secondary market center would you shop and why?

16. Select any two companies described in the readings in this chapter and explain how they differ from one another.

5

$\mathcal{T}$HE $\mathcal{M}$ENSWEAR $\mathcal{I}$NDUSTRY

Until the 1950s, the average man's wardrobe consisted of one or more dark suits with vests, white shirts, subdued colored ties, highly polished shoes, an overcoat, and a hat. Whatever changes in fashion did take place usually expressed themselves in little more than variations in the width of lapels, the style and flap of a jacket pocket, and the location of a vent in the suit jacket. The industry that produced men's garments did not consider itself to be in the fast-changing business of fashion.

Change came dramatically after World War II. Surfeited with khaki drabness, many of the younger men yearned for color, even in undershirts. Suburban living, the shorter work week, and the trend toward family-oriented leisure activities set up a demand for sports and leisure wear and resulted in a much freer style of dress even during business hours. By the 1960s, the presence of a large and highly visible generation of young adults sparked a demand for greater variety, faster change, and new opportunities for expression of individuality. Through the 1970s and on into the 1980s, the winds of fashion change continued to blow up a storm in the men's field. From the late 1980s and into the 1990s, active sportswear has created a casual dress code that has revolutionized and revitalized the menswear industry. Special-purpose wardrobes abound in the closets of fashion-conscious males who want to make a "statement" about themselves, with different wardrobes for work, sports, evenings out, shopping, and just hanging out. (The same is true for females, but this is relatively new for males.)

Today men's interest in fashion has become increasingly pronounced and the industry that serves them has responded accordingly. Obviously then, no book about the fashion business would be complete without a discussion of the menswear industry—the subject of this chapter and the readings that follow it.

ECONOMIC IMPORTANCE _____

The menswear industry's importance as a segment of the U.S. fashion business is demonstrated by such figures as these: More than 3,000 separate companies are engaged in the production of men's and boys' clothing and furnishings. They employ more than 265,000 people, the majority of whom are engaged directly in production activities. Factory output is estimated at above $18.0 billion (wholesale value) for 1989.[1]

Another measure of the importance of the industry is that there is scarcely an area of the United States in which it does not have production facilities. Some segments of the industry, such as tailored clothing, require highly skilled workers. Others, such as shirts and work clothing (including the ever-present jeans), can provide employment even for people with minimal skills, as long as they can guide a seam through a sewing machine.

Still another indication of the industry's importance: Consumer expenditures in 1989 for men's and boys' clothing and accessories were $55.9 billion, exclusive of shoes. Not all of this was domestic production, of course, nor did all of the domestic industry's output necessarily go to consumers in this country.[2]

HISTORY AND DEVELOPMENT _____

The U.S. ready-to-wear apparel industry started with clothing for men; it was born in the early 1800s, almost half a century before women's ready-to-wear had its beginnings. Until that time, all men's apparel in this country either was custom tailored, for those who could afford this service, or was made at home for those less affluent.

Early Beginnings in the Nineteenth Century

Like so many other segments of the fashion industry, menswear manufacturing began with the efforts of some enterprising individuals who saw a need and proceeded to fill it. In this case, the need was to supply clothes for men who either had no access to the then customary source of supply—the housewife's nimble fingers—or could not afford custom-made clothing.

DEVELOPMENT OF MEN'S READY-TO-WEAR

In such port cities as New Bedford, New York, Boston, Philadelphia, and Baltimore, a few venturesome tailoring shops conceived the idea of producing and selling cheap ready-to-wear trousers, jackets, and shirts for sailors who needed to replenish their wardrobes inexpensively and immediately during their brief stops in port. These clothes were poorly made in low-quality fabrics. The cutting was done in the dealers' shops and the garments were then sent out to local women for hand sewing.

This early ready-made clothing was referred to as "**slops**," a term from

1849 Advertisement for Ready-Made Men's Clothing

LABORING MEN, MECHANICS, TEAMSTERS, &C.

WIL FIND BY FAR THE LARGEST ASSORTMENT OF

BAIZE JACKETS, OVERALLS, PANTALOONS, GUERNSEY AND FLANNEL SHIRTS, &c.,

that have ever been collected in any Clothing Warehouse in Boston, at

SIMMONS' OAK HALL,

which the word *sloppy* developed, with the same connotation then as now. It was remarked that these garments "could be readily recognized about as far as the wearer could be seen. Hence, there was a sort of shame in the purchase and wear of such clothing, and it was considered almost disreputable to wear it; it was at once a reflection upon a man's taste and a supposed indication of his poverty."[3] Nevertheless, the market for ready-made clothing soon expanded to serve bachelors who had no one at home to sew for them and plantation owners who needed cheap clothing for their slaves.

FROM TAILORS TO MANUFACTURERS

Since no firms then existed that produced clothing for others to sell, these early shops functioned as both retailers and manufacturers. Some of the proprietors were custom tailors who produced ready-made garments from cheaper grades of cloth in addition to carrying on their primary business of made-to-measure clothing. Others cut the cloth on store premises and contracted to have the sewing done outside by people who worked at home.

As industrialization developed in the early nineteenth century, cities grew and a new mass market began to emerge among middle-class or white-collar city dwellers. To attract these customers, some of the more resourceful shop owners offered higher priced and better made garments. The quality of "store clothes" improved and their acceptance increased. By 1830, the market for "store bought" apparel had expanded so greatly that there were firms specializing in the manufacture of garments for others to sell at retail. The first steps in the establishment of the men's clothing industry as we know it today had been taken. By 1835, some manufacturers in New York City, then the nation's leading center for ready-made men's clothing, reportedly employed from 300 to 500 workers.[4] Boston, Philadelphia, Newark, and Baltimore also progressed rapidly as manufacturing centers, as did Rochester and Cincinnati, toward the middle of the century. Impetus was gained when the sewing machine was developed in the middle of the 1800s.

Among the early producers of men's ready-mades was one of today's most famous and prestigious retailers of men's apparel—Brooks Brothers. Founded in 1818 as a custom-tailoring shop, the company got its start in ready-to-wear during the early period of industrialization. By 1857, it employed 78 tailors who worked on the premises and more than 1,500 outside workers.[5]

WORK CLOTHES FOR LABORERS

A development that contributed in a special way to the growth of the menswear industry was the Gold Rush of 1848, which drew thousands of men to the West to pan or dig for gold. Anticipating that these prospectors would need tents to shelter them, a man named Levi Strauss went to California with a supply of heavy fabrics from which to make tents. Among these fabrics was one from France, then called *de Nime*, later Americanized to denim. Seeing a need for workclothes, he used his fabrics not for tents but to make workpants that featured large back pockets to hold mining tools. When he added metal rivets to the pockets to hold them securely, the success of his pants was ensured. The menswear industry grew in a way typical of American frontier life—with workclothes for laborers. Aside from Levi Strauss's contribution, the industry grew generally as a result of the westward migration. The men who pushed the frontier westward, not just in California but in the prairies and the Mountain states, became a promising market for ready-made clothing. Plants to produce such clothing developed in Chicago and St. Louis to meet the demand.

STANDARDIZATION OF SIZES

The manufacture of ready-to-wear is based on **standardized sizes** in sufficient variety so that almost any figure can be accommodated by one of them. In the early years of the industry, each manufacturer worked out its own set of sizes and made garments to its own specifications, hoping to fit as many people as possible. The fit of these early garments was far from perfect.

One of the biggest boosts to the men's ready-to-wear clothing industry came from the government orders for soldiers' uniforms during the Civil War. Because hand sewing could not keep pace with the Army's needs, factories had to be built and equipped with the then new sewing machines. Also, in order to facilitate the production of its uniforms, the Army surveyed the height and chest measurements of more than a million recruits, and thus provided the first mass of statistical data on the form and build of American men. After the war, the results of the Army study were made available to producers of men's civilian clothing. This put the sizing of men's ready-to-wear on a scientific basis and, by making improved fit possible, hastened the change from homemade and custom-made to factory-made garments.

Twentieth-Century Developments

By the time the menswear business entered the twentieth century, it was no longer an industry of small entrepreneurs; it had its share of large enterprises. As the present century progressed, there came such developments as unionization, public ownership, and, in time, a return to private ownership on the part of some of those who had earlier gone public.

"THE AMALGAMATED" — ACTWUA

Like the women's garment industry, the men's clothing industry presented a dismal labor picture at the beginning of this century, with sweatshops prevalent. Producers contracted to have the sewing of garments done outside their plants, either by individuals who did the work in their tenement homes or by contractors who gathered sewing hands together in equally uncomfortable and unsanitary lofts.

In 1910, a strike that started at the Hart, Schaffner & Marx plant in Chicago spread and eventually drew 35,000 workers from their jobs. Settlement of the dispute brought improved working conditions, reduced working hours to 54 hours a week, and set up machinery for adjusting grievances. A few years later, in 1914, the craft union that formerly represented the men's clothing workers yielded its place to the Amalgamated Clothing Workers of America, an industry union, and one that has established a record of labor peace and pioneering effort.

"The Amalgamated" worked for arbitration and industry-wide bargaining; it sought stable labor relations with management as a means of keeping its people employed. It has encouraged scientific techniques in industry management, and it has provided extensive and innovative social welfare services to its members. The union points with pride to its relationship with that same Hart, Schaffner & Marx, at whose Chicago factory a strike triggered the events that led to Amalgamated's birth. For more than 50 years, that plant, now the world's largest in the men's clothing field, did not have a strike.

In the 1970s, the Amalgamated merged with the Textile Workers of America and the United Shoe Workers of America to form the Amalgamated Clothing and Textile Workers Union of America (**ACTWUA**). Virtually all factories in the United States that produce men's tailored clothing (suits, tailored sports coats, formal wear, top coats, etc.) are unionized today. This is not true, however, of other segments of the men's apparel industry, such as sportswear. In that respect, the Amalgamated does not have control over its industry. In part, this situation arises because production of men's apparel is widespread throughout the United States; and in part, it is due to the varying patterns of production in the different segments of the industry.

PUBLIC OWNERSHIP IN THE 1960S

Until the 1960s, publicly owned firms were the exception rather than the rule in menswear. Just as was the case in women's apparel at that time, most concerns were individually owned enterprises, partnerships, or closely held corporations. During the 1960s, many firms in the men's field went public, for much the same reasons as prevailed in the women's field. In some instances, it was a way for a proprietor with no family successor to ease his way into retirement; in others, it was a need for expansion capital. The lure of expansion capital is a strong one. Without it, firms can expand only to the extent that they plow back the profits of their operations year after year. Drawing on the public's invested capital is a faster way.

PRIVATE OWNERSHIP IN THE 1980S

Like the women's industry, in the ultracompetitive atmosphere of the 1980s, some major men's apparel producers began to see public ownership as more of a liability than an asset. Publicly owned companies have a responsibility to shareholders, and this includes public disclosure of new marketing plans and strategies to the extent that swift, silent changes of course are difficult to execute. Some firms, therefore, decided to go private—that is, to buy back their corporation's stock. Levi-Strauss, Blue Bell, and Palm Beach took this step. By returning a company to the private sector, a firm is freer in decision making; it is no longer in the spotlight turned on public companies by investment experts; it is protected from the possibility of hostile takeovers.

NATURE OF THE INDUSTRY _ _ _ _ _ _ _ _ _ _ _ _ _ _ _

The menswear industry, which also includes garments for boys and youths, resembles the women's wear industry in some ways and differs from it in others. Their points of resemblance include the following: (1) manufacturers usually specialize in clearly definable categories of garments, (2) producers in the various industry branches present seasonal lines, and (3) designer names are featured. Still another point of resemblance is the importance of collections that feature complete, coordinated groups of merchandise, all of which are produced, sold, and ultimately displayed in retail stores under a single brand or designer name. A still later development is the growing importance of classification (pants, tee shirts) merchandising to avoid excessive markdowns sometimes caused by buying complete collections. This development mirrors a prior development from decades ago in women's sportswear as the sportswear market was growing and expanding.

Points of difference from the women's field are numerous: (1) the larger firms account for a greater share of the men's industry's total output; (2) manufacturers' brand names have been long established, are better known, more important to the consumer, and more influential in marketing than they are in the women's field; and (3) the contracting system, so much a part of the women's field, is less common. On the last point, however, the growing importance of sportswear is increasing the use of the contracting system.

Finally, in the menswear field, many firms have expanded into women's wear, by either creating or acquiring women's divisions.

Industry Divisions

The menswear industry differs greatly from women's wear in that the distinctions between its traditional product divisions and the types of firms they encompass are not as clearly defined. Since 1987, however, the U.S. Department of Commerce's Bureau of Census has attempted to rearrange the categories of merchandise included in its industry divisions. In some ways this has improved the situation; in others it has created more confusion. For example, jeans have now been included in separate trousers (which is fine), but separate jackets, although produced by firms that produce separate trousers, are now included in the not-elsewhere-classified category (NEC), as are ties, which previously had their own division.

In the women's wear area, a women's coat firm is not likely to produce separate pants and jackets, but this is all included together as reported under tailored clothing. In women's wear one can readily identify merchandise grouped together under the concept of sportswear, whereas in menswear this is still difficult to do. Be that as it may, the major divisions, as classified by government and industry alike and for which statistics are available, are as follows:[6]

- SIC 2311   *Tailored clothing.* This division includes firms that are primarily engaged in manufacturing men's, youths', and boys' tailored suits, jackets, slacks, and overcoats. Also included in this classification are firms primarily engaged in manufacturing uniforms.

   In the lexicon of the men's apparel industry, the term *tailored clothing* refers to structured or semistructured suits, overcoats, sports jackets, and separate slacks, the production of which involves a number of hand-tailoring operations. This division at one time so dominated the industry that, to the consumer, the term *men's clothing* was synonymous with tailored clothing.
- SIC 2325   *Trousers and slacks* (jeans included).
- SIC 2326   *Work clothes* (includes work shirts, working apparel, and washable wearing apparel).
- SIC 2321   *Shirts, casual and dress* (broken down separately for knit shirts SIC 23213 and woven shirts SIC 23216).
- SIC 2322   *Underwear and nightwear* (includes nightshirts and pajamas).

- SIC 2329   *NEC* (includes nontailored jackets and outerwear, swimwear, and ties).

Dominance of Large Firms

There are more large firms in menswear than in women's apparel. The men's industry has more firms that do half a billion dollars or more in sales a year, and these big companies do a greater share of their industry's total business than the big women's firms do in their field. Nevertheless, although there are a few menswear firms whose individual annual sales figures exceed $1 billion, these are no match in size for companies in other fields such as Procter & Gamble, with its $20.3 billion a year, or Philip Morris, with its $31.7 billion a year.

A table in this chapter lists some of the major menswear firms, along with their respective sales volume figures and an indication of the menswear that they produce.

Many menswear firms have grown large by opening up new divisions, or acquiring other companies, or both. One example is **Levi-Strauss**, which started in the menswear business and expanded into women's and children's jeans and other sportswear separates. Other large menswear producers have also entered the women's apparel field in the course of expansion. Thus, Cluett Peabody, initially simply the producer of Arrow shirts and still the country's largest producer of men's shirts, has expanded through acquisitions and new divisions into sports shirts, underwear, jackets, sweaters, slacks, hosiery, and women's wear.

In 1986, Cluett Peabody was acquired by West Point Pepperell, which was itself acquired in 1989 by Farley Industries, which also own Fruit of the Loom. In 1990, Cluett Peabody was sold by Farley to Bidermann Industries. Ralph Lauren started in menswear, expanded into womenswear and boys' clothing, and then expanded further into retailing by opening his own stores and franchising stores to sell Ralph Lauren, Polo, and Chaps products.

Major Menswear Producers: Selected Examples

Company	1989 Sales (add 000,000)	Principal Menswear Product
Levi Strauss, San Francisco	3,628	Jeans, sportswear
Hartmarx, Chicago	1,297	Tailored clothing
Philips-Van Heusen, New York	732.9	Shirts, sportswear
Russell	687.9	Shirts, sportswear, and tailored clothing
Oxford Industries	566.2	Active wear
Farah	239.0	Tailored clothing, sportswear

SOURCE: Companies' annual reports.

Geographic Locations: Decentralized

Unlike the women's industry, menswear firms are not heavily concentrated in New York City but are widely distributed throughout the United States. The industry's largest, Levi-Strauss, is headquartered in San Francisco. **Hartmarx**, a major producer of tailored clothing, is headquartered in Chicago. Philadelphia is headquarters for Greif & Company, After Six, and Pincus Bros. Maxwell. In the Pacific Northwest are White Stag and Pendleton. Haggar and Farrah are in Texas. Oxford Industries is one of the many companies in the South. Production facilities, as well as headquarters offices, are so widely scattered that the industry is truly national and there is scarcely a state that is not involved in menswear. All the firms mentioned, however, have showrooms in New York City, as do many, many others.

IMPORTANCE OF NEW YORK

New York City is the hub of the industry's marketing efforts and houses the sales office of virtually every important producer in the United States. In just a single building, 1290 Avenue of the Americas, several hundred menswear firms have their offices. As the industry has grown, its showrooms have spilled over into surrounding office buildings on 51st, 52nd, and 53rd streets, from Fifth Avenue to Seventh Avenue. Farther downtown, in the Empire State Building at 34th Street and Fifth Avenue, there are sales offices for a major share of the men's furnishings companies. Meantime, the area around 23rd Street and Fifth Avenue, which was once the heart of the industry, has been abandoned to retail and housing uses.

What draws merchants to New York City is the presence of showrooms, showrooms, and more showrooms. The typical retailer has little need or desire to visit production facilities.

CENTERS OF PRODUCTION

The production of menswear, as has been mentioned, takes place all over the United States. Certain areas, however, are more important than others for specific types of apparel. Tailored clothing is produced primarily in the Northeast, with New York, Pennsylvania, and Massachusetts being the major areas. Together with Georgia, these states produce more than 50 percent of all tailored clothing.[7]

As to other categories: A large percentage of men's and boys' shirts and nightwear are produced in North Carolina, Alabama, Georgia, and Tennessee; almost three-fourths of separate trousers are produced in Georgia, Texas, Tennessee, and Mississippi; and the main production of all men's and boys' neckwear takes place in New York, North Carolina, California, and Louisiana.[8]

DESIGN AND
PRODUCTION PROCEDURES__ _ _ _ _ _ _ _ _ _ _ _ _ _ _ _

The procedures in the design and production of men's tailored clothing and in the design and production of men's sportswear differ greatly. In tailored clothing, changes are simple and subtle; in sportswear, changes tend to be more rapid, more drastic, and more trendy. Throughout the entire menswear field, however, men remain slower and less willing than women to accept radical fashion changes in their wardrobes. What has been changing, however, is men's attitudes toward their bodies, with emphasis on health. Exercise became a fact of life in the 1980s. Fitness, says designer Bill Blass, "is a major preoccupation of people in our time."[9]

This new body awareness manifests itself in menswear in a number of ways. There is, of course, the demand for jogging suits, tennis and running shorts, and workout outfits. So strong is the interest in athletics and athletic clothes that the warmup suit has become known as the leisure suit of the 1980s. At the same time, men's tailored clothing has changed to reflect the interest in fit bodies. Shoulders are wider, waists are narrower, and the drop has increased. The **drop** is the difference between the chest measurement and the waist measurement. Traditionally, this was six inches, but nowadays manufacturers are changing their specifications to seven or eight inches.

Tailored Clothing

The tailored clothing segment of the menswear industry presents a completely different picture from what prevails in other branches, and certainly a picture utterly unlike that which prevails in the women's fashion industry. Production is slow and painstaking; highly skilled operators are required; handwork is still a factor; sizing is complex; emphasis is on selection of fabrics rather than styles alone; and styles change slowly and gradually. With all these elements to consider, it is not surprising that this segment of the industry operates on the basis of only two seasons a year.

SEASONAL LINES

The tailored clothing industry, with its long and complex production methods, traditionally presents its lines to retailers only twice a year. Fall/Winter lines are shown to the trade in December and January; Spring/Summer lines are shown in July and August. This long-established calendar prevails today and continues to do so because the apparel concerned remains largely classic in style. If fashion changes were swifter and more marked in this field, necessitating more frequent introduction of new styles, the calendar would change—and the industry's methods of operation would undoubtedly have to change along with it.

DEVELOPMENT OF A LINE

The development of a tailored clothing line starts with a decision as to the bodies, or basic styles, that will be featured for the coming season. Each major suit and coat manufacturer employs at least one master tailor/designer whose job is to make the subtle changes in last year's bodies that may be needed to produce this year's new shape. Changes may include adding or subtracting length in the jacket and lapels; bringing the garment closer to or farther from the body; making the shoulders fuller or less so; choosing between flap and patch pockets; deciding on whether there will be side vents, back vent, or no vent; and so on.

Once the newly modified bodies are ready, the designer, the piece goods buyer, and the principals of the company set to work to choose the fabric assortment. These assortments are quite extensive, as retailers expect to see a broad range when they come in to make their selections for a major season. Finally, sample garments are made up in a few of the fabrics, so that the bodies can be shown in plaids, stripes, and solids. This is the line that is shown to the retailer, along with a swatch book of additional fabrics that are available.

PRODUCTION OF TAILORED CLOTHING

The process of producing men's tailored clothing is long, complex, and quite different from the procedures followed in women's apparel or in other divisions of menswear. Many hand operations are involved in the construction of structured garments, the sizing system is more complicated, and it is fabric rather than shape or silhouette that differentiates one tailored style from another. The manufacturer commits itself in advance to 100 fabrics or more. These are presented to the retail customers, and the retail buyers select those they want and the basic bodies in which they want them made up. To that extent, the retailer designs its own exclusive line. The producer, moreover, may offer PGR (Piece Goods Reservation), a system whereby the manufacturer sets aside fabric for a specific retailer during or immediately after showing the line. The manufacturer does not begin production until sufficient orders have been accumulated for a fabric to justify a cutting ticket. A quality maker will put a fabric into production, if it has been ordered in one or several different models and runs of sizes, as long as there are at least a minimum number of garments to cut. Each producer sets its own figure, of course.

Even after the cutting has been done, production goes slowly. The hand operations involved in tailored clothing are time consuming; as much as an hour or more may be needed for the pressing operation alone. Quality control is maintained throughout the construction of tailored clothing—a factor that explains why many producers in this division of the industry are inside shops, using their own production facilities rather than those of outside contractors. This is in sharp contrast with the men's sportswear field, where style and design features are emphasized rather than exact fit and meticulous workmanship.

Tailored Clothing for Today's Man

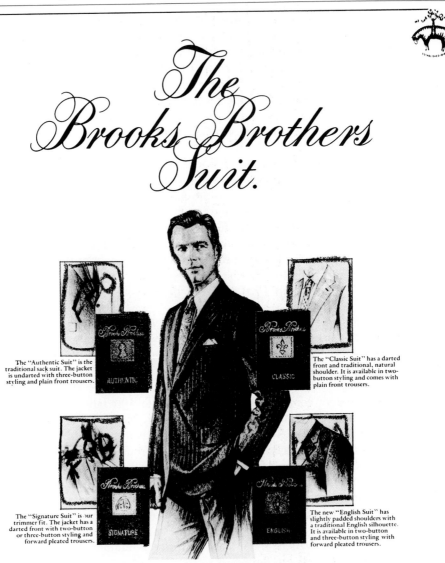

The "Authentic Suit" is the traditional sack suit. The jacket is undarted with three-button styling and plain front trousers.

The "Classic Suit" has a darted front and traditional, natural shoulder. It is available in two-button styling and comes with plain front trousers.

The "Signature Suit" is our trimmer fit. The jacket has a darted front with two-button or three-button styling and forward pleated trousers.

The new "English Suit" has slightly padded shoulders with a traditional English silhouette. It is available in two-button and three-button styling with forward pleated trousers.

THE MORE THINGS CHANGE, THE MORE THEY STAY THE SAME.
AND THE MORE THINGS STAY THE SAME, THE MORE THEY CHANGE.

Around the turn of the century, about the time New York was getting its first subway, the sack suit made its debut at Brooks Brothers. Well, to all of you who have become addicted to its straight lines, to its comfortable fit and to the distinctive roll of its lapels, relax. The sack suit is alive and still very well at Brooks Brothers.

346 MADISON AVENUE   LIBERTY PLAZA   MANHASSET   PARAMUS   SCARSDALE   SHORT HILLS   STAMFORD

Use your Brooks Brothers card, American Express, MasterCard or Visa

COMPLEX SIZING

The dual sizing system that prevails in tailored clothing is a further factor in making production procedures slow and cumbersome. Men's suits are cut in different chest measurements, each one of which is combined with different figure types. This is in sharp contrast with the situation that prevails in the women's apparel industry, in which each producer tends to concentrate on a single figure type, such as misses, junior, or half-size, and cuts possibly five or six sizes for that figure type. A tailored suit producer, however, has to cope with all these sizes for any one number in the line:

- *Short.* 36, 37, 38, up to 42 chest measurement.
- *Regular.* 36, 38, 39, 40, up to 46 chest measurement.
- *Long.* 38, 39, 40, 41, up to 48 chest measurement.
- *Extra Long.* 40, 42, 44, up to 48 chest measurement.
- *Portly.* 39, 40, 41, up to 50 chest measurement.

Even in the case of separate slacks, the sizing is not simple. Many in the tailored category are sized by waist alone, it is true, depending on the retailer or the customer to measure off the inseam length and hem the garment. But there are also many men's pants that are sold finished at the hem, and these are sized in waists from 26 to 42 for the most part, and in inseam lengths of 29 to 36 inches.

This enormous variety of sizes is important to the retail seller, since many menswear stores continue to alter men's suits to fit individual customers and to absorb the cost of such alterations. This, too, is changing, as the mix of stores selling men's tailored clothing changes to include discounters and others who charge for alterations. Also, stores that have traditionally provided free alterations now charge for some types of alteration in order to keep expenses down. Even Brooks Brothers now charges for some alterations.

The enormous variety of sizes necessary to be stocked by retailers that desire to have a presence in the tailored clothing marketplace has necessitated huge investments of capital in slow-turning stock. In January 1989, Sears decided to discontinue the men's tailored clothing departments in its stores, thus abandoning $100 to $150 million dollars worth of business, and to concentrate on the other areas of men's apparel. Sears will remain in men's tailored clothing only in its catalog operations and in its leased Kuppenheimer departments.

The custom of doing free alterations goes back to the made-to-order beginnings of menswear, when accurate fit was expected by the consumer. (In contrast, women, who are supposed by tradition to be competent seamstresses, have always had to pay for any needed alterations.) To minimize alterations, menswear retailers have sought to carry stocks that permit almost any size or figure type to be fitted with a minimum of adjustments. Although it is unlikely that any one style will be carried in all sizes, the average number of sizes bought in one garment ranges from 15 to 25, depending on the type and size of the store and the importance placed on the model and fabric in relation to the total inventory.

SIMPLIFYING SIZES

The growing importance of young men as suit buyers is slowly leading the way into S/M/L/XL sizing, introduced at the MAGIC show in 1986 to poor results, to replace the myriad of sizes carried in traditional tailored clothing departments today. This trend to date is confined to makers that market to the customers who desire a more formal version of the contemporary soft suit, but do not want fully constructed clothing. However, traditional manufacturers such as South-wick, Lanvin Studio by Greif, Joseph Abboud, and Bill Robinson among others are producing soft-construction tailored clothing.

At the base of this S/M/L/XL sizing, which can be done in regulars and longs, is "Small," which has a 40 shoulder and a 38 body; "Medium," which has a 43 shoulder and a 41 body; and "Large," which has a 49 (or equivalent) shoulder and a 44 body. In a way, this is another way of responding to the desire for increased "drop" in tailored clothing. It may also be the retailer's way to respond to the desire to keep inventories as lean as possible without giving up the tailored clothing business.

HAND TAILORING

The production of men's tailored clothing traditionally has involved many hours of hand tailoring. In the past, tailored clothing was given *grades* from 1 to 6+, based on the number of hand operations that went into the production. In recent years, the practice of identifying suits by grades has disappeared, due to technological developments. Today, many hand-tailoring processes have been eliminated because there is machinery that simulates hand stitching of lapels, turning of pockets, or finishing of buttonholes. Such procedures speed up production and reduce costs. However, top-quality men's suits still involve a great deal of hand tailoring.

CUSTOM TAILORS AND TAILORS-TO-THE-TRADE

Because men's apparel required a more precise fit than women's clothes, custom tailoring remained important in the men's field longer than custom dressmaking did in women's wear. Most of the men's tailors who did custom work in this country in the early years of this century had been trained in Europe under the apprentice system; they could design a suit, sponge the fabric to preshrink it, cut the garment, run up the seams, sew on buttons, make buttonholes by hand, and supply the fine stitching on lapels. Until the 1920s, a man could enjoy the excellent fit of a made-to-order suit at prices and in qualities that compared very favorably with ready-made clothing.

The supply of custom tailors, however, began to dwindle in the 1920s and 1930s. Immigration had been restricted and, as the older European-trained tailors died or retired, very few new ones crossed the Atlantic to take their places. Work in the factories of this country did not produce craftsmen capable of making complete garments. Efficient methods of operation required some men to specialize in cutting, others in sewing, and still others in the hand finishing.

The Growing Importance of Made-to-Order Men's Clothing

Today, a growing number of **custom tailor** (made-to-order) shops still exist in the United States, principally in large cities and at the upper end of the price scale. An outstanding example is Dunhill Tailors of New York City, with a sales volume of more than $1 million a year and featuring suits that sell for $1,500 or more each. To quote Leon Block, one of Dunhill's principals: "Custom is bigger than ever; eight years ago, we planned to phase it out but we couldn't because so many clients wanted it."[10] The store's customer list has included such names as Cary Grant, Paul Newman, Walter Hoving, and New York's former governor, Hugh Carey.

In 1989, Sulka, a venerable haberdashery shop that made only custom-made shirts in the past, opened a custom-made suit department selling suits from $1,250 to $3,000. This store is owned by Sy Syms of Syms discount retailing. In Washington, D.C., the traditional men's clothier of Lewis and Thos. Saltz Co. opened a prototype store that offers 500 swatches from which a customer may choose a custom-made suit costing from $500 to more than $1,000, and this company expects to open 100 more such stores in major cities nationwide over the next 10 years. This company, as does Sulka, also offers custom-made shirts. The trend for custom-made clothing is indeed expanding.

In addition to the retail custom tailors who produce a complete garment on their own premises, there are also **tailors-to-the-trade** or *made-to-measure firms*. These are factories that specialize in cutting individual garments according to the exact measurements of customers who place their orders through retail stores serviced by these firms. The customer selects style and fabric from fashion books and swatches that he consults in the retail store; the retailer relays his selection and his measurements to the factory; and in due course the garment is made up. Although there are still some tailors-to-the-trade, their output is only a small portion of the industry's total and is no longer reported separately in census figures. Much of the made-to-order business nowadays is handled by large producers of ready-made apparel that have set up separate division for this special made-to-measure business.

Sportswear Design and Production

It was only a few decades ago when men's sportswear emerged from the dark ages. The mod explosion of the 1960s transformed the business. The old-furnishings-oriented (ties and shirts) business-clothing-only look gave way to the jeans generation of baby boomers.

The designer revolution of the 1960s, which brought names like Oleg Cassini, John Weitz, Pierre Cardin, and Yves St. Laurent to the forefront, later swept in Ralph Lauren and Calvin Klein in the 1970s, and Perry Ellis and Georgio Armani in the 1980s.

From California came the young men's revolution and Brittania (later to become Generra) and Union Bay. The active boom brought in names such as Nike and Adidas to the apparel industry. Names once important, such as

Levi Strauss: Jeans Down — Sales Up

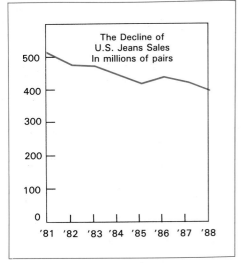

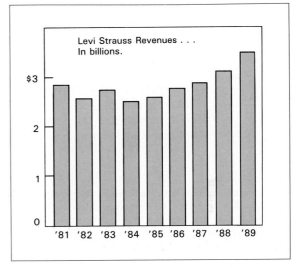

SOURCE: Information Services, Levi Strauss & Co.

Merona, Bruce, and McGregor, lost their luster and gave way to names such as Guess and Levi's/Dockers.

The demand of male customers for a more fashionable look—for clothes suited to the multifaceted multidimensional lives they lead—has made the sportswear segment of the men's clothing industry increasingly important. Clothes for activity, the outdoors, casual evening dressing, biking, hiking, running, and working out all require appropriate clothing. Even "hanging out" needs the right clothes depending on where you do your hanging out. These clothes do not require careful shaping and hand operations; the shape is supplied by the wearer. What is required is more fashion awareness and producers that can quickly respond to changing customer demands.

SEASONAL LINES

In men's sportswear, the quickening desire of consumers for fashion newness has resulted in a quickening pace of style change. Because of its ability to respond to changes in silhouette, pattern, color, and trend, sportswear provides faster inventory turnover.

In the quickening fashion pace of the men's sportswear market, the need has developed for more newness more often. Instead of the three seasons that were prevalent just six short years ago, sportswear now has four seasons. Fall (shown in March) is delivered in August; Holiday (shown in June) is delivered in November; Spring (shown in October) is delivered in February; and Summer (shown in January) is shipped in April or May. Claiborne, the menswear division of Liz Claiborne, offers five men's lines a year: Fall I is shown in March for June delivery; Fall II is shown in June for September delivery; Holiday/Pre-Spring is shown in August for November delivery; Spring I is shown in October for January delivery; and Spring II is shown in January for March delivery.

DEVELOPMENT OF A LINE

The preparation of a sportswear line differs a great deal from the development of a tailored clothing line. In sportswear, as in women's wear, the producer has already preselected the fabrics for the various numbers in the line, and the emphasis is on offering a selection of styles rather than a choice of fabric.

An Example of a Men's Sportswear Line

Merchandise complete outfits on mannequins to show how easy it is to layer these pattern mixes. Use T-stands to merchandise outfits that show how bright color accents spark these black and white looks. Offer customers a variety of ideas for exciting new late-night wardrobing ideas.

In preparing a line of coordinated sportswear, or of men's separates (such as trousers, shirts, or sweaters), there are both similarities and differences between one company and another. Where a designer's name is involved, the designer usually oversees the sketching, selection of fabrics, making of samples, and selection of colors. A company that specializes in separates, such as Haggar, uses house designers who prepare a line of pants by adding or removing front pleats, narrowing or widening pants legs, or making whatever other modifications are needed to achieve the new season's look. Fabric selection is usually handled by the designer, working with the company's principals and the sales manager, each of whom contributes his or her special expertise to the final selection. Pricing is usually done by the same group, but with the production manager replacing the designer on the team for this task.

PRODUCTION

Since no hand tailoring is involved in the production of sportswear, the sewing (and often also the cutting) is likely to be farmed out to independent contractors, much as is done in the women's apparel industry. However, in addition to using outside shops, many large producers such as Haggar and Levi-Strauss also handle some of the production in their own plants.

With fashion changes, the scope of a line expands or contracts. There may be more or fewer sweaters, fewer tee shirts, more or less activewear, and so on. In such cases, it is necessary merely to find new contractors for the expanded categories and to drop those no longer needed for fading areas of demand. And, as in the women's industry, both foreign and domestic contractors are used.

SIMPLIFIED SIZING

The sizing in some sportswear categories is fairly simple; in others, it is becoming so. Men's sweaters are usually sized Small, Medium, Large, and Extra Large. Sports pants are sold by waist measurement in inches. Some trousers carry both waist and length sizes, in inches, such as 29/30, 29/31, and so on. In these designations, the first figure is the waist measurement and the second is the inseam, or length from trouser rise to hem. More expensive trousers often come without hems, so that the leg length can be adjusted for the individual customer.

Sports shirts are produced in only four sizes: Small, Medium, Large, and Extra Large. Sleeve lengths are standard for each size. Makers of men's dress shirts have been following the lead of the sports shirt makers in simplifying their sizes, but with limited success. Manufacturers in this field had been accustomed to making their entire lines with neck sizes ranging from 14 (inches) to 17½ or even larger. For each neck size, they produced sleeve lengths ranging from 31 to 37 inches, at one-inch intervals. Such a wide range of sizes represented a slow production process for the manufacturer and a formidable inventory problem for both retailer and manufacturer.

To permit quicker response to fashion change and to aid operation on lower inventories, shirt producers have sought to pay less attention to fit and increased attention to fashion. They simply produce a very large percentage of their styles with average rather than exact sleeve lengths. This system of producing only average sleeve lengths (ASL) has not been too well received by customers. Today, major men's shirt retailers carry both types — fashion shirts in average sleeve lengths only and classic dress shirts in the customary collar and sleeve length sizing.

IMPORTANCE OF THE COLLECTION CONCEPT

In the past, male shoppers tended to build their wardrobes around tailored clothing and regarded such items as sweaters or sports trousers as merely extra purchases. Today, they may very well make all their purchases in sportswear departments, where they can achieve a look that is properly put together, even if the fabrics in the various garments are different. This has become possible because of the **collection concept**.

Originally in the realm of licensing designers such as John Weitz, Giorgio Armani, and Allan Flusser, the collection concept has grown to the point that it encompasses almost all menswear, whether designer sponsored or manufacturers' brands, and at all price levels. A menswear retailer nowadays buys and presents a collection from a company that produces jackets, trousers, shirts, sweaters, and even ties and belts, thus ensuring that the customer will be offered varied items, all of which can be worn together and are color coordinated.

For example, Henry Grethel, a New York designer licensed by Hartmarx, designs a complete clothing collection including trousers, jackets, shirts sweaters, and tee-shirts, all geared for weekend wear. Perry Ellis America produced by Manhattan Shirt Co., a division of Salant Corp., creates complete coordinated collections, as does Andrew Fezza for GFT America. Other designer collections include those by Barry Bricken, Jhane Barnes, Jeffrey Banks, and Claiborne. Giorgio Armani does three collections, each geared to a separate target market by price and lifestyle: Armani Couture, the highest priced and most elegant; Armani Boutique, moderate to high priced, geared to the man on his way up the corporate and fiscal ladder; and Mani, the most fashion-forward line in department store price ranges.

INCREASE OF CLASSIFICATION MERCHANDISING

"There's a redefinition of what is considered regular clothing. Tailored sport coats are both sportswear and clothing. It's the attitude in which they are worn. Throwing it over a pair of jeans and a T-shirt has a contemporary feel. That's the '90s."[11]

Because of the growth of the menswear customer today who has confidence in his own fashion expertise and taste, and because retailers want the freedom to pick and choose from a line to satisfy their target market, we see a return to classification buying and merchandising. This approach lowers potential markdown, lowers stock investments in slower selling classifications, and speeds inventory turns.

MARKETING OF MENSWEAR

The way to achieve growth is to win business away from competing companies. Thus there is greater emphasis on marketing, instead of on production alone, and this in turn has speeded up the industry's use of contractors to facilitate quick response to the changes in demand. As the apparel industry develops and emphasizes marketing strategies rather than production capabilities alone, the field of menswear becomes an ever more important area of potential growth. Today's menswear customer, at every age and economic level, is more interested and involved than ever before in the building of a wardrobe and in the process of selection. Fashion shopping is no longer for women only; it has truly become an activity for both sexes.

Manufacturers' Brands

Brand names in the men's field are older and better established, and have been longer promoted, than those in the women's field. Men have been conditioned for generations to purchase apparel in terms of grade, quality, fit, and durability rather than style alone. Thus, until a dozen or more years ago, consumers gravitated to brand names that were associated in their minds with quality: Arrow and Manhattan shirts, Hickey-Freeman and Society brand suits, for example, and such stores labels (private brands) as those of retailers such as Brooks Brothers, major department stores, outstanding menswear shops, chains, and mail-order companies.

Some of the brand names still prominent in menswear date back to the beginning of this century or earlier. Hart, Schaffner & Marx, now known as Hartmarx, began promoting its name through national advertising in 1890. In 1901, Joseph & Feiss (now owned by Phillips–Van Heusen) embarked on a national campaign to sell its "Clothescraft Clothes," retailing $10 and upward, by telling their retail customers that "the wearer will be brought to you by judicious advertising. We pay for it."[12] This, of course, was an early and simple form of cooperative advertising.

Responding to a vastly different department and specialty store climate created by mergers and acquisitions on the part of retailers, manufacturers are developing new marketing strategies to maintain the consumer awareness of their brand names. GREIF companies, which include licensed labels such as Chaps by Ralph Lauren and Colours by Alexander Julian among others, has added a new layer of service people who will act as liaison between the retailers and the company to provide marketing intelligence to themselves and their customers, thus keeping their brand names highly visible. Levi-Strauss spends more than $25 million a year to advertise just one style jean, and Guess spends between $15 and $18 million a year to promote what it describes as "image advertising." The Wrangler division of VF Corp. spent $30 million plus to reach

Hartmarx Uses Brand and Licensed Names to Market Its Products

Retail Market Segments	Business Professional	Natural Shoulder Traditional	American Fashion Contemporary
UPPER	Hickey-Freeman Tailored clothing Walter Morton Tailored clothing **Graham & Gunn Stores **Barrie Pace Ltd. Women's stores and catalogs	Hickey-Freeman VSSC Tailored clothing	
UPPER MODERATE	Hart Schaffner & Marx Tailored clothing & rainwear Sansabelt Ltd. Dress slacks **Hartmarx Specialty Stores Thorngate Uniforms	Graham & Gunn Traditional clothing	Society Brand Ltd. Tailored clothing Lady Sansabelt Women's separates Sterling & Hunt Women's tailored clothing
MODERATE	Sansabelt Suit Tailored clothing Sansabelt Slacks **Sansabelt Shops Jaymar Dress slacks Gleneagles Rainwear Fashionaire Uniforms	Briar Tailored clothing, dress furnishings Yorke Shirts H. Oritsky Tailored clothing	Henry Grethel Tailored clothing, sportswear, dress furnishings **Henry Grethel Studio Country Suburbans Women's coordinated separates **Old Mill Retail Stores
POPULAR	Allyn St. George Tailored clothing **Kuppenheimer Total men's wardrobe		*Johnny Carson Tailored clothing

SOURCE: Annual stockholders' reports.
*Licensed label.
**Owned retail stores.
†"Bespoke" means custom tailored; "off the peg" means ready to wear. These are English terms used here for snob appeal.

British Fashion	Italian Fashion	French Fashion	American Sportsman
*Gieves & Hawkes †Bespoke Tailored clothing *Gieves & Hawkes †Off the peg, tailored clothing			*Bobby Jones by Hickey-Freeman Blazers, sport coats, dress slacks
*Austin Reed of Regent Street New Bond Street Collection tailored clothing	*Nino Cerruti Signature Tailored clothing	*Christian Dior Le Connoisseur Tailored clothing *Christian Dior Rainwear	*Bobby Jones Golf Apparel (A sportswear division of Hickey-Freeman) sportswear, jackets *Jack Nicklaus Blazers & dress slacks by Hart Schaffner & Marx
*Austin Reed of Regent Street Tailored clothing, rainwear Racquet Club Wimbledon Tailored clothing, sportswear, dress furnishings	*Nino Cerruti Rue Royale Tailored clothing	*Christian Dior Monsieur Tailored clothing *Pierre Cardin Tailored clothing	*Jack Nicklaus Golf slacks Sansabelt Golf Sportswear Sansabelt Stadium Sportswear
	Confezióni Risèrva Luciano Franzoni Tailored clothing		Escadrille Casual slacks **Kuppenheimer American Sportsman blazers, slacks

"80 million proud working men, who make up the largest jean market in this country."[13]

Targeted Customer Approach

As menswear purchases in apparel changed from replacement purchases to impulse fashion purchases, manufacturers had to develop much more knowledge about their customer. A very focused and targeted approach is developing, and is replacing the commodity thinking that was prevalent in the menswear industry. Major producers such as Hartmarx have developed customer profiles for different divisions of their company,[14] as has Generra, which has separated its business into a young men's market (the 15-to-24 age range) and a men's market (geared to men in the 25-to-45 age range).[15]

Designer Labels and Designer Licensing

National brands contributed to market growth for many apparel companies and a goodly number capitalized on the expanded consumer demand for designer-name clothing as the menswear consumer grew more fashion conscious. This trend was evident from the late 1970s and peaked during the late 1980s. Some designers whose names were well established in the women's wear industry took the logical step of moving over into the menswear area. The first steps were made by designers such as Calvin Klein, Pierre Cardin, and Yves St. Laurent, soon followed by Perry Ellis, Christian Dior, and others who signed licensing agreements with various menswear tailored clothing and sportswear producers for the use of their names. Only occasionally did the name designer have much input into the actual designing of the line. Soon celebrity sports and entertainment names such as Johnny Carson and Bobby Jones, both licensed by Hartmarx, entered the menswear arena. In addition, names such as Indiana Jones and Batman come and go as the movie industry grinds out new licensable heroes. These licensing agreements, of course, have added a great deal of additional income for the designers and, hopefully, luster to the apparel producers' products.

Liz Claiborne is among the more recent entries into the menswear area with the introduction of the Claiborne division in late 1985. Using its designing talent and marketing know-how learned in the women's wear area, this business has emerged as a very successful menswear manufacturer. This is not a licensed arrangement; Claiborne is an example of a designer company that does its own manufacturing rather than licensing its name.

Although designer names continue to be important, the consumer's response is only as strong as the continued importance of the designer's name. The designer business has become more "business than designer."[16]

Selected Examples of Menswear Licensing by Women's Designers

Designer (licensor)	Company (licensee)	Product
Givenchy	Active American Apparel	Active sportswear
	Carter and Holmes	Neckwear
	Cheavers	Tailored clothing
	Keepers Industries	Hosiery
	Koret Inc.	Small leather goods
	Mann and Bros.	Handkerchiefs, scarfs, mufflers
	CAS group	Belts
Aldolfo	Leon of Paris Co.	Tailored clothing
	Aetna Shirt Co.	Formal shirts, cummerbunds, ties
	Jule Long Inc.	Trousers
	Monte Carlo Shirts	Dress and sports shirts
	Stratojac	Outerwear
	Sigallo Ltd.	Activewear, swimwear
	Castle Neckwear	Neckwear
	Cipriani Inc.	Belts
	Fishman Tobin	Boys suits and trousers
Oscar de la Renta	Wembley	Ties
	Oxford Industries	Shirts
	Lanier Clothes	Suits
	Versailles Formalwear	Tuxedos
Perry Ellis	Greif Co.	Suits
	Host Apparel Inc.	Robes, nightwear
	Fairbrooke Enterprises	Coats
	Birger Christensen	Fur coats
	Jockey International	Underwear
	Manhattan	Belts, suspenders, neckwear
	Trimfit	Hosiery
Bill Blass	Royal Robes	Robes, loungewear
	Revlon	Toiletries
	Buxton	Small leather goods
	J. S. Blank	Neckwear
	Gates Shirts	Dress, sports shirts
	PBM	Tailored clothing
	After Six	Formalwear
	Malcolm Kenneth	Coats, rainwear

Retail Channels of Distribution

In the past, the largest percentage of the retail menswear business was done in the strictly masculine confines of the men's specialty stores. As men became more interested in presenting an appearance that reflected both the current fashions and their own personalities, and as they sought alternatives to the conventional business suit, they began to shop in other types of stores. And to enjoy shopping! At the same time, that bastion of men's privacy, the menswear store, began to solicit female customers. Examples include Brooks Brothers, Hastings, Paul Stuart, and Barney's.

A parallel development has occurred in the traditionally feminine environs of the department store and women's specialty shops. Neiman Marcus now devotes a large part of the main floor of its flagship Dallas store to menswear. At Bloomingdale's in New York, menswear gets nearly half the main floor, plus another half a floor in the area that was once a low-priced basement sales area. The same is true of Garfinkel's in Washington, D.C., and the Macy's stores in New York and San Francisco. Bergdorf Goodman in New York spent $10 million to expand and relocate its menswear business into 45,000 square feet of space in a new store across the street from its present location. Filene's opened 11 new all-menswear stores in 1990; Bloomingdale's doubled its menswear space in its Chevy Chase, Maryland, unit; and the Atlanta Mart has now devoted twice the amount of floor space (one whole floor) to men's apparel. Says Neiman Marcus vice president James F. Guerra, "We devote increasing floor space to menswear because it is one of the best performers in the store in terms of sales and margins."[17] At the same time, those specialty chains whose units are primarily located in malls are appealing to young men who shop with young women for the fun of it. Both sexes watch MTV and both react to the same fashion images. Nevertheless, there are still many small men's specialty shops that are an important outlet for men's clothing.

Men's specialty shops, large or small, remain important for several reasons. For one, many men still hesitate to enter the predominantly feminine confines of the department store, or feel so uncomfortable there that even special entrances and special elevators do not entirely break down their reluctance. Another reason is that men's specialty shops are usually arranged in such a way that furnishings and clothing are placed near one another, and a single salesperson can escort the customer throughout the entire store and assist him in all his purchases. Such procedures save time for the customer and make suggestion selling of second, third, fourth, or umpteenth items infinitely easier. Still another reason is the convenience of location; men's shops can be found everywhere and anywhere—in business districts, residential areas, and shopping centers.

The menswear business pie, once heavily weighted toward men's specialty stores, is now giving a slightly larger slice to the discounters, with department stores, specialty stores, and chains each holding its own shares, as illustrated in a chart in this chapter.

Channels of Distribution for Menswear

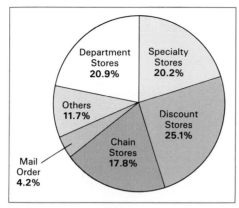

SOURCE: Apparel Marketing Monitor, 1989; AAMA Marketing Committee.

Manufacturer-Owned Retail Stores: Dual Distribution

Firmly entrenched in the menswear field is the **dual-distribution** system, whereby some large menswear manufacturers own and operate retail stores through which they sell their products — the same products that they also sell to other independent retailers for resale. Manufacturer-owned stores include in their assortments merchandise produced by other apparel makers — men's furnishings, for example, and women's wear. A prominent example is Hartmarx, whose 468 stores include such chains as Wallach's, Silverwood, and Hastings.[18] Phillips–Van Heusen, the giant shirt company, also owns many stores, including Harris and Frank, Kennedy's, and Titus MacDuff. As these examples indicate, manufacturer-owned stores are usually given names that do not identify them to the public as belonging to the producer concerned.

Marketing Activities by Trade Associations

An important point of difference between the menswear and women's apparel fields lies in the role of trade associations. In menswear, several trade associations are actively concerned with the marketing of the merchandise, acting more or less as go-betweens for producers and retailers. In the women's field, trade associations generally work only at single levels of distribution — that is, retail organizations work only with their retail members, and industry associations only with producers, as far as marketing is concerned.

FALL/WINTER PRESS PREVIEW
SCHEDULED EVENTS

WEDNESDAY, JUNE 7

2 p.m.
MFA SEMINAR: High Touch Dressing Fall/Winter Overview (Live Fashion Show)
3 p.m.
Cotton Incorporated (Live Fashion Show)
3:30 p.m.
Jeffrey Banks (Live Fashion Show)
4 p.m.
TFW/Chips 'N Twigs (Live Fashion Show)
6:30 p.m.
Perry Ellis/Roger Forsythe cocktails, followed by signature collection show at 7:30 p.m. in the Westchester Ballroom.
"Decades in Denim" sponsored by Jeanswear Communications and Lee Company with live auction of decorated jackets to benefit DIFFA.

THURSDAY, JUNE 8

8 a.m.
Designers' Portfolio breakfast in the Grand Ballroom followed by fashion presentation in the Westchester Ballroom.
9 a.m.
DESIGNERS' PORTFOLIO I:
•Jhane Barnes
•Barry Bricken
•Chose Classique
•Boston Prepatory Co.
•a.b.s. Men
•Falke/Jeff Sayre
•Bill Ditfort
•Zylos by George Machado
9:50 a.m.
Intermission
10:05 a.m.
DESIGNERS' PORTFOLIO II
•Allyn St. George
•Karl Logan
•Marienbad by Patrick Groenendaal, Stanley Steinerg
•Bill Robinson
•M. Julian by Jules Weinsieder
•Cecilia Metheny
•Mondo
•Ronaldus Shamask
11 a.m.
GQ Magazine (audio/visual)
11:30 a.m.
Combe Incorporated, presents Michael Farmer, co-founder of Age Wave, the nation's leading expert on the impact of aging baby boomers on: fashion, grooming, the future ... cookout following.
2 p.m.
Swatch (audio/visual)
2:30 p.m.
Henry Grethel (Live Fashion Show)
3 p.m.
Details Magazine (Walking style file)
3:30 p.m.
J.C. Penney (Live Fashion Show) A visual presentation of India and TEA PARTY with your hosts E.G. Smith and Paige Palmer.
6:30 p.m.
The Wool Bureau's first annual Woolmark Awards for men's wear ... cocktails, dinner, presentation. Black tie or festive dress. (Grand Ballroom Assembly, Patio, and Grand Ballroom.)

FRIDAY, JUNE 9

7:30 a.m.
Esquire Magazine breakfast in the Penfield's Patio followed by fashion video, Westchester Ballroom.

9 a.m.
Timex
9:30 a.m.
Jantzen (Live Fashion Show)
10 a.m.
Hart, Schaffner & Marx (Live Fashion Show)
10:30 a.m.
Nautica (Live Fashion Show)
11 a.m.
John Weitz (audio/visual — "Berlin Summer")
11:30 a.m.
Sears new fashion direction with its new super-stores within a store, called Kids & More and The Men's Store. Luncheon to follow. Grand Ballroom.
2 p.m.
Alfred Dunhill of London (Live Fashion Show)
2:30 p.m.
Pendleton (Live Fashion Show)
3 p.m.
The Arrow Shirt Co. (Live Fashion Show)
3:30 p.m.
National Outerwear & Sportswear Association (Live Fashion Show)
4 p.m.
BASF Seminar, Grand Ballroom
6:30 p.m.
Cultured Pearl Association cocktails party in the Westchester Assembly and preview the latest designs in cultured pearl jewelry with clothing, Westchester Ballroom.
8 p.m.
Alexander Julian celebrates his 15th anniversary with a live fashion show in the theater and dinner to follow in the Grand Ballroom.

SATURDAY, JUNE 10

8 a.m.
Commercial Office of Spain breakfast in the Grand Ballroom, followed at 9 by video highlights of Barcelona Fall '89 men's wear collections narrated by DNR columnist Clara Hancox, Westchester Ballroom.
10 a.m.
Andrew Fezza (Live Fashion Show)
10:30 a.m.
Tony Lambert (Live Fashion Show)
11 a.m.
Dimitri Couture (Live Fashion Show)
11:30 a.m.
Bausch & Lomb 1989 Donna Karan eyewear collection, followed by noon lunch in Grand Ballroom.
2-5 p.m.
PHOTOGRAPHY, INTERVIEW SESSION
(Grand Ballroom Assembly)
6:30 p.m.
Marithe & Francois Girbaud cocktail party in the Westchester Assembly followed by a showing of its collection in the Westchester Ballroom at 7:30.
8 p.m.
Serengeti eyewear by Coming Optics' MFA Masquerade, a dinner dance benefit for DIFFA, the Design Industries Foundation for AIDS.

SUNDAY, JUNE 11

8 a.m.
Breakfast/Grand Ballroom
9 a.m.-Noon
Interview session/Grand Ballroom Assembly

MFA PRESS COMMUNICATIONS
Board Rooms:
WEDNESDAY 9 a.m.-5 p.m.
THURSDAY-SATURDAY 7:30 a.m.-5 p.m.
SUNDAY 8 a.m.-Noon

CLOTHING MANUFACTURERS' ASSOCIATION

The oldest trade association in the menswear field is the **CMA**. This was formed originally by producers of tailored clothing to represent manufacturers in negotiations with the union—the "Amalgamated." Although it still performs this function, the CMA's activities have been greatly expanded. The association coordinates and publicizes the two New York market weeks each year: the January/February showings for Fall/Winter and the August/September showings for Spring/Summer. Twice a year, in January and July, the association publishes, in cooperation with *Newsweek* magazine, a trade periodical for international distribution. Appearing in three languages—English, French, and German—it undertakes to inform retailers about major fashion trends in tailored clothing. Another association function is to compile and distribute periodically to its members statistical and technical reports on developments in tailored clothing. And, of course, like most major trade associations, it is the lobbying voice of its industry.

NAMSB

A second trade association that is very active in marketing menswear is the National Association of Men's Sportswear Buyers (**NAMSB**). This organization was founded and is financially supported by store buyers of menswear as well as owners of men's stores. It was founded in 1953 to give status and identity to a then new category of menswear—sportswear. In its early years, it helped give direction to the styling of men's and boy's sportswear by recommending themes and colors the retailers considered most likely to succeed.

The NAMSB stages four show weeks a year: in January at the Sheraton Center and New York Hilton hotels, and in March, June, and October at the New York Javits Center. At each of these shows, exhibit booths are set up on several floors for the use of manufacturers in showing their lines. Although the association was founded by sportswear buyers and originally concentrated on that single category, its function has expanded to include all types of men's and boys' apparel and furnishings, including accessories and shoes. At each show week, more than 1,200 exhibitors buy space. The opportunity to view so many lines draws more than 25,000 countrywide retailers from establishments of every size and type. NAMSB estimates that more than half of these are store owners and reports that all who come to the shows come to buy. Since show weeks attract more menswear buying power than any menswear trade event, they have become a key marketing tool not only for domestic producers and retailers, but also for importers, foreign producers, and groups of overseas suppliers exhibiting under sponsorship of their governments.

MEN'S FASHION ASSOCIATION OF AMERICA

The Men's Fashion Association of America (**MFA**) is the public relations arm of the industry. It is funded by members drawn from fiber, mill, apparel manufacturing, and retail organizations, and its purpose is to make male fashions newsworthy and to provide information on the subject to the press. Press previews are held three times a year in an area near New York City in June, and in a major southwestern city such as Dallas in January or February. A Press Preview Week is held in September or October, usually on the West Coast. Each preview entails three-day seminars, supplemented by elaborate press kits, to acquaint the media with upcoming trends in menswear fashions. In addition, material is supplied to the press from time to time as the seasons progress. Activity is not limited to the print media; scripts and slides are also provided to television programs. Further encouragement to the media is the award each year of a "Lulu" for outstanding male fashion journalism in various newspaper, television, and radio categories.

THE "MAGIC" TRADE SHOW

Growing in importance is the Men's Apparel Guild of California; this show was once an association and trade show for West Coast producers only, but since 1979 has been a national men's apparel show with emphasis on sportswear. Its "MAGIC" designation is, of course, an acronym for its name. Factors in its development are the energetic promotion of the "California look" by producers, and the attraction of sportswear lines for retailers eager to capitalize on increasing demand from consumers for such apparel. The show's ability to draw retailers from a widening area has enabled it to move from a regional to a national organization. Held in Las Vegas, it is today considered as important as the NAMSB.

CALIFORNIA INTERNATIONAL MENSWEAR MARKET (CIMM)

The latest menswear trade show to make an appearance is **CIMM**, which started up in 1988. This show hopes to give major competition to the MAGIC shows. CIMM meets in Los Angeles; its importance remains uncertain at this time.

MENSWEAR TRADE SHOWINGS

In addition to the menswear group **trade shows** described above, menswear manufacturers also have the opportunity to show their wares at fashion trade shows held in various fashion centers around the world. In the United States, the **Designers' Collective**, a trade association, presents seasonal shows in New York City, with emphasis on fashion newness and innovation. Participants are a constantly growing group of menswear designers, both established and newcomers.

Other trade shows are staged by European menswear trade associations. Among them are the European Menswear Show (SEHM) in Paris, Pitti Como in

Announcement of Major Menswear Trade Show

Florence, the English Menswear Designers' Collection in London, the Scandinavian Menswear Fair in Copenhagen, and the International Men's Fashion Week in Cologne. These are seasonal showings that are presented twice a year for the major seasons — Fall/Winter and Spring/Summer.

COMPETITION FROM IMPORTS

As in the women's wear field, the menswear industry has been faced with the problem of steadily rising imports. Unable to compete with the lower prices of foreign goods, many manufacturers have turned to contracting operations in such low-wage countries as Hong Kong, Taiwan, South Korea, and China.

Although the growth rate of imports has been slowing down in the past few years, the ratio of imports to domestic production is still at historically high levels. Foreign competition has not caused as many disruptions in menswear as it has in the women's branch of the industry; however, imports of some menswear categories represent more than half of the garments available to the consumer — notably shirts, jackets, coats, and swimwear for men and boys.

Since the subject of import competition is discussed in detail in a later chapter, at this point it is sufficient to say that foreign competition is expected to continue.

FASHION EXPLOSION IN MEN'S ACCESSORIES

Great as the impact of fashion has been on men's clothing, the American male still wears essentially the same articles of dress that his father and grandfather did before him: coat, pants, shirts, ties. Color, pattern, line, and other elements may have changed, but not the basic costume. Where men have really broken loose from regimentation, however, is in accessories. Not only do they have their hair styled instead of simply cut, and not only do they use perfumes (whose very presence in the home would have scandalized the earlier generations), but they also have let themselves go in wearing medallions and gold chains, in wearing decorative identity bracelets on their wrists, in carrying shoulder and tote bags if they choose to, or in wearing western-look hats and boots if they like the idea. Not since the days of Beau Brummel have men so much indulged in fun things to wear and in uninhibited colors.

Perhaps the most important development in the total men's market is that fashion has become more important in men's lives than it ever has been before.

Readings

Not too many years ago, menswear was fashion's stepchild. Today men's interest in fashion has become increasingly pronounced and the industry that serves them has responded accordingly.

Brooks on Precedents and Presidents

George Bush is not the first U.S. president to wear Brooks Brothers suits. Practically every president since 1818, when the store was founded, has been a "Brooks Brothers Man." In fact, Abraham Lincoln was wearing a Brooks Brothers coat on the night he was assassinated.

Suit Wars

Competition has been heating up between upscale men's specialty stores as a result of a surprising and unprecedented demand for expensive tailored suits.

Two-Day Sales Trip to Up Sales: Focus on Customer Service

Herb Wallace is a sales trainer who conducts retail sales training courses in which he spreads the gospel on menswear.

Greif Companies: Megastore Trend Gives Rise to Merchandise Coordinators

In addition to its salesmen, this major menswear manufacturer has developed a team of merchandise coordinators whose function is to help their retail accounts sell the merchandise they buy.

How Hartmarx Brands America

Hartmarx, the menswear giant, has transformed itself from a manufacturing company to a marketing company and has designs on dressing almost any available customer.

BROOKS ON PRECEDENTS
AND PRESIDENTS

by Amy M. Spindler

New York—Where would Wall Streeters be without their Brooks Brothers button-down shirts, silk foulard neckwear and classic, natural-shoulder suits?

Naked, probably, since the 170-year-old company is not only responsible for introducing all these corporate staples into the U.S. market but for identifying a lifestyle as well.

And, in addition to protecting the sartorial traditions of stockbrokers in trading rooms across the country, Brooks Brothers' clientele can also thank the venerable store for introducing other classics that have endured for decades.

Included are cotton madras clothing, introduced in 1890, shetland wool sweaters in 1904, camel's hair polo coats in 1910, the lightweight summer suit in 1930, and wash-and-wear shirts in 1953.

Stock analysts who frequent the La-Farge & Morris–designed flagship store on Madison Avenue would probably appreciate the return on investment that Brooks Brothers represents. The first Brooks store, founded by Henry Sands Brooks on Catherine and Cherry streets in New York City, cost $15,250—a far cry from the $750 million that Marks & Spencer laid out for ownership of the 50-store chain last year.

While it is predicted that George Bush's preference for the Brooks Brothers attitude may further popularize its traditional clothing, he won't be the first to receive deliveries at 1600 Pennsylvania Avenue. It's been reported that practically every president since the store's founding (when James Monroe ws president) has worn Brooks Brothers suits. In fact, Abraham Lincoln was wearing a Brooks Brothers coat on the night he was assassinated.

"Bush in office can do nothing but help business over time," says Brooks Brothers' president, William Roberti, who could be mistaken for the captain of a collegiate football team. The eighth-floor executive offices of the Madison Avenue store have an Oval-Office feel themselves, with plush carpeting, wood panelling, and brass fixtures. "We dress all our customers with good taste in the conservative tradition. Jack Kennedy was one of our best customers, as the members of his family still are."

The men's specialty store that was one of the first to deliver men's off-the-peg clothing to a ready and waiting market may be steeped in tradition, but there's more brewing at Brooks than watered-down memories. After introducing a new men's wear idea every decade for almost two centuries, Brooks has returned to the drawing table to keep up one of its longest-standing traditions: innovation.

It may be hard to beat the wash-and-wear buttondown that the company introduced with Du Pont in 1953, but Roberti has high hopes. Behind his desk, a pennant from the latest sales meeting stretches out as if starched. The front reads "Brooks Brothers," illustrated with the blue-ribboned golden fleece, and the reverse reads "Participation in Innovation."

"We're definitely putting an emphasis on innovation," Roberti proudly states.

"There's been a renewed effort on product development—updating clothing

Source: *Daily News Record*, Fairchild Publications, January 19, 1989. Reprinted by permission.

models, styles, focusing on sportswear and accessories. We offer a comfortable atmosphere for our customers to shop — in confidence that the products will be in good taste. Our newest products will keep that in mind."

In short, Roberti is giving Brooks a contemporary dateline.

Any stodginess that may be associated with the gilded "346" over the double doors of the store would have to be credited to the minds of customers who haven't dropped by in the past decade.

Gone are the days when a phone call to the store to request a nightcap reportedly elicited the response, "Tasseled or untasseled?" While a newly remodeled giftware section will offer other eccentric antiquities from a more preppie past, Brooks' apparel is decidedly updated.

The broad-shouldered new president is a model for the versatility of the more youthful Brooks styling, wearing a 7-inch-drop suit in a contemporary classic check, and a wide cuff on the trousers. "Our most

contemporary suit, Brooksgate, begins at $300," he says, highlighting the store's history of carrying a customer along from its boys' department on up the corporate ladder.

Brooks' branches pepper the map like stops on a Fortune 500 travel itinerary, and the store interiors are reminiscent of Ivy League alumni halls. "We may open the stores up a bit more to show the merchandise, but they all have the same environment," Roberti explains. Brooks has replicated its old-school look throughout the chain.

Yet what is perceived as the Brooks environment is gleaned from more than just the ambience. Brooks' customers are far too savvy to be fooled by a shiny brass rack and wishbone wooden hangers . . . though without those esthetic touches Brooks would hardly be Brooks.

Whether he seeks pure cotton pajamas or a striped polo shirt, if he comes to Brooks, he expects to find what Dad found.

SUIT WARS

by Michael Gross

Bruce Newman went on a binge on the first Saturday after Labor Day. He walked out of the sun and crisp afternoon cool and into the soothing twilight of Louis, Boston, the large, new, and very expensive men's store on 57th Street at Lexington Avenue. Newman owns the Newel Art Galleries, an antiques emporium with equally breathtaking

prices, and he was about to engage in the successful man's newest ritual of city consumption — buying an entire fall-season wardrobe.

"Okay, make me look like Robert Redford," Newman said to salesman Ralph Pagano as he tried on a nail-head-woven gunmetal wool suit by Luciano Barbera.

"People will know why my prices are so high if I buy clothes like this," he joked nervously, gesturing at Louis's casually rich displays.

The clothing, presented in an atmosphere every bit as clubby and genteel as Ralph Lauren's 72nd Street shop, is high-priced, even for New York. Sweaters go for as much as $2,400. Suits like the Barbera—which is typical of the Louis stock—cost about $1,700. In fact, suit prices at Louis *begin* at $795. Newman picked out two handsome American-made tweed sport jackets from a selection that starts at about $600. "He wants them to knock around in," Pagano told Newman's wife, Judy. "He might want a better one to wear in a serious vein." The price tag on a sober double-breasted, peaked-lapel blue blazer by Ermenegildo Zegna read $895.

"Unfortunately, the more expensive ones fit better," Newman said, turning to Pagano to be sure that the blazer's sleeve buttons would actually unbutton. They would.

"I'm in a high-luxury business myself," Newman said. "And since the crash, I've seen a strange phenomenon. People are buying higher-priced items. They're more quality-conscious. If you have discriminating taste and care how you look and you can afford it—why not? You might as well have a suit that will last through the next depression." Then Newman turned back to Pagano. "Shouldn't we look at ties?"

Newman has it right. Almost a year after the stock market's plunge sent retailers into a state of shock, a surprising and unprecedented new vogue for opulence in men's clothes has put Manhattan on the front line of a new retail phenomenon—Suit Wars. The same week Louis expanded from a two-store operation in Boston, opening its 20,000-square-foot sybarite's delight

at 131 East 57th Street, Bergdorf Goodman announced that it had leased the former site of F.A.O. Schwartz for a new men's store at 745 Fifth Avenue, just across the street from the mother ship. The store, which will have 30,000 square feet on two sales floors, is expected to be open by spring 1990.

The week after Louis did, Barneys New York opened a 10,000-square-foot store on the second level of 2 World Financial Center. It is already doing big business with people who either work on Wall Street or live in the Battery Park area.

Department stores, too, are touting men's-fashion news. Bloomingdale's on 59th Street has just expanded its men's area—moving designers like Valentino, Armani, Bill Robinson, Andrew Fezza, Perry Ellis, Comme des Garçons, and Jean-Paul Gaultier down to its basement. Saks Fifth Avenue just opened a shop for the English custom tailor Edward Sexton.

Bergdorf's chairman, Ira Neimark, professes to see no trend here, putting the boom down to real-estate serendipity rather than premeditation. "Property became available," he says matter-of-factly. Louis and Barneys are retail anchors in newly developed office buildings. The F.A.O. Schwartz space has been empty since April 1986.

But obviously, there is a new customer willing to spend large sums for clothes—even if he can't do it on the scale of a Henry Kravis, who recently snapped up more than 100 shirts in one visit to Ascot Chang, the Hong Kong shirt-maker with a year-old branch at 7 West 57th Street.

"We're selling better better than anything else," says Ralph Lauren. "Better" generally means suits that start at $700.

"People are crying out," adds Robert Stock, who just launched Finery, an exclusive collection for Ascot Chang featuring exquisite handmade clothes at extravagant prices. Stock thinks fashion is prospering despite economic anxiety because it is "a cheap fix compared to a house or a car."

Most retailers say they welcome the new competition. "I'm not concerned, not at all," Lauren says. "It's good for the city. It's good for awareness." Adds Neimark, "It's a big pond." But off the record and behind the scenes, sniping had already begun before the construction crews left the city's new stores. And it isn't as simple as New York retailers' reacting against the carpetbagger from Boston, because the local teams all regard one another warily, too.

Neimark thinks things will get nasty. "It's going to be very exciting," he says. But that may be true because "there are only so many men in New York who will spend $1,000 on a suit," says Bill Flink, vice-president of Hickey-Freeman, Inc., which sells suits under its own label and that of Britain's Gieves & Hawkes.

In the once-gentlemanly, now-crowded men's-wear world, the gloves are coming off. "I want to be challenged by the best market in the world, and I think it might be here," says Murray Pearlstein, the owner of Louis, who estimates that although his rent in New York will be four times higher than in Boston, the potential market here is "ten times greater."

"It's challenging as hell," says Clifford Grodd, president of Paul Stuart, where a typical suit costs about $700 and the best — an off-the-rack cashmere-and-wool suit — goes for $2,200.

To be sure, men's clothes remain, as they always have been, fashion's stepchild. But now, "women's wear is lagging behind," says designer John Weitz, quickly adding that "the men's wear 'explosion' is a matter of sales, not fashion."

As men's wardrobes have evolved, men's-clothing businesses — especially those selling stylish yet proper tailored suits, jackets, trousers, and coats — have prospered. "The better-men's business hasn't been this good in a decade," says Nick Hilton, president of the century-old clothier Norman Hilton. "A $500 suit looks great when you buy it. Two years later, it's a rat's nest," Hilton claims. But as prices rise, he promises, suits are "palpably different — obviously better."

Many of the differences are in subtleties of manufacture such as stress-point reinforcement and the material used to line the front of the jacket (hand-sewn canvas is more durable and supple than the stiff, glued-in interfacing that characterizes inexpensive suits, for example). Other differences are more obvious. "Ten years ago, you wore scratchy, heavy suits," Hilton says. Today, though, spinning, weaving, and even sheep-farming have advanced to the point where Murray Pearlstein can demonstrate a Louis suit's lightness and quality by taking his jacket off, scrunching it into a tight ball, and then putting it on again, unscrunched. "It's like eating fresh food instead of frozen," says Ermenegildo Zegna, whose Italian label is sold at both Louis and Barneys.

The evolving interest and taste in clothes among men seem at last to have beaten down the notion that fashion is somehow unmanly. Increased newspaper coverage and changes in fashion magazines like *GQ*, which moved away from a perceived gay point of view in the eighties, made men's fashion and its trends more accessible.

Ralph Lauren is often singled out as a man responsible for sparking the men's wear explosion. "I give him a lot of credit for showing how to do it," says Pearlstein. "He merely did what should have been done," says Neimark. "He represented himself properly. Not many take the pain and effort."

The prospering men's specialty stores do, but not so long ago, their movement was out of business, and the same thing was happening to the traditional clothing firms that supplied them. "There are very few really fine producers of men's clothing left in the world," says Bill Flink. "Little merchants couldn't afford to stay in business. That's why the good merchants who have survived are now getting a bigger share of the pie." Their expansion comes after a decline that "left New York understored," says Hilton. "The void became glaring."

Lauren saw that department stores lacked the resources and atmosphere to fill the growing demand for expensive tailored clothing. He saw Paul Stuart, Brooks Brothers, and Barneys doing well by offering both service and well-defined personality. As a retailer, he combined service, atmosphere, and stock in a unified approach to a customer "who was traditional, but with flair," he says.

His stunning success helped promote archetypal American looks around the world. "American influences—Brooks Brothers, L. L. Bean, Lauren, Levi's, preppies—apply worldwide," says John Weitz. "We're too self-effacing as a nation," adds Hilton. "We lead in marketing, merchandise, and look. We're what everyone is doing. Now they can come here to get it." Manhattan is challenging London's Savile Row and Rome's Via Condotti as a source for seekers of masculine style. "We *are* Rome," Grodd declares bluntly.

Even Europeans agree. "There is only one city with so many things going on," says Zegna, who believes that New York has become a showcase "for the best of the world. New York is the flagship. It is leading not only the States but Europe."

Much of this growth has come at the expense of the city's large department stores. Many say those chain stores suffer from a sameness of merchandise, deficiencies in service, lack of stock, and too much reliance on well-known labels that skimp on value. Bruce Newman said he was particularly impressed by the quality of the sales help at Louis. After bantering with a salesman and fitter about dimples, pleats, and cuffs, he said, "Too many stores will hire anyone with a heartbeat." Fashion professionals also cite the recent wave of takeovers, amalgamations, and leveraged buyouts. These factors have all fed the growth of the specialized shops.

To be fair, specialty stores, too, often carry similar merchandise. Both Barneys and Louis have the Zegna, Barbera, and Mariano Rubinacci labels, as well as private-label suits from the same factories. There are sometimes slight price differences. So sales staffs play up slight style differences. Top specialty stores tend to have exclusive fabrics, colors, and details. Louis, for example, is stressing brown in about half its retro-style suits and jackets this season. But the similarities are as striking as the differences. Flink says the Gieves & Hawkes suit sold at Barneys is similar to Hickey-Freeman's, and they are made in the same factory. The "exclusive" Chester Barrie suit sold at Louis is essentially the same—and made in the same factory—as the "exclusive" Turnbull & Asser suit now sold at the London haberdashery's Bergdorf boutique, two manufacturers say.

The Turnbull shop will be a cornerstone of Bergdorf's new men's store. And the fact that there will be such shops—for designers (like Armani) and foreign retailers (like Turnbull and Charvet)—is the one detail that Neimark will reveal. Bergdorf will discuss only its commitment to build—but that was enough for it to be mentioned in every news story about the Louis and Barneys expansions. Though Neimark says he's expanding only because the real estate was too good to pass up, he claims he can see an untapped market from his desk. "Come to the window with me," he says, pointing up Fifth Avenue. "From 57th Street to 96th Street. Every building, easily 25 to 100 people. Untold wealth. Park Avenue. Both sides of the street. Look over here. Central Park West. Three-, four-, five-million-dollar apartments. These apartments aren't empty." Neimark believes that the occupants will happily pay Bergdorf's prices (which range from a typical $600-to-$900 suit to $1,600 for Bergdorf's best Armani or Valentino couture).

But all the city's top-rank retailers are fighting for that customer and to distinguish their stores from the rest. "I'm somewhat amused by firms pushing a look considered stylish 40 years ago," says Paul Stuart's Grodd. "A look that used to say 'right off the boat' is now fashion." Though he doesn't mention names, he's described the current Louis look. Grodd is equally critical of stores—Barneys and Bergdorf, for instance—that take what he calls the supermarket approach. "You don't go to a supermarket if you can afford a butcher," he says, stressing Stuart's consistency and substance. Others sell "the frosting," he says. "We bake the cake [for a customer who] can't be offensive. Who, when the smoke is blown away, is still there, making a statement."

Louis bakes a cake, too, though quite a different one. Pearlstein, whose father and uncle founded the store 65 years ago, readily agrees that his customer likes fashion. "We buy the European taste and mentality," he says. "We are an alternative. A little more individual. A guy can be acceptable and still not look like everybody else. We offer the service and focus of a small store

with the selection of a big store. I don't think anyone carries a more extensive line of high-quality merchandise. With all due respect, they don't do it the way we do. Our eyes are open to what people don't own."

The Louis triplex, created by Stedila Design, is a luxurious study in polished granite, pearwood Biedermeier cabinetry, black ash, mahogany, brass, brushed steel, and glass tile. The ground floor offers American-made clothing, including two- and three-button and double-breasted suits developed by A. H. Freedberg of Boston. Stairs lead to an atrium and greenhouse, a second-floor women's department, and the spacious third floor—featuring 40 windows overlooking the street and an espresso bar, imported clothing, casual- and outerwear, formal clothes (including a $2,500 tuxedo), and such accessories as Borsalino hats and shoes by Lobb's.

At Barneys, the Pressman family members are reacting to Louis the way New Yorkers should, with street-smart pride. Just as Ira Neimark is quick to point out that he "opened" in the World Financial Center first, by sponsoring Christian Lacroix's coming-out party in the Winter Garden, the Pressmans claim first place in the hearts of hometown fans over the Louis-come-lately from Boston.

"It's the range that they love. It's not just going into a particular store with a single point of view," Fred Pressman says, leading a tour of his new antiques- and mahogany-filled U-shaped store, overlooking the Hudson River as well as the construction site of a planned marina.

"We have the pure soft-shoulder customer," he continues. "We have the slightly lower button. The rounded shoulder. The straighter, leaner coat, too. He may buy a natural-shoulder suit and an Armani tie.

That's not Ivy League. That's not boring. They want to mix it all up. That's our reason for being. We cover the looks. It's not like four different stores."

Like Louis, the new Barneys, which was designed by architect Peter Marino, offers both off-the-rack and made-to-measure clothing. The selection is wider, though.

Suits run from $475 to $1,300, shirts from $60 to $155, and ties from $18 to $65. Labels include Brioni; Armani; Gianfranco Ferre; H. Huntsman & Sons; Kilgour, French & Stanbury; and Polo by Ralph Lauren. Several islands on the selling floor offer both new and antique jewelry, sweaters, British barbershop products from Geo. F. Trumper, small leather goods, luxury hosiery, and Swiss underwear.

After encountering many unexpected costs and difficulties in launching their women's store in the eighties, the Pressmans seem content to bask in the sun coming off the river and enjoy the crowds of natural-shoulder Wall Street men learning about Armani ties in their new school of style.

"We built a store on time for a change," Gene Pressman says. "And on budget," adds his brother, Bob.

But when the subject turns to competition, the Barneys family becomes circumspect. "I don't want to mention any names," Fred Pressman says. Other Barneys execs are feistier. "We'd only have competition if we opened a store full of greens, browns, and $1,400 suits," one says. "We thought we'd give them that market."

Louis will also get the uptown men who are "too lazy" to go downtown to Barneys. "I don't have a visa for south of 23rd Street," Bruce Newman said after spending nearly $5,000 at Louis.

But that Saturday another shopper who usually spends his money at Barneys wasn't as keen on the new guy's chances. As luxe as the shop is, it isn't New York, he said: "The least they could do is spell it Looie."

TWO-DAY SALES TRIP TO UP SALES: FOCUS ON CUSTOMER SERVICE

by Jules Abend

Herb Wallace is a gracious host. Herb Wallace is a country preacher. Herb Wallace is a motivating salesman.

In fact, Herb Wallace is all of the above . . . and more. Just ask executives and sales personnel in some of the country's leading department and specialty stores.

What Wallace does is conduct semi-nars on how to sell, presumably for men's department staffs, but actually for the entire store, in a way that lifts his presentation above the commercialism of his product.

Wallace is so fair, and detailed, in the way he delivers the information that the meetings become generic in nature. That alone endears the man representing The Greif Companies to his audiences.

His audiences have been many. He was reached for this article at The Parisian in Birmingham and was moving on from there to entertain and educate other people who manage and sell not only men's clothing, but any variety of quality products, at retail.

Wallace has been giving a Retail Sales Training Course for about two years. During that period, he has been to 225 stores and has seen nearly 9,000 people.

Among his satisfied customers are: Bullock's (the store participated in the first experimental course); Neiman-Marcus; I. Magnin; Dillard's; Macy's; Rich's and Saks Fifth Avenue.

Greif naturally fits into the better stores, making garments bearing the labels of Polo University Club, Chaps by Ralph Lauren, Perry Ellis, Lanvin, and Kilgour French & Stanbury to name a few.

The proof of his success is that Wallace has been invited back by—and has returned to—many of the retailers for subsequent presentations. He is booked through 1989.

Wallace was not always a professional lecture circuiteer. He joined Greif more than a decade ago to organize its career apparel division. He earlier was with Hartmarx.

That division has become a dominant force in its niche, with volume expected to increase $7 million this year. And at one point Wallace was national sales manager as well.

When he turned 65, he relinquished some of those responsibilities, although he's still involved, and concentrated on doing the schools at the behest of the company chairman.

Wallace says: "The chairman and I signed an agreement I won't retire."

The schools aren't a way of being put out to pasture, judging by the money Greif

spends and the personnel it supplies to maintain the program—about $500,000 annually along with two support people who back up Wallace.

But what does he do exactly? To hear store executives tell it, everything to stimulate excellence on the selling floor.

Sue Graham, general manager of Bullock's South Coast Plaza store, says: "The thing that's special about Herb is that he talks the way that selling associates understand.

"He is involved with people who sell. And he can really relate to how we feel when working with a customer, and also, he thinks like a customer.

"He can tell you how a customer perceives the experience by the way you use a certain selling technique. For example, if you show a beautiful necklace on a piece of velvet, that shows the customer you respect it and that it is very special.

"He talks about the way you present merchandise in every detail; that the customer is starting a scorecard the minute the person walks in the door."

Graham notes that a most important aspect of Wallace's school is the way he talks about selling as a profession, stressing, "I think he gives a self-respect and confidence even to people who have been around for 40 years. They need that."

She emphasizes, "We talk about selling a lot, but Herb gets the point across. His communication of selling is very clear. And few people have that kind of background —to be able to talk selling and make it interesting."

Although the effects of any seminar are hard to measure, Graham claims that right after one presentation, her store's sales increased by 50% on that particular day.

She adds that an unproductive salesman increased his self esteem to such an extent that several weeks later he was promoted to a managerial position.

She adds, "Everybody has a program to sell, but Herb just talks to you about taking care of customers and what customers see. He tells you all the ingredients of selling.

"It's more than simply taking care of the customer. It's how the alterations staff works with them, it's the way the sales associates dress and how they're groomed. He's very alive and energetic. When he talks selling, he feels it."

Wayne Meichner and Derrill Osborn couldn't agree more. Meichner, assistant general merchandise manager, Saks Fifth Avenue, is a new fan.

Osborn, vice president, merchandise manager of men's clothing for Neiman-Marcus, who has enjoyed the exposure to Wallace's experience from the beginning, says: "You have a lot of people who talk about product knowledge, but you do not have many who know how to sell it. How do you open a sale? How do you close a sell? What is in-between? How to put on a jacket? How to treat the customer all the while?

"Those kinds of things—things that you can only obtain in men's clothing through experience—that's what he does best. He's a salesman. He knows the subject very well and he talks directly to the sales associates. That is the key to his success."

Osborn reflects that Wallace is the missing link between the standards of the 1940s and '50s and the societal changes that occurred later, saying, "The most important thing today is that there is a new generation of sellers. All the great ones are gone or retired.

"Came the '70s and '80s with no service—so what he has to say through his own experiences is refreshing, surprisingly to management as well as to sales associates.

"Plus, Herb is a great deliverer. He's a great motivator with great inflection in his voice."

Saks Fifth Avenue, with a reputation of being a premier quality store, doesn't impress easily. But management recently accepted Greif's invitation to send 80 people, over four and a half days, to Greif's headquarters in Allentown, Pa., for Wallace's program.

Why? Meichner explains, "It's not a 'Greif' seminar and that's the reason we agreed to do it. It was a presentation that was productive for all the merchandise we carry.

"It was a generic tour of a clothing facility as well as a motivational seminar, really hitting home to some very experienced sales people.

"It was impressive. I put all 25 of my managers through, not just clothing people—the furnishings, women's shoe and collections people were in attendance.

"At least half the 40 sales associates who attended have written Herb personally, thanking him for the day and the information. And my clothing people have an average 25 years in selling and they have heard enough seminars to last a lifetime."

Wallace's response to him, and anybody who asks, is, "If the level of professionalism doesn't improve at retail where sales people can tell a customer why they need to buy quality garments, we're not going to be able to sell better merchandise.

"We said we need to become more of a partner with the retailer in helping him move better garments. And being that partner, we would go and help stores develop the sophistication and a level of professionalism for their sales associates."

In essence, the manufacturer is insuring that the best stores are marketing properly so they continue to provide a healthy business.

Wallace contends there isn't much

meaningful training being done on the floor, and Meichner says, "Typically, there is not a person on the floor who can pass on expertise. So the seminar has a lot of merit.

"Nobody is doing it to the extent Wallace is. Not even close. He's a good extemporaneous speaker. He captures your attention. He knocks you down and builds you back up. He really gets you thinking about what you are doing with yourself."

Wallace's dog-and-pony shows are done with style. His aim is to convince the sales staff they are important and that is reflected in the smallest details; silver coffee urns and silverware and china cups are used during the breaks, as an example.

The program usually runs for two days and Wallace insists that management participate the first day, "because we can get the sales associates highly motivated when they leave but then you send them back to the same old management.

"So we always talk to the managers first about their role as leaders to develop ordinary people to their highest potential.

"We tell them they can be the best buyers in the world with the finest facilities but the only two things that count are products—and everybody can buy the same products—and service.

"The service is dependent upon people. And if the people aren't highly motivated; if they don't understand their responsibility and they don't have a mission or a vision; and they don't understand that they're the conduit from the store to the customer, then nothing is going to happen; that management 'by walking around,' must be a daily thing."

GRIEF COMPANIES: MEGASTORE TREND GIVES RISE TO MERCHANDISE COORDINATORS

by Stan Gellers

New York—Responding to the vastly different department store landscape where fewer merchandisers are making more buying decisions, the Greif Companies is in the process of restructuring its sales organization on a marketing basis.

According to David Pergola, senior vice-president sales and marketing, the "less is more" buying policy and the proliferation of branches is resulting in a new way of doing business.

And it's his belief that with top store management making the major decisions as to whether a clothing label is in or out, the trend will intensify. The payoff? The role of the traditional clothing salesmen—the "Willy Lomans"—will change radically. In the case of dealing with megastores, the real challenge won't be to sell, but to insure sell-through of a line, he claims.

Pergola explains the traditional talents of the so-called "big sellers" will be eclipsed by the need for different skills in the new megastore–vendor relationships.

With product and merchandising knowledge, the new key players will function as account executives and run interference for vendors at point of sale. He calls them merchandise coordinators.

Pergola's proposal is to add a new layer of these service people to the selling hierarchy to the informational liaison between the store and Greif. He admits that the concept has worked in a few spots in the women's business and seemed like a natural in the men's clothing industry.

He reports, "Regular salesmen who chased orders and spent time doing paperwork will be freed up to sell independent specialty stores. The merchandise coordinators, meanwhile, will not perform a selling function, but a marketing function.

"They will go to branches regularly to provide marketing intelligence to the store and to us. In addition, they'll sharpen visual presentation and product display and tackle problems as they arise. All of this will be fed to our newly created marketing department and the information will be relayed back to the buyers."

In addition, he says the department stores will also get input on what's happening in comparable branch operations at other major stores for comparison.

Greif now has 25 salesmen nationally and is building a second team of six merchandise coordinators who will be responsible for all of the company labels: Chaps by Ralph Lauren and Polo University; Perry Ellis and Perry Ellis Portfolio; Colours by Alexander Julian; Lanvin and Lanvin Studio; Kilgour French & Stanbury and Donald Brooks.

The company's strong position with megastores was the main reason for management's search for a better way of getting sell-through. Pergola points out that for spring and fall 1988, 4 percent of the company's major department store customers accounted for half of Greif's business, while an additional 8 percent (including major specialty stores) generated 70 percent of the volume. The remaining volume was done by an overwhelming 88 percent of the customers—independent retailers.

Pergola says point blank, "Our goal now is to get more small specialty store business."

Under the new set-up at Greif, presentations to major store groups will be made by the merchandisers or stylists for each of the company's labels. They report to the head of each division, a salesmanager, and naturally have an intimate knowledge of their own line.

Greif, he asserts, wants to be able to offer the heavy hitters a new kind of package. "The stores want knowledge about the product . . . information about the status of their orders . . . and real help at point-of-sale." That's where the new merchandise coordinators come in. He adds, "We don't want the selling effort to end with a salesman who sells the line."

To get this show on the road, Pergola pulled another switch and began signing on a number of young bloods who were either ex-retailers or from the sportswear business. Some graduated from their customer service jobs. He jokes, "We didn't want any recycled clothing salesmen."

The new crew of merchandise coordinators will grow to seven by February. At this point, to Pergola, they're the eyes and ears which he feels have been lacking. He observes, "Most importantly, the merchandise coordinators will be a new direct link with the consumers. They'll be on the scene to monitor preferences and give us the best reading of how we perform at retail."

HOW HARTMARX BRANDS AMERICA

by Robert Sharoff

Hartmarx, the nation's biggest combined tailored clothing and specialty retailer, is as nimble as a legendary designer or a landmark men's store in staking out and selling its customers.

But the Chicago-based $1.2 billion giant does it for seven different customer types with a string of famous clothing names—from Hart Schaffner & Marx to Pierre Cardin, Nino Cerruti and Johnny Carson.

And the same rifle-shot approach is used for the company's sprawling retail operation, with such venerable nameplates as Basin, Wallachs, Raleighs and F. R. Tripler, and many more.

In all, the Hartmarx stable has 32 apparel brands and 468 retail stores. The manufacturing arm generates 46.6 percent of the volume; retail contributes a whopping 53.4 percent. Each operating division has a distinct fashion attitude and pricing —an innovative marketing approach that took years to define and refine.

The strategy of niche marketing began in the late 1970s after the successful launch of Austin Reed, the British retail and clothing name. Its success soon led Hartmarx into becoming the clothing licensee for Christian Dior and a string of other designer names and brands. All became vehicles for Hartmarx to reshape the way it operates.

Today, niche marketing dictates all decisions of the manufacturing and retail divisions.

Discussing the company's marketing strategy, Bert Hand, president and chief operating officer, explains, "We've gone from a manufacturing to a marketing company." And there's plenty of evidence to support this claim.

He cites a marketing grid in the company's 1988 annual report that divides the clothing market into seven fashion categories and four price segments.

Hartmarx segments its brands and retail stores for each of these target customers by their fashion tastes. And this is further broken out by upper, upper moderate, moderate and popular prices.

- *Business professional:* Hickey-Freeman, Walter Morton, Graham & Gunn Stores, Hart Schaffner & Marx, Sansabelt Ltd. Dress Slacks, Hartmarx Specialty Stores; Sansabelt Suits and Slacks, Jaymar Dress Slacks, Gleneagles; Allyn St. George and Kuppenheimer stores.
- *Natural-shoulder traditional:* Hickey-Freeman VSSC; Graham & Gunn clothing, Briar, H. Oritsky.
- *American fashion contemporary:* Society Brand, Henry Grethel, Henry Grethel Studio stores, Johnny Carson.
- *British:* Gieves & Hawkes, Austin Reed, New Bond Street, Racquet Club– Wimbledon.
- *Italian:* Nino Cerruti, Confezioni Riserva/ Luciano Franzoni.
- *French:* Christian Dior, Pierre Cardin.
- *American sportsman:* Bobby Jones, Jack Nicklaus, Sansabelt Golf.

On the manufacturing side, the company has been restructured to cater to each of these market segments. The Hartmarx Men's Apparel Group, under Hand, now

Source: *Daily News Record*, June 5, 1989. Reprinted with permission.

has three divisions with a combination of national and house brands as well as designer labels: Hart Schaffner & Marx; Intercontinental Branded Apparel and American Apparel Brands.

The retailing side, under the helm of Harvey Weinberg, chairman and chief executive officer, is equally ambitious. In men's wear, there are the Hartmarx Specialty stores; the Graham & Gunn Group (including Henry Grethel Studio); Kuppenheimer Men's Clothiers and the Sansabelt Stores.

Discussing the background of the company's move into marketing, Hand recalls, "Back in the '70s, we were very strong with business and professional clothing with Hickey-Freeman and Hart Schaffner & Marx. Then came the 1973–74 recession and a turning point in the clothing market. "Before that, the business was very fragmented," the executive continues, "and there were a lot of companies run as manufacturing outfits rather than as marketing companies. There weren't a lot of different looks. The choices were mainly different brands."

During the ensuing period of takeovers and closings of many oldtimers, Hand claims Americans were getting exposed to, and began accepting, European clothing influences.

"The result is that the remaining major players began to expand their fashion bases. Our first big post-recession effort was Austin Reed. The problem was we were trying to emulate what we saw in Britain—real British models, very shouldered, very formal.

"We had to do a line together that Americans think British clothing is—rather than what it really is. The result? The line took off like gangbusters and it was our first indication that niching—going after a market where we weren't represented—was do-able."

Reed, the "moderate-priced British fashion" line, now does about $50 million a year. Its success led to the licensing of Christian Dior, the second major label, which was focused between the young and the more mature customer.

Hand adds, "I think both in terms of price points and styles when I think of growth in the clothing market. And this means selection, clothes that fit well and good service in the stores. Otherwise, it's tough to survive in the clothing business."

Fashion is another issue, the executive contends. "Everything ebbs and flows. Back in the late '70s, the French designers, like Yves Saint Laurent, were the hot guys. Then the Italians came in. The British look has been quiet recently, but now the Italians are starting to show British looks, so I think a resurgence of them is on the way."

On niche marketing, Hand asserts, "You have to pick your market, but a comparable fashion can be at different price points. Upper-moderate Austin Reed and upper Gieves & Hawkes are good examples. The key point is to stay focused."

As a marketing company, Hartmarx conducts extensive research on the clothing industry. Hand particularly likes focus groups where consumers air their likes and dislikes to an anchor person. "They're great if you have a specific question you want answered.

"A couple of years ago, I wanted to know why someone—not who—buys an HS&M suit. We conducted focus groups and learned men perceive HS&M to be the correct suit for business situations. That's how we came up with 'The Right Suit' ad campaign."

The moderate-price area is the spot the company has been going after aggressively with its Henry Grethel and Racquet Club labels. Briar, a complete package of traditional tailored clothing, neckwear and dress shirts, is expected to do $20 million this year.

"We're positioning Grethel to become our next big tailored clothing business," asserts Hand, who expects designer clothing, sportswear and furnishings to do about $25 million. Racquet Club sportswear, occupying the same market niche as Austin Reed, is currently being streamlined.

Similarly, the Bobby Jones sportswear line in the upscale Hickey-Freeman division has been expanded substantially for this customer with more leisure time.

Discussing the dramatic changes in the retail landscape, Hand observes, "I see specialty stores coming back. They have the ability to focus in and service customers better than the average department store. Specialty stores have tended to be more traditional. Now, they're more fashion-oriented and contemporary. The changes in our stores show what's happening."

Hart's specialty stores formerly occupied an upper-moderate price niche, but in the last year it has aimed both higher and lower. Expansion has come mostly through acquisition. In 1988, Hartmarx bought Raleighs, Washington, D.C., and Boyd's, St. Louis.

Weinberg admits, "In our expansions, we had to be cognizant of our wholesale customers. We didn't feel we could just go into cities and disturb the channel of distribution by selling the same product as the independents. There is some overlap and we hear about it. But we think our offerings will be better than the stores that are already in the market."

Graham & Gunn, a chain developed by Hartmarx, is the national version of Root's, the traditional store in New Jersey and Massachusetts. Weinberg explains the growing chain "has a very specific look — traditional, upscale, natural-shouldered clothing." Suits range from $395 to $900.

Graham & Gunn, meanwhile, is aimed at midsize markets. The Hartmarx executive reports, "We did a lot of market research and there seems to be a real opportunity for a well-executed traditional store in Memphis, Tenn., and Omaha, Neb., in an upscale environment."

Weinberg adds the expansion plan differs from the usual expansion by acquisition. "There aren't a lot of soft-shouldered stores to buy." The Graham group also gives Hart's the chance to reenter markets previously surrendered to independents.

Weinberg says Hart's regular specialty stores — Wallachs, Baskin, Silverwoods, etc. — while broader in concept, are still very focused. He explains, "They're focused on business people. Essentially, they carry Hickey-Freeman, HS&M, Austin Reed and some private label under the name of International Passport.

"We cater to all kinds of business customers. Some wear Hickey and some like Italian styling. Our slogan is 'We'll dress you for business, the rest is up to you.'"

Kuppenheimer, the new Hartmarx retail cash cow, is also "right on target," according to Weinberg. He calls it the fastest-growing group of stores we own ". . . with a fine product, a good price and in a specialty store ambience." The chain has been renovated and the merchandise reoriented so that the clothing now is mainly all-wool. Prices are in the $175-to-$250 range.

The three Grethel contemporary sportswear stores — something new for the company — are in and around Chicago and at an experimental stage. Confesses Weinberg, "We want to see how the stores do in different retail environments before expanding."

The Sansabelt Stores are geared for another sportswear customer with more mainstream tastes. At this point the complete Jaymar-Ruby line of sportswear, slacks and blazers is carried.

Plans call for broadening of Sansabelt Ltd., a new, upscale traditional collection for a more fashion-conscious customer.

This fine-tuning is typical of Hartmarx, which has to be the most successful company in targeting and selling the biggest pieces of the American men's wear market.

Endnotes

1. *U.S. Industrial Outlook, 1990.* Department of Commerce.
2. U.S. Department of Commerce, Bureau of Economic Analysis.
3. Claudia Kidwell and Margaret C. Christman, *Suiting Everyone.* Washington, D.C.: Smithsonian Institution Press, 1974.
4. Harry Cobrin, *The Men's Clothing Industry: Colonial through Modern Times.* New York: Fairchild Publications, 1971.
5. Kidwell and Christman, p. 53.
6. U.S. Department of Commerce, *Standard Industrial Classification Manual.*
7. U.S. Census of Manufacturers, 1989.
8. Ibid.
9. "The Impact of Fitness on the Cut of Clothes," *New York Times, Men's Fashions of the Times,* September 5, 1985.
10. "At $1500, His Clothes Make the Man," *New York Times,* July 9, 1982.
11. Barry Wishnow, CEO of Hugo Boss, *Daily News Record,* April 5, 1989.
12. Harry Cobrin, *The Men's Clothing Industry,* p. 317.
13. Neal Anderson, Wrangler's vice president of consumer marketing, *Daily News Record,* April 16, 1989.
14. Herbert Blueweiss, "Perspective," *Daily News Record,* March 6, 1989.
15. Rachel Spevack, "Marketplace," *Daily News Record,* March 20, 1989.
16. Nicholas DiPaolo, president of Manhattan Industries, *Daily News Record,* September 1, 1988.
17. "A License to Make Money," *Forbes,* December 3, 1984.
18. Hartmarx, 1989 annual stockholders' report.

Selected Bibliography

Bennet-England, Rodney. *Dress Optional: the Revolution in Menswear.* Chester Springs, Penna.: Dufour, 1968.

Boyer, Bruce. *Elegance: A Guide to Quality in Menswear.* New York, W. W. Norton, 1984.

Carlson, Peter, and William Wilson. *Manstyle: The GQ Guide to Fashion, Fitness and Grooming*. New York: Clarkson, Potter, 1977.

Cobrin, Harry. *The Men's Clothing Industry: Colonial through Modern Times*. New York: Fairchild Publications, 1971.

Cray, Edward. *Levis*. New York: Houghton Mifflin, 1979.

Dolce, Donald W. *The Consumer's Guide to Menswear*. New York: Dodd, 1983.

Dyer, Ron and Spark. *Fit to Be Tied: Vintage Neckwear of the Forties and Early Fifties*. New York: Ron Abbeville Press, 1987.

Editors of *Menswear Magazine*. *75 Years of Men's Wear Fashion 1890–1965*. New York: Fairchild Publications, 1965.

Feldman, Egal. *FIT for Men*. Washington, D.C.: Public Affairs Press, 1960.

Flusser, Alan. *Clothes and the Man*. New York: Villard Books, 1985.

Hyde, Jack. *Esquire's Encyclopedia of 20th Century Men's Fashions*, 2d ed. New York: Abrams Publications, 1990.

Jackson, Carole, and Kalia Luow. *Color for Men*. New York: Balantine, 1984.

Laver, James. *Dandies*. London: Weidenfeld and Nicholson, Ltd., 1968.

Martin, Richard and Harold Koda. *Men's Styles in the Twentieth Century*. New York: Rizzoli International Publications, Inc., 1989.

Molloy, John T. *Dress for Success*. New York: P. H. Wyden, 1975.

Shapiro, H. T. *Man, Culture and Society*. London: Oxford University Press, 1956.

Tolman, Ruth. *Selling Men's Fashion*. New York: Fairchild Publications, 1982.

Wagenvoord, James. *The Man's Book: A Complete Manual of Style*. New York: Avon, 1978.

Wilson, William, and Editors of *Esquire* Magazine. *Man at His Best*. Reading, Mass.: Addison-Wesley, 1985.

Winnick, Charles. *The New People: Desexualization in American Life*. New York: Pegasus, 1968.

Trade Associations

Boys' and Young Men's Apparel Manufacturer's Association, 350 Fifth Avenue, New York, N.Y. 10018.

Clothing Manufacturers Association, 1290 Avenue of the Americas, New York, N.Y. 10004.

Designers Collective, Inc., 3 East 54th Street, New York, N.Y. 10022.

Men's Apparel Guild in California, 124 West Olympia Boulevard, Los Angeles, Calif. 90015.

Men's Fashion Association of America, 240 Madison Avenue, New York, N.Y. 10016.

National Association of Men's Sportswear Buyers, 535 Fifth Avenue, New York, N.Y. 10017.

Young Menswear Association, 1328 Broadway, New York, N.Y. 10001.

Trade Publications

Business Newsletter of Menswear Retailers of America, 2011 Eye Street, Northwest, Suite 600, Washington, D.C. 20006.

California Men's Stylist, 945 South Wall Street, Los Angeles, Calif. 90015.

Custom Tailors and Designers Association of America, Inc., 565 Fifth Avenue, New York, N.Y. 10017.

Daily News Record, 7 East 12th Street, New York, N.Y. 10003.

Made-to-Measure Magazine, 300 West Adams Street, Chicago, Ill. 60606.

Masculines, 225 East 36th Street, New York, N.Y. 10016.

Men's and Boys' Scene, Seymour Middlemark Organization, Inc., Lincoln Building, Suite 631, 40 East 42nd Street, New York, N.Y. 10165.

Men's Apparel News, 110 West 40th Street, New York, N.Y. 10008.

Menswear Magazine, 7 East 12th Street, New York, N.Y. 10003.

CHAPTER REVIEW AND LEARNING ACTIVITIES

Key Words and Concepts

Define, identify, or briefly explain the following:

ACTWUA	Levi-Strauss
CIMM	The "MAGIC" show
CMA	MFA
Collection concept	NAMSB
Custom tailors	"Slops"
Designers' Collective	Standardized sizes
Drop	Tailored clothing
Dual distribution	Tailors to the trade
Hartmarx	Trade show

Review Questions on Chapter Highlights

1. Why were the shops that produced men's ready-to-wear in the early nineteenth century known as "slop shops"?

2. Name two developments of the nineteenth century that contributed to the growth of the menswear industry and explain their effect.

3. How does the menswear industry differ from the women's apparel industry? In what ways are they similar?

4. How do the procedures of the men's tailored clothing segment of the industry differ from those of the other segments of the menswear industry?

5. How do the sizes of men's tailored clothing differ from those of men's sportswear? Why?

6. What is the meaning of the "collection concept" in men's clothing? Why has it developed?

7. Why do male customers continue to be attracted to specialized menswear retailers?

8. What trade associations play an important role in the marketing of menswear? What is their importance?

9. Name and compare two of the major menswear companies discussed in the readings.

10. Why is fashion today more important to men than it was formerly? Is it as important to men as it is to women? Why or why not?

6

FASHION ACCESSORIES AND INTIMATE APPAREL

Like a pebble dropped in a lake, every fashion change in apparel creates a ripple of change in the industries that produce fashion accessories and intimate apparel. The total look that the wearer seeks to achieve demands such change. For example, a blazer jacket may invite the use of a tucked-in scarf; a long skirt may require a long slip; short skirts may focus enough attention on the leg to suggest eye-catching patterns in hosiery; shoes may change shape and heel height to become good companions to current clothes; belts may be wide and colorful when waistlines are important, and vanish when dresses hang straight. Jewelry, too, must conform, playing to the high or low neckline, the short or long sleeve, or whatever are the important features of the garment. Even precious heirlooms may be consigned to the vault for a time if the prevailing "look" is wrong for the treasured pieces. Accessories conform to and accentuate apparel fashions to be viable; they cannot afford to lag or clash with the dress or coat or other garment that is the star of the show.

Accessories, intimate apparel, and the industries that produce them are an integral part of the fashion business. This chapter discusses the economic importance and methods of operation of each of these industries. The readings that follow are concerned with different aspects of this segment of the fashion business.

THE ACCESSORIES INDUSTRIES _____

When designers show their collections on models, and when retail stores put important fashion garments on display, they "accessorize" each dress, or suit, or other featured garment to emphasize the total look that is being presented. Consumers also use **accessories** both to accentuate the important fashion points of their appearance and to give individuality to mass-produced clothes. Jewelry in the newest trend, a color-coordinated scarf, a very special handbag, newly textured hosiery—these and similar touches help each woman feel that the outfit she wears is uniquely her own.

Every fashion in the accessory category changes its look as clothing fashions change. Shoes may go from unadorned flats to elegantly pointed high-heeled styles; scarfs and jewelry may vary in length, color, and materials; hosiery may go from neutral to colorful or from plain to textured—all in terms of what best suits the current apparel fashions. Success in accessories production and sales is a matter of moving quickly and surely in step with apparel fashions. Conversely, no amount of promotion and invention can create acceptance for a particular accessory when it simply does not fit into the current fashion picture.

Many accessories have experienced dramatic ups and downs as fashions changed. Belts, for example, went into eclipse for many years when chemise dresses hung from the shoulder, ignoring the natural curves of the body. Millinery, too, has had its problems, reaping only a thin harvest from its industry promotional efforts at times when women preferred to go hatless. Accessories as a whole have had lean years at times when there was little room for them in the fashion picture.

In recent years the accessories business is being perceived as an ever more vital and important part of the fashion industry. Accessories are considered by some to be the most necessary part of dressing because they define the style and character of the wearer. One retailer referred to the uptrend in accessories as "the great accessories explosion. The customer is hungry for accessories. The sixties was the era of the dress. In the seventies and early eighties timeless sportswear took the spotlight, and I believe the late eighties and the nineties is the time for accessories."[1] Another indication of accessories' growing importance is that the licensing concept has flourished as designers want to increase their share of this rich pie. Examples include Echo Design, which has licensed Ralph Lauren for scarfs, Alpert Nipon for belts and small leather goods, and Sarah Coventry for neckwear; Vera produces Perry Ellis and Anne Klein neckwear; and Victoria Creations holds licenses for Diane Von Furstenberg, Givenchy, and Karl Lagerfeld in jewelry. The list grows monthly.

The Business of Accessories

The design, production, and marketing of fashion accessories are not a single business, but several. Each category of accessories is produced in its own industry, and these individual industries are as diverse as the merchandise

Semiannual Trade Show in the Accessories Industry

Discover the fashion advantage... Fashion Accessories Expo.

Directional and classic accessories

screened to insure impeccable

quality and originality.

FAE FOR SPRING '90

JANUARY 14-16, 1990

Piers 88, 90, 92

New York City

FASHION

ACCESSORIES
EXPO

A new experience awaits you at FAE.

Introducing:

ELITE. An exclusive gallery of better-priced

accessories with specific fashion direction.

CALIFORNIA COLLECTIVE. A unique grouping of West Coast

resources with an attitude all their own.

INTERNATIONAL PAVILION. Designers from around the

world introducing their lines to the U.S. market.

NEW EXHIBITOR PAVILION. Debuts new up-and-coming designers

making their first appearance at FAE

Come to

FAE-LA

FASHION ACCESSORIES EXPO IN LOS ANGELES

FEBRUARY 4-6, 1990
Shrine Exposition Hall
Los Angeles

For the retail trade and press.
Order-writing only.
Two forms of buyer credentials required
on-site to gain admission.
No one under 16 admitted.
For information on attending: (203) 852-0500.
For hotel and airline discounts
call Travel Planners: (800) 221-3531.
Fashion Accessories Expo is
sponsored by Accessories Magazine.
And produced by
Conference Management Corporation.
FAJ30

SOURCE: Reprinted with permission of FAE, Conference Management Corporation.

itself. Some, like shoes and hosiery, are large and dominated by big producers. Others, like gloves, handbags, jewelry, scarfs, and millinery, are the domain of small firms. Some of the industries are highly mechanized; others still use hand operations not much changed from those used 50 or even 100 years ago. Some have plants in or near New York City; others are hundreds of miles from that center and merely have showrooms there.

The accessories industries as a whole, however, do have several elements in common:

1. All are extremely responsive to fashion and very quick to interpret incoming trends. Their success depends on how well they reflect the look of the apparel with which they will be worn.
2. All present a minimum of two new seasonal lines a year.
3. All domestic accessory manufacturers, as is the case with other segments of the fashion industry, are confronted with increasing competition from imports.
4. Almost all major accessory producers have entered into licensing agreements with leading apparel designers to produce and market styles bearing the designer's name.

Economic Importance

According to *Women's Wear Daily*, in its premiere issue of "A" (accessories), dated May 1985, accessories represented about $9.5 billion in retail sales nationwide. This figure covered jewelry, handbags, small leather goods, scarfs, hosiery, hats, and gloves, but does not include shoes. By 1988, sales of accessories, exclusive of shoes and fine jewelry, reached $17.3 billion at retail, with costume jewelry alone accounting for $5.5 billion.[2]

Another indication of the importance of accessories is their importance in terms of volume achieved and space allotted to this business by department and specialty stores. Traditionally, accessory departments were located primarily on the main floor. Although this remains the case, recent years have seen a proliferation of accessory departments as many stores move some classifications to the apparel floors, thereby increasing store space allocated to total accessory business. Cases in point are Bergdorf Goodman, Macy's, and Saks Fifth Avenue. In many cases promotional accessories remain on the main floor and designer accessories are located adjacent to the designer apparel departments to enable the customer to assemble a completely coordinated and accessorized outfit all in one location.

In 1988 Bergdorf Goodman doubled the floor space occupied by accessories and did $2,000 volume per square foot in its accessory departments and $5,000 per square foot in fine jewelry. Macy's has opened accessories outposts on all apparel floors and now does 8 to 10 percent of total store sales in all accessory categories. Lord & Taylor restructured its main floor and added an additional 4,000 square feet of selling space and three new display windows for only accessories in the flagship store in New York City, and increased accessories departments accordingly in the other stores.[3]

In addition, the growing importance of accessories has added a new dimension to the accessories business. More and more previously specialized accessory companies with a strong brand image are expanding by branching out into other classifications. To name a few, Echo—a pillar in the scarf market—is now being recognized as a belt resource, and Carolee, a jewelry firm, has added watches, jewelry, belts, and plans to add scarfs. Monet is another example of a producer capitalizing on strong brand recognition. This long-standing fashion jewelry company has added handbags and small leather goods.

Manufacturers have several reasons for branching out. One is that they hope to increase their business and a second is that some accessory classifications are soft one season and strong another. It still remains to be seen however whether retailers will continue to divide their departments by classification or feature coordinated accessory looks together.

SHOES

If we had no other indication of the importance of the shoe industry, consider the leather industry's estimate that each of us walks the equivalent of twice around the world in the course of a lifetime. No wonder foot protection has always been of prime importance to mankind and shoes take a prominent place in our legends, proverbs, and fairy tales! We are cautioned not to criticize a man until we have walked a mile in his shoes; we grow up on tales of seven-league boots, glass slippers, and red dancing shoes; we tie shoes to the cars of newly married couples as symbols of good luck. Aching feet remind us of the importance of being comfortably shod; a glance into a full-length mirror highlights the importance of shoes appropriate to one's outfit.

The first American shoemaker was Thomas Beard, who landed in the Massachusetts colony on the second voyage of the *Mayflower* and opened his shop to produce made-to-order shoes. Others followed, some of whom became "visiting shoemakers." These men lived with a household until all members had been shod. Leather for the purpose was usually supplied by the farmer or householder and was obtained from the cured skins of animals killed for meat. During the eighteenth century, shoemakers began producing "sale shoes," made without waiting for specific orders and brought to market to be offered for sale. Thus, ready-made shoes were introduced. These, however, were made only in three widths and five lengths. The well-to-do, therefore, almost universally had their shoes custom-made as late as 1880.[4]

The oldest and still active retail shoe organization in the United States is Thomas F. Pierce & Son of Providence, Rhode Island, established in 1767.

Nature of the Industry

The largest dollar volume of business in the accessories group is done by the shoe industry. This is an industry dominated by large firms. It is not unusual to find among them companies with many divisions, each of which produces and

The Shoe Industry Is Dominated by Large Firms

Company	1989 Sales (Add 000)
Reebok International	1,822,092
Brown Group	1,820,547
Nike	1,710,803
Melville	1,697,000
L. A. Gear	617,080
Edison Bros.	479,200
Stride Rite Corp.	454,373
J. Baker	399,230
Wolverine World Wide	323,734
Timberland Co.	156,141
Weyenberg Shoe Mfg.	138,868

SOURCE: Kurt Salmon Associates Inc., *Financial Performance Profile of the Footwear Industry.*

distributes footwear under its own brand name. For example, Joyce is a division of the U.S. Shoe Company, which also produces Pappagallo and Red Cross Shoes. Thom McCann is a division of Melville Shoe Corp., which also produces footwear under several other labels. The Brown Group manufacturers Buster Brown shoes for children, Naturalizer and Airstep for women, and Roblee and Regal shoes for men.

Production facilities are located primarily in Missouri, Pennsylvania, Maine, Tennessee, New York, New Hampshire, and Massachusetts, with total payroll dollars of $1.3 billion in direct manufacturing alone.[5] As with most segments of the fashion industry, the major marketing center for shoes is New York City, and most producers maintain permanent showrooms there. For decades, the 34th Street area was the center of activity for American footwear manufacturers. Headquarters were in the Marbridge Building, at 34th Street and Sixth Avenue, and in the Empire State Building, on the corner of Fifth Avenue. Since the mid-1970s, however, many companies have moved uptown to the 50s, close to the hotels where out-of-town retail buyers stay when they come to attend the industry's semiannual trade showings. Most of those who have remained in the 34th Street area are producers of children's and men's shoes. Companies such as Ferragamo, Golo, and Joan and David prefer the more fashionable 50s.

Development of Athletic Shoes

Not too many years ago, athletically inclined people bought a single pair of sneakers in which to run, jump, bike, or scramble up the side of a hill. Today, all is specialized. There are biking shoes that are stiff enough to direct all the rider's energy into the pedal, cross-country running shoes with spiked soles for traction, high-laced shoes for skateboards, and on and on to a variety of special-purpose sports shoes.

Athletic Shoe Sales 1989

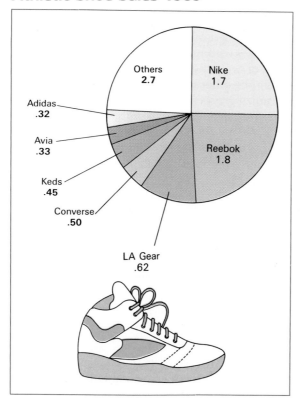

SOURCE: The New York Times.

The phenomenal interest of the American consumer in physical fitness has created an entirely new segment within the formerly traditional shoe industry. This segment has its share of giants, such as Reebok International Ltd. (sales volume of $1.8 billion), whose subsidiaries include Avia and Rockport. Reebok sold more than $1.18 billion worth of athletic shoes and Avia sold more than $140 million worth.[6] Nike's total sales were $1.7 billion, of which over $950 million was sneakers. Also important, but to a much lesser degree, were Converse, L. A. Gear, Adidas, and Keds, as is shown by a chart in this chapter.[7]

The wearing of athletic shoes has also become acceptable with business clothes. The custom began in New York City during a 1980 transit strike, and gradually was picked up as a fashion for commuters in other parts of the country as a mark of the business or professional person's interest in health and body comfort.[8] In the United States, wholesale sales grew to more than $4.3 billion in 1989 from $2 billion in 1984.[9]

Economic Importance

The **nonrubber footwear** industry includes production of all footwear that is deemed to contain more than 50 percent nonrubber in the upper part of the shoe. Thus, athletic shoes with more than 50 percent of the shoe itself made of suede, leather, vinyl, or any other fabric are considered part of the nonrubber footwear industry. On the other hand, shoes such as "jellies," or shoes that are produced by a vulcanizing process, or those that have more than 50 percent rubber in the uppers, are classified as part of the rubber shoe industry. With the enormous growth of athletic shoes, these distinctions are increasingly difficult to perceive. However, a tariff advantage is currently granted to imported rubber footwear, and many canvas-topped athletic shoes contain just enough rubber to qualify for this category.[10]

The domestic shoe industry in 1989 produced 222.2 million pairs of nonrubber footwear and 79.5 million pairs of rubber-and-fabric footwear, for a total of 301.7 million pairs—men's, women's, and children's. The domestic production of nonrubber footwear in 1989 was $4.56 billion. The industry employed 84,000 people, compared with employment of 158,400 in 1978. Meanwhile, domestic consumption reached 1,343,400 pairs in 1989, or the equivalent of almost 5.5 pairs for every man, woman, and child.[11]

Shoe Construction

Shoes consist of a number of different parts, all of which must be joined together with precision to make for a comfortable fit. These parts include the shoe **uppers** (the visible outside material) and linings cut to fit inside the uppers. These two elements are joined and draped over a **last**—the form that gives the finished shoe its size and shape. Also included are the toe box, which protects both the wearer's toes and the shape and contour of the shoe, and the **vamp**, which is the front of the shoe from toe to instep.

The lasting of a shoe is one of the most important processes in making shoes, since it gives the finished shoe proper fit, removes wrinkles, and ensures comfort and good appearance. Each size is made on a different last, and it is not unusual for a shoe manufacturer to have thousands of pairs of lasts in a factory. Originally, lasts were constructed of wood, but today newer lasts are made of lightweight plastic or aluminum.

At the bottom of the shoe is the outsole, the surface that hits the ground with each step. Above this is the insole, the lining on which the foot rests. Between these two layers is sandwiched a shank—a metal, leather, or plastic strip that protects and forms the arch of the foot within the shoe itself. Some shoes also contain additional padding within the two sole layers for further cushioning and comfort.

The method by which the sole of a shoe is attached to the upper varies within the industry. Each method is referred to as a "construction," to identify the process used: stitching, cementing, vulcanizing, injection molding, nailing, or stapling. About 60 percent of shoes made today use the cement process, applying adhesives to attach the sole to the upper with a permanent bond. This construction is found primarily in men's and women's casual and lighter-weight dress shoes. The most expensive shoes are usually of hand-sewn construction and are referred to as "bench made."

Heel heights of shoes vary, of course; the industry builds them and refers to them in terms of eighths of an inch. Flats measure up to $7/8$ inch, low heels are $8/8$ to $14/8$ inch. Medium heels are $15/8$ to $19/8$ inch; high heels are $20/8$ inch and up. Heels are made of many materials, including leather, wood, plastic, and rubber.

A most important distinction in shoe construction is whether the various parts are made of leather or synthetic material. Leather is highly valued, because it molds to the wearer's foot, is supple and resilient, and breathes to allow moisture to evaporate. Thus, leather is generally used in footwear of the finest quality. Shoes are generally labeled to identify the areas in which natural and synthetic materials are incorporated.

Marketing

The shoe industry is extremely fashion and marketing oriented, and each season presents a wide variety of new colors, shapes, and designs, geared to apparel trends. Perhaps this is why many women seem to be intensely susceptible to the lure of new shoes and to buy them as often as or even more often than they buy the other major components of their wardrobes. The industry does not rely on fashion alone to sell its products, however. Major emphasis is also placed on manufacturers' brand names in selling and in trade and consumer advertising.

SEASONAL SHOWINGS

New lines are brought out twice a year. Because shoe production is a slow process, manufacturers develop and show their seasonal lines in advance of ready-to-wear. Fall/Winter lines are shown in January/February and Spring/Summer lines in August. In addition to presenting their lines in their own showrooms, manufacturers participate in semiannual cooperative trade shows, such as the National Shoe Fairs held in New York. These shows attract thousands of shoe store owners and buyers from all over the country, not only to see the new merchandise but also to attend merchandising clinics and discuss new fashion trends with the fashion directors of the participating manufacturers. A regular feature of the New York shows is fashion presentations, at which retailers see how the new shoes coordinate with apparel fashions. All this is done six months before so much as a pair of the new shoes is likely to turn up in a retail store. In addition, there are other, less elaborate regional showings and clinics throughout the country.

LEASED SHOE DEPARTMENTS

Because of the expertise needed to fit and sell shoes, and also because of the tremendous inventory needed to stock a shoe department, department and specialty stores have traditionally leased out some or all their selling space to experts in the field. Many of these are manufacturers of well-known national brands, such as the U.S. Shoe Company, which uses leased departments to stock and sell its Cobbie, Red Cross, and Pappagallo lines, and the Brown Shoe Company, whose leased departments feature its Buster Brown, Regal, and Naturalizer shoes. Other leaseholders are simply shoe merchants, who operate their departments as they would operate free-standing stores, with as many or as few brands as they deem appropriate.

Many of the leased shoe departments, manufacturer-owned or otherwise, also stock related accessories, such as handbags, hosiery, and small leather goods, which they purchase for resale from producers in these various industries.

MANUFACTURER-OWNED RETAIL CHAINS

As has happened in the apparel industry, the growth of manufacturer-owned stores has been a fast-developing trend in the accessories area. The shoe classification, as the largest segment of the accessories industry, was the first to get into this business and remains in the forefront.

The advantages shoe companies see in this type of operation include creating a stronger brand franchise for their stores, protecting their share of the market in the wake of a diminishing number of mom-and-pop specialty shoe stores; and providing target consumers with a tightly focused assortment to fit their needs.

As a result, many of the leading names in footwear including U.S. Shoe, Stride Rite, Jumping-Jack Shoes, and Nike either are operating their own stores or are aggressively pursuing franchisees to operate stores for them. U.S. Shoe operates about 600 stores nationwide, 80 percent of which are franchised. Brands include Joyce/Shelby, Pappagallo, Red Cross, and Cobbie. Stride Rite itself operates 270 stores and additionally has about 400 individual dealers across the country that are licensed to operate a Stride Rite store.[12]

An even newer development is the trend to outfit the targeted consumer from head to toe as shoe manufacturers expand into apparel and activewear. Nike has opened stores where "we're trying to merchandise appropriate footwear and apparel together as a collection, so consumers can see how it coordinates."[13] Others such as Reebok, which in 1987 purchased Ellesse, L. A. Gear, and E. J. Gitano, are opening stores to do the same thing.

Extensive Competition from Imports

In 1989, foreign producers shipped more than 1 billion pairs of shoes into the United States. Stated in a different way, foreign producers supplied more than 79.1 percent of the total U.S. shoe consumption—a constantly increasing share that has caused domestic production to drop to a 50-year low.[14] Thus, the footwear industries suffer from import competition just as the fashion industries in general do. (A full discussion of imports is found in a later chapter.)

The fashion appeal of Italian and other European styling is important; so is

Nonrubber Footwear: Imports Versus Domestic Production

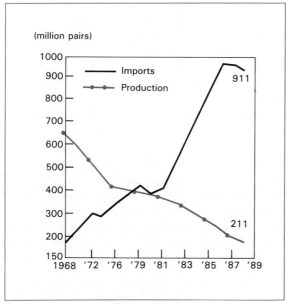

(million pairs)

SOURCE: Footwear Industries of America; compiled from U.S. Department of Commerce data.

their expertise. Important competition is also a result of the price appeal of low-wage-labor countries. A further complication faced by shoe producers is that foreign countries are quick to buy up hides and leather in the United States, where our meat-eating habits make us an important provider of these commodities. Then these foreign producers manufacture shoes and other leather goods in their own countries, at a lower cost than is possible here, and compete on a favorable price basis with domestic producers.

Total imports of nonrubber footwear were 903.1 million pairs compared to 217.2 million domestic. Rubber-and-fabric footwear showed domestic production of 79.5 million pairs versus 160.1 million imported pairs. The five largest suppliers of nonrubber footwear to the United States in 1989 were Taiwan (33 percent of total quantity), South Korea (18 percent), Brazil (14 percent), China (14 percent), and Italy (6 percent).[15] Included in these figures are shoes imported and resold by domestic manufacturers, as well as those purchased directly by retailers. Some U.S. manufacturers, moreover, use offshore producers. There are those who own their own facilities in Italy, Spain, or South America; others contract out their work to foreign producers. An example of this latter type is the extremely fashion-oriented firm of Joan and David, whose shoes are produced by the Martini factories, among the oldest and finest in Italy.

An example of the inroads made by imported shoes was the fashion craze in 1983–84 of the "jelly bean" or "**jellies**," which are plastic shoes made from polyvinyl chloride or nylon. These shoes, the staple footwear of the poor in underdeveloped countries for years, were first imported in cut-out open sandals, styles that overcame their nonbreathing drawback. In 1981, they came into the United States as nonbranded, inexpensive footwear. In 1983, they were colored, restyled, boxed, and tissued, and became a huge retail success. Grendene, a Brazilian factory, produces 200,000 pairs a day, which are shipped all over the world. Jellies are also produced and worn in countries such as Mexico, Greece, and China.

Thus, the footwear industry's problems with foreign competition parallel those of other labor-intensive industries in this country. For shoes, however, there are no import quotas. Because of this, competition from imports is a serious problem to the domestic shoe industry.

Grim as the picture may be, an occasional manufacturer in this country is able, by ingenuity and enterprise, not only to meet foreign competition, but also to sell domestic shoes abroad. There are not yet enough of these rare birds to make a summer, however, and in the meantime the industry presses for government action to hold back at least part of the import flood. The outlook for any such governmental assistance, however, looks very bleak indeed.

HOSIERY

The introduction of nylon stockings in 1938 set the stage for vast changes in hosiery, in the industry that produces it, and in its importance as a fashion accessory. Before nylon, stockings were made primarily of silk and also of wool, rayon, and cotton. Yarns were knitted into pieces of flat fabric, each shaped so that when it was folded in half and seamed down the back, a stocking in the form of a leg results. Colors were limited and fabric surfaces were plain.

Early nylon stockings were made much as silks and rayons had been. Except during the World War II years, when civilian use of nylon was ruled out to make way for military needs, nylon has made steady progress in hosiery, to the point that it has virtually crowded out other fibers for dress wear. With continuing technological progress, nylon stockings became sheerer, took on more colors, were produced in sandal-foot and other styles, and developed patterns and textures undreamed of in earlier years. in the 1960s, the development and popularity of pantyhose substantially added to the growth and fashion importance of hosiery.

Nature of the Industry

The business of hosiery is one of chemistry, filaments, knitting machines, technology, big production, big promotion, and big competition. It is also the second largest industry in the accessories field, after footwear. And like the shoe industry, it is dominated by large firms. Among the largest are Hanes, Round-the-Clock, Bonnie Doon, Hot Sox, and Kayser-Roth.

Most of the plants are in the Southeast—notably North Carolina, a state that accounts for more than half the industry's output. Nevertheless, the marketing center for the industry is New York City. There the larger firms have their showrooms and smaller companies also have sales representation. It is there that retail buyers go during market weeks, not only to select merchandise, but also to learn about national advertising programs that producers plan to run and to assess the opportunities for tying in at the local level.

Economic Importance

The wholesale value of the hosiery industry's output was estimated at approximately $5 billion in 1989.[16] This volume of business represents the output of 325 companies, of which 74 produced women's hosiery and 266 produced hosiery for men, boys, girls, infants, and children. Hosiery consumption was estimated at 17.9 pairs per person in 1989 compared with 15.7 in 1979.[17] The industry provided employment for 70,100 in 1989 compared with 64,400 in 1979, one of the few industries in the fashion-related industries to show any growth in the number of production employees. More than 90 percent of these workers are employed in North Carolina, Alabama, Tennessee and other Southern states.[18]

Hosiery Construction

Hosiery is knitted, either full-fashioned or seamless, and in the greige. Full-fashioned stockings are knitted flat to the desired shape, length, and size; sewn into the shape of the leg; next heat-set or boarded; and then packaged. Seamless hosiery is knitted on a circular machine, at high speed, and then dyed. The same procedure is used for pantyhose, some of which are knitted as stockings and

Total Hosiery — Per Capita Consumption

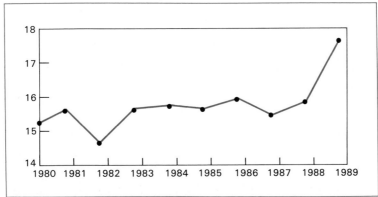

SOURCE: National Association of Hosiery Manufacturers. Reprinted with permission.

then attached to separate panties. Full-fashioned hosiery has the advantage of a better fit than seamless until the introduction of stretch yarns in the 1960s. With them, the fit of seamless hosiery and pantyhose was greatly improved. Stretch yarns also made possible stretch hosiery, support hose, control tops, and comfortably fitted knee-high stockings.

Automation in hosiery production is constantly increasing, to the point that computerized machines can turn out hosiery that features graphics, patterns, and textures and employs many novelty yarns. Such machines were introduced by the Japanese NEGATAS and the British E.T.C.

Marketing of Hosiery

As hosiery moved from almost entirely functional purposes toward becoming an important fashion accessory, the marketing strategies of the industry changed along with its product. Manufacturers' brands acquired new influence; producers' advertising took on greater importance to the retailer; fashion became the watchword of the industry.

NATIONALLY ADVERTISED BRANDS

Manufacturers' brand names in the hosiery field are older and better established, and have been longer promoted than those in other accessories areas. But whereas women had been conditioned to purchase a brand for its fit and durability, they are now bombarded with advertising that stresses the fashion points of the brands. Major producers advertise consistently in national magazines, on television, and, through cooperative advertising with retail stores, in newspapers.

Retailers have capitalized on women's devotion to brand names by not only featuring national brands but also creating their own. This approach gives them greater price flexibility, removes them from direct competition with other stores in the national brand arena, and creates a certain exclusivity for their stores. Usually, the same manufacturer will produce both the store's private brand and its own national brand that is also carried in the same department. For example, Macy's has its Clubhouse but it carries an impressive array of nationally advertised brands side by side with their own. And in that array, the maker of the house brand is sure to be represented. Its source of supply, however, remains the store's secret. The same situation prevails in discount houses, chain drug stores, supermarkets, and others, except that these latter outlets seldom carry as many brands as department stores and major women's specialty shops.

IMPACT OF FASHION AND DESIGNER NAMES

As hosiery has moved into the fashion spotlight, both retailers and manufacturers have been treating legwear much as ready-to-wear is treated. For example, the industry has changed from two to three market weeks a year: March for the presentation of Fall lines; August for the opening of Holiday and Early Spring lines; and November for Spring lines. This change in the marketing calendar is a natural outgrowth of the increased number of fashion items attuned to the seasonal apparel fashions. More and more emphasis is put on decorative legwear in a wide variety of textures, colors, and patterns. To coordinate with active sportswear, the industry offers leg warmers in colors coordinated with the clothes themselves. And in response to women's body-building and other exercise activities, the industry produces bodywear in attractive colors, to be sold in hosiery departments.

Inevitably, as the total look became important in fashion, leading apparel designers, both European and American, moved into designer-name hosiery — for the most part under licensing arrangements with producers of national brands. For example, Round-the-Clock has legwear bearing the name of Givenchy; Bonnie Doon has Geoffrey Beene socks; Kayser-Roth produces the Calvin Klein line; Hot Sox has a Ralph Lauren collection.[19] Newcomers to the hosiery licensing business are Liz Claiborne and Donna Karan, both of whom have jumped into hosiery with both feet.

PACKAGE MARKETING

Hosiery, like so many other products, has been affected by packaging and self-service techniques. For decades, it was sold over department and specialty store counters by saleswomen who slipped their beautifully kept hands into the stockings to show how they would look on the leg. Then came packaging, notably L'Eggs by Hanes. These were pantyhose, folded into egg-shaped containers, for sale from self-service fixtures conspicuously placed near checkout counters in supermarkets and drugstores. With the marketing success of L'Eggs, other producers soon followed the Hanes lead. Kayser-Roth developed the No-Nonsense brand for similar distribution. Presently, the consumer can find a packaged hosiery rack in almost any self-selection store.

The success of these untraditional channels of distribution has led hosiery producers to seek out more innovative packaging and marketing techniques. Department and specialty stores, too, have had to look to their laurels; their share of the market is now quite small. To compete with the price appeal of discounters, supermarkets, and others, they are using a two-pronged attack. One effort is to push their own brands to meet price competition; the other is to emphasize decorative legwear as a major accessory of fashion.

Competition from Imports

Pantyhose, hosiery, and basic socks constitute one area of domestic production that has resisted the inroads of import competition. This is true because the industries involved are capital intensive. Cheap labor, the competitive edge that many foreign merchandise sources enjoy, has little impact in this field. Competition does come, however, from industrialized countries such as Japan, England, and France. These produce goods of high quality, have great technical expertise, and use sophisticated dyeing techniques. Despite attempts by the domestic industry to keep imports to a minimum, some manufacturers say they will bring goods in from offshore because of the quality of foreign yarns, the quality of finishing, and the greater sophistication of dyeing techniques.

As to the figures, in 1989 almost 15 million dozen pairs of hosiery were imported into the United States. This is in comparison with 3.9 million dozen pairs imported in 1979. Of those imported in 1989, 7.09 million dozen pairs were pantyhose—a category in which domestic production is at the 700 million dozen mark.[20]

HANDBAGS AND SMALL LEATHER GOODS

From earliest history, people have needed receptacles of some kind in which to carry with them various personal possessions and necessities. Quite possibly, a pouch made of skin or leather and suspended from a belt or girdle was used by primitive peoples who had not yet ventured into clothes, much less clothing with pockets. Handbags as we know them are a creation of the twentieth century; before that, women had only a belt from which to suspend housekeeping keys, and slit pockets in their voluminous skirts to accommodate whatever a lady wanted to carry with her. As women's activities grew more varied in the twentieth century, and as their garments became slimmer and sleeker, handbags became necessary and developed into accessories that would complement and coordinate with the apparel. Today, most women have a wardrobe of handbags in a variety of materials (leather, fabric, and plastic, for example), and in a diversity of sizes and shapes, such as clutch, envelope, satchel, box, duffle, tote, pouch—and the woman executive's briefcase-like carryall.

Nature of the Industry

For the most part, the handbag industry consists of relatively small specialists, the majority of whom are headquartered in New York—primarily in the 30s, between Broadway and Fifth Avenue. They present their lines in two major showings a year: in May for Fall and in November for Spring and Summer. Supplementary collections, smaller than the main seasonal ones, are shown for Holiday/Transitional in August, for Early Fall in March, and for Summer in January.

The industry has been dramatically affected by a great influx of foreign-produced handbags. Because of this factor, some producers have replaced lost volume by expanding their lines, adding small leather goods, luggage items, or even coordinated belts.

The majority of buyers for retail handbag departments also buy other accessory items, such as gloves, belts, or small leather goods. Such buyers demand and usually get coordination in both color and silhouette among the various markets they shop, and they also seek to purchase accessories that will relate well to the upcoming season's ready-to-wear. The handbag industry, through the National Handbag Association, establishes market dates that dovetail with apparel openings. It also uses its openings as an opportunity to disseminate both industry and fashion information to the retail store buyers.

Economic Importance

Manufacturers in the handbag industry produce women's handbags and purses of all materials with the exception of precious metals. In 1989, the value of shipments was estimated at $441 million, which represented an approximate 8 percent decrease over the past several years. Much of this decrease can be attributed to the rising cost of leather, which is used extensively in the production of handbags and purses. Apparent consumption grew by 12.4 percent in 1988 and most of this growth was satisfied by imports. Industry employment declined in 1989 by 5.6 percent. However, this rate of decline was less severe than that experienced between 1979 and 1986.[21]

Handbag Construction

Years ago, leather was the principal material from which bags were made. This meant a large amount of hand-guided work and demanded considerable resourcefulness in cutting, since the operator had to work with a natural product, irregular in shape and sometimes with scars to be worked around. Today, many bags are made of plastic or fabric with a uniformity in width and quality that vastly simplifies the cutter's task.

1990 Handbag Market Weeks

N·H·A	**SUMMER**
	JANUARY 6
SPRING	**TRANSITIONAL**
HANDBAG	MARCH 10
AND ACCESSORIES	**FALL**
MARKET	MAY 12
opens November 4th...	**HOLIDAY/TRANSITIONAL**
	AUGUST 11
	SPRING
	NOVEMBER 3

SOURCE: Reprinted with permission of the National Fashion Accessories Association.

Today's handbags range from classic, constructed types to unconstructed, unframed bags of leather, canvas, or other materials. The number and difficulty of the operations required varies with the styling. All, however, begin with a design from which a muslin sample is made. From the muslin, a paper or metal pattern is made, and this is used to cut the handbag materials. The actual cutting is done either by hand or with metal dies, depending on the complexity of the design and the quantities to be produced. Each handbag shape, such as the clutch, envelope, tote, and satchel, for example, requires different types of construction and parts. If the design requires a frame, then all of the inside and outside parts must be fitted into the frame; after that, closures and straps are added.

Competition from Imports

The value of imports climbed an estimated 15.6 percent in 1989, to $911.5 million. In addition, the market share of imports reached 70 percent, up from 68.1 percent in 1987 and continuing a decade-long upward growth. China overtook Taiwan as the principal source of supply, capturing an estimated 44.4 percentage of the quantity in the U.S. marketplace. Other important suppliers are Taiwan and South Korea for lower priced merchandise and Italy and France for higher priced goods.[22] According to some major domestic handbag manufacturers, "The only way we can compete is to be more creative" and "by using designer labels."[23] Faced with such intense foreign competition, many domestic handbag manufacturers themselves have become importers. Some design handbags in this country but have them produced abroad.

In fact, one of the few remaining domestic handbag producers has been quoted as saying, "Eighty-eight to 90 percent of our industry has been penetrated by imports. Three years ago, it was only about 60 percent."[24] According to the National Handbag Association, most large retailers buy directly from the factories abroad, primarily in the Far East.

Small Leather Goods

Fashion and changing activities of both men and women have had strong impacts on the industry that produces **small leather goods**, such as wallets, credit card cases, billfolds, key cases, jewelry and eyeglass cases, cigarette cases, and similar items for both sexes. Although historically the largest producers of these types of products were Prince Gardner, Buxton, and Swank, the recent addition of Liz Claiborne Accessories, Bosea, and Bond Street has added to the fashion look of these items.

In today's world of fashion, many women choose to match such items with the handbags they carry. This is especially true of designer-licensed lines, which coordinate the various items by fabric and color. And among women climbing the success ladder in the business world, special needs are developing for which the small leather goods industry is providing some answers: calculator wallets,

Example of Designer Licensing

ANNE KLEIN
HANDBAGS & BELTS*

**The Collections of
ANNE KLEIN & CALDERON** BELTS and HANDBAGS
**are now being shown at our New York Showroom
and thru our Sales Representatives.
Appointments are suggested.**

 **BELTS & BAGS, INC.**
389 FIFTH AVENUE ■ NYC 10016 ■ (212) 684-0253

NORTHEAST: Gabriel Pecci
DALLAS: Harry Weiss • 1434 Apparel Mart
FLORIDA: Jeff Frankel • Miami Merchandise Mart
ATLANTA: Stan Grey • 6-N-302 Merchandise Mart
CHARLOTTE: Stan Grey • A301/K301 Carolina Mart
WEST COAST: Edith Sheppard Assoc • A1073 Calif Mart • Los Angeles
CHICAGO: Bernard Nahm & Associates • 580 Apparel Center
KANSAS CITY: Rose Wasser • Apparel Center

*Excluding Metal Belts

SOURCE: Reprinted with permission by Anne Klein for Calderon.

credit card cases, pocket appointment calendars, work-and-date organizers, notebooks, and all sorts of handbag and briefcase accessories that project both fashion and businesslike efficiency.

This industry's domestic production was estimated for 1989 to be $317 million, a decrease of 8.1 percent in recent years. However, since leather represents more than 60 percent of the value of materials used to produce these items, the increased cost of the leather accounts for decreased value of shipments. Industry-wide employment (approximately 8,000 employees) remained stable in 1989. Imports of personal leather goods rose an estimated 17.7 percent in 1989 on top of a 24 percent rise in 1988 to a total of $398.5 million, thereby bringing import penetration from 33.3 percent in 1984 to an estimated 47.9 percent in 1989. Principal suppliers include China, South Korea, and Taiwan, which together supply two-thirds of the quantity of imported goods in this classification.[25]

GLOVES

One can trace the wearing of gloves before and through recorded history. In ancient times, they were worn as protection and adornment—as they are today. Objects in pyramids dating back to Egypt's twenty-first dynasty include gloves. In ancient Rome, ladies protected their hands with gloves. In medieval times, kings and church dignitaries wore richly ornamented gloves, symbolic of their status. A knight wore gloves, or gauntlets, reinforced with armor. When he threw one down before another knight, that constituted a challenge to battle.

Gloves today have many purposes, many of them functional. Foundry workers use insulated gloves to protect their hands from heat; Eskimos need mittens to keep out the cold; racing drivers wear gloves that give them better wheel grip; skiers use waterproof kinds to protect them from frostbite. In fashion, gloves play a role that changes in importance, taking a share of the spotlight when dress becomes elegant and fading out when the look is at a casual extreme.

Nature of the Industry

The glove industry suffered a severe blow during the 1960s and 1970s, when fashion took on an ultracasual look and gloves became almost obsolete as fashion accessories. The hard times this situation imposed on the glove industry dealt it a blow from which it has not yet fully recovered.

Many of today's gloves, especially those made of fabric, are produced by divisions of multiproduct companies that also manufacture small leather goods and handbags, such as Etienne Aigner, or by firms such as Kayser-Roth that produce intimate apparel and hosiery. There are still, however, some specialists that are glovers exclusively. Among these are Aris Glove, producers of a line of fine leather gloves and also the Isotoner glove. Hansen Gloves is another well-known specialist. Other important names here are Fownes and Grandoe, both important producers of fashion gloves, as is LaCrasia, producer of a line of trendy gloves that are unquestionably more fashionable than functional. Companies such as these, which are glovers first and foremost, flourish or suffer according to whether fashion smiles on or ignores the glove as an accessory to the total look.

The plants that produce leather gloves are located principally in the Northeast. Many are in the city of Gloversville, New York—where, not surprisingly, the National Glove Manufacturers Association makes its headquarters. That association, unlike many in the fashion field, concerns itself primarily with federal regulations affecting its industry, rather than with product and industry publicity. Gloversville was the site of the first glove production facility in the United States, as far back as 1760, and it is where, by 1900, some 80 percent of American gloves originated.[26] Production of fabric gloves, on the other hand, is more widely distributed throughout the country, with 65 percent of the factories being located in North Carolina, Mississippi, Alabama, and Tennessee.[27]

Economic Importance

The U.S. leather glove and mitten industry is composed of two product segments: work gloves and mittens, which account for approximately 85 percent of domestic production, and dress gloves, which account for the remaining 15 percent. Some 3,300 employees produce $167.0 million[28] worth of gloves and mittens at factory value. Although the glove business today is largely a business of warm hands and work gloves, the recent return to a more elegant lifestyle has increased the importance of gloves to complete a fashionable outfit.

Imported gloves have been and still are a serious threat to the domestic glove industry, with 1989 showing a 8.9 percent rise in value of imports to a total of $106.6 million. Principal sources of supply are China, the Philippines, Mexico, and Korea.[29]

Glove Construction

Of all accessories, gloves are probably the most labor intensive to manufacture. Although made on an assembly line, they require the most skill on the part of production workers and involve many steps, since a glove must fit when the hand is closed in a fist and yet not be baggy when the hand is open.

Gloves are made up of numerous small pieces, such as the trank, or hand and finger piece, both front and back; the thumb part, which may be made in any of several ways; the fourchettes, or pieces that shape the fingers between front and back; and quirks, tiny triangular pieces sewn at the back of the fingers to provide flexibility and give additional fit. Only the very inexpensive gloves use few pieces; they consist merely of a front and back sewn together—a procedure that earns them the name of "sandwich gloves" in the trade.

Because there are so many pieces in the usual glove and because they are so small, a great deal of handwork is involved in cutting. This may be done on a table, using a ruler to measure each part, or with the use of a die. The former method is known as table cutting, the latter as clicker cutting. Actual sewing is done on several types of machines and uses lock stitch, chain stitch, and overstitching, depending on quality and style. Since gloves are curved, high-speed production equipment cannot be used.

Glove Marketing

The major marketing center for gloves is New York City, where most glove producers maintain permanent showrooms of their own or use the facilities of sales representatives. These showrooms are usually located in the East 30s, where many of the other accessories industries are also located. Seasonal lines are shown at the same time as the handbag showings. Compared with the promotional outlays and activities of other fashion accessories manufacturers and retailers, the money devoted to promoting gloves is relatively insignificant.

Some of the more aggressive producers, however, have followed the example of the hosiery industry and are packaging "one size fits all" stretch gloves that can be displayed and sold in self-service fixtures. Others are increasing their volume by packaging their gloves with matching hats or scarfs, or both—a combination with strong consumer appeal during cold winter months.

MILLINERY

Until the middle of the present century, it was unthinkable for a well-dressed woman to be seen on the streets or to enter a store or office without a hat. Every department or women's specialty store devoted a great deal of prime space to millinery departments, which featured both ready-made and custom-made hats and were usually located adjacent to apparel departments. In the 1950s, there was an enormous exodus from the city to the suburbs and, with it, an emerging fashion for casual living and casual clothes. The outdoor barbecues of the 1950s called for a very different style of dress from the garden tea party of an earlier suburban generation. Country casual dress spread to the city, and the habit of wearing hats went into a decline. The millinery industry, after many years of prosperity when women had whole wardrobes of hats, went into decline, too—one from which it has just recently begun to recover. Over the past several years many women have once again begun to consider an outfit incomplete without a hat to provide the finishing touch.

Nature of the Industry

The millinery industry today is small, because of the diminished demand for its wares. It is made up, as it always has been, of small firms, numbering fewer than 100, all of which are specialists in this one field. The industry has been untouched by the drive to bigness and diversification that has affected other areas of the fashion business. Smallness is no handicap in this industry, however, as there is little opportunity to mechanize, automate, or develop huge runs of individual styles. The ability to move quickly on a new idea—the strong point of small operations—is an important asset in the millinery field.

The importance of the total look in fashion today has sparked renewed interest in millinery. Designers dutifully put appropriate headwear on their models as they parade the runways; retailers show millinery with other outer apparel; some customers even buy hats. But one still sees few, indeed, on the streets and in other public places. That tide may turn, as tides often do in fashion. Meanwhile, even the most prestigious of fashion retailers gives only minimal space to millinery departments. The day of the huge millinery department—in which expert salespeople helped women choose the right hats for their outfits, or the right hat to enhance their morale for an important date—has not yet returned. Until it does, the millinery industry will remain small.

Economic Importance

The wholesale value of output in 1989 for millinery alone was approximately $180 million, which represents a healthy increase over the $58 million production in the late 1970s.[30] The production of millinery domestically takes place primarily in New York City, although a small number of companies are located in St. Louis, Dallas, and Los Angeles. The fewer than 80 companies operating today represent a continued decline from the more than 400 companies operating in the 1960s when hats were always worn by a majority of the women.[31]

Construction of Millinery

Basically, the millinery industry's output falls into two categories: hats and caps, and millinery. The former category can be made by machine or by hand. Millinery-type hats are made by sewing velvet, satin, or other fabric and trimmings over buckram frames, or by shaping and trimming felt or straw bodies. Millinery made by the latter methods involves a great deal of handwork, and the processes lend themselves readily to custom work for consumers or for sale through retail shops. The industry is headquartered mostly on a single street in New York City: West 37th Street, between Fifth and Sixth Avenues.

At one time, the industry had its share of well-known designers. Adolfo and Halston, for example, began their fashion careers as milliners. These days, however, the glamorous names bypass the millinery industry and concentrate in the apparel field, where opportunities and rewards are much greater.

Marketing of Millinery

An unusual factor in the millinery industry is the millinery syndicate of Consolidated Millinery, which operates 250 leased departments. Such a firm leases space for millinery departments in retail stores across the country and provides these stores with a continuing supply of new styles. In order to obtain such styles, the buyers for these firms are constantly in the wholesale markets, not only to seek out actual merchandise but also to find and develop talented new producers and stylists. Help, advice, and sometimes even operating capital will be made available by the syndicate to potentially creative resources.

Unlike other fashion accessories, millinery does not function on two lines a year. Seasonality has its influence, of course, but the life of a hat as an accessory is usually short and, as a rule, the faster a firm gets into and out of a good selling style number, the better the operation is. In millinery, the important element is an unending procession of new styles or new versions of currently accepted styles. At one time, when millinery was in its heyday, retailers sought to have completely new assortments every three or four weeks, and the term *millinery turnover* was used in retail circles to describe extremely fast-moving merchandise.

Today the millinery market has four specific seasons, currently labeled Fall I, Fall II, Spring I, and Spring II, which roughly correspond to the seasons in ready-to-wear. However, since millinery is such an impulse purchase on the part of most consumers, constant new additions serve to increase the turnover.[32]

The great unknown for millinery today is the customer. It still remains to be seen whether promotion, publicity, and fashion creativity can reverse the trend toward hatlessness and convince her that smart millinery is essential to the total fashion look.

JEWELRY

The wearing of jewelry is believed to antedate the wearing of clothes; in fact, among primitive peoples today, even if one sees little that could be called clothing, there is usually a ring or two or ten on the body, the neck, the ears, or the nose. In modern times, jewelry has become a sign of worth and status—and a very important fashion accessory, indeed. No fashion costume is complete without it, whether it be the understated string of cultured pearls worn with a woman executive's office clothing, or the outrageous four-inch earrings hanging from the earlobes of the latest MTV star.

The jewelry industry divides itself into two distinct parts: fine jewelry, made of precious metals and gemstones, and costume jewelry. In recent years, a third category has entered the picture: bridge jewelry, which spans the gap between the other two.

Precious or Fine Jewelry

The metals used in **fine jewelry** are gold, silver, and platinum, worked alone or in combination with gemstones. The approximately 2,000 firms operating in this field in the United States produced an estimated $4.6 billion a year of merchandise and employed more than 27,100 people in 1989. More than 60 percent of the factories are located in New York, Rhode Island, California, and Massachusetts.[33]

Gold, the metal of first choice for fine jewelry, is too soft to be used by itself and is therefore usually combined with base metals. The gold content is expressed in terms of carats, or **karats**. Solid gold is 24 karats, or **24K**. The most commonly used alloys are rated 18K, 14K, or 12K, and are arrived at by mixing gold with copper (to produce reddish yellow metal), silver (to produce greenish yellow), or palladium or nickel (to produce white gold). Any alloy of less than 10K may not be called karat gold. In the United States, 14K is favored; in European jewelry, 18K is customary.

Platinum, a silvery metal, is rarer, heavier, and more expensive than gold, and is a favorite for diamond settings. It, too, is generally alloyed, primarily to reduce its price, with palladium, iridium, rhodium, or ruthenium—all white and hard metals.

Silver, the least expensive of the precious metals, is usually combined with copper. The term **sterling** may be used where there are at least 925 parts of silver per thousand.

GEMSTONES

Precious stones include diamonds, emeralds, sapphires, rubies, and real pearls. With the exception of pearls, stones are measured in carats, one carat being the equivalent of 100 points. Pearls are measured in millimeters and length.

Semiprecious stones include amethysts, garnets, opals, lapis, jades, topaz, and aquamarines, among others. Today, fine jewelry uses more of these than ever, because of the high prices of precious stones.

In addition to natural gemstones, wide use is now made of synthetic gemstones. Laboratories can produce synthetic corundum to look like garnets and amethysts, and synthetic spinel to look like emeralds, diamonds, and aquamarines, among others.

An important element in the value of a piece of fine jewelry is the workmanship that goes into it. It is a hand-made product, with a jeweler creating each setting for each stone at the workbench, one piece at a time. The creativity and skill of the workman are major factors in the cost of the finished piece.

MARKETING OF FINE AND PRECIOUS JEWELRY

In recent years the fine jewelry industry has seen a major consolidation at the retail level through the steady growth of jewelry store chains. These chains are growing both through internal growth and through acquisitions. Examples here are Kay Jewelers; Peoples Jewelers, a Canadian owned company; Ratner's Group, a British owned company; Reeds Jewelers; and Barry's Jewelers, among others.[34]

Bridge Jewelry

With the price of fine jewelry climbing and the demand for jewelry increasing, a new area of jewelry has developed to fill the need. This is **bridge jewelry**, which involves silver, gold-plated metals, or 14K gold, and which uses less expensive stones, such as onyx, ivory, coral, or freshwater pearls. Much of the fashion leadership comes from designers such as Celia or Karen Sibiri, Elsa Perretti, and M. J. Savitt, who, among others, create hand-made and signed pieces. Also important here are items such as gold chains; gold combined with the less expensive semiprecious stones; and jewelry that sets many small diamonds in a group to create the look of larger stones. Retail prices range from about $100 to $2,000 for these products.

Costume Jewelry

Costume jewelry is mass produced to fill the fashion demand of customers who seek relatively inexpensive jewelry to complete the fashion look of their outfits. The materials used may be plastic, wood, brass, tin, glass, lucite, or any other substance that can be manipulated to achieve the desired effect. Retail prices range widely, from items sold in variety stores to those bearing the names of the such companies as Kenneth J. Lane and Miriam Haskell.

The costume jewelry trade has deep roots in Rhode Island. It dates back to colonial silversmiths, who hammered out teaspoons and thimbles and who developed a method in the early 1800s for reducing the cost of jewelry by rolling a thin sheet of gold over a cheaper base. Today this is done by **electroplating**, the process for coating materials with a thin layer of gold or silver.[35]

The total output of the industry was about $1.4 billion in 1989. Rhode Island manufacturers produce more than 60 percent of the total national output. The industry employs 21,800 people. Ninety percent of the more than 700 American companies that produce costume jewelry are family-owned companies with fewer than 25 employees.[36] Like other accessories producers, the

Costume Jewelry Sales

Imports account for a growing portion of the U.S. costume jewelry market.

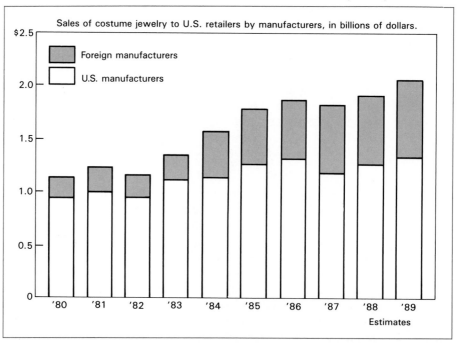

Sales of costume jewelry to U.S. retailers by manufacturers, in billions of dollars.

■ Foreign manufacturers
□ U.S. manufacturers

Estimates

SOURCE: The New York Times.

manufacturers of costume jewelry have showrooms in New York and present two lines a year, timed for the convenience of buyers who expect to coordinate their purchases with what their stores will offer in other fashion departments.

Among the leading names in the costume jewelry field are Monet and Trifari; both are owned by Crystal Brands, whose total volume exceeds $200

Dior Also Licenses Jewelry Manufacturers

Christian Dior only uses the licensee's name in advertising that appears in the trade publication.

SOURCE: Reprinted with permission of Christian Dior/Grossé Jewelers.

million. This company also owns Marvella, Inc., a pearl specialist. In 1988, Monet entered the direct mail-order business (which accounts for an estimated 20 percent of the total costume jewelry business done at retail), to enter into competition with Avon for a portion of the pie. Another big producer is Napier, with annual sales of nearly $70 million.[37] In 1989, Liz Claiborne accessories went into costume jewelry for the first time. A great many bangles and beads indeed!

The costume jewelry industry in recent years has begun to feel the effects of import competition for the first time. In 1989, imports had a 37 percent share of the U.S. market compared to only 19 percent in 1980. During that period imports have more than tripled to exceed $528 million. They mostly come from low-wage countries such as South Korea, Taiwan, Singapore, and Hong Kong.[38]

Unlike other accessories industries, the costume jewelry industry does not yet appear to be harassed by import competition. Pearls usually come from abroad, but the assembling takes place in this country. The threat from low-wage countries is felt, it is true, but as one producer points out, the industry offsets that particular differential by offering the retailer such benefits as advertising, adjustment of stock, and dependable deliveries. It also imports some of its components but designs and produces the finished articles in this country.

OTHER ACCESSORIES _____

Other accessories include sunglasses, scarfs, belts, handkerchiefs, umbrellas, and wigs. Sunglasses came into fashion prominence in the 1960s, when then First Lady Jackie Kennedy wore "shades" constantly. They have remained important in fashion , not only for daytime, functional outdoor wear, but also as accessories for evening. Wigs, falls, and hairpieces, too, have been important accessories at various times, and to some extent their burgeoning popularity coincided with the decline of millinery. Hair ornaments have been an addition to the well-dressed look. Nowadays women have an entire wardrobe of watches to wear for different occasions.

Belts gain prominence when waistlines are in fashion. Scarfs and stoles fill in low necklines, provide a bit of warmth, add a touch of color, or can be worn to accent broad-shouldered or slender looks, according to how they are draped and according to current fashion requirements. Handkerchiefs, whose utilitarian functions have been taken over by tissues, peep in and out of the fashion picture, tucked into breast pockets or sleeves if and when they enhance whatever the "in" look may be. Umbrellas, too, have their fashion ins and outs, sometimes carried with a swagger like a walking stick, sometimes brightly colored to liven up drab days and drab rainwear, or whatever the case may be. Utility sells many umbrellas; fashion, when it touches this field, sells more.

ACCESSORIES DESIGNERS

"Name" designers in the accessories field are almost exclusively those who have made their mark in the apparel field and who license their names to manufacturers of accessories. The designs themselves may or may not originate with the famous individual whose name is attached to them; they may have come from a design studio run by that luminary, or they may have been created by anonymous employees of the producer and then approved by the licensor.

Very few designers become famous through their work in accessories alone. For the most part, manufacturers have design staffs or use free-lancers; in neither case do they feature the names of these designers. Among the distinguished exceptions are Vera, who began many years ago in scarfs; Elsa Peretti, the house designer of jewelry for Tiffany's; and Paloma Picasso and Kenneth Jay Lane, also in the jewelry field.

Apparel designers moved strongly into licensed accessories in the 1970s, when the total "look" became important in fashion and consumers began putting together outfits in which the accessories were quite as essential as the apparel if one was to achieve the desired casual or elegant smartness. This trend has brought almost every famous American and European apparel design name into the accessories area. It has brought glamour and useful promotional tools to the field.

It is interesting to note that Liz Claiborne, Inc., whose name had been licensed to Kayser-Roth for a line of accessories in 1986, discontinued this arrangement and opened a new division, Liz Claiborne Accessories. The decision to do this was explained by Jerome Chazen, co-chairman of Liz Claiborne, Inc., as follows: "Since there has always been a synergistic relationship between apparel and accessories, we have decided to make that relationship closer."[39] Other designers' companies have followed their lead.

INTIMATE APPAREL

The segment of the fashion industry that produces loungewear, nightwear, women's and children's undergarments, and body shapers for women is known as the **intimate apparel industry**. The history of its products is also a history of society's changing perceptions of modesty and feminine beauty. In the nineteenth century and into the early decades of the twentieth, manufacturers in the United States produced, and women wore, an astonishing variety of devices to shape, distort, and even deform the figure to achieve what was considered fashionable for women. It is a matter of amazement that women of the generations that first fought for suffrage and first entered the business world conducted their activities in garments so constricting that people in the trade referred to them in later years as "iron maidens."

Since undergarments in general come into close contact with the body, they have always had sexual connotations. Even though their appearance to the outside observer is secondary, these garments, other than the actual corsets, have generally been characterized by soft fabrics, a great deal of detailing, and many trimmings. The Gibson Girl might have worn a corset of tough fabric reinforced with whalebone, but she wore a dainty camisole and lacy petticoats with it.

Recent years have seen renewed consumer interest in intimate apparel. The industry had hit a low point in the 1960s when young women burnt their bras as a form of protest and declaration of freedom. This was also the era of tight jeans, worn with little or no undergarments. Nowadays, intimate apparel is well on the road back up again, thanks to the return of interest in dresses and the concomitant return of slips and petticoats. Today's concern with fitness, moreover, has created a need for jogging bras among women who exercise strenuously, and has revived interest in bras and girdles and support panties among those who want to look even more trim and fit then they may actually be.

Industry Segments

The industry's products fall into three major categories:

1. **foundations**, which include girdles, brassieres, garter belts, and the shapewear that nowadays replaces corsets;
2. **lingerie**, which includes petticoats, slips, panties, camisoles, and sleepwear such as nightgowns and pajamas;
3. **loungewear**, which consists of robes, negligees, bed jackets, and housecoats. The lines between lingerie and loungewear are not always clear-cut, however, and some in the industry categorize their products as daywear (lingerie and housecoats) and nightwear (sleepwear and negligees, etc.).

Many of the producers in the intimate apparel field have products in all three categories of the industry. Nevertheless, there are separate trade associations for each of the different branches within the industry—namely, the Associated Corset and Brassiere Manufacturers, Intimate Apparel Council of the American Apparel Manufacturers Association, and Lingerie Manufacturer Association. Each of these has its headquarters in New York City.

Economic Importance

The intimate apparel industry is big business in the United States, with a total output of more than $4 billion in 1989.[40] The largest segment of this total is produced by the underwear and nightwear segments of the industry, which employ approximately 53,000 employees and encompass almost 500 companies. Bras and girdles employ approximately 15,000 workers in more than 120 establishments. Robes and dressing gowns employ more than 8,000 workers in 92 establishments.[41] These establishments cover manufacturing facilities only, and each location is separately counted. The leading production states are New York, North and South Carolina, and California.

Marketing

New York City is the major market center for all segments of the intimate apparel industry, and the showings are timed to mesh with those of ready-to-wear. The buyer of intimate apparel is usually a specialist, not involved with the merchandising of outerwear. Nevertheless, the close relationships between undergarments and outerwear fashions, and between outerwear fashions and the various categories of at-home wear, make it essential for the intimate apparel buyer to be guided by what the other segments of the fashion industry are presenting.

The intimate apparel industry, which functioned on two markets a year in the days when its major concern was corsetry, now has five seasonal showings: Early Spring in August, Spring in November, Summer in January, Early Fall in March, Fall and Holiday in May. Market weeks are also held in important regional centers: the Dallas Mart, the Atlanta Mart, the Chicago Apparel Center, and the California Apparel Mart in Los Angeles.

IMPACT OF FASHION

Even in this industry's purely functional garments, the impact of fashion is felt. For example, the length and fullness of outwear skirts necessarily determines the length and shape of the slips to be worn under them; figure-revealing silhouettes enhance the demand for body-shaping undergarments, whereas relaxed lines diminish their importance; emphasis on the waistline brings waist-cinchers back into production, generally briefly. Changes in women's lifestyles

Market Weeks in Intimate Apparel

COMING N.Y. MARKETS
1990

January 8–12
SUMMER AND MOTHERS DAY

March 12–16
EARLY FALL

May 14–18
FALL AND HOLIDAY

August 13–17
EARLY SPRING AND RESORT 1991

November 5–9
SPRING 1991

SOURCE: Intimate Apparel Market Council.

and interests, too, affect the industry's output. A notable example, already cited, is the development of special bras for aerobic dancing, in response to the interest in fitness. In loungewear and nightwear, in which looks are more important than function, the relation to fashion is clear indeed. The customer, consciously or otherwise, tends to seek out the same general effects, the same overall looks, that she has been seeing in apparel displays and on smartly dressed women in her area.

IMPORTANCE OF BRAND AND DESIGNER NAMES

The brand names of producers in this industry have traditionally been so important that store buyers tend to budget their purchases by resource or vendor rather than by merchandise category. This practice goes back to the days when foundation garments had to be carefully fitted to individual customers. Leading manufacturers, in those days, took a major share of responsibility for planning retail stocks and training salespeople in stores that carried their lines.

Among the best-known names in foundations are Warner (the oldest in the field), Formfit-Rogers, Lily of France, Maidenform, Bali, and Playtex. In the lingerie area, well-known brands include Vanity Fair, Barbizon, Vassarette, Natori, Eileen West for Queen Anne's Lace, and Eve Stillman.

As would be expected in a field where brand names are important, producers advertise widely along three fronts: directly to the consumer in print and television, through cooperative advertising with retail stores, and to retail stores through trade publications. Some companies also provide stores with display fixtures, on which their brand names appear, for use in featuring the particular brand in windows and store interiors.

The importance of designer names in marketing fashion merchandise is mirrored in the many licensing arrangements that exist between intimate apparel producers and leading designers of outerwear. Bill Blass, for example, designs robes and loungewear for Evelyn Pearson Company; Christian Dior is licensed to Carol Hochman Designs; Warnaco licenses Olga, Valentino Intimo, and Ungaro; and Calvin Klein licenses his name in underwear and sleepwear to a financial management group that purchased the division from Wickes Cos. in 1988.

According to the designers themselves, their objective is to apply to their intimate apparel collections the interpretation of fashion that they present in their ready-to-wear collections. Thus, the seasons' changes in silhouette and fabrication, as they see them, are reflected in intimate apparel as well as in streetwear.

Competition from Imports

Imports competition has affected the intimate apparel industry, as it has every other segment of the fashion industry, but not yet to as great an extreme as in some other categories. Imports generally play their greatest role where production is labor intensive, as in intricately sewn and embroidered loungewear and sleepwear, because of the quality of handwork and the advantageous pricing. In some of the more basic styles of loungewear and sleepwear, retailers have goods produced overseas for presentation under their private labels. Direct import of European-made bras occurs among some of the prestigious fashion stores such as Saks Fifth Avenue and Bergdorf Goodman, which feature French bras from Prima and LeJaby, and Italian bras from LaPerla. The major offshore bra production center, however, is the Philippines, where such companies as Lovable, Bali, and Warner's are major importers. In second place after the Philippines is Costa Rica. For robes and dressing gowns, Hong Kong and China are the major import sources.

Readings

In the very diverse field of accessories and intimate apparel, many different marketing strategies are used successfully. These readings discuss some of the approaches that have worked for various firms and products.

Carolee: Taking Risks, Moving Ahead

Carolee's interpretation of the Duchess of Windsor's famous jewels brought her company to forefront of the jewelry industry.

Nike's Bright Knight

Nike wants its logo to stand for the very best athletic footwear and apparel that the market has to offer.

Inside Grandoe

Grandoe's glove business is multinational. Its raw materials come from suppliers located all over the world—Nigeria, Ethiopia, Spain, Belgium, and China.

Hanes Hosiery: Runs, Hits & Errors

With a surprising new appetite for risk taking, Hanes Hosiery is shedding its traditional image as a plodding giant.

Industry Focus: The Business of Intimate Apparel: What's Next?

Women are looking for more romantic and more daring intimate apparel. They now consider provocative undergarments a justifiable expense and an investment in self-esteem.

CAROLEE: TAKING RISKS, MOVING AHEAD

by Jill Newman

New York—Carolee Friedlander is a top example of the entrepreneurial impulses that are electrifying the accessories business these days.

The fashion jewelry designer believes in taking chances, and in the past few years her philosophy has paid off.

While Friedlander's firm, Carolee, has been a recognizable name in the jewelry business for years, it was the company's interpretation of the Duchess of Windsor's jewels in fall 1987 that brought Carolee to the forefront of the industry.

Friedlander, who started the firm at her kitchen table about 20 years ago, is estimated to hit a volume of more than $30 million this year.

In 1987, the year of the Duchess of Windsor, Friedlander said her sales increased 30 percent, and then another 15 percent in 1988. For 1989, she projected gains between 10 and 15 percent.

As far as national consumer recognition, Friedlander said it was the Duchess of Windsor–inspired jewelry that "puts us on the map." When she first heard of the plans for the Sotheby's auction of the Duchess's jewels, which took place in April, 1987, she studied the jewelry to develop them for her own line. The collection included mostly pins, which were favorites of the Duchess.

At that time, Friedlander said she estimated that pins represented only 2 percent of fashion jewelry sales. Not sure whether retailers would respond to pins or whether the auction would be a success, Friedlander took a chance when she planned a national advertising campaign with the Duchess jewelry.

The ads broke nationally around the time of the Sotheby's auction, which turned out to be a media bonanza. "Now pins are 30 percent of our business, and easily 15 percent of the retailers' business," said Friedlander.

"We need to take these kinds of risks or else retail becomes flat and dull," she added.

Friedlander said more than 1,000 articles appeared about her Duchess of Windsor–inspired jewelry in publications across the country. The best-selling item in the collection was a flamingo pin, retailing for $75, of which she sold more than 15,000.

On the heels of the Duchess of Windsor collection, she initiated plans for her own freestanding store, which opened last August at the Mall at Short Hills in Short Hills, N.J.

The store was another big investment and risk. The motivation behind opening the 700-square-foot store was to use it as a vehicle to show retailers the best way to merchandise jewelry in order to maximize sales. Friedlander said volume was about $400,000 in the first five months of business.

The idea has clicked. During the accessories market this week, she said she signed agreements to open four in-store boutiques using the concept of her freestanding store.

The boutiques will open in I. Magnin, San Francisco, Bloomingdale's, New York

Source: *Women's Wear Daily*, January 13, 1989. Reprint permission granted.

and Marshall Field's Water Tower Place and State Street stores in Chicago. Friedlander said she is discussing opening more in-store boutiques with many retailers.

Another major growth area for the firm is overseas distribution in the Far East and Europe. Within the next two years, she is looking to open freestanding stores in Paris, Milan and London.

Her strategy is to open the stores and establish brand identity, in this way preparing for the economic unification of Europe in 1992, which she feels will bring expanded opportunities for more retail accounts in these countries.

The company has been distributing in the Far East for 10 years, though Friedlander said the business started to flourish over the past 3 years.

An in-store boutique is scheduled to open this year in Isetan, Tokyo, and Friedlander said she is discussing the possibility of opening more boutiques in other stores in the Far East. She noted about 2 percent of the company's sales are done in the Far East, and she said the potential is "huge."

Amidst all the expansion, Friedlander insists the main focus remains on product. "We are a product-driven company," she said. She has recently added metal belts and a wide range of watches to her line, and is considering other product categories in the future.

"Carolee's belts and jewelry are very strong right now," said Jane Tuma, fashion director of accessories at Saks Fifth Avenue. "The Duchess of Windsor collection brought her to the surface. She has a talent for coming up with merchandise at the right time." Tuma continued, "We have a strong business with her, and it continues to grow."

Friedlander did not always intend to go into the fashion jewelry business. She went to college at Bennington for a degree in architecture.

After getting her degree, she worked in architecture for awhile, and it wasn't until she was married with three children that she started making jewelry for herself. She was doing the lost wax process with a variety of metals casting Oreo cookies. "I made silver, gold and pewter Oreo impressions." Friedlander recalls.

She then decided to try her hand at the business professionally. Friedlander said it was harder starting out 20 years ago than it would be today. "I first went to Providence to meet with people to have my designs made and being a woman, they did not take me seriously," she said.

She said the toughest part about getting started was getting to see buyers. "Back then, there were three giant jewelry firms —Monet, Trifari and Napier. All they sold was classic, tailored jewelry." But her persistence paid off and after several days of waiting in line to be seen on open-house days, Friedlander received her first big order from Bloomingdale's, New York.

Following this, she was able to get a $50,000 bank loan to purchase molds and models, and built what she calls a cabin in the backyard of her Greenwich, Conn. home, "complete with a Telex and everything I needed to run a business." Friedlander admits that for the first 10 years she was concentrating more on raising her three children than on building her business.

In 1985, she took what she considered a major gamble by investing in her first national advertising campaign. "I figured advertising would separate us from the pack, because few jewelry firms had the revenue to advertise," she said.

Her first ad featured fashion jewelry made to look like fine jewelry through the lost wax casting process, which has become her forte. At that time, she said, few firms were doing the look of fine jewelry in fashion jewelry. Christian Dior was a major exception.

As a result of the success of the first ad, Carolee has continued to advertise every year. "With ads we create consumer demand for the product. We have built a strong following, and ads reinforce this and create excitement.

For fall 1988, Friedlander capitalized on the Chanel-inspired look. Again she anticipated the resurgence and her ad featuring multiple chains broke last March and April.

This coming fall the company is extending the Chanel-inspired look, adding "Carolee's Collectibles." This group consists of pendants on chains to be worn along with the chains from last fall.

"It layers the look, which is far from dead," said Friedlander. "What makes the collectibles special is that they are functional. For example there is a magnifying glass and a watch fob. "People like things that are different and have another dimension, things that are conversation pieces," added Friedlander.

She also expects dress clips to be a hot item this fall. She said they have not been around for years. She expects to do a full group of them, borrowing ideas from the Thirties and Forties.

The company launches four new lines a year, and each season has about 3,000 stockkeeping units in the line. Prices run the gamut, starting at $17.50 for earrings and going as high as $125 for a necklace. Friedlander said the line is sold in more than 3,000 department and specialty stores. She said her strongest regions are the Northeast and West Coast.

For most fashion jewelry firms, the bulk of the volume is done with earrings, but for Carolee it varies from season to season.

"We do not put all our research and development money in one area. We want to see all parts of the business grow," she said. This season necklaces will be the biggest portion of the business. "We create new business for the stores. Like pins, pendants and dress clips were negligible businesses."

Private label accounts for 10 to 12 percent of Carolee's volume, and Friedlander said that level should be maintained this year. "Our name is stronger than ever, and we do not look at private label as intensely as we did three years ago. We will only do private label where our product meshes with a store's concept." She noted the firm has been particularly successful doing private label with Ann Taylor and Talbots.

Today she has a 30,000-square-foot factory in Providence employing 300 people, and her Greenwich, Conn., headquarters of 20,000 square feet employs 100 people. In addition, there is a 1,000-square-foot New York showroom at 385 Fifth Ave.

The company has also evolved into a family affair. Although Friedlander's first marriage ended in divorce a number of years ago, her second husband of some eight years, Burt Friedlander, joined the firm as chief operating officer last April.

He left his 20-year career as a trader on the New York Stock Exchange floor. The second generation of Friedlanders is also involved in the business, with Steven Friedlander serving as vice president of sales.

At 47 years old, Friedlander said she has seen a lot of changes in the fashion jewelry business over the years. "At one point there were a lot of cheap imports in the market. But today the customer demands quality. Better merchandise and quality is what sells," she said.

As for the future, Friedlander's goal is to keep creating newness for the stores, which in her mind means keep taking risks.

NIKE'S BRIGHT KNIGHT

by Stuart B. Chirls

Portland, Ore—It's a chilly, overcast autumn morning in the Pacific Northwest, but the boisterous crowd heating up the Portland State University theater isn't there for freshman orientation.

The celebratory mood is part of Nike, Inc.'s annual sales meeting, and the reps and executives greet the opening presentation with standing ovations. Phil Knight, Nike's 50-year-old founder, chairman and driving force, sits in the middle of it all, grinning broadly.

And with good reason. After spending much of the 1980s watching upstart Reebok seize on the aerobic fitness trend and ultimately dominate the market his company helped define, Knight and Nike have rebounded. Earnings shot up to $101,695,000, an 83 percent increase from the previous year, on worldwide sales of $1.2 billion in 1988, up 37 percent. Apparel sales hit $142.9 million in fiscal 1988, and are projected to reach $200 million in 1989. Inventory is down, the company has extended its reach with new product lines and acquisitions, and a 475,000-square-foot headquarters complex is under construction.

Knight admits that the experience has given him perspective. "I've learned some basic lessons," he says. "Appreciating the customer, what a brand stands for, the importance of the entrepreneurial spirit . . . and how to tolerate pain.

"We also learned that a brand has to stand for something. We dabbled in fashion for (retail) shelf space and store presence, but we decided what we want to be. Nike is an athletic, technical product and we want to establish that with the consumer."

Since Nike's Air technology put its footwear back on the beam, the firm's design teams have turned their attention to performance activewear. Like other major footwear companies, Nike has had its share of clothing disasters. "The problems with apparel in the past were our fault," Knight says frankly. "We want apparel to make a profit, which it does. I'm optimistic that we'll be stronger in apparel as far as design and communication with the market are concerned. It's a big area of emphasis for us in 1989."

His mandate calls for Nike to offer the most technically advanced apparel, a line that will compare favorably with its footwear. That means, for example, waterproof, breathable Gore-Tex fitness tights, a must for the serious runner, retailing for a tidy $300 a pair. "We'll sell about two pair of those," laughs Knight, but the point is well taken. He wants the Nike logo to stand for the best the market has to offer.

Apparel and shoes will be marketed as collections, cross-merchandised by colors and graphics, a critical tool for unified retail presentations. "Apparel is a complicated business," says Knight, "and becomes more complicated when tying shoes and apparel together. Apparel should be its own viable business, but, if done right, can also make the shoes stand out."

Cross-training continues to be the most important subcategory within the fitness market for 1989, and Nike's cutting-edge attitude in apparel development has led it down some radical trails.

Terming the outdoors "the ultimate gym," Nike has introduced ACG (All Conditions Gear), a high-tech, layered dressing

Source: *Daily News Record*, January 2, 1989. Reprinted with permission.

system aimed at mountaineers, ice climbers, trekkers and other rugged outdoors people who demand technical innovation. ACG includes Thermax innerwear, Polarfleece jackets, and Gore-Tex parkas, each tailored for sport-specific applications. "It's radical but fits with the Nike definition of advanced product," says Knight. No sales projections have been made, but with only one shoe model currently marketed under the ACG logo, Knight expects big things. "It's tougher to develop as a category. We have a ways to go but I'm encouraged," he adds. Greg Thomsen, formerly with outdoor specialist Wilderness Experience, has been named director of apparel marketing, and Robyn Millet, late of rugged outerwear maker Patagonia, has joined as chief of design.

The line will retail from $55 for the underwear to $125 for the fleece and up to $260 for the Gore-Tex jackets. "Phil told us it had to be the best," says Thomsen. "It's the best all right, but what we don't know is if we can jump right in, not having had a background in the category. To succeed, we'll do what we do well: marketing, advertising, promotions, and point-of-purchase. We'll sponsor a Himalayan expedition in January as well as climbers and climbing contests throughout the year. It's the lifestyle of the future . . ."

Thomsen expects ACG to be in 1,500 specialty shops, outdoor stores and ski shops by July, with a hoped-for network of 5,000 specialty stores nationwide.

Nike's multiphasic marketing plan serves as the linchpin between supplier, retailer and consumer. The no-nonsense "Just Do It" campaign will be reprised in 1989 with a $45-million media campaign, including a series of new TV spots featuring Andre Agassi, Bo Jackson and Nike's top gun, Michael Jordan. Add in sponsorships, promotions and in-store materials, and Nike's annual marketing tab comes to a neat $75 million.

Knight, who in the past rarely granted interviews, knows the value of a good press: "The market will continue to get more competitive in apparel and footwear. The scenario we grew under has been refined. For the first time, our advertising and promotions have an intended public relations aspect. It's now a new industry, a mix of sporting goods, apparel and the old shoe business. Hopefully, we're writing the history."

The effect has been historic, if not downright mind-numbing. Following sales of more than a half-billion dollars for the first quarter of fiscal 1989, an 80 percent increase from a year ago, six-month earnings jumped to $81,761,000, or $2.18 a share, compared with $43,628,000, or $1.15. Six-month sales totaled $832,719,000, a 60.9 percent jump from $517,236,000 in fiscal '88. Knight is pleased, but looks to the future. "We don't want to be overpowered by one quarter. Margins stayed strong, but we don't want to buy shelf space. We'll give it up, in fact, to maintain margins. We're looking to first quarter, 1990."

The volatility of the performance market led Knight to expand Nike's product mix into other diverse areas, acquiring Cole-Haan, a manufacturer of women's better casual footwear, and introducing Side I, a homegrown collection of young women's contemporary shoes. "Our growth in the next five years will come through acquisitions, new lines, and growing our existing products," says Knight. "There're 54 million consumer buying impulses out there, and we believe companies like Cole-Haan give us design strengths and insights into consumers we didn't have before."

Since ending an early retirement in the mid-1980s, Knight has spent most of his time handpicking executives that he feels will fit Nike's management matrix and lead the company into the 1990s. "The biggest challenge is constantly upgrading management, developing them," he says, crediting decentralized group management for the company's independence and creativity. "How well we do that will dictate our future success."

INSIDE GRANDOE

Gloversville, NY—It's about 270 miles up the Hudson from New York to a place known to 18th-century locals as Stump City, because a tanning process developed by the Iroquois and Mohawk Indians left truncated hemlocks and tamaracks to dot the landscape. Since about 1835, however, this village in the foothills of the Adirondack State Park has been called Gloversville, after its main claim to fame, the American glove industry.

Of the more than 300 glove manufacturers populating this part of Fulton County during the Thirties and Forties, only Grandoe still has its headquarters here. But the gray four-building complex accented with the lavender "Grandoe" logo is just the nucleus of an international business that is centralized in the Philippines with operations throughout the Far East and a total work force of about 2,300.

"It's really a multinational business," says Grandoe president, Richard Zuckerwar Jr. who, reporting a growth of 52 percent for 1988, expects his family-owned company to garner figures only slightly lower for 1989.

Stocking up on raw materials for gloves, which wholesale from $12 to $56, takes Zuckerwar all over the world: Ethiopia, Nigeria and the Sudan for skins; Spain and Belgium for rabbit pelts, and China for raw cashmere. "We buy the cashmere there and send it to another country to be spun," he says, refusing to mention the latter location for fear of losing a competitive edge.

For deerskin, however, he travels only as far as his own backyard. Claiming that deer from Vermont and the Northwest are not up to the Grandoe standard, he explains, "We use the skin of the white-tailed deer from the Adirondack region and from Canada for the gloves you would buy at L.L. Bean, Eddie Bauer or Land's End."

Grandoe gloves bear the Grandoe label, that of licensees Bill Blass or Le Sportsac or of any one of several private label customers, including Saks Fifth Avenue, Bloomingdale's, Nordstroms, Neiman-Marcus and I. Magnin. Grandoe also supplies chain-store operations including K mart and Sears.

"We sell some in Canada, but it's really as much as we can handle at this point," says Zuckerwar about prospects of tapping foreign markets. "I think Europe is probably ready for us, because of the condition of the dollar, but we've got as much as we can deal with."

Because the glove business is so closely tied to international politics and the world's economic mood, Grandoe's operations are feeling the effects of the softening dollar.

Source: *Women's Wear Daily*/Accessories, January 1989. Reprinted with permission.

The weak currency translates into higher production costs and more expensive raw materials, specifically leather and cashmere, but according to Zuckerwar, a glove from a domestic company is still more affordable than one from Italy. The main competition for Grandoe right now, according to Zuckerwar, is domestic.

"Stores are placing orders for next fall, and, starting January first, we sit down to begin designing the fall 1989 line," he explains. This kind of lead time means stocking up on inventory far in advance, even if returns on investments aren't seen for two years. Zuckerwar's most recent cashmere purchase was timed just right, he says. "We couldn't have known what was going to happen, but, let's put it this way, I could sell the raw cashmere now and make a lot of money."

The inventory at any given time is worth several million dollars, explains Zuckerwar. Pointing to rows of dozens of bundled, tanned sheepskins, he says, "For the amount of money you could get for just these two rows, you could buy a Rolls-Royce."

Survival in the glove industry today depends on long-established contacts with suppliers from around the world, contacts that, Zuckerwar says, cannot be cultivated today. "The Ethiopian government is only selling to two buyers in the U.S. Grandoe is one. But you could give me $50 million today to start a glove business and that still wouldn't be enough money."

Grandoe has had connections overseas for sourcing since the company's start in 1913, but the company went abroad for production 25 years ago, at first contracting work to factories in Puerto Rico and the Philippines. In 1977, Grandoe acquired its own factory in the Philippines and began with a work force of 35. Today, the total number of employees there is 2,000 and investigations are being made into developing their presence in China. "We conducted our first survey of China just seven years ago," says Zuckerwar. Today, Grandoe has a small operation in the Shanghai area and is looking into building a factory.

The glove industry has moved into the computer age as far as inventory and distribution, but it remains labor intensive. Gloves are cut from skins one at a time. The clicker-cut method, a stamping process using iron pattern pieces, yields eight dozen pairs of gloves daily per cutter. With the slower method of handcutting, which Grandoe also uses, the turnout is only 3 dozen pairs. The company employs 250 cutters.

The sewing process utilizes sewing machines, many of which are Singers from 75 or 100 years ago or French-made Pique machines which stitch in special patterns. With one of these, a woman can turn out only three pairs of hand-sewn gloves a day. "The process of glovemaking is really anachronistic," says Zuckerwar. "A lot of hand craftmanship is involved."

In an industry which combines the old and the new at a time when glove-wearing is no longer de rigueur, Zuckerwar sees Grandoe as making great strides. It's staffed with a relatively young group—his nephew, Eric Friedman, vice president, is 28; Zuckerwar, who's from the fourth generation of the family who founded Grandoe, is 43. And the company is competitive in all areas of the glove market, producing for golf, skiing and driving. Revamping its knitwear division to include a more developed cashmere line and introducing its Activizer line to compete with Aris's Isotoner, Grandoe is one of the top three and getting bigger.

When pressed to find an explanation for its growth, Zuckerwar simply says, "I don't know; we're just making a little more noise than we used to."

HANES HOSIERY: RUNS, HITS & ERRORS

by Marilyn Neerman

In the boardroom of Hanes Hosiery in Winston-Salem, generations of the Hanes family still "preside" from their gilt-framed portraits. "I often look up and wonder what they would be thinking,' says Weldon Schenck, Hanes president since 1985. "And I'm sure they would approve. But this is a very different company than it was just two years ago."

This $200 million hosiery leviathan, once characterized as stodgy, has been moving as fast as a McDonald's counter at high noon.

The company that never saw the fashion or designer hosiery business as "red meat," is now launching sexy lingerie looks. It has penned a licensing agreement with Donna Karan for a line of hosiery with price tags starting at $7 and possibly going up to triple-digit retails for bodysuits. The company that usually worried more about how much space it could grab in each department store is now working on how that space looks and how the merchandise is presented. On its drawing board are plans for Hanes boutiques which include a sales person, or persons, selling nothing but Hanes hosiery. Hanes also plans to have UPC codes on all products by the end of June and is hard at work on a data capture system specifically tailored to the department store hosiery business.

No Risks

In the past, Hanes held its dominant position by staying with what it did best. It identified the hosiery products that would translate into long and profitable production runs; cranked up the machines; turned its awesome 300-strong sales force loose on the stores; and then rolled out the heavy advertising artillery.

In fact, Hanes advertising is so powerful that even competitors credit the launch of Silk Reflections (its Lycra sheer line) and its ad campaign with expanding the entire department store Lycra sheer business.

Notwithstanding its unquestionable success, the launch of Silk Reflections is also an example of what can go wrong with a too strict avoid-all-risk strategy. Hanes, the industry leader, didn't roll out Silk Reflections nationally until 1986. That's about four years after L'Eggs introduced its Lycra sheer entry, Sheer Elegance; three years after J.C. Penney introduced its private label Lycra sheers; and several seasons after its branded and private label department store competition.

Characteristically, Hanes made a late, albeit grand, entrance. While the timing decisions for Silk Reflections were made before Schenck's arrival, he explains that its timing probably reflects the company's traditional practice of test-marketing every new product "until it was bullet proof." As to why department stores didn't loudly complain about their major supplier being late with a product as innovative as Lycra sheers, Schenck says that the stores have really never expected Hanes to be innovative, much less "first."

Line -up Review

But since Schenck left a vp position at a management consulting firm to become

Source: Courtesy of *Accessories* magazine, April 1988.

president of Hanes, he has been constantly reviewing Hanes' brand lineup. This process has led to the reworking of the Fitting Pretty line. Originally slated for large and petite women, the line now focuses entirely on the large size customer; sizes were pared down from seven to five, and fashion colors were added.

During the past year Fitting Pretty outposts were rolled into large size departments with those outposts accounting for roughly 30 percent of the total Fitting Pretty business in those stores that have them. As a result of this retooling, Fitting Pretty is projected for a 35 percent sales gain this year.

The Hanes Too line is also being revamped. Schenck explains that Hanes Too was launched about six years ago when department stores were most fearful of losing more market share to the mass channels of distribution. Hence, the introduction of Hanes Too, a branded product at a moderate price. The major selling feature of Hanes Too was the pricepoint, but it had no other real identity.

Now the Hanes Too mix—with the addition of bold colors and textures and a new ad campaign—is being skewed to capture a young customer, a target that has been missing from both the Hanes and the department stores' strategy.

Last year Hanes struck again with yet another new brand launch: the all Lycra Isotoner line targeted to the working woman. Predictably Isotoner is capitalizing on the strong image of Sara Lee's Aris Isotoner brand, producing gloves and slippers. Now there is Isotoner hosiery which, of course, "fits like the glove."

"We laid down a very strong base for Isotoner this past year," says Schenck. "Next year we're looking at major growth, a 40 to 60 percent sales gain."

Next year's marketing plan for Iso-toner, which Schenck describes as "investment spending," is being set now. Last year's effort included some dramatic billboarding, but the marketing effort was mainly regional. Next year it's going national.

Growing in a Stagnant Market

All of Hanes' strategies are designed to keep its growth juggernaut going and to maintain its leading share in the department stores. A challenge, indeed: the hosiery market is stagnant, growing at the rate of only 1–2 percent a year.

Hanes, with the exception of its Underalls brand, focuses its distribution entirely on the department and specialty stores. Market share erosion in this channel of distribution seems to have come to a halt, settling in at about a 15 percent share of units sold; and there isn't much inflationary pressure driving dollar gains ahead.

Undaunted, Schenck responds, "We are in a super position because there is such a strong base from which to build. We have to help keep department stores competitive because if the department stores don't grow and succeed, we don't grow and succeed. Our future is directly tied to how well we help the stores maximize their sales and profits."

One piece of the plan was set in motion just prior to Schenck's arrival. Turn back the clock a couple of years, mention Hanes to department stores and they would immediately bring up the pebble in their shoe: Hanes' 47 percent margin compared to the loftier 55 to 60 percent margins of the competition.

Hanes' retort was that its heavy spending in marketing its products (specifically, TV advertising) resulted in significantly higher stock-turns, and therefore healthier profits despite a lower margin.

Ultimately, however, Hanes relented. In 1985 it moved its margin up to 50 percent, coinciding with the introduction of Silk Reflections.

Still, Hanes management believes that the stores put undue emphasis on margin when determining which brands are delivering the highest rate of profit return. If Schenck had his way, the stores would base their brand, style and SKU decisions on a combination of margin, turn, investment in space and inventory.

In addition, says Schenck, the stores have too many brands, too many SKUs and an appalling stockout problem.

"It's complex as hell," states Schenck. "Our company alone makes 4,000 SKUs. Multiply that by about 15 hosiery brands, times styles, sizes and colors. I guess a department store is choosing among as many as 40,000 SKUs."

Inventory Management

The process of weeding out brands and SKU's will accelerate as stores install the systems that will provide them with instant, accurate and objective information. And Hanes is in the forefront of developing such a system. Theirs will capture sales data and manage inventory—down to the SKU level—based on the UPC code and point-of-sale scanning.

While many department stores are moving in that direction on their own, Hanes intends to develop a system for the hosiery area that will be better than what the stores develop to cover many product categories.

Schenck envisions a computer-to-computer transmission system—Hanes to the stores and back—that will reduce the currently laborious system of inventory-taking, order-writing and stock replenishment by as much as 50 percent.

"This is critical," states Schenck. "If we reduce that time lag and maintain a perpetually accurate inventory, it will reduce our cost of servicing the stores and allow retailers to put their inventory dollars to better use."

Hanes is working on a system that will accommodate either a UPC or OCR-based system. Some testing is currently being done with a few stores, but completion of the Hanes system is said to be "some months away."

The Boutique Concept

Hanes is also ready to lay down another trump card. During the past it has been spending a lot of time and money looking for ways to present and sell hosiery with more visual impact. The result is that in mid-summer the first test of a complete Hanes boutique will be installed in two to four department stores.

Certainly the idea of a shop within a department stocking the merchandise of just one brand is nothing revolutionary in department stores. Sportswear, cosmetics, just about every other merchandise area has them. But it's a first for hosiery.

Each Hanes shop will contain modular fixtures—which can be rearranged to fit the space given the boutique in each store —its own signing, new display techniques and planogram. The fixtures are designed to cut back reliance on stockroom inventory; the Hanes fixtures skew the inventory to 60 percent selling floor/40 percent stockroom.

Schenck knows that not every store is going to be knocking on his door asking for a Hanes boutique. Nor is Hanes ready for a national rollout. The boutiques are seen, at least initially, as a laboratory in which Hanes and the stores will be able to instantly work on new ideas for displays, product mix, ease of service, shelf versus stockroom inventory, etc. What's learned in this lab can also be adapted in stores with or without the boutiques.

But if the boutiques work, there will be more of them. Hanes is planning to install the boutiques on a joint venture basis with the stores. Details on who is paying for which components of the shop—fixtures, displays and the sales people—are being worked out now.

Becoming a Fashion Insider

Historically, Hanes has had its nose pressed against the window when it came to either the fashion hosiery business or the designer hosiery business. But the company's recent agreement to produce a line of Donna Karan hosiery will change all that. Anyone who thinks that this arrangement is simply a matter of Hanes playing catch-up in the designer area is mistaken.

The addition of Donna Karan hosiery is expected to do the following for Hanes: 1) increase Hanes sales by expanding its distribution into the pricier tier of department and specialty stores it isn't currently selling (i.e., Bloomingdale's, Saks Fifth Avenue and Neiman Marcus); 2) offer the kind of distribution exclusivity that other designer lines do not; 3) increase Hanes' market share in the upscale stores with an expansion of Donna Karan hosiery—when and if Donna Karan sportswear broadens to include prices lower than its current couture levels.

The addition of Donna Karan represents a big shift in direction for Hanes. It used to think of the department stores as one big homogeneous group. Now it's acknowledging that department stores are splitting into a variety of segments, each aimed at a distinct customer group. Hanes has always thought of its own brands as being targeted to a variety of consumers. Now it is focusing on both department store segments and *their* distinct customer types.

The Donna Karan line says something else about how Hanes views its business today. For years it resisted the designer hosiery business. Its arrangement with Oleg Cassini, discontinued last year, was a half-hearted, hesitant move in that direction. Cassini wasn't positioned as a separate brand; it was an "endorsement" which read "Hanes by Oleg Cassini."

Ultimately, the way designer hosiery was being marketed struck a raw nerve. Hanes was spending big money to advertise its hosiery. Along came the designer lines, succeeding in part because of the instant name recognition already afforded them by earlier product entries in sportswear, perfume, sunglasses, etc.

In a determined tone Schenck states, "The designer lines had a name that was known, so you didn't have to spend a lot of money to convince people. As a result they offered the trade a high margin. So you had a brand that automatically had a customer and that presumably turned well. We needed that in our kit bag; we were not going to sit here and not play in that game."

The licensing arrangement with Karan is a first for both parties. Until now, Donna Karan accessories have been produced and sold by the Karan organization.

Another "first" is that with the launch of this line, Hanes is handing over its veto power to Karan. Cathy Volker, Hanes' vp of product development, is responsible for the Karan launch. But when it comes to final decisions on packaging, styling, marketing, it's Donna Karan who is calling the shots.

The plan is to launch the line for fall, start small with a limited distribution to under 1,000 doors (compared to Hanes distribution to about 12,000 doors) that also carry the Karan sportswear line. Initial sales could be small compared to Hanes' other broader-based lines. The line will have its own sales force.

Volker adds: "All the better stores are asking for exclusivity. We're really the only ones who are going to give it to them. And there is a big void in the market for a truly better hosiery brand."

An Open Mind

Hanes isn't saying "no" to any new idea for increasing its business, including the addi-tion of other designer names, as long as they don't compete with the Karan line or target the same customer. Schenck obviously relishes the possibility of growing into a dominant share of the upscale department store business.

It is often said that the most nerve-wracking position a company can be in is that of market leader. Companies like IBM, General Motors and Revlon would probably agree. Hanes, on the other hand, seems to be thriving in—and enjoying—the top spot that is alleged to be a precarious perch.

AN INDUSTRY FOCUS: THE BUSINESS OF INTIMATE APPAREL: WHAT'S NEXT?

Trend Setter . . .
Sleeping Giant . . .
Key to Fantasy

These are but a few key phrases used to describe the intimate apparel industry today at a lively, thought-provoking panel discussion, the first of The Fashion Group's Industry Focus series.

Presented in September to an enthusiastic, sell-out crowd, the program addressed both the problems and the paradoxes of an industry on the brink of self-discovery . . . an industry that has gone from house-dress dowdy to the inspiration for those glamorous clothes seen on steamy soaps and rock-beat soundstages.

In their introductory remarks, Elaine Taylor-Gordon and Norma Reinhardt, co-chairmen and moderators, noted that the innerwear industry, historically accustomed to reacting to ready-to-wear trends, is finding itself setting the trends instead. In the process, the industry has "discovered" marketing.

"Once the province of movie stars and mistresses, fine lingerie has become a treat that women are giving themselves. No longer viewed as kinky or frivolous, provocative lingerie is now considered a justifiable expense and an investment in self-esteem," claimed Elaine Taylor-Gordon.

"Women are looking for—and finding —more romantic, more daring lingerie," added Norma Reinhardt. "They're gleaning them from catalogs and small lingerie boutiques that often project an image of Jean Harlow's walk-in closet."

Source: *Fashion Group Report*, September 16, 1988. Reprint permission granted by The Fashion Group International.

Current Trends . . .

Some of the trends pointed to by the moderators: a resurgence of femininity (noted in the revival of tricot, particularly in trousseau sets) and the trend towards pure comfort (cozy-up loungewear for "couch potatoes").

Teenagers were credited for the "incredible cross-pollinization of innerwear and outer wear," another noteworthy trend. And, according to the moderators, these teens represent a virtually untapped $5.5 *billion* market!

Women are choosing feminine and romantic looks, wearing lingerie and lingerie looks outside, teaming sleepshirts with skirts, using nightgowns for formal wear, pairing bustiers, chemises and camisoles with evening shirts and pants in a manner that appeals to the ever-practical American woman.

"It's glamorous, it makes everybody feel good and . . . it's big business!", concluded Ms. Taylor-Gordon.

Toothpaste and Salad Bars . . .

Jill Gerson, Editor

What do Topol toothpaste, Alcott & Andrews, McDonald's Salad Bar and the sports bra have in common?

Nothing on the surface. But as Jill Gerson pointed out, each was developed to satisfy specific consumer needs.

Ms. Gerson noted that intimate apparel, like many other consumer commodities marketed in the 80's, has experienced growth by identifying specific market needs and then developing products to meet these specific needs. Such "niche marketing" has

paved the way for intimate apparel successes like the sports bra and the minimizer and has brought about the invention of a leisure wear category.

Other successes mentioned by Ms. Gerson were the new-again crinoline petticoat, the padded shoulder camisole, a bonafide underwear revolution spearheaded by brands like Jockey, Calvin Klein and Swipe, plus "alphabet" bras with A, T and Z backs designed to accommodate fashionable sleevelines and necklines. Sales of bras projected at $1.75 million for 1988 could, with the adroit use of niche marketing, reach well over the $2 million mark by the late 90's.

Ms. Gerson suggested that the intimate apparel industry study some of the cosmetics industry's tricks of their trade — creating illusions and then creating markets to fulfill these illusions.

Growth Opportunities . . .

As for growth opportunities, Ms. Gerson pointed to the maturing baby-boomer, the large-size customer, the traveling career woman and the new maternity customer. Other opportunities exist for our disposable-oriented society, for filling the special needs of women who remain active in their later years, even for the growing necessity for different home and office lingerie wardrobes. And, she hinted, even the growing movement towards a more monogamous society could present other growth potential.

Ms. Gerson urged the industry to "think about how old fifty used to be. The fifty-year-old customer of the past was the duster customer, the girdle customer. Today a fifty-year-old woman is very young." Her lifestyle, she added, is active and global and she frequently has more money to spend than ever before. She thinks young and probably will do so for the rest of her life. "We must to think like she does."

Ms. Gerson noted the effect this attitude has had on the robe and loungewear markets. "Almost overnight, the robe business took a dive and a new leisurewear category was born."

"Lifestyle changes have blurred the distinction between sleepwear and loungewear, robes and leisurewear. It is the people who understand these lifestyle changes and their effects who will grow and prosper," concluded Ms. Gerson.

What's Needed . . .

David Gustafson, Wacoal

According to David Gustafson, it's time for intimate apparel to be treated as serious fashion. To be so treated, intimate apparel must itself be truly fashionable.

Mr. Gustafson pointed to a shallowness and lack of quality to life in this country as contrasted with "a certain aesthetic sensitivity that many of our European and Japanese neighbors come by naturally." Mentioning "state of mind and commitment to a higher standard," he complimented the Galeries Lafayette in Paris on "upgrading the whole concept of department store boutiques, making shopping for intimate apparel a pleasurable experience."

He lauded Donna Karan and Calvin Klein, among others, for the use of lycra in body-conscious lingerie fabrications, believing that they showed awareness of the appeal of intimate apparel as true fashion. Even so, he queried, "Why do so many of us relegate intimate apparel to one of the functional necessities of life, somewhere between toothpaste and feminine hygiene? Why are we satisfied with the assumption

that a couple of bras a year and a couple of things to sleep in are sufficient in terms of our own lifestyles? And why are we happy with a $6 million industry six years running?"

His conclusion to such questions: What's needed is a new retail environment . . . one that makes intimate apparel fun to shop for, fun to buy, fun to wear.

Shoppers Speak Out . . .

To support this point of view, Mr. Gustafson presented film clips of focus-group interviews. Some of the shopper's comments:

— "If you don't see it on the wall, they don't have it."
— "With 10,000 panties hanging on the Panty Wall, I don't know how anybody can make a decision . . . it's too overwhelming."
— "When you go into the Intimate Apparel department in Nordstrom's, you have a salesperson . . . you are treated with kid gloves."

These same shoppers criticized stores for lack of sales help, particularly for the young girl buying her first bra and also for such things as permitting only two bras at a time in fitting rooms, creating beautiful displays that entice the customer and then providing no sales help to get merchandise for her.

Although, according to Mr. Gustafson, retail presentation has gone from bad to very bad in the past ten years, some firms have begun to show enthusiasm for change. His advice: Make priorities quality, *not* price alone . . . fashion, *not* function alone . . . ambiance, *not* density and dozens-per-square-foot alone—service *not* abandonment. He also suggested closer cooperation between designers and retailers and urged that manufacturers learn store organization and begin to work as closely with store management as with the merchandising side.

Need and Feel Good . . .

Dr. Judith Kuriansky, Psychologist

Dr. Judith Kuriansky, psychologist, broadcaster, columnist and protege of Masters & Johnson, spoke of the overlap between the intimate apparel and counseling fields . . . that of recognizing people's need to feel good about themselves, then marketing products to meet that need. In her own counseling, she noted, she advises people to change their wardrobes if necessary in order to wear whatever makes them feel good.

People should indulge in such feel-good items by going out and shopping for them, a direct boon to the intimate apparel business. And, she claimed, as women become more comfortable with the notion of living out their fantasies, lingerie becomes a key item. And that, of course, becomes a major thrust in the marketing of intimate apparel. However, Dr. Kuriansky cautioned, the industry must also recognize that trends toward seductivity and sensuality need not be overtly sexual.

Practical Glamour . . .

Dr. Kuriansky noted that she constantly queries women in high-fashion stores about their lingerie selections and the motivations behind those selections. Interviews with women at Saks Fifth Avenue and other stores revealed that more and more women are wearing beautiful lingerie for themselves, not necessarily for a partner. She said that in a discussion with designer Bill Tice, the phrase "practical glamour" surfaced. Kuriansky believes this phrase accurately reflects the attitudes of women today; they would like to be attractive, glamorous, even "glitzy", but want the practicality of a comfortable garment as well. (Teddies fall into the pretty-but-impractical category with some of Kuriansky's clients.)

Lingerie marketers need to be aware, she pointed out, of the multiple roles women have today as careerists, parents and lovers. Combining practicality with glamour should be the thrust of the intimate apparel industry in deciding what goes into stores next.

Swirls and Hooverettes . . .

Bernie Ozer, AMC

Bernard Ozer, a fashion-business veteran of more than thirty years, noted that the business of intimate apparel has come a long way since the days when the robe was a brunch coat, a dress a frock, Swirls twirled and Hooverettes swept the marketplace! Today this department contributes 4% of total store volume and, even more significant, clears up to ten percentage points higher in gross margins in total store. Ozer posed pertinent questions: With intimate apparel such an integral building block to retail's foundation, how do we take it from supporting role to make it a star? How can we awaken this grand sleeping beauty? And how do we take lingerie out of the closet and turn it into a commodity come-on?

Mr. Ozer's one-word answer: Specialization. The success of specialty retailers such as The Gap, The Limited and Victoria's Secret demonstrates that specialization is rapidly replacing generalization as the key to successful wholesaling and retailing.

"Sexy" Sells . . .

When it comes to specialization on the intimate-apparel front, the two areas of opportunity cited by Ozer are those that target 1) the sexy looks, or 2) "couch potatoes". Sexy looks, he said, have gotten a boost from stars like Madonna and Cindi Lauper —rock stars who've "flaunted it, pushed it out, sucked it in, girdled it, corseted it and let it slip." In turn, smart intimate apparel manufacturers echoed the trend with inside-out lingerie—crinolines, teddies and bustiers all meant to show. Scantily-clad soap queens, daytime or prime time, have captured the imaginations of women who daydream about a more glamorous lifestyle. The bottom line on that fantasy? Sex equals seduction equals sales!

The flip counterpart of the sexy consumer is, Ozer reports, none other than the "couch potato"—a self-proclaimed stay-at-home who is a direct by-product of the high-tech environment. In the book "Megatrends", John Naisbett predicted that the high-tech environment would cause a need for more high-touch products. The growth opportunity implied for the intimate apparel industry is in robes and leisurewear, a category that currently represents a 12% penetration level in total intimate apparel business.

Mr. Ozer suggests fleece as a particularly good area for intimate apparel manufacturers to exploit. One idea: "couch potato" fleece shops for the whole family complete with Mr. Potatohead logos, TV sets and potato chips, gift-with-purchase incentives.

Mr. Ozer cited figures saying that 72% of customers are open to coordinate purchases if they are displayed together. This makes a case for the market provision of a more fashion-right concept of two-piece dressing, pairing robes with sleepwear, robes with daywear. He also suggested that robes be thought of as the outerwear department of intimate apparel and suggested that retailers appeal to a contemporary customer with robes that are in tune with fashion's trends.

"Creative Sells" . . .

Mr. Ozer suggested that both manufacturers and merchandisers should turn the creative wheels and offered suggestions such as:

- Set up a main floor "body cosmetics" shop. Include fragrance, cosmetics or bathwear line and offer gift with purchase.
- Offer gift-with-purchase stockings with garter belts to combat the hosiery business' teddy hose.
- Cross merchandise—package intimate apparel for men—silk boxer shorts, for instance—and merchandise them as impulse gift items in high-traffic women's departments. Conversely, package women's silk panties, g-strings and lace camisoles and outpost them in men's departments.
- Offer pre-packed boxes of a week's supply of panties or bras for all her lifestyles.
- Set up a year-round monogramming shop, offering free monogramming on purchases over $50 and place the shop strategically on a his or her outpost.
- Provide retailers with sex education teachers to train sales people in the nuances of fit, style by body type and appropriate merchandising techniques.
- Aggressively pair ready-to-wear and intimate apparel to promote important trends, i.e., short slips for shorter skirts. Advertise and promote such merchandise

with special manufacturer hangtags to illustrate the style, educate the consumer.

- Introduce multiple sales. Be aware of trends. Mr. Ozer predicts a Pucci-print revival for fall 1988 and suggests capitalizing on it with coordinated sheets, sleepwear and robes.
- Begin marketing more intimate apparel to men.

Special Sizes . . .

According to Mr. Ozer, the single fastest growing opportunity for specialization exists in special sizes. Large-size shops, ready-to-wear and accessory departments are growing to the tune of 20–50% per year. He pointed to Brookshire Hosiery's success in translating current sexy lingerie and hosiery packaging to their large-size customers and suggested carrying through with large-size teddies, bustiers, garter belts, camisoles and bikinis. Since the large-size woman doesn't negate her own sexuality, neither should the industry, Ozer advises, recommending more lace, vivid colors, prints and touchable silks in sexy, sensuous lingerie.

Finally, Mr. Ozer pointed out that specialized customer lifestyle marketing and merchandising opportunities are inconsequential if the product isn't trend-right. Here are some of the trends (seen in St. Tropez) that he cited among those that should influence the intimate apparel business:

- Shapes like Empire, flyaway and hourglass, in stretch or puckered fabrics.
- Dayglow colors cutting through neutrals and pastels.
- Logos, from Australian surfer to pinball graphics, a natural for junior nightshirt business.
- Sheer shirts which call for shockingly bright silk camisoles to wear beneath.
- Black and white taken beyond the basics, newest mixed with gingham, dots, stripes, plaids and florals.
- Folkloric looks heralding a return of ethnic prints and textured fabrics, from large baroque tapestries to small provincial prints.
- Pajama parties—celebrating home entertaining with a return to surface interest crepes, silks in pajamas reminiscent of 1930's–40's glamour lingerie.
- Continuing interest in all things British from Victorian velvet robes to monogrammed lapels to tartan bra-and-panty sets to items that recall the 60's, that unforgettable heyday of hip Carnaby Street.

Endnotes

1. Ame Keenes, senior vice president and general merchandise manager of Neiman Marcus, *Women's Wear Daily*, May 19, 1989.
2. Speech given by Renie Brown, publisher/editorial director of *Accessories Magazine*, Fashion Group International Accessories Industry Focus Program, May 17, 1989.
3. *Women's Wear Daily/Accessories*, October, 1988.
4. Harold R. Quimby, "The Story of Footwear," *Shoe and Leather Reporter*, Vol. 216, No. 13, December 30, 1936.
5. Footwear Industries of America, December 31, 1989.
6. *New York Times*, February 14, 1989.

7. Companies' annual reports.

8. "Sneakers Gain as a Symbol of Commuting," *Wall Street Journal*, October 17, 1984.

9. "Footwear Profile for 1989," *Kurt Salmon Perspective*, 1989.

10. Janet Treber, chief statistician of Footwear Industries of America, in conversation with author.

11. *Statistical Reporter*, Footwear Industries of America, April 1990; and *U.S. Industrial Outlook*, 1990.

12. "Footwear: Concept Stores," *Stores*, August 1988.

13. Paul McGuire, Director, Nike's Retail Division.

14. *Statistical Reporter*, April 1990; and *U.S. Industrial Outlook*, 1990.

15. Ibid.

16. Sarah Alexander, chief statistician of National Association of Hosiery Manufacturers, in conversation with author.

17. National Association of Hosiery Manufacturers, Charlotte, N.C., 1988 Hosiery Statistics.

18. Ibid.

19. Cutting Edge, "Hot Sox Spreads Its Empire," *Women's Wear Daily*, May 3, 1989.

20. National Association of Hosiery Manufacturers, 1989 Hosiery Statistics.

21. *U.S. Industrial Outlook*, 1990.

22. Ibid.

23. *Women's Wear Daily*, May 3, 1986.

24. Ibid.

25. *U.S. Industrial Outlook*, 1990.

26. Leslie Ruth Pelz, *Fashion Accessories*, 2d ed. Indianapolis: Bobbs-Merrill Educational Publishing, 1980.

27. Census of Manufacturers.

28. *U.S. Industrial Outlook*, 1990.

29. Ibid.

30. Conversations with publicity directors of Millinery Institute of America, June 24, 1989.

31. Ibid.

32. Norma Galbraith, executive at Consolidated Millinery, in conversation with author.

33. Census of Manufacturers and Current Industrial Reports, 1989.

34. *U.S. Industrial Outlook*, 1990.

35. *New York Times*, April 16, 1989.

36. Ibid.; and *U.S. Industrial Outlook*, 1990.

37. *New York Times*, April 16, 1989.

38. Ibid.

39. "Claiborne Buys Its Accessories Line," *Women's Wear Daily*, December 23, 1985.

40. Fairchild Fact File—Women's Inner Fashions, Nightwear, Daywear, Loungewear 1990; Census of Manufacturers and Current Industrial Reports, 1990.

41. Ibid.

Selected Bibliography

Becker, Vivienne. *Art Nouveau Jewelry*, 1st ed. New York: E. P. Dutton, 1985.

Boehn, Max von. *Ornaments: Lace, Fans, Gloves, Walking Sticks, Parasols, Jewelry and Trinkets*, reprint of the 1929 edition. New York: Ayer Company, 1970.

Clark, Fiona. *Hats*. London: B. T. Batesford, 1982.

Cumming, Valerie. *Gloves*. London: B. T. Batesford, 1982.

Gray, Mitchell. *The Lingerie Book*. New York: St. Martin's Press, 1982.

Johnson, Eleanor. *Fashion Accessories*. Aylesbuey, Bucks, England: Shire, 1980.

Kedley, Lyngerda, and Nancy Schiffer. *Costume Jewelry, The Great Pretenders*. Westchester, Penna.: Schiffer Publishing Ltd., 1987.

Northampton English Museum. *A History of Shoe Fashions*. Northampton, England: Museum Pub., 1975.

Peltz, Leslie Ruth. *Fashion Accessories*, 3rd ed. Encino, Calif.: Elencoe, 1986.

Probert, Christina. *Shoes in Vogue since 1910*. New York: Abbeville Press, 1981.

Schiffer, Nancy. *The Power of Jewelry*. Westchester, Penna.: Schiffer Publishing Ltd., 1987.

Swann, June. *Shoes*. New York: Drama Book, 1982.

Tice, Bill. *Enticements: How to Look Fabulous in Lingerie*. New York: Macmillan, 1985.

The Undercover Story. New York: Fashion Institute of Technology, 1982.

Untracht, Oppi. *Jewelry Concepts and Technology*. Garden City, N.Y.: Doubleday, 1982.

Zucker, Benjamin. *Gems and Jewels: A Connoisseur's Guide*. New York: Thames and Hudson, 1984.

Trade Associations

American Footwear Industry Association, 1611 North Kent Street, Arlington, Va. 22209.

Associated Corset and Brassiere Manufacturers, 535 Fifth Avenue, New York, N.Y. 10017.

Association of Umbrella Manufacturers and Suppliers, 11 West 32nd Street, New York, N.Y. 10001.

Belt Association, 225 West 34th Street, New York, N.Y. 10122.

Footwear Council, 51 East 42nd Street, New York, N.Y. 10017.

Intimate Apparel Council for the American Apparel Manufacturing Association, 1611 North Kent Street, Suite 800, Arlington, Va. 22209.

Jewelry Industry Council, 608 Fifth Avenue, New York, N.Y. 10020.

Lingerie Manufacturers Association, 41 East 42nd Street, New York, N.Y. 10018.

Manufacturing Jewelers and Silversmiths of America, Inc., The Biltmore Plaza, Providence, R.I. 02903.

Millinery Institute of America, 37 West 39th Street, New York, N.Y. 10018.

National Association of Fashion Accessory Designers, 2721 Clayton Street, Denver, Co. 80205.

National Association of Hosiery Manufacturers, 516 Charlottetown Mall, Charlotte, N.C. 28204.

National Fashion Accessories Association, 350 Fifth Avenue, New York, N.Y. 10001.

National Association of Glove Manufacturers, 30 South Main Street, Gloversville, N.Y. 12078.

National Shoe Fair, 230 West 55th Street, Suite 22D, New York, N.Y. 10019.

National Shoe Retailers Association, 200 Madison Avenue, New York, N.Y. 10016.

Trade Publications

Accent (Jewelry), Sugartown News, Devon, Penna. 19333.

Accessories, 22 South Smith Street, Norwalk, Conn. 06855.

Fashion Accessories Magazine, 244 Madison Avenue, New York, N.Y. 10016.

Footwear Focus, 200 Madison Avenue, New York, N.Y. 10016.

Footwear News, 7 East 12th Street, New York, N.Y. 10003.

Glove News, 30 South Main Street, Gloversville, N.Y. 12078.

Hosiery & Underwear, 757 Third Avenue, New York, N.Y. 10017.

Intimate Apparel, 757 Third Avenue, New York, N.Y. 10017.

Intimate Fashion News, 309 Fifth Avenue, New York, N.Y. 10016.

Jewelers Circular—Keystone, 825 Seventh Avenue, New York, N.Y. 10019.

Leather and Shoes, 47 West 34th Street, New York, N.Y. 10001.

Modern Jeweler, 133 East 58th Street, New York, N.Y. 10022.

National Jeweler, 1515 Broadway, New York, N.Y. 10036.

National Shoe Retailer Association Newsletter, 200 Madison Avenue, New York, N.Y. 10006.

Wigs, Hats and Accessories, 22 East 42nd Street, New York, N.Y. 10007.

CHAPTER REVIEW AND LEARNING ACTIVITIES

Key Words and Concepts

Define, identify, or briefly explain the following:

Accessories	Lingerie
Bridge jewelry	Loungewear
Costume jewelry	Nonrubber footwear
Electroplating	Precious stones
Fine jewelry	Small leather goods
Foundations	Sterling silver
Intimate apparel industry	24K
"Jellies"	Uppers
Karats	Vamp
Last	

Review Questions on Chapter Highlights

1. How do fashions in accessories relate to apparel fashions? Give examples.
2. What four factors do all of the accessory industries have in common?
3. What is the difference between rubber and nonrubber athletic footwear? Why is this distinction made?
4. In sequential order, list and explain the steps in the construction of shoes.
5. Why have shoe departments traditionally been leased? What is the current status of leased shoe departments?
6. Why are imports less "threatening" to the hosiery industry than they are to other segments of accessories?
7. How has the handbag industry responded to the deluge of handbag imports?
8. List the various parts and different types of gloves.
9. Give three major categories of jewelry and explain the differences among them.
10. Discuss the statement that "it still remains to be seen whether promotion and fashion creativity can reverse the trend to hatlessness." Will this industry be revitalized?
11. Name the three major divisions of the intimate apparel industry and give one well-known brand name in each.
12. Give examples of designer licensing in each product area of the accessories industries.
13. What changes in the intimate apparel industry are discussed in the reading "Industry Focus: The Business of Intimate Apparel: What's Next?"
14. The readings discuss some of the marketing strategies used by different accessory companies. Name several and explain why they took place.

_7_

_I_MPORTS

A development of major importance in the American fashion business has been the penetration of foreign-made clothing, accessories, and textiles into the domestic markets. Today, even though productive capacity and creative talent abound in this country, importing from foreign sources of supply has become a multibillion dollar activity of the U.S. textile–apparel–retailing complex.

Imports and exports have always been a major consideration of nations. Each country tries to sustain and expand its economy by exporting products it has in abundance or can produce efficiently and importing those it needs or cannot produce efficiently. As far as fashion merchandise is concerned, international trade in the United States dates back to the country's beginnings. As far back as the eighteenth century, the inventories of our sailing ships listed silks from China, woolens and calicos from England, damasks and velvets from Italy, and embroideries and fine laces and fabrics from Paris. In the nineteenth century, dolls dressed in the latest French fashions were imported by American dressmakers to be used as models of the garments they would create for their wealthy clientele. When advanced printing techniques made possible illustrated magazines, dressmakers turned to such early European magazines as _Peterson's_ and _Mrs. Demarest_ to see what was being worn in London and Paris—and copied what they saw. Early American fashion retailers, such as Lord & Taylor of New York and Marshall Field of Chicago, bought the models of leading Paris designers, such as Worth and Doucet, as well as European fabrics and trimmings, to copy couture styles in their workrooms.

This chapter discusses the penetration of imports into the United States, the reasons for it, the procedures involved, and the applicable government regulations. The readings deal with the importing operations of well-known American producers and retailers. The chapter that follows deals with the foreign producers that supply us with our imports.

European   Imports   in   the   19th
Century

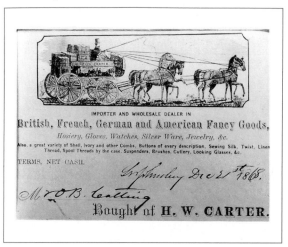

IMPORT PENETRATION BY
FOREIGN PRODUCERS _____

Although competition from **imports** is a problem shared by all consumer-oriented domestic manufacturing industries, the fashion industry has been one of the hardest hit by the penetration of imports. Since 1970, imports have been increasing faster than domestic output, resulting in a decline in consumer purchases for domestically produced fashion goods.

Imports versus Domestic Production

In 1970 we imported $1.3 billion in clothing and textiles for men, women, and children. By 1980 our imports had reached $5.1 billion.[1] In 1989 imports of such merchandise grew to a staggering $32.4 billion.[2]

Impressive as the dollar figures are, attention must also be paid to the percentage relationship between domestic production and apparel imports. This is known as **import penetration**, a way to measure foreign against domestic goods. For example, in 1980 it averaged 31.1 percent for the industry as a whole[3] and by 1989 had grown to an amount equal to 55 percent of U.S. apparel production.[4] What this figure means, as previously noted, is that overall for every 100 garments produced by our domestic industry, an additional 55 are imported from foreign producers. It is estimated that if the growth of imports is not drastically curtailed, import penetration could account for 65 percent of all apparel in the not too distant future.

In some categories of merchandise, however, the market share of imports is even greater than that of domestic output. For example, 75 percent of the

Growth of Imports and Import Penetration in Selected Women's
Garments (Imports in thousands of units: Penetration by %)

Type of Garments	1980		1989	
	Import Units	Import Penetration	Import Units	Import Penetration
Coats, jackets, raincoats	47,441	65.9%	78,701	235.6%
Suits and dresses	26,168	7.2	81,435	39.6
Blouses (woven fabric)	210,960	45.9	271,508	158.3
Knit shirts	168,809	54.3	527,060	130.7
Sweaters	123,106	130.7	307,253	373.5
Skirts	14,774	15.3	85,595	83.9
Slacks and shorts*	168,036	34.8	446,054	93.5
Nightwear & pajamas	8,534	3.2	87,357	28.7
Underwear	53,466	5.8	450,724	34.9
Bras & girdles	200,983	66.6	219,759	101.9

*Includes jeans
SOURCE: *U.S. Bureau of the Census and ILGWU Research Department.*

sweaters available to consumers are imported, as are 61 percent of women's
knitted blouses. In all other categories except dresses, suits (both men's and
women's), and men's trousers, imports are equal to domestic production.[5]

Apparel/Textile Trade Deficit

A **trade deficit** is the amount by which the value of imports exceeds exports. In
1989, the United States imported $26 billion of apparel and $6.4 billion of
textiles, a combined total of $32.4 billion. This compares with exports of textiles
amounting to $3.8 billion and $2 billion worth of apparel, or a total of $5.8
billion. The trade deficit of apparel and textiles combined was $26.4 billion, the
highest in history.[6]

REGULATION OF IMPORTS — — — — — — — — — — — —

The international trading policy of the United States has generally been based
on the principle that high tariffs and excessive restrictions of foreign goods will
lower our standard of living for the following reasons:

- Trade barriers mean high prices for consumers, since decreased competition
  will allow domestic firms to charge higher prices.
- Domestic producers that are incapable of meeting competition are not entitled to special consideration by the government.
- Nations affected by restrictive import measures taken by this country may
  retaliate against what they consider to be American protectionism, and thus
  damage the export prospects of outer industries in this country.

U.S. Apparel and Textile Imports, Exports, and Trade Balance

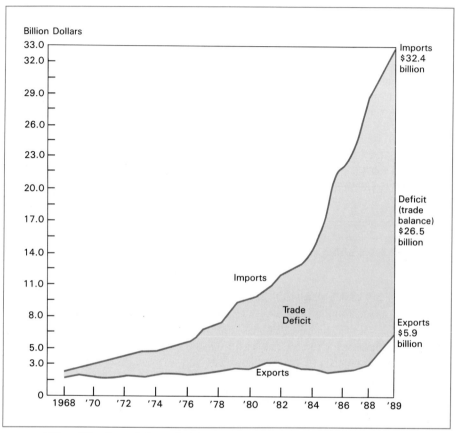

SOURCE: Office of Textiles and Apparel, U.S. Department of Commerce.

• Trade restraints to protect one industry, such as textiles and apparel, may save some jobs but increase unemployment in others as foreign countries retaliate by buying less from the United States. Also, domestic firms that rely on imports would be less able to compete and would lose business.

In 1947, the United States and other major trading nations entered into the General Agreement on Tariffs and Trade (known as **GATT**). This is a multilateral agreement designed to liberalize and govern world trade. Within the framework of GATT, there are many different trading agreements and rules, some of which are entered into by two or more countries, and some of which are unilateral.

The Multi-Fiber and Textile Arrangement

Until the 1970s, the dollar volume of U.S. purchases from foreign producers was relatively insignificant and therefore created little or no real disruption of our domestic textile and apparel industries. As imports began to swell and penetration reached flood level, the U.S. government moved to control the growth rate of imports by keeping it equal to the growth rate of domestic production. The most important outcome of this was the multilateral Multi-Fiber Textile Arrangement (**MFA**). This provides an umbrella under which nations may negotiate and implement bilateral trade agreements.

The MFA first became effective in 1974 and was renewed, with some revisions, in 1977, to cope with the problem of increased penetration into the apparel/textile industry. The MFA sets general rules for the kinds of actions countries can take to protect their industries from disruption by rising imports. Under its provisions, the United States (or any other nation) can control disruptive imports by consulting with the exporting nations individually and entering into bilateral agreements, which establish import quotas. Such agreements provide for a somewhat orderly development of trade and offer some relief to a country that is being overwhelmed by imports.

The MFA, however, is not without shortcomings, and it does not give American producers the measure of relief they need. In many categories of apparel, the permitted level of imports remains high enough to disrupt domestic production. A further weakness is that the MFA assumes levels of domestic growth beyond what is actually occurring, and thus lets imports continue at a disproportionate level. Another shortcoming is that the MFA limits the quantity or number of units brought into the United States rather than the cost value of the merchandise. Foreign producers are thus encouraged to shift into higher-priced items if they choose to do so, thereby cutting even more deeply into the dollar value of the domestic market.

At the time of this writing, the MFA is up for revision. Most of the low-wage apparel-producing nations want it scrapped, whereas the United States and European countries favor a more stringent trade agreement that would include such measures as surcharges on exports from low-wage countries.

The MFA was further revised in the 1980s, but its basic ground rules were not changed. The only major change was the addition of silk, linen, and ramie to the original negotiable categories of wool, cotton, and man-made fibers.

Quotas and Bilateral Trade Agreements

Quotas are quantitative restrictions placed on exporting countries on the number of units of specific items that may be shipped to a particular importing country over a specified period of time. With some regulated exceptions, which are explained below, a foreign producer cannot ship goods into the United States without a quota.

Quotas for Sale

SOURCE: Reprinted with permission of RWP: Hva Shak Company.

The United States negotiates separate bilateral treaties with each of the textile/apparel exporting nations. These **bilateral treaties** establish country-by-country quotas, or annual maximums, on hundreds of categories in cotton, wool, man-made fiber textiles, and apparel. Each bilateral agreement establishes the quota level on a category-by-category basis, specifies the growth factors to be applied to each quota year, and provides for establishing new quotas in cases in which the bilateral agreement does not provide for a particular import category. The negotiating of bilateral agreements is the responsibility of the office of the U.S. Trade Representative. The Customs Service is responsible for keeping track of import levels and quota levels. When more goods are presented for entry into the United States than the quota level allows, that merchandise is denied entry and is warehoused at the port of entry, at the expense of the importer.

Quotas, which vary for different merchandise categories and for different countries, are specified in numerical units first by fiber square yardage equivalents (SYE) and then are translated into apparel categories. For example, Hong Kong has the largest quota allocation for natural fiber garments, whereas Taiwan and South Korea have the biggest quotas for man-made fibers. Usually, the exporting country administers its own quota and makes allocations to individual producers based on their past export performance. Allocations can be lost if they are not used within the designated quota year. Manufacturers, however, can and do sell unused quotas to other companies and thus maintain their export rights for subsequent years.

In Hong Kong particularly, the system has given rise to quota brokers, who deal independently in unused or excess quotas. In some cases, a manufacturer who has large quota allotments can make more profit from selling part or all of its quota than from actually producing apparel.

Several areas in the world, however, have no quota restrictions at all — for example, the European Economic Community (EEC). Exemptions are based on the assumption that (1) these are high-wage industrialized countries whose products are not price-competitive with domestic goods, (2) our exports to these countries balance our imports from them, and (3) their import penetration is not large enough to cause domestic market disruption.

Also exempt from U.S. quotas are countries in the Caribbean Basin or in Central America — this is because the regions are not considered to constitute major apparel-producing centers. Many countries in Africa and Asia that are not yet in the industrialized or even in the developing stage are exempt as well. Our relations with these exempt areas are in marked contrast with the quota restrictions we place on more than 90 percent of the garments imported from Taiwan, Hong Kong, South Korea, and China, our four biggest sources of supply.

"GETTING AROUND" THE QUOTAS

From time to time, the White House has announced programs to tighten the administration of the textile agreements in order to control an excessive influx of imports, yet little has been accomplished toward stemming the tide. U.S. importers, whether retailers, wholesale importers, or manufacturers, have been getting around quotas with impunity. Production has been transferred to countries with unused or excess quotas, or to developing countries without quotas. In addition, countries with used-up quotas are illegally trans-shipping through countries with quota availability.

In a sense, quotas have created opportunities of export growth for many of the low-wage producing countries developing around the world. As the demand for inexpensive imports grows, U.S. manufacturers have of necessity sought sources beyond the quota-limited facilities of Hong Kong, Taiwan, China, and South Korea. However, as the volume of garment production inevitably shifts from the Asian quadrangle to other emerging low-wage countries, new trade agreements are bound to follow. And with them will come the added headache of quotas.

In this day and age, obtaining the best quality and prices is not always the only concern of U.S. buyers. The problem of available quotas now complicates the procedure. For buyers who are interested in importing goods to America, availability centers on quotas—spelled with a capital "Q."

NEW COUNTRY-OF-ORIGIN RULES

To curtail quota evasion by diversion and trans-shipment through second countries on categories covered by treaties, new country-of-origin laws were established by the United States in January 1985. The new rules set up criteria for determining which country was truly the country of origin for incoming merchandise—and thus which country's quota was involved.

Traditionally, it has been accepted as legitimate practice for two or more foreign countries to contribute to the making of some apparel categories. For example, in the case of a knitted sweater, yarn could be spun in one country, dyed in another, knit into panels for back, front, and sleeves in a third, and then finally assembled into a garment, labeled, and exported in a fourth. Hong Kong, for instance, has functioned as the assembler and shipper for much of its knitwear, using panels knitted in mainland China.

The new rules say that the first manufacturing steps determine a garment's origin. It must carry an import label bearing that country's name and be subject to that country's quota limitations. In the example of Hong Kong, cited above, the sweaters are now regarded as having originated in China and would be counted against China's quota, even though Hong Kong does the finishing and shipping. The problem for Hong Kong is that China's quota is insufficient.

These new U.S. rules have affected such countries as Hong Kong, South Korea, and Taiwan. They are now exploring and investing in other low-wage countries that are producing below their quota levels or are quota free. Among this latter category are the Caribbean countries, Sri Lanka, Mauritius, and Thailand. As production shifts, however, quotas for such countries are inevitable, and may even result in some shift of production back to the United States.

Simultaneously with the new country-of-origin laws, a new textile and apparel law was passed which required that all clothing and household fabrics made in this country are now required to carry a label saying "Made in USA." The law also requires that all mail-order ads identify which items are manufactured in the United States and which in foreign countries. The intent of this legislation was to fill a void in existing labeling requirements and to provide the federal government with ways to prevent fraudulently marked or unmarked foreign goods.

Taxes on Imports: Tariffs/Duties

In addition to the restraints imposed by import quotas, most fashion goods are subject to an import tax. Among the rare exceptions are leather and furs. This tax on imports, known as a **duty** or **tariff**, is established and regulated by the

Example of "Made in the USA" Logo

SOURCE: Reprinted with permission of Crafted with Price in the USA Council, Inc.

U.S. government, paid by the importer, and collected by the U.S. Customs Service. The amount varies for different categories of merchandise, but it is generally *ad valorem*, or a percentage of the first or invoice cost. Its primary purpose, of course, is to increase the eventual selling price of imported goods and thus protect domestic industries. For many fashion categories, however, from the low-wage countries, even with the addition of taxes and shipping costs, the final landed cost in the United States is often considerably less than for domestically produced apparel of equal quality.

The countries from which we import tend to impose tariffs that are highly restrictive. They use excise taxes and other trade barriers that make this country's goods economically unsuitable for sale within their borders. Some, like Brazil, for example, keep the products of other countries, including the United States, from entering its country.

Preferential Programs: Exemptions from Tariffs or Quotas

The U.S. government also has a number of programs that are designed to stimulate the trade and economy of developing countries around the world. Such countries receive preferential treatment and exemption from quotas.

GENERAL SYSTEM OF PREFERENCES (GSP)

The GSP, which became effective in 1976 and expired in 1985, allowed merchandise from beneficiary countries to come in without quota restrictions or tariffs. These are **developing countries** or dependent countries and territories throughout the world. The original list consisted of 112 countries in Central America, Africa, Asia, the Caribbean Basin, and the Far East. Since 1976, however, some of those on the original list became highly industrialized and were removed from the preferred group—Taiwan, South Korea, and Sri Lanka, for example. Current lists were maintained and published in *Importing*, a periodical of the Department of the Treasury, U.S. Customs Service.

TARIFF SCHEDULE 807: VALUE-ADDED TAX

Section 807 of the U.S. Tariff Schedule provides for special duty treatment of garments that have been cut within this country, shipped abroad for further processing, and then reimported back into the United States.

Under this program, a domestic manufacturer, using only fabrics made in the United States, can cut the garments in a U.S. plant and ship the cut materials to another country for sewing. The only duty paid on the returning goods is a very low one—a tax only on the cost of labor for the sewing, which is considered the value added. In effect, if $10 worth of cut materials go out of the United States and the overseas labor costs are $1, only that $1 is taxed when the goods return.

807 Production in Costa Rica and Dominican Republic

---

807 PRODUCTION

Open capacity in D.R. for established women's sportswear manufacturer. Top quality, fast production, Florida cutting facilities. Contact Ms. Mandez, 315 666-4433.

807 PRODUCTION

Open capacity for men's suits in Costa Rica. American management available, quality sewing, fast turnaround. Contact Suzanne Wong, 202 123-2439.

THE CARIBBEAN BASIN INITIATIVE

In 1983 Congress passed the **Caribbean Basin Initiative (CBI)**, which permits almost all manufactured or semimanufactured goods produced in Caribbean and Central American countries to come into the United States without quota restrictions. The legislation was intended to industrialize these areas by stimulating their exports into the United States and thus spark a boom in manufacturing investments. In conjunction with the CBI, Caribbean countries recognized this potential for growth and adjusted their laws to provide incentives for industrialization. Among these incentives are duty-free importation of equipment, low factory rentals, and tax-free profits for a specified number of years.

Since the enactment of the CBI in 1983, shipments from that area increased from some $398 million to well over $2 billion in 1989.[7] Recent investment trends in the Caribbean indicate that exports to the United States will continue to grow.

The following reaction of the ILGWU to the increase in 807 operations in the Caribbean is of interest. "The increased resort to off-shore production under 807, a euphemism for imports, has led some to view this form of importing as somehow healthier for the U.S. than other forms of importing. This, of course, is nonsense, except for the individual firm doing the importing."[8] There are others, however, who argue that 807 benefits U.S. industry since all parts that are assembled are fabricated domestically. Among the Caribbean countries that are being used by domestic producers for their offshore production are Jamaica, the Dominican Republic, Haiti, and Costa Rica. Mexico, which is not a Caribbean country, is the largest producer under the 807 program.

Textile and Apparel Trade Bills

Introduced into Congress in 1985, a Textile and Apparel Trade Enforcement Act was presented by its proponents as a way to "promote orderly nondisruptive future growth of world trade in fibers, textiles and apparel products." Essentially, its purpose was to do the following:

- *Roll back imports* from the major exporting nations of South Korea, Taiwan, and Hong Kong from their 1984 levels by some 24 percent and assign them a 1 percent annual growth thereafter.
- *Limit 1985 imports* from China, Japan, Pakistan, Indonesia, India, the Philippines, Thailand, Brazil, and Singapore to 1984 levels, with a 1 percent annual increase in their quotas for 1986 and 1987.
- *Require an import license* as a prerequisite for all imports, including those from Canada, the EEC, and all other quota-free countries.
- *Vary quota restrictions* on imports from nations classified as "nonmajor exporters" of textiles and apparel, depending on whether their exported products equal 40 percent of U.S. domestic production of like merchandise during the preceding year. Whenever the 40 percent threshold is reached, a product would be classified as "import sensitive" and an import quota would be imposed.
- *Expansion of quotas on textiles* so that silk, linen, and ramie would be subject to the square yards equivalents (SYE) quotas imposed on cotton, wool, and man-made fiber merchandise.

Although passed by both houses of Congress, this bill was vetoed by President Reagan in December 1985, an action the industry termed "appalling." After the veto, its congressional supporters rescheduled an override veto on the bill for August 6, 1986, in an attempt to defeat his veto. The attempt failed by eight votes, reflecting the split between protectionists and free traders. In 1988 a somewhat modified textile/apparel trade bill was again passed by the House and Senate and again vetoed by President Reagan.

The industry was vowed to intensify its lobbying efforts and, at the time of this writing, has already announced that it will seek a compromise quota-revision bill that will not be vetoed by President Bush. What the outcome will be remains to be seen.

WHO IMPORTS AND WHY

There are two major categories of fashion merchandise that the United States imports. One is the importation of ready-to-wear fashion merchandise that is totally designed and produced by foreign manufacturers and for the most part is purchased by retail buyers for resale to their customers. The second type of importation is the merchandise that is contracted out to overseas factories for all or part of the production process and is then returned to the United States.

Whenever the domestic market is unable to meet a fashion need, whether it be lower prices, technical know-how, innovation, production capabilities, or whatever, imports have become a means of coping with the need. Each foreign source of supply contributes to the import stream according to its specialized capabilities and its particular area of expertise.

The reasons for the penetration of imports are many and varied. Among them are:

- *Lower prices*: On the price front, the domestic industry has a twofold disadvantage. Labor costs in America are much higher than in the low-wage countries around the world, and the domestic producer does not enjoy the tax exemptions, rebates, preferential financing schemes, and other profit cushions that many foreign governments provide their exporting entrepreneurs.

- *Availability of hand labor*: Many foreign countries have hand-production capabilities and expertise that we do not possess. For example, many foreign countries have generations of skills behind them in such hand operations as laces, embroideries, beading, hand-finished buttonholes, hand-loomed fabrics, and hand-knitted sweaters, to name but a few. They also have a large pool of handicraft workers.

- *Product voids in the United States*: In the category of merchandise that American producers either cannot produce at all or cannot do as well are the cashmeres of Scotland and China, the soft-as-butter leathers of Spain, the linens of Belgium, and the silks of Italy and China. Another example of a product void is the absence of domestically produced fully fashioned sweaters, which is such a labor-intensive process that the American knitwear industry cannot produce them at a salable price.

- *Foreign producers are more adaptable or cooperative*: Many users of imports feel that foreign producers are more cooperative and responsive to their needs than domestic suppliers. For example the president of Jones, NY explained that the firm makes 35 different styles of blouses, which it is able to do overseas without the snafus that would be encountered in the United States. "Here" he said, "they want to mass-produce one style of blouses and factories tell us what their needs are and what we should be doing instead of letting us design and telling them what we want. In the Orient, they are more flexible and less insistent upon large mass cuttings."[9]

  And as Art Ortenberg, the former co-chairman of Liz Claiborne, explained it, "When we show a new design to a Japanese sweater knitter, he says," 'Oh, how simple' but the American knitter says 'Oh, how complicated.' "[10] Many designers also verbalize that it's much easier to work, buy fabrics, and get things done in Europe and the Orient. According to Isaac Mizrahi, Europe has a more nurturing approach toward its talent, and Marc Jacobs says, "It's much easier to work in Tokyo where everyone wants to work with you. Here you go into a fabric company and they give you minimums. How can a young designer be creative here with that kind of attitude. A lot of times I see great fabric but I can't have it because the minimums are so high."[11]

- *Exclusive rights*: Foreign purchases also give American companies an opportunity to avoid sameness—assortments that are too much like those of their competitors. American retailers are always in search of new and different merchandise to which they can get exclusive rights, particularly if they can secure these rights without making the massive purchases often required by large, volume-minded American apparel producers. The exclusive items, not available in competing stores, permit the retailer to generate storewide excitement because the merchandise is free from competition. Similarly, it is almost impossible for apparel producers to obtain exclusivity of fabrics from American textile producers without committing themselves to the purchase of huge runs far in advance of their selling season. Foreign producers of apparel or textiles, which generally are not as large as American manufacturers, do not need or demand big commitments.

- *Fashion cachet of Europe*: Not to be underestimated as a reason for importing fashion goods is the glamour associated with European fashions and labels. From its inception, the U.S. fashion business has been influenced by foreign fashions and has found inspiration across the Atlantic. It is true that today a circle of American designers get adoring treatment from American retailers and their customers, yet what comes from the European fashion centers will probably always have a special cachet just because of its origin.

Imports by Retailers

A retail firm's success ultimately rests on the strength, balance, and competitiveness of its merchandise assortment. A major responsibility of retail buyers and merchandise managers is, therefore, to seek ideal assortments wherever they can find them. In many situations, imports are an essential ingredient of the retail product mix because they can provide distinctive, competitive, and profitable merchandise.

Although exact figures are not available, published estimates indicate that one-third of foreign-made goods are imported directly by American retailers, one-third by import jobbers, and the remaining third is being produced offshore for domestic apparel producers. It is also estimated, however, that goods of foreign origin account for only 10 to 15 percent of store inventories.[12]

IMPORT BUYING METHODS

Not all foreign purchases by retailers are made in a single pattern. Procedures vary and may involve anything from sending representatives abroad to placing an order with a foreign source at a showroom in the United States. Among the most common means are the following:

- *Foreign trade shows in the United States.* Many foreign producers exhibit their collections in the United States. Such showings may be at international trade shows staged in this country, or in single-nation shows sponsored by a particular country to court foreign buyers. Buyers who are unable or unwilling to make trips overseas do their buying at such shows.
- *Foreign producers' showrooms in the United States.* Many large overseas producers maintain their individual sales forces in showrooms in New York

City, as well as in major regional apparel marts, for the convenience of retailers.

- *Store-owned foreign buying offices.* Many large retailers maintain offices, independently or in conjunction with their buying offices in the United States, in major cities of Europe and the Orient, such as Florence, Paris, London, Hong Kong, and Tokyo. These offices keep their principals updated on new producers, important new products, and fashion developments. In addition, they place orders as requested and handle the forms and other procedures that are involved, such as letters of credit, quality control checks, and follow-through on shipping arrangements and delivery dates. Retailers that maintain such offices include, for example, Sears, J. C. Penney, Macy's, The May Company, and Saks Fifth Avenue. Also maintaining foreign offices for the benefit of the retailers they serve are such buying offices as Frederick Atkins and the Associated Merchandising Corporation.

- *Foreign commissionaires and agents.* Retailers, particularly those of smaller size that are not represented by their own foreign offices in a particular country, use **commissionaires** and agents. These functionaries assist store buyers when they make direct visits to the countries concerned. In return for a fee (i.e., a commission), they direct visiting buyers to suitable producers, handle the necessary export forms, and follow through on delivery and shipping arrangements.

- *Foreign trade showings.* Practically every European country and some Far Eastern fashion centers hold seasonal, semiannual group showings in March/April and in October. These shows are attended by thousands of visiting buyers from all over the world who come to buy or observe new developments in foreign fashions and products, or do both. Purchases that are made are followed up by either commissionaires or the foreign buying office serving the store concerned. These shows, which are both national and international in nature are discussed in the following chapter.

Ad by Foreign Commissionaire

SPECIFICATION BUYING FOR PRIVATE LABELS

The move toward import buying by retailers has been accelerated by the renewed retail trend toward featuring private label merchandise. Merchants have become disenchanted with designer-name products and national brands because these widely distributed products have lost much of their exclusivity. Designer names and national brands turn up in off-price discount stores that have multiplied like fried chicken and hamburger outlets.

Such store-name or private-brand goods, more often than not, are made overseas by producers that offer better comparative values in terms of styling or price, or sometimes both. Nearly all private-label merchandise is made to the specifications of the importing retailer (or retail buying group). In **specification buying**, the buyer plans the styles and designs to be produced. This is done sometimes by describing the garment, and sometimes by supplying an actual sample for copying or adaptation. The merchant may even supply the fabric, not necessarily from the country in which the garment is to be made. Also specified by the purchaser are the garment's measurements, its trimmings, the quantity, and the negotiated wholesale price. In effect, the retailer fulfills the function of an apparel jobber, and the foreign producer the function of a

Specification Buying from India

contractor. In this way, U.S. retailers can enjoy both exclusive styles and the favorable prices that are possible when merchandise is made to specifications by lower-cost producers in the Far East.

Imports by Producers

Even if all retailers were to purchase exclusively from domestic sources, imports would still be a major factor in their merchandise assortments, because U.S. manufacturers also import. The retailer that purchases these imports does so, not necessarily because they are imports, but because they satisfy a need in the merchandise assortment and can be sold profitably at a price point attractive to the store's customers.

DIRECT IMPORTS BY PRODUCERS

Producers do direct importing of textiles and apparel for the same reasons that apply to retailers—price advantage, exclusivity of product, foreign expertise, and any other fashion or quality factors that may be absent from domestic markets. Fabric mills import yarns not readily available in this country. Fabric jobbers and apparel manufacturers import silks and certain luxurious fabrics that are not produced here. Many sportswear apparel companies import sweaters or leather items to coordinate with their domestically produced skirts, slacks, and other separates. There are also some U.S.-based companies that specialize in importing finished products, such as dresses and skirts, and market them domestically under their own labels.

OFFSHORE PRODUCTION

Despite their continuing outcry over the amount of direct importing done by retail buyers, American producers have been steadily increasing their own import practices by having their merchandise produced abroad. For example, some 85 percent of Liz Claiborne's merchandise is produced by 26 manufacturers, most of which are located in the Far East.[13]

Imports from India and South America

Pisces Fashions Ltd. India	TEE SHIRTS IN SOUTH AMERICA
Looking for importers/wholesalers for woven sleep and loungewear production. We have 10 years experience with top corporations in U.S. market. NY contact: 212 789-1234. Overseas: 25 W. Gandhi Plaza, Delhi, India. 543-5454. TELEX: 33-7711.	Large tee shirt manufacturer, high-volume production, offers high-quality services in manufacturing or silk-screening tee shirts on any textiles. Contact Tee-Shirts, 8998 Carnation St., Wolfburg, NY 11666.

To manufacture overseas, domestic producers send designs, patterns, and production specifications that must be exact and clear. The three basic methods used when producing overseas are as follows:

1. **Production package:** In this method, everything but the design is supplied by the contractor, including the fabrics, all of the production processes, finishing, labeling, packaging, and shipping.
2. **Cut, make, and sew:** In this method, the domestic producer that supplies the designs buys the fabric from one country and then has it shipped to a contractor in another country to be cut and sewn according to specifications.
3. **Offshore assembly:** In this method, fabric is made and cut in the United States and then sent abroad for sewing as specified. It is then sent back to the originating company for finishing, labeling, and shipping.

PROTECTIONISM VERSUS FREE TRADE

The penetration of imports into the U.S. fashion business has given rise to a highly vocal battle between advocates of protectionism and of free trade. **Protectionism** means the reduction, limitation, or exclusion of foreign goods. **Free trade** means avoiding protectionist measures and letting goods flow freely among countries.

On the protectionist side are the American producers of apparel, accessories, and textiles, the two major industry unions (the ILGWU and the ACTWU), and the industry's trade associations. All are continuously lobbying in Washington for more protection from imports. On the other side are the retailers and their trade associations, and organized consumer groups. These spokespersons adamantly believe that the public wants and should have imported products. Other industries, too, are in the fray—industries that do have entry into markets abroad and fear they will lose them if protectionism is invoked on behalf of fashion industries.

In addition to their lobbying efforts, both sides exhort the general public to add its voice. Statements are made in newspapers and on TV, petitions are circulated, consumer surveys are made, and demonstrations are held.

To finance these efforts, American retailers formed the Retail Industry Trade Action Coalition (RITAC) in 1985 to fight for freer international trade in textiles and apparel. Its membership consists of 20 leading retail firms and 8 retail trade associations. Similarly, the fiber producers, fabric mills, and apparel manufacturers have formed and are supporting the Crafted with Pride in USA Council and launched a public information campaign to heighten consumer awareness of the "Made in the USA" label and to educate retailers on the bottom-line advantages of domestically produced goods. These advantages include timeliness, reduced handling costs, geographic proximity, and flexibility.

How the problem will be resolved is uncertain at this point. The arguments both for and against imports are valid and rational. One thing, however, is

Protectionism: "Crafted with Pride in
USA" Council

SOURCE: Reprinted with permission of Crafted with Pride in
the USA Council, Inc.

certain: The problem will not be easily cured and will continue to involve many
compromises to satisfy retailers, importers, foreign exporters, workers, labor
unions, textile producers, apparel and accessory manufacturers, U.S. legislators
—and the consumer.

GLOBAL SOURCING: AN INTERNATIONAL FASHION MIX

The fashion industry has indeed become a global one, involving a merchandise
mix that ranges from anything to everything, and comes from anywhere to
everywhere. Although the tempo of import growth has been moderating in
recent years, industry observers do not foresee a swing back to exclusively
domestic sourcing. Despite the declining dollar, the tightening enforcement of
quota restrictions, the growing protectionist movement in the United States, and
the shifting from one major foreign supplier to another, imports are still at
historical highs.

Today, American buyers and producers range all over the world to visit
fashion producing markets: to Europe for new ideas or to buy relatively small
quantities of high-priced goods; to major suppliers in the Orient for lower cost
production orders in depth; to emerging producing countries that have not yet

Global Sourcing: An International Fashion Mix

U.S. Imports of Cotton, Wool, and Man-Made Fiber Apparel from Selected Countries, 1974–1988 (in millions of SYE)*

	1974	1978	1982	1984	1986	1987	1988†
Taiwan	422	608	748	931	1,011	942	868
Hong Kong	369	695	690	814	881	871	890
People's Republic of China	8	63	357	445	709	739	763
Korea	294	458	576	685	701	690	717
Subtotal	1,093	1,824	2,371	2,875	3,302	3,242	3,238
% of Total	56%	63%	70%	61%	56%	53%	51%
Japan	164	170	76	138	121	87	54
% of Total	8%	6%	2%	3%	2%	1%	0%
Philippines	102	158	161	234	274	304	319
Indonesia	—	—	38	129	168	192	179
Bangladesh	0	0	2	24	109	179	170
Dominican Republic	6	35	76	95	143	173	221
Singapore	90	85	82	128	182	172	167
Mexico	91	91	56	86	116	160	188
Sri Lanka	1	10	59	108	138	157	139
India	27	77	73	131	124	151	176
Haiti	41	53	54	68	96	109	111
Malaysia	—	—	26	64	113	108	113
Subtotal	358	509	627	1,067	1,463	1,705	1,783
% of Total	19%	17%	19%	23%	25%	28%	28%
All Other Countries	322	398	308	635	973	1,082	1,239
% of Total	17%	14%	9%	13%	17%	18%	19%
Total All Countries	1,937	2,901	3,382	4,715	5,859	6,116	6,314
	100%	100%	100%	100%	100%	100%	100%

*Square yards equivalent; this is a means of measuring quantity by using the fabric content rather than the number of units involved.

†1988 includes new MFA fibers.

SOURCE: Office of Textiles and Apparel, Department of Commerce.

been affected by quotas; and to domestic market centers within the United States.

How effective future regulations, if any, will be in improving the textile/apparel imbalance of trade remains to be seen. One conclusion, however, is fairly certain: The real problem our domestic industry will continue to face is continuing import penetration. No mater how much exports may increase, it is most unlikely that they will ever counterbalance the surge of imports into the American fashion industry. The trade imbalance is not a problem that will be easily solved. It is one that the best minds in industry and government will have to wrestle with, probably for a long time to come.

U.S. PENETRATION OF FOREIGN MARKETS_____

American textile and apparel producers have been unable to match their exports to the rising tide of imports. This is not simply a matter of this country's cost of production versus the costs in other countries. The nub of the textile trade problem lies not just in the price advantage that these textile exporting countries have, but also in the fact that they keep their markets firmly closed to exports from our domestic industry.

Although all major textile and apparel markets protect their domestic industry to a greater or lesser extent, the most liberal trade regimes maintained by major nations are those of the United States and the European Economic Community. Most other markets are heavily protected by trade barriers such as excise taxes, value-added taxes, restrictive quotas, and even import bans on many products.

Joint Ventures and Foreign Licensing Pacts

Some of our major textile and apparel producers have found ways to penetrate foreign markets in spite of the obstacles just mentioned. One method is to license foreign producers in return for a percentage of their wholesale sales. A second is to enter into a **joint venture**, or partnership arrangement, with a foreign producer. A third method is to establish *wholly owned manufacturing plants* in foreign countries. Some U.S. companies use one, two, or all three of these methods, the choice depending on how the particular method works in relation to the international trade rules of the country concerned. A domestic company doing business in three or more foreign markets may use all three methods, each in a different area.

LICENSING AGREEMENTS

Licensing is a relatively uncomplicated way for a domestic manufacturer to cultivate foreign markets, and it is the least costly. Entering into a legal arrangement, the U.S. company gives the right to use its manufacturing process or its trademark name, or both, to a foreign producer. In return, it receives a fee or royalty percentage on wholesale sales.

The foreign producer gains production expertise and the use of a well-known name, or both. The licensing American firm gains entry into a foreign market at little risk or financial investment. Among the firms that have such licensing arrangements are Healthtex and Carter, in the children's wear field. Enormous amounts of women's and men's clothing and accessories are also produced and sold in Japan and European countries that bear the names of well-known French, Italian, and American designers or the brand names of their companies.

JOINT-OWNERSHIP VENTURES

A joint venture in the context of foreign trade consists of a partnership between a U.S. company and a foreign producer. In many countries, such an arrangement is a requirement for penetrating anti-import barriers. Under joint-ownership ventures, the U.S. company provides designs, patterns, technical expertise, and the use of its name. The foreign partner then employs its own country's labor to produce and market the merchandise.

A notable example is the U.S.-based firm of Esprit, which has established Esprit Far East in Asia through a partnership with Michael Ying of Hong Kong. The Asian partner owns half the company and serves as its managing director. Esprit Far East is a major exporter of women's and children's casual apparel. Ninety-five percent of its merchandise is produced in Asia. Hong Kong manufactures the bulk of the output, and the balance is contracted out to factories in Taiwan, Singapore, and to a lesser extent Malaysia, China, and Macao. The U.S. company, however, is involved in every operational step, from design to patterns, to fabric, to quota, to shipping arrangement. Most of the elements that constitute the garments are purchased in Asia—even zippers, labels, and buttons.

Another example of a joint venture is the arrangement between the French silk producer J. Brochier Soieries, based in Lyons, France, and the China Silk Company, to manufacture silk fabrics for export. Still other such joint ventures exist between Blue Bell, Inc., the producer of Wrangler jeans, and companies in Italy and Spain.[14]

Direct Ownership of Production Facilities

The third method of penetrating a foreign market is by a 100 percent investment in a foreign-based assembly or production facility. Some foreign countries, for economic reasons, offer investment incentives to U.S. companies to establish wholly owned subsidiaries within their borders. As in the case of joint ventures, the foreign facility provides employment to the host country's own labor and often uses the local materials.

For example, Burlington Industries has such manufacturing facilities of its own in Ireland, France, England, Germany, Italy, and Mexico. Another example is Wrangler Jeans, which has facilities in Scotland and Malta and, until recently, also had manufacturing units in Belgium and the Ivory Coast.

Direct Exports

Along with foreign licensing, joint ventures, and foreign subsidiaries, some U.S. companies also do direct exporting to other areas where the tariff and other trade barriers are less restrictive. The volume involved is relatively small, because of the high cost of the domestic product and the trade barriers involved. Nevertheless, there are foreign consumers who are eager to buy products that are uniquely American and who covet the "Made in the USA" label.

Our **exports** are so small in relation to our imports of textiles and apparel that our balance of trade (imports versus exports) continues to be alarmingly high.

Seeking to correct this situation, our government has from time to time launched efforts to increase exports. As one example among several, the Department of Commerce's Bureau of Export Development in 1979 formalized and put into effect a Textile and Apparel Export Expansion Program whose purpose was to increase the amount of direct exporting done by U.S. apparel companies.

The ineffectiveness of programs such as this is clearly evidenced by the fact that our apparel and textile trade deficit continued to rise. From a little more than $1.5 billion in 1970, the combined apparel/textile trade deficit reached $26.4 billion in 1989.

Some domestic ready-to-wear manufacturers are doing their bit to battle the U.S. trade deficit by exporting their lines to Europe and cashing in on the allure of American apparel to customers there. Although a few apparel producers have been doing business overseas for several years, the number of firms bringing their lines to Europe seems to be increasing. The weakness of the dollar in the late 1980s against European currencies made American merchandise a better value to the European consumer and domestic manufacturers eager to take advantage of this. Among those that embarked on direct exporting to Europe are Leslie Fay, Nicole Miller, Robert Janan Ltd., and Liz Roberts. Each estimates that at best their European sales could amount to about 10 percent of their domestic volume.[15]

THE EUROPEAN ECONOMIC COMMUNITY: THE COMMON MARKET (EEC)

The **Common Market (EEC)** is an agreement between a group of European countries to establish free trade, a uniform transportation system, and free movement of labor and capital among its member countries. In 1992, all trade barriers (tariffs, quotas, etc.) among the EEC members will be abolished so that in effect there will be a "United States of Europe" for trading purposes. The

Foreign Import Restrictions in Textiles and Apparel

Developed Countries	Form of Restrictions
European Communities	Bilateral agreements pursuant to Multifiber Arrangement
Canada	" "
Sweden	" "
United States	" "
Finland	" "
Austria	" "
Australia	Global tariff quotas
New Zealand	Import licensing subject to global quotas maintained "without GATT cover"
Norway	Global quotas pursuant to non-MFA bilaterals with major LDC suppliers
Japan	Non-MFA voluntary restraint agreements, informal government pressure on distributors

Eastern Trading Area Countries	Licensing requirements; imports must be conducted through foreign trade organizations (FTOs)

Major Developing Countries	
Mexico	Licensing requirements; licenses denied for most products
India	Import ban on most products
China	Trade regulated by FTOs
Korea	Licensing requirement for items on "negative list," sometimes amounts to ban
Taiwan	Periodic import bans, high tariffs
Nigeria	Imports of all textiles and apparel are banned
Argentina	Severe restrictions on items "similar" to those produced domestically
Indonesia	Licensing requirement administered to protect Indonesian producers
Turkey	Import ban on many products
Brazil	High (100% +) tariffs; licensing system amounting to a ban on many products
Egypt	Import ban on some products; licensing requirements
Colombia	Import ban on many products
Venezuela	All clothing imports are banned
Pakistan	Licensing requirements; some items allowed only for barter or if linked to extension of credit

SOURCE: The Reality of World Trade in Apparel and Textiles.

only major problem still to be addressed pertains to whether there will be a uniform currency system. As far as the United States is concerned, it still remains to be seen how the abolishment of trade barriers among the members of the EEC will affect the trade relationship between the United States and the Common Market countries.

Readings

Despite the ample productive capabilities of our domestic fashion producers, imports account for more than one-half of consumer expenditures for textiles and apparel. These articles discuss foreign sources of supply and the efforts of U.S. producers to counterbalance imports with exports.

Allure of Asia Continues High for U.S. Firms

Despite protectionism, quotas, and rising cost of labor, offshore production in low-wage Far Eastern countries continues to have appeal for U.S. apparel companies.

Caribbean Sourcing Poised to Take Off

Predictions are that the Caribbean will become in the future as important an apparel manufacturing center as the Orient is today.

A Visit with Vittadini in Hong Kong

A beaded dress by Adrienne Vittadini that retails for $4,000 when produced in the United States can retail for $300 if produced in Hong Kong.

Why Made in America Is Back in Style

The ability of domestic producers to respond more quickly to customers' needs is offsetting the lure of offshore low-wage producers.

A European Push by Robert Janan

U.S. apparel producers are broadening their customer base by going after the European market.

ALLURE OF ASIA CONTINUES HIGH FOR U.S. FIRMS

by Robert Hartlein

New York—Stumbling blocks facing importers—from the declining dollar to tightened trade pacts with major Asian supplier countries—have mounted significantly over the past two years, severely limiting import growth.

Nevertheless, for several major sportswear manufacturers, sourcing in the Far East continues to hold virtually unshakable appeal.

These executives insist that product quality, greater flexibility and a labor pool that, despite the falling dollar, remains considerably cheaper, still give the Orient a significant edge.

In particular, they point out, the more intricate a garment, the less capable American facilities are of producing it.

"It's more of a cookie-cutter mentality here," one executive said. "If you want 10,000 of one style of white shirt, fine, but once you start adding more detail and special treatments, it becomes less cost-effective to make it here."

This is not to say, however, that the growing array of deterrents isn't having an effect. Perhaps most obvious was the sharp cutback in textile-apparel import growth last year.

Bilateral trade agreements negotiated over the past two years with the five major Asian suppliers—China, Hong Kong, Taiwan, Japan and South Korea—limit to 1 percent or less the current annual growth of exports to the U.S.

In 1987, imports from these five countries were actually down, by 7.4 percent. However, other rising suppliers in the Far East, such as Indonesia, Malaysia and the Philippines, helped take up the slack.

"There are a lot of factors out there, and they're causing shifts in sourcing," said Eugene Milosh, president of the American Association of Exporters and Importers.

"There is more interest in domestic sourcing, and more interest than I've seen before in Latin America, including countries like Ecuador and Bolivia. People are also looking at such countries as Morocco."

Yet, he points out, the Far East still continues to hold sway, although "growth there is going to be limited, and prices will be going up."

Depending on market conditions, 85 percent of Claiborne merchandise is made in contracted facilities around the world.

A lot of it is made in Asia, some in Europe, and there is an increased emphasis on United States production. The company owns no factories outright.

"We are constantly looking for areas to develop, and although price is naturally important, we are also deeply concerned with quality and the time it takes to deliver," he said.

How contractors work with the firm's designs is another important consideration. "It's important for us, the guys in the back room, to be sensitive to what the design team achieves," Listanowsky emphasized.

The Claiborne executive noted that while many U.S. factories may be flexible enough to meet the demands placed upon them, there are shortcomings in domestic availability of fabrics.

Another point of contention, he added,

Source: *Women's Wear Daily*, February 24, 1988. Reprint permission granted.

is that in the Orient, samples are delivered before a production run. "Here, it's 'Let me finish the production run first, and then I'll get the samples in.'"

If at all possible, he said, he would buy piece goods domestically, rather than cull offshore markets, but he asserted he is unable to find U.S. suppliers to meet the firm's needs.

"I can't understand why more American weavers aren't attempting to meet the needs of companies like ourselves," he said.

Ellinger said 95 percent of Basco merchandise is made overseas, and despite the devalued dollar, the traveling distance between the U.S. and the Orient, and lack of hands-on control, Ellinger contends it is still less expensive to produce goods offshore.

At Manhattan Industries, where production of goods is an international and domestic mix, Nicholas P. DiPaolo, president and chief operating officer, noted that as costs rise in established supplier countries such as Hong Kong and South Korea, new areas are drawing both management and labor pools to do the work.

"A lack of talented labor in these developing countries does not appear to be a problem," he said.

Still, the price of labor in the Far East, though it remains relatively cheap today, is not like it was 15 years ago, he noted, and the situation is providing greater opportunity for revival of U.S. manufacturing.

DiPaolo said the company has been reacting to this development by pulling back some production to these shores over the last two years.

"If the product being made is not very labor-intensive, the United States now can compete with many parts of the world because of the increased costs," he said.

Some of Manhattan's production now is also being done in the Caribbean under the Item 807 program in which fabrics are cut in the U.S. and shipped to the Caribbean for sewing and shipment back. Tariffs cover only the value added.

Meanwhile, DiPaolo, like others, expressed general worry over the specter of rising prices, regardless of how ingenious firms may be in finding sources.

"We are very concerned about prices, moving into the second half of 1988," he reiterated.

"And there is talk of heavy increases next year as well, due to the fluctuation in the value of the dollar and restrictions on quota. Most apparel will be more expensive; some substantially so."

Alfred Fuoco, chairman of Palm Beach, said 80 percent of the company's Evan-Picone brand is produced domestically.

However, he said it is more advantageous for categories such as knitwear and blouses to be made in the Orient than on these shores. Sixty percent of knitwear and 80 percent of blouses are produced in the Far East.

"We buy goods in Japan, so it's easier for us to transfer them to Hong Kong to be made," Fuoco said. "Our polyester and rayon are sourced in Japan. We couldn't afford to bring those fibers to the U.S. to have them cut and sewn, so we do it there."

But Fuoco said price is not the only consideration. Quality, as well as sourcing location, is taken into account.

"If we source fabrics in Korea, we will make it in Korea," he said. But what it comes right down to, he asserted, is, "Where can we get the product made the quickest in the best possible way for the least amount of money?"

He lauded the innovative fabrics found in the Orient, and at the same time said the United States has a long way to go in this regard.

Also, "the sewing in Hong Kong is topnotch, and the work done there is as good as any factory in the world," Fuoco said. It's only a matter of time, he added, before Singapore, Manila and Malaysia reach similar levels.

The Jones New York division of the Jones Apparel Group does 60 to 70 percent of its manufacturing overseas, according to Michael D. Treiber, president of the division.

"But we have a desire to pull back as much as we can," he said.

According to Treiber, although the desire may be there, the reality is that for those sportswear makers looking for a higher level of quality, as well as sophisticated technological expertise, the Far East continues to outpace the U.S.

And for sophisticated work in specific categories, such as blouses and sweaters, he said it is virtually impossible to find domestic facilities up to the task.

On the other hand, he said, the U.S. has been more successful in bringing back production of what he calls "hard goods," such as jackets, shirts and pants.

Securing quota, Treiber said, depends on fluctuating business conditions. "You never have enough quota in the right cate-gory, and should you be lucky enough, you pay dearly," he said. "But with categories that are not popular, you have more quota than you know what to do with."

He said factoring in the cost of quota and air fare can add as much as 20 percent to the price of a garment. Nevertheless, even with these costs, Treiber said that, for the companies looking for top quality, the Far East is unmatched.

To benefit from this situation, he said American contractors would have to learn to be more diversified. He pointed out that Jones New York makes 35 different styles of blouses, which it is able to do overseas without the snafus it would encounter in the U.S.

"Here, they want to mass-produce one style of blouse, and factories tell us what their needs are, and what we should be doing, instead of letting us design and telling them what we want.

"The U.S. disdains diversity. All stores should look the same and all people should look alike. It's convenient and easier. In the Orient, they're not looking for those large mass cuttings."

CARIBBEAN SOURCING POISED TO TAKE OFF

by David Orgel

Montego Bay, Jamaica—After years of growth by fits and starts, apparel sourcing programs in the Caribbean region are finally poised for sharp advances.

U.S. apparel executives, while recognizing the formidable difficulties of produc-ing in the Caribbean and Central America, are ready to devote more effort to this location because Far East sourcing programs are saddled with mounting costs and restrictions.

The Caribbean's low labor rates and

proximity to the U.S. market seem more attractive now, as do U.S.-sponsored programs. Item 807, which grants duty savings for apparel production using U.S.-cut fabrics, is an old program that is now gaining momentum.

A newer arrangement, the super 807, has provided a shot in the arm to Caribbean production by granting virtually unlimited access to the U.S. market for apparel made with fabrics both made and cut in the United States.

Not surprisingly, predictions are that in 10 to 15 years, the Caribbean could be as important in U.S. apparel circles as the Orient is today.

Both the growing interest in Caribbean programs and the concerns came out during interviews at the first major Caribbean sourcing trade show, The Caribbean Fashion Carnivale, held here last month and sponsored by the Jamaican government.

Many American apparel manufacturers are overwhelmed by the enormous commitment and research needed to source in this region, unlike in the Orient, where Asian firms produce full apparel packages to order. The logistics of 807 work from warehousing and cutting fabrics to arranging assembly and transport can be prohibitive.

Choosing the right Caribbean nation is crucial. Considerations range from native language to wage rates to political stability, and more than a few producers wish they had foreseen political turmoil in Panama and Haiti. The top six 807 nations are Jamaica, Costa Rica, Honduras, the Dominican Republic, Guatemala and Haiti. Their total apparel exports to the U.S. have grown to $976,800,000 last year from $405,900,000 in 1984, according to Department of Commerce statistics made available by Kurt Salmon Associates.

Other problems threaten the 807 arrangements. The American textile industry is criticized for not providing the right mix of fabrics for 807 and 807-A programs, leading many apparel firms to manufacture without U.S. textiles.

Another concern is that Far East apparel manufacturers are increasingly locating factories in Caribbean nations. This sparks fears of another kind of import threat from Asia.

Nevertheless, more U.S. apparel firms and some retailers are showing increased interests in working in this part of the world. The region is currently used more for basic or mass market production, but the quality of apparel styling is becoming increasingly sophisticated.

"I would say 23 of the top 25 U.S. garment manufacturers are already doing some sourcing in the Caribbean or Central America, and many more will follow," said Gary Finkel, president of Colonial Corp. of America, one of the largest U.S. firms producing apparel in the Caribbean.

Colonial produces private label women's and men's sportswear in Jamaica, the Dominican Republic, Haiti and Costa Rica, and its list of accounts include J.C. Penney, Sears, Roebuck & Co., Target Stores and The Gap.

Manufacturers at the show who will take production to the Caribbean include the BVY Group, women's and men's sportswear. "We'll be switching knitwear souring to the Caribbean," said Joe Miranda, vice president of manufacturing and sourcing for BVY, based in Foster City, Calif.

"We were until recently sourcing in Hong Kong but the quota prices were far too high, we moved production to South America, but now I'd like to be closer to the United States. We're interested in Jamaica, the Dominican Republic, Guatemala and Costa Rica," said Miranda.

Gitano, one of the large branded manufacturers producing in the Caribbean, has found pluses and minuses in working in many countries in the region.

Some 15 to 20 percent of its worldwide sourcing for women's and men's sportswear is conducted in this region, and that figure may grow because of favorable wage structures, Isaac Dabah, executive vice president, said in a telephone interview in New York.

"But you find problems in various nations with local unions and political stability," he emphasized. "It's important to be in the region in order to spread your worldwide sourcing mix and risk, but the Caribbean doesn't yet have the stable climate and well developed apparel markets of the Orient."

The hazards of 807 production became evident to many producers who were investigating this sourcing option for the first time. Typical was Linda Kinback, associate operations manager for Puma USA, who visited factories to produce apparel, including women's poplin shirts and pique tops.

"In one factory they didn't order enough elastic components for shorts, and the 807 production was held up because they had to go back to the States for more," she said. "Moreover, because of the great deal of paperwork required by customs in these 807 programs, if one thing is out of order the whole operation can be delayed or hurt."

But the Caribbean is one location in which U.S. manufacturers still have an edge over retail customers. Although a number of stores are working on Caribbean programs through their U.S. resources, retailers are generally less willing than manufacturers to devote the effort and money to setting up plants, providing technical guidance, and warehousing fabric and components.

"Retailers can't get as involved as manufacturers in all of these steps," said F.Y. Wong, divisional vice president of sourcing for Carter Hawley Hale. "In the Orient, you just place an order and cancel if the goods aren't right. However, I am encouraging my resources to produce in the Caribbean."

A similar tack was noted by Marshall Beere, vice president and division merchandise manager for women's apparel of Penney's. "We have 807 work done on our behalf through U.S. manufacturers, and I'm encouraged with the results in products such as women's shorts, shirts, jeans and pants," he said.

"For the long term, we may even decide to get more involved by working directly with Caribbean contractors, but for now those contractors aren't sophisticated enough for that kind of arrangement," Beere said.

A few retailers have devoted a lot of effort to direct sourcing. Probably most notable is The Gap, which sources in Haiti, Costa Rica and Jamaica for its 800 stores in four divisions. This retailer not only built a major business with contractors, but it pushed for increasingly higher styling on apparel, said Mack Nichols, whose title at The Gap is "807 engineer."

Because of Washington's special breaks for programs using American fabrics, the Caribbean is eyed as a potential gold mine by American textile firms, who exhibited at the Jamaica show in their own pavilion.

"The Caribbean will really help the U.S. textile industry because Super 807 specifies U.S. fabrics, and the region doesn't have its own textile industry for all of this apparel production," said Hank Herbst, marketing director for The WestPoint-Pepperell Apparel Fabrics Division. "We're even considering setting up our own distribution center in Jamaica so that basic fabric styles can be ordered for immediate delivery."

Some of the textile executives countered the complaints of apparelmakers that the mills didn't provide all the types of fabrics, particularly better quality goods, that might be wanted for 807 production.

"Look at these fine fabrics available from the domestic textile industry," emphasized Newell Woodworth, vice president of marketing for lightweight fabrics for Dan River, Inc.

"I'm showing buyers a 50-single pima cotton for shirting weights as good as any you'll find in the world. And here's a pima cotton pinpoint oxford for shirts and blouses. We've had these products on the market for some 18 months now. "Two years ago the criticisms about availability of textiles leveled against us may have been right, but we went back and made the finer fabrics the market needed."

A VISIT WITH VITTADINI IN HONG KONG

Hong Kong—Parked on a sofa in her room at the Regent Hotel, a hazy view of Hong Kong behind her, Adrienne Vittadini has her sleeves rolled up, ready for the siege. Soon the racks will arrive and the campaign to "refine, retouch and edit" her cruise collection begins.

"We work late in the night, going group by group, layering, working on color stories, for each division," says the designer, her voice relaying the drudgery ahead. Outings are limited; a morning workout in the hotel pool (which lured her away from the Peninsula hotel a few years back), required "entertaining" at the factory and maybe a visit to Charlotte Horstmann (for Oriental antiques).

"I always used to go, and go to the warehouse, too, but now the prices are very high," she says. On the same note, she adds, "I went into Chanel (jammed at all hours with Japanese customers) to buy a bag and it was more expensive than in New York."

When she does leave the hotel, a haven for visiting SA folk, she'll take an extended route. "I'll go all the way around the hotel," she says, to avoid bumping into fellow industry people.

Vittadini has been a veteran Hong Kong commuter since 1969. Now she makes three trips a year. "There have been a lot of changes," she notes, "from the attitude to the skyline.

"We always produced in Italy, where an idea could come out of the air and it was understood. Here, you always had to bring something, a sample, as a point of reference. You couldn't be totally creative from scratch."

But the "esthetic sense," she feels, has risen along with the sophistication of the machinery, enabling her to do things here that she can't do anywhere else.

"People here are willing to try new things," she says, citing some of the beadings from her fall collection as an example. There is the craft here, she says, and the right price. A beaded dress that could retail in the U.S. for $4,000, if produced there, "we can retail for around $300," she said.

There are the negatives, however, to

Source: *Women's Wear Daily*, April 27, 1988. Reprinted with permission.

delivering collections for six seasons from long distance. "You have to wear many hats, know your tools," says Vittadini, who will personally adjust tensions and gauges of knitting machines to get what she wants.

"We send total layouts from New York, very detailed sketches that you'd have to be an idiot not to understand."

The designer tells of another current difficulty: mastering the stonewash quality she is trying to achieve with her knitwear.

After her 10-day stint in Hong Kong, Vittadini moves onto Bangkok (for R&R), then back home through Europe to check on more production sites, including one in Portugal.

"I don't enjoy traveling," she says a bit grumpily. "I used to socialize when I was here, but it took too much time. I just want to come here, get the work done and go home."

WHY MADE IN AMERICA IS BACK IN STYLE

The apparel business isn't often singed as sharply as it was this year. Many clothing makers and retailers blamed the miniskirt fiasco. But sales of all women's clothing have been limping. The slowdown has apparel makers vowing never to be caught again with their pants down—and their hems up. They have relearned the lesson that they have to respond quickly to the famous question: What do women want? And that is starting to have a profound effect on how the American apparel industry operates. Little by little the producers are coming home again.

After years of relying on cheap manufacturing bases in distant East Asia—with at least three months between order and delivery—clothing makers now are recognizing the value of faster turnarounds and deliveries in responding to the ever-changing whims of fashion. Even companies from traditionally low-wage countries in the Far East are moving their production to the U.S. to escape rising costs and American import quotas and to get closer to their customers.

Quick-Change Artist

It doesn't amount to droves yet, and the trend isn't tilting the trade balance. But textile and apparel imports are down 8% through August, compared with the same period last year. And employment in apparel and textiles, which had been declining for a decade, has begun to creep up, according to the U.S. Commerce Dept. There are stirrings of a revival in two industries that many had written off forever as a vibrant part of the American industrial landscape. While few statistics are available yet, once-rare garments labeled "made in the

Source: Reprinted from November 7, 1988, issue of *Business Week* by special permission, © 1988 by McGraw-Hill, Inc.

U.S.A." can now be found in stores from K mart to Saks Fifth Avenue.

Competitive pressures are making speed of delivery the key factor in the industry. And apparel makers who come up with the goods most quickly will have the edge with retailers. "The strategy for the '90s is going to be reducing lead times," says Freddie Wood, senior vice-president of Kurt Salmon Associates Inc., a prominent apparel consultant. That means shortening the time spent on everything from designing fashions and changing equipment to reordering popular lines. "It should all play into the hands of the American industry," says Wood, as the bottom line depends more and more on getting to market quickly, whatever the cost.

Take Salant Corp., a $525 million-a-year New York–based apparel company that owns Perry Ellis Sportswear, Manhattan Shirt Co., and other clothing companies. Two years ago every item sold by Perry Ellis' women's division was imported from contractors in Hong Kong, Taiwan, Macau, and other faraway locales. Today 40% of the line is made domestically. A Salant-owned, unionized sewing factory in Americus, Ga., that was operating at one-third capacity and spewing red ink three years ago, is now going full tilt and turning a profit. Says Salant President Nicholas P. Di Paolo: "The spread between productivity in Asia and the U.S. has been narrowing significantly."

Indeed, breakthroughs in faster, more automated sewing machines are bringing U.S. labor costs down. Greif Cos., the Allentown (Pa.) maker of tailored men's suits, has spent about $6 million in the past four years on automation. Its computer-aided design system lays out patterns with minimal waste and taps directly into automated cutting machines. This has helped boost productivity by 30%. And the technology is

solving the local unemployment problem— the job market is so tight that wages at Burger King are on a par with Greif's starting pay: about $5 an hour.

Fifteen years ago, says Salant's Di Paolo, many U.S. manufacturers went offshore because they could make wildly wrong predictions about the market and still come out way ahead. Labor was cheap, and consumers were less changing. A wave of mergers and acquisitions in retail and apparel has left in its wake highly leveraged companies from Campeau to Salant itself, which won a hostile takeover battle for Manhattan Industries this summer. That makes both retailers and manufacturers averse to tying up cash with long lead times, big inventories, and large markdowns.

Steep discounts, which Di Paolo says eat away at least 10% of net sales, are almost inevitable on clothing that must be ordered in bulk and far in advance because it comes from abroad. Items made closer to home in smaller lots for faster delivery allow quicker reaction to fashion—and reduce the markdown bite.

Aiding this are data processing links that can instantaneously report purchases from stores to designers and fabric suppliers. Cluett, Peabody & Co., maker of Arrow and other men's shirts, for example, can take electronic orders from retailers for shirts on Sunday night and have goods shipped out by Tuesday. This has helped the company shift about 20% of its production back to the U.S. Frederick Atkins Inc., a marketing cooperative for 50 retailers, now contracts for half of its private-label lines domestically—a figure that may approach 60% next year. This way, says President Bernard Olsoff, "I don't have to project demand a year in advance, finance it with letters of credit, or worry about the vagaries of a typhoon knocking my ship out."

Quota Quandary

Seminole Manufacturing Co. returned to the U.S. to get better control over quality. The Columbus (Miss.) company had shifted some production of its men's casual slacks to Jamaica to save about $1 per pair. But in reality, "we had a higher rate of rework and higher travel costs," says Chief Executive James D. High Sr. Now 50 workers in Seminole's Evergreen (Ala.) factory turn out an order of pants in less than four weeks, vs. 12 to 16 weeks in Jamaica. CEO High figures that Seminole's offshore work has fallen to 20% from 40% of its total sales.

For Asian apparel makers, quotas, labor shortages, increased protectionism, and rising wages at home are beginning to make the U.S. look good. Hong Kong–based Onwel Manufacturing Inc. opened a factory in Flushing, N.Y., last year to get around a growing problem with the U.S. quota system. The U.S. is no longer allowing any significant growth in imports from Hong Kong, Taiwan, South Korea, and other Asian countries. Many Asian garment manufacturers thus must pay high prices for the right to ship certain categories of garments to their U.S. customers.

When quota prices for knitted skirts, tops, and pants hit $90 per dozen, for example, the items became too costly, and Onwel officials worried that they would lose customers, including Lord & Taylor and its parent May Department Stores Co. Instead, they calculated that by making the goods in the U.S., they could put the money saved from costly quotas toward higher U.S. wages. Onwel workers in Hong Kong make $300 to $400 a month; in Flushing, they take home that much each week.

The ability to respond quickly to customers' needs is also drawing Hong Kong garment makers to the U.S. Two Hong Kong contractors that work exclusively for Liz Claiborne Inc. opened shop in New York's Chinatown last year, mainly to get their popular skirts and blouses to stores faster. Thomas E. Goetz, managing director of Hong Kong–based Goetz Trading Ltd., plans to open a $5 million cut-and-sew sweater factory near Chattanooga next year. A vocal critic of protectionism, he concedes that tariffs and quotas are "the reason it's viable to set up an apparel factory" in the U.S. Asian garment makers won't flock to America, says Goetz, but those that do come will be formidable.

Island-Bound

Even some European clothing companies are moving production to the U.S. Trendy Benetton, taking advantage of the weak dollar and the proximity to major cities, opened its first U.S. plant just 18 months ago in Rocky Mount, N.C. There, 130 employees make sweatsuits and cotton and denim garments, all previously sewn in Italy.

Some of apparel's homecoming isn't quite what it appears to be. Substantial business is also headed for the Caribbean and Mexico. The islands became a big apparel center under President Reagan's Caribbean Basin Initiative, which allows U.S. clothing makers to ship fabric for sewing to low-wage factories in the islands and reimport the finished goods with tax breaks. The same is true of Mexico.

It's a big business: In 1987, 21% more clothing was stitched in the Caribbean than the year before. That represents roughly 10% of all imported apparel, according to the Commerce Dept. And now Canada, soon to clinch a free-trade agreement with the U.S., is gearing up in clothing production, spurred on by the many Asians with experience in apparel who migrate there.

Manufacturers will always want to locate jobs sewing clothes for America's style-hungry consumers in countries with the lowest wages. China, for one, intent on making textiles and apparel exports a big earner of foreign exchange, is quickly becoming a major low-cost center. But now that it's getting more difficult to sell fashionable threads, retailers and manufacturers alike are beginning to see why cheaper isn't always better—or even really cheaper. That realization is breathing life into a U.S. industry long ago left for dead.

A EUROPEAN PUSH BY ROBERT JANAN

by Dianne M. Pogoda

New York—Mel Turkel is sowing the seeds for growth in Europe—not just for his own firm, Robert Janan, Ltd., but for a pioneering handful of other SA resources as well.

Turkel, chairman of the 18-year-old dress and suit company, has had a steady business in England for 12 years. This year he has taken some bold steps to make the European market the bull's-eye in his target for expansion.

In February, he moved the firm's worldwide headquarters from New York to its London office, and in March, opened satellite offices in Zurich, Switzerland, and Duesseldorf, West Germany. He maintains a New York showroom, which is linked to London by computer. Eventually, all offices around the world will be linked.

The Zurich office handles all the Continental European business, with Duesseldorf focusing on the booming West German market.

Just before moving his headquarters to London, Turkel increased his stake as an importer into Europe, bringing dresses from Nicole Miller, Baron Peters, Ciao and Jack Mulqueen to overseas retailers. He started in this venture three years ago, when he brought Liz Roberts dresses to the U.K.

"We'll be adding more lines to bring over," Turkel said. "At first, we concentrated only on dresses, but now we're considering adding separates also.

"Suddenly, the Europeans are letting us into the club in a big way." Turkel stated. "Many of our major designers have broken ground internationally with their advertising and their fragrances. These have paved the way for other American designers and apparel makers." American boutiques appearing in Europe, such as Ralph Lauren, also promote awareness and bring acceptance to U.S. lines, he added.

Last year, Robert Janan's volume was more than $7 million each in the United States and in Europe. Turkel expects his firm to more than double its European volume this year with the addition of the new lines.

American apparel across the board generally sells well in Europe, Turkel pointed out. He said jersey dresses and suits, the cornerstone of the Robert Janan

Source: *Women's Wear Daily*, April 11, 1989. Reprinted with permission.

business, represent about 70 percent of the total volume, and he expects that category to grow tremendously in Europe this year. The polyester print dresses are also doing well, he said, and he sees increases in this area, too.

"The demand for easy-care fabric is tremendous in Europe, particularly because their drycleaning facilities are not as good as they are here," he said. "Polyester has a much better reputation over there than it does in this country."

According to U.S. statistics, the U.K. ranks sixth in the world as an importer of U.S.-made knit apparel. Total value of knit apparel shipped from the U.S. into the U.K. in 1988 was $14.4 million, up from $9.6 million in 1987.

Bill Dawson, a trade specialist in textiles and apparel with the Department of Commerce, surmised the big jumps were probably because of the drop in the dollar in recent years, as compared to the British pound and other currencies.

"Everyone [in Europe] has liked U.S. quality and styling all along, but it was too expensive," Dawson said. "When the dollar dropped, the prices became very competitive. This has been happening across the board, with different products in many countries."

Turkel said that in selecting a line to bring to the European market, it must first be successful in the U.S., as well as the kind of product with a world market.

"It doesn't necessarily follow that a good seller here will do well there," said Eva Shapiro, designer and president of Robert Janan. "It must be absolutely right for that market, and the Europeans are quite fashion conscious. They want something new every year. They don't take last year's styles."

Turkel explained that to be competitive in price and avoid high markups on U.S. garments, he buys apparel directly from the factories in which they are made, both here and in other parts of the world. He pays the same price for a dress from the shop as the dress house, thus cutting out the manufacturer's markup for shipping and warehousing costs. He also cuts out one leg of shipping, in bringing it directly to England without stopping at the maker's facility. However, the manufacturers are paid a royalty for their dresses.

With the dresses coming into England at a lower base rate, the taxes and tariffs are lower, so the dresses can retail for the same price there as they do here.

Turkel said he also intends to start entering joint ventures with European firms for distribution as he expands into different markets.

"Until now, it hasn't been really necessary to do joint ventures, but with 1992 approaching, the joint venture is the essence of efficient working in an international business," he emphasized. "To learn about another country's systems and market, it's mutually beneficial to hook up with someone who knows that market better than anyone else. He benefits from our product, and we benefit from his knowledge of distribution and marketing."

Robert Janan also has been sold in Canada for 18 years, and in Australia for about 10 years.

Liz Roberts, Inc., has been with the Janan group in London for three years, the longest of the outside lines Turkel has brought abroad.

Alan Passeroff, vice president of Liz Roberts, estimated that 5 percent of the firm's overall business is now done in Europe through Janan. With the expansion into other countries, he said, that will probably double over the year. Total annual sales volume for Liz Roberts is nearly $50 million.

Passeroff said Liz Roberts probably would not have gone to Europe on its own.

"Robert Janan already has the team in place, and has overcome a lot of the obstacles involved in going to Europe," he explained. "Although it's the same industry, going to Europe involves learning a whole new sense of fashion, new timing, and new merchandising strategies. Over the course of the three years, we've been able to work out our production and sampling schedules."

He noted, for example, that the Europeans generally show only two seasons—spring and fall—and the stores buy earlier than they do in the U.S. "The Europeans are very cautious; they do a lot of sampling and testing, but once you prove yourself, they're very loyal," he said. "The quality standards in Europe are even higher than in the U.S. Most of the competition is German, and their quality is impeccable."

Bud Konheim, president of Nicole Miller, has been involved in the European market, selling to British retailer Harvey Nichols in London for about six years. He hooked up with Turkel at the beginning of this year to take advantage of the Janan group's base of specialty stores in other parts of England and on the continent.

"We don't know what's going to happen in the next few years, but we can't just burst on the scene in 1992," Konheim said. "We must build gradually an idea of fashion and a customer base. That's what we've done with Harvey Nichols. We've learned a lot about the English market through them, such as the different market times, and that certain colors or styles that will sell here won't sell at the same times of the year over there."

Konheim said the Nicole Miller line won't be sold to any other stores in London, because of his exclusive arrangement with Nichols.

In the three months he's been selling through Janan, Konheim said the better boutiques have shown the most interest. Prior to the arrangement with Janan, Konheim said that less than 5 percent of his overall sales came from Europe, a figure that can only grow with expanded distribution.

Jack Mulqueen, chairman of the better-price dress and sportswear firm bearing his name, is also not new to the European market. From 1978 to 1983, he said his business with retailers in the U.K. and on the Continent totaled about $15 million, or 10 percent of the $150 million sold at that time in the United States.

"We deemphasized the European business when the currency exchange rates became unfavorable for American products," Mulqueen said. "We started to go back to Europe about a year ago, selling to retailers who came here. But it's hard to do it like that. We needed a good channel of distribution and a strong marketing group over there."

Mulqueen's dresses wholesale for $79 to $125 in the U.S., and make up almost half of his overall business. The sportswear half is focused on denim and weekend wear, he noted. The company ran into some bumpy times about six years ago, Mulqueen said, and restructured. Now, volume is building up again.

Baron Peters, Inc., a designer-priced dress and sportswear house that wholesales its dresses for $175 to $420, has been selling through Janan since Feb. 1. The line is basically conservative, classic and for a sophisticated, older customer. It is available in misses' and large sizes.

"One of the main reasons we're going now is because of the 1992 explosion," said Andrew Baron, president. "We see that as a tremendous opportunity. We decided to go with the Janan organization because Mel's knowledge and expertise can give us a first-class entree to that market."

As for other countries, Baron Peters currently sells in Canada, but those retailers come to the U.S to buy the line; it has no representation based in Canada, Baron said, adding that he had been considering going to Europe for a while.

"We were interested in exposing our line to the European market, particularly now that the exchange rates are in our favor," he said. "We shop the fabric lines in Europe extensively several times a year, but we had never exposed our line there."

Dress house Ciao, Ltd., is also on its second round of selling to the United Kingdom. The firm had a distribution network in England for about five years, through a British company. When the principals of the British firm retired about nine years ago, Ciao president Ted Shapiro didn't pursue reestablishing his connections.

"We know our dresses sell in England," Shapiro said. "Our type of customer—over 35, conservative, quality-conscious—never disappeared over there."

Ciao dresses wholesale for $120 to $300, and include many all-wool dresses, which is a favorite among Europeans, he said.

Shapiro said Ciao sells in Canada, Australia and Japan, and he had been considering a move back to European business for about a year or so when the opportunity arose to link with Turkel's organization. He said a prime target for his company is the German market.

He pointed out there's not much difference in the clothes that sell in the U.S. or in other countries, except for colors, occasionally. Shapiro agreed that the allure of the products in Europe must be the quality —not necessarily that it's an American dress.

Endnotes

1. *U.S. Industrial Outlook*, 1981 for 1980 figures; 1970 figures from *Statistical Abstract of the United States*, 1971 ed.

2. *U.S. Industrial Outlook*, 1990; Bureau of Economic Analysis.

3. "Import Penetration in the Apparel Industry," published by the Fiber, Fabric and Apparel Coalition for Trade, September 1989.

4. Ibid.

5. *Industry Surveys, Textiles, Apparel and Home Furnishings*, Standard & Poor's, 1990.

6. *U.S. Industrial Outlook*, 1990; Bureau of Economic Analysis.

7. *Focus*, published by American Apparel Manufacturers Association, 1990.

8. ILGWU, "Conditions in the Women's Garment Industry," September 1987.

9. "Asia's Lure Continues," *Women's Wear Daily*, February 24, 1988.

10. Ibid.

11. Ibid.

12. AAMA, "Report of Technical Advisory Committee," 1988.

13. "Can Ms Fashion Bounce Back," *Business Week*, January 16, 1989.

14. *Women's Wear Daily*, August 30, 1988.
15. "Import Penetration in the Apparel Industry."

Selected Bibliography

Caribbean Economic Handbook. London: Euromonitor Publications, 1985.

China Economic Handbook. London: Euromonitor Publications, 1986.

Cline, William. *Future of World Trade in Textiles and Apparel*. Washington, D.C.: Institute for International Economics, 1987.

Customs Regulation of the United States. Washington, D.C.: U.S. International Trade Commission, 1987.

Global Market Surveys. Washington, D.C.: U.S. Department of Commerce, International Trade Administration, periodically.

Kaye, Harvey, Paul Plaia, Jr., and Michael Hertzberg. *International Trade Practice*. New York: McGraw-Hill, 1986.

Latin America and Caribbean Review. Lincolnwood, Ill.: N.T.C. Business Books, 1987.

Rossides, Eugene. *U.S. Import Trade Regulations*. Washington, D.C.: Bureau of National Affairs, 1986.

Tariff Schedules of the United States. Washington, D.C.: U.S. International Trade Commission, 1987.

Textiles and Apparel. Washington, D.C.: Institute for International Economics, 1987.

Woronoff, John. *World Trade War*. New York: Praeger, 1984.

Trade Associations

Caribbean Business Development, 67 Wall Street, New York, N.Y. 10005.

China External Trade Development Council, 41 Madison Avenue, New York, N.Y. 10016.

French Fashion and Textile Center, 200 Madison Avenue, New York, N.Y. 10016.

Hong Kong Trade Development Council, 548 Fifth Avenue, New York, N.Y. 10022.

Israel Trade Center, 350 Fifth Avenue, New York, N.Y. 10010.

Italian Trade Center, 499 Park Avenue, New York, N.Y. 10022.

Japanese Trade Center, 1221 Avenue of the Americas, New York, N.Y. 10019.

Korea Trade Promotion Center, 460 Park Avenue, New York, N.Y. 10022.

Taiwan Trade Information, 41 Madison Avenue, New York, N.Y. 10016.

Trade Publications

Apparel Import Digest, American Apparel Manufacturers Association, 1611 North Kent Street, Arlington, Va. 22209.

Focus, American Apparel Manufacturers Association, 1611 North Kent Street, Arlington, Va. 22209.

CHAPTER REVIEW AND LEARNING ACTIVITIES

Key Words and Concepts

Define, identify, or briefly explain the following:

Bilateral treaty
Caribbean Basin Initiative
Commissionaires
Common Market (EEC)
Cut, make, and sew
Developing country
Duties
Exports
Free trade
GATT
Global sourcing
Imports

Import penetration
Joint venture
Licensing
MFA
Offshore assembly
Production package
Protectionism
Quotas
Section 807
Specification buying
Tariffs
Trade deficit

Review Questions on Chapter Highlights

1. Why has the traditional international trading policy of the United States been based on the principle that excessive import restrictions will lower our standard of living?
2. What are the regulations that pertain to imports? Explain each one.
3. What countries have quota exemptions and why?
4. What is the Caribbean Basin Initiative, and why would an Asian country own production plants in this area?
5. What types of domestic companies import and why?
6. Describe the various methods used by retailers to buy foreign merchandise.
7. What is specification buying? How is it done, who does it, and why?
8. Name several major American apparel producers who produce "offshore" and explain why they use foreign contractors instead of domestic ones.

9. Are you a "protectionist" or a "free trader"? What are the reasons for your position?

10. In view of the productive capacity and creative talent in the U.S. fashion industry, why is our fashion trade deficit so big?

11. Do you agree with the statement that "U.S. apparel and textile exports will never counterbalance the penetration of imports"? Explain why.

12. Some of our textile and apparel producers have found ways to penetrate foreign markets other than exporting directly. List those ways and explain each one.

$\mathcal{F}$OREIGN $\mathcal{F}$ASHION $\mathcal{P}$RODUCERS

Foreign producers of fashion merchandise have proliferated in almost every country of the world and are competing for an ever-increasing share of U.S. consumer dollars. The race is not limited to countries with creative design talent and high-quality products; those with only sewing skills to offer have acquired the know-how to work their way into the world fashion market. In this they have had the encouragement and support of their respective governments. Eager to promote their foreign trade, their governments have developed export incentive programs as well as help in staging international trade shows to attract buyers from around the world.

This chapter deals with the nature, locations, and fashion operations of the foreign fashion producers that supply us with goods. The readings that follow the text focus on the operations of leading foreign exporting companies.

DIFFERENT TYPES OF FOREIGN PRODUCERS

Foreign fashion producers fall into three basic categories, each of which is discussed in greater detail further in this chapter.

- *Haute couture houses.* As used in the fashion business, an **haute couture** house refers to a firm whose designer (in French, *couturier* for male or *couturière* for female) semiannually creates and presents for sale a collection of original designs that are then duplicated for individual customers on a made-to-order basis. Today the only important couture houses are located in Paris, plus a few in Italy.

- *Ready-to-wear foreign fashion centers.* Whereas some ready-to-wear was being produced abroad before World War II, it was not until after the war that major ready-to-wear design and manufacturing centers in foreign countries developed and expanded. They did not achieve their present level of design creativity, importance, prestige, and fashion leadership until the 1970s. Today, even though Paris is considered the major fashion center in the world, there are now other countries whose manufacturers and products have gained recognition as fashion creators and influentials. Italy, England, and Japan are prominent among them.

- *Foreign contractors—off-shore production.* The system of using independently owned outside production facilities—the **contracting system**—plays a major role in the production of ready-made clothing. Since contractors can be located anywhere in the world where labor is abundant, wages are reasonable, and facilities, machinery, and transportation are available, today there are countless numbers of factories located in low-wage areas such as China, Hong Kong, Taiwan, Korea, India, Sri Lanka, Mexico, the Caribbean, and the like. They are used by both American and foreign manufacturers and retailers to produce goods from the designs and specifications of those that hire them.

PARIS HAUTE COUTURE ———————————————

The fashion leadership of Europe, notably that of Paris, originally derived from a small group of fashion producers known as the haute couture. The founder of the haute couture is generally acknowledged to be Charles Frederick Worth, a brilliant young English designer with a flair for business, who was appointed dressmaker to the Empress Eugenie. He established his house (and the Paris couture) in the mid-1860s, at about the same time that Elias Howe, in the United States, was busy perfecting his sewing machine.

European haute couture garments are completely different from those of the American firms that produce the high-priced ready-to-wear that is often incorrectly called "couture ready-to-wear." That description is, of course, a contradiction in terms, since couture implies clothes made to measure for individual customers, and ready-to-wear means garments produced in standard sizes without regard to the individual measurements of the persons who will eventually purchase them. Haute couture garments, moreover, are made of the finest and most luxurious fabrics, use superb needlework and a great deal of handwork, and command astronomical prices. Nothing produced in the United States bears the slightest resemblance to European couture.

Chambre Syndicale de la Couture Parisienne

Shortly after Worth opened his business, a trade association was formed to determine qualifications for a couture house and to deal with their common problems and interests. This was the **Chambre Syndicale de la Couture Parisienne**, founded in 1868. Membership was, and still is, limited to couturiers who met specified qualifications and agreed to abide by a set of rules governing dates of showings, copying, shipping dates, and so on.

To qualify as an haute couture house today, an establishment must do the following:

A French Couture Directory

BALMAIN
44 Rue François-ler
75008 Paris
Tel. 47-20-35-34

PIERRE CARDIN
Maryse Gaspard
27 Avenue Marigny
75008 Paris
Tel. 42-66-92-25

CARVEN
Mme. Carven
6 Rond-point des
 Champs-Elysées
75008 Paris
Tel. 43-59-17-52

CHANEL
Véronique de Pardieu
31 Rue Cambon
75008 Paris
Tel. 42-61-54-55

CHRISTIAN DIOR
Anne de Cizancourt
30 Avenue Montaigne
75008 Paris
Tel. 47-23-54-44

CHRISTIAN LACROIX
Hélène de Mortemart
73 Rue du Faubourg-
 Saint-Honoré
75008 Paris
Tel. 42-65-79-08

EMANUAL UNGARO
Catherine de Limur
2 Avenue Montaigne
75008 Paris
Tel. 47-23-61-94

GIVENCHY
Caroline Aubry
3 Avenue George V
75008 Paris
Tel. 47-23-73-60

GRES
Jacqueline Eobry
19 Rue de la Paix
75002 Paris
Tel. 42-61-58-15

GUY LAROCHE
Caroline Magny
 29 Avenue Montaigne
75008 Paris
Tel. 47-23-78-72

HANAE MORI
Stéphanie Stepien
17-19 Avenue
 Montaigne
75008 Paris
Tel. 47-23-52-03

**JEAN-LOUIS
 SCHERRER**
Mylena de Liechtenstein
51 Avenue Montaigne
75008 Paris
Tel. 43-59-55-39

LANVIN
Marie-France
 d'Hérouville
22 Rue du Faubourg-
 Saint-Honoré
75008 Paris
Tel. 42-65-14-40

LECOANET HEMANT
Hémant Sajar and
 Didier Lecoanet
5 Rue Lamennais
75008 Paris
Tel. 42-25-24-24

LOUIS FERAUD
Françoise Van Labeck
 and Patricia Yvon
88 Rue du Faubourg-
 Saint-Honoré
75008 Paris
Tel. 42-65-27-29

NINA RICCI
Sophie de Würtemberg
39 Avenue Montaigne
75008 Paris
Tel. 47-23-78-88

PACO RABANNE
Michael Chevalier
7 Rue du Cherche-Midi
75006 Paris
Tel. 42-22-87-80

PER SPOOK
Bouy Katiou
18 Avenue George V
75008 Paris
Tel. 47-23-00-19

PHILIPPE VENET
Chantal Chickoye
62 Rue François-ler
75008 Paris
Tel. 42-25-33-63

SERGE LEPAGE
Lucienne Letellière
29 Rue François-ler
75008 Paris
Tel. 47-20-51-25

TED LAPIDUS
Marie Christine le Sage
35 Rue François-ler
75008 Paris
Tel. 47-20-56-14

TORRENTE
Mme. Torrente
9 Rue du Faubourg-
 Saint-Honoré
75008 Paris
Tel. 42-56-14-14

**YVES SAINT
 LAURENT**
Hélène de
 Ludinghausen
5 Avenue Marceau
75116 Paris
Tel. 47-23-72-71

- Present a formal written request for membership in the Chambre Syndicale.
- Establish workrooms in Paris.
- Present a collection twice a year, in January and July, on dates established and coordinated by the Chambre Syndicale.
- Create a collection of 75 or more original garments designed by the firm's head designer (i.e., without recourse to designs bought from outsiders) and present them on live models.
- Employ a minimum of three models on a year-round basis.
- Employ a minimum of 20 workers in the firm's couture production workrooms.
- Produce only custom-made garments for individuals in its own workrooms (as opposed to the standardized sizes of ready-to-wear garments).

French origin is not a qualification for membership. Many of the most famous Paris couture designers were not French by birth. For example, Balenciaga was a Spaniard, Dessès was a Greek, Mainboucher was born in Chicago, and Molyneux was an Englishman, as was the founder of the French couture, Charles Frederick Worth. Another couturière is Hanae Mori, Japanese by birth.

CHAMBRE SYNDICALE DU PRÊT-À-PORTER

Originally the Chambre Syndicale limited its membership strictly to haute couture houses. As ready-to-wear operations by couture houses burgeoned in France, the Chambre Syndicale expanded its membership to include some designer-named ready-to-wear (prêt-à-porter) companies. Today, there is a subgroup called the *Chambre Syndicale du Prêt-à-Porter des Couturiers et des Créateurs de Mode.* Among the 24 designers who have been designated *créateurs* are Claude Montana, Dorothée Bis, Chloe, Emanuelle Khan, Kenzo, Sonya Rykiel, Thierry Mugler, Jean-Paul Gaultier, Patrick Kelly, Angelo Tarlazzi, and Karl Lagerfeld.

ACTIVITIES OF THE CHAMBRE SYNDICALE

The Chambre Syndicale provides many services for both ready-to-wear and couture members. It represents its members in their relations with the French government, arbitrates disputes, regulates uniform wage arrangements and working hours, coordinates the opening dates and times of the collections, issues admission cards for the openings to the press, and registers and copyrights the new designs of its members. Unlike the United States, France considers the copying of a registered design punishable by law.

Designer-Name Couture Houses

The operations of typical couture firms are fairly uniform. Each establishment is known as a *house*, because it operates in a residential building rather than in a commercial neighborhood. The head of the house is generally the chief designer (the **couturier** or couturière), who more often than not is the owner or co-owner. The house usually carries the name of its designer, and its reputation is essentially a one-man or one-woman affair. Occasionally, however, as in the case of Chanel and Dior, the well-known name is retained after the death of the founder, but a new hired designer takes over. For example, Gianco Ferre designs for the house of Dior and Karl Lagerfeld for Chanel.

There are usually fewer than 25 dressmaking establishments at any given time that are designated as haute couture, and of these, not all achieve world-wide fashion reputations. Among famous couturiers of the past are Paul Poiret, Vionnet, Schiaparelli, Balenciaga, Dior, Chanel, Molyneux, and, of course, Worth. Of those who show collections currently, the best known of all is probably Yves St. Laurent. Among others are Pierre Cardin, Hubert de Givenchy, Emmanuel Ungaro, Christian Lacroix, and Guy Laroche, to name but a few. Among the Paris couturiers, many have made fashion history, each for some innovative contribution.

Semiannual Collections and Showings

Twice a year, the couturiers prepare major collections of sample garments. They work with the most luxurious and expensive materials, some of which cost more than $200 a yard, and trimmings of equivalent quality. Each sample is made to the exact measurements of the model who will show it. In addition, accessories are created for each garment shown — shoes, hats, gloves, perhaps a fur, and generous amounts of jewelry. The cost of preparing such a collection is extreme, as high as $4 million. Showings are held in January for Spring/Summer and in July for Fall/Winter.

The heavy costs of preparing the collections plus the rise in the costs of labor and materials have skyrocketed the prices of the custom-made couture garments. They range from $2,000 to $3,000 for a blouse, $9,000 to $20,000 for a suit, and up to $100,000 for an embroidered evening gown.[1]

Until 1980 different types of customers, who came from all over the world to attend the openings, included the following:

- Wealthy private customers, to choose styles to be made to their order for their own wardrobes.
- Trade or commercial buyers (i.e., textile producers, designers, apparel manufacturers, retailers), to buy one or several models for the express purpose of having them copied exactly or adapted into ready-to-wear styles to be produced in their respective countries, or both.
- Pattern companies, to buy models or paper patterns to copy as commercial patterns for home sewers.
- Representatives of the press, to whom couture openings were and still are a source of fashion news.

ROME AND PARIS COUTURE SCHEDULES

PARIS — The schedules for next month's showings of couture collections in Europe are:

ROME

Monday, July 17

2 p.m.	**Young Designers**
	Group Show
8:30 p.m.	**Rocco Barocco**

Tuesday, July 18

10:30 a.m.	Raniero Gattinoni
3 p.m.	Clara Centinaro
5:30 p.m.	Irene Galitzine
7:30 p.m.	De Carlis
9:30 p.m.	Lancetti

Wednesday, July 19

12:30 p.m.	Fausto Sarli
3 p.m.	Giancarlo Ripa (still life)
7 p.m.	Mila Schon
9:30 p.m.	Renato Balestra

Thursday, July 20

10:30 a.m.	Andre Laug
12:30 p.m.	Raffaella Curiel
3 p.m.	Odicini
6 p.m.	Carlo Tivioli
8:30 p.m.	Valentino

PARIS

Sunday, July 23

Noon	Torrente
2 p.m.	Christian Lacroix
5:30 p.m.	Hanae Mori
7 p.m.	Serge Lepage

Monday, July 24

9:30 a.m.	Pierre Balmain
10:45 a.m.	Pierre Cardin
12:15 p.m.	Jean Louis Scherrer
2:30 p.m.	Nina Ricci

4 p.m.	Christian Dior

Tuesday, July 25

9:30 a.m.	Philippe Venet
10:30 a.m.	Emanuel Ungaro
Noon	Ted Lapidus
2 p.m.	Louis Feraud
3:30 p.m.	Chanel
5:30 p.m.	Guy Laroche

Wednesday, July 26

11 a.m.	Yves Saint Laurent
2 p.m.	Lecoanet Hemant
3:30 p.m.	Gres
4:30 p.m.	Paco Rabanne
6:30 p.m.	Carven

Thursday, July 27

9:30 a.m.	Givenchy
11:15 a.m.	Per Spook

Private customers and the press were admitted without charge, but most houses charged trade buyers a **caution fee** (French for deposit or surety). This right-to-see fee ranged in amount from as low as $500 in some houses to as high as $3,000. In others, the caution took the form of a minimum required purchase, generally one or two models. The caution was then deducted from the amount of whatever purchases were made; if no purchase was made, or if purchases did not equal the caution figure, there was no refund.

Trade buyers were traditionally charged more for a garment than a private customer would be asked to pay. The explanation for the higher price was that retailers and producers were actually buying copying rights as well as the garment, whereas the private customer was simply buying for her own use.

Economics of Couture Today: Other Sources of Income

Today, the astronomical prices of couture garments have become prohibitive to all but a relatively few private clients. Trade buyers no longer attend the openings or buy couture clothing for copying. Even the private clientele—

Famous Haute Couture Designers

Cristobal Balenciaga
de Eisequirre

Captain
Edward Henry Molyneux

Gabrielle Chanel

Paul Poiret

Christian Dior

Mme Vionnet

Elsa Schiaparelli

extremely wealthy women from all over the world, whose purchases accounted for a sizable majority of couture clothes at its peak—has eroded from 15,000 in the 1950s to somewhere between 250 and 500 according to Jacques Mouclier, secretary general of the Chambre Syndicale.[2] Of these customers, about 60 percent are American, 20 percent are from the Middle East, and 20 percent are from other countries. He estimates annual couture sales at $60 million, but this is still a losing proposition for even the most successful houses.[3] This amount involves only the sales of the custom-made apparel produced by the members of the Chambre. Although the semiannual openings of haute couture houses continue to make worldwide fashion news, the sales of couture garments alone have always cost rather than made money for the houses. To survive, therefore, couture houses have expanded into other, more lucrative ventures, making capital of their names to give luster to more profitable activities, including the following:

- *House boutiques.* Most couture houses have established boutiques in or adjacent to their haute couture premises. These boutiques feature very high priced, high quality accessories such as handbags, lingerie, jewelry, and scarfs, all manufactured exclusively for the house by outside producers. Often the accessories thus offered are identical with those worn or carried by the models when the haute couture collections are shown. The merchandise that is carried in the boutiques is designed by the couturier or a member of his staff and bears the designer's prestigious label.

- *Prêt-à-porter.* Beginning in the 1960s, the decline in couture sales, combined with growing competition from an increasing number of talented ready-to-wear designers, both French and other Europeans, led haute couture houses strongly into the **prêt-à-porter** (ready-to-wear) field. Although the ready-to-wear lines of the couture houses are designed by the couturiers, production arrangements vary greatly among the different houses, as do the locations of the manufacturing plants. For example, Ungaro's ready-to-wear is manufactured by an independently owned Italian company that also makes Valentino's ready-to-wear. Givenchy's ready-to-wear is produced under licensing agreements by ready-to-wear manufacturing companies in France. The house of Yves St. Laurent has a separate ready-to-wear division, St. Laurent Rive Gauche, whose merchandise is produced in France by a manufacturing company in which it has a financial interest. In all cases, however, the sales volume of their prêt-à-porter lines is far greater than their couture sales and yields a far greater profit.

- *Franchised boutiques.* Retail boutiques bearing the name of a couturier and featuring his ready-to-wear merchandise made their appearance in the late 1960s and spread worldwide, opening a far-flung consumer market for couturier-designed ready-made clothing. Some of these "name" boutiques are owned and operated by the couture house itself; others are run by independently owned retail stores under a **franchising arrangement**. Under such an agreement, an independent retail distributor—that is, a franchisee

—is given permission by a franchising parent company to sell the producer's product in a store that bears the name of the parent company. Especially noteworthy today are the franchising operations of Yves St. Laurent. He launched his first Rive Gauche ready-to-wear boutique in Paris in 1966, and it met with such enormous success that he now has a worldwide chain of franchised Rive Gauche boutiques that carry only St. Laurent's ready-to-wear. Some of these boutiques are free-standing stores; others are specialized shops within large stores that carry other merchandise as well. Among the couture designers who followed his lead into **franchised boutiques** are Dior, Valentino, and Givenchy, with his Nouvelle Boutiques.

- *Worldwide licensing agreements.* In addition to their ready-to-wear operations, major couture houses also license the use of their names on an enormous variety of products—lingerie, shoes, perfumes, stockings, bed linens, luggage, children's clothing, lower-priced women's and men's ready-to-wear, and anything else that is fair game for a well-known designer's name. As in all such **licensing agreements**, the designer sells different manufacturing companies the right to produce and market specific products bearing his or her name. Although the licensed products are supposedly designed, screened, or edited by the couturier whose name appears on them, it does not always work out that way. However, what does work in all cases is the lucrative royalty percentage of wholesale sales that the licensed manufacturer pays to the designer.

Despite frequent predictions of its imminent demise, Paris haute couture seems destined to remain active in the foreseeable future. Although Yves St. Laurent, for example, claims that his couture garments, each of which sells for many thousands of dollars, are a "gift" to his clients, his business managers do not view his haute couture operation per se as a philanthropic venture. As Jean Szware, general director of Yves St. Laurent, explained it: "As long as the losses align reasonably with the value gained in publicity and image, the couture is worth maintaining. But it is possible, in view of rising costs and declining sales, that a moment could arrive when this is no longer the case."[4] Since Yves St. Laurent is still continuing haute couture clothing, it seems evident that "the moment" has not yet arrived.

At the very least, however, it seems apparent that haute couture garments have a new business function: to publicize the name of the house in order to provide a well-known, prestigious label for use in the house's other, more lucrative business activities. As Pierre Berge, president of Yves St. Laurent, said, "No, we don't make a profit on the couture, but it's not a problem. It's our advertising budget."[5]

Italian Couture

Although other European countries such as Spain and England have at one time had haute couture houses, none has ever approached Paris in importance. Today, the only important couture outside Paris is that of Italy. The Italian couture was organized after World War II along lines similar to those of the Paris couture, but on a much smaller scale. Unlike the French, however, the Italian houses are not headquartered in a single city, but are located in three: Rome, Florence, and Milan. The Italian counterpart of the Chambre Syndicale de la Couture Parisienne is the Camera Nazionale dell' Alta Moda Italiana. Its membership of some 13 haute couture houses includes such famous designers as Valentino, Audre Lang, Mila Schon, Galitzine, and Gianco Ferre. Like the Paris couture, the Italian houses present two collections semiannually—in January for Spring/Summer and in July for Fall/Winter, one week prior to the Paris showings.

The experience of the Italian couture parallels that of the Paris houses: couture prices too high for all but a dwindling clientele of the ultrarich; no more trade buyers; and a largely unprofitable couture operation that is subsidized by income from ready-to-wear divisions, franchised boutiques, and licensing fees from perfumes, accessories, and other goods to which a designer's name adds prestige.

READY-TO-WEAR FASHION CENTERS

Today, there is hardly a country in the world that does not produce some type of ready-to-wear fashion merchandise that is of interest to foreign buyers. Even though creative talent and productive capacity abound in this country, hundreds of U.S. textile producers, apparel firms, retailers, and fashion reporters travel regularly to Paris, Milan, London, Munich, Dusseldorf, and other, less important **fashion centers** in order to observe new trends or buy merchandise for copying or resale. Patriotism and a less than favorable currency exchange not withstanding, European designers and their designs continue to hold a special cachet for fashion-forward consumers on this side of the Atlantic.

French Ready-to-Wear Industry

The production of ready-to-wear has blossomed into a large, full-fledged industry in France. Contributing to its development were such designer-named producing firms as Sonya Rykiel, Daniel Hechter, Dorothée Bis, Cacherel, and Emanuelle Khanh, many of whom had their beginnings as owner-operated retail boutiques. Such designers began to attract the attention of foreign buyers and the press by developing styles and looks of their own, which were quite different and lower in price than the couture garments.

Many other designer-named ready-to-wear firms have since joined their ranks. Among them are Claude Montana, Angelo Tarlazzi, Thierry Mugler, Jean-Paul Gaultier, Castelebajac, and Azzadine Alaia. As was mentioned earlier, many of these ready-to-wear designers have been designated as *créateurs* by the Chambre Syndicale and have been admitted as members.

SIZE OF THE INDUSTRY

The ready-to-wear operations of the Paris couture houses and of the designer-named firms that are members of the Chambre represent only a small part of the industry, in both number of firms and value of output. The **Fédération Française du Prêt à Porter Féminin**, the trade association that represents ready-to-wear producers other than those who belong to the Chambre Syndicale, reports a membership of some 1,200 companies, with sales totaling some $3 billion. The women's industry alone employs some 70,000 people in addition to those employed in menswear. Exports to the United States, their fourth largest customer, amount to approximately $140 million. Belgium is their largest customer.[6]

Innovative fashions and mass production have combined to build a ready-to-wear industry that is a very important resource to the American fashion business. Although our dollar purchases of French ready-to-wear amount to only a small percentage of our total imports, our adaptations and copies of their styles and ideas have enormous impact.

SEMIANNUAL COLLECTIONS AND TRADE SHOWINGS

Unlike the American industry, French ready-to-wear producers prepare and present only two seasonal collections a year, as do all foreign fashion manufacturers. Fall/Winter collections are shown in March, and Spring/Summer collections are presented in October.

In its efforts to court foreign buyers, the French ready-to-wear industry stages week-long semiannual **trade shows** in Paris, which are attended by thousands of fashion professionals ("lookers," buyers, and fashion reporters) from all over the world.

Semiannual prêt-à-porter shows, sponsored and coordinated by the Chambre Syndicale, present the ready-to-wear collections of the couturiers and créateurs. These are held in a central Paris area known as Les Halles—which has developed as a cultural center. In addition to the French designer-name collections, some 20 or so top fashion designers from other countries also present collections at this show.

The mass-producing ready-to-wear companies stage their own semiannual shows—the Salon International du Prêt-à-Porter Féminin in the Porte de Versailles, an exhibition building larger than the New York Javits Center. Some 1,300 apparel firms, most but not all French, exhibit their seasonal lines there. In 1989, the Fédération Française du Prêt-à-Porter Féminin introduced a secondary and smaller seasonal show called the Collection Privées. The French menswear industry also stages its own semiannual seasonal trade shows in the Porte de Versailles. Held in February and September, these are run in conjunction with producers of knitwear and children's clothes.

SALON INTERNATIONAL
PRET-A-PORTER FEMININ
SALON BOUTIQUE

PARIS - PORTE DE VERSAILLES

PROFEM

Promosalons International Trade Exhibitions in France, Inc. 8 West 40th Street Suite 1505 NEW YORK N.Y. 10018

Tel. (1212) 869 1720 Telex 427 565 FRSHOWS

SOURCE: International Trade Exhibitions in France Inc.

The Fédération Française du Prêt à Porter also organizes French participation in international trade shows held in New York, Dusseldorf, Milan, Tokyo, Munich, and Stockholm. It also maintains a permanent office in New York City. This is the French Fashion and Textile Center, whose major purpose is to promote French ready-to-wear in the United States. It represents all branches of the industry except couture and couture ready-to-wear. Additionally, most of the leading couture houses and many of the larger designer-name ready-to-wear companies have established their own offices in New York, along with sales representation at regional apparel marts.

Summing up, it is obvious that the French are not waiting for fashion buyers to come knocking at their doors. They participate in international trade shows, they franchise designer-name ready-to-wear boutiques worldwide, they have global licensing arrangements, and they maintain individual and group sales offices in the United States. It seems apparent that, to the French, although creative designers are important players in the fashion game, the name of the fashion game in France is "MARKETING."

Italy

Today, the most serious challenger to the fashion leadership of Paris is Italy, which has been attracting foreign fashion buyers since the 1960s. Italy's strengths and competitive advantages derive from the superior quality and design of its fabrics, its workmanship, and the innovative, sophisticated styling of its knitwear, sportswear, and accessories—notably leather shoes and handbags. It has also developed a reputation for its interesting and *avant garde* styling of men's apparel and accessories.

The Italian ready-to-wear industry developed simultaneously with its couture industry and did not depend on Italian couturiers for fashion leadership and design talent. As a result, it started exporting earlier. Today the well-being of the industry relies heavily on its foreign sales efforts, in which it receives encouragement and support from the Italian government.

SEMIANNUAL COLLECTIONS AND TRADE SHOWS

When Italy first emerged as a major fashion center, foreign trade buyers went to Florence, where the semiannual collections and showings of ready-to-wear were presented in the luxurious and elegant setting of the Pitti Palace. In the mid-1970s, however, ready-to-wear firms in the north of Italy decided to present their own showings in Milan. The initial handful of firms, among them Basile, Callaghan, Missoni, and Caumont, has grown into an avalanche, and today, Milan has become the major staging ground for Italian ready-to-wear presentations. In fact, many of the Florence ready-to-wear firms have defected to the north and show in both Milan and Florence. Their semiannual showings take place prior to the prêt-à-porter openings in Paris, in early March for Fall/Winter and early October for Spring/Summer. The week-long Milan

EUROPE READY-TO-WEAR SHOW SCHEDULES LISTED

MILAN — The schedules for the European designer fall ready-to-wear collections to be shown next month in Milan, London and Paris are as follows.

MILAN

Saturday, March 3

9:30 a.m.	Andrea Sargeant
10:30 a.m.	x Dieci by Luca Coelli
11:30 a.m.	Paola Marzotto
12:30 p.m.	Marina Spadafora
2 p.m.	Harriet Selling
3 p.m.	Massimo Monteforte
4 p.m.	Maurizio Galante
5 p.m.	Emilio Cavallini
6 p.m.	Alma
7 p.m.	Enrica Massei
9 p.m.	Mariella Burani

Sunday, March 4

9 a.m.	Sanlorenzo
10 a.m.	Emporio Armani
11 a.m.	Complice
noon	Chiara Boni
2 p.m.	Max Mara
3 p.m.	Rocco Barocco
4 p.m.	Mario Valentino
5:15 p.m.	Laura Biagiotti
7 p.m.	Gianni Versace

Monday, March 5

9:30 a.m.	Krizia
11 a.m.	Mila Schon
noon	Missoni
1 p.m.	Gianmarco Venturi
2:30 p.m.	Byblos
3:30 p.m.	Salvatore Ferragamo
4:30 p.m.	Erreuno
5:30 p.m.	Blumarine

Tuesday, March 6

9:30 a.m.	Callaghan
10:30 a.m.	Genny
11:30 a.m.	Gianna Cassoli
12:30 p.m.	Basile
2 p.m.	Gherardini
3 p.m.	Sportmax
4 p.m.	Alberta Ferretti
5:30 p.m.	Gianfranco Ferre
7:30 p.m.	Fendi
9:00 p.m.	Filippo Alpi

Wednesday, March 7

9:30 a.m.	Verri
10:30 a.m.	Luciano Soprani
11:30 a.m.	Trussardi
12:30 p.m.	Moschino
2 p.m.	Bill Kaiserman
3 p.m.	Tivioli
4 p.m.	Maurizio Baldassari
5 p.m.	Giorgio Armani
6 p.m.	Giorgio Correggiari

LONDON

Friday, March 9

3:30 p.m.	Caroline Charles
4:45 p.m.	Edina Ronay
6:15 p.m.	Murray Arbeid

7 p.m.	Bodymap

Saturday, March 10

10 a.m.	Red or Dead
Noon	Betty Jackson
12:45 p.m.	Zandra Rhodes
3 p.m.	Workers for Freedom
5 p.m.	Joe Casely-Hayford
6:30 p.m.	Nick Coleman

Sunday, March 11

10 a.m.	Paul Costelloe
Noon	Jean Muir
1:30 p.m.	Bruce Oldfield
3 p.m.	Arabella Pollen
4 p.m.	Ghost

Monday, March 12

10:15 a.m.	Tomasz Starzewski/Shirin Cashmere
11:30 a.m.	Pam Hogg
5 p.m.	Michiko Koshino
6:30 p.m.	Vivienne Westwood

PARIS

Tuesday, March 13

9:30 a.m.	Claude Barthelemy
11 a.m.	Hiroko Koshino
Noon	Krystyna Bukowska
1 p.m.	Yuki Torii
1:30 p.m.	Corinne Cobson
2:30 p.m.	Kimijima
3:30 p.m.	Emmanuelle Khanh
5 p.m.	Paco Rabanne
6:30 p.m.	Etienne Brunel
7:30 p.m.	Olivier Guillemin

Wednesday, March 14

9:30 a.m.	Barbara Bui
10:30 a.m.	Doby Broda
11:30 a.m.	Elisabeth De Senneville
12:30 p.m.	John Galliano
2:30 p.m.	Junko Shimada
3:30 p.m.	Lolita Lempicka
5 p.m.	Olivier Lapidus
6:30 p.m.	Chantal Thomass

Thursday, March 15

9:30 a.m.	Daniel Hechter
10:30 a.m.	Comme Des Garcons
11:30 a.m.	Angelo Tarlazzi
1 p.m.	Helmut Lang
2:30 p.m.	Yohji Yamamoto
3:30 p.m.	Cerruti
5 p.m.	Jean-Charles de Castelbajac
6:30 p.m.	Thierry Mugler

Friday, March 16

9 a.m.	Givenchy
10 a.m.	Bernard Perris
11:15 a.m.	Karl Lagerfeld
12:30 p.m.	Popy Moreni

2 p.m.	Zucca
3 p.m.	Chloe
4 p.m.	Anne-Marie Beretta
5 p.m.	Jean-Paul Gaultier

Saturday, March 17

9:30 a.m.	Guy Paulin for Tiktiner
10:30 a.m.	Odile Lancon
2 p.m.	Gres
3:30 p.m.	Balenciaga
5 p.m.	Issey Miyake
6:30 p.m.	Dorothee Bis
8:30 p.m.	Romeo Gigli

Sunday, March 18

10 a.m.	Matsuda
11 a.m.	Enrico Coveri
12:30 p.m.	Martine Sitbon
2 p.m.	Agnes B
3:30 p.m.	I.W.S. Woolmark
4:30 p.m.	Kansai Yamamoto
6 p.m.	Sonia Rykiel
8 p.m.	Katharine Hamnett

Monday, March 19

9:30 a.m.	Jean-Louis Scherrer
10:30 a.m.	Chanel
Noon	Hanae Mori
2:30 p.m.	Christian Dior
4 p.m.	Jin Abe
5:30 p.m.	Valentino
7 p.m.	Lanvin
8 p.m.	Claude Petin

Tuesday, March 20

9:30 a.m.	Torrente
10:30 a.m.	Guy Laroche
11:30 a.m.	Emanuel Ungaro
2 p.m.	Frederic Castet
3:30 p.m.	Hermes
4:30 p.m.	Lecoanet Hemant
5:30 p.m.	Jacqueline De Ribes
7 p.m.	Junko Koshino
9 p.m.	Marithe and Francois Girbaud

Wednesday, March 21

11 a.m.	Yves Saint Laurent
1 p.m.	Michel Klein

By Invitation

Christian Lacroix
Claude Montana
Kenzo

By Appointment

Pierre Balmain
Carven
Courreges
Jacques Esterel
Louis Feraud
Nina Ricci
Pierre Cardin
Ted Lapidus
Daniel Olivier Favre

shows include not only those staged by the country's top ready-to-wear designers, but also Modit, an exhibition at which other countries' apparel manufacturers are invited to show.

Also, like their French counterparts, the Italian industry participates in trade shows in many other countries—among them the New York Pret showings held in early fall and spring. There are many other trade presentations such as Uomo Modo, the semiannual show of menswear manufacturers; an Italian shoe fair staged annually in March in Bologna; the famous textile show, Ideacomo, held in May at Lake Como; and the Mipel accessories show, held in Milan, each January and June. These are but a few of the many trade exhibits staged in Italy.

LEADING DESIGNERS

Along with those mentioned above, some of the best-known ready-to-wear designer companies in Italy are Krizia, Gianni Versace, Soprani, Complice, Jenny, Biagotti, and Giorgio Armani. All of these have achieved worldwide reputations for their trendsetting fashions. Consider also the names of Gucci and Ferragamo, internationally known for leather products; and Fendi, renowned for innovative fur fashions. Add these names to those mentioned previously in this section and it becomes clear that the fashion story, Italian style, represents serious competition to Paris as the prime source of fashion leadership.

ITALY'S FASHION INDUSTRY

After tourism, the fashion industry is Italy's largest national industry. There are more than twice as many apparel and accessory firms in Italy as there are in France. Close to 40 percent of their annual output is exported, with their largest customers being West Germany (number 1) and France (second). The United States is Italy's third largest customer.[7]

It is interesting to note that, because Italian workmanship and fabrics are, on the whole, better and cheaper than they are in France, many French designers are steady customers of Italy. Besides the silks from Como and woolens from Biella, large numbers of sweaters, leather garments, and accessories that come from Italy are sold under French labels.

Like their French counterparts, many Italian companies have established retail boutiques around the world that feature their ready-to-wear. Some of these "name" boutiques are owned and operated by the company itself. Others are owned and operated by franchised retailers. Particularly notable is the worldwide chain of the franchised stores of Benetton. And also like their French counterparts, many of the Italian companies are involved in worldwide licensing agreements. A case in point is the $800 million-a-year Gruppo GFT Italian clothing manufacturer that has put Armani, Valentino, Ungaro, Dior, and other licensed designer labels into closets from Melbourne to Manhattan.

London

The British have long been famous for their tweeds and their men's custom tailoring, but it was not until after World War II that reverberations from their ready-to-wear industry were heard around the fashion world. Their couture effort, which was keyed to the conservative tastes of royalty and the peerage, did not succeed, and is nonexistent today.

FASHION LEADERSHIP IN THE 1960s

The British ready-to-wear industry, unlike their couture, did flourish and made a major impact on both men's and women's fashions in the 1960s. The name *Carnaby Street* became synonymous with colorful, uninhibited, *avant garde* clothes for both sexes. The London streets in that area were filled with boutiques carrying unconventional, trendy fashions by new young designers. Their

miniskirted dresses, reflecting the free, young spirit of the decade, sent feminine hemlines soaring to incredible highs all over the world. Especially notable was the work of Mary Quant, a young English designer who understood what many other designers around the world were quite late in recognizing: that the young were setting fashions on their own, and that, instead of the young following their elders, the mature folk were following the young.

CLASSICS IN THE 1970s

In the 1970s, the mood of the "swinging sixties" changed, as did the ready-to-wear offerings of that period. English fashion houses focused on their traditional and classic high-quality woolen fabrics in men's tailored clothing, the excellent workmanship of their rainwear (notably Aquascutum and Burberry), and the fine cotton products of Liberty of London and Laura Ashley.

REVITALIZATION IN THE 1980s

Led by Jean Muir, Zandra Rhodes, and Ossie Clark, the British fashion industry was revitalized in the 1980s. All kinds of young, highly individualized, and even outrageous fashion statements began coming out of England. Today, the new and exciting exists side by side with the traditional, conservative, and classic clothing for which England has always been known. There could not be anything more radically different from the romantic cotton prints of Laura Ashley than the industrial cottons and futuristic silks of Katherine Hamnett, the bold prints of Betty Jackson, or the unconventional, inventive styles of such other trendsetting firms as Wendy Dagworthy, Rifat Ozbek, Body Map, Jasper Conran, and Vivienne Westwood, for example. These and other new designer talents are leading the British fashion parade today.

Even the retail boutiques in London are as inventive as the designers and the styles seen on the streets. For example, there is a shop called the Warehouse, where one can buy white clothes and dye them on the spot, with the dye and washing machines provided for the customer on the premises. In a shop called Spring, clothes are sold Chinese-take-out style.

SIZE OF THE INDUSTRY

There is no question about it: English fashions have captured the hearts of both the young and rebellious and their fashion-conscious elders. What is equally important is that they have also captured the dollars of American buyers. Attendance is on the increase at their semiannual trade showings, in March and October. Sponsored by the Fashion Council of Great Britain, the event fills the Olympia Fashion Center to overflowing with foreign buyers. Overall wholesale figures for the British industry are above $1 billion, and the export figures have been rapidly escalating.[8] Among Britain's foreign customers, the United States has moved from fourth to second place. Whether London will maintain its renewed vitality as the Mecca of the young contemporary market remains to be seen.

International Shows in West Germany

Germany's apparel industry has long been known for its superior knitting technology and its well-made, moderately priced "middle of the road" clothing, much of which it exports to other European countries. It is only in recent years that a few German companies have begun to make their names and design ideas increasingly felt in the U.S. market. Two companies, Escada and Mondi, are leading their emerging fashion parade, and a number of other companies have begun to follow their lead. Among them is Hugo Boss, who produces a line of fashion-forward clothing for younger men. It is interesting to note that both Escada and Mondi have set up their own retail boutiques in the United States and in Europe.

The country's impact on the fashion world, however, arises from a different source. What West Germany is famous for is the international textile and apparel fashion fairs that are staged there and are probably the most impressive events of their kind in the world. For example, in Frankfurt each May and November, there is a huge textile trade show, Interstoff, at which thousands of fabric producers from many different countries exhibit their wares. Apparel producers from every part of the world attend this show.

In **Dusseldorf** each April and September, there is an international women's show, **Igedo**, which is reported to draw some 3,000 producers from 41 countries to exhibit their merchandise to a worldwide audience of more than 50,000 potential buyers.[9]

Each February and August, Cologne offers a week-long International Men's Fashion Week that attracts some 30,000 buyers to see the lines of an estimated 1,000 exhibitors from 27 countries.

In addition to these, there is an annual International Footwear Fair held in Dusseldorf every March; a semiannual international children's fair in Cologne; and semiannual swimwear and underwear shows in Dusseldorf, which are the only trade fairs of their type in the world. And there are still others. Among them is the Overseas Export Fair, held in Berlin every September.[10]

Germany's apparel industry may not be fashion leaders as yet, but their international trade fairs are a major source for new fabric and fashion ideas.

Japan

In the not-too-distant past, a label reading "Made in Japan" was usually associated with cheap and poorly made products that were carried in low-priced stores in the United States. Today, however, the Japanese fashion industry has been transformed. This is partly the result of the enlightened postwar aid of the United States, and partly the fruit of the Japanese determination to become a major industrial democracy. In the process, that country has become an impor-

Semiannual Trade Show

igedo düsseldorf
september 9-12, 1990

europe's biggest fashion fair

The meeting place of "professionals" from trade and industry of all important fashion countries. The scene of international spring/summer 91 collections. Order detailed information on trends, exhibitors, events, designer shows from Igedo Düsseldorf, tel. (211) 439601, fax (211) 4396345, telex 8584823.

In the USA: Düsseldorf Trade Shows, New York, tel. (212) 2393750, fax (212) 2393174, telex 428652.

Information and admission restricted to trade only

Tokyo show schedule

Following is the schedule for spring collections:
April 15: Comme des Garcons; Hiroko Koshino; Itsuko Nakajima; Yohji Yamamoto.
April 16: Nicole; Mariko Koga; Nobuo Ikeda (K-Factory); Junko Shimada.
April 17: Masando Shinzaki; Masahisa Shimura; Yuki Tori.
April 18: Pashu De; Junko Koshino; Kazataka Kato; Yukio Kobayashi.
April 19: Masayuki Abo; Yoshiyuki Konishi; Hiromi Yoshida.
April 20: A.T. (Atsuru Tayama); Issey Miyake.
April 22: Kansai Yamamoto; Takao Ikeda.
April 23: Hanae Mori; I.S. by Chisato Tsumori; Michiko Koshino; Takeo Nishida.
April 24: Jin Abe; Atsuki Onishi; Hiromichi Nakano; Bigi; Noriko Kazuki.
April 25: Yoshiki Hishinuma; Ichiro Kimijima; Kensho Abe; Hanai Sachiko.
April 26: Jun Ashida; Yoshie Inabe-Moga.
April 27: Pink House.
May 21: Studio V.

tant fashion center for medium and high priced goods, thanks to the presence of many bright, talented designers and to the quality of workmanship in Japanese factories. That country's fashion industry today is indeed a modern miracle.

An excellent description of the Japanese industry is to be found in these excerpts from an advertisement in *Women's Wear Daily* of January 8, 1980. It was placed by the Tokyo Industrial Association of Women's and Children's Wear.

Dotted with glistening skyscrapers and a gathering place for people from all over, Tokyo is proud of its ability to absorb foreign culture, and especially of being a stage for world fashion trends. . . . Japanese fashion makers have taken their knowledge of world fashion and added to it the traditional Japanese aesthetic sense of beauty, for a higher level of creativity. They believe that the entire fashion world will appreciate the true value of a uniquely Japanese fashion sense. . . . The fashion industry in Japan is at the top of [Japan's] list of growth industries and it is almost certain that fashion will become the superstar among Japanese growth industries in the 1980s. The Sixties were a period when Japanese trade was internationalized, and in the seventies internationalism became a reality in the Japanese world of finance. Now in the 1980s, Japan will push its fashion industry toward internationalization. As Japan's foremost city, Tokyo is striving to raise itself to a par with the world's great fashion centers—New York, Paris, Milan, London.

That they have already raised their par was evident in 1983, when Japanese designers such as Hanae Mori, Kenzo Takada, Kansai Yamamoto, and Issey Miyake first showed their lines at the Paris prêt-à-porter showings. They became a design sensation overnight, and Tokyo was hailed by buyers and the press as the fashion frontier of the 1980s.

NEW WAVE OF JAPANESE DESIGNERS

The initial enthusiasm over Japanese designers grew out of their highly innovative, nontraditional, androgynous, oversized, and almost barbaric look—called by some the "bag lady" look. Although the original excitement has subsided, no one denies that their unusual shapes, asymmetrical balance, somber color combinations, and use of natural fibers—particularly cotton—continue to be one of the most interesting and influential forces in fashion. Today there are many designer-name firms that are well known for their ingenious concepts. Among them are Rei Kawakubo of Comme des Garcons, and Yohi Yamamoto in addition to those previously mentioned. Many Western designers have adapted features of their untraditional designs as well as their unusual color combinations and fabric concepts.

Although they are still focusing on new ways of constructing clothes, their recent designs are less startling and more conventional than those that first burst on the fashion scene.

JAPANESE MARKETING EXPERTISE

Today, Japan is applying to its textile and apparel industries the same marketing efforts and skills that have enabled it to corner the world market in automobiles and consumer electronics. One indication is that in 1985 the country's fashion industry compressed its semiannual trade shows into a two-week period, instead of the former practice of spacing shows over as many as nine weeks. Those long-drawn-out showings dates had made it virtually impossible for foreign buyers to shop the Japanese market thoroughly; the condensed dates were a move toward accommodating buyers.

A further evidence of their marketing strategies is seen in the action of Renown, the largest apparel manufacturer in Japan and one with licensing agreements with 40 European and American prominent designers. That company now has an office in New York's garment center. In addition, Japanese companies continue to participate in international trade shows and designers have opened their own retail boutiques in this and other countries.

All of these steps, of course, make their clothing more accessible to foreign buyers than if these customers had to go to Japan to see them.

Secondary European Centers

Many other countries, in addition to those just discussed, produce ready-to-wear and textiles that attract fashion-hungry producers and retailers from the United States and other parts of the world. Each of these countries is so eager for export trade that its government has encouraged organizations of manufacturers and has offered cooperation and subsidies to help earn recognition for the creative talents of its designers and to promote its apparel and textile industries. With the support of their governments, these countries have developed fashion trade fairs within their own borders and have participated in international trade fairs throughout the world. They are found at such shows as the New York Prêt show, the Italian Modit show, and those staged in West Germany. In addition, they have established promotional trade offices in both the United States and other major market centers.

Fashion buyers in the United States are not likely to overlook creative talent, wherever it appears on the face of the globe. For example, they shop in the following places:

- Scandinavia, for jacquard wool sweaters in native patterns, suede coats, sportswear, raincoats, and woolen apparel.
- Ireland, for hand-knitted sweaters, and coats and suits of hand-loomed tweeds.
- Scotland, for cashmeres.
- Austria, for knitwear.
- Israel, for swimwear, leather jackets and coats, and knitwear.
- Spain, for leather wear.
- Greece, for inexpensive leathers and furs.

In the Western hemisphere, U.S. buyers shop in Canada, whose fashion industry of some 2,000 firms offers sturdy raincoats, furs, and weather-worthy outerwear for men, women, and children. In shoes, the label "Made in Brazil" is now very common. So is the "Made in Argentina" label on furs and alligator bags that are sold all over the world.

Each nation vies with the others for a share of the world's fashion dollars. None of them, however, has achieved the fashion importance of Paris, Italy, or London to date.

OVERSEAS CONTRACTORS IN LOW-WAGE COUNTRIES

As was explained in Chapter 4, there are very few ready-to-wear apparel producers that handle the entire production process in company-owned factories. Most contract out some or all of their production to independently owned outside contracting facilities that produce according to given specifications.

Beginning in the 1970s, U.S. producers, recognizing that the prime source for low-cost production was to be found in the low-wage countries of the Orient, began to explore their capabilities. The countries initially used for this purpose were Hong Kong and Japan, where ready-to-wear could be produced at a fraction of domestic prices. Today, merchandise produced by **overseas contractors** in low-wage countries around the world constitutes the largest percentage of U.S. imports.

Lower Labor Costs

Apparel production is still one of the most labor intensive and least automated major industries. Labor costs are thus an important element in the manufacturing of clothing. As of 1989, pay, for example, for domestic apparel workers was $7.55 per hour—as compared with $2.11 per hour in Hong Kong, $1.75 in Taiwan, $1.17 in Korea, $.25 in Sri Lanka, and $.25 in India.[11]

An additional factor is that in many other countries, the government offers subsidies and tax incentives to producers of textiles and apparel for exports. Such incentives have no counterparts in this country. Thus, even with import taxes of 16 to 32 percent and with the cost of shipping goods, the landed cost of these goods is less than production costs in domestic contracting factories.

Major Low-Wage Contracting Countries: The Far East

At one time, apparel made in Far Eastern countries was of such poor quality that it was relegated to the lowest price points of the fashion market. This situation no longer holds true. Producers in Asia, although still a source for lower priced merchandise, have also acquired the skills and the modern machinery to produce moderate to high quality apparel, thus closing the technological gap that formerly existed between them and American producers.

HONG KONG

For 30 years, Hong Kong has been producing apparel to order—to the order of the garment trade throughout the world. Today, Hong Kong is the world's largest exporter, and the production of apparel and textiles is its largest industry. Its more than 8,000 garment firms and 5,000 textile companies employ more than 35 percent of its multi-thousand work force and account for more than $8 billion in exports.[12] Among its most popular products have been beaded items, jeans, knitwear, trousers, and other sportswear items.

A decade ago, the "Made in Hong Kong" label generally meant a cheap, poor quality item made in a side street sweatshop. But quota restraints that limit their exports to this country have had their effect. So, too, has the competition from other emerging low-wage apparel-producing countries. To get maximum foreign currency return on its exports, Hong Kong had little choice but to improve the quality of its workmanship and produce garments of higher quality—and higher price.

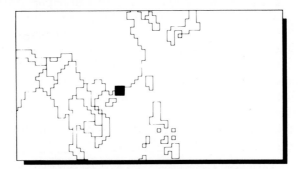

The Hong Kong industry today is noted for its ability to accommodate style changes and for superior workmanship, for which sources generally pay premium prices. Long runs of low priced staple products are no longer Hong Kong's forte. The Hong Kong industry competes more on the basis of service, quality, and flexibility than on low cost.

Some Hong Kong manufacturers are part of multinational Far Eastern companies that have production facilities throughout Southeast Asia. As part of a multiplant, multinational company, a contracting deal made in Hong Kong is often shifted to other locations for manufacture if Hong Kong's prices are not competitive.

Leading designers from all over the world use Hong Kong for top-price designer-name jeans; garments of silk, linen, and ramie; high priced sweaters; and sportswear items. Among those whose garments they produce are Calvin Klein and Oscar de la Renta from the United States; Givenchy, Pierre Cardin, and Christian Dior from Paris; Giorgio Armani from Italy; and Yamamoto from Japan, to name but a few. Hong Kong is also used by mass producing firms such as Esprit and Liz Claiborne, both of which contract almost all of their production out to producers in the country. In addition, almost every important retail store in the United States that offers private label fashion merchandise has some manufactured to its specifications there.

Close to a decade of producing designer-name garments for such discerning customers has given Hong Kong manufacturers a great deal of experience in the production of high quality garments. Today, Hong Kong is also nurturing a fledgling designer crop of its own, who are establishing their own businesses. While the colony has not yet produced an Yves St. Laurent or Calvin Klein, fashions by such Hong Kong–based designers as Eddi Lau, Patricia Chong, Jennie Lewis, Diane Freis, and Hanna Pang are featured in leading retail stores such as Saks Fifth Avenue, Neiman Marcus, and Harrods of London.

Hong Kong's Trade Development Council is promoting the colony's designers in American and European trade shows, including those in Dusseldorf and Paris. They also arranged for some of their designers to make personal appearances at Harrods in London and at the National Retail Merchants Association convention in New York. Further, they support and stage local fashion fairs.

The colony's best designers still have far to go, however, before they become household names. Having their garments on the racks of some of the world's most respected stores is just the beginning. And there is also a local problem to be overcome. Hong Kong's wealthy women, of whom there are many, do not patronize local producers. They often prefer expensive garments bearing the labels of foreign designers. They do not realize that the clothes were manufactured just down the street!

Hong Kong's future as a fashion center is still developing, but it has begun to take its local designers seriously. As Regence Lam, one of the leading designers, explains it: "There's a 30 year gap between the development of their manufacturing and the designers. Making up this difference will take time."[13]

TAIWAN AND SOUTH KOREA

Taiwan, today a major low-wage contracting center, was an agricultural area called Formosa until Chiang Kai-shek escaped from China, declared Taiwan to be Nationalist China, became its first president in 1949, and remained its ruler virtually until his death. Within a decade after installation, he had transformed Taiwan into an industrial nation.

That country's textile and apparel industry, which the United States and Japan helped to develop, is its second largest industry. It is made up of relatively small producers that for the most part do not have the efficiency, quality control, and diversity of Hong Kong's factories. Its main manufacturing capabilities are in the production of polyester fiber and of low to moderate priced men's and women's sportswear separates. As in the case of Hong Kong, quota restrictions on their exports to the United States have encouraged them to upgrade the quality of their work and to develop a more fashion-oriented and higher priced product. Under the aegis of the Taiwan Textile Federation, government-funded programs have been established to train young fashion designers and technicians who have the potential to help their industry achieve these goals. The Federation runs a Design Center which helps keep apparel and fabric makers informed about the latest fashion, technical, and business information. In addition, it sponsors Taiwan manufacturer exhibits at trade fairs around the world.

Expansion of Taiwan's garment production continues to be encouraged by the government through tax holidays and low-interest loans, even though it has been replaced by electronics as a favored industry.

Many industry experts feel that South Korea has the potential to challenge Hong Kong because its factory production is much more efficient than Taiwan's, almost rivaling that of Japan. South Korean fabrics are generally of excellent quality and their suitings, in particular, are considered to be the equal of anything in Asia. The main exporting products consist of knitted tops, men's suits and shirts, and women's sportswear in synthetic fibers that have been fabricated in South Korean textile factories.

Although most of its production is still of a contracting nature, Korea, like Hong Kong and Taiwan, is attempting to develop young Korean designers, who hopefully will add a new dimension to the growing industry.

PEOPLE'S REPUBLIC OF CHINA

In 1970, for the first time there was an experimental Canton Trade Fair, attended mostly by Japanese buyers. In the year following, Americans were invited, but fewer than a hundred showed up. In 1972, the United Nations seated the delegation from the People's Republic of China. Bloomingdale's, New York, hailed the event by opening a shop called China Passage—the first of its kind in the United States, and so well received that the featured Chinese worker's jacket of quilted blue cotton sold out completely. In that same year, many American retailing executives attended the Canton fair and bought Chinese robes, quilted jackets, men's silk shirts and pajamas, plus jade jewelry, straw baskets, porcelains, and other Chinese craft products. Among the stores represented were Bonwit Teller, Saks Fifth Avenue, and Macy's, of New York, Neiman Marcus of Texas, and I. Magnin of California.

By 1975, China had come into fashion—slim side-fastened dresses, long silk tunics over pants, flower-embroidered quilted jackets, intense Chinese colors, and bright satin slippers on high black lacquer platforms—and Saks Fifth Avenue accelerated deliveries of its large fall orders for Chinese-inspired American fashions. In 1980, Bloomingdale's launched a promotion featuring $10 million worth of Chinese imports.

By 1988, China had become America's third largest apparel trading partner (behind Hong Kong and Taiwan), exporting more than $2 billion worth of clothing and textiles to the United States. But in terms of the number of garments, China is the number 1 supplier to the United States.

Chinese-made clothes represent approximately 6 percent of all garments in the country, according to Carl Priestland, the chief economist of the American Apparel Manufacturers Association.[14] Chain retailers such as K mart and J. C. Penney and manufacturers such as Liz Claiborne have become heavily involved with Chinese contractors in the past few years.

Today, China is promoting the expansion of its textile and apparel exporting industries in order to exchange labor (which is plentiful) for badly needed hard currency. In its efforts, it is being aided by investments and technological know-how from Hong Kong in particular. Joint ventures with Hong Kong companies are encouraged by the government in which China supplies the land, facilities, and labor; the Hong Kong partner supplies the machinery, know-how, and markets for the products and generally supplies ongoing supervision of the operation. China has thus become increasingly important to Hong Kong as its principal source of materials as well as being a major customer of yarn and fabric.

Many industry analysts believe that, with the strong entrepreneurial spirit of the Chinese, China is still a sleeping giant with the potential to become, in the not too distant future, the most important apparel production area in the world.

EMERGENCE OF OTHER LOW-WAGE CONTRACTING CENTERS

In the Orient, a void in low priced apparel production was created when Japan, Hong Kong, Taiwan, and South Korea moved into higher priced quality goods. Other developing nations in Asia moved to fill that void—in many instances supported by investments from the four Asiatic countries that vacated that very field. To protect their investments, these same four countries helped the newcomers with production technology and expertise.

Among the countries in the Far East that have developed as low cost apparel producers are the following:

- *Singapore:* for underwear, raincoats, and men's and women's shirts.
- *India:* for cotton, linens, and the coarse gauze fabrics that are popular for dresses and blouses.
- *Sri Lanka:* for sportswear separates.
- *Thailand:* for underwear and brightly colored patterned silks and cottons in dresses, skirts, and blouses.
- *The Philippines:* for children's wear, denim products, embroidered items, gloves, and bras.
- *Malaysia:* for low priced cotton tops for men and women.

Much of the apparel produced in these emerging nations is being subcontracted there by the more traditional sources of Far Eastern apparel—primarily Hong Kong and Japan—in search of either lower labor costs or fewer quota restraints.

Low-Cost Contracting in Latin America

In addition to the Far East, many low-wage contracting facilities have developed in Latin American countries, where labor is abundant and wages are as low as or even lower than in the Far East. Today, there are many contracting factories being developed in Jamaica, Costa Rica, Honduras, the Dominican Republic, Guatemala, Haiti, and Mexico.

Representatives of the Caribbean garment industry are pushing hard to replace the Far East as America's main source of foreign-manufactured apparel. They list among their competitive advantages their proximity to the United States, competitive wage rates, an English-speaking work force, fewer or no quota restrictions, and an abundance of willing trainable—but generally untrained—labor.

However the Far Eastern industrialized nations offer many more advantages. They provide importers with full package programs, extensive fabric choices, skilled operators, experienced and informed management, reliable communication, transportation, banking, and brokerage services—all already in place.

It is interesting to note that there are Far Eastern companies that, plagued by quota restrictions, rising labor costs, and a shortage of labor, have shifted some of their production facilities to the Caribbean in order to gain easier entry into the U.S. markets.

There are those who believe that in 10 to 15 years, the Caribbean area could be as important in U.S. apparel operations as the Orient is today.

Shift of Foreign-Owned Factories to the United States

The drop in the dollar over the past few years together with rising costs of foreign labor and tight U.S. quota restrictions has made direct investment in the United States increasingly attractive to foreign companies. Some foreign producers are using their surplus funds to establish a foothold in the U.S. industry and have shifted some of their production facilities to this country. For example, Tai Apparel Ltd., a Hong Kong apparel producer, bought a 900-employee plant in North Carolina from Burlington Industries. Benetton, an Italian producer, has also opened up a production factory in North Carolina. The Kienja Industrial Co. of South Korea has opened a sweater factory in South Carolina, as has the Jonesville Fancy Yarn Mills, which makes knit yarns. A Hong Kong company that has been producing merchandise abroad has set up a factory near New York's Chinatown district. And other foreign companies have begun to follow suit.

In each case, the branch factories in America are controlled by the main overseas factory, which supplies them with the fabrics, patterns, and designs for their production operations.

Since, at the time of this writing, these shifts are just at the beginning, it will be interesting to watch the development of the penetration of foreign-owned contracting factories into American locations.

FASHION: A GLOBAL BUSINESS TODAY _____

Today, in addition to shopping European countries for new and incoming fashion ideas and for high quality products, knowledgeable American producers and retailers travel the length and breadth of the Orient, from Osaka to Kuala Lampur, and from Manila to Calcutta, with a dozen stops in between, seeking low-wage contracting factories for apparel and accessories.

One top fashion executive summed it all up when she was asked about the foreign fashion producers her company shops and buys from: "Where there is a sewing machine, we'll go."[15] The fashion business has indeed become global in all its aspects—design, production, and distribution. In the process, it has made the whole world into a neighborhood garment center. Boundaries, borders, hemispheres—these present no obstacle if there is an idea or facility that the fashion world can use.

Readings

Fashion is a global business, as these readings discussing some leading foreign fashion producers show.

La Crème de la Hem: An Insider's Guide to the Exclusive World of Haute Couture

Buying haute couture garments is an utterly luxurious experience, and wearing them is an adventure in perfection.

Italy's Fashion Trillionaire

Marco Rivetti has made Gruppo GFT one of the largest manufacturers and marketers of quality designer labels in the world.

Investing in the Nineties

The German fashion industry is coming into its own, and Escada AG is leading the parade.

The Business of Chic

Yves St. Laurent is the golden man of French fashion. Because of his genius and that of other couturiers, Paris continues to command the center stage of the fashion world.

Gotta Have Gottex

Gottex, an Israeli company, is a name that is virtually synonymous with fashion. Donna Karan calls Gottex's swimwear the "Rolls Royce of bathing suits."

CRÈME DE LA HEM: AN INSIDER'S GUIDE TO THE EXCLUSIVE WORLD OF HAUTE COUTURE

by Regan Charles

Lynn Wyatt and Liza Minnelli, Georgette Mosbacher and Nan Kempner, Paloma Picasso and Estée Lauder have at least one thing in common: they are all part of the elite clientele who buy French haute couture. These busy, privileged, high-profile women shop in an archaic way: they travel twice a year, in January and July, to the Paris couture press shows, make their selections based on samples they may never have tried on, pay up to $2,000 for a blouse and $13,000 to $100,000 for a gown, return to the design house as many as three times for fittings, and receive their finished outfits three to eight weeks later — when they may be back in their homes in Houston, Manhattan, Tokyo, Beverly Hills, or Bahrain.

What's in it for them? Exclusivity, prestige, the kind of personal service only royalty can count on day to day — and the knowledge that they are getting the very best. Buying couture is an utterly sybaritic experience and an adventure in perfectionism. Couture clients have the assurance of the designer name and the physical comfort of a garment minutely fitted to more than thirty very personal measurements, cut from exquisite materials, and involving up to eighty hours of handiwork to produce. These customers also receive expert assistance in choosing the proper outfit for their lifestyle. And when they're wearing their new clothes, they know that, thanks to the vigilance of their couture saleswomen, they won't run into anyone in the same outfit at the same occasion.

While many designers claim that they make haute couture, in France the appellation is strictly controlled by the Chambre Syndicale de la Haute Couture, the guild governing the twenty-three couture houses of Paris. To qualify, a house must employ at least twenty workers in its ateliers; it must present to the press two collections a year, each with at least seventy-five outfits on live models; and it must show the collections at least forty-five times a year within the couture house, in a salon designed for that purpose (the fall/winter collections can be seen during the first week of August, then from September 1 through mid-October; the spring/summer collections are shown from early February to mid-May).

The couture houses, in turn, impose some fairly daunting, if unofficial, regulations on their clients. They will not send a videotape of the couture show to anyone they don't know, and prefer to have references for first-time clients. At the major houses, whether or not a purchase is made immediately, customers are assigned a vendeuse for life, based on a rotation inscribed in the *livre de tours*, or appointment book. The customer, too, enters the world of haute couture cautiously. "Most first-time visitors will not buy at all, or will buy one item to test the house," says Pamela Lamotte, *première vendeuse* at Christian Dior.

Things are slightly more informal at the smaller houses, but the friendly personal relationship one builds up with one's vendeuse — or, better yet, one's *directrice de la couture* (the head saleswoman) — is crucial, since clients rarely meet the couturier

Source: *Avenue*, January 1989. Reprinted with permission.

381

himself. Hubert de Givenchy regularly socializes with his clientele and often comes to fittings, but he is an exception. In general, the couturier is consulted only for major modifications and special orders, such as wedding dresses, which he usually designs himself.

Invariably elegant, often a titled princess or baroness herself, the directrice de la couture is the social equal of her client, whom she may befriend and advise. Most directrices travel to New York at least once a year to show the collection, take orders, and fit American clients. Several will travel to the client's home for fittings. It's even possible, once a relationship with a house is established and one's measurements are known, to order a couture outfit by mail, from photographs. But to get the *full* couture treatment, it is essential to come to Paris.

The directrices at the top houses — say, Yves Saint Laurent, Christian Lacroix, or Chanel — take it upon themselves to educate their clients, and offer advice on jewelry, shoes, hair, when to wear what, and even more personal matters. They will not hesitate to speak, diplomatically but clearly, when they feel the client has chosen an unbecoming outfit. The client, notes Hélène de Mortemart of Lacroix dryly, "usually ends up agreeing."

Such relationships make economic sense. Women are often very faithful to their couturiers, where they know who will receive them and whom they are dealing with. But today it's neither unusual nor bad form to make the rounds of the other couture houses as well, shopping at three or even four.

Buying couture is an investment of time as well as money — although customers today give it much less time than their predecessors did. Twenty years ago, a woman would come to Paris with her maid,

settle into a hotel for two weeks, and order an entire wardrobe, which would often be ready by the time she left. Today, volume is lower, the cost of exquisite fabrics higher, skilled artisans a dying breed, and production consequently slower. Clients zip through Paris, resent the time for fittings, and, by the time the outfit is ready a month later, are often halfway around the world.

Yet however expensive a couture garment may be, it is almost certainly created at a financial loss. The house's profits come not from couture but from fragrances, accessories, and manufacturing or licensing of ready-to-wear. For the designer, couture is a laboratory of ideas, free from material limitations. For the client, it's a fantasy. "I don't just want to make a sale," says Véronique de Pardieu, directrice at Chanel, "but to make the client beautiful and happy to have bought Chanel. This satisfaction will come out in her, and it is the best advertisement that the house can have."

Americans are said to be particularly drawn to the prestige of a name. And slim American women are widely appreciated as the group that remains most eager to wear runway designs as conceived — an advantage for them when it comes to sample sales. At the end of each season, it is standard practice to sell many of the runway models — meticulously cleaned, retouched, and fitted — at 25 to 50 percent off, to clients who can get into them. Good clients can even take an option on an outfit, without obligation; Princess Sophie de Württemberg, directrice of Nina Ricci, has several regular clients who dress only in the less costly samples.

But the bulk of the business is in customizing the couturier's designs for each client — a practice that can be fraught with risk. The hang of a garment can be ruined or the spirit of a collection betrayed by too much tinkering. And even changes that have been demanded by a client may be rejected. Each directrice has her own horror story. Mme. de Mortemart of Lacroix recalls one client who didn't like the dress when she opened the box, whereupon she packed it up and sent it back, as if it were ready-to-wear.

Yet all couture houses allow the client some latitude for modification. At Chanel, for instance, a client can simply change a wool crepe to a silk crepe to adapt to a hot climate. And Mme. de Württemberg at Nina Ricci will go so far as to add a floor-length skirt to a day suit so that a Middle Eastern client can wear it one way at home and another when abroad.

Although the houses are theoretically in competition, there is a great deal of cooperation between them. The directrices de la couture will often give one another a call to report that a common client's measurements have changed, or that she's experiencing financial difficulties. They will even deliver a competitor's dress to a client when traveling on business.

New clients to couture usually come with personal references. But with only two to three thousand couture clients in the world, a new customer, whatever her provenance, is a rare and wonderful thing. When five unknown clients bought heavily following the Yves Saint Laurent trunk show in New York last summer, it made fashion headlines. Christian Dior, the only house that will admit to actively recruiting new clients, reported that it acquired ten new ones last year.

In most cases, however, the house wants to know who it is dealing with. A potential client may call to make an appointment, or even walk in and ask to speak to the directrice de la couture. The directrice, however, may ask some leading questions to make sure the newcomer is not a copyist working for a ready-to-wear house,

a trade problem that has inspired a veritable phobia in some houses. "With twenty years in the business, I can usually tell if a client is dishonest," insists Saint Laurent's Hélène de Ludinghausen. "Anyway, couture workmanship is too intricate to be copied. Even a *toile* [muslin pattern] doesn't have all the details."

A bigger problem for the houses is their power to intimidate and thereby discourage potential clients. All take care not to embarrass a new client for her lack of knowledge. As Mme. de Ludinghausen puts it: "Meticulousness, perfectionism, and hospitality are traditions in the house."

Chanel

Chanel, located behind the Ritz Hotel, is synonymous with classic sophistication. Its cream-and-black salons, reached by a mirrored staircase, reflect the distinctively simple hallmark style recently rejuvenated by Karl Lagerfeld.

"A new client here will never feel pushed, cornered, or forced," says directrice Véronique de Pardieu. "We're delighted to welcome back a client who's been absent for years, too. We never forget you." Mme. de Pardieu will send a potential client an invitation to the runway shows held at the Rue Cambon two to three times a week in season. Models, in the traditional way, carry numbered cards, and the client is given a pencil and a notebook to list her selections; she can make an appointment to try on her selections later.

Every September since 1985, Chanel has presented its fall/winter collection to a coterie of "friends" in New York. Mme. de Pardieu goes with one model and two *premières d'atelier* (the head of the workroom) to meet clients who have come from all over the country for a private video presentation of the couture show and a consultation. Afterward, orders can even be placed by telephone. "It's a very personal way to meet the client and get a more precise image of who she is and what she needs," says Mme. de Pardieu, who finds American women very faithful clients.

Most garments can be made with two fittings about ten days apart, and completed within a month. A padded mannequin based on the client's measurements is made when she orders her first outfit, and it remains in the house permanently, along with her vital statistics, including a record of what she bought and when.

Women who buy Chanel are not merely purchasing outfits for given occasions. They are investing in what Mme. de Pardieu calls "the Chanel look and spirit." They usually invest in all the accessories, too, from the legendary white-camelia hair ornament to the handbag and shoes. (Chanel won't divulge prices.) As Mme. de Pardieu puts it, choosing Chanel implies a certain state of mind—a desire to be elegant, refined, and impeccable—as well as an eye for pretty things. Such elegance apparently has no age—the youngest Chanel couture customer in recent years was a three-year-old who had a pink faille dress custom-designed to coordinate with her aunt's.

Christian Lacroix

As the newest and most controversial of the Paris couturiers, Christian Lacroix has been drawing the adventurous and the image-conscious to his couture house on the Rue du Faubourg-Saint-Honoré since it opened in February 1987. "Clients often come to us for a complete makeover," says Hélène de Mortemart, the directrice de la couture. "It's more reassuring to wear a Saint Laurent suit, but more exciting to discover oneself through other images."

A handsome woman with salt-and-pepper hair, Mme. de Mortemart is striking proof that Lacroix is not just for the young and frivolous. She presides briskly and amiably over the couture salon decorated by trendy-chic "barbarians" Elisabeth Garouste and Mattia Bonetti in Lacroix's favorite colors—fuchsia and orange.

Lacroix attracts a very diverse clientele, of which about 40 percent is American. "We are known as a younger, livelier, more open house," Mme. de Mortemart explains. "We get many of the classic couture clients, but also newcomers to couture, who see the house as relatively accessible and unintimidating. Our couture clients range in age from their twenties to eighty-four." They include American socialites renewing their wardrobes, Frenchwomen looking for a single outfit for an important occasion, society daughters in search of wedding gowns, and a sprinkling of show people, such as Faye Dunaway, Bette Midler, and Mrs. Bryan (Lucy) Ferry, who, until Lacroix came along, might have dismissed couture as old hat.

Mme. de Mortemart will show a video of the couture show to selected clients even without an appointment. During couture week, in January and July, Lacroix (who always has his press show on the first day) presents three full shows daily in his house —more than any other couturier—for clients and the press. During the rest of the season, the house does not present its collection on live models, except for specially commissioned shows and the "mitigated video" (a video presentation punctuated by occasional live models) used for both its couture and Luxe (higher-priced ready-to-wear).

Givenchy

Twice a year—in early February and September—Hubert de Givenchy himself takes his entire couture collection to his New York boutique for at least a week, accompanied by two vendeuses, an *essayeuse* (a fittings specialist), and a model. It's an event that draws women from around the country. His clientele is predominantly American, and he is a familiar figure on the streets of New York, where perfect strangers often come up and greet him by name.

During his trips, Caroline Aubry, his directrice de la couture, remains in Paris to receive clients at Givenchy headquarters on the Avenue George V. Some women come for an entire wardrobe of fifteen pieces, others for a single suit or evening gown. The house's strong reputation for cocktail and evening looks is currently attracting a new clientele, women as young as thirty. "There's a recognizable house style that's crisp and streamlined," notes Mme. Aubry. Suits can run more than $10,000, a jersey dress $7,500 to $8,000, a cocktail dress about $10,000, and evening gowns $13,500 and up.

Givenchy clients are high-profile women who, because they travel and entertain a lot, have extensive wardrobe needs. They make flying visits, trying on the *toile* (muslin version), which always precedes the actual garment. "They plan their wardrobes as others plan their workday," remarks Mme. Aubry, who speaks English but finds that most of her clients like to practice their French.

Guy Laroche

At Guy Laroche, references are not a must. "We tend to trust people here," says directrice Caroline Magny, who will simply ask a client whether it's her first visit before showing her the video or sketches of the collection, or taking her into the *cabine*.

Savvy French women, including several political wives, dress at Laroche. A personal mannequin is made with the first purchase. Subsequently, the vendeuse can tell at a glance if a client's figure has changed. She will also make a point of remembering any idiosyncrasies. Petite Mrs. Donald Newhouse, for instance, will never wear pleats—too thickening. Modifications are no problem. "We can create some very beautiful things, even if they're revised," says Mme. Magny. "What matters is that the client be happy and beautiful." It is possible to buy here without fittings, but, says the directrice, "it always breaks my heart."

Laroche is known for lavish evening embroideries, a painterly palette, and form-fitting draping that sets off the waist. If a choice must be made between couture and ready-to-wear, Mme. Magny recommends the couture for day and ready-to-wear for evening. "The woman who dresses in couture from morning to night is simply wealthier. Between the boutique and the couture there's a difference of ten times the price," she says, skirting the issue.

Yves Saint Laurent

Baroness Helene de Ludinghausen has been the directrice de la couture at Yves Saint Laurent for the last eighteen years. Like most of her colleagues at the other houses, this slim, aristocratic woman is courteous yet authoritative, clearly born to give orders graciously.

Two house models are always on hand here to try on gowns for a client, and shows and video screenings are held in the Saint Laurent *maison's* spacious ground-floor salon, whose curving, comfortable red damask sofas and matching curtains recall the Proustian era Saint Laurent so admires.

After the showing, the client can try on the outfits she has chosen. Mme. de Ludinghausen works closely with her to discover the key pieces that will round out her existing wardrobe. "I would rather sell a few outfits each to many women than forty outfits apiece to a handful," she says.

Women like Catherine Deneuve, Liza Minnelli, and Nan Kempner go to Saint Laurent for his classic, constructed elegance and his striking color sense. His exceptionally tailored suits are so highly prized for their enduring, day-into-evening elegance that Mme. de Ludinghausen, who declines to quote prices, is able to say, "A woman today spends almost as much here on day wear as on evening. She may buy her dinner dresses at the boutique, but her suits are couture."

At Saint Laurent, a minimum of two fittings are considered essential.

The collection theoretically provides enough choice for anyone who wants the Saint Laurent look. Rather than change a model drastically, the house can create a variation on the current collection.

The needs, tastes, lifestyles—and budgets—of Americans are quite different from those of their European counterparts. As Mme. de Ludinghausen sees it, the Frenchwoman dresses more soberly and privately, partly because she usually doesn't have as public an image or the same social press to dress up for. The American is wealthier, maintains a hectic social schedule, and has a more extensive wardrobe—with different outfits for different climates.

ITALY'S FASHION TRILLIONAIRE

by Andrew Rosenbaum

Marco Rivetti is something of a maverick among Italian industrialists. As CEO and president of GFT S.p.A., he runs a closely held $800 million-a-year Italian clothing manufacturer that has put Armani, Valentino, Ungaro, Dior, and other designer labels into closets from Melbourne to Manhattan. But executive flash is not his style. Dispensing with the chauffeur-driven Bugatti, he pilots his own modest Citroën. Instead of a palazzo, the forty-five-year-old bachelor lives in a porter's lodge on the family estate outside Turin. And unlike fellow Turinese magnate Gianni Agnelli, head of Fiat, Mr. Rivetti doesn't wear his wristwatch over his shirt cuff. He favors impeccably tailored but sober gray suits and regimental ties.

Mr. Rivetti, who took the helm of Gruppo GFT—a family business—two years ago upon his father's death, has been active in the company since 1969. Because of his vision, Gruppo GFT (for Gruppo Finanziario Tessile, or "Textile Financial

Source: *Avenue*, September 1988. Reprint permission granted.

Group") has grown from a traditional manufacturer with its own labels to one of the largest manufacturers and marketers of quality designer-label clothes in the world —with thirty-six companies, eighteen factories, eight thousand employees in seventy countries, and sixty different clothing lines. In addition, satellite factories have been built—or are about to be—in the United States, Mexico, Germany, the Soviet Union, and China.

Recently, the company's men's wear division moved into a new $10 million headquarters on the Corso Dell'Emillia, in an old industrial quarter of Turin. Designed by Mr. Rivetti's good friend Aldo Rossi (the renowned Italian architect), the Baroque-influenced postmodern building in green stone includes a theater for fashion shows and special sales rooms for each designer collection.

Although Gruppo GFT does as much business as Esprit (one quarter of all Gruppo GFT's consolidated sales come from its GFT USA Corporation of America) it has almost zero name recognition among American consumers. However, no one in the fashion *business* has to ask, "What's Gruppo GFT?" or, for that matter, "Who is Marco Rivetti?" Mr. Rivetti has built a reputation as a man who makes the right clothes at the right time. Perhaps his greatest accomplishment was to foresee, long before his competitors did, a major international market for high-quality designer-label merchandise. "He has remarkable intuition," says Giorgio Armani, who signed a licensing agreement with Gruppo GFT early in his career, before he was the international star he is today.

An Italian company, of course, is in an advantageous position to market luxury clothing. The Italians have the flair, the fine fabrics, and the labor force to produce quality sewing. Not surprisingly, two of the three top manufacturers of designer-licensed clothes are Italian: Gruppo GFT and Genny, which produces Christian Lacroix's ready-to-wear lines. The third is Mendès, the French company that holds Yves Saint Laurent's women's wear licenses. When Christian Dior chose GFT to make its European ready-to-wear lines, the French *Journal du Textile* was up in arms, asking why GFT was "the only manufacturer that can work with European designers."

But much of the credit must go to Mr. Rivetti himself, who has brought to Gruppo GFT not only his legendary fashion intuition, but a hands-on, professional management style that stands in sharp contrast to his father's autocratic rule. The secret ingredient to Mr. Rivetti's success just might be his background, says the Paris-based, Italian-born designer Emanuel Ungaro, who licenses three lines to Gruppo GFT. "He's from the Piedmont. And they are sober, serious people." Indeed, the Turinese are known for their traditional values, their dedication—and their long workdays.

The industrial city of Turin lies eighty-seven miles west of Milan, at the foot of the Alps. Along its wide, tree-lined avenues are gray eighteenth-century palaces, many with shop-lined arcades and cafés. It also has an old aristocratic tradition: although Italy did not become a nation until 1870, Turin has been a capital since the eleventh century, when the kings of Savoy, one of Europe's oldest ruling houses, arrived and held on to power well into the nineteenth century. From 1861 to 1865, Turin was the capital of the Kingdom of Italy. Such is its status that bankers, industrialists, and social climbers all over Italy like to effect the city's distinctive Gallic accent.

Today, Turin is known as the home of Fiat, Europe's leading carmaker, which has been responsible for most of the city's development in the twentieth century. But ever since its founding in 1865, Gruppo GFT has been a major economic force in the city as well. If Milan is the creative brain that shapes the Italian fashion industry, then Turin, thanks to Gruppo GFT, provides the industry's production muscle. Long before Fiat became the city's leading employer, however, Gruppo GFT was turning out uniforms to clothe the king's soldiers. Later, Gruppo GFT would make work clothes for the first autoworkers and suits for Turin's policemen.

In the twentieth century, with the rise of personal consumption, clothing manufacturers no longer had to depend on the army or the commercial sector to succeed. As early as 1887, GFT founder Donato Levi had pioneered ready-made clothing—an act of supreme chutzpah in a country where most people had their suits made at the local tailor shop. But it wasn't until 1930, when Marco Rivetti's father and uncles purchased the company, that Gruppo GFT began using mass-production methods. After World War II, the family got Italian-Americans to bring technology from the large garment factories of the American Midwest, and created a retail chain that sold medium-priced ready-to-wear garments under the men's Facis and women's Cori labels.

In the late 1960s, Marco Rivetti, then in his early twenties, joined the family firm, after receiving his degree in economics and commerce at his hometown university. His father, Franco, and his uncles, Silvio and Piergiorgio, who had been running Gruppo GFT jointly, quickly recognized his abilities. After just three years he was appointed director of Gruppo GFT's women's division.

It was as its director that young Marco earned his reputation for making the right clothes at the right time. Massive social changes made the early 1970s a turning

point in the fashion business. Mass-market retailing was beginning to falter. Education, travel, and greater prosperity made consumers desire more individuality and sophistication in their clothes. The 1960s, it's been said, were a time when stores took labels out of clothes. In the 1970s, consumers wanted the labels back in—and on—everything.

Mr. Rivetti was one of the first Italian manufacturers—if not the first—to grasp the importance of the *griffe* (French for "signature") lines, which are sold under the name of a prominent designer who doesn't have the know-how, the staff, or the desire to produce and market a variety of lines. Mr. Rivetti persuaded his father and uncle to let him use Gruppo GFT's powerful manufacturing and distribution operation to promote designers such as Armani and Ungaro both at home and for the export market.

To work with name designers, Gruppo GFT had to be transformed from a company that made one kind of mass-produced clothing into a diversified, high-quality producer. Staff designers and more sophisticated patternmakers would be needed to interpret the ideas and sketches of fussy star designers. "We had to learn to be elastic, more open to change," says Mr. Rivetti, who admits that "we have learned something from each of the great stylists who've worked with us: from Armani a great deal about the construction of jackets, from Valentino the design of shirts and the use of silk. But I'm modest about it," he feels obliged to add. "I say what we learned from them, not what they learned from us."

He learns from the consumer as well. "When you have to change the product every six months," he says, "you pay attention to what is happening in the rest of the world." Indeed, much as Mr. Rivetti dislikes social life, he makes it his business, when traveling, to do some people watching. In New York, says Maria De Luca, vice-president of marketing and image for GFT USA Corporation, "Doctor Marco"—as the staff calls him—"is not just interested in facts and figures, he wants to know if people are going to clubs. What are the chicest restaurants? He goes to see what people are wearing."

No one could have predicted that Marco Rivetti would start out in designer licensing with Emanuel Ungaro, Gruppo GFT's first big catch—and something of a fluke. "Ungaro was a controversial designer in the seventies; many considered him too florid," says Maristella Vicini, a director of SOGESE, a company that produces Florence's fashion shows. In 1971 Mr. Rivetti's division bought a factory in Turin that had a license for one of Ungaro's lines, and, Mr. Ungaro recalls, "he gave me full reign over production in the factory. I spent months going to Turin from Paris every weekend, and I cut with the technicians. We created a line that was, and remains, successful."

Gruppo GFT does not make the designer's haute couture line (average suit price, $15,000), but it does make his prestigious prêt-à-porter lines, Parallèle ($1,000 and up) and Ungaro Solo Donna ($650–$1,500 per suit); a medium-priced "bridge" line of separates, Ungaro Ter ($110–$500); and his Uomo men's line ($500–$600 per suit). All demanded a level of quality rarely found in the Far East. (Gruppo in America alone makes six lines with Valentino, two with Armani, and one with Dior for distribution in this country.)

But it was Gruppo GFT's collaboration with Giorgio Armani, beginning in 1978, that really put the company on the map. "It was the right historic moment," says Annamaria Luminari Moretti, a professor at the

Rome School of Fashion. "People were tired of the 'country look' of the sixties. Armani gave dignity to the dress of the new woman. He gave the clothes a pure line, in gray, beige, or black and white. It was all part of the new seriousness. And GFT absorbed Armani's values in a kind of osmosis," she explains. "Each took from the other. They created fashion without rigidity, with profits for the designer and for the producer [licensing royalties usually run five to ten percent of net sales]. And it worked for export, because the griffe meant Italian culture, Italian civilization."

"It was really a bit of luck that brought me to know Armani," recalls Mr. Rivetti, in an interview in Gruppo GFT's art-filled Turin boardroom, explaining that GFT needed to revamp its collection for women, and one of his consultants recommended Giorgio Armani. "I told her, 'Go see him, maybe he'll throw you out, but ask him if he'll do some stylistic consulting for us.' Well, Giorgio Armani didn't throw her out, and his partner, the late Sergio Galeotti, said perhaps a company like ours could handle both production and distribution. So we made our first collection for women together."

But the story doesn't end there. The first collection "came out terribly," says Mr. Rivetti, wincing. "Badly made. The memory of it still haunts me, just the way you remember an exam you failed at school. I thought they would say goodbye at this point, but Galeotti saw us through and I've always been grateful to him for that."

Although Giorgio Armani is only eighty-seven miles from GFT's Turin headquarters, he might as well be in a different universe. The interior of his office, located in the most fashionable section of Milan, looks like an Armani creation, its spare, white walls set off by the plain lines of black pole lamps. Mr. Armani, dressed in his trademark dark-blue T-shirt and gray flannel trousers, seems perfectly at home with an antique bust of Marcus Aurelius, the philosopher-emperor.

"People warned me that GFT would *ruin* me," recalls Mr. Armani. "GFT was synonymous with 'commercial,' and no one thought that I could translate my complicated designs into their factories. In fact, the industrial world of GFT was limited — there were many problems with managers and technicians. I had to create a little island of my own in the large world of GFT. But the company has the kind of flexibility that I can work with.

"I had to spend more than two years creating the samples I wanted to produce with GFT," Mr. Armani continues. "Given the complications of my technique — I use very light fabrics with a complicated shoulder — one might have expected problems, but we were able to work together." Mr. Armani says that his American lines, made by Giorgio Fashion Fashion Corp. under the Giorgio Armani and Mani by Giorgio Armani labels, "are valid, intelligent, and, of course, very successful." (GFT USA refuses, however, to release any figures.)

Valentino came to Gruppo GFT nine years ago with an established reputation. With him came his éminence grise, Giancarlo Giammetti, generally considered the strategist behind Valentino's success. Mr. Giammetti has been with the designer from the beginning, building a company that rang up $190 million in sales in 1986. He has worked with Marco Rivetti since 1979, and the two very different men are good friends.

Originally under license to another manufacturer, Valentino switched because, says Mr. Giammetti, "we were having trouble getting the attention we wanted. The Rivettis were thought of as an old family, with extensive experience in the sector. They had their own trademarks and were considered very traditional, successful marketers. We went to Turin and found that Marco Rivetti was interested and eager to take us on. He convinced the rest of the family that it was a good idea." The Valentino contract will run until the year 2000.

Last year, about 60 percent of Valentino's products manufactured and produced by Gruppo GFT were in exports. Mr. Giammetti knows that this is a crucial period for Italian designers in the U.S. market. "Until recently," he says, "the consumer bought the Italian name and high quality without asking the price. Now they are asking. I'm trying to convince Marco, with some success, that this should be a prime consideration."

But whatever their differences, Mr. Giammetti retains his considerable respect for Mr. Rivetti. "Marco has an incredible instinct and an extraordinary flair for fashion. Of course, it's difficult when a person is taken for a prophet."

If Marco Rivetti helped create the Made in Italy mystique, now he is attempting to become an "insider" in the U.S. market. More than a quarter of GFT's sales are in the U.S., where the companies compete with Ralph Lauren, Calvin Klein, Bill Blass, Yves Saint Laurent, and Givenchy. But while sales worldwide rose 10 percent last year to $733 million, profits dropped 5 percent to $29 million. Much of the drop can be blamed on the weak dollar, but it may also signal a trend that most fashion people have spotted already: consumer resistance to rising prices and hemlines, and a certain disenchantment with designer labels, which may have succeeded too well in market penetration. As Ms. Moretti puts it: "Why buy a jacket with a famous signature, when you can go to the bakery and find the baker's daughter wearing something with the same name on it?"

As a hedge against the softening international designer market, GFT bought a factory in New Bedford, Massachusetts, last year and is now adding American designers to its stable of Valentino, Ungaro, Armani, Dior, and Montana. It has entered into joint ventures with Joseph Abboud, Joan and David, a licensing agreement with Andrew Fezza, and has introduced new lower-priced GFT-designed lines aimed specifically at the U.S. market, such as Pferris and Jean-Baptiste Caumont, also sold in Mexico.

Besides branching out from Gruppo GFT's high-fashion base into the higher end of the bridge market to compete with Anne Klein II and Portfolio, he is trying to build the Gruppo GFT name. Banging the drum for GFT will not be an easy task, though, when the publicity-shy Mr. Rivetti doesn't play the media game his top designers have long since mastered.

GFT's grand strategy in the United States, however, doesn't require Mr. Rivetti's presence. The company is pursuing a high-impact advertising campaign designed to catch the eye of the newsmakers and market makers. It is also sponsoring avant-garde cultural events, such as the Claes Oldenburg exhibition in New York last year, which included a production of the play *Il Corso del Coltello*. A highlight of the show was his sculpture *The Knife Ship*, which GFT USA this year donated to the Museum of Contemporary Art in Los Angeles.

Gruppo GFT is following a similar strategy to make its own name known in Europe. The company underwrites Rivoli Castle, Turin's only museum of contempo-

rary art. It has produced multimedia performances on the canals of Venice and has sponsored an exhibition of Russian clothing from the twenties that has toured the Continent.

If for no other reason, the higher profile is necessary to combat what is known in Italy as the "German peril."

"The Germans have succeeded by copying Italians," declares Ferruccio Tinghi, director of international operations for GFT. "They use similar fabrics and similar styles. By approximating our techniques, they have managed to regain a share of the market." To counterattack inside Germany, GFT already has a subsidiary called Oberkassel 1, with offices in Düsseldorf, which markets the group's lines. "And we are seeking to acquire a factory in Germany, as well as looking for new German talent," adds Mr. Tinghi.

Messrs. Rivetti and Tinghi are looking even farther afield for new markets. In January Gruppo GFT set up a joint venture with Pierre Cardin and the Chinese government to make clothes both for the Chinese market. Mr. Rivetti has also been conducting negotiations with the USSR for two years in an attempt to set up a plant there. And, in an effort to diversify even further, Gruppo GFT has formed a joint venture in financial services with fellow Italian garment-giant Benetton S.p.A.

In short, Gruppo GFT is everywhere. A century after its founding, Mr. Rivetti, who put the Armanis and the Valentinos in so many millions of closets, is taking Gruppo GFT out of the Turin closet and turning it into a global fashion player.

But don't invite him to a party to celebrate.

INVESTING IN THE NINETIES

Dornach, West Germany—In 13 years, Wolfgang Ley has built Escada AG into a key player in the game of international fashion. And Ley is determined to keep it that way.

Volume this year is projected to reach about $293 million. Looking ahead, Ley envisions a continuously more competitive environment "simultaneously involving technology and marketing, management and product development.

"The magnitude of investment has gone up drastically," he says, "and there will be no room five years from now for a midsize company that neglects any of these areas."

"The number one factor is good design, but there was a time when it was fashionable to say I only design the line, and the manufacturers are contractors," observes Ley. "And you can see the results in some French and American lines."

Ley, Escada's chief executive officer, and his designer wife, Margaretha Ley, started the company as a contractor of knits in 1976. Today, Escada's spiral of growth and its commitment to the future are evident at its headquarters here.

Among the current three collections developed in-house, Escada is the premier and most upscale. Designed by Margaretha Ley, it accounts for over 50 percent of Escada AG's total sales. Laurel consists of coordinated separates for those the firm terms "quality conscious" business women, and Crisca is geared to a younger, trend-oriented consumer.

"People often ask us why we didn't just concentrate on Escada. It would have made life so much easier," Ley says. "But diversifying cuts risks, and our objective is to have six or seven strong lines, each to be one of the best in its particular market."

Each line has its own management, but shares vertical functions, with Escada AG providing centralized services. These include production, sourcing, central buying, central warehousing, design studios, international distribution, financial services, electronic data processing and logistics systems, most of which are housed at Dornach. Ley suggests this set-up is useful in developing collections, one of which is on the drawing board for 1990, though that's all he would divulge.

"We don't want growth only by expanding existing lines," he says, "for one day we could flood the market. Instead we see so many niches to fill." Acquisition has been part of Ley's diversification strategy as well. In 1987, Escada AG acquired Schneberger, a Munster-based manufacturer of moderate-price, large-size dresses which produces more than 1 million units yearly, and has production facilities in Tunisia, Morocco and Greece. More recently, Escada acquired a 90 percent stake in Kemper, another German women's apparel concern, with additional manufacturing facilities in Portugal. Last June, Kemper, in turn, took over the worldwide distribution and license for the Cerruti 1881 women's collection.

In 1986, the Leys, who hold 76 percent of Escada's common stock, took Escada public in West Germany. In the fiscal year ended in September 1985, the firm had reached a volume of 237 million marks ($129 million), and was heading toward sales of 365 million marks ($198 million) in fiscal 1986.

Ley points out that when Escada hit the

Source: *Women's Wear Daily*, February 22, 1989. Reprinted with permission.

stock market it had "no short, mid or long-term bank liabilities."

"We didn't go public for financing," he says. "We didn't need any, but fashion businesses are usually family businesses, and family businesses have a tendency not to open themselves to outside management. We felt that through a separation of ownership and management, it would be possible to attract a higher caliber of international management.

"We have entrepreneurs and bankers on our advisory board, not Aunt Sally," he quips.

The question of succession was another factor. "We are the first generation, and we are young still," the 51-year-old Ley says, "but we don't have six or seven family members capable to take over the company. That is why we felt we had to open our company, and employ the best people in our industry."

Moreover, Ley notes that a public company does have financial advantages. "If the opportunity to take over an interesting international label arises, a public company has access to capital markets. Yes, you can do it as a private company, but then you build up long-term debts which are impossible for a fashion company."

Like many other industrialists, Ley is quick to stress that growth is not an end in itself. "If we looked at all the applications for licenses, and added up all the proposals, we could double our turnover next year," Ley remarks. "But I fear two years later, the Escada woman wouldn't forgive me. She's used to quality."

All design aspects of the Escada collection come under Margaretha Ley. She is a somewhat retiring woman, far more at ease in working out the intricacies of this massive collection than in describing her creativity. Pressed to described what her husband calls the "Escada woman," she

comments: "The Escada woman is basically a working woman. And I try to help this very busy woman, to give her an easy time from the standpoint of dressing.

"And I try to give her the complete season, which is the way the collection is built."

To keep Escada awareness high, the company pursues a well-funded publicity-advertising profile in both good times and bad. "If you cut advertising and marketing expenses, you lose label recognition. You may have a short-term plus, but two years later you'll have to triple those expenses," Wolfgang Ley declares.

In 1987, when the company lost $2 million in the U.S. market, "we didn't reduce our advertising. Instead, we increased the budget," he says.

Consistency in fabrics and manufacturing is another Ley tenet. In spite of rumors to the contrary, approximately 95 percent of the Escada collection is manufactured in Bavaria, with the remaining 5 percent contracted in Italy. "It's strictly a question of skilled labor," he maintains. Hand intarsia sweaters can't be done in West Germany, and for fine silk blouses, the company turned to contractors in Perugia, Italy.

"But we've never done one piece in Yugoslavia, Poland or Greece for Escada. Last year, we brought in some silk T-shirts from Hong Kong, because a big supplier of ours went sour, and the merchandise was blocked." Nevertheless, the 5,000-piece Hong Kong fill-in was very much the exception, and not the rule.

The Escada collection, which runs to about 1.1 million pieces annually, will continue to be manufactured almost completely in Bavaria, Ley says, because of the flexibility, quality control and ability to coordinate shipments this provides. "It's a huge range, and we have to break it down between 35 and 38 plants."

Eighty percent of Escada knitwear is knitted and assembled in Escada-owned factories, the remaining portion contracted in Bavaria or Italy, depending on the machinery involved. For wovens, the high-technology cutting center in Dollnstein, 75 miles north of Munich, distributes pieces to 35 highly specialized plants in Barvaria, both company owned and contractors.

Contractors, Ley says, must give "a two to three-year guarantee that they will only work for us. But they run themselves. A plant manager is always a partner, and his plant is his business."

Laurel, with total units of about 700,000 annually, is made 60 percent in West Germany and 40 percent in Italy, Portugal and Greece, with some ornamental sweaters and T-shirts (less than 3 percent of sales) sourced in Hong Kong. Crisca's range of about 240,000 pieces is produced 70 percent in West Germany, and 30 percent in an Escada-owned factory in Portugal.

The company prefinances all the coordinates nine to 12 months before they're shipped, Ley says. Escada develops many of its own fabrics and yarns, and last November, the company already had more than 10 million marks worth of yarn in house for the fall 1989 season. "We pay all our invoices within 10 days, or prepay our suppliers, but I expect the highest priority on deliveries," Ley asserts.

The advantage, he says, "is that we can always ship. If we have a dye lot problem or a quality problem, we have a two-week cushion. Our customers are guaranteed goods, but it's a risk."

The risks would seem to pay off in growth. In fiscal 1988, consolidated net income was about 24 million marks ($13 million) on sales of 447 million marks ($243 million), against a net of 12.5 million marks on sales of 365 million marks in 1987.

The projected volume of 540 million marks ($293 million) for 1989 is expected to result in a consolidated pretax profit of 56 million marks ($30 million). In 1988, pretax profit was 44 million marks ($24 million).

There have, of course, been setbacks, most notably in the U.S., where the company suffered the aforementioned $2 million loss in fiscal 1987. The following year, however, Escada's U.S. operation was back in the black, with a $2.5 million profit before taxes on U.S. sales of $46 million, and Ley is estimating $60 million in U.S. sales for 1989, with a 5 to 6 percent profit on sales.

Ley credits Escada U.S.A.'s renewed health to, first and foremost, consumer satisfaction with the collections, and a more efficient restructuring of the company, under Peter Laniak.

In the U.S., Escada services 125 accounts at a total of 153 stores, with shop within shop set-ups in stores such as Gordon Stewart, Oklahoma City, Okla.; Lilly Dodson, Richardson, Tex.; Bergdorf Goodman, New York, and Five Escada corners in Neiman-Marcus. Last September, Escada Retail, Inc., a wholly owned subsidiary of Escada U.S.A., opened what Ley terms a "test project"—that is, a full-range Escada shop in Heritage Center in Boston. Worldwide, Escada owns or is represented by 54 Escada shops and shops within shops, with 16 more planned or under construction in 1989. Escada stores in Chicago, New York and Beverly Hills are on the drawing board, with Beverly Hills set for March 1990. The Laurel division has made retail headway in the U.S., with the fifth Laurel boutique opened, and four more to open this fall.

"We have no strict policy for stores. If we find the right partner," says Ley, "we're happy to have the resident owner as a joint partner, rather than a franchise. The second choice is a good franchise."

Separate Escada stores do not represent

what Ley terms "a policy of growth." Rather, he says, it's a matter of the line needing "showcasing," which helps existing accounts hike their Escada business, he says.

Ley remains a staunch optimist when it comes to the American market. "All markets are our growth markets," he says with conviction, "but North America has 260 million people."

"Our strategy over the next five years," he goes on, "foresees upward proportionate growth in the U.S.," which now accounts for about 21 percent of Escada AG's total volume. The company is also considering producing "new lines, manufactured in America, up to one day even buying U.S. companies. But it's nothing definite," he says.

"We will try to bring in part of our technological and labor skills by setting up our first small operation in the States between spring 1989 and 1990." He describes this proposed operation as a sewing room with between 35 and 40 workers, with two or three skilled engineers brought in from West Germany. It would be geared to simpler elements of Laurel and Crisca.

As for Europe, he feels there are too many expectations for 1992's economic unification, but he says there will be "additional opportunity for strong companies to increase their market share in existing markets."

"In five or six years," he predicts, "there will be only a few market players in Europe." He cites GFT and Steilman in particular as among those that will be in the forefront of the new international gamesmanship, and he concludes: "I hope that Escada will be one of them."

THE BUSINESS OF CHIC

by Nina Hyde

It is 15 minutes past the hour when his show is scheduled to begin, but the guests of Paris *couturier* Yves Saint Laurent are still pouring through the door. Mme François Mitterrand, wife of the president of the republic; Catherine Deneuve, the most beautiful woman in France; and jewelry designer Paloma Picasso, the daughter of the celebrated painter, drift to the gilt ballroom chairs that have been reserved for them in the front row. An American movie star is shown to her seat on the other side of the room.

In homage to Saint Laurent most of the fashionable women up front are wearing several thousand dollars' worth of his creations. Any single part of an original Yves Saint Laurent outfit sewed for the wearer — a skirt, a jacket — costs not less than $3,000. These prices seem fair to his clients, not only for the luxurious fabrics, the matchless workmanship, the perfect fit of the gar-

Source: *National Geographic*, July 1989.

ments themselves, but also for the tradition (Marie Antoinette often exceeded her annual clothing allowance of 120,000 gold livres) and the security of knowing that they look perfect.

Beyond a door framed in grapevines at the far end of the room, Yves Saint Laurent himself waits nervously, surrounded by the wand-like young women who will model his new collection. He makes the final adjustments in feverish silence.

The runway is already lined with photographers, each equipped with several cameras, poised to capture the first moment of glory or disappointment. The world fashion press are poised with notebooks and pencils to record their judgments. Selections from grand opera issue from loudspeakers. At last, after a further 15-minute delay, the first model appears in a sweeping royal blue cape over a bronze suit. The audience breaks into loud applause.

With minor variations this scene is duplicated each July and January in the salons of the other designers of the high-fashion clothes for women that the French call *couture* (literally, "sewing"). For 150 years Paris has been the mecca of couture. Designers have come here from all over the world to show their collections: Charles Frederick Worth (who opened the first couture house in Paris a hundred years ago) from England, Schiaparelli from Italy, Balenciaga from Spain, Mainbocher from the United States, Karl Lagerfeld from Germany, Hanae Mori from Japan.

Needless to say, you can't simply open a shop in Paris and get on the couture calendar. The Chambre Syndicale de la Haute Couture defines a couturier as one who has his own *atelier* (workroom) employing not fewer than 20 people and presenting at least 75 designs on at least three models in each collection. *Haute couture*, the name for the product of such ateliers, can be used

only by the 22 members of the Chambre Syndicale.

Newcomers do exist. In January 1989 the Italian designer Valentino, who has been showing his ready-to-wear clothes in Paris for 15 years and his couture in Rome for 29 years, presented his first couture collection in Paris. "I have *dreamed* of showing my couture collection here," he told me.

Valentino's earlier work may have made him a rich man, but his Paris couture show was the ultimate endorsement of his craft. The couturier is bound by no creative restrictions, no concern for price, no worry as to who will buy the new styles. Originality is all.

Perhaps, however, couturiers are more aware of their customers than other artists: "When there were beautiful bodies to dress, it was my greatest pleasure to dress them," Mme Vionnet, whose venerable couture house was at its peak in the 1920s and 1930s, said to me 15 years ago, just before she died at 98. "For the others I did my best."

Couture now caters to "the others." In the mid-1970s Saint Laurent became the first designer to move his shows from his fashion house, where couture clothes had always been made, to the more spacious ballroom of one of Paris's grand hotels. Before that, models resembled statues, and the audience stared at them in solemnity and silence—no music every played, and applause was seldom heard. Except for the irrepressible Coco Chanel, who watched her shows from the top step of the stairway in her famous house in the Rue Cambon, designers stayed behind the scenes.

Even today applause is saved for the most spectacular creations. But sometimes the simplest garment—an impeccable black suit, for example—will inspire a burst of applause. At the Saint Laurent show last July, the audience clapped for the Lesage grape embroideries on some of his creations.

Only once in 23 years of covering the Paris shows do I recall a negative reaction. That was in the early 1970s, when Christian Dior showed leopard-skin coats in his collection, and American editors and photographers hissed this exploitation of an endangered animal species. Coats made of the skins of leopards and other great cats were shown the next season, but never again.

Customers possessed of the sort of figure admired by Mme Vionnet can buy the clothes worn by models in the shows for half price. Most require different sizes, and these are created, one at a time, by the couturier's seamstresses and tailors. It may take as many as six fittings to make sure that the dress is perfectly draped for the body, that the covered snaps are in precisely the right place, that the gold metal chain (at Chanel) anchors the jacket precisely as it should, that the supple silk lining doesn't pull.

Nothing in a house of couture carries a written price. If the customer thinks that the price is too high, she can say so; occasionally it will be adjusted.

It is a brave soul who suggests changing the look of a design. The rare victories of customer over designer are justly celebrated. Gloria Guinness, wife of the heir to a vast Irish fortune, scandalized fitter and *vendeuse* by demanding changes in the late Balenciaga's pyramid-shaped dress. "Gloria, how dare you change one of my designs?" Balenciaga asked her sternly. "I dare because my husband will be paying the bill and will not like the dress precisely as you have designed it," Mrs. Guinness replied spunkily. "You are absolutely right," Balenciaga agreed with a grin. Mrs. Guinness was photographed frequently in the adjusted style.

Gloria Guinness's triumph was perhaps unique, but regular customers do have certain privileges in addition to a seat in the front row. The Duchess of Windsor, who did as much for the French fashion industry in her time as Nancy Reagan did for its U.S. counterpart in our own day, often benefited from a 40 percent discount. Regulars who missed a collection used to be sent sketches, descriptions, and prices. Nowadays fashionable women who can't attend the shows are more likely to order from videos or photographs.

Most women treat their couture purchases like the treasures they are. Deeda Blair, a medical-research consultant from Washington, D.C., who wears some of her Paris dresses for as long as 16 years, donates garments she knows she will never wear again to museums. Ivana Tump, wife of New York tycoon Donald Trump, packs older designs off to her mother in Czechoslovakia. But the late Lorraine Rowan Cooper, wife of former Kentucky Senator John Sherman Cooper, would occasionally use the sturdy wool from a couture skirt to cover an ottoman.

"Couture is necessary and must be preserved, because it is the last refuge of the craftsman," Yves Saint Laurent once told me. "The rich woman must preserve couture. Maybe that is not a law, but it is her duty. Otherwise couture and its crafts will die, and rich women will be responsible for the decline of this art *extraordinaire!*"

Already some of the crafts are dying out. Saint Laurent is finding it increasingly difficult to get high-quality *passementerie* (trimming) to replace the original trim on clothes inspired several years ago by the costumes of the Russian peasants of tsarist times or the raffia used in his African designs. The fine satin and taffeta needed to stitch together the 16 parts of a glove are also becoming scarce.

Designers live not by couture alone, but by the things that couture makes possible in the mass market—fragrances, ready-to-wear clothes for men and women, shoes, scarves, and other items with the designer's brand on them. This business started less than 25 years ago, when Saint Laurent kicked off his ready-to-wear line. Other designers followed, to their immense profit. Such products are estimated to bring in nearly 200 times the 50 million dollars earned each year by couture itself.

Buyers from all over the world flock to the official ready-to-wear shows that take place twice a year in tents set up in the courtyard of the Louvre. There is nothing ladylike or gentlemanly about these crowded, market-driven shows. Rock music blasts, and ten models come down the runway at one time, wearing fantastic outfits. A designer has to be director and producer, or hire someone who is, in order to compete.

Clothes are often exaggerated, overaccessorized to beam the message loud and clear to the professional audience in the back of the tent. The designer's chosen team of hairstylists and makeup artists changes the models' look to suit the designer's choice of image. At least 50 other designers show their clothes in schools, restaurants, theaters—even their apartments. The first American to make it big in the ready-to-wear shows is Patrick Kelly, originally from Mississippi, who like a coach before the big game always engages his models, assistants, and dressers behind the scenes in a brief prayer session before the show begins.

Ready-to-wear may not be genteel, but it's good business for French fashion and good business for France. The French government and fashion industry are attached by a strong and ancient thread. President Mitterrand encouraged establishment of the Musée de la Mode in the Louvre and still worries whether the elevators work properly.

Louis XIV established dress edicts for his court that pushed upwardly mobile nobles to the edge of bankruptcy. Like the modern designers who loaned dresses to Mrs. Reagan, he understood the trickle-down theory of fashion—that if someone in a special position wears something, others will imitate. The Sun King decreed that only noblemen of a high rank could wear silver bullion on their waistcoats. "This created a vast popularity for lumps of silver," says Harold Koda, curator at the Fashion Institute of Technology in New York City.

Traveling aristocrats brought the styles of the French court to other European courts. French ambassadors carried books of swatches and designs as a way to boost the silk and other luxury industries.

Napoleon understood that the Revolution had virtually destroyed France's silk industry, which was essential to the nation's economy. "I saw you in the same dress two weeks ago," he might say, beginning a conversation with a young noblewoman in the simple cotton dress popular at the time. "Don't you think it would be better to dress more richly, like some of the others who are bedecked in silk and embroidery and lace?" The emperor ordered butlers to keep the fires in the court banked, so that the chill would encourage women to cover themselves with more silk.

One wealthy 19th-century American, a Mrs. Moulton, who had been invited to Napoleon III's court at the Palace of Compiègne, bought 21 dresses from Worth: "Eight day costumes (counting my traveling suit), the green cloth dress for the hunt, which I was told was absolutely necessary, seven ball dresses, five gowns for tea."

About such lavish wardrobe expenditures she once grumbled, "Some compliments were paid me, but unfortunately not enough to pay the bill."

Other American women have been at

the very center of couture. Early in this century Paris designer Jean Patou decided that his "sporting look" was particularly suitable to the long-legged, athletic American woman. According to Patou's grandnephew, Jean de Mouy, who now runs the house on the Rue Saint-Florentin, Patou went to New York City in 1926 and made a deal with Florenz Ziegfeld to hire showgirls to use in presenting his collection. Today many leading models are Americans.

If all this history and current turmoil tells us anything, it tells us that fashion may change, but it never dies. The healthy overstatement of the ready-to-wear shows reassures us on that score, as people come from all over the world in search of clothes that people will buy in the hope of looking perfect.

At the Claude Montana ready-to-wear show last October, there was a wait of more than an hour and a half from the time the show was scheduled until it finally began. Scattered handclapping gave the first hint that the crowd was restless, and before the show started, the rhythmic pounding of feet seemed to rock the tent. But once the show began with a parade of models in wide-legged pants, see-through blouses, jackets, and coats, the audience cheered and the delay was forgotten.

Even the couturiers seem to be getting into the spirit of the future. "It was your best, your best!" one retailer told a dazed Saint Laurent after a recent show. A member of the press kissed the couturier on both cheeks and said, "It's hard to imagine you could do such a brilliant collection again!" And Saint Laurent agreed, "You are probably right."

But he probably will do it again. As the French say, it is his *métier*.

GOTTA HAVE GOTTEX

By Louise Bernikow

It began in Budapest before World War II, a place Diana Vreeland called "the most chic city in Europe" and "the last city of pleasure." While some citizens danced to Gypsy music and others bejeweled themselves for dinner parties, a young woman was thinking about chemistry. When her husband went to buy fabrics for the family's raincoat business, she went along. "I have a feeling for this," she thought. She had a feeling for design and style, but, even more, she had one for chemistry. She hoped to study the subject. Thinking about fabric, she asked herself questions, partly chemical, partly alchemical, about what would happen if you mixed certain things together.

Leah Gottlieb has not stopped thinking about chemistry. Today, more than forty years after her fabric-buying excursions in Budapest, she oversees Gottex, the $50 million-a-year swimwear company whose name is virtually synonymous not only with high fashion but with technical innovations rooted in questions of chemistry. Gottex suits are unique because they use a high proportion of Lycra, which gives them a

Source: *Connoisseur*, June 1988. Reprinted with permission.

tight fit and distinctive line, and because Gottex fabrics shimmer and shine, carry bold colors, and bring to the world of the bathing suit textures—of lace, sequins, velvets—generally associated with evening clothes.

Unlike other designers, including Norma Kamali, who Mrs. Gottlieb has said may be the best swimsuit designer in the world, Gottex concentrates on beachwear, presenting its yearly collection with all the fanfare of the couturiers in Milan or Paris and being received with as much respect. Donna Karan calls them "the Rolls-Royce of bathing suits." "They have an aura, a mystique," she says, "because they're clearly the best, and everybody—especially designers—knows it."

All this is the product of a family business headed by a seventy-ish grandmother who looks like a cross between Helena Rubinstein and Dr. Ruth. "Sexy" is the last thing you expect her to advocate. Chicken soup is more likely. (In fact, her daughter has been known to fly chicken soup on the Concorde to an ailing friend in Paris.) "I have a very sexy aesthetic," she says, "but not vulgar. I am very much watching the limit." She also says that she doesn't "like" money but does like "to make from nothing, something." It's still about chemistry.

Mrs. Gottlieb makes something from nothing in Tel Aviv, where she was often compared to Golda Meir, another small, graying woman with savvy and drive. This is far from the glittering aisles of the Rue Faubourg St.-Honoré. "I hate fashion," Mrs. Meir was quoted as saying. "Fashion is an imposition, a rein on freedom." Mrs. Gottlieb may find operating out of Israel difficult in some ways, but she hardly hates fashion.

Gottex suits clad Diana, the princess of Wales, as she lounged on the yacht of King Carlos of Spain last year. They adorn an unlikely assortment of celebrated bodies, from Elizabeth Taylor's and Brooke Shields's to Barbara Walters's and Yoko Ono's. Harrods, where Gottex has its own boutique, as it does at Galeries Lafayette and other quality stores in sixty-two countries, rushes suits to the princess when she rings up. King Hussein's former wife Muna was not so lucky. Some styles with matching caftans were not at Harrods when she called, but the queen called Tel Aviv and had her suits within forty-eight hours.

The Gottlieb family has been in Israel since its arrival, in 1949, soon after the nation's founding. Armin Gottlieb had survived a Nazi labor camp. Leah Gottlieb and her two daughters had survived years in hiding. The war had prevented her from studying chemistry. At first, the family tried to revive the raincoat business in Israel. "Raincoats in a country with no rain," says Leah. "So I ask myself, What is the most important thing here? What is important is to go to the beach."

Swimsuits for the Israeli market were produced by the family in the midfifties under the label Gottex, which combines "Gottlieb" and "textiles." They began, as other swimwear manufacturers did, with "that elastic, Lastex," but quickly switched to the more versatile Lycra. They were the first to print on Lycra, which, until then, had been used in solid-color suits. Her first hit was a suit in yellow and pink roses, which "people lined up for" and which convinced Leah Gottlieb that her "feeling for it" was real.

With swimsuits, Gottex entered a minefield. No form of clothing produces more anxiety in women than bathing suits do. They represent the supreme test of how a woman feels about her body, a test often failed. Unlike lingerie, where a woman may experiment to her heart's content with skimpiness or plenty, country-plain or bordello-bold, a bathing suit is a public garment. Lingerie, for all the freedom it offers the imagination, remains under a woman's control, under her clothes. Opportunities for fear and loathing in a bathing suit are endless. Nowhere else is the discrepancy between what is seen on the model and what is seen in the mirror so enormous. Pity the designer who becomes the butt of a woman's chagrin at the limitations of her own flesh.

The history of swimwear fashion is a history of progressive revelation—the unveiling, first, of kneecaps and arms, then of shoulders, midsections, thighs, hipbones, cleavage, derrieres. The bikini, which Diana Vreeland called "the biggest thing since the atom bomb," has never much appealed to Gottex designers. It stands at the other end of the spectrum from the classic Gottex suit, in which breasts are generally minimized and legs emphasized, and artifice, as opposed to nature, dominates. For that reason, Mrs. Gottlieb has been called the "matriarch of the maillot," and her design has emphasized one-piece suits, which she considers "more elegant" and more dressed. In the war between the body and the bathing suit, clothes have won.

The focus has shifted in swimwear, in fashion, and in life away from breasts and navels and onto legs. Eighty-five percent of the current collection is of one-piece suits, cut high on the leg and, often, deep in the neckline, draped as adroitly as any dinner dress, in patterns that go from ultrafeminine roses to siren-y metallics to whimsical narratives like the motif of the Orient-Express. Gottex was the first to use lace on bathing suits; then velours; then, in the early 1980s, metallics, which it now considers "old hat." It is also the leader in ensemble swimwear, intensifying the idea that swimwear is dressing. What is seen in the mirror is easily camouflaged by a line of pareos, jackets, and skirts. The palazzo pants of current couture turn up in next season's beach ensembles.

"I don't believe anymore in revealing so much," Mrs. Gottlieb's daughter says. Miriam Ruzow, president of the American operation, says that suits with underwire and those with high necklines are popular. Gottex suits are designed to be filled by a woman with some flex. "Of course we design for bad figures," Mrs. Ruzow says. "Most people have bad figures."

Mrs. Ruzow is herself a small woman who, one day this spring, was wearing a tight black knot bodysuit and short skirt by Donna Karan—"the first American designer whose clothes I'm wearing." Gottex makes Karan's swimwear. "She understands what a woman needs," Ruzow says. "I don't think men designers do." Gottex suits seem to attend to a woman's need not to embarrass herself in a bathing suit. The underwires help. So does the fact that many designs give the illusion of a high cut on the leg but are cut to a reasonable height. In larger sizes, the legs are cut lower.

A Gottex suit today is the product of the collective vision of Leah Gottlieb and her daughters. Miriam Ruzow studied design in Paris at the École Guerre Lavigne and, like her mother, looked at a world of solids and decided it needed prints. For her, the field was lingerie, which, in the early 1960s, was "all pink and white and black." Miriam Ruzow's print lingerie did well, and in the midsixties she joined the family business, becoming president of Gottex USA. Her sister, Judith, is the "technical" expert, involved with the sportswear division in Israel. Armin Gottlieb still oversees the finances.

The team convenes and reconvenes monthly, boarding airplanes to reconnoiter in Paris, Milan, Tel Aviv, or New York.

Some of their fabrics are printed by the Italian factory that also prints fabrics for Christian Lacroix, Valentino, and Armani. They attend the spring and fall collections in Paris and Milan, whence a fashion trend finds its way quickly into a Gottex collection—animal prints, as they did this year, or pouf skirts, which turned up in several bathing suits designed for a younger market.

"My eyes is all the time open," Leah Gottlieb says. Ideas for fabric designs come to her in museums and at operas or ballets. Picasso's colors have been used often. The spring collection features florals drawn directly from Monet. Three years ago, in the Metropolitan Museum of Art, she was taken with van Gogh's paintings from Arles. "I made van Gogh prints," she says, "but people didn't approve. Now Christian Lacroix has brought them out." "Many times," she sighs, "we are too early. People have to be ready for what you have." No animosity here, however. Lacroix remains a favorite designer—"He brings new fresh air"—and his fall show drew the entire family.

Gottex is resolutely European, in love with Italy—"Italians are the most elegant women in the world," Miriam Ruzow declares firmly—and last season's collection climaxed with the Triumphal March from *Aida* playing behind the models. Although Americans are admired for being "much earlier up-to-date, more ready to accept things" than essentially conservative Europeans, the idea of elegance, for mother and daughters, still belongs to "the Old World." The newest navy bathing suits in the collection—"Navy," Miriam Ruzow says, "is this year's black"—are named after the duchess of Windsor. They ride high on the leg and low on the cleavage. What would Wallis Simpson have thought?

Budapest was landlocked, but it had dash and glamour. From Tel Aviv, an unlikely place, from Leah Gottlieb, a somewhat unlikely person, and in swimwear, an entirely unlikely métier, the ghost of Budapest whispers.

Endnotes

1. "Fashion Flash," the Fashion Group Foundation, August 1988 and "Couture's Constant Red Ink," *Women's Wear Daily*, January 18, 1990.
2. Ibid.
3. Ibid.
4. "Designers Grumble But Fashion Goes On," *Women's Wear Daily*, July 26, 1976.
5. "Voice of the Couture," *Vanity Fair*, December 1984.
6. French Fashion and Textile Center, New York City; and *Women's Wear Daily*, August 25, 1988.
7. Italian Fashion Trade Center, New York City.
8. Clothing Export Council of Great Britain, London.
9. *Women's Wear Daily*, September 13, 1989.
10. Ibid.

11. "Industry Surveys," Standard & Poor's, 1990; and U.S. Bureau of Labor Statistics.

12. "The U.S. and Hong Kong," Hong Kong Trade Development Council, New York, September 1988.

13. *Women's Wear Daily*, January 3, 1988.

14. *New York Times*, May 15, 1989.

15. Mary Ellen Bernard, executive vice president of Frederick Atkins, Inc., at a Fashion Institute of Technology's Fashion Seminar, October 1985.

Selected Bibliography

Balmain, Pierre. *40 Années de Creation*. Paris: Musée de la Mode et du Costume, 1985.

Calliaway, Nicholas. *Issey Miyake*. New York: New York Graphic Society, 1988.

Charles-Roux, Edmonde. *Chanel*. New York: Alfred A. Knopf, 1975.

De Graw, Imelda G. *25 Years/25 Couturiers*. Denver: Art Publication, 1975.

Dior, Christian. *Christian Dior and I*. New York: E. P. Dutton, 1957.

Giroud, Francoise. *Dior*. New York: Rizzoli International Publications, 1987.

Leymarie, Jean. *Chanel*. New York: Rizzoli International Publications, 1987.

Lyman, Ruth, ed. *Couture*. Garden City, N.Y.: Doubleday, 1972.

McDermott, Catherine. *Street Style: British Design in the 80's*. New York: Rizzoli International Publications, 1987.

Markowitz, Milton. *The Global Marketplace: 102 of the Most Influential Countries outside America*. New York: Macmillan Publishers, 1988.

Milbank, Carolyn R. *Couture: The Great Designers*. New York: Steward, Tabori and Chang. 1985.

Poiret, Paul. *Kings of Fashion*. Philadelphia: J. B. Lippincott, 1931.

Quant, Mary. *Quant by Quant*. New York: Putnam, 1966.

Rhodes, Zandra, and Anne Knight. *The Art of Zandra Rhodes*. Boston: Houghton Mifflin, 1985.

Rykiel, Sonia. *Rykiel*. Paris: Herscher, 1985.

Saint Laurent, Yves. *Yves St. Laurent*. New York: Metropolitan Museum of Art, distributed by Crown Publishers, 1983.

Saunders, Edith. *The Age of Worth*. Bloomington, Ind.: University Press, 1955.

Schaparelli, Elsa. *Shocking Life*. New York: E. P. Dutton, 1954.

Steele, Valerie. *Paris Fashion. A Cultural History*. New York: Oxford University Press, 1988.

White, Palmer. *Haute Couture Embroidery: The Art of Lesage*. New York: The Vendome Press, 1988.

Trade Associations

Board of Trade, Export Services Division, Hillgate House, 35 Old Bailey, London EC 4, England.

Camera Nazionale della Moda Italiana, 00187 Roma, Via Lombardia, 44, Italy.

Centro Di Firenze Per La Moda Italiana, Vitale Gramsci 9/A, Florence, Italy.

Chambre Syndicale de La Couture Parisienne, 100 Rue Du St. Honoré, 75008 Paris, France.

Clothing Export Council of Great Britain, 54 Grosvenor Street, London, WIXODB, England.

Fédération Française des Industries de Prêt-à-Porter Féminin, 69 Rue de Richelieu, Paris 75002, France.

Trade Publications

Daily News Record, 7 East 12th Street, New York, N.Y. 10003.

Femme-Lines, 225 East 36th Street, New York, N.Y. 10016.

Women's Wear Daily, 7 East 12th Street, New York, N.Y. 10003.

CHAPTER REVIEW AND LEARNING ACTIVITIES

Key Words and Concepts

Define, identify, or briefly explain the following:

Caution fee	Franchised boutiques
Chambre Syndicale de la Couture Parisienne	Franchising arrangement
Contracting system	Haute couture
Couturier	Igedo
Dusseldorf	Imports
Fashion center	Licensing agreement
Fédération Française du Prêt à Porter Féminin	Overseas contractors
	Prêt-à-porter
	Trade show

Review Questions on Chapter Highlights

1. Name the three categories of foreign fashion producers and explain how they differ.

2. What is a haute couture house, and how do its operations differ from those of an American apparel company? Are there haute couture houses in the United States? Explain your answer.

3. What is the prêt-á-porter division of the Chambre Syndicale de la Couture Parisienne, and why did it come into existence?

4. What are the major sources of income for haute couture houses?

5. Which are the secondary European centers and for what are they known?

6. What is the fashion importance of Japan today? Give examples that support your answer.

7. What are the dates of (a) haute couture showings and (b) ready-to-wear showings? Why do you think they differ?

8. Name some low-wage apparel production centers in the Far East; for what is each best known?

9. Discuss the following statement made by a major retailer: "Where there is a sewing machine, we'll go."

10. Why are all foreign governments so eager to develop the apparel industry in their respective countries? Is the United States as active as foreign governments in its support of our domestic apparel industry? Explain your answer.

11. Which reading do you believe to be the most informative and why?

The Retailers of Fashion

Eventually all merchandise that is designed and produced must reach the ultimate consumers, and that is the role and responsibility of **retailers**. In the course of buying and selling goods that are acceptable to their customers, retailers also serve the industry as a series of listening posts on the consumer front. At the same time they act as a medium for disseminating information and stimulating demand for fashion products.

Retailers of fashion outnumber fashion producers by more than seven to one and are the largest source of fashion industry jobs. It is estimated that there are approximately 135,000 retailers that specialize in fashion apparel and accessories, and another 70,000 that include some apparel and accessories in their merchandise assortment.[1] Some retailers are giant companies as, for example, Sears and K mart, which are among the world's largest businesses. At the other extreme are small **"mom-and-pop" stores** run by an owner with few or no assistants.

The first part of this chapter discusses the differing kinds of retail operations and the period and environmental circumstances of their origin. The second part discusses the many changes that have occurred in the retailing of fashion today. The readings that follow the text illustrate the fashion operations of leading companies in their respective fields.

FASHION RETAILING IN THE PAST

In the early 1800s, there were only about 10 million people in the United States, and most were farmers or pioneers moving westward with the frontier. Except for the few cities established along the Atlantic coast, the country was rural.

Transportation was by foot, on horseback, or by horse and wagon. Roads, such as they were, were little more than Indian trails through the wilderness. Retailers that functioned in this environment were small country stores and trading posts, or itinerant peddlers. The last-named group traveled from farm to farm, offering for sale such small conveniences as cutlery, tools, buttons, combs, hand mirrors, needles, and thread. They were welcome visitors to frontier people, because they brought with them bits of news and a touch of civilization. The retailing of ready-to-wear was still in the future, awaiting the development of factory-produced textile and apparel.

It was not until late in the nineteenth century that significant amounts of ready-made clothing became available for sale in stores. Before that, the fashion operations of stores in the growing cities consisted only of selling fabrics, trimmings, and made-to-order clothing. Although custom-made clothing remained important into the 1920s, it was steadily giving way before the growing and constantly improving ready-to-wear manufacturing industry. At the same time, retailers were learning to deal in ready-to-wear. By the 1920s men's, women's, and children's apparel departments were firmly established in all big-city department and specialty stores, and ready-to-wear was also available through mail-order catalogs to customers in outlying areas.

In the early days of ready-to-wear retailing, owners of the great fashion stores worked creatively with manufacturers to produce ready-to-wear designs that would meet the fashion needs of their customers. Many retailers helped manufacturers get started by bringing them Paris models to copy and providing them with substantial orders. The retailer at that time was the main source of fashion information for consumers as well as manufacturers. There were few movies, few telephones, no television, and only a few publications to keep people up to date on what should be produced or worn. Long before the fashion show, the bridal counselor, and the college shop were commonplace, several prominent stores were publishing fashion brochures that they mailed to their customers. Lord & Taylor began such a publication in 1881, John Wanamaker in 1909, Marshall Field and Company in 1914. As fashion traveled its long, slow route from Paris to Podunk, customers looked to their oracles, their favorite stores, for advice on what to wear.

DIFFERENT KINDS OF
RETAIL OPERATIONS _____

In the retailing of fashion, as in fashion itself, customers call the tune. Just as fashion keeps changing to reflect changes in consumer wants and needs, so does its retailing continue to change. Historically, new and different forms of retailing have come into being in response to changes in social and economic conditions, and each has initiated certain operational methods that distinguish it from previously existing types. Today, although many once widely disparate kinds of retailing now overlap, many of their distinctive operational characteristics still exist.

Where America Shops for Clothes
Market share of apparel sales.

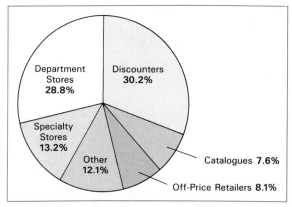

SOURCE: Management Horizons; The New York Times.

DEPARTMENT STORES_____

A **department store** is defined by the Bureau of Census as a retail establishment that employs 25 people or more and that carries a wide variety of merchandise lines, including (1) men's, women's, and children's apparel; (2) furniture and home furnishings; and (3) household linens and fabrics. In the trade, however, several other criteria are applied: related categories of merchandise are offered for sale in separate departments; each department is managed as a separate profit center; responsibilities for stocking the department are delegated to a buyer; customers are offered many services, such as credit, return privileges, deliveries, and telephone and mail order. There are usually also such specialized services as restaurants, beauty salons, and jewelry repair, among others.

The typical department store chooses as its target group of customers people of middle to upper middle class, with fairly large discretionary incomes. The fashion appeal of such a store stems from the breadth of assortment it offers in middle to upper-middle prices and in **national brand** and designer names, often augmented by its own brand name. Browsing among its broad stocks and guided by its advertising and displays, the customer can develop his or her own ideas of what to buy. When the choice has been made, the purchase can be consummated with confidence because of the store's refund policies. The offer of money back if the merchandise fails to please has been a cornerstone of department store policy for more than a century.

It is not uncommon for department stores to stage fashion shows, within the store and also outside for clubs and charities. Their advertising and displays bring customer traffic and, since these stores cover so many fields of merchandise, they can generate more traffic than a specialized clothing store. The combination of customer traffic and appealing displays often prompts, say, a

Organization Chart of a Typical Large Department Store

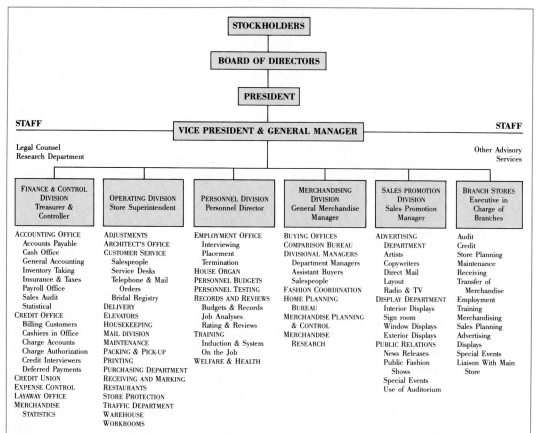

SOURCE: Reprinted with permission by the National Retail Merchants' Association.

woman who has come seeking a lamp for her living room to purchase fashion items for herself, even though these were not on her shopping list. Department stores cater chiefly to women and typically do more than half of their total volume in apparel and accessories for women, men, and children. In the fashion business, the department store not only represents an impressive volume of sales, but also is a medium for exposing merchandise to the customer, often with considerable drama.

Origin of Department Stores

Most of our large, best-known department stores were founded in the middle and late nineteenth century, when mass production was developing and cities were growing. Some of their founders began as peddlers before they opened a store. Some examples are Aaron Meier, whose small general store in Portland,

Oregon, was opened in 1857 and later developed into Meier & Frank; Morris Rich, who peddled notions in Ohio and then moved on to Georgia to open Rich's of Atlanta in 1867; Adam Gimbel, whose descendants built the Gimbel organization on the foundation of the store he opened in Vincennes, Indiana, in 1842. Others had their beginnings as small dry goods stores such as Macy's, New York, which opened in 1858 for the sale of feathers, hosiery, and gloves and added new lines as increasing mass production made them possible.[2]

Branches: From Suburban to National

In retailing, when a store well established in one location opens an additional facility in another but operates it from the original parent or flagship store, the new addition is called a **branch store**. Just as the branches of a tree depend on the trunk for nourishment and growth, so do branch stores depend on the buyers, promotion executives, and other members of the parent store's management team for merchandise and direction.

Where customers go, stores go. When young city families moved out to new suburbs in vast numbers in the 1950s, retailers in the central cities moved out to serve them in branches—free standing at first, but later in the shopping centers that soon developed. By the early 1970s, branches had proliferated to the point that collectively they began contributing more than half the parent firm's total value. By the late 1970s, suitable suburban areas had been exploited to the full by some stores, and these began to expand around the country, into other metropolitan areas. Thus, we find New York's Lord & Taylor with branches in Connecticut, New Jersey, Pennsylvania, Virginia, and Maryland. Dillard's of Little Rock, Arkansas, has branches in Texas, Missouri, New Mexico, Oklahoma, Florida, Kansas, and Ohio. Bloomingdale's of New York has branches in Massachusetts, New Jersey, Pennsylvania, Texas, Florida, and the Washington, D.C. area.

Store Ownership Groups

The founding fathers to today's great department stores operated family-owned and family-run single-unit stores. Today, by means of mergers and acquisitions, nearly every such store is part of a **store ownership group**, which is a corporation that owns a number of autonomously operated retail organizations. Each store division retains its local identity and independence, has its own branches, has its own buyers and merchandise mix, operates under its own name, and presents itself to customers much as if it were still an independently owned institution.

The first and oldest of such groups was the Federated Department Stores, Inc., incorporated in 1929 by a merger of Filene's in Boston, Lazarus in Columbus, and Abraham & Straus in Brooklyn, soon joined by Bloomingdale's in New York. During the decade that followed, other corporate ownership groups were formed such as the R. H. Macy group, Allied Stores, and Associated Dry

May Department Stores: A Store
Ownership Group

Division	Headquarters	Sales (Add 000,000)
Foley's	Houston, Tex.	1,121
Lord and Taylor	New York, N.Y.	1,034
May Co., Cal.	Los Angeles, Calif.	954
Hecht Co.	Washington, D.C.	829
Robinson's	Los Angeles, Calif.	753
Kaufman	Pittsburgh, Pa.	752
Famous-Barr	St. Louis, Mo.	508
Filene's	Boston, Mass.	484
May Co., Ohio	Cleveland, Ohio	436
G. Fox	Hartford, Conn.	426
L. S. Ayres	Indianapolis, Ind.	328
May D. & F.	Denver, Colo.	297
Meier & Frank	Portland, Oreg.	274
Total department stores		8,196
Volume shoe		1,228
Venture		1,339
Total retail operations		10,763

Goods. The trend continued, giving birth to such other groups as Dayton-Hudson, Carter Hawley Hale, and May Department Stores.

In the 1980s, several of these groups were acquired by other groups and merged together. Associated Dry Goods was acquired by the May Department Stores group, and Federated Department Stores and Allied Stores were merged when they were acquired by Campeau Corporation, and their corporate name was changed to Federated/Allied.

Few consumers realize that, for example, Lord & Taylor of New York, Robinson's of Los Angeles, L. S. Ayres of Indianapolis, and the May Company in Cleveland are among the stores owned by the May Stores. Similarly, among the stores of Federated/Allied are Bloomingdale's of New York, Burdine's in Florida, and Lazarus in Ohio. Indeed, few of this country's largest department stores are now independently owned.

APPAREL SPECIALTY STORES: LARGE AND SMALL

In contrast to the department store's wide variety of general merchandise, a **specialty store** is a retail establishment that either deals in a single category of merchandise (such as jewelry, shoes, books, furniture, apparel) or specializes in related categories of merchandise—for example, clothing and accessories for men, women, and children, or sporting equipment and active sports apparel, or television, radios, and VCRs. Compared to the broad appeal of department stores, specialty retailers cater to a particular type of customer and carry narrow lines of merchandise, with a large assortment within each line that is specifically geared for a well-defined targeted customer.

Specialty retailers vary widely in size. Some are single-unit "mom-and-pop" stores, some are units of chains, and some are large departmentalized stores with branches. Among consumers, the larger versions are often mislabeled department stores, because they carry wide assortments in the merchandise categories in which they specialize, offer extensive customer services, and are also organized by departments. To qualify as department stores, however, they would have to carry furniture and home appliances beyond the token assortments of linens and giftwares that some of them offer.

Large and small, the specialty shops play an important role in the retailing of fashion today. The fashion impact of giants such as Saks Fifth Avenue and Neiman Marcus makes a great contribution, but so also does the small, independently owned shop that offers convenience, friendliness, and an assortment carefully tuned to the wants of its clientele.

Large Departmentalized Specialty Stores

Like the department stores, many of today's large and prestigious specialty shops began in the second half of the 1800s as small, independently owned enterprises, in small towns or in the then-developing cities. Some expanded into department stores; others simply broadened their assortments in specialized merchandise categories. Filene's of Boston, for example, was founded in 1873 in Lynn, Massachusetts, by William Filene, who later bought a men's store in that city, a dry goods store in Bath, Maine, and two stores in Boston—one specializing in gloves, and the other in laces. Similarly, I. Magnin of San Francisco had its beginnings in 1880, in the modest home of Isaac and Mary Ann Magnin, where wealthy San Francisco ladies came for Mrs. Magnin's exquisite, handmade, embroidered, and lace-trimmed lingerie, christening dresses, and spectacular made-to-order bridal gowns.[3]

Like the department stores, almost every one of these great specialty stores is now part of a store ownership group. To cite but a few examples, Bullock's and I. Magnin are owned by the R. H. Macy group and Filene's by the May Company group. And also like department stores, they operate branch stores, either in local suburbs or nationally, or both.

Unlike department stores, however, they are completely dedicated to fashions in the rise and peak stages, and their assortments are both broad and deep in the upper-middle to highest price ranges. Therein lies their competitive strength. They can more easily define their targeted customers; they develop salespeople who are fashion knowledgeable and helpful; and they provide personalized services.

Small Apparel Specialty Shops

It would be hard to find a town so small, or a city so big, that it is without independently owned, small mom-and-pop apparel or accessories shops. These are the stores owned and managed by one or two people and employing fewer than three salespeople. Without having branches or being a part of a chain, each of the stores so defined generally has annual sales volume of half a million dollars or less. The attrition rate among them is high, but so also is the rate of replacement by new entrepreneurs. Their collective impact in the fashion business, however, is important. Bureau of the Census figures continue to show that a substantial part of fashion retailing is done in just such outlets.

From the consumers' point of view, small fashion retailers offer convenience of location and intimate knowledge of their customers' needs and tastes. Their owners know the way of dressing in the communities they serve, and more often than not, they will buy with individual customers in mind.

From the producer's point of view, according to manufacturers interviewed by the authors, the importance of these stores goes far beyond the amount of business they place. For one thing, they are loyal to the firms from which they buy. In the larger stores, the buyers may not be the same from one year to the next, and they do not have that same loyalty.

With some quite large manufacturing firms, such as Russ Togs, for example, small specialty shops may account for a major portion of their business. With others, such as Liz Claiborne or Esprit, the minimum quantities demanded on an order will rule out the small retailer entirely. For the industry as a whole, which is a stronghold of small manufacturing firms, the collective buying power of the small, specialized apparel retailers is invaluable.

Boutiques

The term **boutique** is French for *little shop,* and for many years it referred only to those intimate shops within Paris couture houses where the customer could buy perfumes and accessories carrying the house label. In the United States the term *boutique* designates a small shop that carries highly individualized and specialized merchandise intended for a narrow, well-defined customer segment.

The proliferation of boutiques in the United States (and in London, where the trend began) was an outgrowth of the anti-establishment "do your own thing" attitudes of the 1960s. Some of today's boutiques, like their 1960s forerunners, cater to the *avant garde* young, others to more mature customers. Many feature merchandise at astronomical prices; others sell at more moderate levels. Some deal only in designer clothes; others deal in hand-crafted fashions; some deal in trendy accessories; and still others deal in antique clothing.

The early independently owned boutiques of the 1960s were often established by creative fashion enthusiasts to sell merchandise that expressed their individual point of view — even if they had to design or possibly produce the merchandise themselves. Generally the merchandise was too advanced, too limited in appeal, for large stores to handle; only boutiques could do the job.

Independently owned boutiques made such an important place for themselves in the mid-1960s that large stores sought ways to appeal to boutique customers. Many stores established and still maintain groups of small, highly specialized shops on their floors in which they feature merchandise assortments keyed to a particular "total look" in apparel and accessories.

The boutique approach gained further impetus as European couture designers ventured into ready-to-wear and established their own boutiques, either free standing or within stores selected for the franchise, or both. Among the luminaries whose ready-to-wear is offered in boutiques, in free-standing stores, or within larger stores are Cardin, Givenchy, Valentino, Yves St. Laurent for his Rive Gauche collections, and such Americans as Calvin Klein, Ralph Lauren, Anne Klein, and Donna Karan. In addition, many foreign ready-to-wear designers have entered the U.S. market by way of their own boutiques in fashionable areas—for example, the Soprani boutique on Rodeo Drive in Los Angeles and the Giorgio Armani on New York's Madison Avenue.

Today, the boutique concept is widely accepted and used by most large department and specialty stores, not only for current fashions, but also for bath accessories, gourmet food and cookwear, and whatever else captures customer interest.

CHAIN STORE RETAILING _____

A chain is understood to be a retail organization that owns and operates a string of similar stores, all merchandised and controlled from a central headquarters office. Multi-unit chains developed during the late 1800s, as transportation and communication improved. Among the early chains were the A & P (Great Atlantic & Pacific Tea Company), Woolworth's, and J. C. Penney. Each started with a single store, gradually added others, and demonstrated the feasibility of the multistore concept and the economies of centralized buying.

Chains that sell apparel are either (1) general merchandise retailers, such as Sears and Montgomery Ward, whose product categories are similar to those of department stores, or (2) specialized apparel or accessory chains that focus on one or more related categories of apparel. Chains may be national, regional, or local in location. Their highly centralized, uniform store operation is quite different from what prevails among departmentalized stores that have branches or are autonomously operated retail stores that are part of the store ownership groups discussed earlier.

In the trade, the characteristics that distinguish **chain store** operations from those of typical department stores are as follows:

* There is no one big city flagship or main parent store, as in the case of a multi-unit department store with branches.

- The store units are standardized and uniform in physical appearance and in the merchandise they carry.
- The buying is done by buyers in the chain's central office, and each buyer is responsible for a specific category of merchandise—as contrasted with buying for an entire department.
- Merchandise is usually distributed to the units of a chain from its central or regional warehouses.
- The buying function is separate from the selling function.
- Selling is the responsibility of centralized sales managers and the managers of the individual store units.

However, as the number of branches operated by a departmentalized store increases, the parent store usually adapts several of a chain's operations, notably the separation of the selling function from the buying function. Selling becomes the responsibility of centralized store managers.

As an indication of the important role that chains play in the business of fashion, consider the following facts:[4]

- Sears, K mart, J. C. Penney and Wal-mart—the four largest general merchandise chains—are considered to be the "Big Four" of retailing. Their combined 1989 annual merchandise sales of more than $100 billion amounted to almost two and a half times the total $46 billion sales of the 7 largest store ownership groups. Sears, in fact, is the largest retailer in the world, with a retail sales volume of more than $30 billion.
- The combined sales of the top six specialized apparel chains are $8.9 billion. These chains are The Limited, The Gap, Charming Shoppes, Casual Corner, and Ross stores. Their individual sales and number of store units are illustrated in this chapter. The Limited alone has sales of more than $4.6 billion.
- The number of stores operated by chains total more than 20,000 and are spread across the country. All are largely located in shopping malls. The Limited, for example, has 3,381 units and K mart has 4,259 stores.

The "Big Four" General Merchandise Chains

Company	Sales 1989 (Add 000,000)	Number of Stores
Sears, Roebuck	$31,599	1,221
K mart	29,500	4,259
Wal-Mart	25,810	1,528
J. C. Penney	14,469	1,325

SOURCE: Company annual reports.

Selected Specialized Apparel Chains

Company	Number of Stores	Sales (in millions)	Ownership
The Limited	3,381	$4,647,916	Public
The Gap	1,005	1,586,000	Public
Petrie Stores	1,596	1,257,222	Public
Charming Shoppes	1,115	806,637	Public
Casual Corner	737	700,000	U.S. Shoe
Merry Go Round	650	478,923	Independent
Chess King	564	267,027	Melville Shoe

SOURCE: Company annual reports.

Specialized Apparel Chains

In terms of the fashion business, the decade of the 1920s was the beginning of apparel retailing by chain stores. Before then, there were a few retail chains of "waist stores," as blouse shops were then called. Their targeted market was low-income customers seeking prices below those offered in department and specialty stores. In about 1919, as blouses went out of fashion, producers of waists began to make low-priced dresses that the waist chains added to their assortments. With department and specialty stores catering to middle- and upper-middle-income families, there was little competition for chains featuring low-priced apparel. This period saw the start of many low-priced apparel chains that catered to the new class of "working women" who had entered the work force during the manpower shortage of World War I.

A notable example of an early waist chain is the Lerner Shops, which got its start in those years and by 1984 had 800 stores, with sales of $700 million primarily in low-priced fashions.[5] In 1985 this chain was acquired by The Limited stores. Other types of chains that sprang up and developed in the 1920s included millinery chains, men's hat chains, and family clothing stores. Fashion leadership was not their forte.

Chains took a different direction in the 1970s. There are now new **apparel specialty chains**, quite different from any of their predecessors. Regional or national in scope, they operate stores of relatively small individual size, and feature highly selective lines of contemporary and often trendy fashions in middle price ranges. Their aim is toward mainstream American juniors, misses, and young men's sportswear customers.

Today's apparel chains derive their strength from their ability to focus on a particular segment of the consumer market and the fashion interests of that market. Unlike department stores, they are not burdened by the need to serve a broad section of the public; they concentrate strictly on the consumer audience they have marked out for themselves. As in all chain retailing, their operations

Composite Organization Chart of an Apparel Chain

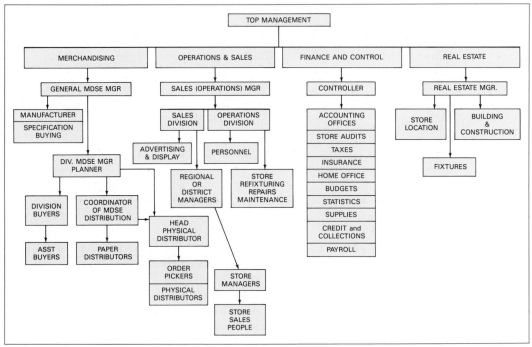

are highly centralized; their store units are generally uniform in design and merchandise presentation; and they usually operate under the same name in all locations. Typical are The Gap, The Limited, and Casual Corner.

Such chains feature mainly their own private brands. Their buying power is so large that they can specify color, patterns, styles, fabrics, designs, and whatever else they consider important. Today, they are not just stores that are selling fashion, but it is their *au courant* fashions that are selling their stores.

These specialized chains became, and still are, a major source of competition to department stores since their merchandise categories and moderate price ranges are within the scope of this older form of retailing. Their competition is felt most directly in casual sportswear for juniors, misses, and young men.

The inroads made on the fashion market by apparel specialty chains have impelled other types of retailers to develop such chains of their own. Specific examples and current developments are discussed in the second segment of this chapter.

Apparel Retailing by General Merchandise Chains

The mass general merchandising chains have also become a factor in fashion distribution. The Penney chain had apparel and accessories from the start, but Montgomery Ward and Sears had functioned primarily as catalog houses until the 1920s. With transportation improving and the rural customer no longer completely dependent on the mails, they moved into store operations. Sears began in 1925, with a single store located in its Chicago mail-order facility. Ward's soon followed. Both companies started with stores that featured equipment and supplies primarily of interest to men. Only gradually did their stores move into apparel, and then it was for their typical customer, of modest means and modest clothing budget.

It was not until the 1960s that the big **general merchandising chains** came of age as major factors in the fashion business. In response to the increased affluence and greater fashion awareness of their targeted customers, they broadened their assortments and extended their price ranges upward. They also gave prime main floor locations to apparel and accessories.

Glamorous names were brought into their stocks through licensing agreements. Where once the customer saw only store-name labels in garments made to the retailer's specifications, now she was offered Halston III collections in Penney's, or Cheryl Tiegs and Stephanie Powers in Sears. Today they are also carrying many well-known national brands.

With their enormous buying power, these great chains can have merchandise produced to their specifications and styled exclusively for them. They may not have, or even attempt to have, the fashion authority and leadership shown by department and specialty stores and by the new breed of specialized apparel chains. But what they can do, and do very well, is move a great deal of merchandise and control a substantial percentage of the fashion market. It is generally estimated in the trade that apparel and accessories represent, at the very least, 30 percent of these chains' total volume. On that basis, the combined fashion goods business of the big chains amounts to many billions of dollars, a decidedly important share of the fashion market.

MAIL-ORDER HOUSES: NONSTORE RETAILING

By Census definition and trade usage today, a **mail-order house** is a retail establishment that does the bulk of its selling to the consumer primarily through the medium of a catalog as a result of orders placed mainly by mail or phone. The concept of selling through a catalog rather than over the counter of a store was pioneered by Aaron Montgomery Ward in 1872, to be followed by Richard Sears, who issued the first Sears Roebuck & Company catalog in 1893, although he had been in business before that time.

Among the conditions that paved the way for this nineteenth-century innovation in retailing was the then predominantly rural nature of the country. Stocks of country stores were limited, and transportation to the developing fashionable city stores was difficult. More to the point, rural free delivery had just been introduced by the Post Office.

These early catalogs were the standbys of rural customers for generations.

1897 Sears, Roebuck & Company Catalog Page

281

1897

TAILOR MADE WALKING AND BICYCLE SUITS

24993
$6.75

24990
$3.75

24980
$3.15

24982
$4.25

SUITS FOR HIGH SUMMER WEAR.

24980 Made of Washable Linen Crash, Blazer style with newest sleeves and cuffs, very finest skirt. Price....................$3.15

24981 Very Stylish, made of high grade plaid washable linen crash, big sailor collar fancy front. Our price, only...........$4.00

24982 This Beautiful Summer Suit, is made of fancy checked washable linen crash, sailor collar and fronts of white linen, newest sleeves and cuffs. Very rich. Price...........................$4.25

24983 $6.00 Would not be too much for this Elegant Suit, made of fancy washable linen crash, big sailor collar, front and cuffs of blue linen, making a very pretty combination.
Price only..$5.00

BICYCLE SUITS.

24989 Consists of five pieces, Jacket, Skirt, Bloomers, Leggins and Cap, made of Austrian covert cloth in brown or gray mixtures. Blazer Jacket very nobby. Price....................................$3.75

24990 This Nobby Suit (illustrated) is made of five pieces in double breasted Reefer style, full skirt in either tan or gray mixed Austrian covert cloth. Would be cheap at $7.50.
Only...$4.00

24991 Very Similar to 24993, made of very stylish novelty cloth, in five pieces consisting of cap, jacket, skirt, leggins and bloomers. Only $4.25

24992 Blazer Style made of Imported Tiger Cloth, consisting of five pieces. Material durable and will outwear any material. Others sell it for $8.00, we sell it for.................................$4.75

24993 This Handsome Suit (illustrated) is made of brown or blue Repellant cloth, bound in leather all around and consists of five pieces, jacket, half lined with silk. Can't be beat...............$6.75

24983 $5.00

24981
$4.00

SOURCE: 1897 Sears, Roebuck & Company catalog.

Although the fashions offered were not exciting, the prices and assortments surpassed those in rural stores and they were a delight to the country clientele they were intended to serve. In the eyes of these customers, the catalogs indeed earned the name that came to be applied to them: "the wish book." So well, indeed, did the mail-order houses meet the needs and broadening interests of rural customers that by 1895 the Sears catalog consisted of 507 pages, and the company's annual sales exceeded $750,000.[6]

As one early mail-order company, Jones Post & Co., told its customers: "Your home, or ranch, or farm, is never so far distant that you are shut out from the great throbbing world with its mammoth commercial establishments. No longer are you forced to be satisfied with the small stock and slim assortment (of country stores) from which to make your selection at exorbitant prices."[7]

Growth of Mail-Order Retailing

Beginning in the 1970s, catalog sales have been increasing rapidly, and show every sign of continuing to do so. Industry estimates are that in 1989 American consumers bought more than $30 billion worth of apparel from more than 12 billion catalogs mailed by some 8,500 different mail-order houses.[8]

This "buying from catalog" phenomenon results from several factors: the rise of two-earner families, in which neither spouse has much time for shopping in stores; affluent singles, whose active working and social lives leave little room for shopping; the time crunch for working mothers; crowded stores and their often inexperienced and hard-to-find salespeople; and the advent of toll-free 800 telephone numbers. The result has been an explosion not only in the number of catalog companies, but also in the variety of goods that can be bought from catalogs. Today mail-order houses range from large, well-known

Growth of Catalog Retailing

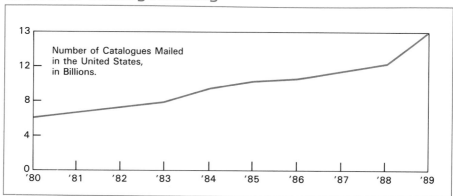

Number of Catalogues Mailed in the United States, in Billions.

SOURCE: Direct Marketing Association; The New York Times.

retailers such as Spiegel, which sells designer-name fashions, to small specialty operations such as the Collins Street Bakery in Texas, which sells fruitcake. In fact, mail-order sellers of both apparel and other consumer products have multiplied to such a degree that there is even a publication called *Shop-at-Home-Directory* for consumers who want information about the various mail-order houses and the merchandise that each features.

The largest in terms of dollar sales are the general merchandise catalogs of Sears, J. C. Penney, and Spiegel. Targeted at mainstream America, they sell everything to furnish a home, clothe a family, and equip every type of activity. Sears reports catalog sales of $3.5 billion. Penney's, which distributes four general merchandise catalogs a year and 15 million smaller specialized books, are $2.5 billion. Among Penney's specialized catalogs are those featuring children's clothing, fitness products, and women's large-sized apparel. Spiegel is in third place with sales of $1.7 billion.[9] In addition to the traditional general merchandise, which features everything from oil paintings to vacuum cleaners, Spiegel puts out a series of specialized books such as designer-name apparel, career clothing, and hard-to-find petite sizes.

Mail-Order Apparel Specialists

Although apparel has been featured in mail-order catalogs since their inception, it is only in recent years that there has been a great emphasis on upscale fashions. Many highly specialized apparel mail-order houses have proliferated, each of which focuses its effort on a clearly defined targeted group of consumers. Some, such as the Horchow Collection, concentrate on high-priced, sophisticated luxury items of wearing apparel and accessories. Other, similar operations of this type are Trifles, J. A. Bank Clothiers, and the specialized fashion-forward books of Spiegel. Another group of catalog fashion retailers specialize in classic and casual wear for men and women. Perhaps among the best known of this type is Land's End, which mails 70 million catalogs annually and whose sales are reported as $545 million.[10] A reading in this chapter describes their operations. Examples of others in this category include Johnny Appleseed, Eddie Bauer, L. L. Bean, and Talbot's. There are also catalogs devoted to off-size apparel, such as King Size for men and Brylane for large-size apparel.

The operations involved in the buying and selling of fashion goods by mail are quite different from those of stores. The preparation of a catalog is a lengthy process, and merchandise must be bought close to a year in advance of a selling season. Since apparel producers do not have their seasonal lines ready that far in advance, mail-order houses must work with fabric suppliers and apparel manufacturers to develop the kinds of merchandise they want for their targeted customers. However, because most catalog retailers print and distribute millions of catalogs, their tremendous purchasing power enables them to have merchandise made expressly for them.

The Store We Mind

Our store is 10¾ inches tall, 8¼ inches wide, and 140 pages deep. **

It has no crowded parking lots, clogged elevators, or hidden rest rooms.

It displays over 600 pieces of merchandise. And by the time you count colors and sizes and shapes and variations, you are up to 10,000 items you can shop from—assembled under one "roof" from the four corners of the earth, wherever quality calls.

Most of these items are shown on or with models so much like you they could live in your neighborhood. Every item is unconditionally guaranteed by the world's shortest guarantee. In two words: GUARANTEED. PERIOD.

We mind our store 24 hours a day, 7 days a week. You can buy from us in the comfort of your own home. But first, remember, we're only a phone call away—wherever you live. The toll-free telephone number: 1-800-356-4444. Or send in the coupon at right for a free look at our "store".

Oh, yes—we accept AX, MC, or VISA. And we deliver by United Parcel Service or U.S. Mail. You name it.

LANDS' END®
DIRECT MERCHANTS

of fine wool and cotton sweaters, Oxford button-down shirts, traditional dress clothing, snow wear, deck wear, original Lands' End soft luggage and a multitude of other quality goods from around the world.

**This describes our "store" for July of '87. The dimensions may vary by season, but you can always count on the quality, price, and service.*

423

Catalog Operations by Department and Specialty Stores

At this point, it may be well to reread the definition of a mail-order house. Some catalog retailers may have one or more retail stores. Talbot's, for example, operates 137 stores across the country. However, if the bulk of a retailer's business is done through catalog sales, it is considered a mail-order house.

Originally, the primary purpose of the catalogs of conventional department and large specialty stores was to attract customers into the store. Nowadays, the same elements that led to the growth of mail-order retailing have encouraged such retail stores to increase the frequency and distribution of their catalogs and improve the efficiency with which they handle mail and telephone responses. These days, although not to be classified as mail-order houses, mail and telephone business accounts for a more and more substantial portion of the conventional stores' business. Precise figures are not readily available, but these may illustrate the point: Bloomingdale's-by-Mail is now referred to as the "second largest store" in their multi-unit operation, with sales of over $100 million. Saks Fifth Avenue handles its Folio catalogs as a separate store and annually mails out 37 specialized catalogs and 4 general catalogs. Neiman Marcus distributes 216 catalogs annually and reported sales of $70 million.[11]

DISCOUNT RETAILING: UNDERSELLING OPERATIONS

Shortly after World War II, discounters added a new dimension to the world of retailing by adopting the operational techniques originated by food **supermarkets** in the 1930s. These techniques entailed offering lower food prices to depression-weary customers by using self-selection selling, low-rent locations, inexpensive decor, and cash-and-carry terms.

As generally understood in the trade, the term **discounter** applies to a retail establishment that *regularly* sells its merchandise at lower prices, concentrating mainly on national brands. By operating with self-service and other expense-saving techniques such as no mail or telephone orders, no free deliveries, low-rent locations, and limited return privileges, they can operate profitably on markups lower than those that prevail among other types of retailers.

The success of discounters in the 1950s stemmed from their selling of nationally advertised branded appliances at prices below the manufacturers' suggested retail prices. This was in the period just after World War II, when men returning from military service spearheaded a boom in family formation, suburban living—and babies. The two-earner household in that period was relatively rare, and incomes had to be stretched to accommodate the pent-up demand for everything young families needed, from refrigerators to ready-to-wear. As the suburban communities burgeoned, so did the discounters. They opened stores in both cities and suburbs, and broadened their merchandise assortments to include low-priced, unbranded apparel.

As these households and their children prospered, many of them retained their active interest in buying at favorable prices. They were in a position to enjoy the good life—but they enjoyed it more at a bargain. This was in marked contrast with the attitude of earlier generations, among whom comfortable incomes were equated with freedom from price consciousness. Underselling retailing in various forms became more and more firmly entrenched in the 1960s, 1970s, and 1980s, without regard to business cycles, employment statistics, or consumer income figures.

Proliferation of Off-Price Specialized Apparel Discounters

Underselling stores that offer quality and fashion apparel have been on the scene for many years, but only recently have they blossomed into a major force in retailing. One of the earliest among them, Loehman's, was founded in Brooklyn in 1920 and is now a national chain of 77 stores. Others that came into the field later followed the same course, starting as individual stores and developing into national chains.

Known in the trade today as **off-price retailers**, the fashion apparel discounters came into their own in the late 1970s, achieving an annual growth rate of 231 percent between 1979 and 1983—a much faster rate than was exhibited by more conventional retailers.[12] What distinguished these new fashion discounters from their predecessors was that they specialized in high-quality brand- and designer-name clothing, at deeply discounted prices—and they still do.

The target customers of these operations are the price-conscious middle class. Among them are also consumers who formerly bought top-quality merchandise without really questioning price. When apparel prices skyrocketed, some of these consumers sought the discounters—not for cheaper grades of merchandise, but for the familiar "names" and qualities at lower prices. For

Big Names in Bargain Clothes

Company	Sales (in millions)	Number of Stores
Marshall's	$1,939,335	347
T. J. Maxx	1,700,000	367
Ross Stores	734,164	156
Burlington Coat Factory	588,542	134
Hit or Miss	400,000	579
Loehmann's	334,000	70
Sym's	300,078	25
Dress Barn	249,201	400

SOURCE: Company annual reports.

example, they are willing to spend $100 on a dress, sweater, or handbag, but they want one that normally sells for $150 to $200 in department and specialty stores.

Currently the largest apparel discounter is Marshall's, which started with one store in Beverly, Massachusetts, and now operates more than 250 stores across the country. The company's financial reports indicate sales of $1.6 billion a year.[13] Other big names in this category are listed in a chart in this chapter.

In addition to the off-priced specialized apparel retailers, there are general merchandise discounting chains that sell very large quantities of "name" apparel and accessories at prices lower than those of the traditionally priced department and specialty stores. They are giving more and more floor space to their apparel departments, and the sales of these departments have been increasing as a percentage of their total sales. The two largest general merchandise discounters are K mart and Wal-Mart. Other giant discounters include T. J. Maxx and Caldor stores. All carry deep assortments of nationally branded sportswear at underselling prices.

The impact of underselling apparel retailing on conventional retailers has been more than just competition. Today one can walk into well-known department and specialty stores at the height of the selling season and find numerous off-price sales being featured. The distinction between conventional and discount retailers has become blurred, and it has become increasingly harder to determine where conventional retailing ends and off-price operations begin.

Off-Price Factory Outlets

Another important form of off-price apparel retailing has been booming across the country—**factory outlets** owned and operated by manufacturers of top brand and designer-name clothing. As mentioned briefly in a previous chapter, these outlets originally served as a dumping ground for out-of-season merchandise and odds and ends of factory stock.

Today, it is estimated that from 1,400 outlets in 1984, there are now 4,800 in all parts of the United States, with projections of 7,000 by 1992. Their store decor, services, merchandise assortments, and locations have been upgraded and they have become good-looking, professionally run retail stores with total sales volume in excess of $2 billion.[14]

Initially located on the factory grounds, these outlets now tend to be clustered in outlying areas not in conflict with the shopping areas of their major retail accounts. In some communities, hundreds of factory outlet stores are set up in specialized shopping centers, where the consumer finds everything from children's clothing to home furnishings. Most such factory outlet areas are in the East, where the greatest number of apparel producers are located. Among the largest such areas are those in Secaucus, New Jersey; Reading, Pennsylvania; Utica, New York; Murfreesboro, Tennessee; and Freeport, Maine.

Factory outlets generally do very little advertising, thus avoiding conflict with their retail accounts, but they do leave labels in the garments. Seasonal

SOURCE: Secaucus Shopping and Services Guide Book.

goods arrive about a month after the producer has shipped to the regular retail customers. For example, fall clothes will be delivered to the outlets in late August rather than in July, as with traditional retailers. Retail selling prices are often lower even than those of the off-price retailers, since the merchandise reaches the consumer directly from the maker.

Among the factory outlets are many run by designer-owned companies: Ralph Lauren in Freeport, Maine; Liz Claiborne and Anne Klein in Reading, Pennsylvania; and Calvin Klein in Secaucus, New Jersey. Manhattan Industries has in its outlets Perry Ellis, Henry Grethel, and John Henry merchandise. Many, if not all, well-known brand-name manufacturers are also in the factory outlet business — among them, Levi-Strauss, Cluett Peabody, Healthtex, and Arrow Shirts. Many producers have several outlets in different areas. Harvé Benard, for example, has 46 outlets throughout the East.

Originally conceived as a way of alleviating manufacturers' problems of excess inventories, their proliferation has become a real force in apparel retailing — and one that seems destined to become an entirely new channel of distribution in the fashion pipeline. Today they have become an established part of many apparel producers' business, and many are even producing "excess clothing" to be sold in their multiplying outlet stores.

The Lowered Costs of Discounting

Regardless of the kinds of merchandise being discounted, the economics of discount operations are basically the same. Operating expenses are kept low by holding customer services (salespeople, telephone ordering, delivery, etc.) to a minimum; locations are in less expensive areas; advertising is minimal; extraneous departments (jewelry repair, travel bureaus, etc.) are eliminated. These economies permit profitable operation at markups far below what conventional retailers require. Merchandise can therefore be priced at from 20 to 30 percent below what prevails in conventional stores.

Both conventional and discount stores often buy from the same wholesale sources, but more often than not the off-price retailers actually pay less than other types for identical merchandise. They are not rigid about sizes, styles, and colors at any given time, nor with continuity of brand and designer merchandise. They simply make opportune buys when and where they are available.

The typical purchasing operation of large discounters was aptly described by Marshall's in an advertising supplement issued when its Dallas store was opened in 1980. Under a headline proclaiming "Brand Names for Less," the copy asked, "What's the Secret Behind Marshall's?" And the supplement answered:

> There's no secret — we pay less, so you pay less. . . . Department store buyers order their merchandise a season ahead. Our buyers wait until the season begins. That's when we can buy the same merchandise at lower wholesale prices. Manufacturers sell at lower wholesale prices during the season because

they've overproduced, missed a delivery date or need to make room for the next season's line. We also keep our overhead costs down. When you're in a department store, notice the carpeting, expensive lighting and elaborate displays. Those extras can add to the cost of your purchase. Our stores are clean, neat and pleasant to shop without the extras. And, we're sure, smart shoppers would rather have value than decor.

Off-price stores also may specify ahead for goods to be made during what would otherwise be a dead, between-seasons time for producers. Sometimes, manufacturers schedule part of their regular production for discounters, but insist that the brand name not be advertised and that it should not be sold in the trading area of the maker's regular accounts. A final virtue of the discounter— they pay promptly, and do not ask for advertising allowances, the privilege of returning slow sellers, or similar concessions that major conventional stores may request.

FRANCHISED RETAILING

Franchised operations are familiar to the public through such organizations as fast-food outlets like McDonald's and Kentucky Fried Chicken, through automobile dealerships, restaurants such as Howard Johnson's, and national networks of real estate offices like Century 21.

In a **franchise** arrangement, the **franchisor** (a parent company) provides a **franchisee** (owner-operator of a retail unit) with exclusive use of an established name in a specific trading area, plus assistance in organizing, training, merchandising, and management, in return for a stipulated consideration. The nature of the agreement varies widely from company to company. For example, the franchising company may provide an operating program complete in every detail, or the agreement may simply specify that the franchisor will provide merchandise for the franchisee. The uniform appearance of many franchised retail outlets often gives the impression to the public that they constitute a chain, but in actuality, each store is run by an individual entrepreneur who owns the business, meets his or her obligation to the franchisor, and retains the remaining profits.

Designer-Name Franchised Boutiques

As described in the previous chapter, European ready-to-wear designers have been operating their own franchised name boutiques for the last two decades, among them the Rive Gauche franchised boutiques of Yves St. Laurent and the Nouvelle Boutiques of Givenchy. Beginning in the 1970s, franchising arrangements began to be visible in the domestic apparel retailing field. Among the earliest and most successful were the maternity shop franchises such as Lady Madonna and Maternally Yours. Other examples are the Tennis Lady shops and the hundreds of Athlete's Foot franchised outlets.

In the 1980s, American name designers began to follow the lead of European designers, and today American designer-franchised boutiques have burgeoned in major cities throughout the United States. An outstanding example is Ralph Lauren, who has pioneered a multimillion-dollar retail business with 106 worldwide franchises, 63 of which are in the United States and others in Stockholm, Antwerp, London, Hong Kong, and South Korea.[15] The growth and future role of retail stores controlled by their designer franchisors is one that bears watching.

SHOPPING CENTERS AND MALLS

A major retail phenomenon growing out of the migration to suburbia that followed World War II was the development and proliferation of shopping centers. A **shopping center** is a preplanned, architecturally coordinated grouping of retail stores, plus a parking area that is generally larger than the area occupied by the stores themselves. Medical facilities, banks, restaurants, and sometimes theaters and skating rinks may be part of the mix offered the shopper. These centers are usually developed by real estate interests and occasionally by the real estate divisions of very large retailers. The centers have their own managements, promotional activities, and merchants' associations to weld their stores into a cohesive group.

Since the 1960s, when shopping centers first hit their stride, they have provided a prime area of expansion for department stores, chain stores, large and small specialty stores, and off-price retailers. By 1988, there were an estimated 33,000 centers.[16] California has the largest number, followed by Texas, Florida, and New York, with some 600 to 700 each.

Numbers alone do not tell the whole story of shopping centers, however. Over the years, they have changed from open-air centers, laid out horizontally with on-site parking, into multilevel, enclosed, and climate-controlled **malls**, where shoppers can spend an entire day shopping, resting, eating, even skating or seeing motion pictures. And they are no longer purely suburban phenomena; they are now in center city areas—often those associated with urban renewal enterprises. An outstanding example of an urban enterprise is Trump Tower, located on Fifth Avenue in New York. This is a 68-story building consisting of 49 floors of apartments, 13 floors of office space, and a 6-floor atrium around which are some of the most prestigious fashion stores in the world. Another example is the Water Tower in Chicago.

Another change—where at first shopping centers contained a heterogeneous mixture of small retail establishments and branches of big-city stores, today there are smaller, specialized centers that contain a homogeneous mix of tenants, all targeted toward the same segment of the consumer market. There are malls containing only factory outlets, such as the Mid-America mall near Chicago. And there are malls whose tenants are all high-priced specialty stores, such as the Galleria in Dallas, the Worth Street Plaza in Palm Beach, Florida, and Design Center in New Jersey. There are even "theme" malls, such as a shopping center in Dallas that specializes in a Hispanic theme, and one in California whose tenants all specialize in early American crafts.

Today, the United States is saturated with malls and centers of many types, differing dramatically from their predecessors in location, tenant mix, and architectural and physical layout. Back in the 1960s, when shopping centers first appeared in numbers, it was feared that their proliferation would "over-store" communities and lead to ruin. Hasn't happened yet!

OTHER TYPES OF RETAIL OPERATIONS _ _ _ _ _ _

One cannot ignore several other types of retailing, even though these do not deal in apparel to any noticeable extent. Among them are the early nonstore operations of producers that sell directly to consumers, the catalog warehouses that developed in the 1970s, the wholesale price clubs that emerged in the 1980s, and the newest type of all—electronic retailing, which is discussed later in this chapter.

Direct Selling: Door-to-Door and Party Plans

Modern versions of the early peddlers are the **direct-selling retailers** who operate without stores. A *direct-selling* establishment is one that sells merchandise by contacting customers through either *door-to-door* approaches or some form of *in-home party plan.* Direct selling is not new in the fashion field; in the period before World War II, silk hosiery and custom-made foundation garments were successfully sold this way.

Door-to-door retailing encompasses many different types of products. Working on commission, a salesperson calls on a customer at home and attempts to make the sale. In the household goods field, such names as Electrolux and Fuller Brush are familiar; they use this method exclusively. In fashion-related fields, Avon is perhaps the best-known operation of this kind. Starting with door-to-door selling of cosmetics, it now includes jewelry as well as other accessories in its merchandise mix.

The **party plan** of selling depends on the company's representative getting a local woman to organize a party of her friends and neighbors, at which the salesperson presents the company's merchandise. The hostess receives a gift, usually provided by the salesperson. This method of selling in the home is most closely associated with Tupperware, but it has also been used effectively in the fashion field by a firm such as Sarah Coventry for jewelry.

In most instances, salespeople who represent direct-selling firms use a company-produced catalog to supplement the relatively limited assortment of samples from which they sell.

Flea Market Retailers

A **flea market** is a location, either indoors or out, in which a wide variety of independent sellers rent space on a temporary basis. Flea markets are growing all over the country, both in number and in size. Some are open every day, others only on the weekend. Any vendor may sell at these markets. All that is needed is merchandise and the money to rent a booth or table.

The merchandise offered for sale may be new or old, antiques and near-antiques, clothing, accessories, furniture, kitchen utensils, hand-crafted and ready-made products, high-priced and penny-priced merchandise. The variety is infinite—and this is part of the attraction for shoppers hunting for possible treasure, bargains, or unique items.

Catalog Showroom Retailing

A **catalog showroom retailer** is an underselling company that sells from a catalog and also maintains a showroom where samples of the merchandise can be seen and ordered. There are no deliveries, but usually the purchases can be picked up immediately at the showroom or from an adjoining warehouse. Very large, prepackaged stocks of the catalog items are on hand.

The mainstay of the merchandise assortment is usually branded house-wares, appliances, TVs, stereo equipment, electronics, toys, and sporting goods at prices well below those prevailing in conventional stores. Items of apparel, cosmetics, children's sleepers, men's underwear, and jewelry are also carried, but often are not featured or listed in the catalogs. Prices reflect the low operating costs. In addition to their bare-bones operation, catalog showrooms are usually in low-rent areas. Few salespeople are needed, because customers select their items from samples and catalogs, then make out purchase slips and pick up their packages from the warehouse.

Retail operations of this type began in the late 1960s and achieved a growth rate ranging from 30 to 40 percent during the 1970s. The largest of these is Service Merchandise, which operates 317 catalog showrooms coast to coast with sales of $3.7 billion. The second largest is Best Products, with sales over $2 billion.[17]

The impact of such stores on the fashion business has been negligible thus far; but so was the impact of other forms of underselling stores at first. Whether or not these minimum-service retailers will make a place for themselves in fashion still remains to be seen.

Warehouse Clubs: Selling in Bulk

Retailers that specialize in bulk sales of nationally branded merchandise at deeply discounted prices are so new that they do not yet have a clearly recognized name. Called "wholesale clubs," "**warehouse clubs**," or "**price clubs**," they are springing up all over the country and selling merchandise in bulk to member customers at an unheard of 10 percent markup. Although they deal primarily in commodities, some are already selling basic apparel and footwear, sheets, towels, and other home textiles.

Membership in these retailing clubs is generally restricted to small businesses, called wholesale members, that pay an initial fee to join, and also to individuals who belong to certain associations and are known as group members. Group members do not pay a membership fee but pay an additional 5 percent above the club's 10 percent markup.

Wholesale members are the backbone of the warehouse clubs' clientele, accounting for approximately 60 percent of their business. These are small mom-and-pop retailers—food stores, drugstores, restaurants, hardware stores —who either cannot meet the minimum-order requirements of conventional wholesalers or want to do fill-in buying.

Little or no advertising, stark industrial decor, low-rent locations, cash-and-carry transactions, and very fast inventory turn keep their expense rate down to 8 percent of their total sales—far lower than for any other type of retailing. The largest and first warehouse club is the Price Club founded in 1976 in San Diego, California, which now operates 40 warehouse stores in the United States and Canada, has sales of $4 billion, and employs 11,000 people.[18]

Inspired by the success of the Price Club, other large and well-established underselling retailers such as K mart and Wal-mart have opened their own warehouse clubs. An editorial in *Stores Magazine*, official publication of the National Retail Merchants Association, asked, "What do warehouse clubs have to do with your business?" and went on to say, "Would anyone venture to say that the $7 billion in new business generated by warehouse clubs are dollars that would not have been spent in conventionally operated stores?"[19]

Current estimates are that there are now 300 warehouse club outlets throughout the United States, generating $15 billion in sales volume.[20] Many have enlarged their store units, expanded their product mix into different categories of merchandise, and have opened stores throughout the country. For example, Sam's Wholesale Club has stores in more than 100 locations and carries drugs, toys, optical goods, and general merchandise in addition to food.

The warehouse atmosphere of these clubs and their low pricing policies serve to attract the value-conscious customer—a category that includes almost everybody who shops for commodities.

THE CHANGING DIMENSIONS OF
FASHION RETAILING _____

Very few periods in history have seen as many changes in the world of retailing as the decade of the 1980s. Although the fundamental role played by retailers in the business of fashion has not changed—the buying and selling of fashion products to the ultimate consumer—almost everything else about them has.

Until 1980, major retailers of fashion could still be easily classified as department stores, specialty stores, chains, mail-order houses, discount houses, and the like, according to their distinctive operational characteristics. During the

1980s, however, retailers moved in so many different directions that they can no longer be so neatly defined. *Acquisitions, verticalization, globalization, buyouts, private labels, electronics, restructuring, consolidation,* and *superstores* became 1980 retailing buzzwords. Today, the retail marketers of fashionable merchandise come in an almost infinite variety of shapes, sizes, corporate ownership, pricing strategies, and merchandise assortments.

The section that follows covers major changes that are revolutionizing soft goods retailing.

Growth of Private Labels: Retailers into Manufacturing

In the late 1970s, as designer and manufacturers' national brand names proliferated, it seemed as if every type of retailer was featuring the same nationally advertised names—department and specialty stores, mail-order houses, chain store retailers, and hordes of off-price apparel specialists that were underselling these well-known names. In order to have merchandise that was unique to their stores and to regain their freedom from price competition, many large department and specialty stores increasingly developed and promoted their own private-label fashion products in men's, women's, and children's apparel and accessories. **Private label** merchandise, as used in the fashion industry, refers to goods that are produced exclusively for one retailer, and it carries only the name of the retailer or one of several brand names that are owned by the retailer. Recent years have witnessed a steady expansion of private label operations, and today the fashion business is inundated with so many different names and labels that it is hard to know whether a specific name is that of a manufacturer's national brand, a designer's name, or a retailer's private label.

Today, as a result of expanding private label operations, large retailers are deeply involved in the production process and have assumed roles that traditionally belong to manufacturers—the purchase of fabrics and the styling and production of merchandise. Most have established special **product development** departments that create their own lines of merchandise and work with manufacturers or contractors in this country and abroad to produce their private brand merchandise according to their specifications. Macy's, for example, whose private labels constitute about 30 percent of their clothing sales, has an 80-person in-house staff and has run help-wanted advertisements for what they describe as "designer merchandisers."[21] Other stores work with producers that specialize in creating and producing private label programs.

Although it is generally estimated that about 70 percent of private label merchandise is produced offshore by contractors in low-wage countries, many major domestic manufacturers with strong national brands of their own are now also producing private label merchandise. Rather than lose business to foreign sources of supply, they are supplying retailers with exclusive merchandise to be sold under the store's own labels. While continuing to produce their

Some Examples of Private Labels

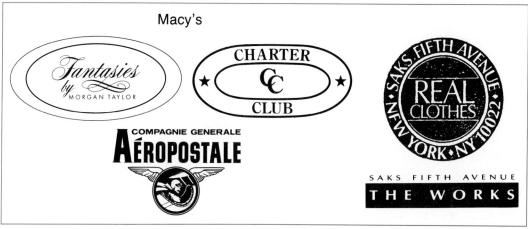

SOURCE: R. H. Macy & Company, Inc. and Saks Fifth Avenue.

own nationally branded products, they are developing private label divisions within their own companies. More often than not, the merchandise is manufactured in the same factories by the same workers who make their national brands and is sold side by side in the same stores. Examples include the Blue Bell American division of Blue Bell (producers of Wrangler jeans) and the Mansco division of Manhattan Industries. Even a high priced fashion producer such as Tahari has entered the field and produces for the Privé-Collection label of Saks Fifth Avenue.

Another development is the licensing and use of a designer or other well-known name as one of a store's private labels. For example, Bloomingdale's has entered into an exclusive licensing agreement with Norma Kamali to design a line of swimwear and sportswear which they have produced. Other examples of such arrangements are the Moods by Krizia line for The Limited chain of stores, the agreement between Sears and McDonald's to feature a McKids children's sportswear line, and the Halston III line sold by J. C. Penney.

Although a few private label merchandising programs have been operating for years, such as the Jaclyn Smith line for K mart and the Winnie the Pooh line for Sears, never before have there been so many store-owned name products, nor have they been such a key issue for retailers. Those private brand products are not intended to completely eliminate the producers' national brands or designer name that retailers feature; they carry these names and their own side by side. The proportion of private labels to other labels varies, of course, from store to store, but industry analysts estimate that private labels account for 20 to 25 percent of all women's apparel sold in this country, with some stores carrying as high as 40 percent of their total stock in privately branded merchandise.[22] It has also been estimated that whereas there were approximately 250 private brands in 1985, today that number has more than doubled, with many

Apparel Manufacturer Seeks Private Label Work

retailers promoting as many as 30 different names for different types of products.[23] Today on the classified pages of industry publications, retailers' help-wanted ads for product developers compete with those of manufacturers for the same designers and production coordinators. It is also interesting to note that among the crowded lofts of New York's garment district, a large department store group has its own design studio, fully equipped with CAD (computer-aided design) terminals that are the envy of its apparel manufacturer neighbors.

The proliferation of retailers' private label operations is progressing on many fronts and has without doubt added a new dimension to the world of fashion retailing.

General Merchandise Retailers into
Specialty Retailing

In the 1980s, the growth and increasing competition of specialized apparel chains exerted tremendous influence on other types of retailing. As the president of R. H. Macy told a stockholders' meeting, "The growing competition

Retail Advertisement for Product Developer

| *Help Wanted* | *Help Wanted* | *Help Wanted* |

DESIGNER/MERCHANDISER

Misses
Ready-to Wear

At R.H. MACY our private label merchandise plays a major role in overall sales and is one of the fastest-growing areas of our business. That growth translates into tremendous opportunity for you, the talented fashion professional.

We're seeking an individual with in-depth knowledge of the ready-to-wear industry — from design and styling to fabric selection . . . from sourcing and production supervision to identifying industry trends. Responsibilities will include product development that YOU initiate.

Your background should include 8 years' of fashion design and merchandising experience with a solid knowledge of wovens, knits, blouses, and related separates. You've worked closely with the fabric markets in the United States, Japan and Europe, and you have the interpersonal skills to deal effectively with MACY'S various levels of management.

If you're the professional we seek, and are ready to accept the challenge, please send your resume and salary history, in strict confidence, to:

R.H. MACY & CO., INC., Corporate Personnel, 151 W. 34th Street, Room 1303, Dept. R.B.L., New York, NY 10001

R. H. Macy & Co. Inc.

Equal Opportunity Employer

from apparel specialty chains, such as The Limited, The Gap, Benetton and countless others, is being felt in the apparel departments that represent 30 percent of our business."[24]

As a result of the inroads made on their business by apparel specialty chains, many general merchandisers have expanded into specialty chains of their own. As is characteristic of all such types of operations, these stores concentrate on specific classifications of merchandise designed for clearly defined targeted markets — their assortments are narrow and deep, they carry mainly their own private label merchandise, and they are located in shopping malls. Some have bought into or acquired existing store chains, others have developed their own chains, and still others have used both methods.

Macy's move into specialty retailing is three pronged, involving three different specializations — Fantasies by Morgan Taylor features European-inspired lingerie in a very frilly, soft environment; Charter Club features women's sportswear; and Aeropostale specializes in adventure-type men's and women's casualwear. Bloomingdale's opened Bloomie's Express stores in New York Kennedy International Airport and in other airports, with more to be located in hotels and shopping centers. Carson Pirie Scott of Chicago has 300 County Seat stores featuring casual apparel and has also opened Corporate Level Career shops catering to career women and men. It also operates Arcadia, a stationery and gifts chain. Bullock's, based in Los Angeles, has started Bullock's Woman, a chain featuring large-size apparel.

Sears, Roebuck and Co. has formed a subsidiary to acquire or develop specialty stores and is already in the arena with a chain of McKids stores featuring children's apparel under a licensing arrangement with McDonald's. J. C. Penney has moved into specialty retailing with its free-standing Mix-it chain carrying moderately priced apparel, and Units, a chain of moderate-priced casual apparel.

With the simultaneous movement into specialized apparel chains by manufacturers (discussed in a previous chapter), mail-order catalog houses, and general merchandise retailers, it has become apparent that, as one industry observer noted, "In the ever-renewing kaleidoscope that is retailing, specialty stores have emerged as the shining knights of the industry."[25]

Acquisitions of American Retailers by Real Estate Developers and Foreign Investors

During the decade of the 1980s the acquisitions of American retailers by real estate developers and foreign investors reshaped the competitive dynamics of the fashion industry. Attracted by a weak dollar, a strong domestic market, and the political stability of the United States, foreign investors apparently came to regard American retailers as profitable investments and foreign ownership of American companies increased dramatically.

FOREIGN BUYOUTS OF AMERICAN RETAILERS

Among the foreign companies that acquired American retailers in the 1980s were the following:

- Marks and Spencer, a major English retailer, bought Brooks Brothers, the prestigious menswear retailer, which was founded in 1818.
- Jusco, a Japanese consortium, acquired Talbots, a multimillion-dollar mail-order retailer.
- Nylex, a Canadian company, acquired the Foxmoor and Brooks Fashion chains.
- Maus Freres, a Swiss company, bought P. A. Bergner/Boston store.

- Hooker Ltd, an Australian real estate developer, bought into a wide array of American retailers, among them B. Altman and Bonwit Teller in New York, the Parisian in Birmingham, Alabama, and Sakowitz, a Texas-based company.
- The Canadian company of Campeau Corporation bought two of the largest American store ownership groups—Federated Department Stores for $6.6 billion and Allied Stores for $3.6 billion—and merged these two acquisitions into Federated/Allied. Federated/Allied owned Bloomingdale's, Abraham and Straus, and Stern's in the New York area, Jordan Marsh in New England, Burdine's and Maas/Jordan Marsh in Florida, Rich's/Goldsmith in Atlanta, Lazarus in Cincinnati, and Bon Marché in Seattle.
- InvestCorp, an Arab company, bought Saks Fifth Avenue.

However, the two largest foreign acquisitions—those of Campeau and Hooker—both involving enormous amounts of borrowed capital at high interest did not pay off and ended up in bankruptcy proceedings. In 1989 Hooker and its B. Altman and Bonwit Teller subsidiaries went into Chapter 11 proceedings. B. Altman was closed and Bonwit Teller was sold in 1990 to Pyramid, a real estate developer, who then closed the chain. In the same year Campeau, having severe cash problems due to insufficient profitability to support his debt load, tried to raise money by (a) putting Bloomingdale's up for sale for $1 billion and (b) borrowing additional monies. When these attempts failed, on January 15, 1990, Federated/Allied filed petitions for reorganization under Chapter 11 of the U.S. Bankruptcy Code, declaring that they had debts of some $7 billion.

Chapter 11 is the legal process that provides an opportunity for reorganization by companies whose individual operations are strong but whose financial structures are burdened by excessive debt at the parent corporate level. The bankruptcy filing enables the companies to continue operations while plans are made to stock merchandise, reschedule debt payments and reorganize the company, and perhaps sell some divisions. All such decisions are made in negotiations with creditor and stockholder committees and are subject to approval and supervision of a Federal bankruptcy judge who oversees the situation.

The eventual outcome of the bankruptcy of the Federated/Allied stores is yet to be resolved as of the time of this writing.

REAL ESTATE DEVELOPERS INTO RETAILING

As shopping centers and malls sprouted all over the country, the real estate developers of these centers have had a dramatic impact by pulling department store operations away from center cities. Many of them have now begun to take over major retail tenants and plan to use the retail companies that they acquire to anchor new shopping centers which they will develop. Among the developers are:

- Crown America Corp., which bought the Hess's Department Store in Allentown, Pennsylvania.
- Alfred Taubman, who acquired Woodward and Lothrop and John Wanamaker.
- Edward de Bartolo, who entered into joint agreements with Dillard's to take financial control of the 12-store Cleveland based Higbee's and the 16-store Jos. Horne group based in Pittsburgh.
- Kevin F. Donohue's real estate company, which now owns Miller and Rhodes.

Hypermarkets: New Era of Superstores

A new type of retailing that originated and is popular in Europe is taking root in the United States—hypermarkets. A **hypermarket** is a gigantic supermarket and discount store rolled into one that sells such products as groceries, meats, clothing, home furnishings, tires, appliances, and even tulip bulbs. In addition to food and merchandise, it offers services such as restaurants, haircuts, banking, and free supervised play areas for children. Prices are extremely low, and well-known "name" merchandise is highly visible in both hard and soft goods. Its estimated 70,000-product mix, consisting of approximately 60 percent food products, are all on one level without any dividing walls and take up 200,000 or more square feet spread across five acres, approximately the size of six football fields.

These sprawling hypermarkets began to appear in France in the 1960s and subsequently spread to a number of other European countries. *Carrefours*, the largest hypermarket operator in Europe, whose sales are reported at $9 billion, has opened a branch in the United States.[26]

To date, two of the largest discount chains in the United States have opened up hypermarkets. Wal-Mart's three *Hypermarkets* USA are located in Arlington, Texas; Garland, Texas; and Topeka, Kansas. K mart's *American Fare* is near Atlanta, Georgia. Both companies are featuring nationally branded casual and active sportswear in upper-moderate prices. Among the brands to be found in K mart's hypermarket are Calvin Klein Sportswear, Bill Blass Swimwear, L. A. Gear, Danskin activewear, and Jones, New York casualwear.

Supercenters are here and are expected to grow and create new excitement in the world of fashion retailing as they inevitably divert millions of dollars in sales from other types of retailers.

Another even larger type of super shopping center is under construction as of the time of this writing. Its official name is the *Mall of America*, but it is being called the Megamall. It is rising up on 78 acres in Bloomington, Minnesota, and will be 10 times the size of the average shopping mall. In addition to 4 anchor stores and 800 specialty shops, it will contain a 300,000-square-foot amusement park, 100 nightclubs and restaurants, 18 theaters, a miniature golf course, and a health club. Bloomingdale's and Macy's of New York, Carson Pirie Scott of Chicago, and Nordstrom of Seattle have already signed on as the four anchor stores. Fall 1992 is the scheduled opening.

Although there is no question that these new supercenters have created excitement in the world of retailing, it still is to be seen whether "bigger is better."

Television Marketing and Home Shopping

Although most goods are still being sold through stores and mail-order catalogs, there are those who believe that **television marketing** is the wave of the future and that many shopping choices will be made through viewing assortments, prices, and brands on television screens. Although they are still in their infancy, different forms of electronic retailing are currently being used to market products directly to consumers.

TV shopping shows have been around for as long as a decade, but most authorities date the real emergence and increasing importance of *home shopping channels* to 1985. Home shopping channels are cable TV channels entirely devoted to selling goods and services. Sales through this medium grew from $450 million in 1986 to $2.5 billion in 1988, and many expect them to reach $7.5 billion by 1992.[27] The largest is the Home Shopping Network (HSN). More than half of all U.S. homes have access to HSN or one of a dozen other home shopping channels such as Cable Value Network, Value Club of America, Home Shopping Mall, or Tel Shop. To date, most feature discounted prices on recognizable brands of jewelry, lamps, power tools, consumer electronics, and other general merchandise, but apparel is becoming a growing category and names such as Pierre Cardin, Oleg Cassini, and Gloria Vanderbilt have already appeared in home shopping offerings. During the 1989 Christmas season, for example, blue fox and mink jackets and 18 karat gold jewelry were among the best selling items on the HSN programs.

The shop-at-home trend is a result of the same social factors that explain the growth of mail-order sales—the rise in the number of working women, and people's interest in spending their spare time in more relaxed ways than shopping. And as other, more traditional types of retailers find the public more interested in shopping from their homes, many major retailers are joining forces with the cable shopping industry. For example, the American Catalog shopping network is offering fashion merchandise from retailers such as Bloomingdale's, L. L. Bean, and Spiegel.

Another form of electronic marketing that is still in an evolutionary stage is the interactive electronic video kiosks where customers can learn about merchandise or order specific sizes and styles. Kiosks made their debut several years ago, but only recently have they started to win acceptance. Now they are cropping up in public spots such as hotel lobbies, shopping centers, airports, and also within stores.

Electronic kiosks are currently being used in a variety of ways. Some in-store kiosks can direct a shopper to a specific product and provide information about it. Some are computer imaging systems that can show a customer how he or she will look in a particular outfit, hair style, or cosmetic. Still others enable customers to view and order merchandise that may not be in stock. For example, Florsheim Shoe Co. and Levi-Strauss and Co, two pioneers in electronic retailing, have installed point-of-purchase interactive video kiosk programs in stores. Florsheim has blanketed its stores across the country with point-of-purchase kiosks that can take orders for every single Florsheim shoe. Levi's also has a network of kiosks that take orders. Another leading experimenter with kiosks is Sears, Roebuck and Co. Sears reported positive results from a tryout of three "Gift Sender" kiosks placed in public spots and is installing more.

Of particular significance to the world of fashion are the stated opinions of highly respected fashion marketing executives. "I think ultimately it (electronic retailing) has a terrific future. If you look at the billions and billions of dollars done in retail, if it only gets 10 percent of the business you are talking big money." And in the opinion of a senior vice president of Saks Fifth Avenue: "The fashion industry will be revolutionized by electronic retailing. . . . If the T.V. picture is sufficiently improved and the consumer becomes fully adjusted to the medium — these will happen eventually — the possibilities for our kind of store are very promising."[28] And last, but not least, "Touch screen at point of sale or other forms of electronic marketing are absolutely the future" is the opinion of Jeff Harlowe, director of retail marketing for Levi's.[29]

Computerized Partnerships with Manufacturers: Quick Response Programs

Emerging in the late 1980s, the new industry-wide strategy of **Quick Response** began to engulf the world of apparel retailers. As discussed in previous chapters, its rationale was to establish a computerized partnership among a retailer, an apparel supplier, and fabric suppliers in order for each to respond rapidly and precisely to the demands of the ultimate consumer.

Since the aim of all QR programs is the quick replenishment of fast-selling items, the selling records of the retailer are the beginning and end of a computerized partnership that has been established. The retailers track their sales by style, size, and color and transmit that information in computer language to the manufacturer of the item. The apparel makers use the information to tailor their production to match retail sales so they can replenish stock quickly and spot trends fast. Linkages also are set up between apparel companies and textile companies so they also are tuned into retail sales.

J. C. Penney Uses Electronics to Develope Private Labels

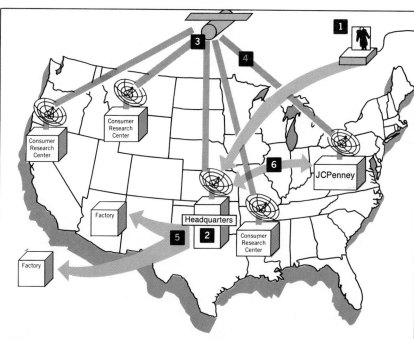

1 J.C. Penney fashion scout in Europe sees a new design, transmits a color photo via telephone lines to headquarters in Dallas.

2 At headquarters, a J.C. Penney version of the product is designed on a computer-aided design system.

3 Using satellite links, designs are shown to consumers at J.C. Penney testing centers around the U.S. The consumers "vote" on the products on personal computers. The results are tabulated at headquarters within 24 hours to help decide if the company should sell the product.

4 Using the company's direct broadcast system, merchandise is shown to buyers at 700 J.C. Penney stores nationwide. They can provide instant feedback.

5 Design and production information about the garment is transmitted electronically to factories in the U.S. and the Far East. Photographs of samples may be transmitted back to headquarters for quality-control checks.

6 Sales results are tabulated daily at J.C. Penney stores and are transmitted to headquarters over phone lines. When sales of a product reach a certain level, a computer in the store may automatically reorder it. In some cases, these reorders are transmitted directly from the store to the manufacturer.

Today many major retailers are participating in a computer-to-computer exchange of information with suppliers about the merchandise their customers are buying. Although apparel retailers have lagged behind food supermarkets in their use of EDI (electronic data interchange) and the identifying bar-coded tickets that record sales data, they are catching up with these supermarket techniques. Bar-coded tickets are becoming increasingly visible on apparel items and may soon become as universal as they now are on food items.

The 25 Top Department and Departmentalized Specialty Stores[a]

Rank	Company Division	Ownership[b]	Volume $ (Add 000,000)
1	Macy's Northeast (New York)	(RHM)	3,350
2	Dillards (Little Rock, Ark.)	(Ind.)	2,769
3	Nordstrom (Seattle)	(Ind.)	2,671
4	Macy's South (Atlanta)	(RHM)	1,875
5	Dayton Hudson (Minneapolis)	(DH)	1,801
6	Macy's California (San Francisco)	(RHM)	1,545
7	Bloomingdale's (New York)	(Camp.)	1,295
8	Saks Fifth Avenue (New York)	(Ind.)	1,224
9	Neiman Marcus (Dallas)	(NMG)	1,230
10	The Broadway (Los Angeles)	(CHH)	1,195
11	Foley's (Houston)	(May)	1,121
12	Marshall Field (Chicago)	(DH)	1,090
13	Lord & Taylor (New York)	(May)	1,034
14	Lazarus (Cinncinati)	(Camp.)	975
15	May Company (Los Angeles)	(May)	954
16	Rich's (Atlanta)	(Camp.)	920
17	Woodward & Lothrop (Washington, D.C.)	(Ind.)	913
18	Burdine's (Miami)	(Camp.)	905
19	Hechts's (Washington, D.C.)	(May)	829
20	Abraham & Straus (Brooklyn)	(Camp.)	775
21	Carson Pirie Scott (Chicago)	(PAB)	770
22	Kaufmann's (Pittsburgh)	(May)	753
23	Robinson's (Los Angeles)	(May)	753
24	Emporium-Capwell (San Francisco)	(CHH)	750
25	Kohl's (Wisconsin)	(Ind.)	750

[a]Companies include traditional department stores and departmentalized specialty stores. Excluded are general merchandise and specialty chains, and discounters.

[b]*Ownership code:* Ind, Independent; CHH, Carter Hawley Hale; Camp., Campeau; DH, Dayton Hudson; May, May Department Stores; NMG, Neiman Marcus Group; PAB, P.A. Bergner; RHM, R.H. Macy & Co.

Author's note: Figures on this listing are either provided by the companies or are estimates based on Stores's research and consultation with retail industry and financial sources.

SOURCE: Adapted from *Stores Magazine*, July 1990.

Readings

The success stories of such different types of retailers as department stores, specialty stores, mail-order houses, and discounters are discussed in these readings.

Watch Out Macy's, Here Comes Nordstrom

In an age when shopping has become a chore, Nordstrom's fervent commitment to treating its customers well is generating big sales and big profits.

Wal-Mart: Will It Take Over the World?

Wal-mart is the house that Sam Walton built. It is an unglamorous, cost-conscious mass merchandiser whose sales have grown at a rate of 40 percent a year for 20 years.

Standout in the Land of Catalogues

Lands' End is a company that is flourishing in response to the boom in mail-order buying. Its folksy catalog and deft use of computers are paying off.

Charivari: New York's Hottest Boutique Causes an Uproar

Charivari is a chain of fashion boutiques whose name is synonymous with the ready-to-wear of famous European designers.

Tomorrow's Buyer: A Production Expert?

As retailers become more private label–oriented and therefore more production-oriented, they are staffing their stores with product development experts and managers.

The Limited: Speeding into the Nineties

The Limited has embarked on an ambitious expansion by means of larger stores, deeper assortments, and wider merchandise selections.

445

WATCH OUT MACY'S, HERE COMES NORDSTROM

by Richard W. Stevenson

It is Sunday morning at the Bel Air Presbyterian Church in Los Angeles, and the subject of the Rev. Carolyn A. Crawford's sermon is the Nordstrom department store chain.

"The Gospel According to Nordstrom," as Crawford calls it, starts with a description of the chain's almost legendary reputation for customer service. Then Crawford tells a story about seeing a Nordstrom saleswoman lavish on a bedraggled bag lady the same type of patient and respectful treatment she might bestow on a Beverly Hills socialite. To judge by their appreciative murmurs, most members of the congregation are Nordstrom shoppers themselves. And if they are somewhat taken aback by Crawford's choice of subject this morning, they seem to know just what she means when she praises Nordstrom "for carrying out the call of the gospel in ways that are more consistent and caring than we sometimes do in the church."

Bel Air Presbyterians aren't the only consumers getting religion from Nordstrom. In an age of sneering, incompetent and elusive service, when shopping has become a chore if not a war, Nordstrom's fervent — some would say cult-like — commitment to treating its customers well is attracting legions of loyal shoppers and generating big profits. It almost doesn't matter that Nordstrom can't always live up to its hype, or that some salespeople complain the corporate culture requires them to subjugate their own personalities to that of the store. So strong is the Nordstrom mystique that within the industry and among the credit-card wielding masses, the company is seen as a powerful engine of change, forcing retailers everywhere to reexamine the way they do business.

Nordstrom — known, in industry jargon, as a "fashion specialty retailer" because it sells mainly apparel, accessories and shoes and not televisions or electric brooms — could hardly be more successful. The company's sales have grown nearly tenfold over the last decade, to more than $2.3 billion last year, the chain having expanded from 15 Nordstrom stores to 42 in that period. (The company also operates a youth-oriented chain called Place Two and a discount outlet called Nordstrom Rack.) Last year's earnings were $123.3 million, up 33 percent from the previous year.

Now, having successfully pushed from its home base in Seattle throughout the Northwest and into California, the company is going national. From their suite of modest offices tucked away atop the Seattle store, the three members of the Nordstrom family who run the company are planning to open stores in Chicago, Indianapolis, Minneapolis and Cheshire, Conn., north of New Haven, with other cities still under consideration. Nordstrom opened its first East Coast store last year, in McLean, Va., outside Washington. And starting in 1990, the chain plans to establish a toehold in the New York market with three stores in northern New Jersey.

The competition has taken notice. After years of concentrating on keeping costs low and luring customers with constant rounds of sale prices, the large department and apparel stores increasingly see competent service from an efficient, cheerful sales staff as the key to success in an increasingly competitive retail environment.

"Nordstrom has been a catalyst for the industry." says Gary M. Witkin, executive vice president of Marshall Field, the retailer in Chicago, where Nordstrom plans to open a store in 1991. One result of a sweeping program to improve its service, Witkin says, is that Marshall Field has reduced to less than two minutes—from more than 10—the average amount of time it takes a salesperson to approach a customer.

In California, where Nordstrom has opened 21 stores in the last 11 years, the chain's success has spurred more established rivals like Macy's and The Broadway to imitate Nordstrom strategies, like putting salespeople on commission, a step they hope will foster more helpful attitudes in their employees.

"All retailers in America have awakened to the Nordstrom threat and are struggling to catch up," says Leonard Lauder, the chief executive of perfume and cosmetics maker Estée Lauder Inc. "Nordstrom is the future of retailing."

If Macy's and Bloomingdale's are fashion theater, slick, flashy and occasionally outrageous in a calculated way, the Nordstrom might be described as country-club chic—classy enough, leaning toward the expensive but restrained and somewhat predictable. In the décor there is lots of polished wood and marble rather than gleaming chrome or bright colors. Most of the stores have an open, airy feel. The design seems in sync with the company's strategy of appealing to the affluent and fashion-conscious shopper without scaring away the middle class, a delicate balancing act.

Nordstrom stores are full of small amenities. Instead of typical retail Muzak, most feature piano players at real baby grands. There is plenty of seating. The dressing rooms are large. The apparel doesn't carry those bulky anti-theft tags that can be annoying when trying things on.

The merchandise is, for the most part, unexceptional for a large, upscale chain. The Nordstrom look is primarily classic and not trendy, the selection limited to styles with broad appeal, what Harry Bernard, an apparel industry consultant in San Francisco, calls "fashion in the safe lane." In women's apparel, that means many of the most popular designers—among them Calvin Klein, Anne Klein, Gianni Versace, Donna Karan and Claude Montana in the middle to upper price ranges, and Carolina Herrera and Carolyne Roehm at the top of the scale. With rare exceptions, the chain does not feature designers in their own in-store boutiques, preferring to emphasize the Nordstrom name rather than that of its suppliers.

Any true competitive advantage in merchandising comes from an enormous inventory (merchandise is generally available in every conceivable size and color; a few Nordstrom stores stock more than 100,000 pairs of shoes), and a regionalized buying system. Buyers are granted significant discretion in selecting apparel that will appeal to local tastes.

Ultimately, though, it is Nordstrom's sales staff that is responsible for the hordes of loyal customers. A typical Nordstrom store has as many as 50 percent more salespeople on the floor than rival stores of similar size, analysts say, with the largest stores employing more than 600.

"Nordies," as employees call themselves, are subjected to a stream of internal morale-boosting and attitude-shaping messages. Nordstrom salespeople often write notes thanking customers for their business. The chain is famed for accepting returns without question, and often without receipts. The hoariest Nordstrom tale, perhaps apocryphal, in circulation concerns the salesman who gave a customer a full refund on a set of snow tires, even though Nordstrom doesn't sell them.

In a pinch, salespeople have paid parking tickets for customers unable to find legal spots, delivered purchases to customers' homes on Christmas Eve and lent a few dollars to customers who have found themselves short at the cash register.

"At a lot of stores, when you're trying things on, you're a prisoner of the dressing room," says Shelley Fariello, an advertising sales manager from Manhattan Beach, Calif., who says she spends several thousand dollars a year at Nordstrom on clothes for herself and her family. "You can walk out and you usually have to scream to get someone to help you. At Nordstrom the saleswoman is always right there."

Fariello recently spent $500 at Nordstrom on a Victor Costa dress. While she was trying it on, she found she didn't have the right kind of bra, so her saleswoman ran up to the next floor to get one for her. Then she wanted to see how the dress would look with high heels, so the saleswoman ran down a flight to borrow some from the shoe department.

When Fariello got home, she found a run in the back of the dress. She called the saleswoman, explained the problem and said she was planning to wear the dress that evening. The saleswoman, without checking with a manager or otherwise delaying, immediately told her she could wear the dress that evening with the run and return it at her convenience for a full refund, or take $100 off the price. Fariello took the price cut.

"They treat you with the most reverence you can imagine," she says. "It's so darn easy to go in there."

To speak of any aspect of Nordstrom's corporate personality is to speak of the three family members who serve as cochairmen. James F. Nordstrom, 49, and John N. Nordstrom, 52, who are brothers, and Bruce A. Nordstrom, 55, who is their cousin, are grandsons of John W. Nordstrom, a Swedish immigrant who, as family lore has it, arrived in New York in 1887 at the age of 16 with $5 in his pocket. Fourteen years later, having made $13,000 panning for gold in Alaska, John W. settled in Seattle and opened a shoe store. By the 1960's, the store was a chain, and under the direction of John W.'s sons, Elmer, Everett and Lloyd, it diversified into apparel.

The current generation of top managers—known around headquarters as Mr. Jim, Mr. John and Mr. Bruce—are polite, self-effacing men who often answer their own phones at work. Ask them about anything but themselves or their business, and they'll probably be helpful to a fault. But ask them about the company, and if you're lucky enough to get an answer, it will be brief, vague, and only slightly helpful in understanding the Nordstrom phenomenon.

Nordstrom would like you to think that the kind of service it offers comes easily, delivered by people who are naturally thoughtful and helpful. "All we do is hire nice people," Nordstrom executives like to say.

Nordstrom employees tend to be young, often college-educated people looking for a career in retailing. They are attracted by relatively high salaries—a reasonably good salesperson can make upwards of $30,000 a year—and opportunities for rapid advancement in a fast-growing company with a policy of promoting from within.

For new hires, the brief training period is largely practical—how to work the cash registers, etc. But once on board, employees are prodded constantly to meet sales quotas and service standards.

The company's formal and informal lines of communication are kept abuzz with tales of salespeople who have made an extraordinary effort to keep the customer happy — "heroics," in Nordstrom parlance. The stories often go all the way to the top of the company. The consultant Harry Bernard recalls sitting in Jim Nordstrom's office as Nordstrom signed a letter of appreciation to a salesperson in Seattle who had unquestioningly accepted for return a $2,500 gown that had been purchased in the Portland store two months earlier.

At monthly store meetings, managers read aloud, to a chorus of whoops and cheers, letters from pleased customers. The salespeople who elicit such written praise are honored as "Customer Service All-Stars." Their pictures are hung on a wall next to the customer-service desk, they receive added discounts on clothing and have notes placed in their personnel files documenting their efforts.

Of course, salespeople are never allowed to forget that even service is a means to an end, namely to keep the merchandise moving. Working on commission — a once-common practice in retailing that disappeared at most stores as they hired more part-time salespeople and looked for ways to keep costs down — is, of course, reminder enough for many salespeople. But in case it's not, Nordstrom managers constantly prod them — to make the next sale, to suggest a belt to go along with those slacks, to call their regular customers when the new spring styles arrive.

The life of a Nordstrom salesperson is defined by goals. Daily, monthly, quarterly and annual goals. Departmental, store-wide and company goals. Qualitative and quantitative goals.

The goal-setting starts at the top. Every year the company's managers gather in meetings where they publicly state their store or departmental goals for the next 12 months. Then their bosses will reveal their own goals for the same manager, sometimes with a dramatic flourish.

Salespeople can keep track of their performances on computer printouts available in back offices that list their sales by an employee identification number. Salespeople often know each other's numbers and so can see how they stand in relation to one another, as well as in relation to their goals. Top salespeople are named "Pacesetters," a label that carries with it roughly the status of a varsity letter on a high school athlete's jacket.

The goal-setting seems to work. Employees at all levels seem always to know precisely what they want and need to achieve. "The first year I consciously set quarterly goals to achieve the Pacesetter requirement," one of Nordstrom's top saleswomen said in a recent interview with one of the company's in-house publications. "My second year my personal goal was $500,000, and I paced myself accordingly. My third year I wanted to achieve $1 million in total sales. To accomplish this I set monthly and quarterly quotas and closely monitored my progress."

Financially well-positioned for an ambitious expansion, Nordstrom is one of the few major retailers without a corporate parent burdened by debt taken on in an acquisition or buyout. Moreover, by selling only apparel, shoes and accessories, which can be densely stocked, and eschewing bulkier goods like appliances, each store is extremely efficient; the chain sells more merchandise per square foot than almost any other retailer — about $380 last year, according to Monroe H. Greenstein, an analyst at Bear, Stearns, more than twice the industry average.

The new Nordstrom store in the Tysons Corner mall in McLean, Va., sold in the range of $100 million worth of merchandise in its first year of operation, making it the most successful fashion or department store opening ever, according to Women's Wear Daily. That record now seems certain to be shattered by a huge, glittering new Nordstrom store that opened in downtown San Francisco last October. Despite its location — on the top floors of an unusually designed vertical mall on seedy Market Street — the store should do at least $150 million in sales in its first 12 months, according to industry estimates.

Having gained confidence at the Virginia store that its strategy will play well in a sophisticated Eastern market, the company has accelerated its original plans for New Jersey. The opening of a store in Paramus next year will be followed by another in 1991 in Edison, with a third New Jersey store opening the following year in Freehold.

The opening of the Virginia store, so far from the rest of the company, provides a clear look at how the company plans to cope with growth. Essentially, Nordstrom wants as many experienced, dedicated Nordies as possible in a new store to serve as examples and trainers. More than 200 Nordstrom employees moved from the West Coast to Virginia, at their own expense, motivated by a chance to get a crack at the management jobs that are opening up as the company grows in the East. The company moved an additional 100 managers to Virginia at *its* expense, and together the groups served to fertilize a new region with the Nordstrom philosophy. On the day the store opened, more than half of its 500 employees were experienced Nordies.

A few company executives admit that their greatest fear is overpromising on the quality of service they can deliver. In the meantime, Nordstrom seems bent on reversing the public perception that shoddy, uncaring service is something we all have to live with in a fast-paced, cost-conscious world. Betsy Sanders, the head of the company's Southern California division, sometimes likes to stand at the doors of one of the stores at night as it closes and say good night to departing customers. One evening as she bade some shoppers farewell, she heard one say to another: "What kind of drugs are these people on? Even the doormen are nice."

WAL-MART: WILL IT TAKE OVER THE WORLD?

by John Huey

Most of the things you've heard about Sam Walton, America's billionaire cotton-sock retailing baron, are true enough — as far as they go. He is rich and homespun and self-made and plain-spoken; he insists you call him Sam. He is a quail-hunting fanatic, and he drives a ten-year-old Ford pickup with cages in back for Leroy and Kate, successors to the late Ol' Roy, his favorite bird dog — now enshrined on the label of Wal-Mart dog food. He is one of the world's great stump speakers, putting all but the best

Source: Reprinted by permission from *Fortune Magazine*, January 30, 1989. © 1989 The Time Inc. Magazine Co. All rights reserved.

evangelists to shame when it comes to delivering a message to his "associates," the term he long ago substituted for "employees." What hasn't yet come through loudly or clearly enough from his lair in Bentonville, Arkansas, however, is just how serious a place this 70-year-old curiosity and his company are likely to hold in the history of American commerce.

No one can pinpoint exactly when an extraordinary company's name, or image, passes from the lumpen mass of corporate entities into a league of its own, but for Wal-Mart Stores the time has come. Not too long ago, even its spectacular results earned it little notice other than for its chairman's wealth. But last year—the first time Wal-Mart was big enough to qualify for FORTUNE's survey of America's most admired corporations—it exploded onto the scene in a tie for ninth place out of more than 300 companies. This year it leapfrogged to No. 5, ranking first in all but one of eight categories among its retailing peers.

It's about time Wal-Mart got some respect. The company's average annual return to investors from 1977 through 1987 was 46%, far ahead of the next-closest company among FORTUNE's ten most admired, Herman Miller at a robust 27.4%. And the next time your broker calls, share this thought: A $1,000 investment in Wal-Mart's 1970 initial public offering would be worth half a million dollars today. If he's so smart, why didn't he put you into that baby?

Before traveling to the foothills of the Ozarks to learn how all this happened, you should know a few more things about America's most admired retailing company. In just a couple of years, Wal-Mart Stores will be the largest retailer in the U.S. The only companies in its way are K mart and the floundering giant, Sears, and the gap is closing fast. Wal-Mart's 1,300 or so discount stores sell nearly $20 billion worth of

goods a year—clothes, shoes, small appliances, cosmetics, and 50,000 other items. Even so, you may never have shopped in a Wal-Mart because the company is really just getting started. Early on, Sam Walton focused on the small-town markets ignored by national discounters, and though the company now operates Wal-Marts in such cities as Dallas, Houston, St. Louis, and Kansas City, its trade area still includes only 25 states.

This year, like last year, Wal-Mart will open 150 or so new stores. David Glass, the company's 53-year-old chief executive who assumed all but the role of corporate inspirational leader from Chairman Sam last year, says there is no state he wouldn't enter. So sooner or later there's bound to be a Wal-Mart in your future. When you do step into your first one, don't get rattled when someone—probably an elderly retiree type—approaches you with a big smile and welcomes you to the store. This is the "people greeter," and every Wal-Mart has one because, well, it's the friendly thing to do, and one of the hourly associates suggested it and the idea worked its way up through the system and Sam liked it.

If all this hospitality makes you think your company might like to sell something to Wal-Mart, a word of caution: Don't expect a greeter, and don't expect friendly. Plan on a tough trip over the river and through the woods and across the rock pile to a low-slung warehouse building in a town of 10,000 people. And even if you're a big deal at your company and have an appointment, don't be surprised if you're kept waiting an hour or two in a lobby filled with 150 molded-plastic chairs and mounted giant fish caught by brother Bud Walton. Unless you like cafeteria food, eat before you come, because Wal-Mart won't let you buy lunch or dinner or anything else for the buyer. And once you are ushered into one of the spartan little buyers' rooms, expect a steely eye across the table and be prepared to cut your price. "They are very, very focused people, and they use their buying power more forcefully than anybody else in America," says the marketing vice president of a major vendor. "All the normal mating rituals are verboten. Their highest priority is making sure everybody at all times in all cases knows who's in charge, and it's Wal-Mart. They talk softly, but they have piranha hearts, and if you aren't totally prepared when you go in there, you'll have your ass handed to you."

Welcome to the house that Sam built, the militantly unglamorous, religiously cost-conscious mass merchandiser that has rewarded true believers and confounded skeptics by growing at a compound rate of over 40% a year for almost 20 years. Wal-Mart's growth has slowed a bit recently, to a mere 30% a year.

Leave the Wall Street eggheads behind and come now to Bentonville, where it is a Friday morning just before Christmas. Some 100 of the company's top managers —senior executives, divisional managers, regional managers—have flown back from visiting stores and are assembled for a weekly, no-holds-barred session with the sole agenda of moving merchandise. We are seated in folding chairs crowded around a big rectangle of tables, and most folks are clutching a thick printout that lists the inventory levels and rates of sale for key items that Wal-Mart stocks. The energy is high, for this is the play-off season of retailing. Conversation crackles; to be heard, one must speak out.

For three hours, the managers pore over the printout. One is concerned that Wal-Mart has priced children's corduroy jeans at $3, while K mart is promoting them at two for $5; this is corrected. CEO Glass worries that a certain videogame isn't moving in stores he has visited this week, and

he wants orders cut off; the buyers have beaten him to it. Then a discussion ensues over knives, which the printout shows are heavily stocked in Wal-Mart's distribution centers. Quickly, a senior manager orders a Christmas gift knife display. Glass sees that only 500,000 sets of cookware are stocked in the stores, while he thinks 600,000 can be sold. Get them out there.

Word on the knives and cookware will reach all store managers by Monday, probably by phone. In more urgent cases, an executive can broadcast the message on TV from Bentonville to all stores over the company's six-channel satellite system, which also gathers store data for the master computer, handles credit card approval transmission in five seconds, and tracks the company's complex distribution system. With the satellite, Glass says, "we can talk to every store at the same time as many times a day as we want, and we've dramatically reduced our phone costs. We train by satellite. But the biggest advantage is the sharing of merchandising information. A buyer can get on and say, 'These are the new items in department 16. Here's how you should display them.'"

The satellite is for efficiency and speed; management of this company is anything but remote control. Almost everyone at the meeting spends Monday through Thursday flying around to stores on one of Wal-Mart's 11 planes—mostly turboprops— then returns to share findings in Friday and Saturday meetings. This is a practice with deep roots in tradition. Sam pilots his own plane, and at one time visited every store at least once a year—often with Ol' Roy.

Nowhere is the technology of Wal-Mart more evident than at its 14 distribution centers, most within a day's drive of the stores they serve. "Our distribution facilities are one of the keys to our success," says Glass. "If we do anything better than other folks, that's it. But the truth is, we were driven to a lot of this technology because the things we needed didn't exist in small-town America." In the early days of discounting, retailers paid distributors a cut, say 15%, to supply merchandise and stock shelves. But there were no distributors available to Wal-Mart in such places as Idabel, Oklahoma, or Van Buren, Arkansas, so it developed its own system, ordering directly from manufacturers and using its own fleet of trucks for delivery.

Consider 35-year-old Jimmy Wright's job as general manager of the 1.2-million-square-foot Cullman, Alabama, distribution center. He oversees 1,042 associates, all working under one 28-acre roof. They load 150 outbound Wal-Mart trailers a day and unload 160. They deliver to each of the center's 165 stores almost every day. Laser scanners route the goods along 11 miles of conveyor belts, which on a heavy day will handle 190,000 cases of goods. Says Wright: "The technology we use is standard—mechanized conveyors, bar coding, computerized inventory. A lot of companies use it. But no one runs it as hard as we do, and no one is as in touch with their business as we are."

Wal-Mart executives chuckle a bit at the irony of all this technology tucked away in the Arkansas foothills. They enjoy the idea that outsiders think they're a bunch of hillbillies and, upon arrival discover a computer-communications complex worthy of the Defense Department. But while the company is near the leading edge in technology, its secret is more in deployment than hardware. As one Wal-Mart executive puts it, "Sam never did like computers. He thinks of them as overhead." But he surrounded himself with controls-oriented people who recognized that technology was necessary to manage Wal-Mart's explosive growth. One of those people was David

Glass, the articulate but reserved company intellectual, who placed computers in all stores in the mid-1970s. Another was Don Soderquist, the 55-year-old vice chairman and chief operating officer, whose effervescent personality belies his background as a data-processing and distribution expert.

Every Wal-Mart associate—from Sam to David to Don to a cashier named Janet at the Wal-Mart on Highway 50 in Ocoee, Florida—will tell you that "better people" are what really make the difference at the company. How Sam Walton and his top managers have motivated 215,000 employees—many of them unskilled workers with starting pay of less than $5 an hour—to work as partners in the process is the most oft-told, least understood chapter of the Wal-Mart saga.

Everyone at Wal-Mart became an "associate." "We," "us," and "our" became the operative words. Wal-Mart department heads, hourly associates who look after one or more of 30-some departments ranging from sporting goods to electronics, see figures that many companies never show general managers: costs, freight charges, profit margins. The company sets a profit goal for each store, and if the store exceeds it, then the hourly associates share part of the additional profit. To control losses from theft and damage—also known as shrinkage, the bugaboo of all big merchants—Sam instituted the shrinkage bonus in 1980. If a store holds shrinkage below the corporate goal, every associate in that store receives up to $200. Wal-Mart's shrinkage is estimated to be just above 1%, vs. an industry average of 2%.

The partnership concept goes beyond monetary participation to open-door policies and grass-roots meetings designed, explains Soderquist, to say, "Hey, if you've got a problem, talk to somebody. Don't talk about it in the lounge or the parking lot.

Come to management." Today at Wal-Mart all this seems so logical and reasonable and is so ingrained in the corporate culture that it is certain to continue long after Sam passes from the scene. "Sam may be the most outstanding talent and the best merchant that I've ever known," says Glass. "But no one man runs a $20 billion company. It is our people that make the difference collectively." But while a lot of people run Wal-Mart today, it all works because one man created it and pushed it, and it is to him that we must look to understand how this all came about.

Sam's explanation is simplistic but to the point: "If people believe in themselves, it's truly amazing what they can accomplish." The Sam Walton story makes this point about as strongly as it can be made. The son of a Depression-era farm-mortgage banker, he grew up in the same four-state heartland where he is today (Arkansas, Missouri, Oklahoma, and Kansas all come together near Bentonville). He graduated from the University of Missouri in 1940 with an economics degree and hired on as a trainee at J.C. Penney. After World War II Army service, he opened a small Ben Franklin five-and-dime in Arkansas and eventually became the company's largest franchisee.

The conventional wisdom, which everybody told Sam over and over, was that a discount store could work only in an area with 50,000 or more people. But in 1962 Walton opened the first Wal-Mart in tiny Rogers, Arkansas, near Bentonville.

So how—from there—did Sam Walton get to be America's most admired retailer? The theory here is that he willed it through sheer force of a complex personality. He is an old-fashioned promoter in the P.T. Barnum style. But he is more than that. He's a little bit Jimmy Stewart, handsome with halting, "aw shucks" charm. He's a little bit Billy Graham, with a charisma and a persuasiveness that heartland folks find hard to resist. And he's more than a little bit Henry Ford, a business genius who sees how all parts of the economic puzzle relate to his business. Overlaying everything is a lot of the old yard rooster who is tough, loves a good fight, and protects his territory.

Sam still comes to Saturday Morning Meeting, a whoop-it-up 7:30 A.M. sales pep rally for 300 managers, complete with Wal-Mart cheers, awards, and occasional appearances by such groups as the singing truck drivers. In November, with the Christmas season approaching, Wal-Mart associates across the country arrived at work to find Sam—wearing his ubiquitous mesh ball cap—waiting to "visit with" them by satellite on a subject he said he was "totally obsessed with": aggressive hospitality to the customers. This isn't just a sales pitch; it's a self-improvement video that Dale Carnegie would have envied.

Sam rambles on about the hunting he's been doing and demonstrates his bird dog whistle, then gets down to his idea. "I don't think any other retail company in the world could do what I'm going to propose to you," he says. "It's simple. It won't cost us anything. And I believe it would just work magic, absolute magic on our customers, and our sales would escalate, and I think we'd just shoot past our K mart friends in a year or two and probably Sears as well." He proposes that whenever customers approach, the associates should look them in the eye, greet them, and ask to help. Sam understands that some associates are shy, but if they do what he suggests, "it would, I'm sure, help you become a leader, it would help your personality develop, you would become more outgoing, and in time you might become manager of that store, you might become a department manager, you might become a district manager, or whatever you choose to be in the company. . . . It will do wonders for you." He guarantees it.

Then, just to make sure, Sam asks the associates to raise their right hands and execute a pledge, keeping in mind that "a promise we make is a promise we keep." The pledge: "From this day forward, I solemnly promise and declare that every customer that comes within ten feet of me, I will smile, look them in the eye, and greet them, so help me Sam."

You city slicker CEOs laugh all you want. This is one of the keys to the magic formula. The same principles apply to Sam's "Bring It Home to the USA" program to replace foreign goods in Wal-Mart with domestic goods. First, the program has created thousands of manufacturing jobs in the U.S. Second, it's a great sales promotion. Finally, every worker in a Wal-Mart-created job becomes a loyal Wal-Mart shopper. "It's the best thing that ever happened to Brinkley, Arkansas, and the best thing that ever happened to me," says Farris Burroughs, an apparel manufacturer whose life changed one day in 1984 when Sam asked him to make 50,000 dozen flannel shirts. "We had a contract with Van Heusen for Penney's and Sears," he says, "and they were moving to China. We were struggling from season to season with 90 jobs. Today we're making two million Wal-Mart shirts, we've got 275 employees, we're adding 70 more next year, and everybody knows what they're getting from the company for Christmas: $25 gift certificates to the Wal-Mart."

In examining the phenomenon of this gargantuan retailing amoeba, three questions naturally arise: How does Wal-Mart keep growing? How can it continue to manage such growth? And what happens after Sam is gone?

"When we were doing $400 million," says Glass, "people said to me, 'Wait till you get to a billion. Things change. You can't do it the way you're doing it now.' So we worked real hard to make sure nothing bad happened at a billion. Then they said $5 billion was the number where everything would fall apart, then $10 billion. Then they said, 'Well, when you move into a new territory you'll have trouble.' So we do all these crazy things to make sure we can still communicate, regardless of our size." Like McDonald's, Wal-Mart has reduced the logistics of growth to a science. The strategy is basically to spread out and fill in. Wal-Mart opens a few stores in a new state or territory, then goes back and saturates that territory, working from a master book of potential sites. The real estate is largely self-financing because institutional investors snap up the stores in sale-leasebacks.

And what of Wal-Mart without Sam? "There's no transition to make," says Glass, "because the principles and the basic values he used in founding this company were so sound and so universally accepted." As for the future, Glass says, "there's more opportunity ahead of us than behind us. We're good students of retailing and we've studied the mistakes that others have made. We'll make our own mistakes, but we won't repeat theirs. The only thing constant at Wal-Mart is change. We'll be fine as long as we never lose our responsiveness to the customer."

STANDOUT IN THE LAND OF CATALOGUES

by Eric N. Berg

Dodgeville, Wis. — In the crowded field of catalogue retailing, Lands' End continues to grow, helped by its folksy approach to selling, devotion to service and deft use of computers.

The Monday after Thanksgiving, Lands' End, whose basic business is selling classic, casual clothing made by others and a line of canvas luggage it manufactures itself, recorded its busiest day ever. Working on a huge selling floor here, Lands' End's 1,350 operators took 78,500 calls on 24-hour toll-free phone lines. Customers ordered everything from brightly colored rugby shirts to Shetland crew sweaters to tartan-plaid boxer shorts.

The holiday season is as important to catalogue houses as it is to other retailers, with up to half of sales made in the month before Christmas.

Now in its 25th years, Lands' End (as a result of a printer's error, the apostrophe turned up in the wrong place in an early catalogue, and the company left it there) has been exceeding even the most optimistic projections by analysts.

In the last four years, sales have grown at a 28.5 percent compound annual rate, reaching $336.3 million in the year ended Jan. 31, while pretax profits have grown at a compound 32.4 percent, to $38.3 million. Return on equity, averaging 45.8 percent, is triple what most big companies earn.

"Lands' End has found a niche, they have stayed with that niche and they have expanded it at a time when mail order is in vogue," said Eric Kramer, a Lands' End customer in Wisconsin who as an investor has followed the company for years.

Lands' End is among dozens of companies that have flourished in recent years in response to a boom in mail-order buying. Unlike Sears, Roebuck & Company, which sells a wide range of merchandise, these companies tend to have specialties.

Some of them are offbeat, mom-and-pop operations like DuSay's, based in Louisiana, which sells sunglasses and hats for pampered poodles, and Life Force, based in Colorado, which sells eavesdropping equipment for the home.

But many others — from L. L. Bean Inc. in camping gear to Sharper Image in high-technology gadgetry — are huge corporations, often publicly held, that mail tens of millions of catalogues a year. Industry experts say an estimated 10,000 companies will mail 11 billion catalogues to consumers this year, up from 4.8 billion in 1980.

"What's happening is a growing confidence that you can buy something successfully without actually touching it," said Richard S. Hodgson, a consultant in Newtown, Pa.

The reasons for the boom are well known: the proliferation of credit cards, the lower cost of toll-free telephone lines, improved printing techniques, widening availability of mailing lists and, most important, a greater emphasis on convenience shopping.

But catalogue merchants are discovering that they have a cost advantage over traditional merchants since they do not need elaborate stores and can locate in low-cost areas. L. L. Bean, for example, is based in Freeport, Me., while J. Crew ships from Lynchburg, Va. Lands' End's huge distribution center here is in a cow pasture.

Copying the Industry Giants

While sales are booming, the industry is also becoming glutted as hundreds of smaller, lesser-known companies try to copy and vie with the giants. With consumers deluged with catalogues, even some of the heavyweights are bowing out.

General Mills, for instance, recently sold its Talbots and Eddie Bauer catalogues. Horchow Mail Order Inc. a gift catalogue, recently sold out to Neiman-Marcus.

"Ultimately, the biggest risk to Lands' End is that a lot of what they do is copyable," said Richard E. Pyle, a managing director at Piper, Jaffray & Hopwood, the Minneapolis-based brokerage. "The $15 turtleneck, the $20 crew-neck sweater, the designer catalogue can all be purchased. So they will have to work harder than the next guy and be smarter, too."

One thing that sets Lands' End apart, however, is its catalogue. The company was founded in 1963 as a sailing hardware company by Gary C. Comer, a former advertising copywriter with Young & Rubicam in Chicago who remains chairman and president. Starting with $30,000 in seed money, Mr. Comer, now 60 years old, was among the earliest to develop the idea of a "magalog"—a catalogue so thick with editorial copy it resembles a magazine.

Essay on Traveling Home

In this year's Christmas issue, Lands' End took a relatively understated approach to the "news" portion of its catalogue: it hired a Chicago Tribune columnist, Eric Zorn, to write an essay about traveling home by train for the holidays, and it included a letters-to-the-editor section and a corrections box. In years past, however, Lands' End's catalogue, which goes to an estimated eight million homes, or one out of 10 households in the nation, has had articles and photographs on everything from wool farming in Australia to cashmere production in Inner Mongolia to madras manufacturing in India.

"The catalogue is extraordinarily persuasive," said Jo-Von Tucker, an industry consultant in New York. "It generates a dialogue with customers that stimulates action."

Sometimes, Lands' End's folksy approach can backfire. A few years ago, for instance, Richard C. Anderson, the company's vice chairman and the editor of the catalogue, got the idea of encouraging customers to call the company's toll-free number just to talk. Lands' End's lines were flooded with calls from lonely hearts and people interested simply in the weather in Dodgeville.

"We even got a couple of heavy breathers," Mr. Anderson recalled, adding that "we get our share of insomniacs and night-shift workers." In fact, the company says that on a good day it receives 30,000 calls, 1,500 between midnight and 6 A.M.

Master of Customer Service

Lands' End is also considered a master of customer service, relying heavily on computers.

Many other catalogue companies, concerned about huge phone bills, encourage operators to keep conversations short. Lands' End authorizes them to stay on the line as long as necessary to close a sale. And the company has spent millions of dollars in recent years writing computer programs that enable its telephone sales representatives to learn, typically in less than a second and a half, whether an item is in stock, and, if not, whether an alternative is on hand.

Of course, Lands' End has its share of problems. Adding names to its eight-million-name mailing list at the rate of a million a year, it has had a mixed record forecasting demand, with the result that it has frequently been saddled with unsold inventory it has been forced to liquidate at low prices through its outlet stores.

But since first being sold to the public in October 1986 at $15 each, Lands' End shares, 60 percent of which are held by Mr. Comer and other insiders, have risen as high as $30, though they have retreated a bit lately amid concerns about weak retail sales in general. The shares closed yesterday at $27.375, unchanged on the New York Stock Exchange.

Bucking the Trend

Lands' End, however, has repeatedly bucked the trend; its sales growth shows no signs of relenting. Indeed, the company will shortly complete a second 250,000-square-foot distribution center, doubling its existing capacity.

The company does not operate any retail stores other than its discount outlets. Even so, summer vacationers regularly travel to Lands' End headquarters in hopes of loading up on the company's clothing. To accommodate them, the company recently set up a limited operation to sell to the public in Dodgeville.

"We'd have carloads of people coming right into our offices looking to buy shirts and sweaters," said Terry W. Wilson, a company spokesman. "Every time you disappoint a customer you've got a problem."

CHARIVARI: NEW YORK'S HOTTEST BOUTIQUE CAUSES AN UPROAR

by Jil Curry

"Of course, the business climate concerns us in 1988. While last year's market collapse didn't affect sales, we're cautious," says Selma Weiser, owner/president of New York's white-hot fashion boutique Charivari.

Weiser, who was on a Spring buying trip in Europe when the stock market began its seemingly never-ending tumble in October, didn't let the collapse unsettle her. She wrote, as planned, the same dollar amount as last year for the six-store operation that attracts the likes of Barbara Streisand, Diana Ross, Diane Keaton and Mariel Hemingway.

Charivari, which celebrated its 20th birthday in 1987, has gained international acclaim among the well-heeled citizens of the world by trafficking in ready-to-wear predominately from the cream of European designers. It was the first store in the United States to stock Yohji Yamamoto clothes.

Source: *California Apparel News*, February 2, 1988. Reprint permission granted, The Apparel News Group.

Today Genny, Montana and Byblos form the backbone of women's wear, which is 55 percent of the store's mix (the rest is men's wear).

Customers have come to rely on the editing genius of Weiser. A former buyer, she admits her greatest asset is her ability to assume many roles. She says, for example, she can picture herself as a banker and project that customer's needs, or she can become a judge, or a gorgeous size 7, or a housewife.

"I buy what I like," she declares. Luckily customers also like the goods—so much so that sales for the six stores, ranging in size from 1,800 to 6,000 square feet, totaled more than $14 million in 1987. All but one of the stores is located within a 20-block radius of New York's fashionable Upper West Side; that unit is off Fifth Avenue on 57th Street, neighbor to Bergdorf Goodman and Henri Bendel.

Despite questions about the economy, Weiser is giving serious consideration to opening "a few stores" on the West Coast. She refuses to be more specific, saying only that "outside influences such as real estate agents have been making some offers that are impossible to refuse."

Evidence for expansion comes from the fact that the operation will shortly be computerized: An SDS computer from Canada will be installed the first quarter of this year. Printouts detailing size, color and number of items sold will give Weiser a daily fix on the business.

So far, Weiser has resisted computers because "our business is very personal," choosing instead to grapple with store tickets at the end of the day to see what's selling. As stores were added, no two were conceived alike. Each was designed to appeal to the multifaceted life styles of monied women. Charivari Workshop, for example, offers the most experimental goods, as typified by Vivienne Westwood and Katharine Hammett, while Charivari Sport features informal wear, and futuristic-looking, multileveled Charivari on 57th Street is rife with the most avant-garde clothes.

Contrary to what most observers think, the mix, says Weiser, consists primarily of "classic, wearable" goods. Only 15 percent, she says, could really be classified as pure fantasy. No matter how you slice it, Charivari merchandise is on the cutting edge of fashion—the one that costs dear. A transitional wool trench coat from Montana, for example, retails for $1,365.

To be part of Charivari's lineup, the merchandise must be "really, really special," says Weiser. New additions this Spring include Italy's Faycal Armor and Helmut Lang (designer for Calla). Also making a (re)appearance is American designer Stephen Sprouse.

As the dollar fluctuates, Weiser would like to sign up more American designers, but claims at this point she is shut out of the market for two reasons. The first concerns distribution. American designers, she notes, have spread themselves too thin and are found in practically every store catering to affluent women. "Why should a customer buy in our store and not another?" the savvy merchant asks. The second reason is even more critical. She has reservations about the quality of American designer apparel. "Our customers have high standards, and these are met by European designers," Weiser emphasizes.

If a line doesn't do as well as she expects, she'll try to find out why by going to the store herself. But with 150 employees, Weiser admits she's finding it harder and harder to get into the stores as she once did.

Weiser puts a lot of time into her job, saying she works six months on merchandise that has a season of eight weeks.

Though she has been in the business for more than 30 years, she still finds it hard to adjust to the fact that she's always working ahead.

Sometimes it also causes her to be removed from the day-to-day doings in the stores. For instance, in the posh 57th Street store friends told her that the salespeople had an attitude problem. "They considered themselves above selling," she explains. "They felt the clothes should sell themselves."

Weiser sees red about this. Salespeople, she says, are as essential as the merchandise. "Customers rely on salespersons' judgment," she stresses. "You'd be amazed how many well-put-together women need assistance." To resolve the problem, she swiftly cleared out the staff and just as quickly brought in new help.

Salespeople have to stay on their toes at Charivari, for sprinkled into the designer merchandise are private label goods and a line that the store wholesales, called Sans Tambours Ni Trompettes, which means "without fanfare." Both lines are sourced abroad.

Sans Tambours, designed by Corinne Delemazure, was introduced this year in women's wear, having made its debut in men's wear a couple of years ago. The line centers around knitwear, jersey dresses and pants. It makes up roughly 20 percent of the store's merchandise mix; private label goods represent less. By nature, Weiser says, the goods are more basic and classic than designer merchandise. While she intends to increase the amount of private label in the store, she says firmly, "We are a designer store."

Each year accessories also become stronger players at Charivari. Sales of hats, gloves and jewelry pushed ahead 20 percent in 1987. And it is here that Weiser lets her imagination run wild. When she was in Florence, for instance, she couldn't resist "big, crazy, floral hats."

Buying responsibilities for women's wear are split between Weiser and her daughter Barbara, who opted to join the business in 1975 after holding a teaching fellowship at Columbia University. Barbara Weiser is perhaps even more fashion forward than her mother. She's the one who scours cities to find merchandise that will inspire customers. She's also the one who discovered Yamamoto clothes in Paris.

But designer merchandise wasn't always synonymous with the name Charivari. When Selma Weiser opened her first store on the Upper West Side, it was filled with Jonathan Logan goods. The year was 1967 and the West Side was the last frontier of New York.

"Young couples and singles were starting to move there," Weiser recalls, "and there was no place to shop." At the time, she was a divorced mother of two, without a job because the New Jersey Chase department store that she worked for had gone out of business.

"Having made a lot of money for other people," she felt it was time to strike out on her own. Of the many stores available, Weiser chose one on Broadway at 85th Street and threw open the doors April 1 — a day that proved auspicious for her.

Her intuition about women wanting to shop near home was on the money. She sold close to 20 percent of the 240 mini-dresses carried and grossed $940. Soon after, the former dress buyer found herself in the sportswear business, securing suede mini-skirts and crepe blouses. These put her on the fashion map in the heady days of mini-dressing.

Today she's come full circle. Short skirts were once more the focus of Charivari this fall. "We couldn't keep them in stock," she says. About 90 percent of the mix was short and it sold, she notes. The 10 percent that was long didn't move out as quickly.

Short will continue to be shown this spring, she says. Beyond that, she won't forecast. "Fashion," she says, "is too unpredictable."

One thing that's not unpredictable is that, no matter what's carried or what shape the economy is in, spirited women who enjoy fashionable clothes will flock to Charivari. It was not for nought that her finger found "charivari" when she was searching *Roget's International Thesaurus* for a name for her store. It means uproar.

TOMORROW'S BUYER: A PRODUCTION EXPERT?

Wanted: "Production Manager/Ladies. The Product Development office of Carter Hawley Hale is currently seeking a manufacturing professional to join our expanding production staff. As Production Manager, you will be responsible for all aspects of production for Ladies woven sportswear and clothing, including pattern-making, factory evaluation and selection, costing, scheduling, tracking, quality control and factory relations. Qualified candidates will have approximately 10 years manufacturing experience and possess a strong knowledge of garment construction, pattern-making and manufacturing operations."

So read a display ad in *Women's Wear Daily*, placed by Carter Hawley Hale Market Services. This ad is a sign of the times. As retailers become more private label-oriented and therefore more production-oriented, they are more frequently staffing offices with product development experts and production managers. This is especially vital as retailers seek to do more sourcing stateside.

As Bernard Wolford, Kurt Salmon Associates, explains, unlike overseas, here there are no agents. "Most department store women's private label merchandise comes from overseas. The agent overseas is a middleman who takes a lot of tasks out of the retailer's hands. But for a retailer who wants to source here, there is no agent to work with contractors of women's wear in Pennsylvania, New Jersey and Chinatown in New York." Believing retailers may get even deeper into production, Wolford makes this prediction: "I see more retailers owning their own manufacturing capability, just as manufacturers are getting their own selling spaces."

Not only are retailers taking production into their own hands, they're also taking on responsibility of creating product from its inception.

A notable change in private label, says Wolford, is "the degree over which the retailer has taken over product development. Rather than producing a knock-off, they are taking it one step farther, with their creative design capability. They're bringing some of the design decision back in house.

"Some are getting quite vertical and ask 'How vertical must I be?' A Marketing

Services Division of Carter Hawley Hale exists to develop and manage execution of their products. At other retail organizations there may be one or two people in-house who speak manufacturing language and talk stitching and wiggles."

Wolford foresees problems if a retailer tries to do all this without people with skills for private label product development. "This person is different from a buyer. There is no co-op money, nobody to take it back," he says.

Ken Sheiffer, a principal of Garland Corp., with both a knit and cut-and-sewn production capability, finds he is dealing more often with retail product development people, a major change from when the knitwear manufacturer first began producing private label apparel several years back. "Before, there were buyers more than product people. Now, buying offices are getting product development people, people who are serious."

He concurs with Wolford about the other important change. Instead of private label programs knocking off brand name or designer styles, as Sheiffer notes was the case as recent as a few years ago, now more original designs are made for private label.

At the same time, Garland's own designers participate in creating retail collections. "A retailer will come in with a design and ask if we can produce it. Once they start talking about cable, we say, 'We have nice cable design our designers found in Europe,' and we start working together on it."

One such product development person fitting the description these men give is Mary Meehan, manager of new product development at Dayton Hudson. There, product development resides in the domain of marketing, so Meehan reports to John Pellegrene, senior vice president, marketing. Meehan, recalling how she had been

"plucked" out of the buying staff four years ago for the post, says enthusiastically, "This has been the greatest job. It has been such an opportunity."

She explains, however, she was not the "business school type buyer." As an art school student in theater design, she had considerable production background and an understanding of how things are made. "I have a whole other point of view. I also know buying. I have more credibility with the buyer. I understand what's going to work and what's not going to work."

Meehan works closely with buyers, who, she explains, make the decisions on what products need to be developed. Buyers also are responsible for sourcing, as Meehan points out, because they travel markets overseas and domestically. "As we get better at doing it, the program gets better. We can really produce the kind of program that makes a private label a success."

Kirk Palmer, Kirk Palmer and Associates, New York–based executive search firm, is on the lookout for product development people, in more demand as retailers develop private label lines from scratch. His clients, who all do private label, some substantial amounts, seek such professionals. This alumnus of The Limited and department stores, observes, "Private label continues to be a growing part of the business. Private label has changed from when a retailer would slap a label on whatever he happened to get. Now the label really stands for something."

He points out that such names as The Limited's Outback Red and The Gap's Hemisphere and Macy's Aeropostale have meaning and identity and that they were developed by the retailers' design and production staffs.

Because of frustrations in working overseas or working here with manufacturers, Palmer predicts: "I wouldn't be at all surprised to see The Limited and others begin to invest in American factories and get factories up to their standards and become partners with them. Most retailers would love to be able to produce domestically. As more of the business they do is private label, they have a vested interest in working with factories. They'll need product development people."

On the new breed of private label people, Palmer says: "I see more opportunity for people with product development and sourcing experience. There are, and will be, a lot of people on the streets. Ones that don't have product development and sourcing experience and extensive overseas background will stay on the streets."

THE LIMITED: SPEEDING INTO THE NINETIES

by Pete Born

New York — Reaching for a more dominant market share, The Limited, Inc., has embarked on an ambitious expansion, driven by larger stores, deeper assortments, a wider merchandiser selection and higher caliber presentation.

After years of patronizing small, tightly focused shops, consumers now prefer to shop in larger specialty stores, The Limited executives believe, and the company's new direction lies in expanded formats. Leslie H. Wexner, chairman and chief executive officer, is building bigger stores with the aim of reaching his previously stated goal of more than doubling volume to $10 billion by the mid-1990s.

The expansion comes at a time when the industry is undergoing what Wexner considers a change to a new generation of retailing, which prizes the agility and quickness necessary to capitalize not only on quicksilver shifts in the consumer taste but new efficiencies and technologies.

"The new era has begun," Wexner told a group of Wall Street analysts meeting at his Columbus, Ohio, headquarters earlier this year. "It will be historic and pivotal. It will be a sunset for some and dawn for others." Last week, The Limited unveiled plans to expand its selling square footage by 18 percent in 1990, adding approximately 2.5 million square feet to its 1989 base of 14.2 million square feet. This represent an addition of 180 to 250 new stores and the remodeling and expansion of 180 to 260 existing units. The bulk of the new units will be built in The Limited Stores, Express, Lerner and Victoria's Secret.

In 1987, The Limited began testing stores two to four times the size of previous formats, and, "results in 1988 and 1989 indicate that the concept is working, in many cases beyond our expectations," Wexner said, adding that the square foot productivity of the new, larger stores already equals the output of the older, smaller stores. Ana-

Source: *Women's Wear Daily*, September 27, 1989. Reprinted with permission.

lysts estimate that figure as approaching $400 a square foot.

Wexner said he sees this development as promising because "I don't think we have yet figured out how to really merchandise, replenish, manage or even design these larger spaces because our skills are in smaller-size stores. So when we can do as well as we're doing on first pass, we see some substantial potential."

Five years ago a typical The Limited Stores division store measured 4,000 square feet. Today, a new store averages 15,000 to 16,000 square feet. Likewise, Express has gone from 3,000 to 7,000 square feet; Lerner from 6,000 to 10,000 square feet, and Lane Bryant from 5,000 to 10,000 square feet. Victoria's Secret stores were opening at 2,400 square feet a year ago. The units now are up to 5,000 square feet.

The shopping center developers were hesitant to lease more space for The Limited stores, although they have since accepted the larger formats. Wexner said the reluctance was understandable since "the generally accepted formula for shopping center space is more stores and less frontage to give a consumer more choices. The industry was and is still largely going in that direction. One hundred feet of frontage gives them one big store or five 20-foot ones. Also the smaller stores could produce greater rents because the smaller tenants pay greater rents," explained Wexner.

Referring to the change in shopping habits, Wexner said, "If you contrast how people shopped 20 years ago, it was almost like one large snake dance going through a shopping center and people just wove in and out of every store, literally going to a shopping center and shopping the entire center."

Now, however, the mood is different. Wexner said that market research by developers indicates that consumers are spending less time in malls shopping fewer stores.

Why consumers are taking to the larger stores, Wexner could only speculate: "People are responding generally to retailers who are offering breadth and depth of assortment in specific categories that provide the consumer with what they perceive to be good service and value.

"I think the physical size of the store relates to a change in preference where people think more about going to what they would perceive as 'the best store for whatever it is'," he said pointing to Toy "R" Us as an example because "they'll have every toy, it'll be in stock and probably at a good price. The same thing is happening in apparel."

The format expansion began in The Limited Stores before spreading to the other divisions. Although The Limited Stores division launched its Casique lingerie and The Limited Too children's business, Wexner maintains that the basic women's assortment has not been expanded dramatically to fill the larger store space. "In the core business without the addition of Casique or Limited Too, the assortment in a 16,000-square-foot store would be a little larger than the assortment in the 4,000-square-foot store. But it essentially is the depth of the inventory and the way the store landscapes.

"What the customer sees is predictability. It's nice to go to A&P and know they are going to have Kellogs cornflakes."

While The Limited's intention is to build large stores wherever possible, the company also is still building smaller units to fit the size of the individual market. "We believe we can build a successful 20,000-square-foot store in Beverly Center. I don't know that Paducah, Ky., would support a 20,000-square-foot store.

"What I believe is the notion of us being capable of flexing the size of the store to the potential of each individual location," he said.

Moreover, the addition of Casique in early 1988 and The Limited Too in late 1987 give shoppers added incentive to visit the store.

"The industry is calling them super-stores," Wexner said, "asserting that what we are really seeing now is maybe a seg-menting of the specialty store business— small, medium and, in fact, large-sized spe-cialty stores."

The Limited's total volume for 1988 increased 15 percent to $4,070,777,000 with a 4 percent increase in net profits to $245,136,000. In the first quarter of this year, net profits boomed ahead by 89 percent to $45,189,000 on a 19 percent sales gain to $964,617,000. For the quarter ended July 29, The Limited's earnings more than doubled from $30,701,000 from $63,781,000.

In a report written by Sosnick and Dorothy Lakner earlier this year, Deutsche Bank estimated The Limited's 1989 sales by division: The Limited Stores, $1,293,000,000; Express, $743 million; Victoria's Secret, $499 million; Lane Bryant, $707 million; Lerner, $966 million; Henri Bendel, $30 million; Abercrombie & Fitch, $50 million; the combined catalog business, $315 mil-lion, and the external sales of the Mast In-dustries apparel manufacturing subsidiary, $25 million. The report also gave a $45 mil-lion estimate for Lerner Woman, which was sold this year. The estimated total sales for 1989 are $4,673,000,000.

Endnotes

1. Department of Commerce, Bureau of the Census, *U.S. Industrial Outlook*, 1990.
2. Leon Harris, *The Merchant Princes*. New York: Harper and Row, 1979.
3. Ibid.
4. Annual company reports.
5. "The Super Specialists," *Stores Magazine*, August 1986.
6. "Merchant to the Millions," Sears, Roebuck and Co. Publication Service, Department 703, Chicago, Ill.
7. Claudia B. Kidwell and Margaret C. Christman, *Suiting Everyone: The De-mocratization of Clothing in America*. Washington, D.C.: Smithsonian Insti-tution Press, 1974.
8. "Targeting Direct Mail," *Stores*, July 1990.
9. Ibid.
10. "Stuffing the Mailbox," *The Wall Street Journal*, June 10, 1989.
11. Ibid.
12. "From Where I Sit," *Women's Wear Daily*, June 20, 1985.
13. Annual company reports.
14. "The Outlet Metamorphosis," a special report by The American Apparel Manufacturers Association, 1990.
15. "Franchising on a Fast Track," *Women's Wear Daily*, March 28, 1989.
16. "From Where I Sit," *Women's Wear Daily*, July 11, 1989.
17. Annual company reports.

18. *Time Magazine*, December 4, 1988.

19. Editorial, *Stores Magazine*, September 1988.

20. "Price Club," *Time Magazine*, December 4, 1988.

21. *Wall Street Journal*, June 9, 1988.

22. Kurt Salmon Perspectives, January 1989.

23. Ibid.

24. "The Super Specialists," *Stores Magazine*, August 1986.

25. "Specialty Shops: King of the Hill," *Women's Wear Daily*, September 16, 1988.

26. "Age of the Superstores," *Morgan Stanley Publication*, January 1989.

27. "A Bargain Basement Where the TV Reception Is Great," *Business Week*, May 30, 1989.

28. *Retailing Technology and Operations*, June 1989.

29. Ibid.

Selected Bibliography

Allen, Randy L. *Bottom Line Issues in Retailing*. New York: Chilton Book Co., 1985.

Brough, James. *The Woolworths*. New York: McGraw-Hill, 1982.

Dressner, Susan. *Shopping on the Inside Track: A Professional Shoppers' Guide to the Best Women's Stores in America's Most Travelled Cities*. New York: Peregrine Smith, 1989.

Fairchild's Financial Manual of Retail Stores. New York: Fairchild Publications, published annually.

Ferkauf, Eugene. *Going into Business, How to Do It, by the Man Who Did It*. New York: Penfield Press, 1977.

Graham, John W. and Susan K. *Selling, Selling by Mail; Direct Response Marketing for Small Business*. New York: Scribner & Sons, 1985.

Guberman, Reuben. *Handbook of Retail Promotion Ideas*. Reading, Mass.: Addison-Wesley, 1981.

Harris, Leon. *Merchant Princes*. New York: Harper and Row, 1979.

Hartley, Robert F. *Retailing: Challenge and Opportunity*, 2nd ed. Boston: Houghton Mifflin, 1980.

Herndon, Booton. *Satisfaction Guaranteed*. New York: McGraw-Hill, 1972.

Hoge, Cecil W. *The First 100 Years Are the Toughest: What We Can Learn from the Century of Competition between Sears and Wards*. Berkeley, Calif.: Ten Speed Press, 1988.

Horchow, Roger. *Elephants in Your Mailbox*. New York: Times Books, 1980.

Katz, Donald R. *The Big Store: Inside the Crisis and Revolution at Sears.* New York: Viking Press, 1987.

Kowinski, William S. *The Malling of America.* New York: Wm. Morrow Publishers, 1985.

McCree, Cree. *Flea Market America: A Bargain Hunter's Guide.* Santa Fe: Muir, 1983.

Mahoney, Tom, and Leonard Sloane. *The Great Merchants,* 2nd ed. New York: Harper & Row, 1974.

Marcus, Stanley. *His and Hers: The Fantasy World of the Neiman Marcus Catalog.* New York: Viking Press, 1982.

Marcus, Stanley. *Minding the Store.* Boston: Little, Brown, 1974.

Marcus, Stanley. *Quest for the Best.* New York: Viking Press, 1979.

National Retail Merchants Association. *The Buyers Manual.* New York: NRMA, 1979.

Nystrom, Paul H. *Fashion Merchandising.* New York: Ronald Press, 1932.

Ostrow, Rona, and Sweetman R. Smith. *The Dictionary of Retailing.* New York: Fairchild Publications, 1985.

Pegler, Martin M. *Stores of the Year,* 4th ed. New York: Fairchild Books, 1988.

Peters, Tom, and Nancy Austin. *A Passion for Excellence: The Leadership Difference.* New York: Random House, 1985.

Segal, Marvin. *From Rags to Riches: Success in Apparel Retailing.* New York: John Wiley & Sons, 1982.

Stevens, Mark. *Like No Other Store in the World: The Inside Story of Bloomingdale's.* New York: Thomas Y. Crowell, 1979.

Stone, Elaine, and Jean A. Samples. *Fashion Merchandising,* 5th ed. New York: McGraw-Hill, 1989.

Stutz, Geraldine. *Designing to Sell: A Complete Guide to Retail Store Planning and Design.* New York: McGraw-Hill, 1985.

Weil, Gordon L. *Sears, Roebuck, U.S.A.* New York: Stein & Day, 1977.

Trade Associations

Direct Selling Association, 1730 M Street, N.W., Washington, D.C. 20036.

International Council of Shopping Centers, Inc., 665 Fifth Avenue, New York, N.Y. 10022.

Men's Retailers Association, 2011 Eye Street, N.W., Washington, D.C. 20006.

Menswear Retailers of America, 390 National Press Building, Washington, D.C. 20045.

National Mass Retailing Institute, 570 Seventh Avenue, New York, N.Y. 10018.

National Retail Merchants Association, 100 West 31st Street, New York, N.Y. 10001.

Trade Publications

Apparel Merchandising, 425 Park Avenue, New York, N.Y. 10022.

Chain Store Age, 425 Park Avenue, New York, N.Y. 10022.

Department Store Guide, Inc., 425 Park Avenue, New York, N.Y. 10022.

Discount Merchandiser, 641 Lexington Avenue, New York, N.Y. 10022.

Discount Store News, 425 Park Avenue, New York, N.Y. 10022.

Franchising Today, 3106 Diablo Avenue, Haywood, Calif. 94545.

Franchising World, 1025 Connecticut Avenue, N.W., Washington, D.C. 20036.

Retail Week, 370 Lexington Avenue, New York, N.Y. 10022.

Stores Magazine, 100 West 31st Street, New York, N.Y. 10001.

Women's Wear Daily, 7 East 12th Street, New York, N.Y. 10003.

CHAPTER REVIEW AND LEARNING ACTIVITIES

Key Words and Concepts

Define, identify, or briefly explain the following:

Apparel specialty chain	Mall
Boutique	Mom-and-pop store
Branch store	National brand
Catalog showroom retailer	Off-price retailer
Chain store	Party plan
Department store	Price Club
Direct-selling retailer	Private label
Discounter	Product development
Factory outlet	Quick Response
Flea market	Retailer
Franchise	Shopping center
Franchisee	Specialty store
Franchisor	Store ownership group
General merchandising chain	Supermarket
Hypermarket	Television marketing
Mail-order house	Warehouse club

Review Questions on Chapter Highlights

1. In what types of retail establishment do you prefer to shop and why? What types do you avoid and why?
2. Describe the targeted customer of the typical department store.

3. What is a store ownership group? How does it differ from chain operations?

4. What are the competitive advantages of apparel specialty stores compared with department stores?

5. Compare the operations of a department store and its branches with chain store operations. How are they similar and how do they differ?

6. Why is mail-order retailing so important today? Name different types of retailers that are in the mail-order business.

7. How can off-price retailers such as Marshall's undersell conventionally priced retailers? What are their sources of supply?

8. How are large department and specialty stores meeting the competition of the underselling retailers?

9. Name the different types of electronic marketing in existence today. Do you use any of them? Why or why not?

10. Describe some of the major changes that are taking place in the field of retailing and illustrate with company names.

11. Name the different types of retailers, give the approximate date of their emergence, and explain the social and economic factors that led to their development.

12. What is a private label and how does it differ from a national brand?

13. What is your opinion about the future importance of apparel selling by electronic retailers, price clubs, catalog showrooms, and others? Why?

14. List the different types of retailing and explain the distinctive operational characteristics of each. Cite an example of each type in your own community.

15. In one of the readings, Wal-Mart is called "America's most admired retailing company." Why?

16. Name and identify the different types of retailers featured in this chapter's readings.

Auxiliary Fashion Enterprises

Of vital importance in the fashion industry are the services of a variety of independently operated auxiliary enterprises that act as advisers, sources of information, and propagators of fashion news. Some of these enterprises devote their full energies to observing and analyzing the fashion scene, and assist producers and retailers in clarifying their own thinking about it. Others aid by getting a coherent fashion message to the consuming public, thus giving impetus to trends that appear to be in the making. Among these fashion business auxiliaries are fashion information and advisory services, the news media, fashion video producers, advertising and publicity specialists, resident buying offices, and others.

This chapter discusses such enterprises, how they function, and the part they play in the fashion business. The readings that follow the text are concerned with the activities of companies that operate in this segment of the fashion business.

FASHION INFORMATION AND ADVISORY SERVICES

Although all fashion producers and retailers of any size have experts of their own within their firms, many use outside specialized sources of fashion information against which to check their own analyses and conclusions.

Fashion Information Services

Beginning in the late 1960s and growing in importance ever since then, a number of comprehensive **fashion information services** have developed. Their clients are worldwide and include fiber companies; textile producers; producers of men's, women's, and children's wear; retailers; buying offices; and accessories and cosmetics companies. So all-pervading is the influence of fashion, however, that their clients also include some producers of small appliances, cars, home furnishings, and other consumer products.

In a business environment where time and timing are ever more important, these services offer specific, timely, concise, and complete worldwide information, often tailored to each client's specific needs.

The number of firms offering these services is constantly increasing, but the following are among the most important:

- Nigel French, headquartered in London. Their fabric reports cover the major fabric seasons — Spring/Summer and Fall/Winter — including the Interstoff and American fabric showings. They also issue separate color and knitwear brochures, report on New York and European designer collections, and present major season styling issues.
- The Fashion Service, known as TFS, whose reports cover fashion information from all over the world. Their specific reports are covered in a reading in this chapter.
- Here and There, whose reports cover U.S. ready-to-wear, couture collections, Japanese Prêt collections, Italian and French knitwear shows, fabric fairs (Interstoff, Ideacomo, Premier Vision, Prato), and a special feature that translates high fashion looks for mass markets.
- Promostyl, which began as a children's wear service in 1967. They now have offices or agents in 23 cities worldwide, and publish 31 different handbooks annually.
- Stylists' Information Service (SIS). Their reports include "The Boutique Forecast" (twice a year), "The Children's Forecast" (twice a year), "The Eveningwear Forecast" (once a year), "The Menswear Forecast" (twice a year), "The Lingerie Forecast" (once a year), "The Women's Actualwear Forecast" (twice a year), and "The Trimming and Finishing Book" (once a year).
- Karten for Kids is published eight times a year and Karten for Little Kids (or infants and toddlers to the age of two) is published twice a year.

Other fashion information services include Pat Tunsky, Color Box, and Fashion Works, Inc. And the list grows from year to year!

Consultants

A **fashion consultant** is an independent individual or firm hired by fashion producers and retailers to assist them in some phase of their fashion operation. Probably the oldest still in existence is **Tobé Associates**, founded in 1927 by

Report from the TFS Fashion Service

Specialized *Activewear/Sportswear* information system for Men, Women and Kids. Summer and Winter Sports. 6 issues per year.

FORECAST:
Advanced Information...
*Colour specially targeted to Activewear
*Fabric: Fashion and Technical swatches
*Trends and Concepts: Styling Ideas, Garments, Details, Trims, Motifs.

WHOLESALE:
Reports on Activewear Fairs..
*ISPO, SISEL, Mode Sport
*200 Colour Slides per year
*Comprehensive Report with Black & White, easy-to-read photos
*Slide Presentations from St. Tropez, the Fairs, and the Street Scenes of Paris and Munich.

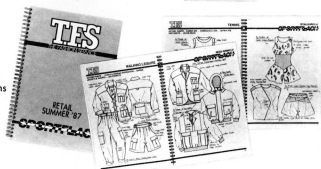

RETAIL:
Detailed Retail Sketches of the HOTTEST items from around-the-world
*Specific ACTIVEWEAR items drawn in detail
*Paris, London, Munich, Amsterdam, New York
*Men's, Women's.

TFS SPORTFLASH

SOURCE: Courtesy of TFS Forecasters.

Mrs. Tobé to service retailers. The firm sends to its paying clients a multipage, illustrated weekly brochure that contains information on current and coming trends illustrated by specific style numbers with the names of the producers and the wholesale prices. As Tobé herself once described the function of her consulting firm,

> We are the reporters and interpreters of the fashion world speaking to the fashion-makers and the fashion sellers. . . . Our job is to tell the makers what the sellers are doing and vice versa. Most of all, we interpret and evaluate for each what is happening to fashion itself. . . . We make it our business to stay abreast of those economic, social, and art trends which I maintain are the great formative currents of fashion. . . . From all these we try to pick the significant trends that will change our lives, and hence our fashions. . . . We keep an eye on what those in the fashion vanguard are wearing and doing and seeing. This not only means reporting on what smart people wear. . . . It also means keeping abreast of what plays, films, and TV presentations they are seeing, which are successful, where they travel, and what books they read. . . . All of this information flows into our offices, where it is digested, sorted out, evaluated, and then disseminated through a weekly report. . . . Our clients— department stores throughout America, specialty stores in Europe, a wool manufacturer in Finland, the Export Institute in Israel—they can all shop the Fifth Avenue stores, the Paris showings, the Seventh Avenue showings, without budging from their desks. They can keep track of resort life without going to Monaco or Florida or the Caribbean. They can read about the fads, as well as the foundations of fashion, without spending much time or effort in research.
>   So it is our business as a whole to interpret the current scene to the makers and sellers of fashion wares.[1]

A reading at the end of this chapter gives specific information about what Tobé Associates does and how it does it.

Another example of a retail consultant is Merchandising Motivation, Inc. (MMI), which is operated on a similar but smaller scale. There are also many other consulting firms, usually headed by former fashion practitioners, whose services are available, for a fee, to retailers or producers, or both. These firms usually deal with specific areas of the fashion industry, such as accessories, fibers, fabrics, children's wear, and menswear.

RESIDENT BUYING OFFICES: MARKET REPRESENTATIVES

The **resident buying office** is almost entirely a twentieth-century phenomenon. It has gone through cycles that faithfully reflect the ups and downs in the fortunes of retailers and manufacturers. It performs a paid service for the retailer in helping him or her locate desirable goods in the market; it performs an equally important but unpaid service for manufacturers by bringing their merchandise to the attention of retailers when it meets their needs and standards.

Originally, almost every large store outside New York City was affiliated with an independent buying office, either serving that store alone or serving many noncompeting retailers. Buying office functions included reporting market information, acting as a representative of its client stores, and performing related services for its retail clients. Today, as it did then, the buying office keeps stores informed of fashion, price, and supply developments, and acts as eyes and ears for the client stores. Buying activities are initiated by the store buyers; the office supplements but does not replace the store staff. The functions of the buying office have expanded over the years, reflecting changes in retail needs and in fashion markets, and they continue to change with the times.

Among the newest and now one of the most important services rendered by buying offices is product development, whereby the design staff of the buying office develops private label merchandise specifically tailored to the needs of their client stores.

Types of Resident Offices

Resident buying offices fall into two major categories: (1) those that are independently owned enterprises and receive fees from the stores they serve and (2) those that are store owned or corporate owned.

INDEPENDENTLY OWNED OR FEE OFFICES

Independently owned offices, also known as salaried or **fee offices**, are run as private enterprises. Member or subscribing stores pay a yearly fee, usually based on a percentage of annual sales volume. Most such offices concentrate on serving specialty stores that carry all or most types of apparel and accessories. Others specialize in such narrow categories as large, petite, or tall sizes; bridal, maternity, or junior wear; off-price apparel; fabrics, accessories; men's and boys' wear, or home furnishings. A few concentrate on filling the needs of small department stores, representing them in all the markets of interest to these clients.

Because buying offices exist at the pleasure of the retail community they serve, the mergers and acquisitions that have changed retailers' ownership in recent years have seen an accompanying phenomenon in buying offices.

Within the past several years, many changes have taken place. Felix Lilienthal and Co., the oldest privately owned buying office, founded in 1909, closed its doors, as did Mutual Buying Syndicate. Henry Doneger Associates, which had acquired Jerry Bernstein, Hilda Bridals, the Buying Connection, and Steinberg-Kass among others, merged with Independent Retailers Syndicate to form the new Doneger Group. This company now operates 11 specialized divisions, including Doneger Menswear, Doneger Kidswear, Doneger Buying Connection, and the Fashion Authority. Each of these divisions is focused to serve the specific needs of specific segments of the client stores' businesses. Other mergers include Van Buren–Neiman Associates and Carr Associates into Van Buren/Carr Associates; Burns-Winkler Associates acquired Young Innovators; and Certified Buying Service and Youth Fashion Guild merged to become Certified Fashion Guild. In 1989, Van Buren/Carr Associates and Burns-Winkler/Innovator merged into VBW Associates.[2]

Specialized buying offices, which can best serve the needs of discounting retailers, include off-price offices such as Price Breakers, Ilene Silver's Good Buys, Brand and Buying Service, O.P.'s Only, and Jerri Pollack. Among other offices are Lee Lorraine, specializing in large and tall sizes, and Betty Cohen, which caters to the "carriage trade" specialty retailers.[3]

When buying offices were first established in New York, they were vital since they offered store owners (outside the marketplace) access to new and current information, increased purchasing power because of their size, and an opportunity to share or exchange information. Today, as major retailers grow bigger and their buying clout also grows bigger, buying offices must change their service menu. One of their major roles now is to facilitate imports and

Logos of Frederick Atkins's Member Stores

private label programs. Another major function is to provide personalized services such as executive searching, and personal market service with and without the presence of the store owner, and to seek out new and unusual resources to provide smaller stores with unusual merchandise.

STORE-OWNED OFFICES: COOPERATIVE OFFICES

Unlike the privately owned, profit-oriented fee offices, the resident offices that are store owned are controlled and supported by the stores they serve. Their major objectives are to provide market expertise and whatever additional services the supporting stores require to assist them in operating profitably.

A **cooperative buying office** is one owned and maintained by a group of stores that it serves exclusively. This type of office is also known as an *associated office*. Membership in the store group is by invitation only, and all the participants in such groups are major retailers within their respective areas.

One of the major and best known of such offices is the Associated Merchandising Corporation (AMC), founded in 1918 by Filene's of Boston; F. & R. Lazarus of Columbus, Ohio; J. L. Hudson of Detroit; and Rike's of Dayton. Other stores, such as Abraham & Straus of Brooklyn, Bloomingdale's of New York, Shillito's of Cincinnati, Foley's of Houston, Sanger-Harris of Dallas, and Burdine's of Miami, soon joined. Membership grew, attracting foreign as well as U.S. stores. In October 1984, however, the Federated Department Stores ceased using the AMC's domestic service in favor of its own corporate office.

Today AMC considers its most vital function to be its long-standing overseas operation with 26 offices located in faraway places such as Paris, London, Montevideo, Osaka, and Casablanca, where more than 1,100 employees find local resources, inspect merchandise, handle orders and bills, and work with store buyers when they shop markets. In 1989, AMC stores imported more than $1 billion worth of merchandise at first cost—almost $4 billion at retail prices. A special team of designers and product developers create three sportswear lines for Sears, Roebuck and Co., one of AMC's clients. Clients include Dayton-Hudson and Casual Corner. When Allied Stores and Batus, Inc. closed their overseas offices, they too became members of AMC overseas, bringing in such stores as Saks Fifth Avenue, Marshall Field, and Jordon Marsh.

The headquarters of AMC are located in the heart of the garment district, where 400 employees including a team of product managers work with AMC design studios to develop its stable of 38 private labels which include Preswick and Moore, and Once Upon a Time for infants and toddlers. Samples are presented at a meeting to all store members, and stores shop AMC apparel lines as they would any vendor's offers.[4] A reading at the end of this chapter gives an inside look at AMC's operations.

The other major cooperative buying office is Frederick Atkins, Inc., which describes itself as an "international research and merchandising organization, jointly owned by 27 department store groups in the United States and five major retailers outside of the United States who are associate members." The combined total annual sales volume of the member stores in the United States only is well over $7 billion. The Atkins office is headquartered in New York City, where it occupies 110,000 square feet on four floors. The office is organized like a department store, with three main divisions: merchandising, operations, and finance. On the staff of more than 400 people are the counterparts of every major executive in a store.[5]

Some of the member stores at Atkins are Adam, Meldrum, and Anderson of Buffalo; and H. C. Prange Co., Elder-Beerman, Dillard's, McCurdy's, Younker's, Hess Brothers, and ZCMI. Overseas members include Harvey Nichols & Co. Ltd.; David Jones, Australia; and Trimingham, Bermuda.

CORPORATE OFFICES

Another very important type of office is the **corporate buying office**, which is owned and financed by a store ownership group and services only the stores of that group. Unlike the homogeneous mix of stores served by cooperative offices, some of the store ownership groups consist of both large and small stores. Examples are May Department Stores, Carter Hawley Hale, R. H. Macy & Co., Mercantile Stores, T. Eaton, Belk Stores, and Batus Corp. In the case of each of these corporate offices, the combined volume of the stores it serves makes it a very important factor in the marketplace.

The large cooperative and corporate buying offices may also maintain branch offices in other U.S. market centers, and in many foreign countries to assist their stores in import buying. R. H. Macy's and May Department Stores maintain and staff their own offices both in New York and overseas, where they employ product developers and design teams to perform the same functions as AMC. They also generally have a presence in the Los Angeles market and an office in Washington, D.C. In addition, they use the services of commissionaires in foreign countries. Frederick Atkins has commissionaires in 27 European, Asian, and South American cities, to "help to develop and maintain foreign resource relationships, assist the office and store personnel on overseas trips set up meetings, and follow through on orders after the buyers have left."[6]

Fashion Merchandising Services Provided

The degree, extent, and quality of services vary from one office to another, depending on its financial capabilities and the needs of its member stores. Essentially, however, they all serve the same function—to make available to their members complete and accurate merchandise information from all parts of the world. The president of Van Buren–Neiman, a major buying office, has said: "The term buying office is an anachronism. Our office is a market researcher and consultant—an additional service tool, not a substitute for the stores we represent."[7]

MARKET INFORMATION

Prior to each major selling season, **market representatives** cover the segments of the wholesale markets for which they are responsible and present written surveys to their member stores. These reports cover market conditions in general and analyze specific fashion classifications by trend, look, price lines, and resources. In addition, many offices hold semiannual fashion clinics or meetings in which they orally present this information and show samples. During the season, news bulletins go out continually, reporting new items, best sellers, price changes, fashion developments, supply conditions, important new resources, and other developments.

BUYING SERVICES

When buyers of member stores are in the market themselves, the market representatives act as advisers and time savers by setting up appointments, recommending important suppliers, and sometimes accompanying them into the wholesale markets. When the store buyers return home, the office representative will, if requested, follow up on shipments of orders that store buyers have placed. During the season, if asked to do so by store buyers, they will place fill-in orders and reorders to ensure faster delivery. In addition, they may send out bulletins with suggested orders attached, to be confirmed by the store buyer. Sometimes store buyers may allocate a small portion of their available open-to-buy to their market representatives to be used at the latter's discretion for an important new fashion item. Some store buyers send copies of their orders to their resident offices to follow up on delivery. It must be emphasized again, however, that the role of a market representative is to service store buyers—not to substitute for or replace them. They do not have the "power to buy" except when given permission by the store to do so. All of the purchasing done by market representatives is ordered under the name of the member store and delivered to and paid for by that store. This procedure prevails in resident offices of all types—fee, associated, or corporate.

GROUP PURCHASING, PRIVATE LABEL, AND IMPORT PROGRAMS

A **group purchase** is an order placed at the same time by a group of stores for the identical merchandise from the same supplier. Through domestic or foreign group purchases, all participants can benefit from the various advantages of large-quantity purchases: lower than regular prices, exclusive rights to the merchandise purchased, production of an item that is not otherwise available, a lower-priced "knock-off" of a fast-selling higher priced style in which the buyers have confidence, the production of merchandise made to the exact specifications of the purchasing group, merchandise for a group mailing piece

Attention: Better Misses Casual Wear Buyers

From: Odile de Candia, Buyer
Judith Loewe, D.M.M. Sportswear

Subject: CALVIN KLEIN SPORT

Style: SS5301 Line Price: $26.00
Description: L/S "classic" shirt w/"monogram CK pocket
Sizes: S–M–L Color: White (only) Fabric: 100% cotton

Style: S42111 Line Price: $26.00
Description: 5 pocket "classic" jean
Sizes: 4–14 Colors: Natural, white, indigo, black
Fabric: 100% cotton

Style: SS2507 Line Price: $42.00
Description: L/S "classic" crew w/"CK" logo
Sizes: S–M–L Colors: Ivory, stone, bisque, straw, rose, melon
Fabric: 100% cotton

Style: S71212 Line Price: $36.00
Description: Country plaid welt pocket trouser
Sizes: 4–14 Color: Brown Fabric: 100% cotton

Delivery: A/R 11/10
Terms: 8/10
F.O.B.: MA

CALVIN KLEIN SPORT
205 West 39th Street, 12th Fl.
New York, NY 10018
Contact: Helaine Elias
(212) 726-8100
Dun# 03-321-1640
FAX #: (212) 869-9891

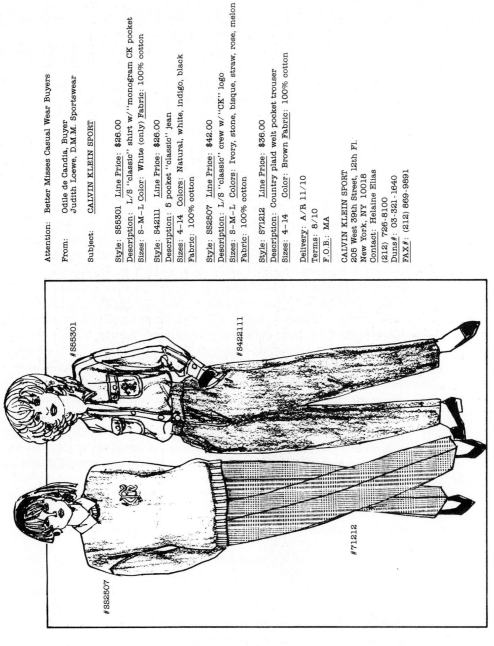

SS2507 #71212 #SS5301 #S422111

CALVIN KLEIN SPORT

SOURCE: Van-Buren-Neiman Associates buying office. Reprint permission granted.

such as a Christmas catalog, merchandise for a private label group program, or a combination of these advantages.

Many resident offices—both independent and store owned—organize, coordinate, and implement such group buying activities for their members. However, such group purchasing programs must be supported by a sufficient number of stores to make them feasible. In addition, the merchandise selected for purchase must be agreed on by (at the very least) a committee of participating store buyers.

In the area of private label, Frederick Atkins has a staff of highly skilled, experienced buyers called **product developers**, whose single responsibility is to develop program merchandise, made to exact specifications, exclusively for member stores.[8] The sourcing for all these private label goods is worldwide.

CENTRALIZED MERCHANDISING

Although declining in importance, some fee offices continue *centralized buying* of budget-priced ready-to-wear and accessories. This means that a market representative of the office makes the selection of styles for each store's stock within the framework of a budget allotment set by that participating store. The office orders the merchandise and, guided by sales and stock reports from the store, reorders some styles and discontinues or replaces others. With the experience of many stores to draw on, the office has a national picture of fashion trends to guide its selections.

SALES PROMOTION

In addition to their buying activities, resident buying offices maintain departments that prepare catalogs and other direct mailing pieces for use by their member stores. Some offices also prepare advertising mats that suggest layouts and copy, supply stores with illustrated suggestions for visual merchandising, and provide a variety of other sales promotion aids. In addition, they prepare visual merchandise aids, develop marketing techniques, and keep member stores advised of emerging media and technology.

EXCHANGE OF INFORMATION

The exchange of merchandise information is a service provided by all types of offices. However, cooperative and corporate offices also consolidate merchandising, operating, and financial figures sent to them by their members and report these cumulative figures back to the stores in a form that enables those participating to compare their operations.

FASHION IN THE NEWS MEDIA _____

Fashion is news, and the news media cover it, both in editorial treatments and in paid advertising messages. This statement applies not only to newspapers and magazines but also to broadcast media. Thus, a vital means of communication between the industry and the consumer, and between related parts of the industry, is activated in the daily newspapers, news magazines, women's and men's magazines, specialized fashion publications, those segments of the trade press that affect the fashion business, radio, and television. The impact is enormous.

Fashion Magazines

Fashion magazines, whose major activity is to report and interpret fashion news to the consumer, together with additional features for balanced reading fare, have been functioning in this country for more than a century. *Godey's Lady's Book*, which was started in 1830, carried pictures of the latest fashions, gave advice on fabrics, contained other helpful hints, and, of course, included advertising. Its distinguished editor, Sara Joseph Hale, gave early proof that a woman could have a successful career in the business world even in the days of hoop skirts and cinched waists. Its masculine counterpart, *Burton's Gentlemen's Magazine*, also had an editor whose name acquired luster: Edgar Allan Poe. His editorial career there was brief, however—from 1839 to 1840.

The present-day roster of fashion magazines is in the midst of an explosive change. The old tried and true magazines such as *Harper's Bazaar, Vogue, Glamour, Mademoiselle,* and *Seventeen* have suddenly been subjected to a barrage of competition from new and exciting magazines. The entrance of *Elle* as an important fashion book started an avalanche that now includes *Mirabella* (headed by Grace Mirabella, the long-time editor of *Vogue*), *Lear, Vanity Fair, Details, M, Inc., Savvy, Model, Taxi, La Style, In Fashion*, and others. How many will stand the test of time is hard to say, but the competition for fashion readership is keen, and the established older books are experimenting with new formats and features to try to keep their circulation and revenue figures up. In menswear, *Gentlemen's Quarterly* and *Esquire* remain the major purveyors of fashion news.

ROLE OF FASHION MAGAZINES

The role of fashion magazines is a many-sided one. As fashion reporters, their editors shop the wholesale markets both here and abroad, to select and feature styles they consider newsworthy for their individual audiences. As fashion influentials, these editors sometimes take an active part in the production of merchandise by working closely with manufacturers to create merchandise that they consider acceptable to their readers. They participate in distribution by contacting retailers and urging them to carry and promote the designs they

Selected Examples of Fashion Magazine Covers

feature and to emphasize the trends endorsed editorially. Finally, they provide their readers with information not only about the styles they recommend, but also about who produces them and who sells them at retail.

An important tool of their activities, and of other consumer magazines that cover fashions to a lesser extent, is the **editorial credit**. This is how it operates: The editors select garments and accessories that, to their minds, exemplify fashion news. They photograph and show these styles in their pages, identifying the makers and naming one or more retail stores in which the consumer can buy them, and usually citing the approximate price. The magazine's sponsorship and the editorial mention encourage the makers to produce the garments in good supply, the retailers to stock them, and the customer to buy. Even in stores that do not have editorial credits for it, a fashion item featured in a strong magazine may be given special attention. If the magazine concerned has a good following among the store's customers, the editorial sponsorship becomes a selling point of the garment not only to consumers but also to the merchant. The style is then stocked, advertised, and displayed, and the magazine's name is usually featured in ads and displays. Hangtags on the garment and magazine blow-ups in the displays remind the customer that this is the style he or she saw in the publication. The magazine, of course, provides the tags and the blow-ups.

DEPENDENCE ON ADVERTISING REVENUE

Like most publications, fashion magazines derive their principal revenue from the sale of advertising space. In 1988, a single black-and-white page in *Vogue*, *Mademoiselle*, or *Glamour* ranged in price from $18,320 too $34,140, and a four-color page began at $23,620 and went up to $48,120.[9] In general magazines such as *Reader's Digest* or women's magazines such as *McCall's*, the rates were about $90,000 a page in black and white. Naturally, a high ratio of advertising to editorial pages means a prosperous magazine. Although conditions vary from issue to issue and from year to year, advertising generally accounts for nearly half the total number of pages in a consumer fashion magazine.

Dependency on dollars from advertisers instead of dollars from subscribers is not always conducive to unbiased fashion reporting; it can result in a conflict between editorial comment and advertising interests. Editorial mentions of merchandise bring to producers highly desirable publicity and prestige, since the editorial pages tend to have more authority in the reader's eyes than do pages devoted to paid advertising. Thus, firms that buy space in a magazine and contribute toward keeping it profitable are likely to protest if they are not given adequate editorial attention. Such a clash of interests often makes objective fashion reportage difficult, if not impossible.

The money the advertiser spends for a page is, in simplest terms, spent to influence customers to buy its product. If a publication can show tangible evidence that it can move merchandise into the retail store and then out into the consumer's hands, its chances of selling advertising space improve.

Magazines confirm that to attract advertisers, nothing is more important to fashion magazines than their relation to stores. This fact accounts for the increasingly large staffs of departments almost unknown to their readers — promotion and merchandising. The merchandising editors act as the liaison between the fashion editors, the advertising staff, and the retail stores. Their job is to ensure that editorialized and advertised merchandise will be placed in retail stores where readers can buy it. They do this by telling the retailers what the magazine is featuring and why — and where to purchase it. Then they list for their readers' information the names of stores where the merchandise can be found. This service to the reader also helps impress the advertisers with the magazine's selling power among retailers.

SERVICES TO THE INDUSTRY

The closer their relationship with both the producers and retailers, the easier it is for magazines to attract advertising. To cement these relationships, many free services are offered by fashion publications. Their staff members keep fabric and apparel producers informed on new trends and advise them on ways and means of selling merchandise. The fashion editors encourage them to manufacture items for which they anticipate a demand and, secure in the knowledge that the items will be featured by the editors, the producers will plunge ahead. The merchandising and promotion departments provide advertisers with "ad advertised" blow-ups to distribute to their retail accounts. In addition, most magazines that are active in fashion prepare, well in advance of each season, fashion forecasts of their color predictions for the guidance of manufacturers and retailers alike. These forecasts show the colors, specific styles, and resources that will be featured in the magazine.

In developing a close relationship with retail stores, the fashion magazines make themselves a source of information for them. To make their editorialized and advertised merchandise desirable to retailers and, ultimately, to their customers, the merchandising departments prepare elaborate retail store kits that, along with the list of sources for featured garments, contain suggestions for advertising, fashion shows, and display. The kits also include selling aids such as hangtags, signs, and other promotional materials. If an important retailer requests the service, the magazine will send a representative to commentate a fashion show. Members of the magazine staff are also available in their offices at almost any time to show samples of merchandise to retailers who call, and thus encourage buyers to visit the producers of the featured apparel and accessories.

Most of the consumer magazines, including those primarily concerned with fashion, also maintain research departments. A function of these departments is to survey the readers of the magazine and compile information about their buying power, living patterns, and merchandise preferences. *Glamour*, for example, surveys young career women and college students periodically and compiles reports for retailers and manufacturers about what these women buy, how much they spend, and similar information. The fashion magazines, then, not only interpret the fashion for their readers but also interpret their readers for their industry. In the process, they serve as a clearinghouse for information in the fashion field.

Compared with consumer magazines of general interest, such as *Reader's Digest*, with a circulation of more than 16 million in 1989, or women's magazines such as *McCall's*, with a circulation of about 5.1 million, the fashion magazines have smaller circulations. *Glamour*, the largest, has a circulation of 2,190,027; *Seventeen* has 1,803,549, followed by *Mademoiselle* with a readership of 1,283,242 and *Vogue* with 1,202,471.[10] Their influence in the fashion business, individually and collectively, is great and far out of proportion to their actual circulation. Fashion editors ignore styles and designers in whom they have little faith but give a great amount of free publicity to those they favor.

Ordinarily, however, what they do is try to pick the most dramatic, the most exciting fashions—not always the most wearable, but the ones that will attract attention.

Newspapers and General Magazines

As mentioned earlier, almost all newspapers devote space to fashion. Coverage varies, of course, in both amount and depth. A paper with the facilities of the *New York Times* may have its experts report on the Paris openings and express opinions that are read by consumers and trade professionals alike. A small-town paper, on the other hand, may assign its society editor to fill out the fashion pages with items about fashion, clipped from what the wire services send, what comes in by way of press releases, or what the local retailers supply. Each paper's policy and the interests of its readers determine how much space the publication devotes to fashion news.

Among magazines not in the fashion-magazine category there is also coverage of fashion, and it varies with the nature of the publication. Fashion editors of such media, looking at the fashion scene through the eyes of their average reader, will select for illustration and comment only the items of interest to the young mother, the working woman, the ageless city sophisticate, the sportsman, the young male executive, or whoever the particular audience may be.

Some of the general magazines show merchandise and give editorial credit; others, like the *New Yorker*, show no merchandise but discuss what the shops are showing. The activities of their fashion editors, as in the case of newspapers, vary according to the importance that each publication and its readers attach to fashion information.

Trade Publications

There is a special field of journalism known as business or **trade publishing**. Some business newspapers and magazines in the fashion field concern themselves with a particular classification of merchandise, from raw material to the sale of the finished product. These publications are not addressed to the ultimate consumer but to the fashion professionals concerned with the manufacturing and distribution of that merchandise. Typical examples are *Textile Age* and *Bobbin Magazine*. Other business publications devote themselves to only one aspect of production or retailing and have a horizontal readership. Examples of these publications are *Stores* magazine, which goes to department store management, and *Chain Store Age*, for chain store management. Fairchild's *Women's Wear Daily*, which is published five times a week, covers the fashion waterfront in the women's fashion business—raw materials, manufacturing, retailing, and how the trend setters among the consuming public dress. Founded in 1890 by E. W. Fairchild, it has headquarters in New York City and maintains offices in cities throughout the United States and Europe—even in Asia. *Women's Wear Daily* reports collections, trade conventions, fashion events,

The Fashion Industry "Bibles"

SOURCE: Mastheads/reprinted with permission of Women's Wear Daily and the Daily News Record.

new technical developments at all stages of production, personnel changes at the executive level, the formation of new fashion businesses—and the wardrobes and activities of prominent individuals. It is often called the industry's "bible" and no women's fashion enterprise is without its copy of *Women's Wear Daily*. The Fairchild counterpart for the textile and men's wear industry is the *Daily News Record*.

Trade publications are not aimed at the general public and are inclined to discourage subscriptions from people not active in the fields they serve. They seldom appear on newsstands, except for the Fairchild dailies in the garment district. Their circulations are quite small compared with those of consumer magazines, and their advertising rates are correspondingly small, approximately $8,200 a page. *Women's Wear Daily*, with a circulation of 65,250 in 1988, is a giant in the field. The *Daily News Record* has a circulation of 22,700, with a black-and-white rate of $7,800 a page.[11]

The capacity of trade papers for disseminating fashion information is out of all proportion to their size. Their readership, it should be kept in mind, is concentrated among people dealing in the merchandise they cover. They talk shop to such people. And, in terms of the amount of merchandise involved, when a manufacturer or merchant responds to information on fashion, that response moves a lot of merchandise.

Trade paper editors are usually in their markets every day of the business year, and they cover every nook and cranny of their fields. They analyze fashion trends for their readers and show sketches or photos of actual merchandise, identified as to source and style number, to assist buyers and store owners in keeping abreast of the flow of new products. In addition, trade publications discuss business conditions and contain articles on how to manufacture, promote, or sell the trade's products. They analyze and report on foreign markets, cover conventions and other meetings of interest to the trade, report on legislative developments of interest, and write up merchandising and promotion operations of retail stores.

Solid market research is also part of a trade publication's work. These magazines and papers make estimates of the size of their markets, survey subscribers on buying responsibilities and attitudes toward current problems, publish directories of manufacturers, help retailers and manufacturers find sources of supply, and report on seminars and conventions appropriate to their fields.

Within their particular fields, trade paper editors and reporters are extremely well informed. Reading their articles is like listening to a group of experts indulging in shop talk.

Television: Broadcast and Closed Circuit Videos

The impact of television advertising is enormous, but the medium is expensive to use and, until fairly recently, one saw and heard little more of fashion advertising on the home screen than the institutional messages of fiber companies or the local promotions of retailers. In the late 1970s, retailers such as J. C. Penney, Kinney Shoes, Macy's, and Carson Pirie Scott, to name but a few, began to use network TV advertising to tell their fashion stories. Today, however, both retailers and producers are harnessing the power of network TV. New brands of jeans, notably Jordache and Calvin Klein, got off to explosive starts through saturation use of this medium.

As the 1980s progressed, a new element was added: video presentations, used both on the TV channels and in the stores themselves to revolutionize customer perception of fashion.

Fashion videos, once perceived as the next major money maker, have not yet lived up to its expected promise. J. C. Penney, which invested in a cable shopping station in 1986, sold its interest in 1989 after it had had disappointing results. Sears, an early user of this medium for in-store promotions, has a number of portable VCR units on which everything from fashion to tractors is sold. Sears produces its tapes in Chicago and sends them out on a monthly schedule coordinated with advertising and display materials.[12]

Designers, among them Donna Karan, Ralph Lauren, Anne Klein, Anne Klein II, and Carolyn Roehm, have used videotape to capture the excitement and sales appeal of their fashion shows for their retail customers, who present the videos on their selling floors with the actual merchandise. "It's almost like a video catalog," says the director of advertising and publicity at Donna Karan. "We gave them away at our Bergdorf Goodman show and people were calling the store ordering clothes." Videotapes are used to support sales in larger stores as salespeople and consumers see the collection from the designer's point of view. Companies such as Keable, Cavaco and Duka, Joan Abraham Fashion

Productions, Inc., and Edward Technologies Video of California are among the many that produce these TV fashion videos.[13]

Since MTV and its superstars such as Madonna, Cindy Lauper, and Michael Jackson have demonstrated how quickly they can create demand for new fashions, stores have been paying close attention to the impact those small screens can have on their customers. Videotapes of models going down the runway are now old hat compared with the new fashion tapes, in which entertainment is the key word and the emphasis is on imagination and excitement, not merely the particular outfits.

Club MTV, for cable uninitiated, is a sort of "American Bandstand" with contemporary verve. The program not only features lifestyle and popular culture, but also has an eclectic mix of designers such as Betsey Johnson and Tommy Hilfiger, sock designer E.G. Smith, and Denise Carbonell among others, who have appeared on the programs speaking about style, dressing some of the dancers, and even introducing records.[14]

The future for this new form of promotion seems as unlimited as the customers' appetite for something new and different. New uses for video are being tested, such as Levi-Strauss's use of transactional and interactional systems, where customers can see merchandise and actually order at the same time. Future uses of videos seem endless.

ADVERTISING AND PUBLICITY AGENCIES _____

There are two ways in which producers and retailers use space in print media or time in broadcast media to get their message across to the trade or to the public. One way is paid **advertising**. The other is **publicity**—time or space given without charge by the medium because it considers the message newsworthy.

Advertising Agencies

An **advertising agency** is a service agency whose original function was simply to prepare and place ads in magazines or newspapers for its clients. Today its job encompasses much more: research of the client's consumer markets, advice on promotional needs, planning of promotional campaigns, preparation of print and broadcast advertising, preparation of selling manuals, and creation of selling aids, labels, signs, and packaging—anything that helps increase the sale of the client's product and makes the advertising itself more effective.

An advertising agency may consist of one talented, hard-working executive with a few small clients, or it may be an organization with a staff of hundreds and clients with hundreds of millions of dollars to spend each year. Approximately 65 percent of agencies' revenue is derived primarily from commissions. These are paid, not by the client, but by the media from which the agencies purchase advertising space or time. Custom has fixed the rate at 15 percent. The balance of their income is received directly from clients, generally in the form of fees for special services such as market research, and as part of the cost for producing a product for the client—for example, photography, typography, art, and layout.

When an advertising agency bids for a client's account, it studies the firm's operation thoughtfully and draws up a presentation that outlines the campaign the agency suggests and the varied services that the agency performs. When awarded the account, the agency may delve into package design, market research, and creation of selling aids and sales training material—plus its original function of preparing and placing advertising in publications, in broadcast media, and, in some cases, in transit and outdoor media.

In the fashion industries, it is usually only the largest producers of nationally distributed merchandise that make use of advertising agencies. These include some makers of finished apparel plus the giant fiber and fabric sources. Retailers whose audience is local or regional, usually maintain their own complete advertising departments that handle their day-to-day newspaper advertisements.

FASHION EXPERTISE

Some agencies, often among the smallest in the field, specialize in fashion accounts. In such agencies, and in those of the larger ones that serve fashion accounts, it is important to have personnel who are expert in the language and background of the fashion business: account executives who work with clients and coordinate what is done, art directors who visualize the fashion advertising, copywriters who are familiar with fashion appeals, and stylists or fashion coordinators who are responsible for the fashion slant of the ads.

The work of the fashion expert in an agency is not necessarily limited to fashion accounts. If a man's or woman's figure appears in an ad for automobiles, cigarettes, or soap, it is most likely that a fashion adviser has checked the model's outfit to make sure it is in tune with the current fashion picture as well as with the occasion and level of society being represented. Agency people also realize that fashion is a quick way to identify with whatever group of customers the advertiser seeks to reach: young, dashing, mature, conservative, or whatever. This is especially noticeable in television advertising, where the advertiser has only a few seconds in which to establish rapport with the particular viewers it wishes to influence. Compare the clothing of the characters in an investment firm's commercials, for example, with those of the characters in commercials for soft drinks. The one seeks to project a conservative image; the other a carefree, young, with-it attitude.

Thus, the advertising agency, whether or not it has a fashion account on its roster of clients, becomes involved, directly or indirectly, in the business of fashion.

Publicity and Public Relations Firms

Publicity, unlike advertising, cannot be controlled in relation to where, when, and how a particular message will appear—if, indeed, it appears at all. The publicity practitioner's control over the fate of the story he or she wishes to place with a medium rests primarily in the ability to convince the particular editor that the material is truly news of interest to that medium's audience.

Publicity's purpose, like that of advertising, is to enhance the client's sales appeal to potential customers. The space or time supplied by the media, in this case, is free, but the public relations firm's services are not. Working on a fee basis, with provision for expenses, the publicity agency develops news stories around the client's product or activities and makes these stories available to editors and broadcasters.

The key word in effective publicity is *news*. The publicity expert's first job is to find or "create" news value in a product, activity, or personality to be publicized. Next, he or she considers the media that might conceivably find this news of interest to their readers and writes the story (called a press release) in a form appropriate to the media that constitute the target. If they are likely to use illustrations, a suitable photograph may be included.

Typically, publicity activities include getting editorial mentions in consumer and trade publications, "plugs" on television and radio, school and college tie-ins, running fashion shows or other events (often with admission charges that go to a charity organization), feature articles in newspapers and magazines, and anything else that makes the products or the client's name better known and more readily accepted by the consumer—or by an industry, if that industry is the client's customer.

The publicity firm does more than merely use its contacts to place material for its client. It also prepares press releases, distributes photographs, writes radio and TV scripts, sometimes works out an elaborate fashion show, and hires and coaches professional actors to sing, dance, and model for the audience. If a medium, whether print or broadcast, is working on a special feature touching the client's field, the public relations people swing into action to provide the writer of the feature with facts, photos, and other help. Many fashion editors in smaller towns depend on press releases and photographs for the content of their fashion pages.

A broader term than publicity is *public relations*. A public relations firm does not limit its efforts to getting the client or the product mentioned in the media through press releases and similar efforts. It may supply expert advice on how to improve the client's public image and may develop some potent but less obvious ways of getting publicity for the client: suggesting him or her as a speaker at conventions of appropriate groups, or having the client give scholarships and establish awards and foundations, for instance.

There are many independent publicists and public relations agencies that specialize in fashion publicity. As in the case of advertising agencies, their clients are generally fiber, fabric, or apparel producers instead of retailers, since retailers usually maintain their own internal publicity staffs. Insofar as the fashion business is concerned, the public relations and publicity fraternity performs the very useful function of feeding information about the industry to the news media and thus stimulates business by keeping fashion in the limelight.

THE FASHION GROUP _____

The Fashion Group is a professional association of women who represent every phase of fashion manufacturing, retailing, merchandising, advertising, publishing, and education. Organized in 1930, its purpose was, and is, to serve as a national and international clearinghouse for the exchange of information about what is going on in the business of fashion.

Headquartered in New York, it has 34 regional chapters in major cities throughout the United States and in foreign countries. Its membership exceeds 5,000. The Fashion Group reading following this chapter gives detailed information on their membership and activities.

OTHER FASHION ENTERPRISES _____

There are enterprises of many other types that play important behind-the-scenes roles in the business of fashion. Their activities, however, are too varied and too highly specialized to be described in detail. For example, display consultants design and construct fashion display materials for manufacturers, retailers, and fashion magazines. Consultants in the fields of sales promotion and marketing are also retained on a fee basis by manufacturers and retailers. Market research agencies do consumer surveys for retail stores, publications, and manufacturers, or retail surveys for producers. Among the research agencies that do work for the fashion field are Audits and Surveys, which has made some interesting studies of the buying patterns of retail store customers, and Yankelovich, Skelly and White, which is noted for its demographic and psychographic research.

There are many **trade associations**, each one serving businesses and business executives with interests in common. Each organization is set up as a medium for such purposes as, for example, disseminating trade and technical information, doing research into markets or methods of operation, analyzing relevant legislation, doing public relations work for the industry or trade, and lobbying on political matters. In addition to those that have been mentioned in preceding chapters, other examples are the National Retail Merchants Association (to which most department and apparel specialty stores belong), the American Apparel Manufacturers Association, the American Textile Manufacturers Institute, and too many more to be enumerated here. There are also associations of publicity and advertising specialists, of menswear buyers, and of fashion designers, among others.

In short, there is a whole arsenal of auxiliary services that contribute to making the fashion business what it is today and that will undoubtedly contribute to its growth in the future.

Readings

The readings in this section give an inside view of some of the auxiliary enterprises that work behind the scenes to serve the fashion business. They analyze and report on fashion trends early and help producers and retailers respond to these trends.

T.F.S. — The Fashion Service

A major fashion information service, with a reputation for being fast to spot new trends, T.F.S. describes the services it offers to its subscribers.

The Tobé Report

More than 300 leading retailers subscribe to the weekly Tobé Report which analyzes, evaluates, and reports on every facet of the women's and children's apparel and accessories market from top designers to moderate-priced manufacturers.

We Are AMC

The AMC is a major cooperative buying office that services leading department stores and specialty operations around the globe.

The Fashion Group

The Fashion Group is a global nonprofit association of influential professional women who represent different segments of the fashion business.

Mademoiselle: Editors and Departments and What They Do

Because this reading outlines everything you have always wanted to know about a fashion magazine—who does what and how—we are repeating it in this section.

T.F.S. — THE FASHION SERVICE

Info-Flash Womenswear

Monthly reporting of important fashion information from the fashion capitals of the world, that keeps abreast of current and ongoing trends in the industry. Tracking, reporting and editing those trends into fashion action points.

- Unique T.F.S. folio format!
- Sketches, photos, slides, audio cassettes, samples, swatches.
- Colour 'chips', posters!
- Monthly!
- Slide presentations of the big current events!
- Fast! On the spot!

REPORTING ON:

Retail: A sketched report of the hot fashion merchandise almost every month from a selection of fashion cities (London, Paris, Milan, Rome, Florence, Tokyo, New York). A focus on the hot looks and the hot items for the season. Twice yearly, at the beginning of the major retail seasons, a bonanza retail report.

Street Scenes: Black and white photographs or colour slides of what the avant garde and trendy fashion set are wearing now.

Samples: A selection of merchandise that reflects the current hot looks and items at retail now and that go forward. On figure illustrations show the item as part of the important total look, ad flat pattern drawings give all the measurements and details. Actual garments can be viewed in the New York Fashion Office. Minimally five times a year. Special 'Samples Flashes' for instant hot items.

Wholesale: Written text, sketched or photographed and fabric or colour swatched (when appropriate) reports covering the major fabric, ready-to-wear and accessory fairs around the world. (Includes Premier Vision, Interstoff, Pitti Filati, Porte de Versailles PRET, Igedo, SEHM, Parisian Haute Couture, European Designer Collections, New York Designer Collections.) Reported on as the events happen!

Memo: A special feature included several times a year, consisting of a written and illustrated and/or swatched editorial on important fashion ideas that should have extra emphasis and development.

SPECIAL ISSUES:

Part of the yearly schedule, but issues that deal primarily with single subjects as highlighted below:

Designer R-T-W Collections: Twice yearly coverage of the designer shows in Milan, London and Paris. 100 colour slides, with drawings of those slides for easy reference; text report on the fashion news in silhouette, looks, items, fabrics and colours (separate colour swatched section). Audio cassette gives recorded commentary for slides. Complete and released one week after collections!

St. Tropez Resort Report: An annual issue that deals with the big fashion news from this trendy summer hot spot. In-

Source: T.F.S. promotional brochure. Reprinted with permission.

cludes colour slides (with drawings) and black & white photographs of the major looks and items as worn by the fashion set on the street; major coverage of what's retailing in the boutiques; a selection of samples. Audio cassette gives recorded commentary for slides. Released July 1!

SLIDE PRESENTATIONS:

Twice yearly presentations of European design ready-to-wear collections. Twice yearly presentations of New York designer shows. Twice yearly presentations of Parisian Haute Couture collections. Annual presentation of the hot looks on the streets and in the boutiques in Saint Tropez. (Available in the New York Office, or by special arrangement with the London Office.)

Forecast Womenswear

Quarterly forecasting of important advance fashion colours, fabrics, trends & items. Informs of future trends in the industry on a seasonal basis. Projecting, creating, merchandising and visualizing that information into fashion action points.

- Unique T.F.S. folio format!
- Sketches, swatches, colour yarn, posters, audio cassettes!
- Seasonal consultation!
- Advanced! Accurate!

FORECASTING:

Colours: Four seasonal Folios containing advanced colour projections for Spring, Summer, Autumn and Winter. Each folio includes colour cards swatched with yarns, plus an extra set of yarns. Three to six cards per season. Five to ten colours per card. Merchandised into fashion colour stories and enhanced with colour mood photography.

Fabrics: Four seasonal Folios containing advanced fabric projections for Spring, Summer, Autumn and Winter. Each folio includes mini posters with sketches, text and swatches. Ten to fifteen mini posters per season. Three to four swatches per poster. Merchandised into fashion fabric stories on fibre, base cloth, print and pattern direction.

Trends/Looks: Four trends per season for Spring, Summer, Autumn and Winter. First previewed in mini poster format, contained in a folio. Highlighting the key information about advanced fashion looks. Fully developed in individual booklet format containing comprehensive information on colour, fabric and styling. Accompanied by an audio cassette trend seminar and illustrated poster as overview.

Items/Design: Original T.F.S. designs throughout the Forecast. On-the-figure illustrations and off-figure croquis sketches visualize all the trends and looks. Each trend booklet contains a "Design File" section, organized by merchandising classification: Tops, Bottoms, Jackets/Coats, Dresses, Knits, Body-Lounge-Swimwear, Accessories & Footwear.

Seasonal Consultations: Personal meetings with a T.F.S. director to focus advanced seasonal information on colour, fabric and trends for clients' individual needs.

What & When . . . Two-part information kits, each season:

Part One: includes colour folio, fabric folio and trend preview folio.

Part Two: includes trend and design booklets, audio cassette, poster.

Spring Part One: January 15

Spring Part Two: February 5

Summer Part One: May 15

Summer Part Two: May 30

Autumn Part One: June 25

Autumn Part Two: July 20

Winter Part One: October 5

Winter Part Two: October 30

Info-flash Menswear

Monthly reporting of important fashion information from the fashion capitals of the world, that keeps abreast of current and on going trends in the industry. Tracking, reporting and editing those trends into fashion action points.

- Unique T.F.S. folio format!
- Sketches, photos, slides, audio cassettes, samples, swatches, colour 'chips,' posters!
- Slide presentations of the big current events!
- Fast! On the spot!

REPORTING ON:

Retail: A sketched report of the hot fashion merchandise almost every month from a selection of fashion cities (London, Paris, Milan, Florence, New York). A focus on the hot looks and the hot items for the season. Twice yearly, at the beginning of the major retail seasons, a bonanza retail report.

Street Scenes: Black and white photographs or colour slides of what the avant garde and trendy fashion set are wearing now.

Samples: A selection of merchandise that reflects the current hot looks and items at retail now and that go forward. On figure illustrations show the item as part of the important total look, and flat pattern drawings give all the measurements and details. Actual garments can be viewed in the New York Fashion Office. Minimally five times a year. Special 'Samples Flashes' for instant hot items.

Wholesale: Written text, sketched or photographed and fabric or colour swatched (when appropriate) reports covering the major fabric and ready-to-wear fairs around the world. (Includes Premier Vision, Interstoff, Pitti Filati, SEHM, European Designer Collections). Reported on as the events happen!

Memo: A special feature included several times a year, consisting of a written and illustrated and/or swatched editorial on important fashion ideas that should have extra emphasis and development.

SPECIAL ISSUES:

Part of the yearly schedule, but issues that deal primarily with single subjects as highlighted below:

Designer R-T-W Collections: Twice yearly coverage of the designer shows in Milan and Paris. 80 colour slides, with drawings of those slides for easy reference; text report on the fashion news in silhouette, looks, items, fabrics and colours (with colour swatches).

St. Tropez Resort Report: An annual issue that deals with the big fashion news from this trendy summer hot spot. Includes colours slides (with drawings) and black & white photographs of the major looks and items as worn by the fashion set on the street; major coverage of what's retailing in the boutiques; a selection of samples. Audio cassette gives recorded commentary for slides. *Released July 1!*

SLIDE PRESENTATIONS:

Twice yearly presentations of Italian and French designer ready-to-wear shows. Annual presentation of the hot looks on the streets and in the boutiques in Saint Tropez. (Available in the New York Office, or by special arrangement with the London Office.)

T.F.S. Show-time

Timely slide showings covering the major events in the fashion calendar. Tracking, reporting and editing current and ongoing trends into fashion action points.

Nine important shows annually!
Multi-screen!
Timely!
Succinct & scintillating!

PROGRAMME:

European Designer Collections (Womens): Twice yearly presentation of the latest, most important and fashion forward information from the designer ready-to-wear shows in Paris, London and Milan. Trended and edited for fashion action! Featuring 280 colour slides.

European Designer Collections (Mens): Twice yearly presentation of the latest, most important and fashion forward information from the Italian and French designer ready-to-wear shows. Trended and edited for fashion action! Featuring 160 colour slides.

New York Designer Collections (Womens): Twice yearly presentation of the latest and most important information from the New York ready-to-wear showings. Trended and edited for fashion action! Featuring 280 colour slides.

Parisian Haute Couture Collections: Twice yearly presentation of the most important looks from the most prestigious names in fashion. Trended and edited for fashion action! Featuring 280 colour slides.

Saint Tropez Resort (Womens & Mens): Annual presentation of the hot looks on the streets and in the boutiques of this trendy fashion hot spot! Trended and edited for fashion action! Featuring 160–280 colour slides.

AVAILABLE TO PURCHASE AS SELF-CONTAINED PRODUCTS . . . OR VIEWING AVAILABLE ON AN ANNUAL SUBSCRIPTION BASIS.

AS SELF-CONTAINED PRODUCTS:

Each show package includes 160 to 280 colour slides (numbered and ready for traying), audio cassette with voice over commentary, typewritten script of same commentary.

Special Fabric Package

Specially selected segments of T.F.S. forecast and info-flash publications regarding advanced and current fabric information.

- Unique T.F.S. folio format.
- Seasonal fabric forecast.
- Premiere Vision and Interstoff newsflashes and swatched reports.

- Slide presentations of the big current events!
- Seasonal consultations!

Fast! On the spot! Advanced! Accurate!

FORECASTING:

Fabrics: Four seasonal Folios, taken from the T.F.S. Forecasts, containing advanced fabric projections for Spring, Summer, Autumn and Winter. Each folio includes mini posters with sketches, text and swatches. Ten to fifteen mini posters per season. Three to four swatches per poster. Merchandised into fashion fabric stories on fiber, base cloth, print and pattern direction.

REPORTING ON:

Major Fabric Fairs: twice yearly issues, taken from T.F.S. Info-Flash, covering Premier Vision and Interstoff. Written text, colour photo collages and fabric swatches that report on those seasonal fabric exhibitions.

Consultations & Presentations: Four seasonal consultations with T.F.S. directors on advance trend information, an overview of the seasons. Nine slide presentations annually (includes— Designer Shows, St. Tropez, Couture, Menswear).

THE TOBÉ REPORT

Who we Are

THE TOBÉ REPORT was founded in 1927. It is the industry's major fashion/merchandising vehicle. Published weekly, it contains over 100 pages of editorial, illustrations and photos which evaluate and analyze every facet of the women's and children's apparel and accessories markets, from top designers to backbone moderate manufacturers. THE TOBÉ REPORT is sold to retailers throughout the United States, Europe, Japan and Australia, the fees based on total store volume. THE TOBÉ REPORT contains no advertising or advertorials, thus allowing its team of editors to submit unbiased weekly reports on quickly changing fashion trends and merchandising strategies. TOBE's prestigious client list of more than 300 retailers includes: Bloomingdale's, Macy's, Dayton's, Bullocks, The Gap, The Limited, Ann Taylor, Bergdorf Goodman, Saks Fifth Avenue, Neiman-Marcus, Robinson's, The Broadway. In addition, advertising agencies, magazines, newspapers, fabric companies, pattern companies and major shopping centers subscribe (but TOBÉ accepts no manufacturers as subscribers).

What we Do

TOBÉ's staff of 10 editors are specialists in their market areas, covering **European and**

Source: Tobé Associates Inc. Reprint permission granted.

American designer labels, Better, Contemporary, Moderate, Junior, Outerwear, Large Sizes, Petites, Swimwear, Intimate Apparel, Children's and all Accessory classifications.

TOBÉ is the only retail merchandising service that enjoys entree to manufacturers' design rooms and access to their business plans, as well. Our professional relationship with the marketplace is unparalleled.

Each week, TOBÉ's editorials, which are geared to specific markets, offer in-depth discussions on the problems—from pitfalls to profit margins, fashion to finance. These articles are written for retailers exclusively, not for designers or for manufacturers.

The retailer is our client. Our point of view is a realistic analysis of changing consumer patterns and their lifestyle demographics, vendor structuring, up-to-the-minute merchandising strategies, fashion forecasting, private label planning and pin-pointing, with proven accuracy, potential growth areas.

Where Tobé Makes Its Impact

Over the last decade, specialty store apparel retailers have experienced tremendous growth. Their focused merchandise assortments, their understanding of value equals price, and their ability to create unique shopping environments in prime locations have successfully challenged the department store.

During this period, TOBÉ's business has expanded, as our editorial content was positioned to provide clear and concise direction for the changing complexion of retailing. The Gap, The Limited and Contempo Casuals, three of the most elite mass-producing specialty store retailers,

have benefited from their subscriptions to THE TOBÉ REPORT since 1975.

At the same time, TOBÉ has been instrumental in aiding Spiegel's in their transition from low-end catalog merchandisers to their now respected place in the market as upscale specialty retailers.

TOBÉ's editors have also worked closely with Macy's to insure they remain competitive by maximizing the benefits of their full-service women's wear departments.

Growth by acquisition is a strategy we have backed away from for another client, JC Penney. Instead, we have encouraged growth from within, focusing on fashion leadership and product image.

Where Tobé Impacts Your Business

1. Identifies your customers.
2. Develops merchandising concepts for specific market areas.
3. Targets growth product classifications through vendor analysis and segmentation of style, price and distribution potential.
4. Forecasts significant fashion changes which will affect across-the-board business.
5. Increases the productivity of private label merchandise through proposed product assortments that are distinctive to your business and merchandising image.
6. Builds a consumer niche which is unique to your business, through buying strategies that minimize product sameness and maximize display and environmental potential.
7. Increases catalog performance by narrowing assortments, projecting best-

sellers and focusing on those fashion items that project product uniqueness.

8. Private consultations with TOBÉ's market specialists provide a competitive edge for buyers and management alike. These meetings offer TOBÉ clients a unique perspective of the current marketplace, and also focus on "how-to" build an image that will mean a difference to you and your customer.

WE ARE AMC

This is to introduce you to the AMC, the world's oldest and largest retail merchandising, marketing and consulting organization, with offices located throughout the world. A vast international network of services exists under the Associated Merchandising Corporation umbrella, all with one overrriding objective—to advance our clients' profitability and market share.

AMC is a not-for-profit corporation, owned by its shareholders, who are leading department stores and specialty operations around the globe. These shareholders are also AMC's principal clients. In addition, AMC's client roster includes major mass merchandisers and promotional department stores.

With the world at our fingertips, we provide our clients the most comprehensive market coverage available. Our focus is on the future as we seek to predict what's ahead: in merchandise trends and fashion direction; in our development of exclusive products and merchandise/marketing concepts; and in incisive research and analysis of conditions which influence the retail marketplace.

In the years since the end of World War II, the AMC has grown and changed as times and retail circumstances have dictated. We still serve our clients from our New York headquarters at 1440 Broadway, but AMC stores and offices now span the globe. Clients in the United States, Canada, Europe, the Far East, and Australia are serviced by AMC offices on five continents. This permits in-depth coverage of markets the world over, plus the speedy identification of new sources.

The AMC also maintains two additional offices in the United States. The Washington, D.C. office keeps member stores and AMC staff up-to-date on significant changes in international trade regulations, new legislation and related matters. The AMC Secaucus, New Jersey office houses AMC Financial Services, Store Statistics, Management Information Systems (MIS), Reproduction Services, and International Transportation.

We believe the international aspect of the AMC is its unifying force. Our long history of merchandising successes, which have contributed significantly to increased market share and profit for our shareholders, reflects the vast expertise of our worldwide staff. It is from these wide and diverse talents that we derive our strength

Source: "AMC Bulletin." Reprint permission granted.

—a "One World" approach to our business that also distinguishes the AMC from any other comparable business.

One World Merchandising

If the international aspect of AMC is its strength, then merchandise is its lifeblood. A One World Merchandising philosophy embodies our commitment to check the pulse of the world's markets constantly — investigating, evaluating and reporting our findings to our clients, to provide them with a competitive edge in their merchandise selection.

The AMC also develops merchandise specifically tailored to our clients' needs for important group programs. In addition, it creates concepts and new products based on our perceptions of consumer wants and fashion direction.

Moreover, the collective buying power of the AMC stores enables them to make the most advantageous purchases in terms of quality and price, almost anywhere in the world.

From the communication of a fashion concept, through the design, manufacture and delivery of products, the AMC One World approach to merchandising works to keep our clients in the forefront of the retail industry.

In the United States

Behind the wide variety of services offered by the AMC are teams of specialists. Organized into merchandising divisions which correspond to our stores, and support teams to back up both staff and clients, the AMC worldwide organization is the most extensive and professional available from any one source. Its reputation for integrity and leadership is unequalled.

The New York merchant team is divided into two complementary functions: merchandise analysis and product management. Underscoring the entire merchandising function is a sense of urgency that translates into swift tracking and reporting of trend and key items.

Merchandise Analysts (MAs) are consultants to AMC department stores in the United States. They canvass the domestic market, evaluating resources and merchandise, spotting trends and reporting opportunities to the stores. The MAs also study and interpret store sales data, translating their conclusions into actionable strategies for their retailer counterparts.

One of the most important consulting services the MAs offer is their analysis of their pre-and-post store visits. In addition to an examination of the merchandise mix, this is an evaluation of the store's position relative to similar stores, other competition, department adjacencies, visual merchandising and presentation, customer profile identification and all relevant market data.

The MAs also manage AMC's Domestic Group Buying (DGB) programs, one of the fastest growing parts of our business. Here early planning and group purchasing allow us to offer exclusive items and volume discounts on wanted, nationally accepted merchandise.

Divisional Merchandise Analysts, a new management level, have been added to the domestic staff structure, to provide a strong supervisory arm and to help assure adequate coverage and development of the United States markets.

The **Director of Domestic Sourcing**, also at management level, is charged with identification and development of United States resources, further strengthening the AMC commitment to building domestic sources.

Product Managers (PMs) develop

merchandise for group programs tailored to the specific needs of AMC clients and their customers. Focusing their energies on overseas markets, PMs work with their colleagues in the AMC stores to plan objectives for seasonal import programs. They travel to appropriate overseas markets, assessing and selecting vendors who manufacture quality merchandise. The PMs know the technical aspects of their commodities, and they are highly skilled at negotiating the best prices for the stores they represent.

The samples are subsequently presented to all of the stores by merchandise segments — often at One World Merchandising Meetings. However, in our increasingly competitive retail world, *exclusive* product development has become more than an option — it is a marketing imperative. If we feel an item or group of items demands immediate development, we *will not wait* for seasonal meetings, but move forward to beat the competition.

The **Design Studios**, an extraordinary source of talent, help support the product managers with fresh merchandise concepts and original product designs. One design group concentrates on apparel and the other is devoted to home furnishings. Both help present concepts, product ideas or specific items via visual designs and prototypes, so that everyone involved is on the same wave length.

On par with the most creative design teams in the field, each group represents the new breed of designers who are knowledgeable about the market; understand the development, production and presentation of merchandise; and can meld aesthetic considerations with the needs of the real world.

These teams have contributed to several of the now-famous AMC brands (Preswick & Moore, Once Upon a Time, Smythe & Cook) in tandem with Product Managers, the Fashion Office, the Art Department,

and AMC merchants, both in the U.S. and overseas — illustrating the continuous interaction of creative forces throughout the AMC.

The **Overseas Merchandising Services** (OMS) division is the newest of the AMC merchandising areas, formed in 1983 to handle the unique foreign market needs of mass merchandisers, promotional department stores and specialty operations.

Because the AMC is committed to protecting the confidentiality of both our department store and OMS shareholders, a separate OMS staff is maintained. By understanding this need and observing discretion in all client matters, AMC has won the respect and confidence of its members.

The **AMC Overseas Stores Services/ U.S. Export Division** serves the needs of the Overseas Shareholder Stores. Working directly with these stores, this division provides the critical link to major United States and Canadian merchandise sources with a steady flow of key merchandise and fashion information. A wide range of supplementary services includes regular up-dating of business news, and other matters related to U.S. retailing. In addition, the division administers purchase orders by overseas stores and supervises the export of merchandise from the North American hemisphere to their stores.

Merchandise Coordinators (MCs) in this area provide overseas affiliates with timely information on merchandise opportunities in the North American hemisphere, facilitate order placement, and confirm the details of merchandise delivery.

International Operations

All told, AMC is represented in 32 locations outside of the United States, with the longest established, retail merchandising office in most of these markets. Overseas offices may be headed by a Divisional Vice President, a Director, or a Manager, with a core of seasoned merchants to provide the most comprehensive coverage possible of their markets.

In addition, each office is supported by experienced Quality Control people (approximately 200 throughout the world), and an administrative team, responsible for all aspects of overseas business, including transportation, customs, freight and consolidation. Future planning includes a network of sophisticated systems and equipment to speed information and merchandise from individual regions to the stores.

Overseas Merchandise Representatives (OMRs) in local overseas offices make major contributions to product management, both in the selection of merchandise for One World meetings and the development of other merchandise. Their great strength derives from their knowledge of the markets; their understanding of the competition, and their ability to detect emerging new markets.

Frequently, these OMRs work "one-on-one" with individual store merchants, who travel the world markets in search of unique product assortments and look to AMC's overseas staff for guidance and direction.

Regional Staffs are responsible for supplying sourcing information in various product categories, determining the most appropriate country for specific needs. Their knowledge provides AMC with the ability to look at the world with an unbiased perspective, to discern the optimum areas for sourcing a product, and to offer our clients a wide range of options.

Behind the Scenes

A strong network of support services, for AMC staff and stores, represents the back-bone of our organization. Some, like our Financial Services and Store Statistics, operate quietly in the background. Others, like AMC Research, are highly visible.

RESEARCH

The AMC Research division tracks developments in consumer and competitive markets, as well as in the general economy. By probing the past and present, it seeks to forecast the future, providing AMC staff and member stores with in-depth analyses of psychographic and demographic trends, major business opportunities, competitive threats, and other issues of concern. Many of the studies represent a joint effort between AMC Merchandising and Research divisions.

THE MARKETING DIVISION

In recognition of today's intensely competitive retail climate, AMC has built a talented marketing team to help give stores a selling edge in the presentation and promotion of their merchandise and message. Actually, the marketing division functions on two levels — it provides general support services to the AMC staff and member stores, and it creates complete marketing packages for AMC private label programs to help them achieve national brand recognition on the selling floor.

The marketing division consists of three principal areas: The Fashion Office, Art, and Audio Visual Services. Acting in concert, they gather information from sources throughout the world, cross-pollinating concepts, and translating them into merchandising/marketing strategies. With a philosophy rooted in merchandise, the group is unusual in its ability to provide guidance in merchandise sourcing, selection, and development.

In short, the marketing group serves as the idea center for trend information, merchandise concepts, advertising, point of sale material, merchandise presentation, special in-store shops, and more. It has had notable success in identifying vital consumer issues and in devising tactics that respond to these issues effectively.

The Fashion Office

Headquartered in New York, with overseas offices in both London and Paris, the Fashion Office is charged with providing actionable fashion direction to AMC stores.

Staff members travel the world to identify trends well in advance of the market, communicating their findings in a lively flow of newsletters, meetings, and multimedia presentations. These cover a wide spectrum of topics—from color and fabric forecasts to reports on street styles worn in the fashion capitals of the world. In this evaluation process, definite positions are taken so that direction is clear and actionable.

Working closely with AMC Merchandise Analysts and Product Managers, each fashion coordinator participates in ongoing dialogue, for fashion forecasts that are substantial and realistic, assuring trackable sales.

As part of this interchange, fashion coordinations are heavily involved with the Product Development Advisory Committees (consisting of both AMC and store people), contributing early information on color, fabric, and silhouette; and later, to the final evaluation and editing process—sometimes traveling with committees in overseas markets.

To keep AMC staff ahead of the trends, the Fashion Office also holds monthly "translation" meetings, offering both long and short term overviews for all merchandise areas—from home to children's. While the AMC staff and stores rely on the Fashion Office for leadership direction in both soft and hard lines, its influence extends far beyond.

Because of the worldwide scope of AMC's fashion research and intelligence, the manufacturing community places a high value on AMC input. AMC color forecasts are much in demand; staff members are often called upon to evaluate wholesale lines pre-season.

The Audio-Visual and Art Departments

Audio-Visual and Art work in a variety of media to communicate the many messages of AMC, interfacing with its different departments on an almost daily basis.

With an in-house video studio, it is not unusual for the A-V team to be assigned the production of a sales training video program one day; a multi-screen presentation of fashion trends on the next; and on the third, a visual interpretation of a major research project, incorporating consumer demographics, survey statistics, and merchandise illustrations.

The challenges to the Art group are equally diverse, ranging from the design of AMC communications and fashion publications to the development of original labels, packages, posters and hang tags in support of the exclusive AMC private label programs. The strong focus on private label marketing material is vital to the continuing expansion of AMC's leadership role in the private label arena and in the development of national brands. As part of the marketing division, the Art team creates a variety of other sales promotion material and is also involved with display activities for One World meetings.

THE FASHION GROUP

Knowing the Fashion Group:

In 1930, the founding members created The Fashion Group as a forum, a stage, and a force to serve the growing need of executive women to exchange ideas and resources in the fashion business.

Today, transition and development are a constant at The Fashion Group and result in strong, dynamic, industry-oriented programming which provides a broad base of current business information from the world of fashion, beauty and home furnishings.

Unique programs and trend-setting industry events are made possible by the collective clout and diverse accomplishments of its members, who range from corporate presidents, owners of advertising manufacturing, and marketing businesses, to retailers and editors-in-chief of major publications.

The Fashion Group met many industry challenges and changes in the past as it built one of the largest fashion networking structures in the world: forty active regional groups in ten countries.

The Fashion Group is special because of the quality of its leadership and because of its mission to keep its members in touch with all aspects of the rapid changes in the volatile fashion business.

Joining The Fashion Group means:

1. . . . keeping company with the most successful women executives and entrepreneurs in a wide field of fashion-related businesses, who are a source of information and a source of action.

Source: The Fashion Group. Reprinted with permission.

2. . . . belonging to an organization that provides a social role through an extensive network of peers, as well as an educational and cultural role.

3. . . . being in touch with the business, marketing and distribution of fashion through the new Forum series created to expand the area of business programming with industry leaders.

4. . . . viewing the original clothes selected from designers' collections, straight from the European runways of Milan, London and Paris, exclusive to The Fashion Group each spring and fall, plus the best of the American collections immediately after the spring and fall market weeks.

5. . . . belonging to the only organization that is privileged to have the first showing of the European Haute Couture to the American fashion community following the designers' shows in Paris and Rome.

6. . . . joining women presidents of major fashion or cosmetic corporation, who are members of The Fashion Group, in their offices for a box lunch and informal business talk.

7. . . . attending a series of "Industry Focus" programs with well-known speakers, geared to specific markets such as accessories, intimate apparel, cosmetics, children's wear, menswear, visual marketing, home fashions, etc.

8. . . . sending officers of each regional group worldwide, to a conference in New York once a year to discuss business, exchange ideas, and review events.

9. . . . receiving The Fashion Group "FG," with news of the regional

groups, new members, major events, and The Fashion Group network calendar.

10. . . . having access to Fashion Group members in all regions for information and assistance when traveling for business in major cities of the USA, Canada, Mexico, Europe, Australia and the Orient.

11. . . . presenting The Fashion Group annual Night of Stars award to outstanding designers, members of the fashion press, and fashion executives, at a gala dinner attended by the luminaries of the international fashion community.

12. . . . presenting special events such as Premiere Vision, the prestigious European textile show, immediately following its presentation in Paris.

13. . . . being listed in The Fashion Group Membership Directory, the Who's Who of the fashion business around the world.

14. . . . participating on committees that plan and develop programs, generate membership, create and edit publications, and interact with all regional groups.

15. . . . addressing the concerns of women in the fashion industry as they face career choices and changes, with counseling, job referrals, and workshops.

16. . . . participating in the nomination and selection of officers of the international organization and the regional groups, as well as the by-laws and guidelines of the organization.

17. . . . meeting the incoming officers and Board of Directors at the Annual Meeting in New York followed by a net-working session and an industry keynote speaker.

18. . . . participating in sessions on trends, focus groups, etc., in various areas of the fashion business for large corporations.

19. . . . having newsflashes, industry reports, and slide presentations from main events of The Fashion Group available for use in a member's own business.

20. . . . supporting The Fashion Group Foundation activities: scholarships, fashion education projects, community service, and special events.

Membership Criteria

A candidate should have a strong interest in the purposes of The Fashion Group and a willingness to become an active participant.

ELIGIBILITY:

A candidate should have a record of achievement and have held an executive position in the fashion business for at least 3 years.

PROCEDURE:

A candidate must be sponsored by a member of The Fashion Group of one year's standing and be known to the sponsor for one year.

A candidate, with the sponsor's endorsement, submits the application form to the Membership Committee.

Notification of acceptance is made to the candidate by letter from the New York office, accompanied by an invoice for annual dues and initiation fee.

MADEMOISELLE: EDITORS AND DEPARTMENTS AND WHAT THEY DO

The Editorial Staff

The EDITOR-IN-CHIEF heads the magazine. She has the final editorial word and determines the final result of the magazine. She reads every piece of copy, sees every proof, approves every photograph, sketch and layout, presides at most office conferences, and is liaison between management and the other editors. Her job is to create, together with the staff, a profitable product for MADEMOISELLE's publishers, The Condé Nast Publications Inc. The profit comes from attracting—and holding—readers and advertisers. With the staff, she must create editorial themes, feature ideas and beauty, health and fashion portfolios for forthcoming issues. She must also spot upcoming trends far enough in advance to make production deadlines. (MADEMOISELLE works roughly three months ahead of actual publication.) The Editor-in-Chief has other varied duties. They include fashion plans with manufacturers, discussing business problems, talking with experts in every field, meeting with staff and freelance writers, and attending fashion shows. She is the chief representative for the magazine—speaking before fashion organizations, making guest appearances on radio and television programs, and serving on various boards and committees.

The MANAGING EDITOR focuses and coordinates the efforts of all the magazine's departments. She works closely with the Editor-in-Chief in planning and organizing the magazine from cover models and cover copy to theming issues to mapping out each issue's format. She keeps track of budget, or the number of pages allotted each issue, supervises deadlines, and keeps art, layouts, copy and proof moving. She edits all copy (including beauty and fashion) and often writes for the magazine. In the absence of the Editor-in-Chief, she becomes head of the staff.

Features are supervised and handled by the FEATURES EDITOR. These include articles that are of general interest, preferably those that are controversial and devoted to women's current concerns of work, relationships and sense of self. A staff of feature writers contributes ideas and articles; some articles are commissioned from freelance writers. Chapters from forthcoming nonfiction books, articles from agents and occasionally unsolicited manuscripts are also used. The Features Editor is responsible for the monthly columns and contributors.

The ART DIRECTOR is responsible for the physical appearance of the magazine. She works closely with the Editor-in-Chief, Managing Editor and department editors in planning editorial features. The Art Department is responsible for the "face" of MADEMOISELLE, and constantly strives for exciting typographical approaches to layouts. The Art Director selects photographers and/or free-lance artists for each feature, approves the selection of models for fashion layouts, chooses the illustrations or photographs to be used with each feature, and arranges these with blocks of copy to form the layouts. This department prepares a maquette (a small diagram organizing the space allotted each month to each department). From the resulting paste-ups and through several series of photostats a loose-bound version of the issue (the dummy) is prepared. In addition, the Art Director sees the portfolios of dozens of aspiring illustrators and photographers.

The FASHION EDITOR's basic function is to interpret fashion news in terms of MADEMOISELLE's readership interest and salability. The department is made up of several Associate Fashion Editors and each one is responsible for a specific area of the fashion market (shoes, lingerie, sportswear, coats, dresses, suits, accessories and men's wear). This department helps select clothes and models, presides over photographic sittings, works with the Art Department and the fashion copy writers, and makes presentations to the fashion trade and retail executives.

The BEAUTY AND HEALTH EDITOR and the BEAUTY MARKETING EDITOR and their assistants are responsible for the editorial beauty pages, as well as many health, diet and fitness pages. They help select models, supervise photography sittings, work closely with the Art Department on photographs and layouts, approve beauty copy and conduct beauty makeovers. The Beauty Editors report and create new looks which complement the new fashions. The Beauty Marketing Editor is specifically responsible for keeping MADE-MOISELLE in touch with the ever-expanding beauty industry. She keeps abreast of the endless developments in the field of beauty and researches new products.

The CAREER EDITOR and her assistant keep track of women and their careers as they write in-depth profiles of young women in specific job fields, research and write articles about job trends, salary scales, management training courses and techniques for finding a job or leaving one.

The MEDICAL EDITOR and her assistant supervise the "Health Guide" that's in each issue and keep tabs on medical trends.

The articles include the latest information on contraception, nutrition, infertility, diet, how to prevent a cold or survive one, how to talk back to your doctor, as well as tips on exercise and sports, beating the heat or cold, how often to have a checkup, etc.

The COPY EDITOR and her associates are in charge of writing some of the health and all of the fashion, beauty and home furnishings copy that appears on the editorial pages of the magazine. The department receives all of the essential information (description, prices, fabric credits, stores) from various departments and layouts from the Art Department to help them write the text copy and blurbs.

The HOME & FOOD EDITOR is responsible for MADEMOISELLE's pages which cover the at-home life: entertaining, table settings, gift ideas, food, decorating, and furniture. The Environments Editor interprets merchandise and decorating trends to the readers, covers the home furnishings market and represents MADEMOISELLE at trade functions.

The FABRIC EDITOR and her assistants are responsible for reporting and developing trends in the fabric market. They work closely with fabric mills and designers, offering suggestions for fabrics or reporting on their discoveries. The Fabric Editor may design material herself, which is then manufactured by a mill and sent to a ready-to-wear house to become a garment that is rightfully called MADEMOISELLE's own. This department usually works a year in advance, making predictions about fabric trends for upcoming seasons. They prepare a fabric bulletin board for use by the garment industry, designers and stores throughout the country who come to MA-DEMOISELLE rather than cover the market themselves.

The ENTERTAINMENTS EDITOR covers the arts: theatre, film, dance, music, literature and visuals. She researches and writes material for the Entertainments section and some other features in the magazine.

The TRAVEL EDITOR and her assistant report on the most interesting vacation possibilities here and abroad in a monthly column. They present in-depth pieces on places to visit, ways to travel, things to buy, the "in" spots of a particular season, or little-known locales of surprising interest. They also advise readers requesting information on any aspect of travel. This department often ties in with the Fashion Department to illustrate, for example, "Where to Ski and What to Wear." They are also invaluable in feeding information on the young women's travel habits and plans to all members of the travel industry.

The FICTION EDITOR spends hours upon hours reading all material submitted to this department—unsolicited manuscripts as well as those sent by agents, college literary magazines, galleys of forthcoming book and European fiction. MADEMOISELLE has the reputation for discovering new writers and for publishing stories that are later selected for inclusion in anthologies. MADEMOISELLE is always on the lookout for new talent and sponsors the annual College Fiction Competition. Fiction entries number close to a thousand.

The SHOPPING EDITOR is responsible for MADEMOISELLES's monthly "Mailway Catalogue" section, selecting merchandise from the best and most original products available through specialty stores, boutiques and mail-order houses.

The PRODUCTION EDITOR and her department are responsible for the physical execution of every page of MADEMOISELLE. They edit all copy for errors in spelling, punctuation, construction and grammar, serving as a liaison between the editorial staff and the printers in Chicago.

They take the copy from original edited text to the final proofs by ordering type, assuring adherence to alloted space and coordinating the type and illustration. The Production Editor must also see that all proofs are approved by the proper editors and that all deadlines are met.

The EDITORIAL PRODUCTION CO-ORDINATOR is responsible for the magazine's release on time. Coordinating corporate production schedules for the art, copy and production departments, she makes sure that the schedules are adhered to. She coordinates the art and editorial units through all stages of production, acting as a liaison between departments as well as a link between the corporate production department and the magazine staff.

The READER MAIL CORRESPONDENT deals exclusively with the readers—the magazine's continual source of feedback opinion. She answers any queries readers might have about MADEMOISELLE—from fashion advice to circulation figures. In addition, she selects reader mail for publication in the column, "From You to Us."

The Business Staff

The PUBLISHER of the magazine works very closely with the Editor-in-Chief but specifically represents the financial, business end of MADEMOISELLE. He is the final "decision maker" for the magazine's relations with the business community. His primary goal is to increase advertising revenue, thus keeping the profit margin healthy.

The ADVERTISING DIRECTOR and his staff of ADVERTISING REPRESENTATIVES have the responsibility of selling advertising space in MADEMOISELLE. Sales representatives solicit business from companies whose products can best and most logically be merchandised to the 18-to-34-year-old age group, MADEMOISELLE's readership. Each sales representative covers a specific market—fashion, beauty, travel, schools, etc. The sales representative is a good-will ambassador, the legman between client and magazine.

The Promotion Staff

The PROMOTION DIRECTOR and her assistants, together with the PROMOTION ART DIRECTOR and the PROMOTION COPY CHIEF, maintain a department that is much like a small advertising agency with MADEMOISELLE as its sole account. It consists of copy writers, publicists, artists and liaison people, and a marketing staff, who work with stores, manufacturers and advertisers. The general purpose is to promote the magazine at every possible level. Promotion pieces, trade ads and presentations are directed to advertisers and potential advertisers. This department also prepares all the sales tools for the advertising department. Merchandising aids specialists carry on a campaign to supply manufacturers and retailers with tie-in material—counter cards, blowups, reprints for mailing, hang tags, etc. The Promotion Director supervises all special projects such as fashion shows, exhibits and promotional films.

The PUBLICITY/CAREER MARKETING MANAGER's job is two-fold. As Career Marketing Manager she works with a panel of college students and career women who do product research for MADEMOISELLE's advertisers, keeping them up-to-date on their likes and dislikes. As Career Manager she reports to advertisers on MADEMOISELLE readers' shopping habits, product preferences and services they may require. She also heads MADEMOISELLE's "Career Network," a panel of successful working women in 25 major cities across the country. In her Publicity Manager capacity, she and her assistant publicize each issue of the magazine at every possible communications level. She prepares news releases for the media—newspapers, syndicates, trade publications, radio and television. She initiates special publicity projects, as well as publicizes the magazine's regular features. She is the official hostess for the magazine—and does everything from giving tours to planning parties.

The Merchandising Department

The MERCHANDISING DIRECTOR and her **merchandising editors** work with retail stores across the country that use MADEMOISELLE promotions throughout the year. MADEMOISELLE maintains a showroom where top store executives come to preview merchandise that will be featured in future issues of the magazine. (MADEMOISELLE was the first magazine to offer on-page merchandising for fashions, i.e., to list retail stores, colors, sizes, fabrics, prices, etc. If the stores decide to carry the merchandise shown in the fashion editorial pages, they may be credited in the magazine.) For each garment, five retail stores across the country and one New York store are listed. MADEMOISELLE also helps retail stores promote the magazine's editorial choices via fashion shows, window displays and other promotional aids. The MERCHANDISE CREDIT COORDINATOR keeps in constant touch with stores across the country checking and rechecking to make certain the clothes shown editorially are readily available to readers. This department also keeps in contact with manufacturers to make sure clothes are actually made and delivered.

The WESTERN EDITOR works with stores and shop markets for editorial merchandise so that the New York City branch is aware of fashion markets and retail patterns across the country. The Western Editor keeps up good public relations with both manufacturers and retailers in addition to keeping the New York staff alerted to market and fashion news in their territory. MADEMOISELLE's fashion directions are passed on to markets and stores by this editor.

Endnotes

1. Address before Harvard Graduate School of Business Administration, Cambridge, Mass., April 25, 1957. Reprinted with permission of the late Tobe Coller Davis in the 1965 edition of this book.
2. Buying Office Status Report, *Stores*, May 1989; *Women's Wear Daily*, October 18, 1989.
3. Samuel Feinberg, "From Where I Sit," *Women's Wear Daily*, September 9, 1988.
4. "AMC's Comeback Wielding a New Kind of Clout," *Women's Wear Daily*, June 12, 1989.
5. Frederick Atkins, Inc., "Handbook."
6. Ibid.
7. Samuel Feinberg, "From Where I Sit," *Women's Wear Daily*, December 22, 1985.
8. Frederick Atkins, Inc., "Handbook."
9. The Standard Rate and Data Service (a reference service for advertisers) provides information on rates and circulation and brings figures up to date periodically. These amounts are from the November 24, 1989 issue.
10. *Standard Periodical Directory*, 13th ed. (New York: Oxbridge Communications, 1990).
11. Ibid.
12. "Dressing Up with FTV," *Newsweek*, January 7, 1985.
13. Woody Hochswender, "Patterns," *New York Times*, August 23, 1988.
14. "Club MTV," *Women's Wear Daily*, June 5, 1989.
15. *Fortune* magazine, April 1989.

Selected Bibliography

Beaton, Cecil. *The Best of Boston*. New York: Macmillan, 1968.

Brady, James. *Superchic*. Boston: Little, Brown, 1974.

Cahan, Linda, and Joseph Robinson. *A Practical Guide to Visual Merchandising*. New York: John Wiley & Sons, 1984.

Ehrenkranz, Lois B., and Gilbert R. Kahn. *Public Relations/Publicity: A Key Link to Communication*. New York: Fairchild Publications, 1983.

Howell, Georgina. *In Vogue; Sixty Years of International Celebrities and Fashion from British Vogue.* New York: Schocken, 1976.

Kelly, Katie. *The Wonderful World of Women's Wear Daily.* New York: Saturday Review Press, 1972.

Pegler, Martin M. *Visual Merchandising and Display.* New York: Fairchild Publications, 1983.

Snow, Carmel. *The World of Carmel Snow.* New York: McGraw-Hill, 1962.

Winters, Arthur, and Stanley Goodman. *Fashion Advertising and Sales Promotion*, 7th ed. New York: Fairchild Publications, 1988.

Trade Associations

American Advertising Federation, 1225 Connecticut Avenue, Northwest, Washington, D.C. 20036.

American Association of Advertising Agencies, 666 Third Avenue, New York, N.Y. 10017.

The Fashion Group, Inc., 9 Rockefeller Plaza, New York, N.Y. 10020.

Magazine Publishers Association, Inc., 575 Lexington Avenue, New York, N.Y. 10010.

Public Relations Institute, 350 West 57th Street, New York, N.Y. 10019.

Public Relations Society of America, 845 Third Avenue, New York, N.Y. 10022.

Trade Publications

Advertising Age, 740 North Rush Street, Chicago, Ill. 60611.

Fashion Calendar, 185 East 85th Street, New York, N.Y. 10028.

Public Relations Journal, 845 Third Avenue, New York, N.Y. 10022.

Standard Rate and Data Service, Inc., 5201 Old Orchard Road, Skokie, Ill. 60076.

Visual Merchandising, 407 Gilbert Avenue, Cincinnati, Ohio 45202.

CHAPTER REVIEW AND LEARNING ACTIVITIES

Key Words and Concepts

Define, identify, or briefly explain the following:

Advertising	Group purchase
Advertising agency	Market representative
Corporate buying office	Merchandising editor
Cooperative buying office	Product developer

Daily News Record   Publicity
Editorial credit   Resident buying office
Fashion consultant   Tobé Associates
The Fashion Group   Trade association
Fashion information service   Trade publication
Fashion magazine   *Women's Wear Daily*
Fee office

Review Questions on Chapter Highlights

1. List the different types of information provided by a fashion information service. What types of firms subscribe to them? Why and how are they used?

2. Why would a Japanese company and an American company subscribe to and utilize the *same* fashion information service?

3. Name and briefly explain the different types of buying offices. What common function do they all serve?

4. Could the services of a New York buying office help you, as an out-of-town store buyer, do a better job, and if so, how? Could the services of a New York buying office help you, as a New York store buyer, and why or why not?

5. Using the reading "We Are the AMC," describe the specific types of merchandising and fashion information that they send to their stores.

6. Explain the relationship and services of a fashion magazine to each of the following: (a) apparel producers, (b) retailers, (c) consumers.

7. What types of information are found in trade publications such as *Women's Wear Daily* and *Daily News Record*? How does a trade publication differ from a fashion magazine?

8. Why and how are retailers using closed circuit television?

9. Citing an example of each, explain the similarities and differences between advertising and publicity. Do you think that one is more effective in selling fashion merchandise than the other? Why or why not?

10. What is a trade association? Give the names of trade associations that have been mentioned in previous chapters in this book and describe their activities.

$\mathcal{T}$HE $\mathcal{I}$NFLUENTIAL $\mathcal{D}$ESIGNERS

These are the people who have had the greatest design impact on the fashion industry during this century. Some of them are superb craftsmen and women whose knowledge of fabric, cut, and production have enabled millions to be clothed with taste and style. Others have raised fashion design to the level of art. In all cases, they have either created lasting trends, established standards of excellence, or been a major influence on future generations. (*Authors Note*: The name of Geoffry Beene, considered by many to be America's most creative designer, was inadvertently omitted from this article. Known for his innovative combination of textures, fabrics and unusual designs. Among other influential designers who emerged in the 80's are Christian Lacroix, Isaac Mizrahi, Patrick Kelly, Romeo Gigli, Matsuda, and Byblos.)

ADOLFO Began as milliner, added separates, custom blouses, long skirts in late '60s . . . devoted following of status dressers.

GILBERT ADRIAN MGM's top designer, 1923–1939, for stars such as Crawford, Hepburn, Garbo . . . wide shoulders, tailored suits.

AZZEDINE ALAIA Sexy clothes that cling to every curve from this contemporary Paris ready-to-wear designer.

WALTER ALBINI Early Italian rtw designer.

HARDY AMIES British couturier for men and women, noted for his tailored suits, coats, cocktail and evening dresses.

GIORGIO ARMANI Major Italian rtw force for men and women . . . beautifully tailored clothes . . . now at peak of his powers.

LAURA ASHLEY Romantic Victorian looks in fabrics and fashion . . . built a London-based empire in clothes and home furnishings.

CRISTOBAL BALENCIAGA One of century's greatest . . . innovations include semifit jacket, cocoon coat, balloon skirt, bathrobe coat, pillbox hat . . . desciples include Givenchy, Courreges, Ungaro.

Source: *WWD: 75 Years in Fashion 1910–1985.* Reprint permission granted.

PIERRE BALMAIN   Opened own Paris house in 1945 . . . classic daytime looks, extravagant evening gowns.

PATRICK DE BARENTZEN   "Daring" member of Italian couture in the '60s . . . whimsical . . . enormous Infanta skirts.

JEAN BARTHET   Influential milliner of the '50s and '60s . . . customers ranged from Princess Grace to Sophia Loren.

BILL BLASS   Mr. Fashion Right . . . taste, durability and a consistent high level of talent since the late '50s.

MARC BOHAN   Joined House of Dior in the early '60s and was there until 1989. Replaced by Gianfranco Ferre (couturier for Dior).

DONALD BROOKE   Most successful period was the '60s . . . also did much work for Broadway stage.

STEPHEN BURROWS   Body-conscious clothes in vibrant colors . . . noted for his draped matte jerseys.

ROBERTO CAPUCCI   Started in Rome at age 21 . . . very hot in the '50s . . . known for drapery, imaginative cutting.

PIERRE CARDIN   King of the licensing game . . . top innovator of the '50s and '60s, became first Paris couturier to sell his own rtw . . . now involved in everything from rock to restaurants.

HATTIE CARNEGIE   Influential in the '30s and '40s . . . began as milliner, then designed custom and rtw . . . influenced Norell, Trigere, McCardell.

BONNIE CASHIN   An American sportswear original — casual country and travel clothes in wool jersey, knits, tweeds, canvas, leather.

ANTONIO DEL CASTILLO   The Infanta silhouette . . . designed for Lanvin from 1950 to 1963, then opened his own house in Paris.

JOHN CAVANAUGH   One of Britain's best in the '50s . . . headed Curzon St. . . . known for nipped-waist, full-skirt New Look.

COCO CHANEL   Chanel No. 5 . . . the house on the rue Cambon . . . the Chanel suit: braid-trim, collarless jacket, patch pockets . . . feminism before it was fashionable . . . the one and only.

ALDO CIPULLO   Jeweler for Cartier's in the '70s . . . elegance, but with a light approach.

LIZ CLAIBORNE   Contemporary sportswear . . . executive dressing . . . great commercial success.

OSSIE CLARK   Enfant terrible of British fashion in the '60s . . . HotPants, maxi coats . . . started '40s revival in 1968.

SYBIL CONNOLLY   Ireland's most prestigious designer.

ANDRES COURREGES   The Basque tailor . . . hot in the '60s, with suits and roomy coats . . . Tough Chic . . . the great white way.

ANGELA CUMMINGS   Designed jewelry for Tiffany's, now on her own . . . inventive and tasteful.

LILLY DACHE   From the '30s to '50s, U.S.'s top milliner . . . draped turbans, brimmed hats, snoods . . . fantasies for films.

DONALD DAVIES   English shirtmaker who is based in Dublin and went to shirtdresses in the '60s . . . he used featherweight Irish tweed in a variety of colors.

CHRISTIAN DIOR   Launched the New Look in 1947, becoming fashion's most famous name until his death 10 years later.

JEAN DRESSES   Designed from 1925–1965 . . . his Jean Dresses Diffusion, a lower-price line for America, the start of mass production by a French couturier.

PERRY ELLIS   Appeared in the '70s as one of the avant-garde young sportswear designers . . . gave classics a high-fashion twist.

ALBERTO FABIANI   One of Italy's top couturiers of the '50s . . . "surgeon of coats and suits" . . . conservative tailoring . . . wed Simonetta Visconti.

JACQUES FATH   Enfant terrible, showman, ran own Paris house from 1937–1954 . . . sexy clothes, hourglass shapes, plunging necklines.

SALVATORE FERRAGAMO   Italian shoemaker who became international success . . . pioneer of wedge heel, platform sole, Lucite acrylics heel.

GIANFRANCO FERRE   Architectural approach has turned him into one of Italy's leading rtw designers.

ANNE FOGARTY   Spearheaded the revolution in junior sizes in the early '50s.

FONTANA SISTERS   One of Italy's leading couture houses in the '50s, started by mother, Amabile, in 1907, continued by daughters Zoe, Micol and Giovanna.

FEDERICO FORQUET   Big in the '60s in Rome, noted for coats and suits in blocks of bold color . . . went into interior design in 1972.

MARIANO FORTUNY   Mushroom-pleated silk tea gowns . . . his clothes now are collectors' items.

JAMES GALANOS   Born in Philadelphia, studied in New York, worked in Paris, opened own business in Los Angeles . . . one of America's most elegant fashion creators.

IRENE GALITZINE   Palazzo pajamas of the '60s an important concept . . . now in cosmetics, furs, linens.

JEAN-PAUL GAULTIER   One of Paris's trendiest and more controversial rtw designers for men and women.

RUDI GERNREICH   Avant-garde sportswear . . . maillots . . . topless swimsuit, 1964 . . . see-through blouses . . . the No-Bra.

HUBERT DE GIVENCHY   A major couturier since he opened own House in Paris in '52 . . . influenced by Balenciaga . . . most famous client: Audrey Hepburn.

ALIX GRES   Originally a sculptress . . . couturiere since 1934 . . . known for statuesque and molded gowns "sculpted" on live model.

ALDO GUCCI   Head of Florence-based family business . . . Manufacturer and retailer of leathers, luggage and apparel . . . GG.

HALSTON   Began as milliner at Bergdorf's, did Jacqueline Kennedy's pillbox hat, 1961 . . . opened couture business in '68, rtw in '72 . . . simple classics . . . name licensed by J. C. Penney.

NORMAN HARTNELL   London's biggest couture house in the '30s . . . coronation gowns for Queen Elizabeth.

EDITH HEAD   Probably Hollywood's best-known designer.

JACQUES HEIM   Successful Paris couturier from 1923 until the early '60s . . . designer of Atome, the first bikini.

BARBARA HULANICKI   Mod look, the early '60s . . . a founder of Biba . . . the Total Look: coordinated color in clothes, cosmetics, hose.

IRENE   Top designer for movie stars for many decades, also had own rtw business in the '60s.

CHARLES JAMES   The Eccentric One . . . ran own custom business in the '40s and '50s . . . innovative shapes . . . the Dali of design.

MR. JOHN   One of America's best-known milliners, especially in the '40s and '50s—the heyday of hats.

BETSEY JOHNSON   Big in the '60s . . . low prices, off-beat fashions . . . designed for Paraphernalia, co-founded Betsey Bunky, Nini.

STEPHEN JONES   London's extraordinary milliner who designs hats for such notables as Lady Di.

NORMA KAMALI   Her contemporary sweatshirt clothes made high fashion affordable by a young audience.

JACQUES KAPLAN   Headed Georges Kaplan, New York furrier . . . innovator and promoter . . . a pioneer of "fun" furs.

DONNA KARAN   Anne Klein's assistant, then her successor . . . now on her own . . . high-fashion, elegant sportswear.

REI KAWAKUBO   Comme des Garcons . . . one of the first of the New Wave from Japan in the '80s.

KENZO   Left Japan for Paris in 1965 . . . light, whimsical rtw.

EMMANUELLE KHANH   One of the first major rtw designers in Paris in the '60s . . . kicky, young clothes.

CHARLES KLEIBACKER   Journalism, show business, then fashion . . . opened own business in New York in 1960 . . . known for bias cuts.

ANNE KLEIN   A major American sportswear designer . . . associated with Junior Sophisticates, 1951–1964 . . . classic sportswear.

CALVIN KLEIN   Pure American looks in sportswear and rtw . . . clean lines, sophistication and a wide range of prices.

KARL LAGERFELD Outspoken, controversial, avant-garde . . . designed for Chloe, now for Fendi and Chanel.

JEANNE LANVIN One of earliest Paris couturiers . . . peak years between two World Wars . . . her perfumes: My Sin and Arpege.

RALPH LAUREN Noted for his Americana-influenced designs . . . the western look for men and women.

LUCIEN LELONG Great name in Paris couture from the '20s to '40s . . . didn't design, himself, but inspired workers such as Dior, Balmain, Givenchy and Schlumberger.

JEAN LOUIS Not only a successful Hollywood designer, but also headed his own couture firm.

CLAIRE McCARDELL Perhaps the most profound influence on American sportswear design . . . hot in the '40s and '50s.

MARY McFADDEN Socialite who first started designing exotic jewelry . . . her pleated evening dresses became the rage in the late '70s.

MAINBOCHER One of America's first custom designers in Paris . . . dressed Duchess of Windsor . . . specialized in quiet quality.

GERMANA MARUCELLI Avant-garde Milanese couturiere of the '50s and '60s.

VERA MAXWELL Pioneer of American sportswear.

MISSONI One of the early Italian rtw families . . . known for knits in original colors and designs.

ISSEY MIYAKE Avant-garde Japanese designer, predated Japan's New Wave.

CAPT. EDWARD MOLYNEUX From the '20s to '40s, his purity of line drew the rich and famous to his Paris salon. Brief revival in the '60s.

CLAUDE MONTANA Contemporary French rtw . . . big shoulders . . . leathers . . . architectural shapes.

HANAE MORI Comes from Japan, shows in France . . . tasteful clothes in beautiful colors . . . innovative beading.

DIGBY MORTON Early British couturier . . . opened house in 1933 . . . specialized in tailored suits, cableknit sweaters, Donegal tweeds.

THIERRY MUGLER Tongue-in-chic fashion from one of Paris's New Wave designers.

JEAN MUIR Started in the '60s in London . . . elegant, intricately detailed young clothes.

NORMAN NORELL Brought American fashion to the level of Paris couture.

FRANK OLIVE Sophisticated and slick hats have been his forté since the '60s.

ANDRE OLIVER Associated with Pierre Cardin since 1955 . . . created clothes for men and women.

PAQUIN   One of the first Paris couturiers . . . house opened in 1891 and lasted until 1956.

MOLLIE PARNIS   One of the most successful women designers and manufacturers on SA.

JEAN PATOU   A businessman and showman as well as a designer of elegant, ladylike couture clothes in the '20s and '30s.

MME. PAULETTE   Leading American milliner in the '50s and '60s . . . associated with Saks Fifth Avenue.

SYLVIA PEDLAR   Put high fashion into loungewear . . . founded Irish Lingerie and designed there 40 years.

ELSA PERETTI   Revolutionary jewelry designer . . . diamonds by the yard . . . made small diamonds fashionable . . . innovator in silver.

ROBERT PIQUET   Ran his Paris couture house from 1933 to 1951 . . . influenced Givenchy and Dior, both of whom were employed by him.

PAUL POIRET   One of first French couturiers to free women from constraints of underpinnings . . . leader of early 20th century.

THEA PORTER   Anti-establishment London designer of the '60s and '70s . . . fantasy long clothes . . . Orientalia.

ANNA POTOK   A key influence in fur design . . . founder of Maximilian.

EMILIO PUCCI   His prints on thin silk jerseys revolutionized Italian fashion in the '50s and '60s.

LILLY PULITZER   Her printed-cotton shift, the "Lilly," swept the nation in the '60s and '70s . . . floral prints . . . Palm Beach.

MARY QUANT   A miniskirt pioneer synonymous with the "swinging London" look of the '60s . . . Carnaby St.

MADELEINE DE RAUCHE   Renowned sportswoman who created sports clothes for herself and friends . . . made functional clothes in the '30s.

OSCAR DE LA RENTA   Came to U.S. to work for Elizabeth Arden in the early '60s . . . one of SA's "luxury" designers.

ZANDRA RHODES   A London original . . . outrageous evening looks . . . fantasy colorings for hair and makeup.

JACQUELINE DE RIBES   A socialite-turned-designer . . . her love of couture quality is reflected in her rtw.

NINA RICCI   Opened her house in Paris in 1932 . . . dressed mature, elegant women . . . pioneered showing lower-priced clothes in a boutique . . . her fragrance: L'Air du Temps.

MARCEL ROCHAS   Elegant French Couture of the '30s and '40s . . . packaged a perfume called Femme in black lace.

SONIA RYKIEL   The genius of sweater dressing.

YVES SAINT LAURENT   One of the century's greatest influences on fashion and taste.

COUNT FERNANDO SARMI Beautiful evening clothes . . . chief designer at Elizabeth Arden, 1951–1959, then head of his own business.

JEAN-LOUIS SCHERRER His soft, refined dresses popular in the '60s . . . opened own Paris house in 1962.

ELSA SCHIAPARELLI The Great Schiap . . . one of the true avant-garde designers in Paris from the '30s to '50s.

JEAN SCHLUMBERGER Legendary jeweler whose exuberant fantasies have pleased women such as Bunny Mellon and Babe Paley since the late '40s.

MILA SCHOEN Important Italian designer of the '60s and '70s.

KEN SCOTT Expatriate from Indiana who settled in Milan . . . fabric and dress designer since 1956 . . . Art Nouveau influenced.

SIMONETTA One of the first of the Italian couture designers . . . married Albert Fabiani.

ADELE SIMPSON One of SA's durables . . . in her own business since 1949 . . . known for conservative good taste.

STEPHEN SPROUSE Contemporary, controversial designs, strongly influenced by the '60s.

GUSTAVE TASSELL Started own business in Los Angeles, 1959 . . . refined, no-nonsense clothes.

PAULINE TRIGERE A pioneer American designer . . . started own business in 1942, still going strong.

EMANUEL UNGARO Once known as "the young terrorist" of fashion, now does some of the most seductive clothes in Paris.

VALENTINA Russian-born, opened own couture business in America in 1928 . . . dramatic clothes . . . dressed Garbo, whom she resembled.

VALENTINO The Chic . . . one of the most important European couturiers since the mid-'60s . . . taste, elegance, timelessness.

PHILIPPE VENET Givenchy's master tailor, 1953–1962, then opened own business . . . noted for lean suits, rounder shoulders.

GIANNI VERSACE Italian rtw . . . an innovator for men and women in leathers and other fabrics.

SALLY VICTOR From mid-'30s to mid-'60s, one of America's most prominent milliners.

MADELEINE VIONNET The inventor of the bias cut and a major influence on fashion since early in the century.

DAVID WEBB Known for his enamel-and-jeweled bracelets in the '60s.

JOHN WEITZ Women's sportswear with menswear look . . . big in the '50s and '60s . . . now only in men's wear . . . once "designed" a cigar.

VIVIENNE WESTWOOD Contemporary, controversial English designer . . . runs World's End, off-beat London boutique.

CHARLES FREDERICK WORTH   Dressmaker for Empress Eugenie and "founder" of French couture when he opened his own house in 1858.

B. H. WRAGGE   Owner-designer of Sydney Wragge, pioneered concept of sportswear separates . . . important in the '40s and '50s.

YOHJI YAMAMOTO   Oversize, dramatic Japanese clothes.

BEN ZUCKERMAN   The master tailor . . . major influence on American coats and suits.

APPENDIX *B*

*S*OURCES OF *C*URRENT *S*TASTISTICAL *I*NFORMATION

FROM THE U.S. GOVERNMENT_____

- *Statistical Abstracts of the United States.* Annual. Provides historical as well as fairly current data on a wide variety of subjects. Uses both government and private sources. From the U.S. Department of Commerce, Washington, D.C. 20233. In most libraries.
- *Survey of Current Business.* Monthly. Provides little historical data but much fairly current data from a variety of sources. U.S. Department of Commerce.
- *U.S. Industrial Outlook.* Annual. Provides quite current figures and interpretive comment on many industries, but may not cover every industry each year. U.S. Department of Commerce.
- *Population Profile.* Annual. Summarizes data on population by age, sex, area, income level, and so on. U.S. Department of Commerce.
- *Monthly Labor Review.* Contains data on the work force, consumer price index, wholesale prices, and so on. U.S. Department of Labor, Washington, D.C. 20212.

The listed publications are a good starting point for research. For greater detail about specific subject areas, consult the following sources:

- *Industry production:* Write the Bureau of the Census, U.S. Department of Commerce, Washington, D.C. 20233, for whatever is currently available on the particular product, industry, or retail or wholesale operation with which you are concerned.

- *The consumer:* Contact the Bureau of the Census for its most recent population reports on whatever phase interests you most (income, education, ethnic origin, metropolitan area versus nonmetropolitan, etc.). For information on how much the public spends on various categories of goods and services, ask the Office of Business Economics, U.S. Department of Commerce, for its latest annual report on personal consumption expenditures. Also check the Bureau of Labor Statistics, U.S. Department of Labor, Washington, D.C. 20212, for possible studies of urban family budgets and expenditures.
- *Foreign trade:* Monthly reports, with annual figures in the December issue each year, from the Department of Commerce, Bureau of the Census. FT110 on imports, and FT410 on exports are good starting points.

PRIVATE RESEARCH ORGANIZATIONS _ _ _ _ _ _ _

Supported by their subscribers, private research organizations often develop useful research publications, some of which may be compendiums of statistics gathered from many sources.

- *Dun & Bradstreet Companies, Inc., 299 Park Avenue, New York, N.Y. 10171.* This is a credit reporting agency, primarily concerned with business enterprises. It makes special studies of various industries and publishes *Focus*, the economic profile sponsored by the Apparel Manufacturers Association of America.
- *The Conference Board, 845 Third Avenue, New York, N.Y. 10022.* Funded by business firms, makes studies of economic conditions, consumer attitudes, and so on. Presents statistics from government sources in graphic form.
- *Standard & Poor's, 25 Broadway, New York, N.Y. 10047.* A service subscribed to by financial and investment concerns to provide information on individual companies whose stocks are listed on the various exchanges. Has detailed information on producers and retailers; makes annual studies of textile and apparel industries, "Textiles, Apparel and Home Furnishings."

Each chapter of the text includes a list of associations functioning in the field covered. For additional organizations, check with your library for its latest available directory of trade associations.

PERIODICALS _ _ _ _ _ _ _ _ _ _ _ _ _ _ _ _ _ _ _

Publications that sell advertising usually have research departments, which are sources of information on the publication's readers and on the market it serves. Each chapter of the text includes an appropriate list. For additional sources, check with your library for its latest directory, such as *Ulrich's International Periodicals Directory, Standard Rate and Data Service,* or *IMS/Ayer Directory of Publications.*

APPENDIX *C*

*C*AREER *O*PPORTUNITIES IN *F*ASHION

Fashion is everywhere, and so are career opportunities for those who combine a knowledge of the fashion business with their own talent, ambition, and ability. Consider that a fashion career may open up anywhere along the road from raw materials to the final consumer purchase; stores, mail-order houses, other forms of retailing, manufacturing companies, advertising agencies, newspapers, magazines, commercial photography studios, and public relations firms are among the student's targets in the quest for a foothold in fashion.

Personal attributes suggest the direction a beginner should take. An outgoing personality helps in sales work at all levels, in showroom work, in public relations, and especially in jobs such as that of fashion coordinator, in which one often needs persuasive skills to sell one's ideas to other executives in the organization. The gift of a great figure or a photogenic face can make modeling a possibility, and through that work, a chance to learn from inside many other phases of the fashion business. Visually creative people do well in design, display, advertising, photography, and sketching for designers and fashion information services. Analytical minds adapt well to the multiple problems of managing retail fashion assortments or planning factory production, and thrive on market research.

The rewards of fashion careers are as varied as the jobs themselves. Some pay fabulously; others provide only a modest living. Some positions demand worldwide travel, to buy or observe, or to do both. Others permit one to live at home and commute to an office, retail store, or manufacturing establishment. But all of them, and hundreds more, offer the student of fashion a chance to work, learn, and grow in the endlessly exciting, unceasingly stimulating business of fashion.

The following is a guide to entry-level jobs in the fashion industry. It was prepared by Phyllis Madan and Marilyn Henrion of the Placement Department of the Fashion Institute of Technology, New York, which is affiliated with the State University of New York.

ENTRY LEVEL JOBS FOR FASHION DESIGN GRADUATES _____

- Assistant designer
- Cutting assistant
- Sketching assistant
- Sketcher (assistant to designer)
- Sketcher/stylist
- Junior designer

The personal qualities needed for all of the following jobs in the design room are similar. Applicants must be well-organized, flexible, fast workers, and must have the ability to work under pressure in often cramped working conditions. Fashionable grooming and neat appearance are essential. Most jobs require creativity and a good eye for trends in silhouette, color, and fabric.

Assistant Designer

Responsible for executing designers' ideas by creating a first pattern from slopers or draping. Instructs and supervises the work of samplehands. Often required to keep records, order fabrics and trim, and do follow-up and clerical work. Although job is primarily technical in nature, one may be asked to shop stores for trends, sketch, possibly consult with designer about fabric choices and designs.

Requirements: Fashion Design degree, good knowledge of garment construction (sewing), strong technical skills (making first patterns, draping, and sketching). Beginners must have a portfolio.

Cutting Assistant

Beginning assistant position in companies where there are several assistant designers. Cuts samples, alters patterns, generally assists in design room. Once ability is proven, may have opportunity to assist patternmaker or do draping.

Requirements: Fashion Design degree preferred, good patternmaking skills, draping skills helpful, knowledge of garment construction.

Sketching Assistant

Sketches principally for designers' records—precise technical sketches of constructed garment swatched with fabric and trim. May sketch freehand or with croquis. May sketch and prepare artwork for presentations. Writes specification sheets on how garments are constructed. Usually orders fabric, handles a variety of clerical and follow-up duties. May do market research.

Requirements: Fashion Design degree necessary. Ability to do precise technical sketches rapidly. Portfolio required.

Sketcher (Assistant to Designer)

Sketches freehand illustration-quality sketches for designers' ideas, may be asked to contribute own design ideas, may deal with buyers, do promotional work. Hours are often long and irregular. Must be available to run errands, and generally assist the designer.

Requirements: Fashion Design degree a must. Ability to do freehand illustration-quality sketches at a fast pace. Outstanding portfolio required.

Sketcher/Stylist

Works directly with principals of firm. Shops stores for current trends, sketches ideas, works with patternmaker in developing these ideas, may not do technical work of draping and patternmaking. Participates in fabric selection, coordination of the line; may be involved in working with buyers in merchandising the line.

Requirements: Fashion Design degree, excellent portfolio, good eye for trends in silhouette, color, and fabric.

Junior Designer

Sketches original designs, executes own first pattern, frequently sews sample. Does market research in fabrics and trends. Must be able to provide company with new design ideas and make accurate predictions on what will be salable in coming season. Must be able to design garments within company's price range. Job is fast paced and a high-risk position since continuation of employment may be based on success of line.

Requirements: Fashion Design degree required. Strong creative ability as well as excellent technical skills (draping, patternmaking, sewing). Good eye for trends (silhouette, color, fabric). Portfolio must show evidence of strong creative ability in designing coordinated line of apparel.

ENTRY LEVEL JOBS FOR TEXTILE/ SURFACE DESIGN GRADUATES_____

- Textile/surface designer
- Colorist
- Assistant to stylist
- Lace and embroidery designer
- Screen print artist
- Woven fabric designer
- Painted woven designer
- Knit designer
- Computer aided designer
- Assistant stylist

Jobs for Textile/Surface Design graduates are available in textile converting houses, vertical manufacturing (garment manufacturers that produce their own fabric), textile/surface design studios, department stores (private label), architectural firms (interior fabrics, wall coverings, carpeting), rug manufacturers, contract manufacturers/consultants, paper products manufacturers, china and giftware companies, color forecasting services, and computer graphics design firms.

Requirements: Degree in Textile/Surface Design. Excellent portfolio of designs exhibiting versatile skills and ability to meet professional standards. Other requirements include initiative, reliability, following instructions, and meeting deadlines.

Textile/Surface Designer

Does original textile designs; may also do color combinations and repeats.

Colorist

Does various combinations for existing designs or products and may do original designs.

Assistant to Stylist

Not to be confused with assistant stylist, an upper-management position. Sets up appointments for stylist, acts as liaison with mills, works with clients and salespeople in stylist's absence, keeps clerical records.

Lace and Embroidery Designer

Does detailed technical drawings on graph paper of designs for lace and embroidery. Limited use of color.

Screen Print Artist

Executes designer's ideas through screen print process. Knowledge of color separations, layouts, repeats, and sample printing is required. An understanding of color and a knowledge of color formation is mandatory. Designers express themselves through the screen print process as a means of executing screened croquis and custom printing (limited or exclusive yardage) for both home furnishings and apparel.

Woven Fabric Designer

Does original designs and executes designer's ideas on handloom. Acts as an aid to stylist, sends out mill specs, does quality control, research, and resource work.

Painted Woven Designer

Executes painted woven designs and colorations using ruling pen and airbrush.

Knit Designer

Executes knit swatches and designs on knit machines for apparel. Knitting skills are required. An understanding of the production process is necessary.

Computer Aided Designer

Executes textile/surface designs, colorings, and repeats through use of computer as a design tool. Computer skills required.

Assistant Stylist

A managerial position in a design firm or studio. Works with stylist in compiling lines, preparing storyboards, and forecasting; acts as liaison among stylists, designers, and clients.

ENTRY LEVEL JOBS FOR ADVERTISING DESIGN GRADUATES _ _ _ _ _ _ _ _ _ _ _ _ _ _ _ _ _ _

- Paste-up and mechanical artist
- Layout artist
- Assistant art director

Jobs for Advertising Design graduates can be in either advertising or graphic design areas.

Advertising artists may work on trade or consumer accounts in advertising agencies, in-house advertising departments, or printing firms. They may work in print (magazines or newspaper) or television advertising.

Graphic designers develop "collateral material" which may consist of brochures, annual reports, packaging, logos and trademarks, corporate image projects, and so forth. They also may work in publishing, doing editorial layout for books and magazines.

Board persons do the finished art to prepare it for the printer. They may work in either advertising or graphic design companies.

Paste-Up and Mechanical Artist

Prepares art for printer by pasting together elements of layout (type, illustration, photography), does color separations using T-square and ruling pen. May work for advertising agency, graphic design studio, service studio, printer, publication, or in-house corporate art department.

Requirements: Advertising Design degree or Illustration degree. Must have taken course in paste-ups and mechanicals, and have portfolio demonstrating precision and accuracy in executing mechanicals and color separations.

Layout Artist

Designs layout for ads, usually under the supervision of the art director. Specifies typeface, does "comp" rendering to indicate what finished ad will look like when printed. May do own mechanicals.

Requirements: Advertising Design degree, portfolio demonstrating advertising layouts, thorough knowledge of typefaces, skill at "comp" rendering and mechanicals, neat and precise work habits.

Assistant Art Director

Works directly with art director. May perform any or all of the following duties depending on the size and structure of the agency or firm: assist in developing concepts for advertising campaigns, rough and finished "comp" renderings, specifying type, mechanicals, paste-ups, layout, and graphic design.

Requirements: Advertising Design degree, strong portfolio indicating thorough development of creative concepts through fast, crisp "comp" rendering.

Alternate Entry Jobs for Advertising Design Graduates

Because of the highly competitive nature of most of the jobs just noted, graduates sometimes begin their careers by accepting nonart positions in the field such as Guy or Gal Friday, advertising assistant, or advertising production/traffic assistant. This is an excellent way to gain experience and contacts and get a foot in the door.

ENTRY LEVEL JOBS FOR FASHION ILLUSTRATION GRADUATES_____

- Free-lance illustrator
- Staff illustrator
- Sketcher

Free-Lance Illustrator

Jobs in illustration tend to be free-lance rather than full-time. Free-lance illustrators may do work for advertising agencies, retail stores, manufacturers, textile and fiber houses, pattern companies, display houses, and publications.

Requirements: Illustration degree required. Must have excellent portfolio indicating distinctive illustration style and creativity. Should be well organized and have ability to run own free-lance business (negotiating contracts, setting rates, billing, keeping own records). Must work successfully from photographic references, as models are not provided in the industry.

Staff Illustrator

Staff illustrators may work for buying offices, retail stores, pattern companies, and some publications. However, most illustration work is done on a free-lance basis.

Requirements: Illustration degree required. Must have excellent portfolio.

Sketcher

Apparel manufacturers may hire sketchers on a free-lance or full-time basis to sketch garments for their records. These sketches are not used for reproduction and are not considered illustrative. They are tight sketches showing clear details of garment construction. In full-time positions other duties such as clerical work may be included in the job.

Requirements: Illustration or Fashion Design degree, knowledge of garment construction, ability to do detailed sketches with tight hand.

ENTRY LEVEL POSITIONS FOR FASHION BUYING AND MERCHANDISING (FBM) GRADUATES _____

Career possibilities for FBM graduates fall into two general categories:

- Retail stores and central and resident buying offices
- Manufacturers

Retail Stores and Central and Resident Buying Offices

EXECUTIVE TRAINEE

Most department stores and some specialty chains have formal executive training programs. Firms recruit trainees as potential managers and buyers. Each store has a limited number of openings for the training program, and competition is keen. For the majority of training programs, a bachelor's degree is necessary (especially with department stores). Each training program is unique and includes components of on-the-job training and formal instruction. Trainees are given exposure to merchandising as well as management areas.

Requirements: A high grade point average (especially in math), analytical ability, strong communication skills, leadership ability, initiative, high degree of motivation and energy, maturity, fashionable grooming.

Long-Range Career Goal: Buyer or retail store manager.

DEPARTMENT MANAGER

Many stores hire candidates directly for managerial positions. Previous experience in sales and management in the store for which they are hired is desirable. A bachelor's degree may be necessary depending on the prerequisites of the firm. Responsibilities are training and supervising sales associates, handling all department operations such as opening and closing the register(s), scheduling, merchandising and displaying goods, some direct customer contact.

Requirements: Similar to that of executive trainee.

Long-Range Career Goal: Retail store manager or buyer.

ASSISTANT STORE MANAGER

These positions are available with specialty chain stores. Duties vary depending on the size and structure of the company and store, but usually involve assisting the manager in all phases of running the store. Positions *do not* usually lead to buying careers.

Requirements: Strong retail sales background. Duties are similar to those of department manager. With a small chain store or boutique, the manager must understand the needs of customers and provide buyers with feedback about sales and inventory. After a proven success record of store management with a specialty chain store, career growth into a district or regional manager position is possible. (Ultimately, the responsibility for growth and volume with a designated number of stores rests with the district manager.)

Long-Range Career Goal: Store manager.

BUYERS CLERICAL

This is usually an entry level position more commonly found in a large central buying office (CBO) or larger resident buying office (RBO). The job duties are often consistent with clerical duties of an assistant buyer trainee in a smaller firm and include keeping accurate records, scheduling appointments, follow-up work, possibly answering phones.

Requirements: A high degree of detail orientation is essential as well as strong math aptitude and communication skills.

Long-Range Career Goal: Assistant buyer.

ASSISTANT BUYER TRAINEE (or ASSISTANT MARKET REPRESENTATIVE)

Often an entry level position in an RBO or small CBO. The trainee works directly with the buyer and performs a variety of duties such as keeping unit control records, accompanying the buyer to the market, scheduling appointments, placing reorders, and following up on shipments. Usually the position is a five-day workweek, although overtime may be required during peak seasons.

Requirements: Necessary qualifications are similar to those of buyer's clerical.

Long-Range Career Goal: Market representatives (or buyers)—make trips to the market and spend a large portion of time researching trends, merchandise, and resources. Qualifications include a high degree of communication skills, solid math aptitude, ability to analyze data and make sound business judgments. A good fashion and color sense is also important.

DISTRIBUTION PLANNER

Usually a position found in a large CBO. Includes working with computer to determine distribution of merchandise to branches of chain store firm. Additional responsibilities include keeping records of unit-control, communicating with buyers and merchandise coordinators. Knowledge of computer entry can be helpful.

Requirements: Strong problem-solving and analytical skills as well as figure aptitude are essential.

Long-Range Career Goal: Head distribution planner, buyer, or controller.

PRODUCT DEVELOPMENT TRAINEE

Jobs in product development combine business, technical, and creative aspects and can be found in large retail organizations, private label apparel manufacturers, or independent consulting firms. Entry level jobs may include preparing specs, handling paperwork and follow-up, dealing with clients, overseas communications, and fashion research. As training progresses, additional responsibilities will include working with product development manager and buyers in coordinating garment styles or lines that meet buyers' expectations in regard to delivery, quality, and price point. Once orders are placed, duties include completing the necessary paperwork, providing breakdown information (sizes, colors, quantities) and approving samples for fit, color, and quality. Communications with overseas or domestic production facilities, approval of production samples, and development of yarn and fabric blends and resources are also included in product development. The job may eventually involve travel overseas, negotiating with factories on pricing, working out delivery schedules, and investigating new factories for possible future sourcing.

Requirements: Understanding of merchandising and fashion trends, basic knowledge of garment construction, textile science, and apparel manufacturing processes. Ability to do flat technical sketches, excellent communication and organizational skills, analytical and problem-solving ability, strong business sense, high energy level.

Manufacturers

Positions with manufacturers involve work in the following general areas: (1) promoting or selling the product line, (2) merchandising or planning the line, and (3) overseeing the production and operations of manufacturing the line. In smaller companies, career positions may include duties in several of those areas, such as sales plus merchandising. In a larger firm, positions may fall more neatly into one particular area. Many jobs involve on-the-job training with regular workweeks (occasional overtime during peak seasons).

ENTRY LEVEL POSITIONS

- Showroom sales trainee
- Showroom receptionist
- Clerical assistant
- Product development trainee

All of the positions just listed may be very diversified depending on the size and nature of the firm. Responsibilities include any of the following—showing and selling the line to clients, dealing with buyers in person and on the phone, reception, greeting clients, keeping sales records, faxing, follow-up on deliveries, writing up orders, possibly modeling garments, and attending meetings.

Requirements: Necessary qualifications include fashionable appearance, assertive personality, excellent oral and written communication skills, and a high level of organization. Light typing skills and past sales experience are often helpful.

Long-Range Career Goals: Showroom sales and showroom manager—responsible for sales with own list of clients. If manager, supervise showroom sales force and staff; coordinate sales meetings. Road salesperson—sales outside of showroom in a particular geographic territory. Usually occurs with a large company after proven showroom sales record.

RETAIL SALES COORDINATOR

These positions are unique in that they provide an opportunity to gain exposure to manufacturing as well as retail. One facet of the job involves duties in the showroom (usually serving as the home base) such as showroom sales, coordinating sales among retail store locations, analyzing inventory reports, and ordering and reordering goods for retail store locations.

A second facet of the position includes promoting the manufacturer in a retail department store setting through customer service, displaying and merchandising the goods, and preparing sales and inventory.

Requirements: Excellent interpersonal and communication skills, high energy level, math aptitude, flexibility, sales ability. Past sales experience can be helpful.

Long-Range Career Goal: Potential growth as merchandiser or in sales.

MERCHANDISING ASSISTANT

Duties include working with the merchandiser in planning upcoming product lines; researching the market for trends and colors; keeping records; dealing with sales force, design staff, and customers.

Requirements: Ability to be highly organized and detailed is essential. Good fashion and color sense, team worker, analytical aptitude, and follow-through ability are important. Sketching skills may be helpful.

Long-Range Career Goal: Merchandiser responsibilities are planning the overall line, investigating colors and fabrics, giving direction to the design staff, estimating prices. In a smaller firm the owner or designer usually fulfills the role of merchandiser.

ASSISTANT PIECE GOODS AND TRIM BUYER

Assist with ordering fabrics and trims, keep track of inventory and records, maintain swatch file and samples, accompany buyer on trips to fabric market to learn resources.

Requirements: Interest in textiles, detail oriented, well organized, ability to make good business judgment. Course work in textiles or garment construction may be helpful.

Long-Range Career Goal: Piece goods and trim buyer—to resource piece goods and trim market, price and cost goods, make purchases in conjunction with needs of design staff, possibly give direction to design staff for fabrics and trims.

PRODUCTION ASSISTANT

Duties involve assisting production manager in keeping records relating to production, sales, shipping, and inventory; keeping track of orders; writing up cutting tickets; costing garments; acting as liaison among factory, sales staff, and customers; heavy phone contact with factory. If production is done overseas, may assist in coordinating imports.

Requirements: Important qualifications include high degree of organization, tolerance for stress, communication skills, planning, follow-up and problem-solving ability, math aptitude.

Long-Range Career Goal: Production manager—coordinates and supervises all aspects of producing the line. Usually works out of factory. If overseas manufacturer, makes regular visits to factory to coordinate production and importing.

ADMINISTRATIVE ASSISTANT

Position can be very diversified and usually involves assisting an executive of the firm (vice president, sales manager) in the following capacities: scheduling appointments, keeping records, filing, follow-up work, coordinating information, typing memos.

Requirements: The ability to organize efficiently is essential. Detail orientation, strong communication skills, and potential for advancement are also important.

Long-Range Career Goal: Upper level management—position in a specialized area (sales manager, operations manager) involved in policy making and overall managing of the firm.

ENTRY LEVEL JOBS FOR APPAREL PRODUCTION MANAGEMENT GRADUATES _____

- Production control assistant
- Import coordinator
- Junior industrial engineer
- Costing analyst
- Quality control specialist
- Assistant plant manager

Graduates of the Apparel Production Management program generally work for apparel manufacturing and importing firms. The work site may be based in a corporate office or at a manufacturing plant. Jobs in the office may or may not involve some travel to factory sites, domestically or overseas.

Production Control Assistant

Working in the corporate office as assistant to the production manager, this entry level position may include any combination of the following responsibilities: serving as liaison between marketing and production, expediting orders, preparing cutting tickets, maintaining production records, piecegoods and trim inventory, ordering piecegoods and trim, following up on and coordinating shipments, receiving and allocating goods, dealing with contractors, production scheduling and follow-up, maintaining telex communications with overseas resources, preparation of cost sheets, overseeing of sample production, quality control, entering and retrieving computer data.

Requirements: Organizational ability, figure aptitude, accuracy, thoroughness, assertiveness, high stress tolerance, good communication skills, detail oriented, problem-solving ability.

Import Coordinator

Coordinates and monitors overseas production and shipments. Constant interface with shipping, warehousing, merchandising, and design areas. Makes certain production schedules are met, coordinates deliveries with sales orders, and meets completion dates. Prepares specifications and documentation, obtains duty rates, adds quotas, figures markups, prepares data for computer entry. Maintains daily telex communications with overseas resources and contractors.

Requirements: Organizational ability, figure aptitude, accuracy, thoroughness, assertiveness, high stress tolerance, good communication skills, detail oriented, problem-solving ability.

Junior Industrial Engineer

Works at apparel manufacturing plant studying operations and practices. Does time and motion studies, methods analyses, rate setting, plant layout, monitors efficiency of plant. Reports findings to management and makes recommendations for improvements.

Requirements: Maturity, organizational skills, strong analytical problem-solving and mathematical ability, good at details and follow-through.

Costing Analyst

Breaks down cost of manufacturing garments, taking into account such factors as piece rates, materials costs, import duties, and so forth.

Requirements: Good mathematical skills, analytical ability, good at details.

Quality Control Specialist

Usually works for apparel manufacturer or importer, though jobs may also be found in large retail organizations with centralized buying. Examines garments (may include fiber, textile, color, as well as sewing construction) to see that production specifications are met. Checks assembly operations, identifies problems, works with production staff and management to correct problems. May develop specifications and inspect merchandise as it comes in from overseas as well as from domestic sources. Job often involves travel to factories.

Requirements: Detail oriented, good at followthrough, ability to work under pressure, high energy level, good communication skills, analytical and problem-solving ability.

Assistant Plant Manager

Assists in running factory—oversees work flow, maintains production schedules, distributes and keeps track of work. Assists in staffing plant and supervising various plant operations including cutting, sewing, pressing, warehousing, shipping.

Requirements: Must be a self-starter, have strong interpersonal skills, supervisory and organizational ability, high energy level, ability to work well under pressure, problem-solving ability.

ENTRY LEVEL JOBS FOR TEXTILE DEVELOPMENT GRADUATES _____

- Assistant converter
- Assistant stylist (fabric or yarn)
- Product development assistant (textiles)

- Textile technologist
- Sales trainee
- Fabric librarian

Since textiles constitute a key component of the apparel industry, graduates of this major have a broad range of career options related to both business and technology. The entry level jobs listed here represent some of the more typical ones available, but by no means cover the entire range of possibilities.

Assistant Converter

Assists converter in overseeing and expediting the various processes involved in the transition of greige goods to finished fabric (dyeing, printing, finishing). Serves as liaison among mills, dyeing and finishing plants, knitters, and clients; heavy phone work. Projects greige goods needs, figures yardage and poundage, prepares dye orders, schedules printing, tracks yarn and finished goods. Processes customer orders and follows up on orders to see that deadlines are met. Figures costs, losses; maintains inventory control.

Requirements: Good at details and followthrough, problem solving, gathering and analyzing data, oral communications, working with figures, memorizing, confronting, mediating.

Assistant Stylist (Fabric or Yarn)

May work for textile firm or yarn producer. Assists in developing seasonal lines and colorations. Duties may include any of the following, alone or in combination: surveys competitors and forecasts, researches market trends. Assists in preparing presentation boards and sales aids. Works with customers on development and refinement of patterns and colors. Places lab dips, follows up on sample yardage. Works with artists to make sure work is done on time. Obtains approval from customers. Maintains fabric library, keeps it current and organized, locates samples and data. Handles administrative and follow-up details related to line development.

Requirements: Excellent color sense, fashion awareness, organizational ability, communication skills, good at details and followthrough.

Product Development Assistant (Textiles)

May be involved in knit or woven fabric development. Helps develop product from technical point of view, prepares specifications graph layouts to be executed at mill level and art room level. Translates clients' and salespeople's ideas into what is technically feasible, advises as to machine capabilities. Has samples made up, checks yarns, follows up on production, sees that finished goods are executed properly. May involve some travel to mills. Utilizes market research findings, maintains records, handles follow-up work, serves as liaison between design room and mill.

Requirements: Analytical ability, organizational skills, fashion awareness, color sense, strong communication skills, problem solving purchase orders and reorders. Maintains phone contact with mills and factories to make certain piece goods shipments are met. Reviews fabric lines brought in by textile salespeople or may go out into market to assist in piece goods selection. May order piece goods, trims, and notions, and may make substitutions when goods are unavailable. Maintains telex communications with overseas resources.

Requirements: Oral communications, negotiating, confronting, record keeping, handling details and followthrough, gathering and analyzing data, problem solving, memorizing, organizational ability, color sense.

Textile Technologist

May work for testing laboratory, retailer, or manufacturer. Responsibilities may include any of the following duties, depending on the setting: performs various lab tests on fabrics, yarns, fibers, and garments to determine color fastness, washability, shrinkage, and so forth. Analyzes fabric construction, fiber content, finishing properties; compiles data; prepares reports on findings. Identifies problems, helps maintain standards. Develops and verifies care labeling.

Requirements: Systematic, good at details, well organized, able to follow instructions and work alone. Good communication skills; oral, written, and analytical ability.

Sales Trainee

May work for textile mill, converter, or yarn producer. Calls on manufacturers (or textile firms) to sell the line and service accounts. Training may include visit to mill or assisting in showroom. Initially will be given list of accounts to work with, ultimately will be expected to generate new accounts. May deal with designers, merchandisers, piece goods buyers, or production people. May suggest end uses for product, explain properties. Gathers information and provides feedback to management on customer needs in terms of styling, product development. Follows up on orders and shipments, services accounts.

Requirements: Initiative, outgoing personality, excellent communication and interpersonal skills, problem-solving ability, good memory, color sense, high energy level, self-starter, competitive spirit.

Fabric Librarian

May work for fiber or textile firm, trade association, or pattern company. Responsibilities may include any combination of the following duties: maintains up-to-date fabric library, prepares sample cards and seasonal presentations. Works with color file system, runs groups of colors in response to requests.

Researches and compiles fabric resources list, may go out to review fabric lines at various resources and select appropriate fabrics for library. Assists users in locating, identifying, and selecting appropriate fabrics for library. May work in a setting that serves as a resource for internal design staff only, or may deal with clients representing other firms.

Requirements: Knowledge of textiles, excellent color sense, design and fashion awareness, organizational ability, systematic, good memory, good communication skills.

ENTRY LEVEL JOBS FOR PATTERNMAKING TECHNOLOGY GRADUATES

- Assistant patternmaker
- Assistant designer (technical)
- Technical designer trainee
- Quality control analyst
- Grader trainee

Assistant Patternmaker

Works as assistant to head patternmaker. Beginner's duties may include working on sample patterns, cutting, grading, marker making. May also work with spec sheets, quality control, fittings, yardage calculations. As skills are evidenced, will assist in making perfect patterns for production.

Requirements: Excellent patternmaking skills, precision oriented, ability to follow instructions and work under pressure.

Assistant Designer (Technical)

Works as technical assistant in design room. Executes designer's ideas from sketches or garments, making first patterns through draping or pattern drafting. May also cut samples, prepare specifications, and supervise sample hands. Job may also include other design room functions such as sketching for spec sheets or records (flat detailed technical sketches), trim purchasing, maintaining design records.

Requirements: Pattern drafting skills; draping (where required); flat, detailed technical sketching (should have sample sketches to show); style sense; organizational skills; problem-solving ability; communication skills; computer grading skills.

Technical Designer Trainee

Job is usually found in retail buying offices that maintain extensive private label manufacturing programs. Assists in developing size specifications, participates in fit meetings, measures and approves sample garments, maintains contact with production facilities (overseas or domestic) and buyers. May also be called on to write reports.

Requirements: Precision oriented, thorough knowledge of garment construction, analytical ability, good communication skills, decision-making ability.

Quality Control Analyst

Evaluates garments for sizing and construction based on specifications. May deal with production facilities to follow up on corrections or report to liaison for follow-up. May also be involved in preparation of specifications.

Requirements: Precision oriented, thorough knowledge of garment construction, good communication skills, analytical ability.

Grader Trainee

Prepares production patterns in various size ranges. May work with computerized grading system or manual system. Job may be combined with marker making, which is the process by which production patterns are laid out onto fabric for maximum fabric usage (computerized or manual system).

Requirements: Precision oriented, strong sense of spacial relationships.

*F*ASHION *B*USINESS *L*ANGUAGE *G*UIDE

ACCESSORIES All articles ranging from hosiery to shoes, bags, gloves, belts, scarfs, jewelry, and hats, for example, worn to complete or enhance an outfit of apparel.

ACCESSORIZING The process of adding accessory items to apparel for display, for models in fashion shows, or for customers' clothes on request.

ACWTU Amalgamated Clothing Workers and Textile Union.

ADAPTATION A design that reflects the outstanding features of another design but is not an exact copy.

ADVERTISING A nonpersonal method of influencing sales through a paid message by an identified sponsor. Advertising appears in media such as newspapers, magazines, television, and radio.

ADVERTISING CREDIT The mention of a store name (one or several), in a producer's advertisement, as a retail source for the advertised merchandise.

APPAREL An all-embracing term that applies to men's, women's, and children's clothing.

APPAREL JOBBER A firm that generally handles all the processes but the sewing, and sometimes the cutting, and that contracts out these production processes to independently owned contractors.

APPAREL MANUFACTURER (i.e., inside shop) A firm that buys fabrics and does the designing, patternmaking, grading, cutting, sewing, and assembling of garments in factories that it owns.

APPAREL MART   A building that houses the regional showrooms of apparel companies.

AVANT GARDE   In any art, the most daring of the experimentalists; innovation of original and unconventional designs, ideas, or techniques during a particular period.

BAR CODE   A series of vertical bars that identify a merchandise category, the manufacturer, and the individual item.

BILATERAL TREATY   A treaty between two countries.

BOARDING (HOSIERY)   Heat-setting process used to give hosiery a permanent shape.

BOUTIQUE   From the French word meaning "little shop." A free-standing shop or an area within a retail store, devoted to specialized merchandise for special-interest customers.

BRANCH   In retailing, an extension of a parent or flagship store, operated under the same name and ownership.

BRAND   A trade name or symbol that distinguishes a product as that of a particular manufacturer or distributor.

BRIDGE JEWELRY   Jewelry that in price and materials is between costume and fine jewelry.

BUYER   An executive (retail) who is responsible for the selection and purchase of merchandise.

CAD   Computer assisted design.

CATALOG   A promotional book or booklet in which merchandise is offered for sale.

CATALOG SHOWROOM RETAILER   An underselling establishment that prints and distributes a catalog and maintains a showroom where samples of the merchandise can be seen and ordered.

CAUTION   French term for admission or entrance fee charged to trade customers by haute couture houses.

CHAIN STORES   A retail organization that owns and operates a string of similar stores that are merchandised and controlled from a central headquarters office.

CHAMBRE SYNDICALE DE LA COUTURE PARISIENNE   The French trade association that represents the haute couture houses of Paris.

CLASSIC   A particular style that continues as an accepted fashion over an extended period of time.

CLOSEOUT   An offering of selected discontinued goods by a vendor to a retailer at reduced prices.

COLLECTION   A manufacturer's or designer's group of styles or design creations for a specific season. The season's total number of styles of designs, accumulated for presentation to buyers, constitutes a collection.

COMMISSIONAIRE An independent retailer's service organization that is foreign based and is used to represent importers abroad.

COMPETITION In its marketing context, it is a form of business activity in which two or more parties are engaged in a rivalry for consumer acceptance.

CONFINED A line or label that is sold to one retailer in a trading area on an exclusive basis.

CONGLOMERATE A company consisting of a number of subsidiary divisions in a variety of unrelated industries.

CONSUMER The ultimate user of goods or services.

CONSUMER OBSOLESCENCE The rejection of something that retains utility value in favor of something new.

CONTRACT TANNERS Business firms that contract hides and skins to the specification of leather converters.

CONTRACTOR (APPAREL) A manufacturing concern that does the sewing and often the cutting for other apparel producers (so called because this work is done under a contractual arrangement).

CONVERTER (LEATHERS) A company that buys hides and skins, farms them out for processing to contract tanneries, and sells the finished product.

CONVERTER (TEXTILE) A firm that buys or handles the greige goods (i.e., unfinished fabrics) from mills and contracts them out to finishing plants to have them finished (i.e., dyed, printed, etc.).

COOPERATIVE ADVERTISING Advertising, the cost of which is shared by a firm and its customer for the benefit of both.

CORPORATION An artificial legal entity.

COST PRICE The price at which goods are billed to a store, exclusive of any cash discounts that may apply to the purchase.

COSTUME JEWELRY Jewelry made of nonprecious materials.

COUTURIER French word for (male) designer, usually one who has his own couture house. Couturière (female).

CRAZE A fad or fashion characterized by much crowd excitement or emotion.

CUSTOM MADE Apparel made to the order of individual customers; cut and fitted to individual measurements as opposed to apparel that is mass-produced in standardized sizes.

CUTTING-UP TRADES The segment of the fashion industries that produces apparel (i.e., apparel producers).

DATA BASE An information system, generally computerized, in which a variety of factual data are organized and stored.

DEMOGRAPHICS The study of vital and social statistics of a population.

DEPARTMENT STORE A retail establishment that employs at least 25 people and that carries a wide variety of merchandise lines, including home furnishings, apparel for the family, and household linens and dry goods.

DESIGN An arrangement of parts, form, color, and line, for example, to create a version of a style.

DIRECT MARKETING A term that embraces direct mail, mail order, and direct response.

DIRECT SELLER A retailer that sells merchandise by contacting customers either through door-to-door approaches or through some form of in-home party plan.

DISCOUNTER (off-price) An "underselling" retail establishment that utilizes self-service combined with many other expense-saving techniques.

DISPLAY A visual presentation of merchandise or ideas.

DOMESTIC MARKET When referring to origin of goods, *domestic* means manufactured in one's own country as opposed to foreign-made.

DOMESTICS Merchandise essentially for the home including sheets, pillows, towels, blankets, table linens, and other textile products.

DUTY A tax on imports.

EDI Electronic data interchange: the exchange of business data between two parties electronically.

EDI MAILBOX Where data are stored on a third party's computer, when a receiving computer is incompatible with a sending computer.

EDI THIRD PARTY A company that provides EDI mailboxes.

EDI TRADING PARTNER A company with which one exchanges data electronically.

EDITORIAL CREDIT The mention, in a magazine or newspaper, of a store name as a retail source for merchandise that is being editorially featured by the publication.

ELECTRONIC RETAILING Selling by means of an electronic device such as television or interactive computers.

ENTREPRENEUR A person who organizes, launches, and directs a business undertaking and assumes the financial risks and uncertainties of the undertaking.

EUROPEAN ECONOMIC COMMUNITY (EEC) Also known as the Common Market. Sharing of common agricultural practices, free movement of labor and capital between members, and a unified transportation system. Most tariffs between members have been abolished.

EXCLUSIVITY Allowing a business company sole use within a given trading area of a product.

FACTOR Financial institution that buys accounts receivable from sellers, assumes the risks and responsibilities of collection, and charges a fee for this service.

FACTORY   A manufacturing plant.

FACTORY OUTLET   A manufacturer-owned retail outlet whose major purpose is to dispose of the manufacturer's excess inventory.

FAD   A minor or short-lived fashion.

FASHION (OR FASHIONS)   (1) The prevailing style(s) at any particular time. When a style is followed or accepted by many people, it is a fashion. (2) a continuing process of change in the styles of dress that are accepted and followed by a large segment of the public at any particular time.

FASHION BULLETIN   Written report on significant fashions prepared by fashion specialists.

FASHION CLINIC   Meeting of a group of persons interested in fashion (under the direction of a fashion specialist) for the purpose of presenting or discussing significant fashion trends. Clinics are usually held at the beginning of new fashion seasons.

FASHION CONSULTANT   A person who gives professional fashion advice or services.

FASHION COORDINATOR (OR DIRECTOR)   A person charged with the responsibility for keeping abreast of fashion trends and developments, and acting as a source of fashion information to others in his or her organization. Other responsibilities vary from place to place, as do job titles.

FASHION FORECAST   A prediction as to which fashions or styles will be popular during a future period.

(THE) FASHION GROUP   A national association of women engaged in the fashion business.

FASHION IMAGE   The impression the consumer has of a retailer's position on fashion leadership, quality, selection, and prices.

(THE) FASHION PRESS   Reporters of fashion news for magazines, newspapers, broadcast media, and so on.

FASHION RETAILING   The business of buying fashion-oriented merchandise from a variety of resources and assembling it in convenient locations for resale to ultimate consumers.

FASHION SHOW OR SHOWING   Formal presentation of a group of styles, often in connection with showing the season's new merchandise.

FASHION TREND   The direction in which fashion is moving.

FLEA MARKET   A location in which a wide variety of independent sellers periodically rent space.

FRANCHISE   A contractual agreement between a wholesaler, manufacturer, or service organization (the franchisor) and an independent retailer that buys the right to use the franchisor's product name or service for a stipulated fee. In return, the parent company provides assistance, guidelines, and established business patterns.

GARMENT CENTER (SA)   The area to the East and West of Seventh Avenue in New York City, in which many of the women's ready-to-wear industry showrooms are located.

GATT   General Agreement on Tariffs and Trade. A multilateral trade treaty between countries that spells out reciprocal rights and obligations for member countries.

GEMSTONES   A mineral found in nature that is used in jewelry because of its beauty, clarity, rarity, and other attributes.

GENERAL MERCHANDISE STORES   Retail stores that carry a wide range of merchandise lines including apparel, hardware, furniture, home furnishings, and many other products.

GLOBAL MARKETING   International operations carried on in which produced goods are exported and marketed in foreign countries.

GLOBAL SOURCING   Utilization of worldwide production.

GREIGE GOODS   Unfinished fabrics.

HAUTE COUTURE (literal French translation: "the finest dressmaking")   As used in the fashion business, this refers to a firm whose designer creates a collection of original designs that are then duplicated for individual customers on a made-to-order basis.

HIDES   Animal skins that weigh more than 25 pounds when shipped to a tannery.

HIGH FASHION   A fashion that is in the stage of limited acceptance.

HYPERMARKET   A superlarge retailing establishment that brings food and general merchandise together in an immense area.

I.L.G.W.U.   International Ladies' Garment Workers' Union.

IMPORT   Merchandise brought in from a foreign country for resale or other purposes.

IMPORT BROKER   An agent middleman who brings buyers and sellers together to facilitate the buying and selling of foreign goods in a domestic market.

INCOME   The returns that come in periodically from business, property, labor, or other sources (i.e., revenue).

INITIAL MARKUP (Mark on)   The difference between the cost price of merchandise and its original retail price.

INTERNATIONAL MARKETING   See Global marketing.

JEWELRY   Articles of personal adornment made of either precious or nonprecious materials.

JOB LOT   A broken, unbalanced assortment of discontinued merchandise reduced in price for quick sale. Also called odd lot.

JOBBER   See Apparel jobber.

KIPS   Animal skins weighing from 15 to 25 pounds when shipped to a tannery.

KNOCK-OFF   The copying of another manufacturer's fashion design.

LANDED COST   The cost of an imported product, which includes the cost of the merchandise, transportation, and duty.

LAST   A form in the shape of a boot over which shoes are built.

LEAD TIME   Time necessary to produce merchandise from receipt of order to delivery time.

LEVERAGED BUYOUT (LBO)   The purchase of a public company's stock made by a group of investors who borrow money from an investment firm using the company's assets as collateral.

LICENSEE   The person or organization to whom a license is granted.

LICENSING   An arrangement whereby firms are given permission to produce and market merchandise that bears the name of a licensor, who receives a percentage of wholesale sales (i.e. a royalty) in return for the use of his or her name.

LICENSOR   The person or organization who grants a license.

LINE   A collection of styles and designs shown by a producer in a given season.

LINE-FOR-LINE COPY   Exact copy of a style originated by a foreign couturier.

MAIL ORDER   A firm that does the bulk of its sales through a catalog.

MAIL-ORDER HOUSE   A retailing organization that generates the bulk of its business through merchandise catalogs.

MALL   See Shopping centers.

MARKDOWN   Reduction from an original retail price.

MARKET   (1) A group of potential customers. (2) The place or area in which buyers and sellers congregate.

MARKET REPRESENTATIVE   A market specialist in a resident buying office who covers a segment of the wholesale market and makes information about it available to client stores.

MARKET SEGMENTATION   The subdivision of a population (frequently ultimate consumers) whose members share similar identifiable characteristics (e.g., age, wealth, education level, marital status, lifestyle).

MARKET STRATEGY   A long-range plan of action calculated to achieve the objectives of an organization.

MARKET WEEKS   Scheduled periods during which producers introduce their new lines for an upcoming season.

MARKETING   The total business interaction that involves the planning, pricing, promotion, and distribution of consumer-wanted goods and services for profit.

MARKETING CONCEPT   Recognizing the importance of the ultimate consumer in the buying and selling process.

MARKUP   The difference between the cost price of merchandise and its retail price. Usually expressed as a percentage of retail.

MART   A building or building complex housing both permanent and transient showrooms of producers.

MASS MERCHANDISING   The retailing on a very large scale of goods.

MASS PRODUCTION   Production of goods in quantity—many at a time rather than one at a time.

MERCHANDISING   The activities involved in buying and selling: finding customers, providing them with what they want, when they want it, at prices they can afford, and are willing to pay.

MERGER   Acquisition of one company by another.

MODE   Synonym for a fashion.

MOM-AND-POP STORE   A small store generally operated by husband and wife with limited capital and few or no hired assistants.

MULTINATIONAL COMPANY   A firm that conducts a portion of its business in two or more countries.

NATIONAL BRAND   Brand owned by a manufacturer, which is a trade name or symbol, that is nationally advertised.

NEEDLE TRADES   Synonym for apparel industry.

N.R.M.A. (NATIONAL RETAIL MERCHANTS ASSOCIATION)   A trade association of the leading department, specialty, and chain stores in the United States.

OCR-A   Optical character recognition, a special type of font that is both human- and machine-readable.

OFF-PRICE RETAILING   The selling of brand and designer-named merchandise at lower than normal retail prices.

OFFSHORE PRODUCTION   Production of goods by a domestic manufacturer in a foreign country.

OPENINGS   Fashion showings of new collections by apparel producers at the beginning of a season.

OPEN-TO-BUY   The amount of money that a buyer may spend on merchandise to be delivered in a given period.

OUTSIDE SHOP   See Contractor.

PELT   Skin of fur-bearing animal.

PLU   Price look-up.

POLICY   A clearly defined course of action or method of doing business deemed necessary, expedient, or advantageous.

POS   Point-of-sale. In retailing, that area of the store or department where the customer pays for the merchandise and the sale is recorded.

PRESS KIT   A collection of facts, figures, photographs, and other promotional materials assembled into a compact package and distributed to the press.

PRESS RELEASE   A written statement of news that has occurred or is about to occur, specifying the source of the information and the date after which its use is permissible.

PRÊT-À-PORTER (French term meaning, literally, "ready-to-carry")   French ready-to-wear apparel, as distinguished from couture clothes, which are custom made.

PRIMARY MARKET   Producers of fibers, textiles, leather, and furs.

PRIVATE LABEL   Merchandise that is produced exclusively for one retail firm and identified by one or more "names" or brands that are owned by the retailer.

PRODUCT DEVELOPER   A person employed by a company to create private label merchandise for their exclusive use.

PRODUCT MANAGER   An executive who functions as the head of the product development team responsible for the planning and development of a particular product, product line, or brand.

PROFIT   Total revenue and sales less all costs and expenses.

PSYCHOGRAPHICS   The study of people's attitudes and values.

PUBLIC CORPORATION   A business that sells shares of its stock on the public market to the public.

PUBLICITY   A nonpaid message — verbal or written — in a public-information medium about a company's merchandise, activities, or services.

PUBLICLY OWNED   A corporation whose shares are available for sale to any person who chooses to purchase these shares.

QUOTA   Quantitative restrictions placed on exporting countries on the number of units of specific categories that may be shipped to a particular importing country over a specified period of time.

QR (QUICK RESPONSE)   A computerized partnership between different segments of the industry. Its purpose is to supply customers with products or services in the precise quantities required at exactly the right time.

READY-TO-WEAR   Apparel that is mass produced in standardized sizes as opposed to apparel made to a customer's special order (custom made).

REORDER NUMBER   A style number that continues to be ordered by buyers.

RESIDENT BUYING OFFICE   A service organization located in a major market center that reports market information, acts as market representative, and renders other related services to a group of stores who have their own buyers.

RESOURCE   A vendor or source of supply.

RETAILING   The business of buying goods from a variety of resources for resale to ultimate consumers.

ROYALTY   A compensation paid to the owner of a right (name, brand, etc.) for the use of that right.

SALES PROMOTION   Any activity that is used to influence the sale of merchandise, services, or ideas.

SAMPLE   The model or trial garment (may be original in design, a copy, or an adaptation) to be shown to the trade.

SEASON   In retailing, a selling period.

SECONDARY MARKET   Producers of finished consumer fashion products (dresses, coats, suits, accessories, and the like).

SELL THROUGH   A measurement of the amount of merchandise sold of a particular merchandise category or style.

SEVENTH AVENUE   An expression used as a synonym for New York City's women's apparel industry (actually, a street on which the showrooms of many garment manufacturers are located).

SHOPPING CENTERS   A group of retail stores and related facilities planned, developed, and managed as a unit.

SHOWING   See Fashion show or showing.

SILHOUETTE   The overall outline or contour of a costume. Also frequently referred to as "shape" or "form."

SKU   Stock-keeping unit.

SMART   Having a fashionable appearance.

SOCIOECONOMICS   Pertaining to a combination or interaction of social and economic factors.

SOURCING   In fashion marketing, the geographic location of suppliers of merchandise.

SPECIALTY STORE   A retail establishment that deals either in one category of merchandise or in related categories of merchandise.

STORE OWNERSHIP GROUP   A retailing organization consisting of a group of stores that are centrally owned and controlled in terms of broad policy making but are operated autonomously.

STYLE (noun)   A type of product with specific characteristics that distinguish it from another type of the same product.

STYLE (verb)   To give fashion features to an article or group of articles (as to style a line of coats and suits, for example).

STYLE NUMBER   An identification number given to an individual design by a manufacturer. The retailer uses the number when ordering the item and for stock identification.

STYLE PIRACY   A term used to describe the use of a design without the consent of the originator.

STYLIST   One who advises concerning styles in clothes, furnishings, and the like.

TARGET MARKET   A particular segment of a total potential market selected by a company as the object of its marketing efforts.

TARIFF   A tax leveled against imported products.

TELEMARKETING   Sales of products and services via an interactive system or two-way television or via telephone.

TRADE ASSOCIATION   A nonprofit voluntary association of businesses having common interests.

TRADE DEFICIT   A condition in international trade in which the value of a country's imports is in excess of the value of its imports.

TRADE PUBLICATIONS   Newspapers or magazines published specifically for professionals in a special field.

TRADE SHOW   Periodic merchandise exhibits staged in various trading areas by groups of producers.

TRIANGLE FIRE   A fire that occurred in the Triangle Shirtwaist factory in 1911 and took 146 lives. The tragedy was the turning point in the "sweatshop" era because it awoke the public conscience to the labor conditions in the garment industry.

TRUNK SHOW   A producer's or designer's complete collection of samples brought into the store for a limited time to take orders from customers.

UPC   Universal product code. A special bar-code symbol that has been adopted as a standard for the retail industry. The code consists of a one-digit merchandise category code, a five-digit UPC vendor number, a five-digit item number, and a one-digit check digit.

VENDEUSE   French term meaning saleswoman.

VENDOR   One who sells; resource from which a retailer buys goods.

VIDEO SHOPPING   In-home shopping using cable television or interactive home computers.

VOLUME   Amount of dollar sales done in a given period by a retail store or other mercantile establishment.

WAREHOUSE CLUB   A retail establishment that specializes in bulk sales of nationally branded merchandise at discount prices.

WOMEN'S WEAR DAILY   Trade publication of the women's fashion industries. (The textile and menswear counterpart is the *Daily News Record*.)

Photo Credits

$\mathcal{I}$NDEX*

Abboud, Joseph, 214
Abraham & Straus, 411, 439
Accessories, **254**
Accessories industry
  designers, 281
  economic importance of,
    256–257
  gloves, 272–274
  handbags, 268–271
  hosiery, 264–268
  jewelry, 276–280
  licensing, 254
  men's accessories, 232–233
  millinery, 274–276
  nature of, 254, 256
  shoes, 257–264
  small leather goods, 270–
    272
  see also specific types of
    accessories
Acetate, 90, 91
Acrylic, 90, 91
Adidas, 216
Administrative assistant, job
    description, 535
Adolfo, 275, 514
Adrian, Gilbert, 514
Advertising
  advertising agency, **489**–490
  cooperative advertising, **150**

fashion magazine revenues,
    484
fashion videos, 488–489
general magazines, 486
newspapers, 486
publicity, 490–491
retailer/manufacturer
    arrangements, 150–151
trade publications, 150
Advertising agency, **489**–490
  fashion accounts as specialty,
    490
  role of, 489–490
After Six, 209
Air jet shuttless looms, 109
Alaia, Azzedine, 360, 514
Albini, Walter, 514
Allied Stores, 411, 412
Amalgamated Clothing and
    Textile Workers Union of
    America (ACTWUA), rise
    of, 205–206
American Fur Information and
    Fashion Council, 113
American Printed Fabrics
    Council, 123
Amies, Hardy, 514
Andre Richard Company, 124
Animal rights, fur industry and,
    110, 114

ANSI X 12, 107–108
Apparel jobbers, role of, **154**
Apparel marts, 170–173
  Atlanta, 171–172
  California, 171
  Chicago, 172–173
  Dallas, 171
  market weeks, **170**, 172
  regional showrooms, **170**
Apparel specialty chains,
    417–418
Aquascutum, 367
Arctic Dream, 113
Aris Glove, 272
Armani, Giorgio, 220, 365, 514
Artificial silk, 88
Ascot Chang, 236
Ashley, Laura, 177, 367, 514
Assistant art director, 529–
    530
Assistant buyer trainee, 632
Assistant converter, 538
Assistant designer, 525, 540
Assistant patternmaker, 540
Assistant piece goods/trim buyer,
    535
Assistant plant manager, 537
Assistant store manager, 632
Assistant to stylist, 527
Assistant stylist, 528, 538

*Bold face page indicates definition term or brief description about designers and companies.

Associated Corset and Brassiere Manufacturers, 282
Associated Dry Goods, 411–412
Associated Merchandising Corporation (AMC), 477
operation of, **500–504**
Associated office, 477
Athletic shoes, 258–259
Atlanta Apparel Mart, 171–172
Audemars, 88
Austria, specialties of, 372
Avant garde, **38**
Awards
Coty Awards, 59
Cutty Sark Award, 60
Lifetime Achievement Award, 59–60
Ayres, L. S., 412

B. Altman, 439
Balenciaga de Eisequirre, Cristóbal, 354, 355, 396, 397, 514
Bali Co., 284, 285
Balmain, Pierre, 514
Banks, Jeffrey, 60, 220
Bar coding, 55, **106**
Barbizon, 284
Barentzen, Patrick de, 514
Barnard, Kurt, 28, 31
Barnes, Jhane, 220
Barney's, 226, 236, 238, 239–240
Baron, Andrew, 345
Baron Peters, Inc., 345–346
Barry's Jewelers, 277
Barthet, Jean, 515
Battery-Street Enterprises, 185
Beard, Thomas, 257
Beene, Geoffrey, 59, **78–79**, 159
Beere, Marshall, 338
Belts, 280
Benetton, 177, 365, 437
Bergdorf Goodman, 226, 236, 238–239, 256
Berge, Pierre, 359
Best Products, 432
Betsy Johnson, 152
Better price level, 159
Biagotti, 365
Bidermann Industries, 208
Bilateral treaties, **314**
Bis, Dorothée, 354, 360
Blass, Bill, 59, 123, 143, 159, 161, 192, 515
Block, Leon, 216
Bloomingdale's, 66, 161, 226, 236, 411, 412, 438, 439
Bloomingdale's-by-Mail, 424
Blue Bell, Inc., 107, 330
Bobbin Magazine, 486

Body Fashions/Intimate Apparel, 150
Body Map, 367
Bohan, Marc, 515
Bon Marché, 439
Bonnie Doon, 264, 267
Bonwit Teller, 439
Boss, Hugo, 368
Boston Apparel Mart, 173
Bottom-up theory, of fashion leadership, 46
"Boutique Forecast, The," 472
Boutiques, **414–415**
designer-name boutiques, 429–430
Boxer, Leonard, 179, 182
Branch store, **411**
Brand and Buying Service, 476
Brand names
hosiery industry, 266
intimate apparel, 284
menswear, 221–223
specification buying, **324–325**
synthetic fibers, **91–92**
Bricken, Barry, 220
Bridge jewelry, **277**
Bridge price level, 159
Brigance, Tom, 138
Brittania, 187, 216
Brooke, Donald, 515
Brooks, Henry Sands, 234
Brooks Brothers, 204, 213, 226, **234–235**, 238, 438
Brown Group, 258
Brown Shoe Company, 262
Browning, William C., 133
Buchman, Dana, 159, 182
Budget price level, 159
Bullock's, 107, 413, 438
Burberry, 367
Burdine's, 412, 439
Burlington Industries, 95, 96, 98, 107, 124–125, 330
Burns-Winkler Associates, 476
Burrows, Stephen, 515
Burton's Gentlemen's Magazine, 482
Bush, Barbara, 49
Butterick, Ebenezer, 135
Buyers clerical, job description, 532
Buying merchandise
buying services, 479
entry level careers in, 532
merchandising services, 478–481
resident buying offices, **474–478**
BVY Group, 337

Cacherel, 360
Caldor, 426
California Apparel Mart, 171
California Apparel News, 150
California International Menswear Market (CIMM), 229
"California look," 229
Calitzine, 360
Calvin Klein cosmetics, 67
Camera Nazionale dell' Alta Moda Italiana, 360
Campeau Corporation, 412, 439
Canada, specialties of, 372
Canadian Majestic Mink Association, 113
Canton Trade Fair, 103, 376–377
Capital, factoring, **163**
Capucci, Roberto, 515
Cardin, Pierre, **17–31**, 355, 515
Care Labeling of Textile Wearing Apparel Act (1972), 16
Career dressing, 63
Careers in fashion
advertising design graduates
assistant art director, 529–530
layout artist, 529
paste-up artist, 529
in apparel production
assistant plant manager, 537
costing analyst, 537
import coordinator, 536
junior industrial engineer, 537
production control assistant, 536
quality control specialist, 537
buying/merchandising graduates
assistant buyer trainee, 532
assistant store manager, 532
buyers clerical, 532
department manager, 531
distribution planner, 533
executive trainee, 531
product development trainee, 533
fashion design graduate
assistant designer, 525
cutting assistant, 525
junior designer, 526
sketcher, 526
sketcher/stylist, 526
sketching assistant, 526
fashion illustrator graduates
freelance illustrator, 530
sketcher, 530–531
staff illustrator, 530

in manufacturing
  administrative assistant, 535
  assistant piece goods/trim
    buyer, 535
  entry level positions, 534
  merchandising assistant,
    534–535
  production assistant, 535
  retail sales coordinator, 534
patternmaking graduates
  assistant designer, 540
  assistant patternmaker, 540
  grader trainee, 541
  quality control analyst, 540
  technical designer trainee,
    540
textile development graduates
  assistant converter, 538
  assistant stylist, 538
  fabric librarian, 539–540
  product development
    assistant, 538–539
  sales trainee, 539
  textile technologist, 539
textile/surface design graduates
  assistant to stylist, 527
  colorist, 527
  lace/embroidery designer,
    528
  screen print artist, 528
  textile/surface designer, 527
woven fabric designer, 528
  assistant stylist, 528
  computer aided designer, 528
  knit designer, 528
  painted woven fabric
    designer, 528
Caribbean, sourcing in, 315,
  336–339
Caribbean Basin Initiative (CBI),
  319, 342
Carnaby Street, 366
Carnegie, Hattie, 515
Carol Hochman Design, 284
Carolee, 257, **287–289**
Carolina Trade Center, 173
Carr, Zack, 65
Carson Pirie Scott, 438
Carter, 174, 330
Carter Hawley Hale, 412
Cashin, Bonnie, 515
Cassini, Oleg, 297
Castelebajac, 360
Casual Corner, 416, 418
Catalog showroom retailer, **432**
Catalogs
  department stores, 424
  see also Mail-order houses
Caution fee, **356**
Cavanaugh, John, 515

Celia, 277
Celler-Kefauver Act (1950), 16
Cellulosics, 90
Central America, 315
Centralized buying, **481**
Certified Fashion Guild, 476
Chain Store Age, 486
Chain stores, **415–419**
  apparel specialty chains,
    417–418
  "big four," 416
  compared to department
    stores, 415–416
  general merchandise chains,
    418–419
Chambre Syndicale de la
  Couture Parisienne, 28,
  352, 354
Chambre Syndicale du
  Prêt-à-Porter, **354**
Chanel, 47, 355
  operation of, 383–384
Chanel, Coco, 63, 396, 515
Chaps, 208
Chardonnet, Hilaire de, 88
Charivari, **458–461**
Charming Shops, 416
Chaus, Bernard, 179
Chazen, Jerome, 152, 179, 281
Chemical fiber producers, 89–90
  impact on fashion, 89
Chicago, 209
  Apparel Mart, 172–173
  as market center, 169–170
Children's apparel industry
  imports, 177
  licensing in, 176–177
  marketing, 175–177
  Miami, 168
  nature of, 174
  specializations in, 175
  trade publications, 175
  trade shows, 175–176
"Children's Forecast, The," 472
China, 315, 316
  overseas contracting
    arrangements, 376–377
China Silk Company, 330
Chloe, 354
Chong, Patricia, 375
Christian Dior, 28
Ciao, Ltd., 159, 346
Cipullo, Aldo, 515
Civil War, 94, 97
Claiborne, Liz, 7, **143**, 152, 153,
  157, 159, **179–183**, 224,
  281, 334, 377, 515
Clark, Ossie, 367, 515
Clark-Schwebel Fiber Glass
  Corporation, 122

Classics, **37**
Clayton Act, 15
Clinics, fashion presentation, 103
Clothing Manufacturers'
  Association (CMA), **228**
Cluett, Peabody & Co., 26, 208,
  341
Cohn Hall Marx, 98
Collection Privées, 361
Collections
  haute couture, 355, 360
  menswear, collection concept,
    220
Collins and Aikman, 96
Colonial Corp., 337
Colonial era, imports, 93–94
Color
  color expert, role of, 120–121
  decision-making about,
    100–101
  furs, 112
  prediction services, 100–101
Color Association of the United
  States (CAUS), color
  prediction, 100–101
Color Box, 472
Color climate, 100
Colorist, job description, 527
Colours, 185, 187
Commissionaires, 323
Complice, 365
Computer-aided design (CAD),
  108
Computer-aided designer, job
  description, 528
Computer-aided manufacturing
  (CAM), 108, 147–148
Concord Fabrics, 98
Cone Mills, 96
  Quick Response (QR), 126–127
Connolly, Sybil, 515
Conran, Jasper, 367
Consumer, role in fashion
  business, 8–9
Consumer expenditures, 5
Consumption communities, 29
Contracting system, **352**, 372–
  379
Contractors
  historical view of, 155
  outside shops, 155–**156**
  overseas, **352**, 372–379
    China, 376–377
    Hong Kong, 373–375
    Latin America, 378
    reasons for, 373
    South Korea, 376
    Taiwan, 376
  role of, **154–156**
  specialization and, 155

Converters, 98–99
  converter-jobber, **99**
  independently owned
    company, 98–99
  integrated converter, **99**
Converting, 98
Cook, Arthur, 66
Cooperative buying office, **477**
Corporate buying office, **478**
Costa, Victor, 62, 168, **188–190**
Costing analyst, job description,
  537
Costume jewelry, **278–280**
Cotons de France, 105
Cotton, 86, 87, 88
Cotton gin, 94
Cotton Incorporated, 88
Coty Awards, 59
Council of Fashion Designers of
  America (CFDA), 59
Council News, 117
Country-of-origin rules, **316**
Courreges, Andres, 48, 515
Couturier, 355, **396**
Crafted with Pride in USA
  Council, 107, 326
Cranston, 98
CRK Advertising, 66
Crystal Brand, 279
Cummings, Angela, 515
Custom Designs, 122
Custom tailors, **214–216**
Customer surveys, 56
Cut/make/sew, **326**
Cutting assistant, job description,
  525
Cutting ticket, **144–145**
Cutty Sark Award, 60

Dache, Lilly, 515
Dagworthy, Wendy, 367
Daily News Record, 487
Dallas
  Apparel Mart, 171
  as market center, 168
Dan River, 96, 98, 100
Davies, Donald, 515
Dawson, Bill, 344
Dayhoff, Richard, 170
Dayton-Hudson, 107, 412
de la Renta, Oscar, 59, 143, 159,
  162, 192, 519
de Rauche, Madeleine, 519
de Ribes, Jacqueline, 519
de Seymes, Geoffroy, 28
*Decline of Radicalism: Reflections
  on America Today, The*
  (Boorstin), 29
Del Castillo, Antonio, 515

Demographics, expected trends,
  17–22
Denim, 204
Department manager, job
  description, 531
Department stores, **409–412**
  branch store, **411**
  catalog operations of, 424
  fur sales, 113
  leased shoe department,
    261–262
  manufacturer's shops in,
    152–153
  menswear apparel, 226
  nature of, 409–410
  origin of, 410–411
  specialty shops by general
    merchandise, 436–438
  store ownership group,
    411–412
  top U.S. stores, 442
Design Center, Taiwan, 376
Designer names
  designer-name boutiques,
    429–430
  hosiery, 266–267
  see also Licensing
Designer price level, 159
Designers
  accessories, 281
  American, rise of, 137–138
  listing of influential designers,
    514–521
  as owners versus employees,
    141, 143
  role in fashion creation, 47–48
  women's apparel
    responsibilities of, 143
    role of, 141, 143
Designers' Collective, 230
Designs, **36**
Dessès, 354
Details, 482
Developing countries, 318
Dillard's, 149
Dior, Christian, 41, 47, 355, 359,
  383, 397, 516
DiPaolo, Nicholas P., 335, 341
Direct ownership of production
  facilities, U.S. and foreign
  markets, 330–331
Discount retailers, **424–429**
  factory outlets, **426**, 428
  off-price retailers, **425–426**
  origins of, 424–425
  purchasing operations of,
    428–429
Disney Enterprises, 161
Distribution channels, 6–7

primary markets, **5**
  retailers, 5
  secondary markets, **5**
  vertical operations, **7**
Distribution planner, job
  description, 533
Dixie Yarns, 98
Dockers, 184–185, 186–187, 217
Doneger Group, 475–476
Door-to-door retailing, **431**
Dow Chemical, 89
Dressers, **111**
Dresses, Jean, 516
Drop, menswear, **210**
Du Pont, 88, 89, 90
Dual-distribution system,
  menswear apparel, **227**
Dunhill Tailors, 216
Duplicate hands, **144**
Dusseldorf, 368, 375

Earnshaw's, 175
Eastern Mink Breeding
  Association, 113
Eastman Chemical, 89
Echo Design, 254, 257
Editorial credit, **483–484**
Electronic Data Interchange
  (EDI), **106**
Electroplating, **278**
Elle, 482
Ellis, Perry, 516
Entry level positions, job
  description, 534
Erlanger Blumgart, 98
Escada AG, 368, **392–395**
Esprit, 152, 174, 330
Esquire, 482
Etienne Aigner, 272
European Economic Community
  (EEC), 315
European Menswear Show
  (SEHM), 229
Evans & Co., 113
Evelyn Pearson Company, 284
"Eveningwear Forecast, The," 472
Events, fashion creation and, 49
Evolutionary changes, fashion, 40
Executive trainee, job description,
  531
Exports, 111, 114
  direct exports, 331
  leather, 118
  textiles, 109
  trade deficit and, 110

Fabiani, Alberto, 516
Fabric librarian, job description,
  539–540

Fabric mills, 97
Factoring, **163**
Factory outlets, **426**, 428
Fads, **37**
Fair Packaging and Labeling Act
    (1966), 16
Fairchild, E. W., 486
Falk, Harvey, 182
Farley Inc., 96
Farley Industries, 208
Farrah, 209
Fashion
    definition of, 36–37
    intrinsic aspects of, 62–64
    power of, 9–10, 35
    terms related to, 36–38
Fashion advisory services
    fashion consultants, **472**, 474
    fashion information services,
        472
Fashion business, **4**
Fashion centers, 360
Fashion change
    fashion cycle, **41**–43
    as gradual process, 40–41
    merchandising and, 43–44
    psychological reasons for, 39
    rational reasons for, 39
Fashion consultants, **472**, 474
Fashion Council of Great Britain,
    367
Fashion creation
    designers, role in, 47–48
    newsworthy personalities and,
        49
    social movements and, 49–52
    social values/attitudes and, 48,
        52
    technological developments
        and, 52–53
Fashion Group, 492
    business staff, 509–510
    editorial staff, 507–509
    merchandising department,
        510–511
    operation of, **505–506**
    promotion staff, 509–510
Fashion industry
    consumer and, 8–9
    demographic trends related to,
        17–22
    distribution channels, 5–7
    economic importance of, 5
    federal legislation related to,
        15–16
    imports and, 14–15
    marketing, 11–13
    product development, 7–8
    scope of, 4–5

socioeconomic factors
    affecting, 10–11
Fashion information services, **472**
Fashion leadership
    bottom-up theory, 46
    marketing implications, 46–47
    trickle-across theory, 45–46
    trickle-down theory, 44–45
Fashion magazines
    advertising revenue, 484
    circulations of, 485
    editorial credit, **483**–484
    major magazines, 482
    role of, 482–484
    services to industry, 485–486
Fashion Pleat, 122
Fashion preferences
    analysis of, 54–56
    point-of-sale analysis, 54
Fashion Service, The (TFS), 472,
    494–498
Fashion trends, **38**
Fashion Works, Inc., 472
Fath, Jacques, 516
"Father of American
    Manufacture," 94
Federal Fur Products Act, 114
Federal Trade Commission, 95
Federal Trade Commission Act
    (1914), 15
Federated/Allied, 412, 439
Federated Department Stores,
    Inc., 411, 412
Fédération Française du Prêt à
    Porter Féminin, **361**, 363
Fee offices, **475–477**
Felix Lilienthal and Co., 475
Fendi, 365
Ferguson, Kathy, 186
Ferragamo, Salvatore, 365, 516
Ferre, Gianfranco, 355, 516
Fezza, Andrew, 220
Fiber
    fiber to fabric process, 85–86
    griege goods, **86**
    man-made fibers, **85**, 88
        brandname, **91–92**
        chemical fiber producers,
            89–90
        development of, 88
        flexibility of, 90
        generic names for, **90–91**
    natural fibers, **85**, 88
        suppliers of, 86–87
    solution-dyed fiber, **86**
    yarn dyeing, **86**
Fiber glass fabrics, 122
Fieldcrest Cannon, 96
Filene's, 226, 411, 413

Fine jewelry, **276–277**
Finery, 236
Finkel, Gary, 337
First Issue, 152
Flame-resistant fabric, 90
Flammable Fabrics Act (1953),
    16
Flax, 86
Flea markets, **432**
Florida Children's Wear
    Manufacturers Guild, 168,
    176
Florsheim Shoe Co., 442–443
Fogarty, Anne, 516
Foley, Caroline, 45
Fontana Sisters, 516
Fontenot, M. L., 123
Foreign buyouts, of retailers,
    438–439
Foreign producers
    contracting system, **352**,
        372–379
    haute couture, **351**, 352–360
    ready-to-wear, 360–372
    in United States, 379
    see also specific topics
Formfit-Rogers, 284
Forquet, Federico, 516
Forstman and Co., 96
Fortune Furs, 111
Fortuny, Mariano, 516
Foundations, **282**
Fownes, 272
France
    ready-to-wear, 360–363
        Fédération Française du Prêt
            à Porter Féminin, **361**, 363
        scope of industry, 360–361
        trade shows, 361, 363
    see also Haute couture
Franchised retailing, 429–430
    designer-name boutiques,
        429–430
    franchisor/franchisee, roles in,
        429
Franchising arrangement, haute
    couture, **358–359**
Frederick Atkins, Inc., 341,
    477–478
Free trade, versus protectionism,
    326–327
Freelance illustrator, job
    description, 530
Freis, Diane, 375
French Fashion and Textile
    Center, 363
Friedlander, Burt, 289
Friedlander, Carolee, **287–289**
Fuoco, Alfred, 335

Fur garments
  designer names, 114
  fashion influences on, 114
  legislation related to, 112, 114
  manufacturing process,
    111–113
  marketing of, 113
Fur industry
  conservationists and, 110, 114
  department store sales, 113
  imports/exports, 110–111, 114
  market considerations,
    110–111
  retailers, 113
  trade associations, 113
  trade shows, 113
Fur Products Labeling Act, 16,
  112

Galanos, James, 59, 60, 143, 159,
  516
Galitzine, Irene, 516
Gap, The, 338, 416, 418, 437
Gap Kids, 177
Garfinkel's, 226
Gaultier, Jean-Paul, 354, 360,
  516
Gay Nineties, 49
General Agreement on Tariffs
    and Trade (GATT), 312
General merchandise chains,
    418–419
General system of preferences
    (GSP), 318
Generic names, synthetic fibers,
    90–91
Generra, 216
Gentlemen's Quarterly, 482
Geographic location, textile
    industry, 96–97
Gernreich, Rudi, 516
Gerre, Gianco, 360
Gerson, Jill, 299
GFT America, 220
Gimbel, Adam, 411
Girls and Boyswear Review, 175
Gitano, 159, 337
Givenchy, Hubert de, 355, 359,
    382, 385, 516
  operation of house, 385
Glamour, 482, 485
Global sourcing, 327–329
Glove industry, 272–274
  economic importance of, 273
  glove construction, 273
  imports, 273
  marketing, 273–274
  nature of, 272–273
  seasonal lines, 274
  trade association, 272

Gloversville, New York, 272–
    273, 292
Godey's Lady's Book, 135, 482
Goetz Trading Ltd., 342
Gold, in jewelry, 276
Gold Rush of 1848, 204
Good Buys, 476
Gottex, 399–402
Gottlieb, Leah, 399–402
Graber Industries, 122, 123
Grader trainee, job description,
    541
Grading, 146
Graham & Gunn, 247
Graham's Magazine, 135
Grandoe, 272, 292–293
Great Lakes Mink Association,
    113
Greece, specialties of, 372
Greenberg, Frank S., 125
Greif Companies, 209, 241,
    243–244, 341
Gres, Alix, 516
Griege goods, 86
Grodd, Clifford, 237
Group purchase, 479, 481
Gruppo GFT, 365, 386–391
Gucci, 365
Gucci, Aldo, 517
Guess, 174, 217
Guilford Mills, 96
Gustafson, David, 300

H. H. Collectibles, 159
Haggar Apparel Company, 107,
    149, 209, 219
Hair ornaments, 280
Hairpieces, 280
Hairstyles, 52
Hale, Sara Joseph, 482
Halston, 48, 275, 517
Hand, Bert, 245–246
Hand tailoring, 214
Handbag industry, 268–271
  economic importance of, 269
  handbag construction, 269–270
  imports, 270
  nature of, 268–269
  seasonal lines, 268–269
  trade association, 269
Handkerchiefs, 280
Hanes Hosiery, 149, 264, 267,
    294–298
Hansen Gloves, 272
Harper's Bazaar, 482
Hart, Schaffner & Marx, 205
Hartmarx, 209, 224, 227, 235–248
Hartnell, Norman, 517
Haskell, Miriam, 278
Hastings, 226

Haute couture, 351, 352–360
  Italy, 359–360
  mass-market ventures, 398
    franchising arrangement,
      358–359
    house boutiques, 358
    licensing, 359
    prêt-à-porter, 358
  Paris
    caution fee, 356
    Chambre Syndicale de la
      Couture Parisienne, 352,
      354
    Chambre Syndicale du
      Prêt-à-Porter, 354
    collections, 355
    directory of, 353
    house, operation of,
      354–355, 381–386
    showings, 355–356
    prices of garments, 355, 382,
      397
    showings, 395, 396–397, 399
    types of customers, 355, 358,
      381, 383, 395, 397
Hawes, Elizabeth, 138
Head, Edith, 517
Healthtex, 174, 330
Hechter, Daniel, 360
Heim, Jacques, 517
Henry Doneger Associates, 475
Henry Grethel, 247
Hepburn, Katherine, 60
Here and There, 472
Herrera, Caroline, 143
Hester, Harris, 26
Hester, Mark, 170
Hide Training School, 117
Hides, 116
High fashion, 38, 41
Hilton, Nick, 237
Hoechst-Celanese Fiber
    Industries, 89, 90
Holograms, 109
Home shopping, 441
Home Shopping Network (HSN),
    441
Hong Kong, 315, 316
  overseas contracting
    arrangements, 373–375
Hong Kong International Leather
    Fair, 118
Hook, J. G., 152, 161
Hooker Ltd., 439
Horst, 60
Hosiery industry, 264–268
  economic importance of, 265
  hosiery construction, 265–266
  imports, 267–268
  marketing

brand names, 266
  designer names, 266–267
  package marketing, 267
  nature of, 264–265
  seasonal lines, 266–267
Hot Sox, 264, 267
House boutiques, 358
Howe, Elias, **136**, 163
Hulanicki, Barbara, 517
Hypermarkets, **440–441**

I. Magnin, 191, 413
Ideacomo, 103, 365
Igedo, 368
Immigrant labor, women's
  apparel industry, 136
Import coordinator, job
  description, 536
Imports, 14–15, 318
  children's apparel, 177
  colonial era, 93–94
  versus domestic production,
    311
  European Economic
    Community and, 315,
    331–332
  furs, 110–111, 114
  global sourcing, 327–329
  gloves, 273
  growth of women's garments,
    310
  handbags, 270
  historical view, 309
  hosiery, 267–268
  impact of, 15
  import penetration, **311**
  intimate apparel, 284–285
  leather, 118
  menswear, 232
  preferential programs
    Caribbean Basin Initiative
      (CBI), **319**
    general system of
      preferences (GSP), **318**
    Section 807, **318**
  by producers
    direct imports, 325
    offshore production,
      325–326
  protectionism versus free
    trade, 326–327
  reasons for importing,
    320–322, 334–336,
    339–340
  regulation of, 311–316
    country-of-origin rules,
      316
    General Agreement on
      Tariffs and Trade (GATT),
      312

Multi-Fiber Textile
    Arrangement (MFA), **313**
  quotas, **313**–316
  by retailers
    buying methods, 322–323
    specification buying,
      324–325
  rise of, 14
  shoe industry, 262–264
  small leather goods, 271–272
  taxes, tariffs, **316**, 318
  textiles, 109
  trade bills, textiles/apparel,
    319–320
  trade deficit, **311**
  U.S. foreign markets
    direct exports, 331
    direct ownership of
      production facilities,
      330–331
    joint-ownership ventures,
      330
    joint ventures, **329**
    licensing, 329–330
  U.S. trading policy, rationale
    for, 311–312
In Fashion, 482
Independent Retailers Syndicate,
    475
Independently owned company,
    converters, 98–99
Industrial Revolution, **94**
Integrated converter, **99**
Intercolor, color prediction, 101
International Color Authority
    (ICA), color prediction, 101
International Footwear Fair, 368
International Ladies' Garment
    Workers' Union (ILGWU),
    rise of, **139**–140
International Men's Fashion
    Week, 232, 368
International Wool Secretariat, 86
Interstoff Textile Fair, 103
Intimate Apparel Council of the
    American Apparel
    Manufacturers
    Association, 282
Intimate apparel industry
  economic importance, 282–283
  historical view, 281
  imports, 284–285
  industry segments, 282
  marketing
    brand names, 284
    fashion influences, 283–284
    licensing, 284
  present/future view of,
    298–303
  seasonal lines, 283

trade associations, 282
Ireland, specialities of, 372
Irene, 517
Isotalo, Leo, 185–186
Israel, specialties of, 372
Italy
  haute couture, 359–360
  ready-to-wear, 363–365
    leading designers, 365
    nature of industry, 363, 365
    trade shows, 363, 365

J. Brochier Soieries, 330
J.C. Penney, 161, 377, 416, 422,
    438
Jackson, Betty, 367
Jacobs, Marc, 321
James, Charles, 517
Jantzen, 159
Japan
  ready-to-wear, 368–371
    leading designers, 371
    marketing, 371
    scope of industry, 370–371
"Jellies," 260, **264**
Jenny, 365
Jerri Pollack, 476
Jewelry industry, 276–280
  bridge jewelry, **277**
  costume jewelry, **278**–280
  fine jewelry, 276–277
  precious stones, **277**
Jindo, 111
John, Mr., 517
John Wanamaker, 408
Johnson, Betsey, 517
Joint-ownership ventures, U.S.
    and foreign markets, 330
Joint ventures, U.S. and foreign
    markets, **329**
Jones, Kate, 170
Jones, Stephen, 517
Jones New York, 159, 321, 336
Jones Post & Co., 421
Jordan Marsh, 24–25, 439
Judy Bond, 159
Julian, Alexander, 60, 185, 187
Junior designer, job description,
    526
Junior industrial engineer, job
    description, 537

K mart, 107, 377, 416, 426, 433,
    435, 440
Kamali, Norma, 161, 400, 435,
    517
Kansas City Trade Center, 173
Kaplan, Jacques, 517
Karan, Donna, 47, **68–70**, 143,
    159, 191, 294, 297, 517

Karats, gold, **276**
Karten for Kids, 472
Karten for Little Kids, 472
Kasten, Tom 186
Kawakubo, Rei, 371, 517
Kay Jewelers, 277
Kayser-Roth, 264, 267, 272
Kelly, Patrick, 354, 398
Kennedy, Jackie, 49
Kenzo, 30, 354, 517
Khan, Emmanuelle, 354, 360, 517
Kids Fashions, 175
King, Charles W., 45
Kiosks, 441–443
Kips, **116**
Kleibacker, Charles, 517
Klein, Anne, 59, 159, 162, 517
Klein, Calvin, 59, **64–67**, 143,
        152, 159, 162, 517
Klopman, William A., 125
Knight, Phil, **290–292**
Knit designer, job description, 528
Knitting, **86**
Knitting Yarn Fair, 105
Knock-offs, **159–160**
    reasons for practice, 160
Konheim, Bud, 345
Krizia, 365
Kuppenheimer, 247
Kuriansky, Dr. Judith, 301
Kurt Salmon Associates Inc., 341

La Style, 482
Labeling laws, examples of, 16
Lace/embroidery designer, job
        description, 528
LaCrasia, 272
Lacroix, Christian, 63, 121, 355
    operation of house, **384**
Lagerfeld, Karl, 354, 383, 396, 517
Lam, Regence, 375
Lambert, Eleanor, 60
Land's End, **456–458**
Lane, Kenneth Jay, 278, 281
Lang, Audre, 360
Lanvin, Jeanne, 518
Lanvin Studio, 214
Laroche, Guy, 355
    operation of house, **385**
Larsen, Jack Lenor, 100
Lasnick, Jules, 123
Latin America, overseas
        contracting arrangements,
        378
Lau, Eddi, 375
Lauren, Ralph, 59, 63, **70–73**,
        143, 152, 153, 159, 162,
        237–238, 518
Layout artist, job description, 529
Lazarus, 411, 412, 439

Lear, 482
Leased shoe departments,
        261–262
Leather
    hides, **116**
    kips, **116**
    legislation related to, 116
    marketing of, 117–118
    processing process, 116
    skins, **116**
    small leather goods, 270–272
    splits, **116**
Leather Industries of America,
        117
Leather industry
    imports/exports, 118
    nature of, 115–116
    trade associations, 117
    trade shows, 118
    types of companies in, 116
    see also Handbag industry;
        Shoe industry
Lee Lorraine, 476
L'Eggs, 267
Legislation
    Celler-Kefauver Act, 16
    Clayton Act, 15
    Federal Trade Commission
        Act, 15
    imports
        country-of-origin rules, **316**
        General Agreement on
            Tariffs and Trade (GATT),
            12
        Multi-Fiber Textile
            Arrangement (MFA), **313**
        quotas, **313–316**
    labeling laws, 16
    Robinson-Patman Act (1936),
        15
    Sherman Anti-Trust Act
        (1890), 15
Lelong, Lucien, 518
Lerner Shops, 417
Leslie Fay, 139, 331
Letting-out process, 113
Leveraged buyouts, women's
        apparel industry, **139**
Levi-Strauss, 25–26, 107, 139,
        148, 157, 159, 174,
        183–188, 208, 209,
        442–443
Lewis, Jennie, 375
Lewis and Thos. Saltz Co., 216
Ley, Margaretha, 392
Ley, Wolfgang, **392–395**
Liberman, Alexander, 60
Liberty of London, 367
Licensing, **160–162**
    accessories, 254

    advantages to licensee,
        161–162
    Cardin and, **27–31**
    children's apparel, 176–177
    company names in, 161
    furs, 114
    haute couture, **359**
    hosiery, 266–267
    intimate apparel, 284
    licensee in, **160**
    licensor in, **160**
    menswear apparel, 224–225
    private labels, 435–436
    royalty fee, **160**
    social assessment related to, 29
    types of arrangements, 161
    U.S. and foreign markets,
        329–330
Lifetime Achievement Award,
        59–60
Lily of France, 284
Limited, The, 177, 416, 418, 435,
        437, **463–465**
Lingerie, **282**
"Lingerie Forecast, The," 472
Lingerie Manufacturer
        Association, 282
Liz Roberts, Inc., 331, 344–345
Loehman's, 425
London
    ready-to-wear, 366–368
        nature of industry, 367
        1960s through 1980s,
            366–367
        trade shows, 367
Looms, shuttless weaving,
        108–109
Loomskill, 98
Lord & Taylor, 138, 256, 408, 412
Los Angeles, as market center,
        167–168
Louis, 235–236, 238, 239, 240
Louis, Jean, 518
Loungewear, **282**
Lovable, 285
Lowell, Francis Cabot, **94**
Luler award, 229

McCardell, Claire, 138, 518
McFadden, Mary, 59, **75–77**,
        100, 193, 518
McKids, 161, 435, 438
Macy's, 437
"Made in USA" label, 316, 326,
        339–340
Mademoiselle, 482, 485
Magazines
    general magazines, 486
    see also Fashion magazines
"Magic" Trade Show, 230

Maidenform, 107, 284
Mail-order houses, 419–424
  catalog operations of stores, 424
  growth of, 421–422
  historical view, 419–421
  specialized houses, 422–423
Mainbocher, 354, 396, 518
Mall of America, 440–441
Malls, 431
Manhattan, Inc., 482
Man-made fibers, **85, 88**
  brand name, 81–92
  cellulosics, 90
  chemical fiber producers,
    89–90
  development of, 88
  flexibility of, 90
  generic names for, **90–91**
  guide to major trade names, 91
  noncellulosics, 90
Manhattan Industries, 335
Manhattan Shirt Co., 220
Manufacturer's retailing,
    151–153
  manufacturer-owned stores,
    152
  manufacturer shops within
    stores, 152–153
  shoe companies, 262
Manufacturers, role of, **154**
Marbridge Building, 258
Marcus, Stanley, 25
Margolis, Jay, 182
Marker, **146**
Market, **12**
Market centers
  Chicago, 169–170
  Dallas, 168
  Los Angeles, 167–168
  Miami, 168
  New York, 163–167
Market representatives, 479
Market segmentation, **12–13**
  factors in, 13
  prediction of fashion and,
    53–54
Market weeks, **170**, 172
Marketing
  children's apparel industry,
    175–177
  consumer orientation, 11–12
  fashion leadership theories
    and, 46–47
  gloves, 273–274
  hosiery
    brand names, 266
    designer names, 266–267
    package marketing, 267
  intimate apparel
    brand names, 284

fashion influences, 283–284
  licensing, 284
Japanese ready-to-wear, 371
manufacturer-owned retail
  chains, 262
marketing concept, **12**
menswear apparel
  brand names, 221–223
  designer labels/licensing,
    224
  dual-distribution system, 227
  retail distribution channels,
    226
  targeted customer approach,
    224
  by trade associations,
    227–230
  trade shows, 230–232
millinery, 275–276
shoes
  leased shoe departments,
    261–262
  seasonal lines, 261
women's apparel
  advertising, 150–151
  presentation of line, 149
  publicity, 151
  sales force, 149–150
  trunk shows, **151**
Marshall Field and Company, 408
Marshall's, 426, 428
Martin, Peggy, 170
Marucelli, Germana, 518
Marvella, Inc., 280
Mass fashion, **38**
Maternity shop franchises, 429
Maxim's de Paris, 31
Maxwell, Vera, 138, 518
Maxx, T. J., 426
May Department Stores, 412
Media
  fashion magazines, 482–486
  newspapers, 486
  television, 488–489
  trade publications, 486–488
Megamall, 440–441
Meichner, Wayne, 242
Meier, Aaron, 410
Meier & Frank, 411
Melville Shoe Company, 258
Men's Apparel Guild of
  California, 229
Men's Fashion Association of
  America (MFA), 60,
  228–229
Menswear apparel industry
  accessories, 232–233
  comparison to women's field,
    206–207
  economic importance of, 202

geographic areas for, 209
historical view
  nineteenth century
    ready-to-wear, 202–204
  private ownership, 206
  publicly owned firms, 206
  standardization of sizes,
    204–205
  union, growth of, 205–206
  work clothes, 204
imports, 232
industry divisions, 207
large firms, dominance of, 208
marketing
  brand names, 221–223
  designer labels/licensing,
    224
  dual-distribution system, 227
  retail distribution channels,
    226
  targeted customer approach,
    224
  by trade associations,
    227–229
  trade shows, 229–232
sportswear
  collection concept, **220**
  development of line,
    218–219
  production process, 219
  seasonal lines, 217–218
  sizing, 219–220
tailored clothing
  custom tailors, 214–216
  development of line, 211
  hand-tailoring, 214
  production process, 211–220
  seasonal lines, 210
  sizing, 213–214
Menswear Designers' Collection,
  232
"Menswear Forecast, The," 472
Merchandising, fashion cycle
  and, 43–44
Merchandising assistant, job
  description, 534–535
Merchandising Motivation, Inc.
  (MMI), 474
Merchandising services, 478–
  481
  buying services, 479
  centralized buying, **481**
  group purchase, 479, **481**
  information exchange, 481
  reports of market
    representatives, 479
  sales promotion, 481
Mergers/acquisitions
  menswear apparel, 208
  textile industry, 96

Miami
  as market center, 168
  Merchandise Mart, 173
Mickey and Co., 152
Microfiber polyester, 90
Miller, Nicole, 345
Milliken & Co., 96, 107, 120
Millinery industry, 274–276
  construction of millinery, 275
  economic importance of, 275
  marketing, 275–276
  nature of, 274–275
  seasonal lines, 275–276
Milosh, Eugene, 334
Mipel accessories show, 365
Mirabella, 482
Missoni, 518
Miyake, Issey, 371, 518
Mizrahi, Isaac, 321
Modacrylics, 90, 91
Model, 482
Moderate price level, 159
Modernization
  computer-aided design (CAD),
    108
  computer-aided manufacturing
    (CAM), 108
  holograms, 109
  Quick Response (QR), 105–108
  shuttless looms, 108–109
Molyneux, Edward, 354, 355, 518
"Mom-and-pop" stores, 407
Mondi, 368
Monet, 279, 280
Monsanto, 89
Montana, Claude, 30, 354, 360,
    399, 518
Montgomery Ward, 415, 418
Moods by Krizia, 435
Mori, Hanae, 354, 371, 396, 518
Morton, Digby, 518
Mugler, Thierry, 354, 360, 518
Muir, Jean, 367, 518
Mulqueen, Jack, 345
Multi-Fiber Textile Arrangement
    (MFA), **313**
Murjani International, 161
Mutual Buying Syndicate, 475
Mystrom, Dr. Paul, 9

Napier, 280
National Association of Men's
    Sportswear Buyers
    (NAMSB), **228**
National brand, 409
National Glove Manufacturers
    Association, 272 -273
National Handbag Association,
    269, 270
National Kids Fashion Shows, 175

National Retail Merchants
    Association, 375, 433
National Shoe Fairs, 261
Natori, 284
Natural fibers, **85, 88**
  suppliers of, 86–87
Nealz, Leann, 66
Neiman-Marcus, 25, 66, 171, 226
Neimark, Ira, 236, 237
New York City, 97, 99, 105
  decentralization of production
    and, 167
  future view, 173–174
  intimate apparel industry, 283
  as market center, 163–167
  menswear apparel, 209
  millinery industry, 275
  Seventh Avenue, **165–167**
  shoe industry, 258
New York Fabric Show, 103
Newman, Ed, 100
Nicole Miller, 331
Nigel French, 472
Nike, 216, **290–292**
Nipon, Albert, 192
Noncellulosics, 90
Nordstrom, **446–450**
Norell, Norman, 59, 159, 518
Norman Hilton, 237
Not-elsewhere-classified category
    (NEC), 207
Nouvelle Boutiques, 359, 429
Nylon, 90
Nylon hosiery, 88
Nylon reflective yarn, 90
Nystrom, Dr. Paul H., 37

O.P.'s Only, 476
O'Brien, Donald, 24
Obsolescence, 9
Odessey Partners, 96
Off-price retailers, **425**, 428
Offshore assembly, **326**
Offshore production
  cut/make/sew, **326**
  offshore assembly, **326**
  production package, **326**
Olive, Frank, 518
Oliver, Andre, 518
Olsoff, Bernard, 341
Onwel Manufacturing Inc., 342
Ortenberg, Arthur, 179,
    181–182, 321
Osborn, Derrill, 242
Oshkosh, 174, 193–195
Outside shops, 155–**156**
Overseas Export Fair, 368
Oxford Industries, 107, 209
Ozbek, Rifat, 367
Ozer, Bernard, 301–303

Pacific, 122
Pacific Silvercloth, 122
Package marketing, hosiery, 267
Page, Vern, 25
Painted woven fabric designer,
    job description, 528
Pang, Hanna, 375
Paquin, 519
Paris. *See* Haute couture
Parnis, Mollie, 519
Party plans, **431**
Passementerie, 397
Passeroff, Alan, 344–345
Paste-up artist, job description,
    529
Pat Tunsky, 472
Patou, Jean, 399, 519
Patternmaker, **144**
Paul Stuart, 226, 237, 238, 239
Paulette, Mme., 519
Pearls, 277, 280
Pedlar, Sylvia, 519
Pelts, **111**
Pendleton, 209
Peoples Jewelers, 277
Peretti, Elsa, 277, 281, 519
Performance, 122
Pergola, David, 243–244
Periodicals, statistical
    information, 523
Perry Ellis America, 220
Personalities in news, fashion
    creation and, 49
Phillips–Van Heusen, 227
Physical fitness, fashion creation
    and, 49
Picasso, Paloma, 281
Picone, Evan, 159
Piece Goods Reservation (PGR),
    211
Pincus Bros. Maxwell, 209
Piquet, Robert, 519
Piracy
  knock-offs, **159**–160
  reasons for practice, 160
Pitti Como, 229
Platinum, in jewelry, 276–277
Playtex, 284
Point-of-sale analysis, fashion
    preferences, 55
Poiret, Paul, 41, 48, 355, 519
Polo, 208
Polyester, 90
Porter, Thea, 519
Potok, Anna, 519
Potter, Clare, 138
Powers, Steve, 184, 186
Precious stones, **277**
Prediction of fashion, 53–
    59

analysis of fashion preferences, 54–56
evaluation of trends, 57–58
market segmentation, 53–54
sources of information for, 58
Preferential programs for imports
 Caribbean Basin Initiative (CBI), **319**
 general system of preferences (GSP), **318**
 Section 807, **318**
Première Vision, 103
Preselling, textiles, 103
Pressman, Fred, 239–240
Pressman-Gutman, 98
Prêt-à-porter, **358**
Pretanning, leather, **116**
Price Breakers, 476
Price Club, 433
"Price clubs," 432–433
Price specialization, 159
Pricing, wholesale compared to retail, 147
Primary markets, **5**
Private labels, **434–436**, 461
Private research organizations, statistical information, 523
Producers
 apparel jobbers, **154**
 contractors, **154–156**
 manufacturers, **154**
Product developers, 481
Product development, timing of, 7–8
Product development assistant, 538–539
Product development trainee, 533
Product line specialization, 158–159
Production assistant, 535
Production control assistant, 536
Production package, **326**
Production process
 menswear
  apparel, 211–220
  sportswear, 216–220
  tailored clothing, 210–216
 women's apparel
  chart of manufacturing process, 145
  computer-aided manufacturing (CAM), 147–148
  cutting ticket, **144–145**
  grading, **146**
  marker, **146**
  Quick Response (QR), 148–149
Projectile looms, 109
Promostyl, 472

Protectionism versus free trade, 326–327
Public relations firm, 491
Publications. See Trade publications
Publicity, 490–491
 activities of, 491
 creation of news, 491
 public relations firm and, 491
 purpose of, 490–491
Publicly owned firms
 menswear apparel industry, 206
 textiles, 95–96
 women's apparel industry, 138–139
Pucci, Emilio, 519
Pulitzer, Lilly, 519
Puritan Fashions, 66, 139
Puritan Inc., 161

Quality control analyst, job description, 540
Quality control specialist, job description, 537
Quant, Mary, 367, 519
Quick Response (QR), 27, 105–108, **148–149**, 443
 bar coding, **106**
 at Cone Mills, 126–127
 effectiveness of, 148–149
 Electronic Data Interchange (EDI), **106**
 goal of, 105
 process in, 105–106, 148
 scanners, **106–107**
 seasonal merchandise and, 149
 standards, 107–108
 supporting industry groups, 107–108
 Universal Product Code, **107**
Quotas, 313–316
 bilateral treaties, **314**
 exemptions from, 315
 getting around quotas, 315–316
 specifications for, 314–315

R.H. Macy group, 411, 413
Racquet Club, 247
Radisson Center, 173
Ramie, 86
Rapier shuttles looms, 109
Ratner's Group, 277
Rayon, **88**, 90
Ready-to-wear, **135**
 foreign, 360–372
 France, 360–363
 historical view, 134–136, 202–204

Italy, 363–365
Japan, 368–371
London, 366–368
secondary European centers, 372
West German trade shows, 368
Reagan, Nancy, 49
Real estate developers into retailing, 439–440
Reebok International Ltd., 258
Reed, Austin, 246
Reeds Jewelers, 277
Regional showrooms, **170**
Reinhardt, Norma, 298
Renown, 371
Resident buying offices, 474–478
 cooperative buying office, **477**
 corporate buying office, **478**
 fee offices, **475–477**
Resources Council, 123
Retail Industry Trade Action Coalition (RITAC), 326
Retail sales coordinator, job description, 534
Retailers, **5**
 catalog showroom retailer, **432**
 chain stores, **415–419**
 current developments
  foreign buyouts, 438–439
  hypermarkets, **440–441**
  kiosks, 441–443
  Quick Response (QR), 443
  real estate developers into retailing, 439–440
  television marketing, **441**
 department stores, **409–412**
 discount retailers, **424–429**
 door-to-door retailing, **431**
 flea markets, **432**
 franchised retailing, 429–430
 historical view, 407–408
 imports
  buying methods, 322–323
  specification buying, 324–325
 mail-order houses, **419–424**
 malls, 431
 manufacturers retailing, 152–153
 party plans, **431**
 private labels, **434–436**
 shopping centers, 430–431
 specialty stores, **412–415**, 437–438
 warehouse clubs, **432–433**
Rhode Island, 278–279
Rhodes, Zandra, 367, 519
Ricci, Nina, 519
Rich, Morris, 411
Rich's of Atlanta, 411

Rive Gauche, 358, 359, 429
Rivetti, Marco, **386–391**
Robert Janan Ltd., 331, 343–344
Roberti, William, 234–235
Robinson, Bill, 60, 214
Robinson-Patman Act (1936), 15
Robinson's 412
Rochas, Marcel, 519
Roche, June, **120–121**
Rodriguez, Maria, 170
Roe, John, 45
Ronlee, 111
"Roscoe" award, 123
Ross stores, 416
Rossi, Gina, 170
Round-the-Clock, 264, 267
Royalty fee, licensing, **160**
Russ Togs, 159, 174, 414
Rykiel, Sonia, 354, 360, 519

St. Laurent, Yves, 355, 358, 359,
　　385–386, 395–396, 519
　Rive Gauche, 358, 359, 429
Saks Fifth Avenue, 66, 424, 439
Salant Corp., 341
Sales force, role of, 149–150
Sales presentation, textiles, 103
Sales promotion, by
　　merchandising services,
　　481
Sales trainee, job description, 539
Salon International du Prêt-à-
　　Porter Féminin, 361
Sam Yang Enterprises, 111
Sam's Wholesale Club, 433
Sample hand, **144**
San Francisco, 209
　Fashion Center, 173
"Sandwich gloves," 273
Sansabelt Stores, 248
Sarah Lee, 158
Sarmi, Count Fernando, 520
Savitt, M.J., 277
Savvy, 482
Scassi, Arnold, 143
Scandinavia, specialties of, 372
Scandinavian Menswear Fair, 232
Scandinavian mink and fox
　　breeders, 113
Scanners, **106–107**
Scarfs, 280
Schenck, Weldon, 294–297
Scherrer, Jean-Louis, 520
Schiaparelli, Elsa, 355, 396, 520
Schlumberger, Jean, 520
Schoen, Mila, 360, 520
Scotland, specialties of, 372
Scott, Ken, 520
Screen print artist, job
　　description, 528

Sears, Richard, 419
Sears Roebuck & Company, 25,
　　107, 213, 415, 416, 418,
　　419, 435, 438
　catalog, 419–422
Seasonal lines
　gloves, 274
　handbags, 268–269
　hosiery, 266–267
　intimate apparel, 283
　menswear
　　sportswear, 217–218
　　tailored clothing, 210
　millinery, 275–276
　price and presentation, 141
　shoes, 261
　women's apparel industry, **141**,
　　149
Secondary markets, **5**
Section 807, **318**, 337, 338, 339
Semaine du Cuir, 118
Seminole Manufacturing Co., 342
Service Merchandise, 432
7 Days, 482
Seventeen, 482, 485
Seventh Avenue, **165–167**
Shadid, Sam, 66
Shapiro, Ted, 346
Shaver, Dorothy, 138
Shaw, Gerald, 192
Sherman Anti-Trust Act (1890),
　　15
Ship 'n' Shore, 159
Shoe industry
　athletic shoes, 258–259
　economic importance of, 260
　historical view, 257
　imports, 262–264
　marketing
　　leased shoe departments,
　　261–262
　　manufacturer-owned retail
　　chains, 262
　　seasonal lines, 261
　nature of industry, 257–258
　production centers, 258
　shoe construction, 260–261
　trade shows, 261
Shopping centers, **430–431**
Shows
　haute couture, 355–356, 360
　to present line, 149
　trunk shows, **151**
　see also Trade shows
Shuttless looms, 108–109
　types of, 109
Sibiri, Karen, 277
Silk, 86, 88
Silver, in jewelry, 277
Simmel, George, 45

Simonetta, 520
Simpson, Adele, 520
Singer, Isaac, **136**
Size of companies, 156–158
　menswear apparel, 208
　women's apparel, 156–158
Size specialization, children's
　　apparel, 175
Sizing of menswear
　sportswear, 219–220
　tailored clothing, 213–214
Sketcher, 526, 530–531
Sketcher/stylist, 526
Sketching assistant, 526
Skinner, 122
Skins, **116**
Slater, Samuel, **94**
Slops, **202–203**
Small leather goods, **270–272**
Smelser, Neil J., 42
Social movements, fashion
　　creation and, 49–52
Social values, fashion creation
　　and, 48, 52
Socioeconomic factors, effects on
　　fashion business, 10–11
Solution-dyed fiber, **86**
Soprani, 365
South Korea, 315, 316
　overseas contracting
　　arrangements, 376
Southwick, 214
Spain, specialties of, 372
Spandex, 90
Specialists, fashion staff, 99–100
Specialization
　children's apparel, 175
　by price, 159
　by product, 158–159
　textile firms, 98
Specialty stores, **412–415**, 437,
　　438
　boutiques, **414–415**
　general merchandise stores,
　　436–438
　large departmentalized stores,
　　413
　menswear apparel, 226
　small shops, 414
Spiegel, 422
Spinning mill, **94**, 97
Splits, **116**
Sportswear, menswear
　collection concept, **220**
　development of line, 218–219
　production process, 219
　seasonal lines, 217–218
　sizing, 219–220
Springmaid, 122
Springs, 122–124

"Springs of Achievement"
  program, 122
Springs Industries, 96
Springs Mills, 96
Sprouse, Stephen, 520
Staff illustrator, job description,
  530
Standardization of sizes,
  menswear apparel
  industry, 204–205
Standards, Quick Response,
  107–108
Statistical information
  periodicals, 523
  private research organizations,
  523
  U.S. Government sources,
  522–523
Sterling, silver, **277**
Stern's, 439
Stevens, J. P., 96, 98
Stillman, Eve, 284
Stock, Robert, 236
Store ownership group, **411–412**
Stores Magazine, 433
Strauss, Levi, 47, 204
Street fashions, 47–48
Style, 36, 37
Style number, **36**
Stylists' Information Service
  (SIS), 472
Suit Wars, 235–240
Sulka, 216
Sunglasses, 280
Sweatshops, **139**
Syms, 216
Syms, Sy, 216
Synthetic fibers, 52
System Updated Retail Feedback
  (SURF), 183
Szware, Jean, 359

Tai Apparel Ltd., 379
Tailored clothing, **207**
  custom tailors, 214–**216**
  development of line, 211
  hand-tailoring, 214
  production process, 211–220
  seasonal lines, 210
  sizing, 213–214
  tailors-to-the-trade, **216**
Taiwan, 315, 316
  overseas contracting
  arrangements, 376
Taiwan Textile Federation, 376
Takada, Kenzo, 371
Talbots, 438
Tanners' Apparel and Garment
  (TAG) Show, 118
Tanning, leather, **116**

Targeted customer approach,
  marketing, 224
Tariffs, **316**, 318
Tarlazzi, Angelo, 354, 360
Taroma Inc., 29
Tassell, Gustave, 520
Taxes
  tariffs, **316**, 318
  value-added tax, **318**
Taxi, 482
Taylor-Gordon, Elaine, 298
Technical designer trainee, job
  description, 540
Technology, fashion creation
  and, 52–53
Television, 488–489
  fashion views, 488–489
  television marketing, **441**
Texitalia, 103
Textile Age, 486
Textile and Apparel Export
  Expansion Program, 331
Textile-Apparel Linkage Council,
  107
Textile and Apparel Trade
  Enforcement Act, 319–320
Textile design, process in, 101
Textile development, 99–105
  color decisions, 100–101
  dessemination of information,
  101, 103
  open-line goods, **103**
  preselling, 103
  sales presentation, 103
  specialized staff for, 99–100
  textile design, 101
  trade shows, 103, 105
Textile Fiber Products
  Identification Act, 16, 88,
  90
Textile industry
  converters, **98–99**
  economic importance of, 93
  geographic location, 96–97
  historical view, 93–96
  mergers/consolidation, 96
  publicly owned firms, 95–96
  sales of largest firms, 95
  specialized firms, 98
  vertically integrated firms,
  97–**98**
Textile/surface designer, 527
Textile technologist, 539
Textiles, **92**
Theory of the Leisure Class
  (Veblen), 39
Thigpen, Peter, 25–26
Thomas F. Pierce & Son, 257
Tighe, Susan, 184–185
Tobe Associates, 472, 474

operation of, **498–500**
Tracy, Ellen, 159
Trade associations
  fur industry, 113
  glove industry, 272
  intimate apparel, 282
  leather industry, 117
  menswear marketing activities
  by, 227–229
  role of, **492**
Trade deficit, imports and, **311**
Trade publications, 4, **486–488**
  advertising in, 150
  children's apparel industry, 175
  circulations, 487
  content of, 487–488
  examples of, 486
Trade shows
  British ready-to-wear, 367
  children's apparel industry,
  175–176
  foreign, 322, 323
  French ready-to-wear, 361, 363
  fur industry, 113
  furs, 113
  Italian ready-to-wear, 363, 365
  leather industry, 118
  menswear, 229–232
  textiles, 103, 105
Treiber, Michael D., 336
Trends, evaluation of, 57–58
Triacetate, 90, 91
Triangle Shirtwaist Fire, **139**
Trickle-across theory, of fashion
  leadership, 45–46
Trickle-down theory, of fashion
  leadership, 44–45
Trifari, 279
Trigere, Pauline, 520
"Trimming and Finishing Book
  The," 472
Trogdon, Dewey, 126–127
Trump Tower, 430
Trunk shows, **151**
  designers attitudes, 191–193
Turkel, Mel, 343–344

U.S. Government sources,
  statistical information,
  522–523
U.S. Shoe Company, 258, 262
Ultrasuede, 122
Umbrellas, 280
Ungaro, Emmanuel, 355, 520
Union Bay, 216
Unions
  Amalgamated Clothing and
  Textile Workers Union of
  America (ACTWUA),
  205–206

Unions (*Continued*)
    International Ladies' Garment
        Workers' Union (ILGWU),
        139–140
    protectionist position, 326
Universal Product Code, **107**
Uomo Modo, 365
Uppers, shoes, 260

V.F. Corporation, 107
Valentina, 520
Valentino, 359, 360, 396, 520
Van Buren/Carr Associates, 476
Van Buren-Neiman Associates,
    476, 478
Vanity Fair, 157–158, 284
Vanity Fair, 482
Vassarette, 284
VBW Associates, 476
Veblen, Thorstein, 39, 45, 47
Venet, Philippe, 520
Vera, 254, 281
Versace, Gianni, 365, 520
Vertical operations, **7**
Vertically integrated firms,
    textiles, 97–**98**
Victor, Sally, 520
Victoria Creations, 254
Victoria's Secret, 120–121, 301
Videos, fashion videos, 488–489
Vionnet, Madeleine, 47, 355,
    396, 397, 520
Vittadini, Adrienne, **73–75**, 143,
    159, 339–340
Vogue, 482, 485
Volker, Cathy, 297–298
Voluntary Interindustry
    Communications
    Standards, 107

"Waist stores," 417
Wallace, Herb, **230–243**
Wal-Mart, 107, 148, 416, 426,
    433, 440, **450–455**

Walton, Sam, **450–455**
Wamsutta, 122, 124
Ward, Aaron Montgomery, 419
Warehouse, 367
Warehouse clubs, **432–433**
Warnaco, 157, 284
Warner, 284, 285
Water jet looms, 109
Water Tower, 430
Weaving, **85**
Webb, David, 520
Weinberg, Harvey, 246
Weiser, Selma, **458–461**
Weitz, John, 237, 238, 520
West, Eileen, 284
West Germany, international
    shows, 368
West Point Pepperell, 96, 208
Westwood, Vivienne, 367, 520
Wexner, Leslie H., 463–465
White Stag, 159, 209
Whitney, Eli, 94
Wickes Co., 96, 284
Wildrick, Bob, 186
William Rosenfeld Furs, 111
Wintuk Yarns, 98
"Women's Actualwear Forecast,
    The," 472
Women's apparel industry
    apparel marts, **170–173**
    designers
        responsibilities of, 143
        role of, 141, 143
    factoring, **163**
    historical view
        immigrant labor, 136
        leveraged buyouts, **139**
        machine production, 136
        nineteenth century
            ready-to-wear, 134–136
        publicly owned firms,
            138–139
        twentieth century, 136–140
        union growth of, 139, 141

knock-offs, 159–160
licensing agreements, 160–162
manufacturer's retailing,
    151–153
market centers, 163–170
marketing
    advertising, 150–151
    presentation of line, 149
    publicity, 151
    sales force, 149–150
    trunk shows, **151**
producers
    apparel jobbers, **154**
    contractors, **154–156**
    manufacturers, **154**
production process, 144–149
seasonal lines, **141**
size of companies, 156–158
specialization, by price and
    product, 158–159
Women's Wear Daily, 150, 175,
    486–487
Wong, F. Y., 338
Wood, Freedie, 341
Wool, 86, 87
Wool Products Labeling Act
    (1939), 16
Woolmark Award, 60
Work clothes, for men, 204
Worth, Charles Frederick, 352,
    354, 355, 396, 521
Worth Street, **97**
Woven fabric designer, job
    description, 528
Wragge, B. H., 521
Wrangler, 159, 331

Yamamoto, Kansai, 371
Yamamoto, Yohi, 371, 521
Yarn dyeing, **86**

Zuckerman, Ben, 521
Zuckerwar, Richard, Jr., **292–293**